CRITICAL PEDAGOGY

"*Critical Pedagogy: Where Are We Now?* is, without a doubt, an impressive volume given the daring challenge of its contributing authors to the perverse reality of the world that mines the ontological directions of men and of women—a perversity shaped by the neoliberal thinking and the globalization of the economy. Each of the authors in this volume write from different perspectives as they follow closely or recreate the critical pedagogy proposed by Paulo Freire.

The contributors courageously denounce the condemnation to a life of hopelessness that has been ruining peoples and nations—a hopelessness that negates the concretization of a possible utopia of a better and more just world—a hopelessness that destroys without clemency or compassion the greatest riches of human existence leading them to question: where are we now? Like Paulo Freire, they propose that we recapture and safeguard the greatest patrimony that justifies and gives meaning to life itself: our humanity."

Ana Maria Araújo Freire

CRITICAL PEDAGOGY

Studies in the Postmodern Theory of Education

Joe L. Kincheloe and Shirley R. Steinberg
General Editors

Vol. 299

PETER LANG
New York • Washington, D.C./Baltimore • Bern
Frankfurt am Main • Berlin • Brussels • Vienna • Oxford

CRITICAL PEDAGOGY

Where Are We Now?

Edited by
Peter McLaren & Joe L. Kincheloe

PETER LANG
New York • Washington, D.C./Baltimore • Bern
Frankfurt am Main • Berlin • Brussels • Vienna • Oxford

Library of Congress Cataloging-in-Publication Data

Critical pedagogy: where are we now? / edited by Peter McLaren,
Joe L. Kincheloe.
p. cm. — (Counterpoints: studies in the postmodern theory of education; v. 299)
Includes bibliographical references.
1. Critical pedagogy. I. McLaren, Peter. II. Kincheloe, Joe L.
LC196.C759   370.11′5—dc22   2006101074
ISBN 978-0-8204-9730-3 (hardcover)
ISBN 978-0-8204-8147-0 (paperback)
ISSN 1058-1634

Bibliographic information published by **Die Deutsche Bibliothek**.
Die Deutsche Bibliothek lists this publication in the "Deutsche
Nationalbibliografie"; detailed bibliographic data is available
on the Internet at http://dnb.ddb.de/.

Cover art by Jesse Kriegel; photo of cover art by Giuliana Cucinelli
Cover design by Lisa Barfield

The paper in this book meets the guidelines for permanence and durability
of the Committee on Production Guidelines for Book Longevity
of the Council of Library Resources.

© 2007 Peter Lang Publishing, Inc., New York
29 Broadway, 18th floor, New York, NY 10006
www.peterlang.com

To Nita Freire, our dear sister and colleague
and in honor of the birth of The Paulo and Nita Freire International
Project for Critical Pedagogy

Table of Contents

Part 2: The Pedagogical Dimensions of Critical Pedagogy

Part 3: The Political Dimensions of Critical Pedagogy

Preface

Where are we now?

SHIRLEY R. STEINBERG

Answering the question, I would say that wherever we are now, we are being insubordinate—at least I hope so. Refusing to compromise to the standards-wielding, neo-liberal, pedagogical pundits, the contributors gathered in this book are engaged in a pedagogy of insubordination. Insubordination borne by the fact that we have been pedagogically violated by conservatives, liberals, quasi-critical pedagogues, and just about everyone else who just doesn't get *it*. And therein, lies the proverbial rub: there is no *it*. Critical pedagogy isn't formulaic, it isn't stagnant, and it isn't an *is*. I believe it is what isn't. Critical pedagogy is not guided by do-gooders, not guided by liberal groupies, or rayon-clad teachers who want to save needing students from pedagogies of prescription, administration, state standards, or even the latest flashdance pedagogical method. Critical pedagogy can be theoretically-based scholarship, grounded in the understanding of the origins and underpinnings of power within society and in the fabric of schooling. Critical pedagogy has the right to be angry, and to express anger, anger at the uses of power and at injustices through the violations of human rights. Critical pedagogy isn't a talk—liberals talk. Critical pedagogy takes language from the radical—radicals must do.

As a transgressive discourse, practice, and fluid way of seeing the world, those engaged in critical pedagogy continually attempt to redefine themselves through the context in which they find themselves. Once we slow down and stop fluidity, the criticality is gone, and we bog ourselves down in the quicksand of compromised liberalism.

Those engaged in critical pedagogy don't need to agree with one another, rather, they need to passionately engage in the radical fire of discursive disagreement. Allowing students to realize that critique is the weft of the weave within democracy, those who espouse a critical pedagogy must constantly be alert and attuned to the context in which politics, power, and pedagogy intersect. Through the critical pedagogy of disagreement, as critical pedagogues, we do not seek popularity, only to express anger and indignation.

Empowered by the anger we feel from socially unjust practices in the world, we are able to use this anger within the radical practices of our own critical pedagogy. By naming the practices, people, and ideologies that infect our schools with dishope, test-driven expectations, and socio-economic insults to our students, we create a space for critique and insurgency.

By asking the question of critical pedagogy: *where are we now?*, I believe the editors and authors of this volume have already moved from the now in which the book was written and have continued to practice naming the neo-liberal curricular "innovations," the racial, class, sexual preference, and gender contradictions within society, and the institutionalized socio-mental paralysis that has become the twenty-first century school. Only as insurgents within the system will we be able to transgress with our critical pedagogy. Critical pedagogy: where are we now? We are in the schools, we are in the classroom, we are in the teacher education program, we are in grassroots organizations, we are in communities—we are naming ourselves, and we aren't being quiet anymore.

The editors of this volume have attempted to contextualize critical pedagogy in a way in which both scholars and students can negotiate through the pages with ease. Henry Giroux introduces the volume as he discusses the dangers of a critical pedagogy and the consistent attacks it warrants. It would be negligent to not mention the impact of Henry's work: in depth, in impact, and in his refusal to apologize or capitulate for his theoretical pedagogy and its importance in laying the foundation from which the authors in this volume build.

The first section of the book addresses the theoretical dimensions of critical pedagogy. Often critiqued as a deficit of critical theory and pedagogy, theoretical discourse is essential in order to both legitimize and to make sense of the praxis we espouse. Refusing to dumb down to the essentialist comments of scholars past, critical pedagogy demands scholarly rigor which draws heavily upon social theories, literary criticism, philosophy, and pedagogy in order to clarify itself.

The second section of the book addresses the pedagogical. Do not mistake the division of these sections to imply that the theoretical/pedagogical/political dimensions do not intersect and entwine in critical pedagogy. The sections merely organize the chapters for ease in both studying and teaching the book.

The third section of the book deals with the political dimensions of critical pedagogy. Peter McLaren begins this section with passionate prose calling for the pedagogical revolution demanded by critical pedagogy. Completing the book is the afterword by Donaldo Macedo. Donaldo calls for a reinsertion of what he calls criticity into critical pedagogy.

Sit down, open the pages, and do not expect to be relaxed—do plan to be uncomfortable: it is with that uncomfortability that we will teach.

Introduction

Democracy, Education, and the Politics of Critical Pedagogy

HENRY A. GIROUX

What makes critical pedagogy so dangerous to Christian evangelicals, neoconservatives, and right-wing nationalists in the United States and Canada today is that central to its very definition is the task of educating students to become critical agents who actively question and negotiate the relationships between theory and practice, critical analysis and common sense, and learning and social change. Critical pedagogy refuses the official lies of power and the utterly reductive notion of being a method. On the contrary, paraphrasing Bill Moyers, it is, in part, part of a project whose purpose is to dignify "people so they become fully free to claim their moral and political agency."[1] Critical pedagogy opens up a space where students should be able to come to terms with their own power as critical agents; it provides a sphere where the unconditional freedom to question and assert is central to the purpose of the university, if not democracy itself.[2] Pedagogy also makes a space available for an argument about the responsibility of the present for a democratic future. And as a political and moral practice, pedagogy should "make evident the multiplicity and complexity of history," as a narrative to enter into critical dialogue with rather than accept unquestioningly. Similarly, such a pedagogy should cultivate in students a healthy skepticism about power, a "willingness to temper any reverence for authority with a sense of critical awareness."[3] As a performative practice, pedagogy should provide the conditions for students to be able to reflectively frame their own relationship to the ongoing project of an unfinished democracy. It is precisely this relationship between democracy and pedagogy that is so threatening to conservatives such as David Horowitz. Pedagogy always represents a commitment to the future, and it remains the task of educators to make sure that the future points the way to a more socially just world, a world in which the discourses of critique and possibility in conjunction with the values of reason, freedom, and equality function to alter, as part of a broader democratic project, the grounds upon which life is lived. This is hardly a prescription for political indoctrination, but it is a project that gives education its most valued purpose and meaning, which in part is "to encourage human agency, not mold it in the manner of *Pygmalion*."[4] It is also a position that threatens right-wing private advocacy groups, neoconservative politicians, and conservative extremists because they recognize that such a pedagogical commitment goes to the very heart of what it means to address real inequalities of power at the social level and to conceive of education as a project for democracy and critical citizenship while at the same time foregrounding a series of important and often ignored questions such as: Why do we [as educators] do what we do the way we do it? Whose interests does higher education serve? How might it be possible to understand and engage the diverse contexts in which education takes place? In spite of the right-wing view that equates indoctrination with any suggestion of politics, critical pedagogy is not simply concerned with offering students new ways to think critically and act with authority as agents in the classroom; it is also concerned with providing students with the skills and knowledge necessary for them to expand their capacities both to question deep-seated assumptions and myths that legitimate the most archaic and disempowering social practices that structure every aspect of society and to take responsibility for intervening in the world they inhabit. Education is not neutral, but that does not mean it is merely a form of indoctrination. On the contrary, as a practice that attempts to expand the capacities necessary for human agency and hence the possibilities for democracy itself, the university must nourish those pedagogical practices that promote "a concern with keeping the forever unexhausted and unfulfilled human potential open, fighting back all attempts to foreclose and pre-empt the further unravelling of human possibilities, prodding human society to go on questioning itself and preventing that questioning from ever stalling or being declared finished."[5] In other words, critical pedagogy forges both critique and agency through a language of skepticism and possibility and a culture of openness, debate, and engagement, all elements that are now at risk in the latest and most dangerous attack on higher education.

The attack on pedagogy is, in part, an attempt to deskill teachers and dismantle teacher authority. Teachers can make a claim to being fair, but not to being either neutral or impartial. Teacher authority can never be neutral, nor can it be assessed in terms that are narrowly ideological. It is always broadly political and interventionist in terms of the knowledge-effects it produces, the classroom experiences it organizes, and the future it presupposes in the countless ways in which it addresses the world. Teacher authority at its best means taking a stand without standing still. It suggests that as educators we make a sincere effort to be self-reflective about the value-laden nature of our authority while taking on the fundamental task of educating students to take responsibility for the direction of society.

Rather than shrink from our political responsibility as educators, we should embrace one of pedagogy's most fundamental goals: to teach students to believe that democracy is desirable and possible. Connecting education to the possibility of a better world is not a prescription for indoctrination; rather it marks the distinction between the academic as a technician and the teacher as a self-reflective educator who is more than the instrument of a safely approved and officially sanctioned worldview.

The authority that enables academics to teach emerges out of the education, knowledge, research, professional rituals, and scholarly experiences that they bring to their field of expertise and classroom teaching. Such authority provides the space and experience in which pedagogy goes beyond providing the conditions for the simple acts of knowing and understanding and includes the cultivation of the very power of self-definition and critical agency. But teacher authority cannot be grounded exclusively in the rituals of professional academic standards. Learning occurs in a space in which commitment and passion provide students with a sense of what it means to link knowledge to a sense of direction. Teaching is a practice rooted in an ethico-political vision that attempts to take students beyond the world they already know, in a way that does not insist on a particular fixed set of altered meanings. In this context, teacher authority rests on pedagogical practices that reject the role of students as passive recipients of familiar knowledge and view them instead as producers of knowledge, who not only critically engage diverse ideas but also transform and act on them.[6] Pedagogy is the space that provides a moral and political referent for understanding how what we do in the classroom is linked to wider social, political, and economic forces.

It is impossible to separate what we do in the classroom from the economic and political conditions that shape our work, and that means that pedagogy has to be understood as a form of academic labor in which questions of time, autonomy, freedom, and power become as central to the classroom as what is taught. As a referent for engaging fundamental questions about democracy, pedagogy gestures to important questions about the political, institutional, and structural conditions that allow teachers to produce curricula, collaborate with colleagues, engage in research, and connect their work to broader public issues. Pedagogy is not about balance, a merely methodological consideration; on the contrary, as Cornelius Castoriadis reminds us, if education is not to become "the political equivalent of a religious ritual,"[7] it must do everything possible to provide students with the knowledge and skills they need to learn how to deliberate, make judgments, and exercise choice, particularly as the latter is brought to bear on critical activities that offer the possibility of democratic change. Democracy cannot work if citizens are not autonomous, self-judging, and independent—qualities that are indispensable for students if they are going to make vital judgments and choices about participating in and shaping decisions that affect everyday life, institutional reform, and governmental policy. Hence, pedagogy becomes the cornerstone of democracy in that it provides the very foundation for students to learn not merely how to be governed, but also how to be capable of governing.

One gets the sense that conservative educators from Lynne Cheney to Ann D. Neal to Horowitz believe that there is no place in the classroom for politics, worldly concerns, social issues, and questions about how to lessen human suffering. In this discourse, the classroom becomes an unworldly counterpart to the gated community, a space for conformity in which the meaning of education is largely reduced to respecting students's "comfort zones" and to perpetuating current governmental and social practices, however corrupt and antidemocratic. This is a form of education, as Howard Zinn notes, where scholars "publish while others perish."[8] This is not education; it is a flight from self and society. Its outcome is not a student who feels a responsibility to others and who feels that her presence in the world matters, but one who feels the presence of difference as an unbearable burden to be contained or expelled. The importance of academics as engaged intellectuals, the necessity of making education worldly and pedagogy a moral and political practice, has been captured in a different context by Edward Said in his discussion of the role of the public intellectual. He wrote:

> So in the end it is the intellectual as a representative figure that matters—someone who visibly represents a standpoint of some kind, and someone who makes articulate representations to his or her public despite all sorts of barriers. My argument is that intellectuals are individuals with a vocation for the art of representing . . . And that vocation is important to the extent that it is publicly recognizable and involves both commitment and risk, boldness and vulnerability. . . . The intellectual . . . is neither a pacifier nor a consensus-builder, but someone whose whole being is staked on a critical sense, a sense of being unwilling to accept easy formulas, or ready-made clichés, or the smooth, ever-so-accommodating confirmations of what the powerful or conventional have to say, and what they do. Not just passively unwilling, but actively willing to say so in public.[9]

Given the seriousness of the current attack on higher education by an alliance of diverse right-wing forces, it is difficult to understand why liberals, progressives, and left-oriented educators have been relatively silent in the face of this assault. There is much more at stake in this attack on the university than the issue of academic freedom. First and foremost is the concerted attempt by right-wing extremists and corporate interests to strip the professoriate of any authority, render critical pedagogy as merely an instrumental task, eliminate tenure as a protection for teacher authority, and remove critical reason from any vestige of civic courage, engaged citizenship, and social responsibility. The three academic unions have a combined membership of almost 200,000, including graduate students and adjuncts, and yet they have barely stirred. In part, they are quiet because they are under the illusion that tenure will protect them, or they believe the attack on academic freedom has little to do with how they perform their academic labor. They are wrong on both counts, and unless the unions and progressives mobilize to protect the institutionalized relationships between democracy and pedagogy, teacher authority and classroom autonomy, they will be at the mercy of a right-wing revolution that views democracy as an excess and the university as a threat.

The current assault on the academy is first and foremost an attack not only on the conditions that make critical pedagogy possible, but also on what it might mean to raise questions about the real problems facing higher education today, which include the increasing role of adjunct faculty, the instrumentalization of knowledge, the rise of an expanding national security state, the hijacking of the university by corporate interests, and the increasing attempts by right-wing extremists to turn education into job training or into an extended exercise in patriotic xenophobia. Pedagogy must be understood as central to any discourse about academic freedom, but, more importantly, it must be understood as the most crucial referent we have for understanding politics and defending the university as one of the very few remaining democratic public spheres in the United States today.

Notes

1. Bill Moyers, "Discovering What Democracy Means," TomPaine.Com (February 12, 2007). Online: http://www.tompaine.com/articles/2007/02/12/discovering_what_democracy_means.php

2. Jacques Derrida, "The Future of the Profession or the Unconditional University," p. 233.

3. Edward Said, *Reflections on Exile and Other Essays* (Cambridge: Harvard University Press, 2001), p. 501.

4. Stanley Aronowitz, "Introduction," in Paulo Freire, *Pedagogy of Freedom* (Boulder: Rowman and Littlefield, 1998), pp. 10-11.

5. Zygmunt Bauman and Keith Tester, *Conversations with Zygmunt Bauman* (Malden: Polity Press, 2001), p. 4.

6. Chandra Mohanty, "On Race and Voice: Challenges for Liberal Education in the 1990s," *Cultural Critique* (Winter 1989-1990), p. 192.

7. Cornelius Castoriadis, "Democracy as Procedure and Democracy as Regime," *Constellations* 4:1 (1997), p. 5.

8. Howard Zinn, *On History* (New York: Seven Stories Press, 2001), p. 178.

9. Edward Said, *Representations of the Intellectual* (New York: Pantheon, 1994), pp. 12-13, 22-23.

PART ONE

The Theoretical Dimensions of Critical Pedagogy

CHAPTER 1

Critical Pedagogy in the Twenty-first Century

Evolution for Survival

JOE L. KINCHELOE

I am dedicated to the basic themes of critical pedagogy. I have been for years and assume I will continue to be for the rest of my life. At the same time because I am dedicated to the principles of criticality, I am by necessity a vehement critic of the tradition. Adherence to such critical notions, many believe, requires those of us within the tradition to criticize and move it to new plateaus while recognizing our own failures and the failures of the domain. It is in this spirit that Peter and I entered into our work on *Critical Pedagogy: Where Are We Now?* Bound by our enduring friendship and common commitment to a wide range of critical concepts, together we move into the next phase of critical pedagogy. As I reference my role as a "vehement critic" of the critical tradition, I offer such criticism in the spirit of Paulo Freire's radical love. I don't want to assess the successes and failures of critical pedagogy in the posture of one who knows best where we should be going—I don't possess such prescience. In the spirit of Paulo I offer my critiques humbly, painfully aware of my own shortcomings as a teacher-scholar.

Concurrently, I refuse to attack my fellow critical pedagogues in some mean-spirited, ad hominem way simply because they might disagree with me. I find that on the vast majority of issues I am a committed ally of proponents of critical pedagogy with whom I have profound disagreements. In such contexts I seek a synergistic conversation, knowing that any disagreement we have around a theoretical or social action-oriented concept can be analyzed within a larger context of sociopolitical and pedagogical solidarity. With this critical harmony and radical love as the foundation that grounds my conception of critical pedagogy, I offer this chapter as a call for critical solidarity in an era that might be described as "less than friendly" to many of our perspectives on social, cultural, political, economic, epistemological, ontological, psychological, social, theoretical, and pedagogical issues of the day. Didn't Ben Franklin once say something about it being better to hang together than to hang separately? In this era of a new U.S. Empire, political economic globalization, a corporatized politics of knowledge, a "recovered" dominant race, class, gender, sexual, and religious supremacy, and a grotesque anti-intellectualism, I would argue that Franklin's eighteenth-century perspective on the dynamics of hanging is quite relevant for twenty-first-century practitioners of critical pedagogy.

Keeping Critical Pedagogy Relevant: Diverse Dialects—Open-Access Writing and Speaking

If critical pedagogy is to matter as we move toward the second decade of the twenty-first century, if it is to be more than a historical blip on the educational landscape of the late twentieth and early twenty-first centuries, then it must meet several contemporary challenges. From my perspective a vibrant, relevant, effective critical pedagogy in the contemporary era must be simultaneously intellectually rigorous and accessible to multiple audiences. In an era when open-access publishing on the Internet is a compelling issue in the politics of knowledge (Willinsky, 2006), I contend that open-access writing and speaking about critical pedagogy are also profoundly important. Such a populist form of criticality does not in any manner undermine our intellectual rigor and theoretical sophistication; instead, it challenges our pedagogical ability to express complex ideas in a language that is understandable and germane to wide audiences.

Make no mistake, there is a central place in the lives of academic critical pedagogues for scholarly, peer-reviewed publications—such an enterprise is a dynamic dimension of being a scholar and improving our intellectual skills. Such a practice occupies a central place in the cultivation of the intellect and in all of our efforts to become adept transformative intellectuals. In the research and scholarship of every critical pedagogue there is an important role for both scholarly peer-reviewed journal publication *and* writing aimed at diverse audiences: teachers, social workers, parents, students at a variety of grade levels, labor groups, women's groups, sexual groups, racial/ethnic groups, religious organizations, etc. Our imagination is the only limit to the audiences critical pedagogues might address. Indeed, we have important insights to pass along to diverse groups; consequently we need to seek out these audiences, publish for them, and convince university tenure and promotion committees of the significance of such work in our larger research and publishing agendas.

Critical pedagogues are public intellectuals, public activists, and as such we need to develop diverse languages to address divergent audiences. Many African Americans,

Latinos/as, indigenous peoples, and first-generation college students from all racial backgrounds know that the language they speak at the university is significantly different from the "dialect" they speak at home and in their communities. As a Southern Appalachian, I knew that the way I spoke with my three Aunt Effies back in Tennessee and Virginia was profoundly different from my presentation on critical postformal thinking at an academic conference. And when I screwed up and talked in too academic a language for my Aunt Effie Kincheloe Bean, she let me know it. "Think you're pretty smart, don't you, Mr. Professor," she would tell me in her best exaggerated East Tennessee mountain accent. I listened to her loving chiding carefully, trying to devise a better way to tell her about the topic at hand. Though she is long departed from this planet, I often write to her in some of my books and essays about critical pedagogy. Some folks see dead people; I write to them.

In a related context I analyze why critical pedagogy as a discourse doesn't speak to many different subcultural groups in divergent societies. When I attend and speak at critical pedagogical conferences around the world, I see far too few indigenous peoples, individuals of African descent, and Asians. In the North American context I am simply appalled by the small numbers of African Americans at critical pedagogical events. Indeed, one of the greatest failures of critical pedagogy at this juncture of its history involves the inability to engage people of African, Asian, and indigenous backgrounds in our tradition. I call for intense efforts in the coming years to bring more diversity into our ranks for two purposes: 1) Critical pedagogy has profound insights to pass along to all peoples; and 2) Critical pedagogy has much to learn from the often subjugated knowledges of African, African American, Asian, and indigenous peoples.

Indeed, a significant dimension of the future of critical pedagogy rests with the lessons to be learned from peoples around the world. Thankfully, critical pedagogy is supported and informed by numerous Latin and South American peoples. My fear, however, is that critical pedagogy has become too much of a North American (and often European) "thing," as White North American scholars appropriate a South American discourse. North Americans must be demanding in their efforts to make sure that Paulo Freire and his South/Latin American colleagues and progeny are viewed as the originators of this hallowed tradition. In the spirit of Paulo, a confident yet humble approach to our work—a critical humility—seems to serve us well. Critical pedagogy does not find its origins as a North American phenomenon, and if critical pedagogues cannot learn this simple lesson then they will have little positive impact on the world.

In addition, despite what proponents of different positions might argue, critical pedagogy is not simply for one interest group. Critical pedagogy serves both teachers and cultural workers who engage in social activism outside the boundaries of schools. Some of the most depressing moments I have spent engaged in critical pedagogy have occurred either when teachers view the classroom as the central if not only domain for critical pedagogical analysis and action or when cultural workers see schools as "lost places" where nothing matters because the institution is flawed. In these cases, I have actually seen cultural worker/social activists roll their eyes at one another when teachers reference classroom practice. My god, the activist labor that critical pedagogically informed cultural workers perform is profoundly important and has much to teach teachers—and teachers, of course, have much to teach such cultural workers.

Those academics who study the politics of knowledge, the macrodynamics of education, cultural pedagogies promoted in the twenty-first-century global marketplace, and many other ideological/educational phenomena have much to teach everyone. My point here is obvious: until we come to see the work of these different groups of critical pedagogues as synergistic rather than hierarchical, the achievements of the tradition will be acutely undermined. Qualitative hierarchies of importance segregating those who engage in critical pedagogy into status-laden groups will destroy our efforts to address power inequities and the human suffering such disparity causes. We are too smart to allow such egocentric status seeking to subvert our struggle for justice. If we're not able to overcome such pathology, then to hell with us—we don't deserve to survive.

Getting Started: The Origins of Critical Pedagogy and Its Uses in a Conflicted, Complex World

With these concerns in mind, let's briefly examine the origins of critical pedagogy. In the early twenty-first century it has become a cliché among many pedagogical scholars to describe education as a Janus-faced institution with its two faces looking toward opposite goals and outcomes: in one direction, a democratic, inclusive, socially sensitive objective concerned with multiple sources of knowledge and socioeconomic mobility for diverse students from marginalized backgrounds; and in the other, a standardized, exclusive, socially regulatory agenda that serves the interest of the dominant power and those students most closely aligned with the social and cultural markers associated with such power.

Thus, in the contemporary era educational scholars on faculties of education at colleges/universities and educators in elementary and secondary schools walk through a complex terrain of contradictions in their everyday professional pursuits, as educational researchers tend to find evidence of both progressive and regressive purposes in most educational institutions. As critical pedagogues observe such phenomena, they understand that the notion of "becoming a teacher" or a cultural worker concerned with social justice involves far more complex bodies of knowledge and conceptual insights than is sometimes found in teacher education and educational research programs, not to mention the knowledge that the mass media make available to the public.

Emerging from Paulo Freire's work in poverty-stricken northeastern Brazil in the 1960s, critical pedagogy amalgamated liberation theological ethics and the critical theory of the Frankfurt School in Germany with progressive impulses in education. Critical pedagogy gained an international audience with the 1967 publication of Freire's *Pedagogy of the Oppressed* and its English translation in 1970. By the mid-1970s several scholars in education and other disciplines adapted Freire's conception of critical pedagogy into a so-called first-world context. Over the next decade, critical pedagogy influenced pedagogical practice, teacher education, and sociopolitical and educational scholarship in South and North America. In the twenty-first century, the field is at a conceptual crossroads as researchers contemplate the nature of its movement to the next phase of its evolution. *Critical Pedagogy: Where Are We Now?* is intent on providing a series of speculations and tentative answers to questions concerning where we are now and where we go from here.

In my own work I have explored this "next phase" of critical pedagogy in relation to the issues raised at the beginning of this chapter and in recognition of the complexity of everyday life (Kincheloe, 2004). Attention to this complexity with the rigorous scholarship it demands—multiple forms of knowledge coming from around the globe as well as diverse research methodologies—forces proponents of critical pedagogy to ask revealing questions about the purposes of existing educational practices and their consequences. Such questions and the answers scholars provide will help shape the next phase of critical pedagogy. In this context we move to a new terrain of intellectually rigorous and highly practical cultural and educational work.

What is the relation between classroom practice and issues of justice? How do schools reflect or subvert democratic practices and the larger culture of democracy? How do schools operate to validate or challenge the power dynamics of race, class, gender, sexuality, religion, indigenous/aboriginal issues, physical ability-related concerns, etc? How do such processes play out in diverse classrooms located in differing social, cultural, and economic domains? How do the knowledges schools and other social institutions choose to transmit replicate political relationships in the larger society and affect the academic performance of students from dissimilar socioeconomic and cultural backgrounds? What roles do diverse media play in the ideological education of societies? What is the pedagogical role of popular culture? What are the hegemonic and counter-hegemonic dimensions of new technologies? How do we use critical methodologies and understandings to tap into the libidinal energy of individuals in a way that will produce joy and happiness as they pursue learning and transformative social action? The ability to provide well-informed and creative answers to such questions that lead to practical educational policy and practice is a key dimension of critical pedagogy.

As we look back from the perspective of the first decade of the twenty-first century to the innovative scholarly work on epistemology and research of the last several decades, one understanding becomes increasingly clear: producing knowledge about the world and understanding the cosmos are more complex than we originally thought. What we designate as facts is not as straightforward a process as it was presented to us. Critical pedagogues operating with this understanding of complex multilogicality or what many have called "the bricolage" (Kincheloe, 2001; Kincheloe and Berry, 2004; Kincheloe, 2005) know that what most people consider the natural social world is a conceptual landmine wired with assumptions and inherited meanings.

Critical researchers have learned that what is unproblematically deemed "a fact" has been shaped by a community of inquirers and sociopolitical forces. All of these researchers accept, often unconsciously, a particular set of theoretical assumptions. Engaging in knowledge work without a deep understanding of the tacit sociopolitical rules of the game is not a manifestation of rigor. Indeed, such a lack of knowledge profoundly undermines the effort to produce compelling and useful data about the world around us (Horn, 2004; Fischer, 1998). Great scholars in diverse historical and cultural settings have admonished individuals not to take fixed viewpoints and concepts as reality (Varela, 1999). Critical pedagogues as bricoleurs heed such a warning as they move into a zone of critical complexity.

Roymeico Carter (2004) extends this critical complex concept into the world of the visual. The complexity of researching the visual domain is often squashed by the formal methods of Cartesian aesthetics. Carter reminds us that the intricate layers of visual meaning must be studied from numerous perspectives as well as diverse cultural and epistemological traditions. But such diversity of perception lets the cat out of the bag; it relinquishes control of how we are to see the world. According to Ilya Prigogine, complexity demands that researchers give up the attempt to dominate and control the world. The social and physical worlds are so complex that they can only be understood like human beings themselves: not machine-like, but unpredictable, dependent upon context, and influenced by minute fluctuations (Capra, 1996). Thus, bricoleurs focus their attention on addressing the complexity of the lived world, understanding in the process that the knowledge they produce should not be viewed as a transhistorical body of truth. In this framework, knowledge produced by bricoleurs is provisional and "in process." Bricoleurs know that tensions will develop in social knowledge as the understandings and insights of individuals change and evolve (Blackler, 1995).

A critical researcher, for example, who returns to an ethnographic study only a few years later may find profound differences in what is reported by subjects. The categories and coding that worked three years ago may no longer be relevant. The most important social, psychological, and educational problems that confront us are untidy and complicated. As we wade through the swamp of everyday life, research methods that fail to provide multiple perspectives at macro-, meso-, and microlevels do not provide the insights that we need.

It is one thing to find out that schools, for example, do not provide many poor students a path to social mobility. It is quite another thing to take this macro finding and combine it with the mesodynamics of the ways particular schools and school leaders conceptualize the relationship between schooling and class mobility. It is also important that these findings be viewed in a context informed by everyday classroom and out-of-classroom interactions between teachers and students and students and their peers. Obviously, different research methodologies will be used to explore the differing questions emerging at the different levels. Once data from these diverse layers are combined we begin to discern a picture of the multiple dynamics of the relationship between socioeconomic class and education. Only a multidimensional, complex picture such as this can help us formulate informed and just strategies to address such issues.

Critical Complications: A Research and Pedagogical Agenda for a Globalized, Multilogical World

If critical pedagogical scholars/researchers refuse to move into the multileveled swamp of complexity or to integrate the diverse forms of data found at its different levels, they may find themselves asking pedestrian questions of profoundly complicated issues. Simple, unproblematic questions about the domain of schooling and socioeconomic class, for example, tend to be the least significant to the society at large. Positivistic standards of rigor as presently employed by many social, psychological, and educational researchers actually preclude the complex, multidimensional, multimethodological work necessary to producing meaningful and usable research data (Schon, 1995). Francisco Varela (1999) writes about "the situated embodiments of simple acts" (p. 8), maintaining that such complexity in everyday life undermines total reliance on computational methods where "knowledge is a manipulation of symbols by logic-like rules, an idea that finds its fullest expression in modern digital computers" (p. 7).

In the domain of cognitive science, Varela concludes, even the simplest acts—even those performed by insects—rest outside the understanding of the computational strategy. Varela's pronouncements tell critical bricoleurs not to throw out computational strategies but to understand what they can and cannot tell us and to carefully consider how we might use them in the bricoleur's pursuit of complexity in the social, political, psychological, and educational spheres. As we examine "where we are now" in critical pedagogy, we must understand these elements of complexity in order to become more rigorous scholar-researcher-educators and more effective agents of socially just political and educational change. We have no choice if we want to remain relevant in the emerging era. Hyperreality, with its bombardment of communicative messages and ideologically inscribed images, demands no less.

Even simple acts of cognition, social interaction, learning, and textual analysis are more complex than researchers first suspected. "Just give me the facts," is not as simple a command as it seemed to appear to Cartesian sensibilities. The situated nature of knowledge questions a variety of Cartesian assumptions. When we pick particular attributions of meaning about specific phenomena, we must consider a variety of factors. Such choices are inevitably political and ideological and have nothing to do with efforts to be objective. Even the decisions researchers make about what to study reflect these same political and ideological dynamics. In the highly ideologically charged first decade of the twenty-first century, do educational researchers study how to improve student test scores in the suburbs or the impact of racism on lower-socioeconomic-class African American students in urban schools? The problems and issues that are chosen by researchers are marked by subjective judgments about whose problems are deemed most important.

These interpretative decisions are always complex and influenced by a plethora of social, cultural, political, economic, psychological, discursive, and pedagogical dynamics. As a critical discourse, the bricolage always considers the normative dimension of what should be as well as what is. When Horkheimer and Adorno's concept of immanence (the examination of what is in relation to what should be) is added to the complex dynamics surrounding decision making and interpretation in the realm of research, critical pedagogues as bricoleurs move to yet a higher domain of complexity. Reflecting on the research process from a perspective shaped by these concerns, critical bricoleurs gain new insights into the ideological consequences of reductionism. For example, when rational inquiry is positioned in opposition to the emotional, affective, and value-laden dimensions of human activity, then it has removed itself as a means of gaining insight into the social, psychological, and educational domains. Life in these domains simply cannot be understood without careful attention to the emotional, affective, and value-laden aspects of human behavior (Williams, 1999; Reason and Bradbury, 2000). Indeed, a rational inquiry that devalues the role of irrationality will sink under the weight of its own gravitas.

Because of this damned complexity, advocates of a critical pedagogy understand that no simple, universally applicable answers can be provided to the questions of justice, power, and praxis that haunt us. Indeed, such questions have to be asked time and again by teachers and other educational professionals operating in different historical times and diverse pedagogical locales. Critical pedagogy understands that no educator who seeks to promote individual intellectual development, sociopolitical and economic justice, the production of practical transformative knowledge, and institutional academic rigor can escape the complex contextual specificity of these challenging questions. The pedagogical and research agenda of a complex critical pedagogy for the twenty-first century must address these realities as it constructs a plan to invigorate the teaching and study of such phenomena in the new phase of critical pedagogy that I am proposing for North America and around the world.

Proponents of a complex critical pedagogy appreciate the fact that all educational spaces are unique and politically contested. Constructed by history and challenged by a wide variety of interest groups, educational practice is an ambiguous phenomenon as it takes place in numerous settings, is molded by numerous and often invisible forces and structures, and can operate under the flag of democracy and justice in oppressive and totalitarian ways. Practitioners of critical pedagogy report that some teacher education students, educational leaders, parents, and members of the general public often have difficulty appreciating the fact that schooling can be hurtful to particular students from specific backgrounds in unique social, cultural, and economic settings—for example, indigenous and aboriginal students. Many individuals often have trouble empathizing with students harmed by such negative educational dynamics because schooling in their experience has played such a positive role in their own lives.

Thus, a complex critical pedagogy is a domain of research and practice that asks much from those who embrace it. Critical pedagogical teacher education and leadership, for example, involve more than learning pedagogical techniques and the knowledge required by the mandated curriculum. In addition to acquiring teaching methods, teachers and leaders steeped in critical pedagogy also understand the social, economic, psychological, and political dimensions of the schools, districts, and systems in which they operate. They also possess a wide range of knowledge about information systems in the larger culture that serve as pedagogical forces in the lives of students and other members of society: television, radio, popular music, movies, the Internet, podcasts, and youth subcultures; alternative bodies of knowledge produced by indigenous, marginalized, or low-status groups; the ways different forms of power operate to construct identities and empower and oppress particular groups; and the modus operandi of the ways sociocultural regulation operates.

Democracy is a fragile entity, advocates of critical pedagogy maintain, and embedded in educational policy and practice are the very issues that make or break it. Understanding these diverse dimensions and structures that shape schooling and the knowledge it conveys is necessary, critical pedagogues believe, to the very survival of democratic schooling—not to mention the continued existence of democracy itself. The analysis of the ways these complex forces evolve in a globalized, technological, electronic communications-based era marked by grand human migrations is central to the complex critical pedagogy proposed here.

The future of critical pedagogy involves addressing this complexity head on and making sure—as I maintained at the beginning of this chapter—that critical pedagogues listen carefully to marginalized groups from diverse corners of the planet. In such a context, a complex, humble critical pedagogy for a new era promotes research, analysis, and the use of subjugated, repressed, and indigenous knowledges in relation to the academy in general, teaching and learning, and epistemological and ontological understandings central to educational policy and practice. Indigenous knowledge has been and continues to be difficult to define. Always aware of the possibility of Western exploitation of particular forms of indigenous knowledge, this new phase of critical pedagogy views its usage with respect and reverence for its producers. For the millions of indigenous peoples of Africa, Latin America, Asia, Oceania, and North America, indigenous knowledge is an everyday way of making sense of the world, the self, and the relationship between them that rewards individuals who live in a given locality.

In this context indigenous knowledge reflects the dynamic way in which the residents of an area have come to understand themselves in relationship to their natural environment and how they organize their knowledge of flora and fauna, cultural beliefs, history, and teaching and learning to enhance their lives (Keith & Keith, 1993; Dei, 1995; Semali and Kincheloe, 1999; Dei and Kempf, 2006). Paulo Freire—among many other scholars—was committed to the potential transformative power of subjugated and indigenous knowledges and the ways that such information and its accompanying conceptual frameworks could be used to foster empowerment and justice in a variety of cultural contexts—for both indigenous peoples themselves and Western scholars who came to understand indigenous epistemologies and ontologies.

As Paulo Freire and Antonio Faundez (1989) wrote, indigenous knowledge is a rich social resource for any justice-related attempt to bring about social change. In this context, indigenous ways of knowing become a central resource for the work of academics, whether they be professors in the universities or teachers in elementary and secondary schools. Intellectuals, Freire and Faundez conclude, should "soak themselves in this knowledge . . .

assimilate the feelings, the sensitivity" (p. 46) of epistemologies that move in ways unimagined by many Western academic impulses. Thus, a central dimension of the new phase of critical pedagogy involves researching subjugated and indigenous knowledges, incorporating them into the development of the discipline of critical pedagogy, and using them to enhance education in general and indigenous/aboriginal education in particular in a multilogical, globalized world.

Critical Pedagogy and the Contemporary Challenge to Democracy

Critical theory—especially in the post-9/11 era of global political, economic, and military empire building—questions the assumption that societies such as the United States, Canada, Australia, New Zealand, and the nations in the European Union, for example, are unproblematically democratic and free. Over the twentieth century, especially after the early 1960s, individuals in these societies were acculturated to feel uncomfortable with equality and independence and more content with relations of social regulation and subordination. Given the social and technological changes of the last half of the century that led to new forms of information production and access, critical theorists argued that questions of self-direction and democratic egalitarianism should be reassessed. In this context critical researchers informed by the "post-discourses" (e.g., critical feminism, poststructuralism, post-colonialism, indigenous studies) came to understand that individuals' views of themselves and the world were even more influenced by social and historical forces than previously believed. Given the changing social and informational conditions of late twentieth-century and early twenty-first-century media-saturated Western culture, critical theorists have needed new ways of researching and analyzing the construction of identity and selfhood (Agger, 1992; Flossner & Otto, 1998; Leistyna, Woodrum, & Sherblom, 1996; Smith & Wexler, 1995; Sünker, 1998; Steinberg, 2001; Wesson & Weaver, 2001). Thus, one begins to understand the need for an evolving notion of criticality—a critical social theory—in light of these changing conditions.

In this context it is important to note that a social theory as used in this context is a map or a guide to the social sphere. A social theory should not determine how we see the world but should help us devise questions and strategies for exploring it. A critical social theory is concerned in particular with issues of power and justice and the ways that the economy, matters of race, class, and gender, ideologies, discourses, education, religion and other social institutions, and cultural dynamics interact to construct a social system (Beck-Gernsheim, Butler, & Puigvert, 2003; Flecha, Gomez, and Puigvert, 2003). Critical theory and critical pedagogy—in the spirit of an evolving criticality—is never static; it is always evolving, changing in light of new theoretical insights, fresh ideas from diverse cultures, and new problems, social circumstances, and educational contexts.

The list of concepts making up this description of an evolving critical theory/critical pedagogy indicates a criticality informed by a variety of discourses emerging after the work of the Frankfurt School of Social Theory in post-World War I Germany. Indeed, some of the theoretical discourses, while referring to themselves as critical, directly call into question some of the work of Frankfurt School founders Max Horkheimer, Theodor Adorno, and Herbert Marcuse. Thus, diverse theoretical traditions have informed our understanding of criticality and have demanded understanding of diverse forms of oppression including class, race, gender, sexual, cultural, religious, colonial and ability-related concerns. In this context critical theorists/critical pedagogues become detectives of new theoretical insights, perpetually searching for new and interconnected ways of understanding power and oppression and the ways they shape everyday life and human experience. They become sleuths on the trail of those ever-mutating forces that threaten power-sensitive forms of democracy around the world.

Thus, criticality and the knowledge production and pedagogy it supports are always evolving, always encountering new ways to engage dominant forms of power and to provide more evocative and compelling insights. It is in this context that a pervasive theme of this chapter and book emerges yet again: criticalists must engage with diverse peoples around the world and listen carefully to and humbly learn from them. Employing these diverse cultural knowledges, the forms of social change an evolving critical pedagogy supports position it in many places as an outsider, an awkward detective always interested in uncovering social structures, discourses, ideologies, and epistemologies that prop up both the status quo and a variety of forms of privilege.

In the epistemological domain White, male, class-elitist, heterosexist, imperial, and colonial privilege often operates by asserting the power to claim objectivity and neutrality. Indeed the owners of such privilege often own the "franchise" on reason, rationality, and truth. An evolving criticality possesses a variety of tools to expose such power politics. In this context it asserts that criticality is well served by drawing upon numerous discourses and including diverse groups of marginalized peoples and their allies in the nonhierarchical collection of critical analysts. Here rests the heart of critical multilogicality, with its feet firmly planted in an understanding of political and economic conditions and its ear attuned to new ways of seeing the world. Moving these ideas to the cognitive domain, I have worked over the last couple of decades to produce a new mode of thinking, an alternate rationality labeled "postformalism" (Kincheloe and Steinberg, 1993; Kincheloe, Steinberg, and Hinchey, 1999; Thomas and Kincheloe, 2006; Kincheloe, 2007).

Obviously, an evolving criticality does not promiscuously choose theories to add to the bricolage of critical theories/pedagogies. It is highly suspicious of theories that fail to understand the workings of power, that fail to critique the blinders of Eurocentrism, that cultivate an elitism of insiders and outsiders, that do not understand the complexities and complications of what is referred to as democratic action, and that fail to discern a global system of inequity supported by diverse forms of hegemony and violence. It is uninterested in any theory—no matter how fashionable—that does not directly address the needs of victims of oppression and the suffering they must endure.

Indeed, the very origins of criticality—the tradition that lays the groundwork for critical pedagogy and is concerned with power and its oppression of human beings and regu-

lation of the social order—are grounded on this concern with human suffering. Herbert
Marcuse, one of the founders of the Frankfurt School of Critical Theory, and Paulo Freire
were profoundly moved by the suffering they respectively witnessed in post-World War I
Germany and Brazil of the 1950s and 1960s. The brilliant and *critical* racial insights of W.E.B.
Du Bois, Ida B. Wells, Carter Woodson, Horace Mann Bond, and many others in the early
decades of the twentieth century were grounded on their understanding of the suffering of
their fellow African Americans. The insights these scholars produced constitute a powerful compendium of critical theoretical data—even though the scholars themselves did not
employ the term critical.

Though my own notion of a critical pedagogy is one that continues to develop and operates to sophisticate its understandings of the world and the educational act, this evolving
criticality in education should never lose sight of its central concern with human suffering. One does not have to go too far in this world to find people who are suffering: battered
women, indigenous peoples attempting to deal with Western efforts to destroy their cultures, working-class people unable to find jobs, victims of racism and ethnic bias, individuals subjected to religious persecution, dirt-poor colonized peoples in poor nations, children
with AIDS, men and women punished by homophobes, young women in developing
countries working for less than subsistence wages from North American-owned transnational companies—unfortunately, the list goes on and on.

In the North American context suffering is often well hidden, but a trip to inner cities,
specific rural areas, or indigenous reservations and reserves will reveal its existence. Outside
of the North America context we can go to almost any region of the world and see tragic
expressions of human misery. My articulation of critical pedagogy asserts that such suffering is a humanly constructed phenomenon and does not have to exist. Steps can be taken
in numerous domains—education in particular—to eradicate such suffering if the people
of the planet and their leaders have the collective will to do so. In recent years, however,
globalized political economic systems with their de-emphasis on progressive forms of education and social policy have exacerbated poverty and its attendant suffering. An evolving criticality develops new ways to deal with such developments and new modes of
education and political action to subvert their effects.

Critical Pedagogy in the Era with No Name:
The Intersection of the Macrosocial
with the Microindividual

If Clint Eastwood played "The Man with No Name," then we now live in an era with no
name. Most of us by now understand that we live in a *new* era—but even after several decades
of trying we still don't know what to call it. The postmodern condition? Hyperreality? Late
capitalism? Late modernity? The post-9/11 world? The age of empire? The globalized
world? The era of neocolonialism? Pax America? ad infinitum. Many will probably agree

that this new era demands a new form of education that deals with macroglobal changes and the recursive dimension of the sociopsychological construction of the individual. In an evolving criticality, critical pedagogues have to come to terms with this new complex and unnamed world, developing insights and modes of praxis in the process that help educators, parents, students, and individuals around the world understand the complicated relationship between the larger sociopolitical domain and the life of the individual. As I asserted at the beginning of this chapter, this is where open-access publishing, speaking, and writing become central to our larger critical project. In this context, critical pedagogy works to develop both in-school and larger cultural pedagogies, always keeping in mind the omnipresent relationship between the social and individual.

I believe that a successful critical pedagogy for the future must be deeply concerned with the relationship between the sociopolitical domain and the life of the individual. A compelling synthesis of these provinces is necessary to catalyzing critical social action, civic contribution, and successful teaching from elementary to graduate school. In order to begin a rigorous analysis of a macro-micro evolving criticality—a critical pedagogy concerned with the sociopolitical realm, the individual, and the relationship that connects them—an appreciation of its critical social and educational theoretical traditions, its culture and the forces that are changing it, and its identity and the increasingly complex ways in which it is being shaped is necessary. I believe such an analysis will be helpful in the first chapter of *Critical Pedagogy: Where Are We Now?* to situate our book in the larger critical literature and conceptually situate the chapters that follow.

The attempt to make sense of contemporary culture and identity formation is enhanced by an appreciation of the critical social theoretical tradition. Peter and I have published versions of the following points elsewhere (Kincheloe, 2004; Kincheloe and McLaren, 2005) in our attempts to introduce critical theory to a wide audience. The following is an abbreviated version of the central points of critical theory. Keep in mind that in the spirit of an evolving criticality the subsequent points are part of an elastic, ever-evolving conceptual matrix. It changes with every theoretical innovation, integration of new cultural knowledge, and shifting of the zeitgeist. The points that are deemed most important in one time period may have little in common with the important points of a new era.

1. *Critical enlightenment.* In this context critical theory analyzes competing power interests between groups and individuals within a society—identifying who gains and who loses in specific situations. Privileged groups, criticalists argue, often have an interest in supporting the status quo to protect their advantages; the dynamics of such efforts often become a central focus of critical research.

2. *Critical emancipation.* Those who seek emancipation attempt to gain the power to control their own lives in solidarity with a justice-oriented community. Here, critical research attempts to expose the forces that prevent individuals and groups from shaping the decisions that crucially affect their lives. In this way greater degrees of autonomy and human agency can be achieved. In the first decade of the twenty-

first century we are cautious in our use of the term "emancipation" because, as many critics have pointed out, no one is ever completely emancipated from the sociopolitical context that has produced him or her. Concurrently, many have used the term to signal the freedom an abstract individual gains by gaining access to Western reason—i.e., becoming reasonable. Our use of emancipation in an evolving criticality rejects any use of the term in this context.

3. *The rejection of economic determinism.* A caveat of a reconceptualized critical theory involves the insistence that the tradition does not accept the orthodox Marxist notion that "base" determines "superstructure"—meaning that economic factors dictate the nature of all other aspects of human existence. Critical theorists understand that in the twenty-first century there are multiple forms of power, racial, gender, and sexual axes of domination. In issuing this caveat, however, an evolving critical theory in no way attempts to argue that economic factors are unimportant in the shaping of everyday life.

4. *The critique of instrumental or technical rationality.* An evolving critical theory sees instrumental/technology rationality as one of the most oppressive features of contemporary society. Such a form of "hyperreason" involves an obsession with means in preference to ends. Critical theorists claim that instrumental/technical rationality is more interested in method and efficiency than in purpose. It delimits its questions to "how to" instead of "why should."

5. *The impact of desire.* An evolving critical theory appreciates poststructuralist psychoanalysis as an important resource in pursuing an emancipatory research project. In this context, critical researchers are empowered to dig more deeply into the complexity of the construction of the human psyche. Such a psychoanalysis helps critical researchers discern the unconscious processes that create resistance to progressive change and induce self-destructive behavior. A poststructural psychoanalysis, in its rejection of traditional psychoanalysis's tendency to view individuals as rational and autonomous beings, allows critical analysts new tools to rethink the interplay among the various axes of power, identity, libido, rationality, and emotion. In this configuration the psychic realm is no longer separated from the sociopolitical one; indeed, desire can be socially constructed and used by power-wielders for destructive and oppressive outcomes. On the other hand, critical theorists can help mobilize desire for progressive and emancipatory projects.

6. *The concept of immanence.* Critical theory is always concerned with what could be, what is immanent in various ways of thinking and perceiving. Thus, critical theory should always move beyond the contemplative realm to concrete social reform. In the spirit of Paulo Freire, our notion of an evolving critical theory possesses immanence as it imagines new ways to ease human suffering and produce psychological-well being. Critical immanence helps us get beyond egocentrism and ethnocentrism and work to build new forms of relationships with diverse peoples.

7. *A reconceptualized critical theory of power: hegemony.* Our conception of a reconcep-

tualized critical theory is intensely concerned with the need to understand the various and complex ways that power operates to dominate and shape consciousness. Power, critical theorists have learned, is an extremely ambiguous topic that demands detailed study and analysis. A consensus seems to be emerging among criticalists that power is a basic constituent of human existence that works to shape both the oppressive and productive nature of the human tradition. In the context of oppressive power and its ability to produce inequalities and human suffering, Antonio Gramsci's notion of hegemony is central to critical research. Gramsci understood that dominant power in the twentieth century was not always exercised simply by physical force but also through social psychological attempts to win people's consent to domination through cultural institutions such as the media, the schools, the family, and the church. Gramscian hegemony recognizes that the winning of popular consent is a very complex process and must be researched carefully on a case-by-case basis.

8. *A reconceptualized critical theory of power: ideology.* Critical theorists understand that the formation of hegemony cannot be separated from the production of ideology. If hegemony is the larger effort of the powerful to win the consent of their "subordinates," then ideological hegemony involves the cultural forms, the meanings, the rituals, and the representations that produce consent to both the status quo and to individuals' particular places within it. Ideology vis-à-vis hegemony moves critical inquirers beyond explanations of domination that have used terms such as propaganda to describe the way media, political, educational, and other sociocultural productions coercively manipulate citizens to adopt oppressive meanings.

9. *A reconceptualized critical theory of power: Linguistic/discursive power.* Critical theorists have come to understand that language is not a mirror of society. It is an unstable social practice whose meaning shifts, depending upon the context in which it is used. Contrary to previous understandings, criticalists appreciate the fact that language is not a neutral and objective conduit for description of the "real world." Rather, from a critical perspective, linguistic descriptions are not simply about the world but serve to construct it. With these linguistic notions in mind, criticalists begin to study the way language in the form of discourses serves as a form of regulation and domination.

10. *Focusing on the relationships among culture, power, and domination.* In the last decades of the twentieth century, culture took on a new importance in the critical effort to understand power and domination. Critical theorists have argued that culture has to be viewed as a domain of struggle where the production and transmission of knowledge is always a contested process. Dominant and subordinate cultures deploy differing systems of meaning based on the forms of knowledge produced in their cultural domain. Popular culture, with its television, movies, video games, computers, music, dance, and other productions, plays an increasingly important role in critical research on power and domination. Cultural studies, of course, occu-

pies an ever-expanding role in this context, as it examines not only popular culture but the tacit rules that guide cultural production.

11. *The centrality of interpretation: Critical hermeneutics*. One of the most important aspects of a critical theory-informed education and scholarship involves the often-neglected domain of interpretation. The critical hermeneutic tradition holds that in knowledge work there is only interpretation, no matter how vociferously many analysts may argue that the facts speak for themselves. The hermeneutic act of interpretation, in its most elemental articulation, involves making sense of what has been observed in a way that communicates understanding. Not only is all research merely an act of interpretation, but (hermeneutics contends) perception itself is an act of interpretation. Thus the quest for understanding is a fundamental feature of human existence, as encounter with the unfamiliar always demands the attempt to make meaning, to make sense.

12. *The role of cultural pedagogy in critical theory*. Cultural production can often be thought of as a form of education, as it generates knowledge, shapes values, and constructs identity. From the perspective of a book on critical pedagogy, such a framing can help critical teachers and students make sense of the world of domination and oppression as they work to bring about a more just, democratic, and egalitarian society. In recent years this educational dynamic has been referred to as cultural pedagogy. "Pedagogy" is a useful term that has traditionally been used to refer only to teaching and schooling. By using the term "cultural pedagogy," criticalists are specifically referring to the ways dominant cultural agents produce particular hegemonic ways of seeing. In our critical interpretive context, the notion of cultural pedagogy asserts that the new "educators" in the electronically wired contemporary era are those who possess the financial resources to use mass media. This is very important in the context of critical pedagogy, as teachers in the contemporary era must understand not only the education that takes place in the classroom but also that which takes place in popular culture.

Informed by these points, we are better able to conceptualize a critical pedagogy that cultivates a rigorous, intellectual ability to acquire, analyze, and produce both self-knowledge and social knowledge. Grounded by such knowledge and scholarly facility, individuals would be equipped to participate in the democratic process as committed and informed citizens. A basic assumption in this civic context involves the belief that, in terms of a democratic social education, Western public life and public education have failed. Corporations, transnational organizations, and other power-wielders have gained increasing control over the production and flow of information. Here, public consciousness is aligned in a complex and never completely successful process with the interests of power.

One of the most important goals of public life over the last few decades has been the cultivation of more and more social obedience and less democracy. The effort to win the consent of the public (hegemony), via appeals to both logic and affect, for privatization projects that may not be in the public's best interests has been frighteningly successful. In the same context, and driven by many of the same forces of power, public schooling has failed to promote a rigorous, democratic social education. Operating in the shadow of Frankfurt School critical social theorist Theodor Adorno, we reference his notion of "half-education" in which he described the way mainstream education perpetuates students' alienation from knowledge of the social and the self. In this process, the possibility of agency, of self-direction, is lost in a sea of social confusion (Sünker, 1994). To confront this alienation, social analysts must provide specific examples of formal and informal educational programs that promote a progressive education that fights alienation. Understanding the affective dimensions of these programs, educators analyze why students and other individuals are emotionally invested in specific programs, why energy is produced and absorbed by participants, and why the disposition to imagine and create new projects is cultivated in some programs and not in others.

Schools as Venues for Critical Democracy: The Triumph of Standardization and Pseudo-democracy

In the contemporary Age of Empire—or whatever we may call it—Western schools have not been concerned with educating democratic citizens. Indeed, schools have not been particularly concerned with any positive public role in the larger society. The traditional public role of pedagogy has been undermined by a private corporate view of the role of education. In addition to their role as supplier of regulated labor to the economy, schools in this privatized view have come to be seen as commodities, subject to the dictates of the free market. In this milieu, students are transformed from citizens into consumers, capable of being bought and sold. The logic of this right-wing social reeducation involves the replacement of government service agencies with private corporate services, the redistribution of wealth from the poor to the wealthy, and the construction of a private market system that promotes the values of isolated individualism, self-help, corporate management, and consumerism in lieu of public ethics and economic democracy. Thus, the social curriculum being taught in twenty-first-century Western schools often involves a sanctification of the private sphere in a way that helps consolidate the power of corporations and the interests of the empire. In this context, the freedom of the corporation to redefine social and educational life in ways that serve its financial interests is expanded.

This conservative reeducation project with its corporatized politics has been difficult for critical pedagogy to counter because it has been adeptly couched in the language of public improvement and democratic virtue. The public sphere has failed, the apostles of privatization proclaim. The private market is a much more effective mechanism in the effort to achieve socioeconomic improvement. Since market forces govern the world, students, citizens, and schooling itself must learn to adapt to this reality. A key element of this conservative social education involves this adaptation, the attempt to promote a market philosophy. Corporations now sponsor schools or enter into school-business partnerships. Upon analysis, one begins to perceive a pattern in the lessons taught to students in the corporate curriculum of privatized schooling. Imperial education is grounded on a set of free-market goals. Schools are expected to graduate students who will help corporations: 1) increase worker output for the same wages; 2) reduce labor turnover; 3) decrease conflict between management and workers; 4) convince citizens that labor and management share the same goals; and 5) create a workforce loyal to the corporation and the goals of the empire. Unfortunately, critical pedagogy must enter the conversation about the purposes of schools with these realities in mind.

This political process of privatization grounds a well-hidden ideological education embedded in the information environment of twenty-first-century Western societies (Sünker, 1994). In these societies, such an education occurs both in and outside of schools in a variety of social and cultural venues. Thus, the imperial ideological education takes into account the changing social conditions of an electronically mediated society, especially the new conditions under which information is produced. In this context, an imaginative critical pedagogy must understand that contemporary education and knowledge production emerge at the intersection of the political economy and the culture. Understanding these dynamics, an important aspect of a transformative critical pedagogy, is its analytic project, its mapping of the ways political meanings are made in both schools and sociocultural locales. Here advocates of critical pedagogy initiate the important task of interpreting how domination takes place on the contemporary political economic, informational landscape. In an interpretive sense, an evolving critical pedagogy becomes a holographic (a dynamic where the whole is contained in all of its parts) hermeneutics that analyzes the ways oppressive ideologies produced by sociopolitical structures (the whole) embed themselves in the individual (the part). What is the relationship between macro-power and the subjectivity of individual human beings?

Understanding the Sociopolitical Construction of the Individual in Contemporary Education

This intersection of the social and the individual—the macro and the micro—is a central dimension in an evolving critical pedagogy. Indeed, as critical pedagogical analysis reintegrates the political, the economic, and the cultural on the new historical plane of the globalized, imperial, and "recovered" society of the twenty-first century, we work to rethink and reassert the importance of subjectivity (pertaining to the domain of personhood, consciousness) in this context. In many ways, such a move is controversial in the critical tradition, as numerous social analysts criticize—many times for good reason—the contemporary concern with individualism, self-actualization, and identity politics. Understanding the problems inherent within these often liberal dynamics, I still believe that there are emancipatory possibilities embedded within this emphasis on self-development. Drawing upon the work of Philip Wexler (1997) and my own work in developing a critical ontology (Kincheloe, 2003), a key feature of an evolving criticality involves the effort to extract the transformative elements in the education of the individual in the Age of Empire.

Since ideological education takes place in a variety of domains, study is demanded of not only the social (macro-) and individual (micro-) level but the institutional (meso-) one as well. In this integrative approach, the interactions of these three levels in the process of ideological education, the ways they operate in the construction of the social and individual, are significant. In such analysis, these multilevel concerns induce educators to avoid one-sided approaches of any variety. For example, I am concerned with not only the social construction of the individual's knowledge but also with the individual's responsibility for his or her actions. This attention to individual volition is often missing from some articulations of critical education. This notion of individual volition must be carefully reconsidered in light of liberal celebrations of individual freedom and deterministic laments of a totalized domination. Individuals frequently defeat the power of capital, White supremacy, homophobia, and patriarchy; at the same time, however, the structures of oppression too often induce individuals to acquiesce to dominant power's ways of viewing the world.

There is nothing simplistic about ideological education. How does one get across an understanding of the complementarity of the self-directed (autonomous) and the social individual? Such a complementarity refuses the collapse of the social and the collapse of the individual; instead, it seeks a third way. This third-way critical pedagogy embraces the complexity of the topic rather than avoiding it. It addresses head-on the contradictions inherent in the interaction of autonomy and belonging. The essence of this notion of the ideological education of selfhood involves the nature of the relationship between independence and interaction. The sociability of the individual within this complex relationship involves much more than just understanding the social context. While an appreciation of context is necessary, this articulation of ideological education involves the development of individual human senses. In this context, Philip Wexler's concept of "revitalization," emanating from the concern with "enlivenment" in contemporary society, is added to the critical theoretical mix. An evolving critical pedagogy takes Wexler's revitalization seriously, analyzing its problems and potentialities in relation to our larger concerns with equity and justice. The possibilities for social change and self-transformation offered by revitalization are compelling in this context.

The Ideological Construction of Subjectivity: Three "Takes"

The reconceptualized notion of the intersection of the social and the individual offered here can be used by critical teachers. Informed by the critical theoretical tradition as articulated by German social analyst Heinz Sünker (1994, 1998), the reconstruction of individual identity as developed by Philip Wexler (1997, 2000) and critical ontology (Kincheloe, 2003), and my own concerns with cultural pedagogy, a new concept of critical pedagogy for a hyperreal Age of Empire emerges.

Tradition

Heinz Sünker (1994, 1998) maintains that education is one social practice connected to and mediated by other social practices; in this context, he asks what is "good" in a good upbringing of youth. Utilizing theorists from both the Frankfurt School as well as German critical educational theorists Heinz-Joachim Hadorn and Georg Theunissen, a critical canon of ideological education is constructed. This body of work takes seriously one's contribution to the good life as a member of society, a contribution based on an awareness of the nature of the social construction of both consciousness and the social fabric. Such a canon understands the importance of intersubjectivity (relations of various individuals, interpersonal interaction) in the construction of subjectivity. In this context, historical educational efforts to act on such understandings are analyzed. Questions are asked about the reasons for their failures and successes and their relevance for contemporary practice. To better answer these questions, Sünker (1994) introduces Hadorn's articulation of *Bildung*, focusing on its concern with emancipation, maturity, and self-determination.

The tradition of *Bildung* is especially important to ideological education in its interest in the production of subjectivity in the context of intersubjective relations. Sünker advocates the relevance of *Bildung* to contemporary criticality by emphasizing two dimensions: 1) the mediating processes between the individual and society; and 2) the processes involved with the construction of the subjectivity of the individual. In this way, *Bildung* transcends hegemonic education's effort to normalize the individual so as to adjust him or her to the existing social order. Rejecting bourgeois liberalism's effort to form the individual without referencing extant social conditions, *Bildung* is interested in individual development in the context of relational consciousness and the development of social competencies. In this context, *Bildung* mediates materialist (political economic) understandings of the world and concerns with everyday life, connecting the macro to the micro in the process. According to the concept of *Bildung*, learning is conceived of as an activity taking place as part of a larger democratic struggle, with one eye on the cultivation of the intellect and the other on democracy.

With our critical canon of ideological education firmly grounded on a knowledge of *Bildung*, we move to other traditions for insights into our conception. As previously mentioned, our multidimensional model of critical education is also informed by Philip Wexler's efforts to reclaim ancient knowledges abandoned since the European Enlightenment and the birth of Cartesianism in the seventeenth and eighteenth centuries. If the modern era is ending (or at least changing), the problems we are called on to solve are mutating as well. As these social/cultural/political changes have occurred, Wexler points out the way religion has returned to the forefront of social practice and cultural consciousness. Moving in different directions simultaneously, religion moves backward, before modernity, and forward, past imperial hyperreality, to provide differing grounds for ways of seeing and acting. Wexler warns progressives and critical theorists not to reject such religious insights in a materialist knee-jerk presumption of religion as merely a tool of dominant ideology. Through the theological window, social educators can explore premodern modes of sacralization and mystical insights. Carefully avoiding commodified and distorted "New Age" articulations of these traditions, Wexler views them through the lenses of an exacting and rigorous critical sociological tradition. In his hands, new applications for such knowledge emerge.

Picking up on Wexler's theoretical move, I attempt to contribute to the canon of a transformative ideological education by bringing previously referenced subjugated and indigenous knowledges to the pedagogical table. Derived from dangerous memories of history that have been suppressed and information that has been disqualified by social and academic gatekeepers, subjugated and indigenous knowledges play an important role in a critical pedagogy concerned with the way dominant power inculcates ideology in the contemporary era. Through the conscious cultivation of these "low-ranking" knowledges, alternative democratic and emancipatory visions of society, politics, cognition, and social education are possible. The subjugated knowledge of Africans, indigenous peoples from around the world, women in diverse cultural contexts, working-class people, and many other groups have contested the dominant culture's view of reality. At the very least, such subjugated knowledges inform students operating within mainstream schools and society that there are multiple perspectives on all issues. A critical pedagogy that includes subjugated ways of seeing teaches a lesson on the complexities of knowledge production and how this process shapes our view of ourselves and the world around us.

Individuals from dominant social formations have rarely understood (or cared to understand) how they look to marginalized others. As a result, women often make sense of men's view of women better than men understand women's view of men; individuals from Africa, or with African heritages, understand the motivations of White people better than the reverse; and low-status workers figure out how they are seen by their managers more clearly than the managers understand how they appear to workers. Obviously, such insights provide critical pedagogues and their students with a very different view of the world and the processes that shape it. Critical educators who employ such subjugated viewpoints become transformative agents who alert the community to its hidden features, its submerged memories, and in the process help specific individuals to name their oppression or possibly understand their complicity in oppression.

In this context, transformative critical educators search out specific forms of subjugated insights, such as indigenous knowledges. Indigenous knowledges are special forms of subjugated knowledges that are local, life-experience-based, and not produced by Western science. Such knowledges are transmitted over time by individuals from a particular geographical or cultural locality. Only now, in the twenty-first century, are European peoples just starting to appreciate the value of indigenous knowledges about health, medicine, agriculture, philosophy, spirituality, ecology, and education. Traditionally, these are the very types of knowledges Western ideological education have tried to discredit and eradicate. A transformative critical education works hard to save such knowledges, which are, unfortunately, disappearing from the face of the earth. Thankfully, many individuals from indigenous backgrounds and their allies are working to reverse this trend.

Culture

This section focuses on the expanding role of the cultural realm in the domain of contemporary ideological education. If a new era has dawned, then critical educators must search for the places where new ways of ideological education are taking place. The emergence of a new role, an expanded political and educational function for the cultural domain is a cardinal feature of the new social condition. The contemporary era confronts critical pedagogy with new contradictions and new ways of thwarting emancipation. In this new era, cultural capital has reorganized itself in ways that make it more flexible, innovative, and powerful. New technological and organizational developments have allowed capital greater access to both the world at large and human consciousness in particular. Reorganized transnational capital has embraced an aesthetic that celebrates the commodification of difference, ephemerality, spectacle, and fashion. In this observation, we uncover the central concern of the ideologically reorganized cultural realm: this new flexible aesthetic of capital gains its hegemonic force from its ability to employ the cultural realm for ideological indoctrination. Thus, the cultural domain emerges as a central political venue, a place where ideological consciousness is constructed, a new locale for ideological education.

Thus, in this context contemporary critical educators learn an invaluable lesson: everyday life takes place on a new ideological template—a semiotic matrix shaped in part by corporate-produced images. A new ideological education is produced by capital that is designed to regulate the population, as affectively charged consumers operating in a privatized domain lose consciousness of what used to be called the public sphere. This privatized domain is both globalized and decentralized/localized at the same time, distorting traditional concepts of space and time. The past is commodified and politicized, turning public memory into Disney's "Frontierland"—a powerful ideological educational venue. In this context, time is rearticulated and everyday life becomes an eternal present. Without critical intervention, the public space deteriorates and critical consciousness is erased. The disorientation that the informational overload of the new cultural condition induces moves individuals to seek more expert help, more therapeutic involvement in their everyday affairs. In the HBO series *The Sopranos*, for example, Tony, the Mafioso leader, is so distraught and confused by changing cultural conditions that he seeks psychological therapy and is prescribed Prozac for his depression. Even those who pride themselves on being self-sufficient outlaws cannot escape the effects of cultural disequilibrium. Working in the realm of information control and the production of pleasure, capital embeds positive images of itself at the deepest levels of our subconscious. Many come to associate the "good things in life" and happiness with the privatized realm of consumption. As powerful as crime boss Tony Soprano may be, for example, he cannot get his own son's attention while the boy (A.J.) plays his Nintendo video game.

Pleasure is a powerful social educator, and the pleasure produced by capital teaches a very conservative political lesson: since corporations produce pleasure, we should align our interests with them. In this way our "affect" is organized in the service of capital: lower corporate taxes, better business climates, equation of the corporate bottom line with social well-being, larger executive salaries, lower labor costs, fewer environmental regulations, and support for imperial wars, to name just a few. Hegemony in this new context operates where affect and politics intersect: the cultural realm. The revolutionary feature of this repressive, capital-driven ideological education is that culture shapes the political. Critical pedagogues have sometimes failed to appreciate this circumstance, not to mention its dramatic impact on the shaping of political consciousness and subjectivity.

Thus, transformative critical educators must understand the new affective dynamics at work in the production of selfhood. When we speak of the cultural realm, of course, a central feature of this domain involves popular culture and its relationship to power. Popular culture involves television, movies, video games, music, Internet, instant messaging, iPods, shopping malls, theme parks, etc. These are the sites of a contemporary cultural pedagogy of commodification that meets people where they exist in their affective fields. As it provides fun, pleasure, good feelings, passion, and emotion, this capital-inscribed ideological education connects ideology to these affective dynamics. In contemporary society, ideologies are only effective to the degree that they can be articulated along the affective plane. Affect is complex in that both pleasure and displeasure are affective responses. One's affective dislike of hip-hop, for example, can be inscribed ideologically with particular meanings about youth with African heritages around the world. Though complex, the power produced and deployed along this affective plane is profound in its ability to shape subjectivity and ways of seeing the world.

Our critical vision of a transformative education, an evolving critical pedagogy recognizes these contemporary politicocultural dynamics and analyzes their consequences at both the macro- and microlevels. One of the most important effects of this corporate colonization of affect has involved, of course, the phenomenon of depoliticization. At the heart of this phenomenon exists a paradoxical reality: while many Westerners have invested affectively in the emerging privatization of the social order, they do not rationally buy into the political-economic policies of conservatism. In this bizarre context, individuals remain politically uncommitted and civically inactive. Except for a significant minority of citizens on the Right, individuals have removed themselves from the political realm. I don't want to discount the importance of struggles such as janitors' fight for economic justice, protests against the World Trade Organization, and the brief outpouring of antiwar sentiment before the U.S. invasion and occupation of Iraq, but these actions are still the exceptions. In addition, the depoliticization process has produced a staggering illiteracy around political language and concepts, especially among the young. This ideological dynamic is so important that critical educators simply cannot do their jobs if they don't understand it.

In the electronic mediated culture of the twenty-first century, youth are no longer shielded from the esoteric knowledge of adulthood. Young people, in a sense, know too much to retain the idealism traditionally associated with this phase of life. In their knowledge of the world, many young people have become jaded to the point that they know of nothing worthy of their faith outside the intrinsic value of pleasure and affect in and of themselves. In their unshockability, many young people (and many adults as well) become emotional only about emotion—certainly not about some complex political issue. In such a culture-driven context, political discourse is reduced to "gut-level" emotion, to affective investments directly tied to self-interest. Politics becomes successful only when it is represented as "not politics." Questions of racial justice become important only when many White citizens perceive that Blacks and government leaders, via affirmative action, are taking their jobs away. Issues of social policy and public morality are irrelevant in this context: "Non-Whites, aided by big government, are stealing 'our' jobs." Rational political debate is irrelevant; affirmative action is an affective issue. Effective television campaign advertisements do not make a rational case for ending affirmative action; they depict a Black hand taking a job application away from a working-class White hand. Professional political consultants chant their mantras: "Keep it on the affective plane, stupid." A transformative ideological education in this media-saturated context can never be the same.

Identity

After having established a critical canon for a transformative ideological education and explored the changing cultural conditions of a twenty-first-century electronic, globalized society, attention needs to be focused on questions of identity and the production of the individual. In this context, Philip Wexler's (1997, 2000) argument catalyzes our notion of an evolving criticality in an age of dominant power's highly successful ideological education. The affect-centeredness of electronically mediated reality, Wexler posits, contains within it a decentered social movement that offers possibilities for emancipatory social education.

There is, he contends, an alternative rationality that often operates affectively to revitalize those caught in the commodified information environment of the present—a revitalization ignored by critical pedagogy. Just as affective measures can be used by power to hegemonize individuals and social groups, they can also be deployed by individuals to make certain things matter in ways that assert their self-direction and group solidarity by using the positive productive ability of power. From this conceptual foundation, Wexler moves to take critical advantage of what is available on the contemporary cultural landscape. If the self is the locus of historical change in the twenty-first century, then an evolving critical pedagogy must seize the opportunity to produce meaningful selves.

Aware of the politicocultural dimensions previously described, critical educators study the various ways individuals protect their identities from the power flows of capital. In such defensive actions, individuals not only shield themselves from the social earthquakes shaking the cultural terrain on which they live, but also forge new forms of collective alliances. Examples of such actions can be found on the Internet, as individuals morph their identities and connect with a wide range of similar web surfers. In such virtual lives, traditional boundaries of self are blurred in the interactions of dematerialized beings. In the electronic informational cosmos, Wexler's recognition of a retreat to a defensive inner world becomes an important understanding for the critical educator.

The revolution of social being described by Wexler is grounded on the possibilities offered by such an inward turn and the effort to reshape consciousness that accompanies it. At this important point there is a convergence of Sünker's *Bildung*-based assertion that consciousness is the central element of the educational process, new cultural technologies of consciousness construction, and Wexler's analysis of the consequences of the opportunities provided by the "inner turn." At this intersection, the new ideological education finds its purpose and the possibility for the construction of a new critical ontology—a transformative, self-aware way of *being* human. Central to this synthetic dynamic is Wexler's understanding of the potentialities of alternate rationalities and enlivenment in the emancipatory reconstruction of consciousness and identity.

Picking up on Wexler's theoretical move, I attempt to contribute to the canon of a transformative ideological education in a larger critical pedagogical context by bringing critical ontology to the recipe. In this context, critical educators engage in the excitement of attaining new levels of consciousness and "ways of being." In a critical ontology, individuals who gain such an awareness understand how and why their political opinions, religious beliefs, gender roles, racial positions, or sexual orientations have been shaped by dominant perspectives. They understand the nature and complexity of the ways dominant power works to construct subjectivity/consciousness via education, the media, and other cultural sites.

A critical ontological vision helps us in the effort to gain new understandings and insights as to who we can become. Such a vision helps us move beyond our present state of being—our ontological selves—as we discern the forces that have made us that way. The line between knowledge production and being is blurred, as the epistemological and the ontological converge around questions of identity and the social construction of selfhood. As we employ the ontological vision we ask questions about ethics, morality, politics, emotion, and gut feelings, seeking not precise steps to reshape our subjectivity but a framework of principles with which we can negotiate. Employing the insights of ontology, we explore our *being in the world*. Thus, we join the quest for new, expanded, and more just and interconnected ways of being human.

A key dimension of a critical ontology involves freeing ourselves from the machine metaphors of Cartesianism. Such an ontological stance recognizes the reductionism of viewing the universe as a well-oiled machine and the human mind as a computer. Such "ways of being" subvert an appreciation of the amazing life force that inhabits both the universe and human beings. This machine cosmology has positioned human beings as living in a dead world, a lifeless universe. Ontologically, this Cartesianism has separated individuals from their inanimate surroundings, undermining any organic interconnection of the person to the cosmos. The life-giving complexity of the inseparability of human and world has been lost and social/cultural/pedagogical/psychological studies of people abstracted—removed from context. Such a removal has exerted disastrous ontological effects. Human beings, in a sense, lost their belongingness to both the world and to other people around them.

The importance of indigenous (Semali and Kincheloe, 1999) and other subjugated knowledges reemerges in this ontological context. With the birth of modernity and the scientific revolution, many premodern, indigenous ontologies were lost, ridiculed by Europeans as primitive. While there is great diversity among premodern worldviews and ways of being, there do seem to be some discernible patterns that distinguish them from modernist perspectives. In addition to developing systems of meaning and being that were connected to cosmological perspectives on the nature of creation, most premodern viewpoints saw nature and the world at large as living systems. Western, Christian observers condescendingly labeled such perspectives as pantheism or nature worship and positioned them as an enemy of monotheism. Not understanding the subtlety and nuance of such indigenous views of the world, Europeans subverted the sense of belonging that accompanied these enchanted views of nature. European Christomodernism transformed the individual from a connected participant in the drama of nature to a detached, objective, depersonalized observer.

The Western modernist individual emerged from the process, alienated and disenchanted. As Edmund O'Sullivan (1999) puts it, Cartesianism tore apart "the relationship between the microcosmos and the macrocosmos" (p. 18). Such a fragmentation resulted in the loss of cosmological significance and the beginning of a snowballing pattern of ontological imbalance. A critical ontology involves the process of reconnecting human beings on a variety of levels and in numerous ways to a living social and physical web of reality, to a living cosmos. Critical pedagogues with a critical ontological vision help students connect to the civic web of the political domain, the biotic web of the natural world, the social web of human life, and the epistemological web of knowledge production. In this manner, we all move to the realm of critical ontology where new ways of being and new ways of *being connected* reshape all people. In a critical ideological education, critical ontology sets the stage for alternative identities in a Western world with truncated possibilities for selfhood.

Here we can see the merger of Wexler's ideas and critical ontology. Grounded on his understanding of these ontological issues, Wexler contends that an intuitive disenchantment with this Cartesian fragmentation and its severing of the self-environment relationship are fueling a diffuse social revaluation. He employs the term, revitalization, for this mass, decentered movement taking place throughout Western societies. It constitutes an attempt, he contends, to resacralize our culture and our "selves." Such an effort exposes the impact of Eurocentrism and Cartesianism on what human beings (or our identities) have become, as, at the same time, it produces an ontological "change from within." Understanding the problems with Cartesianism's lack of self-awareness or concern with consciousness and interconnectedness, Wexler's resacralization picks up on wisdom traditions, both premodern and contemporary, to lay the foundation for profound ontological change. In the emerging ontology the Cartesian bifurcation of the mind and body is repaired, and new relationships with the body, mind, and spirit are pursued. In the transcendence of modernist notions of bodily ego-greed, a new understanding of the body's role in meaning making and *human being* is attained. A new world of identity formation is constructed.

Picking up on these insights, a critical ontology positions the body in relation to the complexity of cognition and the process of life itself. The body is a corporeal reflection of the evolutionary concept of *autopoiesis*, self-organizing or self-making of life (Varela, 1999). Autopoiesis involves the production of a pattern-of-life organization. Cognition in this ontological context involves the process of self-production. Thus life itself, the nature of being, is a cognitive activity that involves establishing patterns of living, patterns that become the life force through self-organization. If life is self-organized, then there are profound onto-logical, cognitive, ideological, and pedagogical implications. By recognizing new patterns and developing new processes, humans exercise much more input into their own evolu-tion than previously imagined. In such a context human agency and possibility are enhanced—we *can* overcome the neofascist elements of contemporary Western ideologi-cal oppression.

With these ideas and this hope in mind, it is important to note that Wexler maintains that one aspect of the electronic informational culture of the contemporary era involves the emergence of a new concern with the worldview and methods of classical mysticism. Even though this mediated culture has often served to shatter identities, Wexler identi-fies a new power in people's minds. Moving past the Cartesian Enlightenment, the new con-sciousness of social being emerges around a resacralization of cultural codes, the globalizing synthesis of cultural expressions that exposes the ethnocentrism of European science and epistemology, and a new historicism that reengages the premodern, the ancient, and the archaic. Revitalization of the self and the new identities it encourages takes shape in this synthetic context. Directly responding to the fragmenting effects of informational hyper-culture, revitalization uses imaginative power to protect the self from threats posed by infor-mationalism in hyperreality. Fueled by these recognitions and an understanding of the traditions of critical theory and cultural studies, Wexler conceptualizes the synergy between a resacralized self-realization and a critical education.

The emancipatory power of this synergy hinges on the articulation of these concep-tual intersections and the consciousness, agency, and praxis that emerge therein. Wexler understands that self-realization, in both its bodily and psychic expression, must transcend its roots in narcissism and plant itself firmly in the transcendent or the cosmological to be of benefit to what I call an evolving critical pedagogy. Employed at the sacred level, self-realization, à la revitalization, provides a compelling strategic grounding in the struggle against the alienation of commodification, rationalization, and ideological indoctrination. As it embraces desire and vitality in everyday life and discerns how to use them in an eman-cipatory rather than a manipulative way, self-realization reexamines the relationship between self and environment. A transformative ideological education takes advantage of this conceptual opening, drawing upon the vitality of this new individualism and connect-ing it to Sünker's canon and my own cultural concerns. Here self engages other in a strong union that constructs a vision for a reinvigorated, ever-evolving critical practice.

Key Dimensions of the Critical Synthesis

In a contemporary culture that finds it increasingly difficult to mobilize itself for political action, advocates of critical pedagogy must take place on uncharted social and cultural ter-ritory. In the complexity and high-speed change of hyperreality, efforts to address alienation, oppression, and ideological indoctrination seem somehow outside the spirit of the times. Our synthesis of these diverse domains must be not only conceptually compelling but also sufficiently contextually aware to operate on the bizarre sociocultural landscape that confronts us in the twenty-first century. The central features of our new evolving critical pedagogical synthesis of the critical theoretical tradition, an understanding of the power of dominant cultural pedagogies, and the importance of identity construction include:

1. *The development of a socioindividual imagination.* At the basis of our multilevel evolving critical pedagogy rests the ability to imagine new forms of self-realization and social collaboration that lead to emancipatory results. An important aspect of these emancipatory results involves the rethinking of educational practice, knowledge production, and engaged forms of citizenship. These dynamics interact to help us imagine new forms of consciousness and cognition grounded on creative images of a changing life. These new forms of consciousness cannot be separated from the educational realm and the democratic effort to reframe learning as part of the struggle against multiple forms of domination. Framed in this manner, an evolving criticality plays a central role in the development of our individual imagination. Here, an ideologically aware education induces individuals to rethink their subjectivities in order to emphasize the role of democratic community and social justice in the process of human development. An education for individual imagination becomes increasingly more important in a society torn asunder by commodified informationalism (McLaren, 1994, 2000, 2006).

2. *The reconstitution of the individual outside the boundaries of abstract individualism.* The reconstitution of the individual that is connected to our evolving critical pedagogy's celebration of self-realization must be articulated carefully in light of the use of the concept of individualism in the Western tradition. Our notion of self-realization is a corrective of both a critical tradition that rejects the possibilities of an authentic individuality and a market-based individualism that rejects the importance of social context. In critical communitarianism, the importance of the community consistently takes precedence over the interests of the individual—a position that poses great danger to the health of the democratic impulse. In the market context, egocentrism is equated with action for the common good, creating in the process powerful forms of regulatory power that ultimately destroy the social fabric. When our notion of criticality expresses its concern for individualism, this should by no means be interpreted as a naïve acceptance of the Cartesian notion of the "abstract individual." This individual subject is removed from the effects of complex power relations and endowed with abstract political rights that mean little when disconnected from the regulatory and disciplinary aspects of economic, social, and cultural forces.

3. *The understanding of power and the ability to interpret its effects on the social and the individual.* Of course one of the most important horizons within which critical educators analyze the world and its actors involves the context of power. Transformative educators are interested in both how power operates in the social order and the ways

it works to produce subjectivity. In this context they focus on the nature of ideology and the process by which it imprints itself on consciousness, the ways hegemonic forces mobilize desire in the effort to win the public's consent to the authority of various power blocs, the means by which discursive powers shape thinking and behavior via the presences and absences of different words and concepts, and the ways that disciplines of knowledge are used to regulate individuals through a process of normalization. In this context an evolving critical pedagogy studies the methods individuals and groups use to assert their agency and self-direction in relation to such power plays. With this in mind, critical pedagogy is especially concerned with the complex relationship connecting individuals, groups, and power. Such an interaction never occurs around a single axis of power, and the ambiguity of the subjectivity that is produced never lends itself to simple description or facile prediction of ways of seeing or behaving. Mainstream forms of Western education have consistently ignored this effort, trivializing, in the process, the role of social analysis.

4. *The provision of alternatives to the alienation of the individual.* A central concern of our evolving critical pedagogy involves providing an alternative to social and educational alienation. Individuals in contemporary society experience social reality mainly as a world of consumerism and not as the possibility of human relations. In a consumerist hyperreality, both young people and adults are alienated from daily life and cultural and educational capital. Such alienation affects individuals from different social locations in divergent ways. Men and women from more dominant locales suffer an informational alienation that erases issues of power, justice, and privilege. Those from less-dominant locales are denied access to institutions that provide tickets to social mobility by the use of a rhetoric of standards, excellence, and values.Less-privileged individuals are induced to blame themselves for their lack of access to various forms of capital via the deployment of such discursive strategies and regulatory forms. Such a reality can be described as a form of "second-degree alienation," a state that is unconscious of the existence of alienation. In this alienated circumstance, the possibility of self-direction fades. In this context, our social education, drawing on the German *Bildung* tradition, provides individuals alternatives to their alienation. Here again Philip Wexler's concepts of resacralization and enlivenment and my concept of critical ontology become central to the generation of empowering alternatives.

5. *The cultivation of a critical consciousness that is aware of the social construction of subjectivity.* An evolving critical pedagogy produces conscious individuals who are aware of their self-production and the social conditions under which they live. With this in mind, our critical pedagogy is concerned not just with how individuals experience social reality but how they often operate in circumstances that they don't understand. A critical consciousness is aware of these dynamics, as it appreciates the complexity of social practices and their relationships with other practices and

structures. Indeed, our education promotes a critical consciousness of self-production that not only understands the many planes of history on which an individual operates but how subjectivity is specifically colonized on these various planes. In this context, questions of the social construction of identity are viewed through the lenses of affect and emotion. Empowered by such knowledge, individuals with a critical consciousness are able to use their insights to overcome alienation and construct social and individual relations with other social actors. If democracy is to succeed, then large numbers of individuals need to reflect on the effects of the social on the individual. Via this consciousness-producing activity, the public space/political cultural is reconstructed.

6. *The construction of democratic community-building relationships between individuals.* The development of the individual coupled with the construction of a democratic community is central to a transformative pedagogy. Embracing a critical alterity (an awareness of difference) involving responsiveness to others, the new social education works to cultivate an intersubjectivity that develops both social consciousness and individual agency. The notion of an individual's relational existence becomes extremely important in this context as we focus attention on the power of difference in social education. Utilizing its understanding of how power relations shape individual subjectivity, an evolving critical pedagogy explores the power-inscribed nature of group difference. In this context, students learn how power shapes lives of privilege and oppression in ways that tear the social fabric and deny community. Students, workers, and other citizens who belong to diverse socioeconomic, racial, ethnic, gender, and sexual groups can learn much from one another if provided the space to exchange ideas and analyze mutual difficulties. As such a powerful force, difference must not simply be tolerated, but cultivated as a spark to human creativity and evolution. Relational existence is not only intrinsically important in a democratic society; it also holds cognitive and educational benefits for self-development. Understandings derived from the perspective of the excluded, the culturally different, or the colonized allow for an appreciation of the nature of justice, the invisibility of the process of oppression, and the difference that highlights our own social construction as human beings.

7. *The reconceptualization of reason—understanding that relational existence applies not only to human beings but concepts as well.* Drawing upon its critical roots, an evolving critical pedagogy understands the irrationality of what has sometimes passed for reason in the post-Enlightenment history of Western societies. Thus, an important aspect of our transformative education involves the reconstruction of reason. Such a process begins with the formulation of a relational reason. A relational reason understands conventional reason's propensity for conceptual fragmentation and narrow focus on abstraction outside of a lived context. The point here is not to reject rationality but to appreciate the limits of its conventional articulation in light of its relationship to power. Such a turn investigates various rationalities from the sub-

jugated to the ancient, as it analyzes the importance of that deemed irrational by dominant Western power and its use-value in sociopolitical affairs and the construction of a critical consciousness. Such alternative ways of thinking are reappropriated via the realization of conventional decontextualization: individuals are separated from the culture, schools from society, and abstract rights from power. An evolving critical pedagogy critiques traditional Western reason's tendency—based on a Cartesian ontology—to view an entity as a thing-in-itself. All things are a part of larger interactive dynamics, interrelationships that provide meaning when brought to the analytical table. Indeed, our evolving critical pedagogy finds this relational reason so important and so potentially transformative that we see the interaction between concepts as a living process. These relational dynamics permeate all aspects of not only our social education but also of critical consciousness itself.

8. *The production of social skills necessary to active participation in the transformed, inclusive democratic community.* As a result of an evolving critical pedagogy, teachers and students will gain the ability to act in the role of democratic citizens. Studying the ideological in relation to self-development, socially educated individuals begin to conceptualize the activities of social life. Viewing their social actions not only through the lenses of the political but also the economic, the cultural, the psychological, the epistemological, and the ontological, individuals analyze the forces that produce apathy and passivity. In this manner, critical pedagogy comes to embody the process of radical democratization, the continuing effort of the presently excluded to gain the right and ability to have input into civic life. As individuals of all stripes, ages, and backgrounds in contemporary hyperreality search for an identity, critical pedagogy provides them an affective social and individual vision in which to invest. Making connections between the political, the economic, the cultural, the psychological, the epistemological, the ontological, and the educational, individuals gain insight into what is and what could be as well as the disposition to act. Thus, as political agency is cultivated, critical pedagogy becomes a democratic social politic. Once again, social consciousness and the valorization of the individual come together to produce an emancipatory synergy.

Conclusion

These are just a few of the ideas that can be used to get the conversation started and to introduce *Critical Pedagogy: Where Are We Now?* I am always amazed with how quickly the world changes, the acceleration of the pace of change, and the expansion of the power of power. Given such dynamics it is inconceivable that critical pedagogy would not be ever-evolving, changing to meet the needs posed by new circumstances and unprecedented challenges. Peter and I hope that this book will provide us a basis for better understanding the possible forms such changes in critical pedagogy might take in the bizarre new era in which we find ourselves—an era where the smell of a new and more effective form of fascism seeps into every room of our apartments and houses and into our (un)consciousnesses. In such dire circumstances we need critical pedagogy more than ever. Where are we now? Wedged between an ideological rock and a hegemonic hard place with a relatively small audience. I believe critical pedagogy contains the imaginative, intellectual, and pragmatic power to free us from that snare. Such an escape is central to the survival of not just critical pedagogy but also to human beings as a species.

References

Agger, B. (1992). *The discourse of domination: From the Frankfurt School to postmodernism*. Evanston, IL: Northwestern University Press.

Beck-Gernsheim, E., Butler, J., & L. Puigvert (2003). *Women and social transformation*. New York: Peter Lang.

Blackler, F. (1995). Knowledge, knowledge work, and organizations: An overview and interpretation. *Organization Studies, 16, 6*.

Capra, F. (1996). *The web of life: A new scientific understanding of living systems*. New York: Anchor Books.

Carter, R. (2004). Visual literacy: Critical thinking with the visual image. In J. Kincheloe & D. Weil (Eds.) *Critical thinking and learning: An encyclopedia for parents and teachers*. Westport, CT: Greenwood.

Dei, G. (1995). Indigenous knowledge as an empowerment tool. In N. Singh & V. Titi (Eds.) *Empowerment: Toward sustainable development*. Toronto: Fernwood Press.

Dei, G. & Kempf, A. (Eds.). (2006). *Anti-colonialism and education: The politics of resistance*. Rotterdam: Sense Publishers.

Fischer, F. (1998). Beyond empiricism: Policy inquiry in postpositivist perspective. *Policy Studies Journal, 26(1)*, 129–46.

Flecha, R., Gomez, J., & Puigvert, L. (2003). *Contemporary sociological theory*. New York: Peter Lang.

Flossner, G., & Otto, H. (Eds.). (1998). *Towards more democracy in social services: Models of culture and welfare*. New York: de Gruyter.

Freire, P. & Faundez, A. (1989). *Learning to question: A pedagogy of liberation*. New York: Continuum.

Horn, R. (2004). Scholar-practitioner leaders: The empowerment of teachers and students. In J. Kincheloe & D. Weil (Eds.) *Critical thinking and learning: An encyclopedia for parents and teachers*. Westport, CT: Greenwood.

Keith, N. and Keith, N. (1993, November). *Education, development, and the rebuilding of urban community*. Paper presented at the Annual Conference of the Association for the Advancement of Research, Policy, and Development in the Third World, Cairo, Egypt.

Kincheloe, J. (2001). Describing the bricolage: Conceptualizing a new rigor in qualitative research. *Qualitative Inquiry, 7(6)*, 679–92.

Kincheloe, J. (2003). Critical ontology: Visions of selfhood and curriculum. *JCT: Journal of Curriculum Theorizing, 19 (1)*, 47–64.

Kincheloe, J. (2004). *Critical pedagogy*. New York: Peter Lang.

Kincheloe, J. (2005). On to the next level: Continuing the conceptualization of the bricolage. *Qualitative Inquiry. 11(3)*, 323–350.

Kincheloe, J. (2007). *Critical pedagogy and cognition: An introduction to a postformal educational psychology.* Dordrecht, Netherlands: Springer.

Kincheloe J. & Berry, K. (2004). *Rigor and complexity in educational research: Conceptualizing the bricolage.* London: Open University Press.

Kincheloe, J. & McLaren, P. (2005). Rethinking critical theory and qualitative research. In N. Denzin and Y. Lincoln (Eds.), *Handbook of qualitative research* (3rd ed.). Thousand Oaks, CA: Sage.

Kincheloe, J. & Steinberg, S. (1993). A tentative description of post-formal thinking: The critical confrontation with cognitive theory. *Harvard Educational Review, 63(3),* 296–320.

Kincheloe, J., Steinberg, S., and Hinchey, P. (1999). *The postformal reader: Cognition and education.* New York: Falmer Press.

Leistyna, P., Woodrum, A., and Sherblom, S. (1996). *Breaking free: The transformative power of critical pedagogy.* Cambridge, MA: Harvard Educational Review.

McLaren, P. (1994). An interview with Heinz Sünker of Germany: Germany today—history and future (or dilemmas, dangers and hopes). *International Journal of Educational Reform, 3(2),* 202–209.

McLaren, P. (2000). *Che Guevara, Paulo Freire, and the pedagogy of revolution.* Lanham, MD: Rowman and Littlefield.

McLaren, P. (2006). *Rage and hope: Interviews with Peter McLaren on war, imperialism, and critical pedagogy.* New York: Peter Lang.

O'Sullivan, E. (1999). *Transformative learning: Educational vision for the twenty-first century.* New York: Zed.

Reason, P. & Bradbury, H. (2000). Introduction: Inquiry and participation in search of a world worthy of human aspiration. In P. Reason & H. Bradbury (Eds.), *Handbook of action research: Participative inquiry and practice.* Thousand Oaks, CA: Sage.

Schon, D. (1995). The new scholarship requires a new epistemology. *Change, 27,* 6.

Semali, L. & Kincheloe, J. (1999). *What is indigenous knowledge? Voices from the academy.* New York: Garland.

Smith, R., & Wexler, P. (Eds.). (1995). *After post-modernism: Education, politics, and identity.* London: Falmer.

Steinberg, S. (Ed.). (2001). *Multi/intercultural conversations.* New York: Peter Lang.

Sünker, H. (1994). Pedagogy and politics: Hadorn's "survival through education" and its challenge to contemporary theories of education (Bildung). In S. Miedema, G. Bieste, & W. Wardekke (Eds.) *The politics of human science.* Brussels, Belgium: VUB Press.

Sünker, H. (1998). Welfare, democracy, and social work. In G. Flosser & H. Otto (Eds.), *Towards more democracy in social services: Models of culture and welfare.* New York: de Gruyter.

Thomas, P. & Kincheloe, J. (2006). *Reading, writing, and thinking: The postformal basics.* Rotterdam: Sense Publishers.

Varela, F. (1999). *Ethical know-how: Action, wisdom, and cognition.* Stanford, CA: Stanford University Press.

Wesson, L. and Weaver, J. (2001). Administration—educational standards: Using the lens of postmodern thinking to examine the role of the school administrator. In J. Kincheloe and D. Weil (Eds.), *Standards and schooling in the United States: An encyclopedia: 3 vols.* Santa Barbara, CA: ABC-CLIO.

Wexler, P. (1997). Social research in education: Ethnography of being. Paper presented at the International Conference on the Culture of Schooling, Halle, Germany.

Wexler, P. (2000). *The mystical society: Revitalization in culture, theory, and education.* Boulder, CO: Westview.

Williams, S. (1999). Truth, speech, and ethics: A feminist revision of free speech theory. *Genders, 30.* http://www.genders.org

Willinsky, J. (2006). *The access principle: The case for open access to research and scholarship.* Cambridge, MA.: MIT Press.

CHAPTER 2

Religion as Socio-Educational Critique

A Weberian Example

PHILIP WEXLER

Location

I feel a kinship, but also a difference, with the critical pedagogy movement. We share a common ancestor in the Frankfurt School, which, as both Kincheloe (2005) and Gur-Zeev (2003) have argued, is a central theoretical resource for work in critical pedagogy. As a sociologist with a theoretical education, I have been fortunate to be able to return to so-called "classical sociology," as an additional resource for the work of social criticism and the imagination of alternative forms of social life. Despite an earlier dismissal of this tradition as irretrievably conservative, the depth of dissent among the classical European sociologists— despite their commitments to secularism, scientism, and individualism—from modernity, has become increasingly recognized. The other side of the textbook scientism taught to young sociologists was the profound radical distaste of the founding sociologists for the emerging anomic, bureaucratic, exploitative, and alienated world of capitalist modernity. Simultaneous with the continuing hegemony of empiricist sociology, there is now a renaissance of interest in classical sociology (Ritzer and Smart, 2000) and a recognition of its critical impetus and lineage (McCarthy, 2003).

Here, I want to take up one aspect of Weber's work, especially since critical pedagogy and the radical sociology of education (however limited in scope and influence), particularly within the U.S. sociological domain, has naturally drawn on other sources (see Kincheloe, 2005), largely from within Western Marxism. Weber did not focus on educational questions, and I want to show that his work, including the brief allusions to charismatic education, has critical theoretical value for us now. My way of doing this, however, rests on the belief that we social and educational critics have unwittingly limited our cultural and theoretical resources for the development of historically relevant critique and practice.

Sacred Critique

"Closing the universe of discourse" (Marcuse, 1964) also shut out the sacred, which was already an historical fact for both Durkheim and Weber, even while they acknowledged the religious basis of the broader, secular, scientific and individualist culture that was closely interwoven with capitalist social structure and dynamics. I have tried to show how, despite their predictions, but in accord with their flickering hopes, the power of the sacred, of prophets and prophecy, of ritual assemblies, and transcendental belief, has been reignited, in a resacralization, reenchantment, and reversal of sociology's evolutionary assumption of natural secularization (Wexler, 2000). Of course, the resacralization is not all to the good, at least from the vantage point of critical theorists. But that it is a potentially critical, and already actual, historical social and cultural movement, is widely acknowledged by contemporary critical sociologists, such as Castells (1997) and Melucci (1996). Whether this broad movement takes fundamentalist or spiritualist new-age forms depends on, in terms of Weber's sociology of religion, its "carriers," or in Marxist terms, their class position, and more generally, on the interaction of social movements and structures within a networked, global informational society.

When critical language, like the capitalist culture that spawns it, becomes, in Weber's term, "petrified," and the sacred is pushed back onto the social stage, then we have the possibility of a new dialectic; where religion is not only a soporific, ideological opiate, but also an Archimedes point, and a powerful source of social mobilization and critical thought. The more effective the hegemonic process, the deeper we need to dig to find what is at once resistant to its logic of incorporating reterritorialization, and also capable of giving language and imagery to historical, social, cultural, and personal alternatives. I agree with Kincheloe (2005) and Bekerman (2006) that indigenous language and thought is a powerful other to commodified social life. At the same time, the resurgence of religious interests, in all its various forms, desublimates—with all the attendant dangers—the historical unconscious of mystical spirituality, of magic and prophecy, which has repeatedly proven its imaginative and practical power (Wexler, 2007).

The cheap, commercial new age is an enhancement of commodity culture. But its other side is an opening to the great traditions of the sacred, in all the world religions, and their power to imagine things otherwise, as well as to offer transformative practices that simultaneously change the self and the world. My own work has increasingly drawn on antinomian traditions of Jewish mysticism, in Hasidism and Kabbalah, as a resource for social and educational critique and for the envisioning of alternative forms of social life. The recovery of the dissenting, mystical traditions of the sacred is occurring from within the world religions (see, for example, Hattam, 2004, on Buddhism and critical theory). In my work, I have been trying to develop a nonincorporative language of analysis and alternative models of social life. In Israel, for example, there is a powerfully public mixture of secular new-age forms and contemporary variants of Jewish mysticism (Garb, 2005; Werczberger, 2006, in Hebrew). Here too, the dialectic of incorporation and critique is at play, and the power of the bureaucratic state is no less tangible than the renaissance of the collective, sacred spirit.

Education

Nevertheless, a new vocabulary of social analysis and critique is emerging, as a theory of "mystical sociality" (Wexler, 2007). It is less clear what this will mean for imagining and specifying the practices of an alternative, critical education, a "mystical education," though there are practical, critical examples even in social movements with fundamentalist elements, like Habad Hasidism (Wexler, 2005). There are ecologically, cosmically oriented educational critiques based broadly in Christian traditions (O'Sullivan, 1999), and there are various secularizations of Western and Eastern religious practices in models of "holistic learning" (Miller et al., 2005). For now, these are marginal developments, work on the periphery, both of mainstream education and critical pedagogy.

For Durkheim (1995), the dynamics of the sacred were the energic source of all social categories, as "collective representation," and of social interactional vitality, generally. Education was the conveyor of this "moral" force of the social—a social powered by collective, ritual, sacred practice. Collins (1998), in his majestic effort to transpose a Durkheimian sociology to intellectual life, replays this social dynamic as an explanation of intellectual creativity and productivity, across time and space, as a sociology of mind. This work is suggestive too, in what a Durkheimian sociology, drawn not from the textbook scientism of a narrow, Western empiricist appropriation, but rather from his sociology of religion, might mean for a new sociology of knowledge.

In a small way, that is what I aim to do here, for Weber. To build, not from the definitional and methodological face of Weber taught as canonical, but from his sociology of religion, as Collins creates a general model of intellectual creation and social life from Durkheim's analysis of the sacred, energic social center. Religion, in Weber, can offer an alternative model to both socially reproductive, ideological functionalism, and its sometimes positivist partner, in Marxist-sounding critique. I try to use Weber's own analysis of religion to at once reach for a way to describe an educational alternative, and, at the same time, to turn his analysis against his own pessimism of the "iron cage"—the social, historical dead end.

In this way, I return to my kinship with critical pedagogy, in the effort to go beyond the present, to realize that humanity that is historically repressed, to redeem the redemptive moment, by a cool-headed look toward a sociology of redemption. This effort is undertaken with a warm heart and a willing spirit, reaching out again, to be part of our common project. But it insists, as history is again teaching us against both positivism and Weber himself, that mysticism is WITHIN this world. It is the sacred of the sacred, and in that sense, the source of social power. Weber gives us a hint about how to tap this power, and go beyond the iron cage of education, as it is ordinarily thought and lived, by sociologists of education.

Toward a Weberian Sociology of Education

I think that it is possible to demonstrate that the main currents of theory and research in the sociology of education are derived—either directly, almost personally, as a lineage, or indirectly and conceptually—from the canonical classics of sociology. The mainstream—from Durkheim through Parsons and Dreeben and their more quantitative heirs in the American school, and Bernstein's growing, posthumous international influence, beginning in England, on the one hand; and the dissidents, from Marx to contemporary American and British economic, social, and cultural analysts of education, on the other—has set the main lines of thinking about education socially.

I want to raise the spectre of Weber, instead, and to suggest, perhaps ironically, that it is the Durkheimian structuralist-functionalist and Marxist labor theories of reproduction and resistance which have made education accessory to what Marcuse (1964) called the "closing of the universe of discourse," and that it is Weber who shows the historical way out of what he called the "iron cage."

Against the structuralist tradition, in its systemic and linguistic pure forms, or in its qualified versions as variable analysis, reproduction, or symbolic agency, Weber's sociology provides an explicit, though only briefly developed, understanding of education that is embedded within his more general analysis of authority, social action, and religion. Weber's condensed "sociological typology of pedagogical ends and means" provides an opportunity to develop an historical, cultural model of education as a social process. The specific contents of his types appear quite relevant to our own historical, cultural situation, and to both the "pedagogical struggles" and the wider sociocultural movements to which they belong. The most radical direction of a Weberian sociology of education, however, goes beyond the provision of an alternative analytic vocabulary, useful cultural typology of education, or historically relevant thesis about social change and education. I want to offer the speculative suggestion that the character of historical changes in society and culture has made the transposition of Weber's sociology of religion to the field of education an empirically heuristic analytical strategy.

Conceptual Setting

Durkheim's sociology has been taken in at least two directions in the sociology of education. The first is toward the analysis of social systems, where education performs core institutional functions in allocation for the division of labor and socialization for the integration of the normative order. Parsons (1959) has taken this view to the level of the school classroom, and Dreeben (1968) has specified what forms the behavioral ritual of reinforcing the specific normative order takes in the modern school. Examples of the quantitative continuity of this tradition can be found in a number of papers in Hallinan's (2000) reader in the sociology of education. Gamoran et al.'s (2000) careful review and synthesis of research relating organizational variables to student achievements is a fine example, showing that unpacking "the black box " of the school organization reveals not only a complex internal technology of teaching but a powerfully determinative societal surround of societal norms and expectations.

The second, Durkheimian direction is British, and indisputably centered on Basil Bernstein's work (1996) and its increasingly pervasive applications, well beyond the British context (Morais & Neves, 2001). Bernstein early on acknowledged Durkheim's theory of social solidarity as the model for his own typology of social educational language. He carries his theory of codes from the family to the school, providing a systematic language of description for both curriculum and pedagogy, based on criteria of structural differentiation and integration that are reminiscent not so much of Durkheim's division of labor, but of his sociology of religion: collective representation and an emphasis on the centrality of boundary differentiation between the sacred and the profane (Wexler, 1996). Bernstein is clear that however much wider social processes are relevant to education, the internal, educational analysis of curriculum and pedagogy as representations of power and control is what must be analyzed, in terms of the differentiation of the structure of knowledge.

The Marxist antithetical tradition might be claimed to be less structuralist and more oriented to Marx's own view of incessant movement, "mors immortalis." In education, however, the Marxist appropriation has fought against an overintegrated, normative, "oversocialized" Durkheimianism with a decided bent toward the reproduction of the social relations of labor and alienated class relations by education. The social character of education is found in the degree to which, as a practice, "learning is labor," and as a form, it is not only isomorphic to the structure of production but serves, even in its moments of apparent relative autonomy and resistance to the hegemonic order, the reproduction of the structure of capitalism, as labor, exploitation, and inequality, and as alienation.

Instances of this central Marxist tendency mark the path of the "critical" paradigm. The early works of Bowles and Gintis (1976), Apple (1979), Willis (1977), and even Bourdieu (1977), show how unequal power in the labor process, the class nature of social knowledge that functions as ideology, the totalizing inclusion of dissent within the culturally hegemonic forms of the dominant class, and the production of capital in the cultural sphere to insure the reproduction of economic and political inequality, all work though the organization, content, and practice of education. Later works, particularly of Bourdieu (1990), introduce concepts of contradiction, reform, practice, and "habitus," as qualifications of a monolithic, automatic apparatus, in which education as correspondence, ideology, or symbolic capital works as a "misrecognition" of power relation in cultural fields, in order to serve the reproduction of societal structure (see, for example, Swartz, 1997).

Critique from the vantage point of gender and race (Ladwig, 1995) extended the horizon of education as reproduction, even as they challenged the assumptions of the Marxist "new" sociology of education.

I have entered the debates and analyzed the historical contexts of these paradigmatic discourses in the social analysis of education, at a relatively early point in the development of the postmodern challenge (Wexler, 1987). But even then, with all discursive and semiotic sensitivity to the emerging decentralization from structures to networks and from simple ideology to the discursive and semiotic complexities of multiplicity, education remained, in sociological analysis at least, within the ambit of a qualified structuralist approach to society and education.

Enter Weber

Weberian sociology takes another path. To put it very schematically, it is authority, rather than either normative integration or economic power alone, that is the prism and opening toward the alternative nature of Weber's approach. Authority, or domination ("herrschaft" vs. "macht") is more than and different from power: " Hence every genuine form of domination implies a minimum of voluntary compliance, that is an interest based on ulterior motives or genuine acceptance and obedience" (Weber, 1978, p. 212). The point of authority or domination is that "voluntary compliance," or obedience, entails a social relationship and one based on belief ("vorstellung") in the "existence of a legitimate order." The belief or motivated aspect indicates that authority is, first of all, a social action, which is to say that it is meaningful: "We shall speak of 'action' insofar as the acting individual attaches a subjective meaning to his behavior—be it overt, or covert, omission or acquiescence. Action is 'social' insofar as its subjective meaning takes account of the behavior of others and is thereby oriented in its course" (Weber, 1978, p. 212).

Weber develops his famous ideal types of authority, which rested on claims to legitimacy: rational, traditional, and charismatic. It is important to note here that both traditional and charismatic authority rest on different forms of "sanctity." Charismatic authority—which I prefigure here as of special interest—is, in addition, different from both rational and traditional authority: "Both rational and traditional authority are specifically forms of everyday routine control of action, while the charismatic type is the direct antithesis of this" (1947, p. 351). Bureaucracy, of course, " has a 'rational' character"(1946 p. 244) and represents " . . . the most rational means of exercising authority over human beings. It is superior . . . precision, stability . . . reliability . . . calculability of results" (1978; p. 222). Charismatic authority, on the other hand " . . . is thus specifically outside the realm of everyday routine and the profane sphere . . ." (1947, p. 361) and " . . . repudiates the past, and is in this sense a specifically revolutionary force . . ." (p. 362). "The concept of 'charisma' ('the gift of grace') is taken from the vocabulary of early Chrisitanity" (p. 328).

These ideal types of authority, based on the subjective, taking-account-of-the-other character of social action, are of general social importance, not simply in their analytical derivation from a general theory of action, but because they empirically affect other spheres of life: "The structure of domination affected the general habits of the people more by virtue of the ethos which it established than through the creation of the technical means of commerce" (1978, p. 1104). Or, even more directly: "The scope of determination of social relationships and cultural phenomena by authority and imperative coordination is considerably broader than appears at first sight." This includes, Weber continues, " . . . the formation of the character of the young, and hence of human beings generally" (1947, p. 327). Authority represents that empirical exemplification of the theory of action that affects—as ethos—a broad swath of social life, including formation of the young, or "bildung" (and "erziehung").

The types of authority, then, are linked to education in two ways. First, as a modal, influential form of social action; and second, in the historical conflict between types of action, authority, and ethos. The overall societal tendency that favors rational action, the rationalization of all social spheres, affects education, and the societal change and conflict in education are part of the wider historical, cultural conflict: "Behind all the present discussions about the question of the educational system, there lurks decisively the struggle of the 'specialist' type of man against the older type of 'cultivated' man . . ." (1978, p. 1002).

We shall see that the "struggle" between rationalism's specialist and traditionalism's cultivated types of person is finally not the primary axis of the historical conflict of ethos. Rather, it is between the rational (bureaucratic) and charismatic cultural interests that the battle lines are drawn. And this makes good Weberian sense, since the historic roots of these types of authority and social action, effective across the social sphere as ethos, are in the hovering ghosts of the religious originary determination of culture. This, most famously in the case of rational action, develops from Protestant asceticism: " . . . a religious basis of rationalism—which is mediated through the triumph of ethical asceticism in the West, at least" (1978, p. 1143). Moreover: "The clear and uniform goal of this asceticism was the disciplining and methodical organization of the whole pattern of life . . ." (1963, p. 183).

The nexus of authority, social action, religion, and education is the place where a Weberian sociology of education can develop and replace the basic terms of reproduction-resistance or classification and framing, or habitus (an anemic version of Weber's ethos of social action). This, however, is not only a question of applying these terms as a conceptual resource to education. Rather, the interest is importantly an historical one. The conflict of ethos is ultimately between rationality and mysticism, with each representing a broader form of life. The "iron cage" is rationalism's unsavory triumph, tinged with Weber's hope for some reprieve. But the relation between the types is not one of unilinear development, and change in historical and material conditions can reverse the order of conflict.

I want to take this hopeful Weberian hint as an historical hypothesis, and as a way of showing that his analysis of religious action is not merely of archaic interest, nor is it restricted to a limited social sphere. On the contrary, the triumph of rationalism may be incomplete, temporary, and reversible, and *if* it is, all social spheres, including education, are implicated again in the originary ethos of religious complexities. Weber's sociology of religion is relevant to education. But, of course, he already knew that.

Education and Religion

Both in his typological positioning of Confucian education and, not surprisingly from our point of view, in the discussion of bureaucratic and charismatic authority, Weber contextualized education within cultural dynamics, as an aspect of an ethos, and as part of an historical, cultural conflict: "Historically, the two polar opposites in the field of educational ends are: to awaken charisma, that is heroic qualities or magical gifts; and to impart specialized training. The first type corresponds to the charismatic structure of domination; the latter type corresponds to the rational and bureaucratic (modern) structure of domination" (1946, p. 426).

In-between is the "cultivation" type of education, which "educates," compared to the rational, specialist type of education, which "trains," and the charismatic education that wishes to "awaken." The historical context of these types, in the modern period, is: ". . . the irresistibly expanding bureaucratization of all public and private relations of authority and by the ever-increasing importance of experts and specialised knowledge" (1978, p. 1002). In contrast, ". . . genuine charismatic education is the radical opposite of specialized training as it is espoused by bureaucracy" (p. 1144). Weber describes the "elements" of this type of education in terms reminiscent of rites of passage, transformational rituals, or practices of liminality: "The real purpose of charismatic education is regeneration . . . a regeneration of the whole personality . . . to awaken the capacity for ecstasy and regeneration . . ." (p. 1143).

It is worthwhile to emphasize that the types of education, like ". . . the three basic types of domination cannot be placed into a simple evolutionary line: they in fact appear together in the most diverse combinations. It is the fate of charisma, however, to recede with the development of permanent institutional structures" (p. 1143). The volatility of charisma does not obviate either that Weber saw the rational ethos as the basis of a destructive ("mechanical petrification") iron cage, and that ". . . genuine charismatic education is the radical opposite of specialized training . . ." (p. 1144). His own historical interest is clearly to find a way out: "No one knows who will live in this cage in the future, or whether at the end of this tremendous development entirely new prophets will arise, or whether there will be a great rebirth of old ideas and ideals, or if neither . . ."(p. 124).

Religion appears not only in the rhetoric of Weber's opposition, but in the assertion that religion may again play a role in the current cultural defeat: "The modern man is in general, even with the best will, unable to give religious ideas a significance for culture and national character which they deserve" (p. 125). The foundational relevance of religion for culture, for authority, and for education, is also present as the religious influence in the development of theory itself: "The religious problem of prophets and priests is the womb from which non-sacerdotal philosophy emanated, where it developed at all" (1978, p. 451).

What if we are indeed "at the end of this tremendous development," of rationalization? And what if its educational expression in "specialized training" encounters again its "radical opposite" in the awakening of the ecstatic capacity of regenerative, charismatic education?

Theodicy and Ecstasy in Education

The social, cultural, and educational antipode of rational action is charisma. And charisma, that extraordinary personal power, is at first intimately linked to ecstasy and to magic, and later evolves into religious cult, theodicy, and metaphysics. According to Weber, " . . . ecstatic states . . . are viewed, in accordance with primitive experience, as the pre-conditions for producing certain effects . . ." (1978, p. 400). The embodiment of this power is, at first, the magician, for " . . . the magician is permanently endowed with charisma . . ." and the subjective state of "ecstasy," which represents a "removal" from the ordinary, mediates charisma for the magician, though it is only "occasionally" available to the layman (p. 401).

The power exercised by the magician who embodies charisma or "mana" or "orenda," which enables "a direct manipulation of forces" (magic), is historically transformed into a manipulation of the world through symbols, which is to say, symbolic activity (p. 403). This early displacement of naturalistic magic by symbolism and its professional masters leads to no lesser performative efficacy, but " . . . all areas of human activity were drawn into this circle of magical symbolism" (p. 405). This symbolic, performative efficacy in the world, which Weber calls "magical coercion," is, though not entirely, the original base of the cult, which defines religion: "By and large this is the original though not exclusive, origin of the orgiastic and mimetic components of the cult—especially of song, dance, drama, and the typical fixed formulae of prayer." The additional elements of religion, "divine worship, prayer and sacrifice have their origin in magic" (p. 422). The evolution from sorcery, which is direct magical coercion, is to religion, which is the cult that includes prayer, sacrifice, and worship, and where: "Correspondingly, those beings that are worshipped and entreated religiously may be termed gods, in contrast to demons, which are magically coerced and charmed" (p. 424). The magician is complemented by the priest and prophet, who though they may also carry forward magical elements—especially in the case of the prophet—are religious practitioners. Their education is also different, and Weber differentiates the " . . . rational training and discipline of priests from the different preparation of charismatic magicians . . . the latter preparation proceeds in part as an 'awakening' using irrational means and aiming at rebirth" (p. 425).

Prophets are an interruption of the theological rationalism of the priests who administer the cult and the doctrine, but they have both priestly and magical aspects. Like the priest, the prophet teaches a "doctrine or commandment, not magic." But, unlike the priest, his authority is not based in cultic tradition and scripture, but "on personal revelation and charisma" (1978, p. 440). Like the magician: "Prophets very often practiced divination as well as magical healing and counseling" (p. 441). Jesus claimed his legitimacy on the basis of "the magical charisma he felt within himself . . . this consciousness of power . . ." (p. 440). But the prophet, while basing his claim on personal revelation and charisma, espouses a revelation that has a "certain systematic and coherent meaning . . . this meaning always contains the important religious conception of the world as a cosmos which is challenged to produce somehow a 'meaningful,' ordered totality . . ." (p. 450).

The development from magician to priest, from magical coercion to cult, with prophetic interruptions that draw on magic and advance meaning, includes an educational development: "When the guild of magicians finally develops into the priesthood . . . secret lore recedes and the priestly doctrine becomes a scripturally established tradition . . . Such a scriptural tradition subsequently becomes the basis of a system of education, not only for the professional members of the priestly class, but also for the laity, indeed especially for the laity" (p. 458). Weber refers to: "The development of priestly education from the most ancient charismatic stage to the period of literary education . . ." This is not, however, a simple linear development in education, since priestly education as forbear of literacy generally may be in conflict with the education of other social strata; notably, "warrior nobles [who] have developed their own system of education and have taken it into their own hands. Later on we must discuss the bifurcation of educational systems which may result from this process" (p. 460).

The prophet, who speaks on the basis of personal charisma and who is "usually a magician" (1978, p. 467), by his doctrinal revelation also serves the goal of articulating rational meaning. This is the general role of "the intellectual" who, facing a world disenchanted and losing magical significance, seeks an "order that is significant and meaningful" (p. 506), and so helps to create the theodicies necessary for salvation. But this quest for salvation continues to include the requirement of sanctification, and sanctification is also accomplished by a "rebirth"—an ecstasy of removal which insures the possession of magical power. Generally, however, the earlier unity of theodicy and ecstasy or experience in the here and now and ordered, cosmic meaningfulness, has ceased to characterize the ever-rationalized meaning of the world: "The unity of the primitive image of the world, in which everything was concrete, magic has tended to *split* [emphasis added] into rational cognition and mastery of nature on the one hand, and into 'mystic' experiences on the other" (1946, p. 282).

The Elementary Forms of Religious Education

Weber's discussion of the evolution of religious practices is interesting not only in the attempt to link the apparently heterogeneous elements or types of activities—magic, charisma, ecstasy, cult, theology, prayer, worship, sacrifice, and prophecy (and their "carriers": magicians, priests, prophets, and warriors)—but also, especially for us, because education is embedded within ethoi of authority and social action and rooted in religion.

The apparent effect of rationalization, and the concomitant split of rationality and mysticism, is also, at the analytical, interpretive level, an effort to separate educational practice from the historical multiplicity of types of authority and action—and from religious practice. Among others, I have suggested, however, that the iron cage is porous, and that the ghosts of religion are reembodied in a world that is not entirely "disenchanted," which is to say, in Weber's language, emptied of magic and charisma (Wexler, 1996, 2000). Whether we speak of reenchantment, resacralization, or a mystical society, spiritual renaissance, or a new age, social and cultural analysts and researchers increasingly argue for the heterogeneity of cultural orientations, and the contemporary empirical expression of the sacred within, rather than outside and in flight from, the everyday social world (see, for example, Forman, 2004). Indeed, the social analysis of identity and meaning in the historical condition of informationalism centers on current social practice as representing various efforts to overcome "the split" and to unite wisdom traditions of spiritual integration with the rational practices of postindustrial technology to create new forms of social solidarity, as well as shared individual meaning (Mellucci, 1996; Maffesoli, 1996). The so-called "new social movements" are spiritual movements, invoking not only an innerworldly mysticism of everyday sanctity (Wuthnow, 1998) but also archaic practices of shamanism and magical prophecy. Weber's anxious hypothesis about the disappearance of magic and mystery from social life has been historically invalidated, and his hopeful hint—or prophecy—about the new prophecies and ideals, and rebirth of the old, can be persuasively and empirically argued (Wexler, 2000).

Education, however, in theory, research, and practice, has remained on one side of modernity's split, without apparent acknowledgment of the broader social movements for reintegration of the ethoi of reason and mystery. The reenchantment of education, or what I have called education in a "mystical society," while perhaps not the "mainstream," is being expressed in a variety of formal and informal educational examples (nor does Weber's caveat about the ephemerality of charisma hold, when the "noninstitutional" is a significant part of everyday social practice). Certainly, part of the work of a Weberian sociology of education is the empirical description and analysis of such examples, relating educational practice to types of authority and social action and also to the social strata who are its carriers. New-age social movements are particularly fertile sites for such research, when they are understood as meaningful social action that significantly fuses the religious and educational interests—as does every type of social action, and not simply "charismatic education." Rational, bureaucratic education on the one hand, and traditional education, on the other, are also expressions of original, and diverse, religious practices of the sacred in the intellectualization of asceticism and the sanctification of immemorial, traditional authorities, particularly in texts.

The current social reintegration is a renewed fusion of the "primitive image of the world," only in that the charismatic, magical, and cultic elements are not ineluctably severed from the rational elements, which remain embedded in efficient organization and precise calculation of instrumental action. This revitalized *hybridization* of types of action, which opens the "one-dimensional universe of discourse," means that the elementary forms of religious action are found within the social world, which counter to Weber's suggestion that this is not "a world robbed of gods," a world, "denuded of irrationality" (1946, p. 282).

The analytical implication which follows the "simple" requirement of empirical research of the emergent educational practices of new religious movements (Yakob, 2006; Werczberger, 2004), is to go beyond social conceptualizations of education that are predicated on an historical "disenchantment." Without magic, charisma, or prophecy, the "rational" instrumental aspects of action and authority can be analyzed in education within one type of social action or ethos of authority. The Marxist emphasis on structural reproduction through cultural reproduction, however contradicted, resisted, or enacted as agents of an habitus, and the Durkheimian emphasis on the normative organization of the functions of allocation (school-effects research) and socialization (moral education) exclude, a priori, the recognition of social and educational charisma and innerworldly mysticism.

Weber's interest in the possibility of an innerworldly mystical alternative to the iron cage of rationalism was limited, in his view, to personal, intimate life, and now socially impossible in the wider public sphere. Likewise, charisma, which he called "the revolutionary force in history," which "revolutionizes . . . from within," (1978, p. 1116), recedes in the face of a combined movement of rationalization and institutionalization. But, if innerworldly mysticism becomes a public practice (Wexler 2000), and institutionalized religion is superseded by "unchurched—which is to say non-institutional religion—spirituality" (Parsons, 1999, Roof, 1993), then Weber's integrative analysis of education as an element of cultural actions, which are deeply religious, becomes the basis for a sociology of education that goes beyond the "newness" of a sociological dissent that merely remains within the rationality of modern capitalism.

In practice, charismatic education promises to break the iron bars of cultural reproduction and system maintenance. In Weber's terms: "Charismatic belief revolutionizes men 'from within' and shapes material and social conditions according to its revolutionary will" (1978, p. 1116). In theory, we want to go beyond Weber's tripartite distinction of the types of authority, and by extension, of education. If we follow the developmental, historical path that he traced, but in reverse, then we can see that indeed "charisma" is only an "ideal type" of education. The elementary forms of educational practice in a reenchanted social world are at least shaped, if not identical, with all the elementary forms of religious practice described by Weber. *The constituents of education*, though in "diverse combinations," include: magic, sacrifice, formulaic and nonformulaic prayer and worship, cultic rituals, scriptural creation of meaning, ecstatic "removals," prophetic "interruptions," and the antinomic, heroic practices of war charismas, which, as Weber wrote of his examples of charisma, are understood in a "value-neutral" way.

The current interest in Jewish education—in the hermeneutic traditions of textual interpretation that can serve as education models (Fox, Scheffler, & Marom, 2003), for example—is a good example of an analytical resacralization. But, this is an appropriation of the priestly tradition for understanding education, which, however valuable, remains silent with regard to magical charisma, prophecies of various types, and contemporary practices of ecstasy, in addition to theodicy. To create a broader model, we shall have to explore not only scriptural traditions of religion as education, but also ask about the emergence of magical charisma, prophecy, and ecstasy in an education that may, in the "knowledge society," come to work, beyond postmodernism, as a polyvocal, this-worldly practice of the sacred.

References

Apple, M. 1979. *Ideology and Curriculum*. Boston & London: Routledge & Kegan Paul.

Bekerman, Z. (Ed.). 2006. *Diaspora, Indigenous, and Minority Education: An International Journal*. Mahwah, New Jersey: Lawrence Erlbaum Associates.

Bernstein, B. 1996. *Pedagogy, Symbolic Control and Identity*. London: Taylor & Francis Ltd.

Bourdieu, P. 1977. "Cultural Reproduction and Social Reproduction," in J. Karabel & A.H. Halsey (Eds.), *Power and Ideology in Education*. New York: Oxford, pp. 487–510.

Bourdieu, P. 1990. *In Other Words: Essays Towards a Reflexive Sociology*.Stanford, CA: Stanford University Press.

Bowles, S. & Gintis, H. 1976. *Schooling in Capitalist America*. New York: Basic.

Castells, M. 1997. *The Power of Identity*. Oxford: Blackwell.

Castells, M. 1996. *The Rise of the Network Society*. Cambridge, MA: Blackwell.

Collins, R. 1998. *The Sociology of Philosophies: A Global Theory of Intellectual Change*. Cambridge, MA: Harvard University Press.

Dreeben, R. 1968. *On What Is Learned in School*. Reading, MA: Addison-Wesley.

Durkheim, E. 1960. "Prefaces of L'Annee Sociologique." In K. Wolff (Ed.), *Essays on Sociology and Philosophy*. New York: Harper and Row, pp. 341–353.

Durkheim, E. 1995. *The Elementary Forms of Religious Life*. Translated by Karen E. Fields. New York: Free Press.

Forman, R. 2004. *Grassroots Spirituality*. Exeter, U.K.: Imprint Academe.

Fox, S., Scheffler, I., & Marom, D. 2003. *Visions of Jewish Education*, Cambridge, UK: Cambridge University Press.

Gamoran, A., Secada, W., & Marrett, C. (2000). "The Organizational Context of Teaching and Learning: Changing Theoretical Perspectives." In M. Hallinan (Ed.), *Handbook of the Sociology of Education*. New York: Kluwer Academic/Plenum Publishers.

Garb, Y. 2005. *"The Chosen Will Become Herds": Twentieth Century Kabbalah*. Jerusalem: Carmel Press. (In Hebrew).

Gerth, H. & Mills, C., 1946. *From Max Weber: Essays in Sociology*. New York: Oxford University Press. .

Gur-Zeev, I. (Ed.). 2003. *Critical Theory and Critical Pedagogy Today*. Haifa, Israel: Haifa University Press.

Hallinan, M. T. (Ed.). 2000. *Handbook of the Sociology of Education*. New York: Kluwer Academic/Plenum Publishers.

Hattam, R. 2004. *Awakening Struggle: Towards a Buddhist Critical Social Theory*. Flaxton: PostPressed.

Kincheloe, J. L. 2005. *Critical Pedagogy Primer*. New York: Peter Lang.

Ladwig, J. G. 1995. *Academic Distinctions: Theory and Methodology in the Sociology of School Knowledge*. New York: Routledge.

Maffesoli, M. 1996. *The Time of the Tribes: The Decline of Individualism in Mass Society*. London: Sage Publications.

Marcuse, H. 1964. *One Dimensional Man: Studies in the Ideology of Advanced Industrial Society*. Boston: Beacon Press.

McCarthy, G. 2003. *Classical Horizons: The Origins of Sociology in Ancient Greece*. Albany, NY: SUNY Press.

Melucci, A. 1996. *Challenging Codes: Collective Action in the Information Age*.Cambridge, UK: Cambridge University Press.

Miller, J. P., Karsten, S., Denton, D., Orr, D., & Colalillo Cates, I. (Eds.). 2005. *Holistic Learning and Spirituality in Education*. Albany, NY: SUNY Press.

Morais, A. & Neves, I. 2001. *Towards a Sociology of Pedagogy: The Contribution of Basil Bernstein to Research*. New York: Peter Lang.

O'Sullivan, E. 1999. *Transformative Learning: Educational Vision for the 21st Century*. Toronto: Zed Books.

Parsons, T. 1959. "The School Class as a Social System: Some of its Functions in American Society." *Harvard Educational Review* 29 (Fall): 297–318.

Parsons, T. 1947. "Introduction," in Weber, M. 1947. *The Theory of Social and Economic Organization*. New York: Oxford University Press.

Parsons, W. B. 1999. *The Enigma of the Oceanic Feeling: Revisioning the Psychoanalytic Theory of Mysticism*. New York: Oxford University Press.

Ritzer, G. & Smart, B. Editors. 2003. *Handbook of Social Theory*. London: Sage Publications.

Roof, W. 1993. *A Generation of Seekers*. New York: HarperCollins.

Swartz, D. 1997. *Culture and Power: The Sociology of Pierre Bourdieu*. Chicago: The University of Chicago Press.

Weber, M. 1946. *Essays in Sociology*. H. Gerth & C. Wright Mills, Ed. New York: Oxford.

Weber, M, 1963. *The Sociology of Religion*, Boston: Beacon Press.

Weber, M. 1947. *The Theory of Social and Economic Organization*. New York: Oxford University Press.

Weber, M. 1978. *Economy and Society*, Volumes 1 & 2. Berkeley, CA: University of California Press.

Werczberger, R. 2006. New Age Movements and Judaism in Israel. Ph.D. Dissertation. Hebrew University of Jerusalem (in Hebrew)

Wexler, P. 1987 *Social Analysis of Education: After the New Sociology*. New York: Routledge and Kegan Paul.

Wexler, P. 1996. *Holy Sparks: Social Theory, Education and Religion*. New York: St. Martin's Press.

Wexler, P. 2007. *Mystical Interactions: Sociology, Jewish Mysticism and Education*. Los Angeles: Cherub Press.

Wexler, P. 2000. *Mystical Society: An Emerging Social Vision*. Boulder, CO: Westview Press.

Wexler, P. 2005. "Chabad: Social Movement and Educational Practice," pp. 196–207 in Nisan, M. & Schremer, O. (Eds.), *Educational Deliberations*. Jerusalem: Keter.

Willis, P. 1977. *Learning to Labour*. Westmead, England: Saxon House.

Wilson, R. & Creswell, J. 1999. *New Religious Movements: Challenge and Response*. London & New York: Routledge.

Wuthnow, R. 1998. *After Heaven: Spirituality in America Since the 1950's*. Berkeley, CA: University of California Press.

Yakob, O. 2006. The Revelatory Beliefs of Spiritual Healers in Israel. Ph.D. Dissertation. The Hebrew University of Jerusalem. (in Hebrew).

Note: An earlier version of the Weber section of this paper appeared in *Searching for the Meaning of Education*, edited by M. Sabour and L. Koski, Joensuu, Finland, 2005. Excerpts included with publisher's permission.

CHAPTER 3

Critical Pedagogy and the Crisis of Imagination

ERIC J. WEINER

Critical pedagogy, a critical theory of education and schooling built upon, at least initially, the philosophical work of the Frankfurt School, has evolved over the past 35 years through a serious integration and consideration of other theoretical work, some that directly challenged many of its main assumptions. Post-structural and feminist theories of identity, power, subjectivity, and culture, for example, challenged critical pedagogy's modernist claims generally, and its neo-Marxist articulations specifically. Critical race theories and postcolonial theories also presented challenges to critical pedagogy's class-oriented theory of reproduction and its emphasis on a universal experience of oppression/liberation as opposed to a more localized critique of "difference." There were still others who saw the tenet of negative critique in critical theory betrayed in critical pedagogy's attention to possibility. Some critics took issue with what they saw as an attempt on behalf of critical pedagogy theorists to colonize competing theories, while others argued that these theories were, in many significant ways, contradictory and could not be integrated into a cohesive theory of schooling and education. For this last group, critical pedagogy's legitimacy as a theory of education and schooling suffered from its own internal contradictions.

I am not going to rehash in detail the debates and arguments that informed the evolution of critical pedagogy over the years, briefly summarized above. In spite of and because

of its critics, critical pedagogy is today a much more complex theory in its design and articulations of schooling and education than it was at its inception. Yet it suffers from what I
call "imaginative inertia." Imaginative inertia describes a state of intellectual paralysis which,
if not remedied, will be the beginning of the end of critical pedagogy's struggle to attract
educators and students, thereby curtailing its influence in educational theory and practice.
Ironically this is occurring during a time in history when critical pedagogy, if reconceptualized, might be the most powerful weapon teachers and other educational workers have
in the fight against the hegemonic forces of neoliberalism, neoconservatism, and what Henry
Giroux sees as a burgeoning "proto-fascism"[1] in the United States. As these ideological forces
bear down with increasing tenacity on schools at all levels, from elementary to higher education, we are confronted with the enormous challenge to teach against and imagine
through the formative proto-fascist discourse of corporate and religious power brokers
which "scorns the present while calling for a revolution that rescues a deeply anti-modernist
past as a way to revolutionize the future."[2]

In what follows, I will provide a critique of what I see as some of the forces within the
discourse of critical pedagogy as well as forces operating outside the discourse that have
helped cause this paralysis. I will then provide an alternative critical discourse that attempts
to rewrite—to (re)imagine—in the service of an inventive and dynamic social imaginary,
"categories of the real."[3] Rejuvenating the imagination—social, cultural, political—
becomes a means that has no foreseeable end; that is, it always represents a state of becoming in the construction of a new critical imaginary. Nonlinear in nature, the process of
becoming is cyclical, yet non-repeating.

Constructing a new critical imaginary is about rejecting the imperatives of realism. This
is different than embracing fantasy; rejecting the imperative of realism—rewriting the categories of the real—means, on one hand, questioning the very epistemological foundation
upon which our most cherished social and political assumptions rest, while, on the other,
developing new categories from which to design new theoretical models of thought and
action. This process requires a rewriting/renewing/reviving of our epistemological imaginations; only from this activity can we begin to radically intervene into the fetish of realism; a fetish which reduces imagination to the practice of escape. Radicalizing the
imagination in this way takes its cues from Bachelard's comment that "every fruitful scientific revolution has forced a profound revision of the categories of the real. What is more,
realism never precipitates such crises on its own. The revolutionary impulse comes from elsewhere, from the realm of the abstract."[4] Imagination then is, in part, manifested in the act
of seeing what is not yet there, speculating how it might come about, rewriting what has
come before, and breaking through "the real"; it is thinking the improbable as possible,[5]
just as it is feeling, seeing, hearing, sensing, and doing that which is not supposed to be felt,
saw, heard, sensed, and done.

In Through the Out Door

The subtitle of this collection asks "Where are we now?" In the context of theoretical/practical development I believe "we" are stuck in the sloppy mud of dying theories and as a consequence are increasingly absent both pedagogically and theoretically in public debates about schooling and education. The evidence of this can be found, in part, in the question itself. More than a reflective pause in the evolutionary life-trajectory of critical pedagogy, the question for me begs another, more disturbing question: "Where aren't we?" As a professor in a well-regarded college of education, I find that where we are is much less impressive than where we are not. Indeed, critical pedagogy is almost completely absent from the debates on schooling as they take place in institutions of power. This might be an unfair way to assess critical pedagogy, given that it never made claims to being anything but a marginal discourse. Yet, I also believe that it aspired to become a counterhegemonic discourse, and that its marginality was not a place of strategic engagement to be protected and reproduced but rather was a temporary space of operations to be vacated as a new hegemonic culture took shape. In its more post-structural articulations, notions of margin and center would, of course, fall away. But in either sense, it is important to consider where we are not against where we might want to be.

We are not well represented in any formal body of organizational power. Aside from a relatively small group of loosely connected scholars and practitioners, there is not a journal dedicated to critical pedagogy, nor are there any, with a few exceptions, degree programs at the undergraduate and graduate levels. It would be a great shock to most academics to see a job posting for a scholar of critical pedagogy. It is not unusual in my university for graduates, never mind undergraduates, to never have read or, in some cases, even of heard of Paulo Freire, Henry Giroux, or Michael Apple, to name just a few of the major contributors to the discourse (at least until they take my course or a course from a few other "critical" teachers). Outside of individual teachers and researchers who are dispersed throughout various departments and colleges, critical pedagogy as an epistemological paradigm has failed to reach or attract a critical mass. This is a terrible irony since it is supposed to be, in part, a theory/practice of liberation and freedom for the masses.

Some have argued, most notably Michael Apple, that this failure is due, in part, to the jargon of the discourse. Again, I will not repeat the argument here, or the counter argument made, most notably, by Henry Giroux and to a lesser degree Donaldo Macedo. I will say that language matters and if an epistemological paradigm is going to use language in a way that is unique or, at the very least, different from the way the people who you want to reach use language, then you better teach your desired audience the language. This is easier said than done, but it can, I believe, be accomplished by including glossaries of terms in each book and/or article that uses the language of critical pedagogy. During presentations of material at professional conferences, speakers could translate terms and concepts as they give their talks. This can be done in a way that is not awkward and does not disrupt the flow of a good presentation. But even in these examples, "language use" seems to be a referent for a more difficult reality; that is, rarely is critical pedagogy spoken and discussed outside of academic institutions or with people who operate outside the discourse itself. This is no small matter.

If critical pedagogy has become a ghettoized paradigm of liberation and freedom, then it no longer can be considered a paradigm of liberation and freedom, only its opposite. Theory, in this context, becomes academic in the worst sense of the word. It becomes disconnected from thought and imagination, as these things intermingle in material ways with the struggles that people engage in throughout their days and lives. It should not be lost on the "we" of critical pedagogy that what was/is valued in the academic ghetto (i.e., in epistemological terms) in terms of research and theory, particularly in the social sciences, is not work that is "public" and/or "popular" in nature. Yet this is exactly what critical pedagogy must be in order to fulfill its promise. In this sense, critical pedagogy is in double trouble; it didn't become a public discourse or public pedagogy on one hand, while, on the other hand, it also suffered from a significant degree of marginalization and devaluation in the academy despite its development as a complex theoretical paradigm of schooling and education.

The point, in the end, is that it does not matter if what you say or write is brilliant if no one who you want to communicate with can understand a thing you say. This is not an argument for clarity, but a simple acknowledgement that people need to learn new languages before they can be expected to understand them. If creating a new language or critical vocabulary is vital to the analytical power of the paradigm (and I think there are persuasive arguments in support of this), then the producers of that language have a responsibility to both translate it as well as teach it to new audiences. Language matters because it is the primary material we use to interpret experience, thereby constructing both our personal and social realities. When we fail to measure our own language's capacity to speak to experiences of oppression, with oppressed people, from the position of the oppressed, we will fail to help oppressed people make sense of their oppression. These failures buttress the walls of the academic ghetto, just as they help to perpetuate the ghettoization of critical pedagogy.

This brings me to the important point of audience. Early critics of Freire's *Pedagogy of the Oppressed* were often impressed by the work but argued that conditions in the industrialized West were so different from the conditions in rural Brazil that it could not be reproduced in a Western context. The response from Freire was twofold. First, the West had its fair share of oppressed people. From the rural poverty in places like Appalachia to urban degradation in the major cities of the United States, poverty, sexism, and racism helped to produce and reproduce generations of people who, it was hard not to argue, were oppressed. Second, Freire's pedagogy of the oppressed was not supposed to be transferred to the United States or anywhere else; it was to be invented and reinvented for new audiences and in the service of new liberatory projects. In this important sense it was not a method of teaching but a theoretical paradigm by which educators and other political workers could find some guidance.

Western educators who were drawn to Freire's work tried to do just that in theory and in practice, producing a large body of significant work. But the subjects of this work, in my estimation, became ambiguous. In other words, critical pedagogy was no longer a pedagogy of or for the oppressed, but rather a working theoretical paradigm for those educators who might or might not want to work with oppressed people. Many educated in the language of critical pedagogy, I would argue without any numbers to support the claim, were educated in graduate programs, especially doctoral programs. As such, the recipients of these degrees, particularly Ph.D.'s, would get positions in colleges and universities. Colleges and universities in the United States at the undergraduate level are rarely accessible to oppressed people, and the degree of representation of oppressed people in graduate schools is even less than it is at the undergraduate level. Consequently, the primary audience for critical pedagogy becomes not the oppressed but the privileged. This is even true if we consider the limited influence critical pedagogy might have in teacher education programs. Unless these programs are geared specifically around the needs and interests of poor urban and rural schools and other oppressive institutional structures of schooling, and the teachers in the programs are committed to teaching in these institutions, then the theoretical provocations of critical pedagogy remain at the level of an intellectual challenge with little to no transformative effect.

Not to be misunderstood, privileged students and teachers with a decidedly progressive bent can and do benefit from working within the paradigm (those with a conservative and liberal bias will dismiss the discourse out of hand). However, how they benefit does not necessarily translate to liberation for oppressed people. It might translate into a more complex understanding of how oppression works in all its forms, but this is much different than transforming conditions and relations of oppression. Privileged people, generally speaking, do not give up their privilege voluntarily, and in the United States have rationalized their privilege by internalizing the myth that hard work, fair assessment, and equal access to institutions of power create equal opportunities for success and failure. As such, oppression is an excuse for one's personal failure just as privilege is a sign of hard work, while the existence of both proves that the system is functioning as it should.[5]

But even those who are angry about oppression don't often want to do what needs to be done to create equity if that means they will potentially lose their privileges of race, class, sex, and/or gender. For example, many progressive Whites want to eradicate racism, a violent and caustic system of exclusion that brutalizes people of color. But Whites benefit handsomely from racism, and to truly eradicate it they would need to relinquish their White privilege by, in part, working to dismantle the social, political, and cultural institutions that both support and reproduce White supremacy. So, what we find in liberal circles especially are Whites fighting against racism (generally framed as a fight for equality of access based on politically "color-blind" multicultural policies), while reinforcing White supremacy through the normalization and silence that surrounds and supports their institutionalized White privilege. Consequently and tragically (in an ironic sense), combating racism in this way ends up supporting White supremacy. It seems to me that the most White people who are serious about eradicating racism can do is to use their privilege toward the goal of destroying their privilege. But in the end, and as history has repeatedly shown,[6] it will not be the privileged who liberate the oppressed, but the oppressed who will wrest power away from the privileged. This is why I think the ideal audience for critical pedagogy should not be the privileged and powerful, but rather oppressed peoples. In this regard we should take our cues directly from Myles Horton's work at Highlander Folk School. People oppressed by poverty, racism, and sexism have the most to gain from this work, while those who are most often exposed to critical pedagogy, at least in formal institutional settings in the United States, have the most to lose (in terms of power, privilege, and authority).

Critical pedagogy, in its current articulations, however, lacks the imagination to speak with oppressed and privileged peoples in technologically advanced capitalist societies, in part because it has not taken into account the deep levels of affective and psychic investment that they have made in current spatial and temporal arrangements. For some people, a serious rewriting of time/space relations has begun to change as Internet involvement gets more advanced. Yet, even in these cases, terrestrial modes of consciousness tend to dominate, and as such new technologies become ensnared and limited in their capacity to launch the imagination off into new and unexpected directions. In this sense, rewriting categories of the real in the service of rejuvenating the social and political imaginary is directly connected to the development of a critical imaginary. Paradigmatically, the development of a critical imaginary can help critical pedagogy speak more effectively to the goals of freedom and individual power, because it will no longer be speaking to these issues as they are defined within current affective and psychic arrangements; that is, these goals will be measured against a different set of possibilities, ones that exist beyond that which we already know.

A Crisis of Imagination

At the risk of oversimplifying, my own working definition of critical pedagogy is born out of the intellectual history of the discourse yet diverts from it in some significant ways. The history, as I have come to understand it, has two distinct trajectories.[7] The first definition could be said to come out of the earlier days of the discourse's theoretical development: critical pedagogy is a way of seeing, analyzing, and intervening into operations of power within various sites of learning, but most specifically schools; it is a critical theory of education born out of the need to better understand how domination, wrapped in educational policy, pedagogy, curriculum development, and assessment oppresses, marginalizes, and/or silences students, especially those from working-class backgrounds. It is particularly concerned with the issues of (false) consciousness and capitalism's hegemony. Embracing the dialectic, it also attempts to understand how students and educators resist the domination that lay hidden within curriculum, assessments, normative practices of knowledge transmission, and behavioral standards.

The second definition, which is on some level an extension of the first, while in another sense a departure and significant rewriting of it, says that critical pedagogy converges with cultural studies.[8] As such, schooling as the primary site of learning and the nurturing of social myth is replaced with a sustained critique of popular culture, alternative cultural production, the development of alternative public spheres, corporate media, consumption, postcolonial subjectivity, racism, sexual repression, and ecological survival. There is a decidedly cultural and discursive turn in this articulation of critical pedagogy. Theorized as important sites of public pedagogy, these spheres of knowledge production represent primary formations of learning and, as such, the primary sites of struggle over power, authority, and consciousness.

The first suffers from the problem of totality. It attempts to be a radical grand theory, providing answers, *in the last instance,* to questions of oppression and schooling. But people's lives and the problems that they experience on the ground don't know from "in the last instance." Theory of this kind can seem quite distant from the complexities and contradictions of working-class life. This position struggles under the weight of ideology itself, for even if it is true that everyday life is shaped by ideologies, it is less clear that solutions to troubles caused by ideology will be discovered in ideology.

Until we can teach people to use theory so that it helps with the immediate problems and concerns of their lives—private and public—the larger theoretical questions will dissolve, not simply in abstraction, but will potentially cause alienation and bitterness about the process of theorizing itself. The anti-intellectualism of educators that so frustrates many who work within this trajectory of critical pedagogy is, in part, shaped by certain forms of intellectual production, specifically those that fail to speak effectively to the needs of those that theorists want to help.

The second suffers, in my estimation, from a different problem; it also claims to know where it stands and what it stands for, yet the theoretical ground upon which it rests and the future it envisions, is, itself (by design), unstable. Although this might make it a more responsive theory in terms of its localized perspective, it struggles on one hand to articulate a social project beyond the pragmatic, while on the other (ironically), it too often seems purely academic in its pragmatism. Ghettoized in the academy, this articulation of critical pedagogy/cultural studies has also lost its capacity to help oppressed people and others who are struggling for a sense of humanity under the enormous dehumanizing forces of capitalism, nationalism, White supremacy, patriarchy, hetero-normativity, and Western-style democracy.

Like cultural studies, critical pedagogy has evolved into a theory that has no clear disciplinary borders, which in and of itself is not bad. But it seems to me that we have lost, as a consequence, a clear sense of what it means to be pedagogically critical in theory and practice. Indeed, the fluidity of our postmodern, globalized times makes the slope of criticality appear quite slippery. We take positions without standing still. We critique ideologies while some of us try to avoid becoming ideological. The nature of "we" suggests a certain degree of exclusivity, yet we aspire toward a greater degree of inclusiveness. We supposedly speak with the oppressed, but in a language they often do not understand. Contradictions, it has been argued, can energize intellectual development, dialectically pointing to a new consciousness, yet our own contradictions often seem to overwhelm many of the best-intentioned pronouncements. Fallibility and the specter of no guarantees nips at the heels of what is argued *should* be done, *must* be done. From above, the view of what is wrong politically, economically, socially, culturally, and pedagogically is abstract, fuzzy, and without a sense of proportion; it too often ignores or undervalues the deep emotional and psychological contradictions that make shifting the optic of domination to one of liberation improbable. From below, the social forces imbricate themselves into speech patterns, modes of interaction and thought that seem entirely personal, internal, like the combustion patterns of a Harley V-Twin engine; perfectly imperfect. In our neoliberal times, the social becomes only personal, just as the individual is severed in mind and body from everything that might offer an alternative to her/his deep psychic frustration and atomization. "In this vocabulary," writes Camaroff and Camaroff,

> it is not just the personal is political. The personal is the only politics there is, the only politics with a tangible referent or emotional valence. By extension, interpersonal relations . . . come to stand, metonymically, for the inchoate forces that threaten the world as we know it. It is in these privatized terms that action is organized, that the experience of inequity and antagonism takes meaningful shape.[9]

Perhaps this is why we are seeing from some corners of the critical spectrum an attempt to reestablish a center, to stop the slide, or—stated in another way—to retheorize critical pedagogy as a radical (i.e., Marxist) discourse. From this perspective, critical pedagogy, once a radical discourse, has lost its teeth. Acknowledging that economic and educational reformation is not to be dismissed out of hand, or vulgarly juxtaposed to "radical" work, reforms and reformers are seen as needing a severe push to the edges of "bourgeois social and economic relations." Peter McLaren, Gregory Martin, Ramin Farahmandpur, and Nathalia Jaramillo argue:

> In the face of such a contemporary intensification of global capitalist relations and permanent structural crisis (rather than a shift in the nature of capital itself), we need to develop a critical pedagogy capable of engaging all of social life and not simply life inside school classrooms. We need, in other words, to challenge capitalist social relations whilst acknowledging global capital's structurally determined inability to share power with the oppressed, its constitutive embeddedness in racist, sexist, and homophobic relations, its functional relationship to xenophobic nationalism, and its tendency towards empire. It means acknowledging the educational left's dependency on the very object of its negation: capital. It means struggling to develop a lateral, polycentric concept of anticapitalist alliances-in-diversity in order to slow down capitalism's metabolic movement—with the eventual aim of shutting it down completely. It means developing and advancing an educational philosophy that is designed to resist the "capitalization" of subjectivity, a pedagogy that we have called (after the British Marxist educator, Paula Allman, 2001) revolutionary critical pedagogy.[10]

A revolutionary critical pedagogy tries to shore up what it identifies as the "runny yolk of critical pedagogy." This runny yolk is characterized by any and all theories of education and schooling that make a claim to being critical without being, *first and foremost*, anticapitalist and prosocialist. As such, the yolk of a revolutionary critical pedagogy is anticapitalist/prosocialist, whilst other theories of social and educational change based, for example, in antiracist or antisexist theories and practices are not "critical" per se, nor, if logic follows, revolutionary. One role for revolutionary critical pedagogy from this perspective is to "formulate principles of solidarity with new networks of organs of popular participation, including social movements that advocate anti-racist, anti-sexist, and anti-homophobic practices while at the same time deepening its anti-capitalist agenda."[11]

Although I understand the need and desire to firm up a discourse that of late has become, from one perspective, watered down by liberal-minded reforms and reformers, I am troubled by the return to a neo-Marxist discourse, even one that begrudgingly acknowledges cultural forces and bio-identities as significant in the reproduction of economic and social relations. For me, a return to a neo-Marxist center signals a crisis of imagination in the critical imaginary. Is there no other way to radically intervene into the hegemony of global capitalism than to resurrect socialist ideals from the ashes of the twentieth century, ideals that reject on a significant level the anarchistic desire for individual freedom, for radically unique expressions of imagination? Is there no other way to retheorize critical pedagogy other than entrenching oneself in a discourse whose contradictions and absences make it a blunt and admittedly dangerous tool of political economy (as capitalism's foil); yet, at the same time, make it a poor choice for theorizing a speculative future complicated by the development of new technologies, cultural integration and segregation, diasporic identities, cosmopolitan subjectivities, new psychic formations based upon new spatial and temporal relations, genetic geographies, religious-political fractures/integration, and ecological degradation?

These complications, as I'm calling them, lead me to align myself with intellectuals like Maxine Greene and Noam Chomsky in rejecting "inclusive rational frameworks in which all problems, all uncertainties can be resolved. All we can do . . . is cultivate new ways of seeing and multiple dialogues in a world where nothing stays the same."[12] This does not mean that we do nothing in the face of oppression, hypocrisy, and fascism, but is rather an acknowledgement that experience is fractured and multiple, and that we do not know who the subjects of the revolutions that will assuredly come will be. As such, we must be diligent in our rejection of certainty (ours and others), yet unyielding in our commitment to rejuvenating the imagination in a way that makes freedom, taking cues here from Erich Fromm, more than an escape from oppressive regimes of thought and behavior; it should also become our marker for social and self-actualization. We must make freedom irresistible in a world where resistance to freedom is encouraged in the form of fear and the promise of security and comfort. One way to do this is to create the conditions, however localized, for people to freely imagine what different conceptions of freedom might look like under various historical arrangements.

Henry Giroux suggested to an audience at Penn State one day in 2001 that it seems we can more easily imagine the end of the world than the end of capitalism. Indeed, for some, the end of capitalism would mean the end of the world. But the provocation in this sentiment, for me, lies in the space it creates for a resignifying of a critical imaginary. Instead of juxtaposing these two possible ends, what might it mean to think about their relationship dialectically? What might our world look like—culturally, socially, politically, economically—after its end? Stated another way, what comes after the end of our world? What if critical pedagogy's project was neither the end of capitalism nor the radicalization of democracy (both projects supported by accepted categories of the real), but rather the end of the world as we have learned to *know* it?

This question begs another equally important question, one that has to be considered before the former can be addressed. That is, have we lost the capacity (or have we ever possessed it) to imagine beyond that which we know? If we can get beyond that which we already know, will this process be helpful to people who are personally suffering the implications of impersonal and often violent social, political, economic, and cultural forces? This is a fundamental question—a radical question—on which the entire project rests; for if it becomes just another exercise in theory, then it cannot be said to be a rejuvenation or resignification of anything, let along a critical imaginary.

Rewriting categories of the real in an effort to jump-start the imagination has to, in the end, offer real people in real situations real tools by which they (we) can make their (our) lives more free. This does not mean, however, that all intellectual work, for it to matter, has to be immediately reduced or translated into some kind of political practice. This is particularly true for the work of imagination. As such, its relevance should be measured not against what it does, like a hammer to a nail, but rather what potentialities it generates, either in the imagination or on the ground.

Let me posit that if, in imagination, we cannot get beyond that which we know (categories of the real), critical pedagogy will suffer a fool's death, for it will have forsaken its authority for dreams past, while the future stares impatiently into an empty mirror. For it is not reason or even an acknowledgement that affectivity plays a significant role in consciousness that can release critical pedagogy specifically and theory more generally from its indolence, but the idea that only imagination itself can free the critical imaginary from its dank cell. Resolving this paradox is at the center of understanding how we can begin to rewrite categories of the real in an effort to construct, investigate and live in—live *through*—alternative realities.

From Practice to Epistemology

My own version of critical pedagogy, the way I "think pedagogy," critically draws from both epistemological trajectories summarized above, while diverting from them in some significant ways. First (at the risk of creating a false dichotomy), I think there needs to be a distinction between critical pedagogy as a way of framing one's pedagogy as it takes form in the context of schools and other sites of "formal" learning, and critical pedagogy as an epistemological paradigm that frames pedagogical projects, educational critique, and social/political/cultural critique more generally. The former I will refer to as "critical teaching" so as to avoid confusion.

As a pedagogical project, critical teaching—as I see it—should be creative, multiperspectival, culturally relevant, emotionally responsive, political, contextual, and psychological in mood and orientation. The best critical teachers combine intellectual and imaginative rigor with deep levels of psychological and emotional connectedness with their students to address the political, social, and cultural nature of power and knowledge. It is a subtle process which can be exercised methodologically in any number of ways: performance, dialogue, cultural production, experiential learning, and inquiry are popular choices. The most important aspect of being an effective critical pedagogue, however, is the ability to recognize in those whom you are teaching the complexity of their emotional and psychological investments in the various institutional arrangements that support a worldview that might or might not provide them with a sense of security, belonging, and identity. In this sense, critical teaching is an art that is sensitive to the unconscious investments in "unfreedom" that we all, on some level, make. It is equally important that critical pedagogues are able to recognize their own ideological blind spots and the emotional and psychological shadows that make these blind spots difficult to identify. Critical teaching is a creative practice that looks different in different contexts and is sensitive to the subtle yet powerful investments students make about their own commonsense assumptions about the world.

As a pedagogical project, the goal is to inform, provoke the imagination, heighten the senses, support interpretive experimentation, provide tools of conceptual/creative analysis, produce new formulations of knowledge, and challenge assumptions; it does not exclude the goal of creating social and political agents that will gain a new and/or deeper understanding of power and its often brutal effects, nor does it exclude the possibility of educating people how to go about transforming their social and political conditions. However, these objectives, when placed within the context of schooling at the exclusion of the project outlined above, risk short-circuiting the learning process. In other words, successful critical pedagogues working within the sphere of public education must be careful to avoid becoming pedantic and authoritarian, just as they are trying to disrupt hegemonic assumptions about the world and their students' place in it. More difficult, however, is the fact that the successful critical teacher must accept, at some point, student resistance to radical ideas as a possible expression of free thinking.

If thinking critically is, indeed, the goal of critical teaching as opposed to thinking progressively or radically, then we must admit that conservative thinking on some issues might be achieved through a critical process. This is only true, of course, if critical teaching and the learning it provokes has, as one of its goals, students' ability to think critically and imaginatively about their own thinking and then, as a consequence, produce thoughts that cut through official knowledge, which more often than not lies in the shallow pool of common sense. If the goal, however, is to persuade or convince students to think progressively or radically, then we have drifted willy-nilly into the muddled practice of pedantic teaching. Pedantic teaching, as opposed to critical teaching, is characterized not by indoctrination (an impossibility given the structures of schooling), but by its opposite; that is, in its attempt to persuade or convince, it will simply help to reinforce the ideas and attitudes that students have before they ever took the class. From this perspective, pedantic teaching is the opposite of critical teaching, not because no learning is being done, but because it creates an environment in which little *unlearning* is being done.

To avoid pedantic teaching, the critical pedagogue might sometimes have to sacrifice what s/he thinks or knows to be right in an effort to create the conditions for students to investigate the conditions, relations, and contradictions that make things appear right or wrong. To "think pedagogy" critically from this perspective is to place learning about power and its effects not at the center of the project per se, but as a specter of inquiry; that is, they drift in and through pedagogical relations, helping to create the context for a rejuvenated imagination and its development. This occurs through an investigation of how power and knowledge place limitations around the imagination, trapping it in an iron cage of probability. The critical pedagogue should help students learn more about what they are not "allowed" to know, either through knowledge production or experience, as well as help them unlearn previous lessons that might limit their ability to see not simply beyond the normal and acceptable, but to think that which has not been thought; to get outside the parameters of probability by taking a detour through the imagination. Critical teaching, then, is in part a pedagogical process that helps to release poisonous social toxins by kneading away at the points where the buildup of power/knowledge and myth has made thinking critically about our social, emotional, and psychic relations near impossible.

Short-circuiting the development of imagination is one of the reasons why critical teachers should not be teaching in the service of a particular ideological project but rather should be teaching in the service of the creation of free and imaginative thinkers. Not to be misunderstood, teachers are political beings with political vocations, and we are always involved in working against entrenched ideologies just as we are always working in the service of some vision of the future, however fuzzy. But acknowledging these realities is quite different than immersing oneself pedagogically in an ideological project, which (as I understand the concept) suggests a degree of blindness in one's own perception of what is as well as what should be.

An intellectual project of this sort differs from an ideological project in the context of critical teaching in its ability to put the goal of free and imaginative thinking above the goal of ideological persuasion. Learning, from this perspective, refers to a process by which students and teachers have the opportunity to coconstruct new knowledges and ideas that might otherwise be constrained by a priori ideological investments made before the imagination has had an opportunity to imagine something wholly other in its epistemological nature and design. By introducing their own ideological project directly into their classrooms, teachers risk dampening the intellectual creativity that can occur in dialogue and social inquiry. This is not to say that ideological critique should be absent, nor is it to suggest that the institution does not operate in the service of ideological interests. On the contrary, ideological critique should continue to be the backbone of critical teaching, just as teachers should avoid becoming ideologues. I believe critical teachers have to recognize that being positioned ideologically is not the same thing as teaching in the service of ideology.

Critical teachers recognize the political nature of their vocation and the impossibility of political neutrality in the class or in the development of curriculum, but instead of an ideological project the critical teacher teaches in the service of creating free and imaginative thinkers and sociologically competent subjects who, through a critical process, can have thoughts of their own and can act in ways that make life more satisfying and just. Some free thinkers, after developing the skills and dispositions that allow for the possibility of having thoughts free from the constraints/possibilities of ideology (this occurs when students both learn what those constraints/possibilities are and break their own affective, intellectual, and psychic investments in those constraints/possibilities), might then indeed choose to work toward a socialist future, while others might choose to fight for a more radically democratic state. Others may be attracted by the promises of anarchistic theory, while some might fight for some kind of synthesis of existing radical, liberal, and conservative formulations of government and the economy. Yet all of these choices, aside from the last, are on one important level problematic; they all trouble what it means to think freely and imaginatively. In other words, I do not believe that thinking freely should be reduced to choosing—through some kind of evaluative process, however reflective it might be—that which is already available. Free and imaginative thinkers, to be considered truly free and imaginative, have to be involved in coproducing new ways of thinking about the world and their place in it. The critical teacher works in the in-between spaces of persuasion, production, reflection, discussion, feeling, sensing, reasoning, and creating; s/he must be intimately aware of both the internal and external forces that limit her/his students' (as well as her/his own) ability to imagine beyond the possible, to think beyond what has already been thought. The critical teacher makes freedom irresistible by creating the conditions for students to experience what it means to be free.

Rewriting Imagination

To rewrite the imagination in the service of a new critical imaginary—to provoke free and imaginative thinking—we must find ways to challenge the hegemony of realism, to engage the improbable through transgressive acts of imagination. The hegemony of realism can be described as the process by which we come, as a matter of common sense, to believe (with serious risk to our own freedom) in a future that looks and feels quite similar to the present. By using common and familiar social, political, and pedagogical categories to organize our lives, we become trapped in thought and action by the categories themselves. Critical pedagogy, even in its most "radical" articulations, has suffered this fate; although the move toward cultural studies, I believe, was a positive advancement in the development of a new imaginary. The future, a fertile time/space, has been emptied of its potential to radically rewrite the imagination, in part, because it exists within accepted categories of the real.

One potential path we might take for breaking into and through the hegemony of realism, as well as one justification for taking it, comes from science-fiction writer extraordinaire Olaf Stapledon. In the preface to his novel *Last and First Men*, first published in 1931 and republished in 1968 with *Star Maker*, he writes:

> To romance of the future may seem to be an indulgence in ungoverned speculation for the sake of the marvelous. Yet controlled imagination in this sphere can be a very valuable exercise for minds bewildered about the present and its potentialities. Today we should welcome, and even study, every serious attempt to envisage the future of our race; not merely in order to grasp the very diverse and often tragic possibilities that confront us, but also that we may familiarize ourselves with the certainty that many of our most cherished ideals would seem puerile to more developed minds. To romance of the far future, then, is to attempt to see the human race in its cosmic setting, and to mould our hearts to entertain new values.[13]

In my estimation, this is as relevant today, if not more so, than when he first wrote it. He goes on to say that "the merely fantastic has only minor power" and that to prophesize is

a futile undertaking, but to write the future as art—as myth—goes beyond a futuristic orientation to history as well as the creation of sheer fiction. "A true myth," he writes, "is one
in which, within the universe of a certain culture (living or dead), expresses richly, and often
perhaps tragically, the highest admirations possible within that culture."[14] The point of creating myth in the service of rejuvenating a social imaginary inert from the weight of "reality," as he does in his provocative story of the future-past of humankind, is to disrupt the
continuity of plausibility as it has been shaped by contemporary Western thought. Working
in the realm of myth creation, he uses the admittedly fantastic literary trope of making the
narrator of his story a "human" from the distant future, a member of the "last men," who
is speaking to "us" telepathically in the present, the book itself the product of his influence
over the author. Stapledon explains:

> Only by some such radical and bewildering device could I embody the possibility that there may
> be more in time's nature than is revealed to us. Indeed, only by some such trick could I do justice
> to the conviction that our whole present mentality is but a confused and halting first experiment.[15]

The making of myth in this formulation, unlike theorizing a utopia that is often the end
result of methodical human advancement, takes into account the potential tragedy of human
destruction and ecological degradation as well as grasps the making of history as both a nonlinear process and one that extends beyond recognized time/space parameters. It is this
tragedy that the creation of myth of this sort might help us to avoid.

Stapledon's myth begins with a direct message from the "last man," communicating
through the narrator/author of the novel. The first person pronoun, readers are told, refers
not to the author, but rather to the "last man" speaking through him. The last man's ultimate goal is to historicize history, thereby transforming human consciousness about space,
time, and place and how, when reconfigured, to articulate with a new sense of human
agency. Recognizing the first human's (our) spiritual and intellectual immaturity, his (pro-
nouns are inaccurate in the context of the story, but alas we have yet to invent English linguistic constructions that describe humans beyond the muddled categories of he and she)
mission, communicated with a profound sense of urgency as the distant future is admittedly
affected by the immediate present, is to help the first humans "to feel not only the vastness
of time and space, but also the vast diversity of the mind's possible modes. But this I can only
hint to you, since so much lies wholly beyond the range of your imagination."[16]

The power of this myth to expand the mind's possible modes comes, in part, from the
specificity of the narrative; its abstraction lies not in broad strokes, but in its exacting descriptions and interpretations of future events, communicated as the past. The book begins with
the political and social struggles of the "First Men," which eventually lead to a collapse of
its civilization. The account of the collapse reads like the most detailed of history and anthropology books combined, citing, for example, major wars and conflicts between competing
nation-states, individual blunders of human ("racial") consequence, human tragedy, and
cultural norms and values. Indeed, a quick purview of the table of contents, called "The
Chronicle," suggests that the contents of the first five chapters deal with the political and
cultural history of the first humans.

Chapters entitled "Balkan Europe," "Europe's Downfall," and "America and China" are, in fact, not historical excavations or cultural genealogies (although this is closer), but rather exercises in myth construction. Constructing myth fractures reality by suggesting possibilities thought to be improbable. More than just a suggestion, however, Stapledon's work represents a detailed articulation of the improbable, thereby making it seem not only possible, but probable. It's hard not to read this work without thinking, at least for a second, that maybe someone far into the future was whispering in his ear.

Avoiding a sense of the fantastic, in part, by being written in a style more suited to empirical research, the imagination is released by the abstraction of specificity. For example, in the chapter "America and China," he writes:

> After the eclipse of Europe, the allegiance of men gradually crystallized into two great national or racial sentiments, the American and the Chinese. Little by little all other patriotisms became mere local variants of one or other of these two major loyalties. At first, indeed, there were many internecine conflicts. A detailed history of this period would describe how North America, repeating the welding process of the ancient "American Civil War," incorporated within itself the already Americanized Latins of South America; and how Japan, once the bully of young China, was so crippled by social revolutions that she fell a prey to American Imperialism; and how this bondage turned her violently Chinese in sentiment, so that finally she freed herself by an heroic war of independence, and joined the Asian Confederacy, under Chinese leadership.[17]

It goes on and on, covering epistemological and religious trends and contradictions, cultural norms and attitudes, national identity and the particular ideologies that these emboldened, changes in power relations and orientation, etc. It is quite impossible to give a fair accounting of the trenchant description and analysis that Stapledon produces in the name of myth creation. Suffice it to say that the myth is in the details.

The first humans perish in an explosion, the causes of which can only be grasped as they played out as a set of integrated moments in the totality of all histories. "Of the two hundred million members of the human race, all were burnt or roasted or suffocated within three months—all but thirty-five, who happened to be in the neighborhood of the North Pole."[18] The remaining humans struggled to survive and after a few hundred thousand years increased in number and diversity. But it was "some ten million years" after the explosion that initially decimated humanity, aside from the 35 survivors, that "the first elements of a few human species appeared, in an epidemic of biological variations, many of which were extremely valuable. Upon this raw material the new and stimulating environment worked for some hundred thousand years until at last there appeared the Second Men."[19]

And so it goes, with time being measured in millions and billions of years, a rewriting of the possibilities of time/space, culture, history, politics, society, education, civic agency, social responsibility . . . humanity. Some species are barely recognizable as humans, possessing the ability to fly or to think telepathically. Each has, in its diversity, a shared culture and means of organizing itself socially. Humans go through 16 iterations of development, only some of which occur on earth. Every iteration possesses different complexities of mind/body/spirit, fantasy, hope, concern, knowledge, and value. The "Second Men," for example: "They even conceived that the ideal community should be knit into one mind by each unique individual's direct telepathic apprehension of the experience of his fellows.

And the fact that this ideal seemed utterly unattainable wove through their whole culture a thread of darkness, a yearning for a spiritual union, a horror of loneliness, which never seriously troubled their far more insulated predecessors." The Fourth Men, a human species of great brains, figuratively and literally, and in part created by the Third Men, "probed the material universe and the universe of mentality . . . He casually solved, to his own satisfaction at least, the ancient problems of good and evil, of mind and its object, of the one and the many, and of truth and error." The Fifth Men, although not immortal, could live between 3 to 50 thousand years, and were the first humans to "attack" the nature of time. During the history of the Fifth Men, we learn that thousands of years could pass without an insight, but, alas, telepathic time travel eventually became a reality.

This kind of myth-making risks falling into sheer fantasy but avoids it by its detailed account of not only the future, but how the far future continually is connected to the distant past. As such, we can read this kind of myth-making as an attempt to reconfigure our imaginative capacities so that the improbable *feels* possible. Myth-making of this type encourages the reader to transgress the parameters of what counts as official knowledge. Transgressions of imagination teach us how to imagine beyond the limits of official expectation, to break the bonds that connect our imaginations to that which has been determined a priori as possible. This correspondence is pedagogic and, when broken, can translate into new ways of thinking and feeling about what is possible. New ways of thinking can and often do lead to new ways of acting. This is no small matter when a combination of cynicism and feelings of powerlessness generated and supported by structures hostile to human agency has placed a vice grip around our social and political imaginations. To think of the improbable as possible is to affectively rewrite categories of the real. This rewriting of the real has the potential to release the mind/body/spirit from its inertia, to be free from the hegemony of realism, to imagine beyond that which we know.

Not to be misunderstood, being imaginatively engaged at this level within this genre of literature does not mean that I am suggesting that people begin to believe in the fantastic. Rather I am suggesting that the power of Stapledon's myths to rewrite categories of the real in a way that challenges readers to imagine what might be is metaphorical. As metaphor, myth creation brokers a new relationship between how we understand reality on one hand, and how we conceptualize possibility on the other. For example, when he discusses the ability of the Fifth Men to travel through time, the power to rejuvenate the imagination lies in its capacity to be read as a metaphor for our own thinking about the possibilities, within our own time, of the relationship between space, time, and mobility. How, with the invention of new technologies, has the very geography of terrestrial space changed, especially in relation to time? Certainly time has become relative, just as space is reduced under the pressure of digitization of information and the means by which that information circulates the globe.

In political terms, the incredible spans of time and the corresponding rewriting of space provides readers with a new way of conceptualizing time's relationship to space by highlighting the equation that force plus time equals a change in spatial constructs, instead of the more common equation that makes spatial constructs a constant in the space/time contin-

uum. Aronowitz's ideas about how class formations arise out of different historical arrangements seem on the surface to be far away from Stapledon's myth of time, which is, at the
same time, a myth of humanity's capacity to destroy itself and rewrite itself in a new form.
But this is not unlike Aronowitz's diachronic framing of class and history. This is not to
suggest that Aronowitz ever read Stapledon, but his ideas about time and space show an
unusual degree of imagination, marked by his ability to break free from established paradigms of thought.[19]

He begins to radically rewrite class theory by arguing that neo-Marxist and other
functionalist theories of class formation failed to consider the historicity of social class. As
such, social class was described and understood as the stratification of economic and social
indicators. The actors of social class might (or might not) move around the board, but in
all cases—whether Karl Marx's "notorious two," Talcott Parson's "income grid," or even
Pierre Bourdieu's conceptualization of cultural capital—social class has been fixed theoretically in a predetermined spatial reality, thereby ignoring the historicity of class formation and "class power":

> Many from marxist and nonmarxist persuasions stipulate the power of the ruling class over eco-
> nomic, political, and ideological relations, but, in their practical activity engage in the same work
> of social cartography—their work is making maps—even if their maps differ in details. What is
> often supposedly marxist or radical about these maps is that, unlike mainstream sociology, inter-
> locking networks between the political and economic directorates are revealed, which explicitly
> or tacitly constitute a critique of the traditional liberal separation of corporate power and the state.
> But both become classifications and draw up charts that show where social groups are placed in
> atemporal social grids.[20]

In contrast, Aronowitz's radical theory of class suggests that time should no longer be
considered a function of space, but instead "presupposes that space is produced by the activity of social formations and as a function of time."[21] This simple, yet important intervention into how class is theorized situates history as the embodiment of class struggle and
fractured class interests. Time, or more accurately the movement of time, signals not only
the dynamic condition of historical memory, but the futurity of change as well. Beyond a
politics of hope, Aronowitz's "diachronic" framing of class formation situates the activities of social movements as modalities of class struggle and class formation. The activity
of these social formations, made up of the combined activity of social movements as they
struggle over class formation, have historically shaped political and cultural life through
direct action, such as strikes, sit-ins, rallies, and, in extreme cases, violent uprising.
Similarly, Stapledon's warping of time/space relations also highlights "historicity" by situating our time in time, giving us a new way of imagining time (our own and others), while
troubling the hegemony of fixed spatial relations.

Another path for critical pedagogy that I think is fruitful to take has been championed
most forcefully by Maxine Greene. Imagination, for Greene, is the key to critical reflection, as well as a way to conceptualize a future in light of realities henceforth unknown; it
is a means "through which we can assemble a coherent world [because imagination] is what,
above all, makes empathy possible . . . [it is the one cognitive capacity] that permits us to

give credence to alternative realities. It allows us to break with the taken for granted, to set aside familiar distinctions and definitions."[22] Her ideas correlate in significant ways with Stapledon's, yet how she goes about provoking these breaks with the "taken for granted" does not involve creating myth as much as it involves becoming immersed in the arts; media that for her and me as well "often lead to a startling defamiliarization of the ordinary."[23]

In my mentorship with Henry Giroux, he often talked about the need to "make the familiar strange and the strange familiar" in an effort to disrupt deeply rooted assumptions about various social, cultural, and pedagogical contingencies. Through this kind of optical as well as affective disruption we see the world and each other anew. This speaks to our sociological imaginations as much as it speaks to our poetic and cultural imaginations. Jean-Paul Sartre writes, "It is on the day that we can conceive of a different state of affairs that a new light falls on our troubles and our suffering and that we *decide* that these are unbearable."[24] Freedom, in this discourse, has an aesthetic dimension that speaks to our relations with the ecology of the world and each other; it suggests a profound beauty in our capacity to imagine a different set of personal/public arrangements, an exquisite asking, "in all the tones of voice there are, 'Why?'"[25]

Critical pedagogy, as it stands, misses for the most part this dimension of imagination. Too directed toward political freedom, even when it is considering culture, critical pedagogy risks a kind of vocationalization of imagination; that is, it can slip into an ascetic understanding of the potential of culture to stir the passions of imagination in terms that might be outside of a narrow conception of freedom. Freedom, as a state of becoming, will not arrive as a train does to the station. Rather, it might float along erratic winds, landing unexpectedly at a time and in a place no one can anticipate. As Greene writes, "There are always vacancies: there are always roads not taken, vistas not acknowledged. The end can never be quite known."[26] This does not mean that we give up the search for freedom. It simply is to suggest that we might find it in the most unusual places and at the most unusual and inconvenient times. It is also to suggest that the seeds of political freedom might be born out of our involvement in activities that have little to do with politics or education directly.

For educators especially, this kind of searching is antithetical to the kinds of knowledges and literacies that dominate the thinking in colleges of education. It reminds me of a recent graduate seminar in which a student was asking me what book she should read for an assignment I gave for a scholarly book review. Explaining the parameters of the assignment, I told them that they could pick any book they wanted, but I encouraged them to pick a recently published book exploring topics about which they were interested. As they shared with me titles of books that they had found to review, I was amazed at how many dealt explicitly with teaching methodologies generally and/or studies that took up themes directly related to their professional disciplines. Few, if any, took up themes outside of their disciplines. The course, entitled "Critical Thinking and Literacy," is wide-open in terms of how we explore these two broadly interpreted concepts; but nevertheless, art, music, poetry, theater, or dance were not chosen as relevant topics. I asked if they had any interest in any of these topics, and indeed most of them did. But they considered them outside the purview of education generally and critical thinking and literacy more specifically. This is in the face, mind you, of discussions that explicitly bring in these cultural spheres as fodder for critical reflection.

For me, this reaction signals a crisis of imagination as well. It was enormously difficult for these students to imagine how doing research about Picasso or reading the poetry of Frost or the literature of Toni Morrison was going to help them be better teachers, let alone better people or more affective civic agents. The capacity to imagine beyond official knowledge production and sanctioned literacies in too many cases has been short-circuited by the official discourse of schooling. More disturbing, however, is the fact that they were resistant to investigating the arts, as doing so might help lead them "to a startling defamiliarization of the ordinary." In this sense, the official discourse of schooling attempts to fix the meaning of being a teacher as well as end the discussion as to what constitutes an educated person.

Conclusion

As an epistemological paradigm as well an orientation to teaching, critical pedagogy's project should be guided, in my estimation and in light of the discussion above, by the following considerations. First, it must reassert itself as a paradigm for liberation of oppressed people throughout the world. This means that oppression in all its forms, from class issues to sexual exploitation of young girls and boys, should be its object of consideration and research, especially how formal and informal institutions of learning and knowledge production either explicitly or inadvertently help produce and reproduce conditions of oppression. Theoretically, critical pedagogy should operate not only as a synthesizer of developed or developing theories, but should place most of its intellectual resources into developing new ways of thinking and seeing, new ways of imagining what is possible. This positions critical pedagogy as a place and space where art and imagination mix with political and sociological concerns in an attempt to provoke inventive ways of perceiving what is as well as imagining those things that have yet to be seen.

This subtle shift that I am recommending is significant in that it is a realignment of critical pedagogy's social optic. While eradicating oppression remains its concern, the optic of possibility no longer rests on withering paradigms of hope and possibility. Beyond the modern and postmodern and outside the feminist and post-structural, critical pedagogy's new role, as I see it, should be artistic, inventive, speculative; it should embrace the abstract and lead the way in rewriting categories of the real. In this role, critical pedagogy can help shape the process by which the social and political imaginary redefines what is so that we can, in turn, develop new ways of seeing what might be.

Second, the pedagogical dimension of this epistemological paradigm ideally needs to be geared to those that it hopes to help. This means recalibrating the discourse so that it "speaks" to the immediate problems and concerns of workers and others who struggle under the daily grind of time edicts, low salaries, disrespectful work environments, etc. From the basic material needs as they are determined against one's agency—political, cultural, social—to the more global problems of ideology and systemized and rationalized structures of domination, becoming pedagogically critical means working with oppressed people so that they can take control over their lives, fight against oppressive enemies, feel and experience a deep sense of agency, and engage in imaginative practices of thinking and feeling otherwise. Critical pedagogy must become a way of touching people where they live and love, for if it doesn't it will never meet its own standards of criticality and creativity.

Third, intellectual pursuits with affective goals and affective pursuits with intellectual goals should overwhelm ideological pursuits, particularly in the classroom. If critical pedagogy is going to attract anything close to a critical mass, it must start to reach beyond what it already claims to know. Questions of economic, political, social, and cultural importance, as they are born out of current institutional arrangements, will not be answered by old paradigms of thought and analysis. The hard truth, I'm afraid, is that critical pedagogy never obtained a critical mass of supporters because, in addition to some of things already discussed above, it did not answer in a compelling way for many on the (New) Left questions of power and oppression that were arising out of new historical conditions, created by (new) historical agents. It would be condescending at best to dismiss these concerns as false consciousness.

Fourth, critical pedagogy should be as concerned with developing complex theoretical research as much as developing vehicles by which to disseminate the research to audiences that would benefit from it the most. This means that critical pedagogy should be driven by public intellectuals, not academics or theoreticians, even though a public intellectual might also be both of these things. But a public intellectual must also be able to speak to the issues and with the people that are the objects/subjects of their concern. Cornel West, bell hooks, Michael Moore, Robin D.G. Kelley, Howard Zinn, Gloria Steinem, Stanley Aronowitz, and Noam Chomsky all embody, in different kinds of ways, what it means to be a public intellectual.

I do believe that critical pedagogy as both a paradigm and practice can regain its footing, but not without a serious rewriting of some of its own assumptions about what it means to be critical. Developing a critical imaginary is one initial step in revitalizing the paradigm. The development of such an imaginary will not come, as Blanchard notes, from the realm of reality, but rather by taking a detour through the abstract. As Greene writes:

> To tap into imagination is to become able to break with what is supposedly fixed and finished, objectively and independently real. It is to see beyond what the imaginer has called normal or "commonsensible" and to carve out new orders in experience. Doing so, a person may become freed to glimpse what might be, to form notions of what should be and what is not yet. And the same person may, at the same time, remain in touch with what presumably *is*.[27]

Notes

1.   Henry Giroux. 2004. *The Terror of Neoliberalism*. Boulder, CO: Paradigm Publishers, pp. 14–32.

2.   Ibid., p. 16.

3.   Stanley Aronowitz and Peter Bratsis. *Situations Manifesto* (p. 7) retrieved on March 30, 2006 from http://ojs.gc.cuny.edu/index.php/situations/article/view/10/11.

4.   Quoted in Stanley Aronowitz and Peter Bratsis, op. cit.

5.   Stanley Aronowitz. 2003. *How Class Works*. New Haven, CT: Yale University Press.

6.   Ibid.

7.   For the first trajectory see Henry A. Giroux. 1983. *Theory and Resistance in Education*. New York: Routledge.

8.   For the second trajectory see Henry A. Giroux. 1992. *Border Crossings*. Boulder, CO. Westview Press.

9.   Jean Camaroff and John L. Camaroff. 2001. "Millennial Capitalism: First Thoughts on a Second Coming." (p.14). In *Millennial Capitalism and the Culture of Neoliberalism*. Durham, NC: Duke University Press.

10.   Peter McLaren, Gregory Martin, Ramin Farahmandpur, and Nathalia Jaramillo. 2004. "Teaching in and Against the Empire." *Teacher Education Quarterly*, No. 1 (Winter): p. 139.

11.   Ibid., p. 140

12.   Maxine Greene. 1995. *Releasing Imagination*. New York: Jossey-Bass, p. 16.

13.   Olaf Stapledon. 1968. *Last and First Men* and *Star Maker*. New York: Dover Publications, p. 9.

14.   Ibid.

15.   Ibid., p. 10.

16.   Ibid., p. 15.

17.   Ibid., p. 41.

18.   Ibid., p. 90.

19.   Ibid., p. 100.

20.   Stanley Aronowitz, op. cit., p. 48–49.

21.   Ibid., p. 52.

22.   Maxine Greene, op. cit., p. 3.

23.   Ibid., p. 4.

24.   Quoted in Greene, ibid., p. 5.

25.   Ibid., p. 6.

26.   Ibid., p. 15.

27.   Ibid., p. 15.

CHAPTER 4

Locations (or Not) of Critical Pedagogy in *Les Petites et Les Grandes Histoires*

KATHLEEN S. BERRY

Prologue

Many professionals and academics professing to be critical pedagogues have, I assume, many tales to tell; theoretically at least. Where are the stories that reveal personal and local examples of where critical pedagogy exists or doesn't exist in action? This chapter will present personal and local realities as an archaeological genealogy to materialize some sense of where we've been, and where we are and aren't now as critical pedagogues. Each petite narrative will be connected to and contextualized within *les grandes narratives* of modern history and society. *Les petites narratives* will act as a challenge to grand narratives such as capitalism, scientific rationality, bureaucracy, bourgeois values, colonialism, patriarchy, Christianity, liberalism, and corporatization. Furthermore, *les petites narratives* will tell tales of struggle, exclusion, marginalization, abuse, lack of agency, and other social injustices against the often-times invisible, discursive powers of *les grandes narratives*.

Needless to say, the purpose of the storytelling is to address actual accounts of the state of critical pedagogy today with implications of where we need to go tomorrow. The title of the book—*Critical Pedagogy: Where Are We Now?*—obviously has entrenched in it a time frame of where are we coming from and where we are going. To freeze the moment of |

"now" time is something that dramatists work with. What the audience sees and the actors perform on stage may include moments from any time and any place, but the story always unfolds in the "now" time. The audience watches as if present at the time and place. To ask "where are we now?" resonates with this sense of a past, present, and future collapsed into "now" time. So I write this chapter as a performance piece where the reader is seeing critical pedagogy on stage but staging the time frame in the presentation of the question, where are we now?

Another clarification includes the use of the word "pedagogy." I use it in the European sense of the word, which doesn't just refer to schooling but rather a relationship of responsibility with and to another. With the attachment of critical, the meaning of pedagogy problematizes the definition of "Other," thus attempting to avoid "Othering," that is, the various ways in which the discourse of power produces its subjects, and constructs its others in order to confirm its own reality (Ashcroft et al., 1998).

Several methodological discourses and practices are threaded throughout the "now" time of the script. Auto-ethnographic data are employed, as selections of personal history are made political by embedding my moments and memories in the larger picture of society, institutions, and Eurocentric constructions. The personal is presented as *les petites histoires* (little narratives); examples drawn from the local that are daily and immediate, concrete and lived. To avoid the essentializing, normalizing, generalizing, and universalizing and, as stated previously, to show how the personal is political, *les petites histoires* are connected to genealogy and contextualized within *les grandes histoires* (big narratives) of modern Western history and society. *Les petites histoires* act as a challenge to *les grand histoires* such as capitalism, scientific rationality, bureaucracy, bourgeois culture, colonialism, patriarchy, Christianity, liberalism, and so forth while *les petites narratives* will tell tales of struggle, exclusion, and so on. (Please note that I use the English word "narrative" and the French word "*histoire*" interchangeably, as I live in an officially bilingual state. Although I am English, my neighbours are French Acadians, and they move between the two languages with an ease of which I would like to honour in my small way).

Other theoretical lenses are used to analyze the *petite narratives* for signs of critical pedagogy or its nonexistence. I adapt features of Foucault's archaeological genealogy to bring my *petite histoire* into the question of *Critical Pedagogy: Where Are We Now?* In examining the *petite narratives*, the archaeological genealogical principles of Foucault ask the writer as researcher to track how, when, where, and why the social construction being studied—in this case, critical pedagogy—moved (or not) from an everyday, informal existence into formalized texts and practices such as institutions; to deconstruct how Eurocentric constructions of race, gender, class, sexuality, and so forth are marked in certain practices; to excavate (archaeology) how the constructed knowledge (about critical pedagogy) existed at certain temporal points (dates) and in certain spatial locations (local) that are carried forth unnoticed or unexamined into the present (now), and without disruption would be carried into the future; to connect (genealogy) to the political, economic, social, historical, and intellectual climate and conditions that created, circulated, and legitimized certain knowledge and not other knowledge; and to critique the continuation and reproduction of power. Of course, the purpose is not only to address the question of where critical studies is now, but to articulate strategies, policies, and practices for the future of critical pedagogy.

In addition to a Foucauldian lens, discourses and practices are borrowed from several areas of critical studies such as feminist studies and the "post-"discourses to expose locations where critical pedagogy exists or not. Together, all the different discourses and lenses mingle among *les petite histoires* and mix with *les grandes histoires* in a manner similar to bricolage (Kincheloe and Berry, 2004) to produce an unfolding script for staging critical pedagogy. The purpose of bricolage as critical research is not to offer a sampling of texts and methodologies but to engage different discourses and methodologies when needed to highlight certain features of critical pedagogy and as different ways to critique the texts employed.

Act One: Scene One

Une Petite Histoire

The moment I first entered the dramatic staging of critical pedagogy was in the late 1940s, at the age of four, when I contracted polio. To live through that period was a training ground in critical pedagogy for many including myself, my family, the surrounding society, and local and state institutions. I learned about the need for critical pedagogy from my parents, relatives, local society, and institutions such as schools, churches, and hospitals. At the time, there was no socialized Medicare in the country (Canada) and a very small lower-end middle class. Neighbors, in an ad hoc manner, donated winter coats for my parents and drives to the doctor's appointments. My parents sold homes to pay for the medical bills; kind doctors shook hands as payments when my parents couldn't pay. My father was given toys or extra days off by his employer, who knew that his paycheck hardly covered rent and medical bills, let alone toys for a sick child. Uncle Paul crossed the quarantine signs to deliver groceries usually left at our door when other relatives wouldn't. Other neighbors ignored us or reported my mother to child-care authorities when she put donated bob-skates on me, dropped me at a nearby backyard skating rink, and made me struggle home by myself—covertly defying, at great cost to her, the gaze of neighbors who classified her as a "bad" mother.

My mother was subject to many such contradictions in societal and institutional practices of social justice. For example, she developed physiotherapy equipment (unknown and unavailable treatment at the time) from living-room furniture, resisting the medical profession's insistence that the "best practice" was for her to slap rags soaked in boiling water on my body (the "Sister Kenny" treatment). Kindergarten classes were available to children, but my parents could not afford to pay for them, and the institutions of schooling did not know what to do with a child in braces with one "lame" arm. Because they understood how marginalized I felt, my parents withdrew me from kindergarten and bought *Reader's*

Digest condensed books (which was all they could afford), and took me to the small local library and read both to and with me. My grandfather (who had only a fourth-grade education) sat and developed a dictionary of words in a soft-covered leather-like scribbler by looking at the answers for crossword puzzles (I can still see, feel, and smell that cover today).

The Christian church our family attended preached brotherly love, said that the poor shall inherit the earth, and sang "Jesus Loves Me" and "God Sees the Little Sparrow Fall," but they were ambivalent in their responsibility to care for others. It seemed that the foreigners the missionaries took care of received more brotherly love than my family. I can remember minimal, if any, support from the church for my family, especially when they knew that my parents, along with many other members of the congregation, were suffering financially. What an unfair and mean place, I thought at the time, as I watched collection plates fill with money to build stained-glass windows and plush red carpeting for the kneeling boards. But if you wanted to live harmoniously and be accepted in that society, you *had* to attend church.

Young fighter pilots, scarred emotionally and physically by World War II, helped my grandfather build a playground for me, because the neighborhood playground was for "normal" children. There, I could exercise on bars and swings, ride 10-gallon-drum broncos, and be hoisted up on rubber tires and pushed for hours (it seemed) by fighter pilots, parents, and grandparents. They redirected my consciousness away from feeling left out from neighbourhood activities and created an imaginary world where I could be a fighter pilot, a cowgirl, an engineer, or a race-car driver. These people taught me to resist the binary world of ability/disability and build a world where anybody can participate. Needless to say, my playground became the envy of the neighbourhood. On my playground, I was normalized. Outside that world, I was "abnormalized." And, as I learned later, many worlds were not built for me. Where was critical pedagogy then?

Act One: Scene Two

Les Grandes Histoires

I was an actor in Act One: Scene One. Now, I am the audience reflecting on that 1940s scene. When the editors, Kincheloe and McLaren, submitted the prospectus for this book, I realized that they tended to assume that education meant schooling, placing critical pedagogy within the institution instead of ways of coming to know and act in the world. That is not to say critical pedagogy cannot, does not, or should not exist in schools. With this in mind, I summarize how my petite narrative taken from the 1940s reveals how social, institutional, and Eurocentric practices, informed by the *grande narratives* of individualism, the free market, capitalist economics, liberalism, and imperialism, have slipped into the early twenty-first century and continue to circulate and reproduce the dominant powers. Furthermore, as an advocate of critical pedagogy, this summary sheds some understanding as to why and how some constructions of social realities from the 1940s have disappeared from mainstream knowledge, or been co-opted by right-wing neoliberals and corporations to legitimize the dismissal of critical pedagogy in all locations of society and institutions, including schooling.

My *petite histoire* describes a certain time and place that cannot be generalized to other times and places and speak as if it were the same for all. The personal as political does, however, contain a history of the late 1940s as an indication of where and how critical pedagogy did or did not exist in the past. In other words, where are we coming from that informs where we are now? Has there been a precedence for critical pedagogy? What practices does the audience recognize or relate to as critical pedagogy at the individual, societal, and institutional levels? Where do the *grande narratives* (those oppositional to critical pedagogy) such as capitalism, individualism, scientific rationality, bureaucracy, bourgeois values, colonialism, patriarchy, Christianity, liberalism, and existentialism create or contradict constructions and practices of critical pedagogy in which the personal *petite narrative* is embedded? Which *grande histoires* that inform critical pedagogy are evident in the *petite narratives*, such as ideology, deconstruction, feminism, antiracism, Marxism, and the "post-" discourses? What practices and discourses in the *petite histoire* are already at work in shaping the identities and subjectivities of a critical pedagogue that are complicit, in conflict, contradictory, and resistant to the agendas of the *grande histoires?*

The purpose of addressing these questions and analyzing the *petite narrative* using the *grande narratives* of Western civilization provides a focal point for the question, "Where are we now?" The personal narrative is embedded with several indications of critical pedagogy at the individual level, both overt and covert. Individuals did take responsibility for producing practices and creating time that opened spaces for critical pedagogy. Parents, relatives, and some neighbours overtly resisted material signs of exclusion such as quarantine posters and societal norms that existed for months, long after the supposed dangerous period of contact was over. Unbeknownst to those crossing the borders of quarantine, they actually were building immunity to the polio virus. None of those who resisted medical authorities ever caught the virus, and that was long before the Salk or Sabine vaccine was administered 10 years later. Others were complicit with the institutional regulation set by Department of Health authorities of isolating the "sick," even to the point where many designated as sick (in many ways meaning "abnormal") were placed into the isolation ward of the local hospital: elderly people with dementia (senility, as they were classified then), Down's syndrome people (mentally retarded as was the discourse then) of all ages, little people (in the 1940's they were labelled dwarfs/midgets), people with physical, mental, and emotional side effects from the war—and physically handicapped me (only one of two cases of polio in the province that year) in my metal cage-like bed.

Those images and practices marked me for life in terms of "now." Those constructions of the "Other" as abnormal, crippled, different, excluded, and isolated from mainstream society still reverberate as legitimate in institutional discourses and practices "now." The institutions that produce policies and discourses also circulate and maintain that authority in a way that even "now" sustains institutional authority and becomes taken for granted or supported as common sense by individuals and society.

The hegemonic processes and discourses that were at work in the 1940s still exist in institutional and societal practices today. Educational psychology and neoliberalism work discursively with a host of special education classifications such as individual educational plans (IEPs), and the discourses and practices of learning/physically/mentally disabled, and ADHD that continue binary practices and classifications such as my mother experienced in the 1940s. Some neighbours legitimized their practices of exclusion and societal abuse by calling in further institutional support from welfare agencies, reporting my mother as neglectful, cruel, and not "fit," and my father as weak. The discourse of the time that positioned me as crippled and my mother as unfit created binary distinctions for which my mother and father (both 90 years of age) still carry a large package of blame and guilt, similar to many parents both then and now.

The discourse and responses of many individuals in the neighbourhood were rationalized by the hospitals, medical profession, and generalized societal norms and standards of the day. The resistance of a few—including some individuals within the Foucauldian surveillance and control mechanisms of institutions (such as quarantine and isolation wards)—resonates as critical pedagogy. But leaving social justice, inclusion, and equity at the individual level does not produce and maintain power for critical pedagogues at the societal and institutional levels. Those individuals that donated their time, space, and expertise to my family and me resisted the power of institutional authority and created practices of inclusion. But these individual acts were ad hoc, localized, and unrecognized. Their actions did not necessarily impact other individuals or the society and institutions where economic, political, intellectual, and cultural power resided, and where the power to make changes and transform knowledge and practices existed.

Partial acts of social justice and inclusion were created in the 1950s with the rise of socialized Medicare, public health nurses in schools, financial support for (predominantly male) veterans to return to school and university, low-cost housing, and a host of other social policies for children and women such as baby bonuses. These social programs were created mainly in response to post-World War II economic and social conditions and requirements. I say partial because unfortunately the gendered and classed social policies of that time worked hegemonically to allow women to stay in the domestic world but not receive support to join the employment market, receive free day care, or go to university—practices still in effect "now."

I speculate that social programs in the 1940s and 1950s were rushed through government bureaucracies and agencies to produce a national state agenda for movement from a labor-intensive workforce to an increasingly needed middle-classed workforce. In the archaeological time and space of my *petite histoire*, the genealogical connections to *les grande histoires* are there, hegemonically and discursively. These social programs were constructed discursively to privilege knowledge, values, and practices along lines of class, race, religion, gender, sexuality, and age, and between the colonizers and the colonized. In fact, they can be seen to have created a large middle-classed, White, patriarchal, Christian, Eurocentric, heterosexual, and youth-obsessed society throughout North America. The residue of these social programs of the 1940s and 1950s are built on the backs of those excluded categories that didn't fit, at both the individual and collective levels. How can critical pedagogy enter the arenas of economic, political, intellectual, institutional, and global power with claims and practices of social justice and exclusion when the historical background of even an individual *histoire* exposes the hegemonic power of the elite? Today, social consciousness and related programs dwindle under the power of an individualism that feeds capitalism, which feeds corporatization, that in turn gradually takes and is taking power away from collective action (of unions and voters, for example), women, children, public education, and public health.

But this is how hegemony works; a gradual process of rejecting social justice and inclusion for the many, and the establishment of invisible works and structures created by the elite (collectives such as governments, policy makers, media, special interest groups, church and religious institutions, big business, and corporations) to maintain their power and authority. Thus, as demonstrated in my *petite histoire*, individual neighbours, relatives, parents, teachers, or doctors might act as critical pedagogues, but it was ad hoc, by chance, selective, and immediate. Critical pedagogy has to reach further and deeper into society, institutions and Eurocentric, Western constructs to have any impact, to fulfill promises of social justice, equity, and inclusion, both in theory and in practice.

Act Two: Scene One

Les Petites Histoires

Critical pedagogy as education is borderless but contained by actions, by movements and transformations for social justice. To have impact and to be included in schools as critical pedagogy, many *petite narratives* as social movements need to be tracked, deconstructed, examined, excavated, connected, critiqued, and articulated. To do so, I move the staging from the 1940s and 1950s to another *petite histoire*.

When the *grande narratives* of the 1940s and 1950s produced the imperial power of the United States; a large middle class (bourgeoisie)which decreased the gap between the very rich and the very poor; realized independence for formerly colonized nations; desegregated schools, and brought about feminist and sexual liberation in the 1960s and 1970s, where was critical pedagogy? During those decades, I worked in an inner-city elementary school (the discourse of the time, which really meant conditions of poverty, high unemployment, welfare, low-quality rental housing and the projects, cement playgrounds, and latchkey children), a growing immigrant population from several Caribbean islands (that had recently gained independence from European colonizers), several immigrants from Eastern European nations, and a small number of Asian immigrants, mainly from Vietnam (the "boat people"). The First Nation population had left the reserves, mainly because Native women who married nonnative men did not receive "Indian" status, and were thus stripped of the economic and social benefits that Native women married to Native men living on the reserve received.

The immigrant male population mostly held low-paying jobs and, from my memory, immigrant women were either dependent on their husbands, working at part-time jobs, or on social assistance. The nonimmigrant population consisted mainly of White, single mothers living on welfare. Each student was categorized based on a point system of economic status in the district. For a student whose single parent (meaning mother) was living on welfare, the school received one point. If the student's mother was living on welfare and an immigrant, the school received two points. If the student's mother was single, an immigrant, non-English speaking, and living on welfare, the school received five points, and on it went. Because the points accumulated for the school were the highest in the district—in other words, the students were living in poor conditions and were of non-Eurocentric ancestry— the school received additional aid; some financial grants, but mainly additional personnel for remedial and second-language teaching. The strap was still used as a disciplinary action, and if I remember correctly, boys were strapped for behaviour problems (i.e., swearing, physical fighting, name-calling, defiance of school authorities, skipped classes, and unfinished homework). I do not remember any girls receiving the strap, although I am sure there were a few who did. Some parents, very concerned about their children receiving a "good" education (as a means to integrate into middle-class society and enter the middle-income job market), tried to help with their children's homework unless the language of the home was not English.

Several parents, mostly single mothers, did not or could not help at home or show up for parent-teacher interviews. The conditions of poverty in which they were raised and were raising their children, their own repeated school failures (failing grades, repeated grade levels), their lack of middle-class socialization and experiences, and their high dropout rates made school an institution that failed them more than they failed it. So why submit to further intimidation and watch their children be subjected to the same processes of failure?

After-school programs were unheard of for many of these students. Sports, music, art, and dance classes, and travel and other experiences outside their community were limited or nonexistent. A paved playground was provided for some ad hoc after-school basketball or softball games when it was warm enough, and there were snowball fights and forts in the winter. I didn't know any students who were able to play hockey; the cost of equipment, access to rinks, and travel to tournaments was prohibitive for this community. Some students were able to join the local Boys and Girls Club (membership was free) but not the Young Men's Christian Association (the Y.M.C.A. had registration fees). For many, not only did the B & G Club provide access to swimming pools and lessons, theater clubs, buses to visit other places, and community gatherings but also to warm-water showers and toilets for those whose water supply and facilities at home were cut off because the bills could not be paid.

Tony (a pseudonym) spent hours in the showers at the B & G Club. He said, "Ms. Berry, it's the only time I get to feel hot-water clean." He was the same student who was sent to detention by a teacher for not doing his homework in grade four. Living with earth flooring and, quite often, no heat, no water, and the constant noise of traffic and police and ambulance sirens at all hours, he cried in that detention hall. "Young man," said his teacher, "you have no excuse for not doing your homework." These moments are personal but were representative of the conditions for so many students in that school.

And yes, there was standardized testing, and IQ tests, and behavior-modification programs, and report cards, and curriculum guides. Individual teachers and principals administered the tests, used behavior-modification strategies and punishment, followed the curriculum, and failed students from kindergarten to grade six. Many students were required to repeat a grade, and by grade six had failed two to three times. The test scores were always in the bottom two or three schools for the district. The schools in the middle-class areas were always statistically near the top of the ratings. Where was critical pedagogy then?

Act Two: Scene Two

Les Grande Histoires

I was an actor in Act Two: Scene One. Now I am in the audience. As a teacher in that school and others with very similar characters, setting, conditions, and experiences during the 1960s and 1970s, I was living in several contradictory and inconsistent worlds. I attended university courses part-time in order to complete my B.A. At the same time that I was studying theories in sociology, psychology, child psychology, history, geography, and statistics courses, I was facing the context of schooling described in the previous section. There were matches between the academic theories and the daily practices involved in educating students at the inner-city school. Was there critical pedagogy?

In psychology, I studied and took part in behaviour modification experiments developed by B. F. Skinner especially for his fictional Walden II community that employed his methods. Next day, at the school, I could point to the control mechanisms such as points, names on the blackboard, standardized testing, and counseling, and food or other stay-after-school bribes for "behavior problem" students. In retrospect, I realize those devices were systematic and universal assumptions about students and how they are to act and learn in schools, no matter what their gender, racialized identities, and especially classed status. In school, the theories and practices of behaviour modification were normalized and naturalized under the weight of psychology's authority, exactly the same authority applied to military training and prison inmates.

At the university, I participated in experiments based on Milgram's theories and research on human subjects (see the documentary *The Human Behaviour Experiments*, shown on the Canadian Broadcasting Corporation's program *The Big Picture*) where resistance to applying electric shock treatment, deception, and lies to humans was almost nonexistent. The next day, I watched students pushed into cycles of failure and intimidation by individual teachers whose actions were supported at the societal and institutional levels. The discourses, which governed and legitimized certain school policies and practices, included, to name a few: "he needs strict disciplining" (meaning punishment); "he'll/she'll never amount to much, look at the parents"; "he deserves the strap/detention/low marks/to be failed"; "he/she never behaves properly, punish him/her"; "he/she needs to be punished for stepping out of line/being noisy/being late for school/failing to do homework [like Tony]/forgetting to bring his/her gym clothes"; "go sit in the cloakroom/the hallway/the principal's office until you can act 'properly'"; and on and on—pushing the students into the same situations as Milgram's experiments—until the students complied with the legitimate practices of the sanctioned authorities; individual actions sanctioned by the authority of the power elite and institutional policies. Resistance by either individual teachers or a collective group to unfair, unjust, and exclusionary practices in that inner-city school, and I suspect many others, was met with threats of dismissal and accusations of professional misconduct or disrespect for authority and the authorities.

My early years (described in the personal narrative of Act One) taught me creative ways to resist and challenge, but mostly at the individual level. Luckily, there were colleagues and principals who also worked as allies for critical pedagogy. Sometimes we were informed by academic theory and could employ critical discourse borrowed from feminism, Marxism, labour unions, and even literary works and films; sometimes by personal experience; and many times by a social conscience shaped by a history and society that thought we were doing the "right thing." (Ironically, those who used behaviour-modification and Milgram-like practices also thought they were doing the "right thing.") For critical pedagogues, it was the means that did not justify the objective, scientific rationality nor the end of classifying, categorizing, and shaping our students to meet the standards of the dominant White, patriarchal, middle-class, Christian, Eurocentric world (that was not the discourse we used at the time, but we knew who and what was dominant); teaching and covering curriculum so that "they" could get a job; and testing and retesting to legitimize failing students and repeating grades until they "became" and "knew" what and whose standards counted as valued. Parents did not question the large numbers of failures and repeated grades of their children. Not only did they accept the hegemonic discourse that they were not "smart enough" when they went to school, or their children must not be "smart enough" either, based on biological determinism. Rarely did the discourse of many parents and teachers recognize the conflict between the social conditions and socializing processes of the home and community, and those that counted for success in school. Until a recognition of the forces at work in society, and how institutions are ruled by an elite who regulate who gets educated and how will parents, teachers, administrators, marginalized cultures, and societies be able to challenge and change systems of social injustice and exclusions.

In the 1960s and 1970s, university courses in child psychology were based mainly on developmental theories; especially Piaget's, which he based on observations and records of his own children (privileged by being Swiss, male, White, European, middle/upper class, having both parents, their mother fit into a domestic ideology and their father was a university professor, etc.). The authority, rationality, objectivity removed from subjectivity, the explicit organization in steps and according to ages, and the measurability of stages of child development were seductive for the institution of schooling. The theory and practices that followed were assumed to be natural, normal, universal, and generalizable for all children. From a critical pedagogue's perspective, however, they are apolitical, essentialistic, and erased any considerations of context, class, race, gender, and so forth. Ideal, in other words, for avoiding the politics of difference, identity formation, and subjugated knowledge.

The authority of Piaget's developmental theories was so pervasive that it overrode any alternative or different ways of thinking about teaching and learning, or about teachers and students. It slipped into the discourse and curriculum documents so readily and discursively that the practices in academic disciplines, classroom control and management, school organization, curriculum theory and development, assessment, and evaluation of classroom work and students became saturated with a Piagetian world. Developmental theories rampantly objectified teaching and students to the point of ludicrousness, ridiculousness, and oppression. Teachers and students were reduced to fitting into a stage and category, and even after insistent, repetitive lessons to get a student into the next developmental stage and category, many students at that inner-city school soon became labeled as developmentally deficient or "suffering from a developmental lag."

Kincheloe and Steinberg (1993) and many other critical pedagogues have questioned the justice of these developmental theories, exposing them as sexist, racist, class-based, and so forth. In the inner-city school where I taught, we novice critical pedagogues tried to creatively resist applying developmental theories and practices to and with our students. We cheated on tests by giving them the answers, completed worksheets and workbooks with and for many students, lied about what "stage" a child was working at, and refused to fail students on the final report card. I know there were principals, superintendents, and other teachers who knew what we were doing but supported us by remaining silent. A few times, some of us were caught and called before a board, chastised verbally, and marked as defiant and uncooperative (we were partially protected by permanent contracts and union membership). But the price for our resistance was small compared to what we would now call practicing critical pedagogy; teaching students and teachers to "misbehave" in a behavioral world/institution (as Shirley Steinberg once told me).

My first formal introduction to the principles, discourse, and practices of critical pedagogy was through an undergraduate university course called "The Politics of Literacy." The required text was Paulo Freire's *Pedagogy of the Oppressed*, first published in 1970. George Martel, a social activist, creator of a school for inner-city students, and founding editor of a left-wing magazine called *This Magazine Is About Schools*, was the professor. Class after class, week after week, I found ways of thinking about teaching, students, and learning that were liberating for me and, I hoped, for my students. When I went back to school the day after a university class, I was filled with the spirit of critical pedagogy. But individual resistance has limited power against those of the society, the institutions, the times, and spaces in which one practices. I learned to be complicit with the injustices of the *grande narratives* and structures of schooling rather than challenge and change them.

During my Ph.D. studies in 1983, Paulo Freire taught a course at the university. Colleagues and I were mesmerized by his compassion and spirit. We found it disconcerting, however, that the theories and practices used were informed by Marxism. What was problematic in this case was that most of us were privileged by our class, race, and education, and the contexts in which many of us worked outside the academy did not seem to be "oppressive." In addition, most thesis and research methodologies acceptable at that time were statistics based, thus legitimizing empiricism, objectivity, positivism, and scientific rationality—major enemies of critical pedagogy. The opportunity for critical pedagogy to access a status among *les grande histoires* of theory and research was limited if not impossible. Although Freire, William Pinar, Valerie Suransky-Polokow, Madeline Grumet, and Maxine Greene were visiting scholars at that time (thanks to the visionary leadership of Ted Aoki and Max Van Manen), research and scholarly work, the departments of educational foundations and administration, educational psychology, and curriculum and instruction still based their studies mainly on the theories and practices of the *grande narratives* of the Enlightenment, modernism, colonialism, the imperialism of the West, and the quantitative analysis of text, individuals, society, and institutions. The struggle for critical pedagogy to enter mainstream academic and school culture at that point was like trying to sail a boat without wind. Where is it now?

Act Three: Scene One

Les Petites Histoires

The first two acts located critical pedagogy (or lack of) personal and institutional settings in the past. This next act places critical pedagogy at the local level of society in the present time. Currently, several community events are unfolding; the drama is still being written, so to speak. The setting is in a small state, in a rural area with a saltwater ocean on most of its border. In summer it is heavily populated with tourists; in winter, just a few permanent residents are left. The population is White, with ancestry from France and England. There are hardly any residents of national, racial, and ethnic ancestry other than European and, if so, they are only there in the summer. So racial diversity is almost nonexistent in this local narrative.

Most people are working-class fishers and farmers, seasonal workers in industries that supply goods to Wal-Mart and other corporations. Class diversity is increasing, as middle-class urbanites are gradually building permanent homes on ocean waterfront and waterview properties. The power of the Church has dwindled, but two area churches—one large Catholic Church and a small Anglican church—are part of the religious landscape, a further indication of the Eurocentric history of the area. Small farms and fishing sustain some local residents, while many drive 30 kilometers to the nearby urban area for employment. To get to school, children as young as five sit for an hour on a bus. Where is critical pedagogy located (or not) in this setting?

Social justice, inclusion, diversity, plurality, and equity are just a few of the major claims made by critical pedagogy. So too is antisexism, antiracism, anticlassist elitism, antihomophobia and antidominance. Have those claims transformed individual, societal, and institutional knowledge, beliefs, values, and practices in the setting described in the previous paragraph, the same world presented in Act One's personal *histoire* only 59 years later? Have the discourses and practices of critical pedagogy entered the everyday discourses and practices of individuals, society, and the institutions of this ocean-side world and time, indicative of "Where Are We Now"?

Ten years ago, I returned to this area after a 46-year absence to build a permanent home as I neared retirement age. Over the past 20 years, I have been exposed to the theoretical tenants of critical pedagogy, first during my Ph.D. studies and currently as a professor of critical studies in a faculty of education at a state-run university. I view the world through the lens of critical studies, attempting to put its theories into practice and assuming the rest of the world is too. Has this world changed since the days of my personal *histoire* of the 1940s?

Social justice, inclusion, and equity are as applicable to the natural world as they are to the human one, although humans construct and change the natural world. In this area, the natural environment acts as a signifier or site for needing critical pedagogy. The relationship between humans and the natural environment requires social justice, diversity, and responsibility. To track, examine, and critique this local relationship and the local relationships between people provides some insights into the question, "Where Are We Now?"

As an ocean-bordered community, it is the condition of our water sources that tests our practices of critical pedagogy. If water is the source of the economy and the community, then both are in grave danger. Needless to say, the saltwater ocean, the freshwater streams, and the water table and the wells are polluted or close to dangerous levels. Outdated septic systems; cottages and homes crowded together on spaces meant for 1930s and 1940s middle-class owners; a rising urban blight; erosion of waterfront land; entropic beaches overrun by huge, environmentally unfriendly boulders; breakwater walls built with railway ties filled with creosote (a kerosene-based chemical to prevent wood from rotting); and even a nearby urban community stealing water from this local area and trucking it to their community are just a few actions imposed by humans on the natural environment.

Several local grassroot committees have been formed to address these issues and to provide a collective voice to approach the local community and the government for funding and action. Like many situations of social injustices, very few at the individual, societal, and institutional (municipal and state government) levels are willing to "get involved," "rock the boat," spend time and money, implement policies and procedures, look for creative and alternative ways to protect the water, or be responsible for future generations—our children (excuse the political cliché and liberal discourse that actually depoliticizes and dismisses the conditions).

Local fishers clash with nearby First Nations fishers over "rights" to fish the waters anytime and anywhere, as legally stated in treaties and Indian Acts produced a century ago. The newspaper media, owned by a corporate family, circulates the situation as a fishing "dispute," as with the lumbering "dispute," while the First Nations people talk of fishing and lumbering "rights." Local people and state government accept the discourse of dispute, thus placing the social and legal rights of the First Nations and their right to action (agency) in jeopardy. Authority is given to the discourse of "dispute" by the media and governments, thus maintaining the discursive power of nonnatives. Some individuals in the community recognize the "rights" but still ally with the local nonnative fishers. Societal discourse includes, "They [the First Nations people] already get too many handouts"; "What rights should they have, they don't even pay taxes"; or, "Isn't it time they got off their butts and worked hard like everyone else." One local resident said how her son has to work hard to get into university, whereas his First Nations' friend does not have to because he gets "his way" paid to go to university. No one ever seems to ask or discuss how nonnative individuals, their relatives, their society, their government, their nation, and their European ancestors benefit(ed) from the wealth of the land and waters since the time of colonization.

In fact, a large corporate family, once identified as the fifteenth-richest family in the world, owns a large portion of the lumbering land in the state and several industries including the ships and trucks that haul the finished products. They don't pay taxes either or allow unions, but the discourse switches when talking of the corporate giant. They become legitimized by the discourses of hero worship "because they provide jobs for the local people"; or dependency discourse of "we [those living in this State] need them because we can't do it [create jobs, bring money to the state, support our families]"; or martyr discourse of "the founder came from nothing and worked so hard to get where he/they are today"; or dismissive discourse of "somebody has to do it." Each insertion of these discourses into daily conversations of the society and in institutional discourse such as newspapers, business meetings, capitalist agendas, and government offices legitimizes the unjust and exclusionary practices of the elite. The discourses are circulated at these different levels of culture and work to maintain and legitimize hegemonic practices of the elite over the very masses that consent to their own discourse as truth and without question. And no one seems to have the power to stop environmental injustices and corporate power—or do they?

A local grassroots movement spent their own money and several years building a portfolio of facts (i.e., cancer rates, noise levels, erosion, and displacement of private residents), constructing arguments, and documenting support from the local community/society to stop the corporation from building and expanding a gravel pit using the land and water sources of the community. At the meeting, the local group dressed in mud-covered work boots, running shoes, plaid hunting shirts, jeans, Zeller's coats, and dollar-store plastic rain hats. They arrived in trucks and small cars. They carried dog-eared file folders and dollar-store notepads scratched with pen or pencil questions and comments. The group consisted of local people—post-office workers, carpenters, farmers, housewives, small business owners, and service-station attendants. There was a close balance of women and men, younger and older. The corporate representatives dressed in London Fog coats and grey, brown, or black suits, wore shoes so polished you could see your face in them, and carried umbrellas (they don't mess the hair). They drove up to the meeting doors in large, expensive, executive-level cars ("fancy-dancy," as one local called them). They carried real leather briefcases and laptop computers. Their reports and notes were typed and carried in hard-covered folders with tabs and slots. Their group consisted of personnel advisors, engineers, scientists, contractors, public and media relations representatives, lawyers, and professional report writers and statisticians. They were almost entirely male, and most of the group seemed to be in their late 40s to early 60s. What a setting for a drama!

The meeting began. The local people talked of personal damage to their health, their homes, and their children, and of the loss of jobs and community services. The corporate people talked about providing jobs (not mentioning the outsourcing), environmental impact surveys done by the leading authorities in the field, and other building they did near water that has been recognized as a model "around the world." When a local man asked about the drilling (not oil-related) into local private properties, a corporate engineer came forward with an explanation of how the drilling would be monitored by leading experts, including himself. He elaborated further by stating that this practice had been done before without any damage being done; how he had reports in his briefcase that confirmed/proved the success of the particular drilling practices by leading scientists and engineers. After overwhelming the crowd with statistics, charts of procedures, and reports stating "conclusive" evidence/proof and "global" success, a young local man at the back of the hall stood up. "Fuck your mighty scientist and engineers. What about the drilling and damming at the Chocolate River? It was known before building it, all the damage it would cause. And today we'll take your goddamn engineers and scientists and show you the fucking proof of the damage during and after the drilling." Needless to say, the locals cheered. The engineer had no response except to retreat to his seat while his colleagues huddled around him. The corporate emperors wore no clothing of authority at that time.

Weeks later, after the local county officials reached a decision in favour of the local grassroots movement to stop the corporate power, the issue was to be voted on in Parliament, an institution filled with representative of taxpayers in a state where non-tax-paying corporate power controls economic systems. The grassroots movement continues to fight for personal, local, social, and environmental justice.

Intermission

To continue the metaphor of staging critical pedagogy through *les petite histoires* brings me to a point of intermission after the presentation of the first three acts. There are more acts and scenes about critical pedagogy to follow this intermission, so many more to be presented. They have been created, produced, and performed in the past, at present, and will be in the future. The "now" time of drama captures those acts in lived and reflective scripting. I have presented three *petite histoires*; a personal one, an institutional one, and a local one, as examples of the complexity of identifying what counts as critical pedagogy and its relationship with historical, political, economic, and intellectual contexts. The *petite narratives* also expose struggles against established systems of power created by the discourse and practices inherent in the *grande narratives*. *Petite histoires* were also presented over three different time periods: the 1940s, 1960s, and 2006. Because critical pedagogy is not a technique or method that can be fixed or total, as empiricism, scientific rationality, and positivistic objectivity want to be, *petite* and *grande narratives* as locations of power relations and structures present the shifting and problematic conditions that have arisen and changed throughout time and space. When *petite* and *grande histoires* collide, connectedness happens. Reflexivity, informed by critical theories, becomes the practice of articulating where and how changes are to be made. Social justice, equity, inclusion, plurality, diversity, and multiplicity are neither means nor ends. They are processes towards creating those conditions for everyone; a never-ending process, perhaps.

The previous *petite narratives* are not necessarily representative of the principles and practices of critical pedagogy. They are, however, an attempt to materialize the abstractness of the theories, discourses, and practices that constitute critical pedagogy. Also, they show the complexity, connectedness, contradictions, and resistance in each isolated situation. This same grassroots group, like many of us in this local area, shifts in our applications of critical pedagogy. Sometimes we are complicit with certain practices that are seen to be racist, sexist, homophobic, and classist. A neighbor in his 70s who mows elderly people's lawns for free, fought single-handedly in court against corruption at his workplace, at a great cost to him financially and emotionally. He was isolated by neighbors and colleagues long after the court found board members had stolen large amounts of money from clients. He supports local committees to save our beaches and water supply. But like many of us, he shifts and contradicts his Christian belief of "love thy neighbour" when he isolates a transgendered person or makes derogatory remarks about a lesbian couple, all of whom live on the same street as he does.

Critical pedagogues are not consistently and continuously struggling against societal and institutional powers. If we did, the sheer political inertness and intellectual exhaustion would prevent us from impacting on individuals, society, and institutions to transform practices and systems of injustice, exclusion, and "Othering." Critical pedagogy is not something that totalizes, finalizes, unifies, and draws conclusions. It does not solve problems. What is seen as a problem or issue is examined and critiqued, even questioning what and who makes it a problem in the first place, how did the problem get to this point, and surrounding the questions with connections to historical, political, economic, and intellectual conditions that created the problem/issue. Once tracked, deconstructed, examined, excavated, connected, and critiqued, the text (problem, issue) can provide articulation of strategies, policies, and practices that will transform individual, societal, and institutional knowledge, beliefs, values, discourses, and structures.

In the context of schools, critical pedagogues are making increased use of digital technologies such as computers, cameras, and recorders; by producing DVDs about unjust social conditions and practices both factual (note the increasing presence of documentaries in mainstream movie houses) and fictional and informed by critical theories and structures that reshape modern constructions of knowledge and values. Teaching students of all ages how to extract multiple readings of a text decenters the cultural heritage orientation with its strong roots in a Eurocentric analysis of text. The "post-"discourses provide different ways of thinking about where and how individuals and texts are positioned in the world by formalism, modernism, and colonialism.

Critical pedagogues bring a variety of material sources, such as oral histories and oral storytellers, print, CDs, film, magazines, music videos, television, video games, art, and photographs into the classroom for critical analysis; everything from classical to popular-culture texts. Students engage in finding the intertextuality of a single text; peeling back layers to find the existence of other texts within the single text, requiring a very rigorous and complex pedagogy. In a critical pedagogue's classroom, digital technologies and multimedia overlap to produce hypertexts. Together teachers and students access knowledge and values from different socially constructed cultures, based on class, gender, race, sexuality, and so on. Critical pedagogues recognize how identity formation floats, rests, and shifts by rejecting evaluations and record-keeping that freeze a student's identity for purposes of controlling, isolating, excluding, and failing. The combinations and permutations of these practices are unlimited, creating a pedagogy of complexity and possibility. Most importantly, however, is that this is not done as entertainment or busy work. Critical pedagogues concern themselves with content first but not as accumulation of knowledge. The concern is always to engage the texts, the students, and the learning in a manner that questions, challenges, and resists unequal relations and conditions of power, be it social, textual, political, economic, and so forth.

So where is critical pedagogy now? In theory, it is ahead of many areas of study and growing each moment, year, and decade, but hopefully not to become hegemonic in and of itself. Critical pedagogy is continuously borrowing and developing discourses that question and challenge dominant powers. In practice, critical pedagogues are sometimes complicit with the regulations and actions of individual, societal, institutional, and the imperialist powers. Sometimes we avoid the conflicts and contradictions between words and actions; between oppositional discourses and ideologies; between people. Most times we work in those spaces between the conflicts. Many times foregoing complicity and resistance as the options, critical pedagogues negotiate borders of conflict, difference, and indifference. Critical pedagogues are continuously tracking and examining *les petite histoires* at the individual, societal, institutional, and civilizational levels for conditions and structures of oppressive privilege and power produced by *les grande histoires*.

References

Ashcroft, B., Griffiths, G. and Tiffin, H. (1998). *Key Concepts in Post-Colonial Studies*. New York: Routledge.

Kincheloe, J.L. (2002). *The Sign of the Burger: McDonald's and the Culture of Power*. Philadelphia: Temple University Press.

Kincheloe, J. L. and Berry, K. S. (2004). *Rigour and Complexity in Educational Research: Conceptualizing the Bricolage*. Maidenhead, UK: Open University Press.

Kincheloe, J. L. and Steinberg, S. R. (1993). A Tentative Description of Post-Formal Thinking: The Critical Confrontation with Cognitive Theory. *Harvard Educational Review*, 63, n3, pp. 296–320.

CHAPTER 5

Neoliberal Non-sense

PEPI LEISTYNA

Even though exclusionary practices and social unrest in the United States are being discussed within the discourse of social and educational reform, both the conservative and liberal efforts to restructure public schooling are severely limited by the paradigm from which they work, and are thus inadequate and ineffective in dealing with the plethora of today's societal dilemmas and tensions.

This is the opening passage of a book called *Breaking Free: The Transformative Power of Critical Pedagogy* that I put together with some colleagues at the *Harvard Educational Review* in 1996. In looking back on the historical context within which this book was conceptualized, while simultaneously asking the question "Where are we now?," the following chapter reveals how, over the past decade, educational policies and practices informed by the logic of neoliberalism have exacerbated rather than ameliorated this "ineffectiveness," and have moved further away from rather than toward the transformative power of critical pedagogy.

Neoliberalism is a political and economic ideology that works to largely eliminate government's power to influence the affairs of private business. In the name of privatization, the goal is to maximize profits—with the vague promise that wealth and prosperity will eventually make their way down to the rest of society. In order to achieve this end, standards such as a minimum wage, job security, health insurance, collective bargaining rights, and environmental protections are replaced with an unrestricted flow of production and trade, and a global division of labor.

It's ironic that elite private powers obsessed with neutralizing government regulations have been successful in using the state to protect their own interests. It is important to take a critical look at the blatant contradiction embodied in downsizing government while expanding its powers to limit democratic participation; that is, how government is being used by corporate powers to establish discriminatory and exclusionary policies and practices that work to justify today's gross inequities, especially those caused by capitalism and its class structure.

No Corporation Left Behind

Most people in the United States are unaware of the extent to which public schools over the past decade have been increasingly influenced by private interests such as publishing, food, and pharmaceutical companies, for-profit education management organizations, and corporate lobbyists (Kohn & Shannon, 2002; Molnar, 2005; Molnar et al., 2006; Saltman, 2000, 2005). In fact, in 2006 alone lobbying monies used to influence the government topped $2.4 billion. Meanwhile, "some 80% of all political contributions now come from less than 1% of the population" (Collins, Hartman, & Sklar, 1999, p. 5). As a consequence, most of the public policy debate in this country remains in the confines of the Wall Street agenda.

> The stealth onslaught of privatization and commercialization of this vital institution should come as no surprise, given that education reform has been masterminded—in large part behind closed doors—by a handful of corporate executives, politicians, and media moguls who have already profited handsomely from the over $600 billion-a-year educational-industrial complex (Bacon 2000; Gluckman, 2002; Miner, 2004/2005).

> It's a pretty simple equation: when you have a captive audience, given that K-12 education is mandatory in the U.S., private interests within the logic of capital can't help but salivate and pounce. But as all good capitalists know, the overriding objective of corporations is to maximize their profits. So what they have to do in order to shape public policy in their own interests—and gain consent on those rare occasions when the general public is involved in the process—is disguise their "profit over people" mentality by wrapping themselves in an image of expertise and compassionate concern for the education and future of our children.

Since President George W. Bush signed into law the Elementary and Secondary Education Act of 2001, better known as *No Child Left Behind (NCLB)*, standardized curricula and high-stakes testing have been officially embraced as the panacea of academic underachievement in public schools in the United States. The Act, ushered in by big business interests (for a detailed version of the history of this corporate story, see Suchak [2001]), engenders a hitherto unheard of transfer of power to the federal government, granting it the right to largely determine the goals and outcomes of these educational institutions. As a direct result of this new agenda, school administrators, teachers, parents, labor unions, and communities are stripped of any substantive decision-making power in the nation's public schools.

This social movement has been spearheaded by a political party that, in the not-so-distant past, called for the dismantling of the federal Department of Education. Neoliberals figure if they can't defeat the system, they can nonetheless control it. But under Article I of the U.S. Constitution, the "founding fathers" gave Congress no power to legislate when it comes to public education—leaving decisions of this matter in the hands of individual states. In blatant disregard for the Constitution, *NCLB* required that by 2003, students in third through eighth grade be evaluated in mathematics and reading, and then reevaluated once in high school. By 2007–08, federal requirements also demand that states administer tests in science in elementary, junior high, and high school. By the year 2014, all students must be proficient in these subject areas. Schools that don't meet these criteria will be stripped of their government funding, threatened with closure, or placed in the hands of charter schools or other such private management companies.[1]

Under pressure to produce results on these standardized tests or face the consequences, many school administrators have been forced to drastically narrow their curriculum and cut back on anything and everything that is perceived as not contributing to raising test scores. In many cases, this includes the elimination of two-way bilingual education, creative writing, interdisciplinary studies, music and art, community, and athletics programs. Within this "one size fits all" standards approach to schooling, the multifarious voices and needs of culturally diverse, low-income, racially subordinated, and linguistic-minority students are simply ignored or discarded. In fact, the concept of multicultural education that was flourishing in many forms in the 1990s has virtually disappeared from public discourse and policy debates.

A key characteristic of the new "highly qualified teacher," according to *NCLB*, is the ability to pass a subject-matter test administered by the state. Reducing teacher expertise to a fixed body of content knowledge, middle and high school teachers are expected to meet an extremely narrow range of skill requirements under the new policy. Any concern with pedagogy—not what we learn, but how we learn it—has virtually disappeared. As a direct consequence of this political climate, public schools are being inundated with prepackaged and teacher-proof curricula, standardized tests, and accountability schemes. Needless to say, a critical pedagogy that calls for nurturing educators and students into analyzing the values, beliefs, and relations of power that shape the world around them is by no means welcome.

In his bid for the presidency in 2000, George W. Bush, as governor of Texas (1994–2000), effectively used what was referred to as the "Texas Miracle"[2] to spearhead his educational policy plans based on standards and high-stakes testing. Declaring himself the "education president," Bush would also use this "miracle" to help push through the *No Child Left Behind* legislation.

The Texas Education Agency (TEA) and Texas school districts had implemented standardized assessments to measure student knowledge of the state's curriculum in 1980. By 1990, the Texas Academic Assessment Skills (TAAS) program had been developed— through a five-year coordinated effort between TEA and the publishing giant Harcourt Brace—in order to measure students' abilities in writing, mathematics, reading, science, and social studies. The exam would be fine-tuned over the years to meet the Texas Essential Knowledge and Skills curriculum standards, which were approved by the State Board of Education in 1997. Success on the TAAS is required in order to graduate from high school in Texas.

While spokespersons for conservative organizations, studies funded by advocates of the testing industry, and much of the mainstream media raved about the work being done in Texas and the fantastic decrease in drop-out rates and increase in academic achievement that occurred since TAAS had been implemented, the so-called "miracle" was in fact a scam (Valadez, 2005; Haney, 2000; McNeil, 2000). Those students who were perceived as potentially lowering the overall test scores were retained in grades where testing was not required, especially ninth grade; or they were placed in special education classrooms or labeled Limited English Proficient (LEP) and were thus exempted from taking the exam. Coupled with a long list of discriminatory practices that predate the standardization movement but continue to fester, this "miracle" has resulted in extremely high drop-out rates in Texas.

It's not as if Rod Paige, the superintendent of the Houston Independent School District (HISD), could have been unaware of allegations of discrimination related to the TAAS exam, or the mass exodus of students from his schools, given that he was elected to the district's Board of Education in 1990, had been the superintendent of HISD since 1994, was listed by *Inside Houston Magazine* as one of "Houston's 25 most powerful people in guiding the city's growth and prosperity,"[3] and the fact that:

> On October 4, 1995, the Office for Civil Rights (OCR) received a complaint filed by the National Association for the Advancement of Colored People (N.A.A.C.P.), Texas State Conference against the Texas Education Agency (TEA), Austin, Texas. The complaint raised concerns pertaining to the Texas Assessment of Academic Skills (TAAS) and its alleged discriminatory impact on African-American and Hispanic/Limited English Proficient (LEP) students. (Texas NAACP, 1995)

High drop-out rates are fantastic for raising test scores, but they simultaneously call into question the overall success of the standards program in place, so while they are often encouraged by corrupt administrators, they need to be hidden from public view. In a self-serving and malicious move, Paige and members of his administration cleverly manipulated the numbers and claimed that the drop-out rate of local schools was 1.5%, rather than the actual figure of 40% (CBS News, 2004). In reality, Texas schools, in particular those in Houston— the 7th largest school district in the country—have some of the worst drop-out rates nationwide.

There were also widespread stories of teachers encouraging students to cheat on the TAAS in order to raise the scores (Valadez, 2005), as well as reports of the monopolization of the entire curriculum by prep classes that were teaching solely to the test (Haney, 2000).

Praised for his "success," in 2001 Paige was named National Superintendent of the Year by the American Association of School Administrators and was appointed Secretary of Education by President George W. Bush.

Conservatives insist, ad nauseam, that "scientifically based research" informs and sustains the nation's educational practices, policies, and goals. However, under close scrutiny, the empirical studies that are used to buttress the Bush agenda are easily stripped of any legitimacy. The well-funded think tanks that produce much of the research and literature to support conservative causes have an obvious, ideologically specific perspective.

A recent example of how data can be manipulated, packaged, and presented as "scientific research" is the official report signed and circulated by the congressionally appointed National Reading Panel (NRP). This report, which informed Bush's *Reading First* literacy campaign, is replete with inconsistencies, methodological flaws, and blatant biases (Allington, 2002; Coles, 2000). For starters, G. Reid Lyon, who was Bush's educational advisor when he was the governor of Texas, headed the NRP. A staunch phonics advocate, Lyon hand-selected the panel and made certain that virtually all of the participants shared his views. There was only one reading teacher on the NRP. However, by the end of the group's investigation into effective literacy practices, she refused to sign the panel's final report, maintaining that it was a manipulation of data, and that the cohort failed to examine important research that did not corroborate its desired findings. As Stephen Metcalf (2002) reveals:

> Widmeyer [the public relations firm hired by the government to promote the panel's work] had represented McGraw-Hill's flagship literacy product Open Court during the Texas literacy drive, and now it counts McGraw-Hill and the Business Roundtable among its most prominent clients. "They wrote the introduction to the final report," says NRP member Joanne Yatvin. "And they wrote the summary, and prepared the video, and did the press releases."

McGraw-Hill has been laughing all the way to the bank ever since, tapping into the $6 billion that the President has set aside to fund his "literacy" campaign. And guess who's been recruited to hold the federal purse strings: Christopher Doherty, the guy who spearheaded the move to bring McGraw-Hill's DISTAR (Direct Instruction System for Teaching Arithmetic and Reading) to public schools in Baltimore (Metcalf, 2002).

Embracing what is in fact an old neoliberal approach dressed up as innovative reform, the political machinery behind *NCLB* has effectively disguised the motivations of a profit-driven industry. Schools now give nearly 50 million tests a year, and the annual value of this market ranges from $400 million to $700 million ("The Testing Industry's Big Four," 2006). The General Accounting Office estimates that by 2008, up to $5.3 billion will be spent by states trying to meet the requirements of this legislation (Miner, 2004/2005). However, this figure doesn't include the enormous costs of prep sessions, practice tests, scoring and reporting, data storage, and let's not forget the nearly $7 billion-a-year market for instructional materials. But the enormous expense doesn't end there. Ben Clarke (2004) reminds us of another lucrative market:

> Under *NCLB*, if a school fails to improve math and reading test scores within three years, a por-
> tion of its federal funding will be diverted to "parental choice" tutoring programs. . . . These out-
> sourced programs are run by private companies such as Educate Inc., owner of Sylvan Learning
> Centers whose revenues have grown from $180 to $250 million in the past three years and whose
> profits shot up 250% last year.

The potential for funneling taxpayers' money into private pockets is astounding. This is precisely why it is important for the public to watch closely how money is earmarked when
politicians increase the federal budget for education: what often appears to be a concerned
call to increase spending to improve schools for our nation's youth is actually a ploy to
increase profit potential for those kingpins playing the standards game.

The ultimate contradiction that the high-stakes testing movement seems to be in no
hurry to reconcile is that, in this era of accountability and "scientifically proven methodologies," the private firms that are benefiting from this trend have little to no oversight in
terms of their daily operations and the quality and performance of their products and services. Unlike other areas of industry that are highly regulated—though not for long, if
neoliberals have their way—there is no federal agency that independently investigates testing company products and practices. It's not even clear in the research what these high-
stakes tests evaluate in terms of student competence. While a score may be indicative of
how well prepared a student is for a particular testing instrument, it reveals little to nothing about his or her overall abilities (Haney, 2000; Kohn, 2000; McNeil, 2000; Sturrock,
2006; "High Stakes Testing and Its Effects on Education," 2000). In other words, the
entire industry is built on theoretical ambiguities and empirical uncertainties rather than
"scientifically based research." Louisiana conducted a study of 91 of its school districts and
"found that $300 million was paid to tutoring companies in one year 'with almost no sci-
entific evidence that this spending has contributed to academic achievement'" (Horn, 2005).
To add insult to injury, unlike public school teachers, those "educators" who work for private schools or tutorial companies that are receiving federal money under *NCLB* do not
need to be credentialed.

It is also important to know who the actual power brokers are that are reaping the ben-
efits of this movement. While many corporations (e.g., Edison Schools/Newton Learning
Corporation, Educational Testing Service's ETS K-12, Advantage Learning Systems,
Measured Progress, Data Recognition, Questar Educational Services, Kaplan, Princeton
Review, BP, AT&T, Tribune, IBM, and Dupont) are in the race to get a piece of this pie,
there are four big publishing houses that have virtually monopolized the industry: Harcourt
Brace, Houghton Mifflin, Pearson, and McGraw-Hill. As Metcalf (2002) notes, "the so-
called Big Three—McGraw-Hill, Houghton Mifflin and Harcourt—[were] all identified as
'Bush stocks' by Wall Street analysts in the wake of the 2000 election." It is interesting to
note that three of the four publishing giants are internationals, and given the conservative
pitch on global competitiveness and national security, it's not clear why such companies
would have any vested interest in improving the education of students in the U.S. other
than for financial gain.

By the end of the millennium, when the testing movement was really heating up, Harcourt Brace's educational division was pleased to inform its shareholders of an almost 30% increase in sales. An international conglomerate that also owns Holt, Rinehart and Winston, Harcourt Brace boasts annual revenues of over $5 billion. Willing to go to almost any length to maximize its profits in Texas, Harcourt Brace pitched its course materials as being published by "the same company that helps to write the TAAS tests" (Bacon, 2000). What is unethical and self-serving about this practice is that any use of prep materials that developmentally coincide with the content of the exam compromises the validity of the scores (Gluckman, 2002). In other words, prepping of this kind is a subtle form of cheating, but for Harcourt, student success on the exam means guaranteed contracts.

Houghton Mifflin also gained from the early race to nationalize standards, as its testing division's profits grew by almost 18% in 1999. With a keen understanding of how information processing is a key component of the standards market, in 2003 Houghton Mifflin purchased Edusoft, a profitable company that specializes in data storage and online tests. The conglomerate now boasts more than $1 billion in annual sales.

Pearson currently has long-term contracts with more than 20 states, and its 2005 profits were up 29%. Since the implementation of NCLB, their sales on assessments alone are up more than 20%. In its 2005 "Performance Report" under the subtitle "Continued Investment for Future Growth," Pearson reassures its shareholders that it will greatly increase its profits from U.S. schools by a steady investment in school publishing; basal-curriculum programs for reading, science, and social studies; and school testing (where it already maintains contracts in Texas, Virginia, Michigan, and Minnesota that have a life-time value of $700 million). It also mentions the creation of Pearson Achievement Solutions to target the growing market for professional teacher development and integrated school solutions. It's interesting to note that there is not a single word in the report about the academic achievment of students.

When Congress allocated $3 billion per year for teacher training in its reauthorization of the Elementary and Secondary Education Act in 2001, Pearson decided to take a big bite out of that market share by acquiring National Evaluation Systems, Inc. (NES), which produces assessments for teacher certification. Teacher burnout, a serious side effect of this era of standards and accountability, is actually a virtue in a profit-driven industry. As Pearson notes in its 2006 press release:

> There are approximately three million public school teachers in the U.S. Approximately 2.5 million new teachers will need to be hired in the current decade, as 700,000 current teachers retire and 1.8 million are expected to leave the profession prior to retirement. On average, nearly 6% of the teacher workforce does not return for each new academic year and half of all new teachers leave the profession within five years.

With 280 offices in 40 countries, McGraw-Hill is a major player in the publishing world. A simple look at this New York-based company's website and one can see how profits have consistently soared since the advent of the standardization craze. With contracts in 23 states, McGraw-Hill's Terra Nova, CTBS, and California Achievement tests are the most lucrative of its assessment instruments. Trying to expand its $1.4 billion textbook sales, "McGraw-Hill lobbyists used the statewide results on their own California Achievement Tests to convince the state legislature that California schools needed the McGraw-Hill Open Court and Reading Mastery program to improve students reading performance" (Clarke, 2004). Expected to teach at least part of the day from the McGraw-Hill Open Court materials, "according to Ben Visnick [president of a local teachers' union in California], 'School district employees and instructional facilitators—we call them Open Court police—inspect the classrooms to verify that the right posters are on the walls and they want everyone in the district on the same page every day'" (as cited in Clarke, 2004). While the California Department of Education guidelines prohibit the use of test-prep materials written for a specific test, the practice is common nonetheless (Gluckman, 2002).

In the 2006 ranking of the Fortune 500, McGraw-Hill comes in at 359, with over $6 billion in annual revenues. But perhaps what's most interesting about this corporation is its deep connection to the Bush dynasty. In his article in *The Nation*, "Reading Between the Lines," Metcalf (2002) lays out the depth of this nepotism, describing how the two families have been chummy since the 1930s, when they vacationed together in an exclusive area in Florida. He is worth quoting at length here:

> Harold McGraw Jr. sits on the national grant advisory and founding board of the Barbara Bush Foundation for Family Literacy. McGraw in turn received the highest literacy award from President Bush in the early 1990s. . . . The McGraw Foundation awarded current Bush Education Secretary Rod Paige its highest educator's award while Paige was Houston's school chief; Paige, in turn, was the keynote speaker at McGraw-Hill's "government initiatives" conference last spring. Harold McGraw III was selected as a member of President George W. Bush's transition advisory team . . . An ex-chief of staff for Barbara Bush is returning to work for Laura Bush in the White House—after a stint with McGraw-Hill as a media relations executive. John Negroponte left his position as McGraw-Hill's executive vice president for global markets to become Bush's ambassador to the United Nations.

And of course, under Bush Jr., Negroponte would go on to be U.S. ambassador to Iraq (2004–05), and is now the Director of National Intelligence. The word "intelligence" here has two frightening implications: a scary thought in terms of national security, given the well-documented horrors that Negroponte was involved in while trying to subvert the growth of democracy in Latin America when he was U.S. ambassador to Honduras (1981–85) under Reagan; and a scary thought in terms of what our children learn in schools that are under the influence of a standards regime that works diligently to engineer history as it sees fit, much in the way that Negroponte himself worked to keep his actions in Latin America from becoming public knowledge.[4]

McGraw III, as part of a group of "education leaders," was invited to speak at the White House by George W. Bush on his first day in office.

Bush Jr. and McGraw-Hill have been partners in crime before. As governor, Bush joined forces with the publishing giant in order to pitch their proposed phonics-based literacy program to the Texas Education Agency, which was trying to establish a statewide reading curriculum.

> For a period of roughly two years, most often at the invitation of the governor, a small group of
> reading experts testified repeatedly about what would constitute a "scientifically valid" reading cur-
> riculum for Texas schoolchildren. As critics pointed out, a preponderance of the consultants were
> McGraw-Hill authors. (Metcalf, 2002)

As to be expected, these experts tooted their own horns in front of the TEA, calling for a reading program that was right in tune with a slew of new textbooks and materials from McGraw-Hill—a market that the company easily cornered with the support of the governor (Clarke, 2004).

In the world of crony capitalism, these kinds of deals are made all the time. Look at how Bill Bennett, the former Secretary of Education under Reagan (1985–1988), and drug czar under Bush Sr. (1989–1990), has been cashing in lately. Bennett's online home/school company, K-12 Inc., recently received $4 million in grants from the U.S. Department of Education. The funds are intended for an online charter school in Arkansas—Arkansas Virtual Academy ("X U.S. Secretary of Education Bill Bennett," 2006).

Not only is it morally questionable how Bennett's for-profit business came about getting the grant, especially since other programs that had been turned down had better independent reviews, but it is also disconcerting that federal funds are being diverted away from public schools in order to subsidize education for home-school students. Sure, *NCLB* has set aside money for its Voluntary Public School Choice Program with the expressed purpose of giving students a chance at a better education; however, only 25% of the students who have participated in K-12 Inc.'s program are from public schools (Ohanian, 2004). Meanwhile, Bennett has been working his inside contacts to cut deals in other states around the country.

Though he extols universal morality in his *Book of Virtues* (1993), it is important to remember that this is a guy who has a multimillion dollar gambling addiction, and who on his syndicated radio talk show expressed to a caller: "If you wanted to reduce crime, you could—if that were your sole purpose—you could abort every black baby in this country and your crime rate would go down" ("Bennett Under Fire," 2005). This is a guy who doesn't even support public education and yet uses taxpayer's money for his own business ventures. As Intel director and former FCC chairman Reed Hundt revealed about the former Secretary of Education:

> . . . I asked Bill Bennett to visit my office so that I could ask him for help in seeking legislation
> that would pay for internet access in all classrooms and libraries in the country. . . . He told me
> he would not help because he did not want public schools to obtain new funding, new capabil-
> ity, new tools for success. He wanted them, he said, to fail so that they could be replaced with vouch-
> ers, charter schools, religious schools, and other forms of private education. Well, I thought, at
> least he's candid about his true views. (Hoffman, 2005)

It's also important to remember that Bennett used start-up money from Knowledge Universe to get K-12 Inc. up and running. Knowledge Universe is owned by Michael Milken, the "Junk Bond King" who ripped off investors for billions of dollars in the 1980s and consequently spent a couple of years behind bars—though there were no actual bars where Milken did time. And when he was done with his sentence, a period during which he learned how to prepare traditional French dishes from the prison chef, he was allowed to keep over $2 billion that he had accumulated from his criminal escapades. It certainly doesn't seem virtuous for Bennett to use blood money for any purpose, let alone to profit from the very taxpaying public from which it was ultimately stolen. It is also hypocritical for a staunch supporter of neoliberalism—an opponent of government influence and assistance—to apply for a federal grant in the first place.

There is ample room for nepotism in state and federal politics, especially when it comes to family connections. As revealed in a *USA Today* article by Jill Lawrence, "Congress Full of Fortunate Sons—and Other Relatives" (2006), there are more than 50 U.S. senators and representatives that are closely related to governors and other members of Congress. But what better position is there to be in when it comes to old-boy networks than to be the grandson of a former senator, the son of a former CIA director and president of the United States, the brother of the incumbent governor of Florida, and the brother of the former governor of Texas—now president of the country.

In the spirit of *NCLB*, Neil Bush, the president's youngest brother, is pushing to sell online, multimedia educational products and test-prep software produced by his Austin-based company, Ignite Inc., to states around the country. Founded in 1999, one of Ignite's first targets was Florida's public schools, where the company has been pitching its products as helping to prepare students for the Florida Comprehensive Assessment Test (FCAT). While the Florida Education Association has expressed some concern about a potential conflict of interest in developing a business relationship with Neil Bush (given that his brother is the governor), the youngest sibling adamantly denies any discussion about his business affairs with either of his brothers.

Ignite's materials are currently being used in a pilot program in Orlando, and the company hopes to be able to market an early-American history course throughout the state at a cost of $30 a year per student. It is looking to sink its teeth into what looks to be a $60 million deal. The company has already come under some heavy criticism for its "dumbed down" version of history, which includes a lesson on the Seminole Wars that presents, in cartoon form, a football game with "the Jacksons vs. the Seminoles." One can only imagine how history will be engineered by Neil Bush when it comes to U.S. foreign policy.

The company also plans to develop software for math, science, and the language arts, as well as programs for special needs and linguistic-minority students. Ignite has already successfully pedaled its educational wares in California, New York, Ohio, Georgia, New Jersey, Pennsylvania, Nevada, Oklahoma, and Arizona. But, the majority of its 40,000 users are in Texas.

Much of the over $20 million that Ignite has generated to materialize and sustain its operations has come from international oil and technology companies in such undemocratic countries as Kuwait and China that have a long history of human rights abuses. However, some of the financial support has actually been arranged for by his mom—the former First Lady who campaigns around the country rallying business leaders about the virtues of her sons' education policies and curriculum packages. She recently made a donation to the Katrina Disaster Fund stipulating that some of the money had to be spent on

Ignite's educational products and their implementation in public schools in Houston, the city where many of the hurricane evacuees found high ground (Garza, 2006). Not only is this inappropriate in the general practice of nonprofit donations, but it provides yet another example of how the rich are brilliant in getting tax breaks for themselves while simultaneously profiting.

If everything goes as planned, Neil Bush could use more than just his family name for influence and access. Given that the government has agreed to fund a portion of state costs for technological products and services for the classroom, and the president is being heavily lobbied to increase the $1.5 billion already allocated for private research and development of educational technology, Ignite will be eligible for federal dollars. The company certainly has an advisory board fit for the job of soliciting these monies:

> Ignite has loaded its advisory committees with Bush loyalists, assuring the company a sympathetic ear in Washington. According to the company, its big-name consultants include Bill Brock, a former senator from Tennessee who chaired the Republican National Committee; Bob Stearns, a Houston investor appointed to a Texas technology board by George W.; Peter Su, a former campaign adviser of the president, and two executives from Bessemer Trust, an exclusive investment firm that manages a portfolio for Neil's dad. (Scherer, 2001)

But put aside for a moment the gross conflict of interest here, as well as the possibility of international firms giving Neil Bush money in order to gain access to the president of the United States. Let's even put aside his testimony during divorce proceedings that revealed his marital infidelity with prostitutes while on business in Asia, and instead focus on the financial track record of the man behind this education project and why the public should have no confidence in his management skills, let alone in a financial endeavor that involves the youth of this nation.

The reason that most people don't know much about the youngest Bush heir is largely because his political career died in the late 1980s—during his father's tour as president—when he was the acting director of Silverado Savings and Loan in Colorado, a company that went down with the S&L ship. Neil Bush's scandalous behavior cost the taxpayers over $1 billion. While angry protesters picketed outside his home demanding prosecution and retribution, a grand jury investigation never pursued the case to that end and young Bush was thus never charged with a crime. His banking activities were nonetheless restricted by federal regulators and he was ordered to pay a $50,000 fine. A civil lawsuit was eventually settled against Bush and other Silverado executives for the sum of $49.5 million.

Neil Bush has a long track record of failed business ventures and a history of wheeling and dealing with sketchy characters, including people that he solicited money from in order to start Ignite Inc. (Bollyn, 2005; Carlson, 2003; Goodman, 2004). This includes dealings with the Saudi Binladen Group; Russian tycoon Boris Berezovsky, who has been prosecuted for fraud; and the Reverend Sun Myung Moon, leader of the controversial Unification Church.

And why all this talk about helping to give the children of the United States a fighting chance to compete in a competitive global economy? In spite of all the rhetoric about lending a hand to the youth of this nation by fighting for a better system of public education, U.S. corporations are huge fans of outsourcing jobs and exploiting cheap labor both domestically and internationally. Neil Bush has actually augmented Ignite's profit structure by outsourcing 70 jobs to Mexico in a partnership that he forged with Grupo Carso Telecom (Carlson, 2003).

With capital flight and global outsourcing, both blue-collar and white-collar jobs have been and continue to be exported by U.S. corporations to nations that pay below a living wage and that ensure that workers have no protection under labor unions or laws that regulate corporate interests and power. As the Federal Reserve has acknowledged, these jobs won't be returning even if there is a major upswing in the U.S. economy. It is important to note that by cheap labor, we're often talking between 13.5 and 36 cents an hour; we're also talking about a total disregard for child-labor laws and environmental protections.

American workers are being blamed by corporate heads for not being educated enough to compete in a global economy, and yet we have one of the most educated and productive workforces in the world, regardless of the fact that our public education system is highly class based. In this era of globalization, with enormous job loss, outsourcing, and off-shoring, corporations need a scapegoat for their avarice. That scapegoat is the nation's workforce; one that is not working hard enough—and yet, since 1975, productivity is way up (163%)—and who are asking for too much money, though wages have been stagnant (115%) while corporate profits have risen through the roof (758%).

It's ironic that corporations are simultaneously claiming that public schools are not doing an adequate job of preparing a qualified labor force in the U.S., while moving their operations to "third world" countries where there is enormous illiteracy and where, in the spirit of neoliberalism, they can exploit the seemingly endless pool of low and semiskilled labor. And of course, these are the same forces, à la Negroponte, that influence a U.S. foreign policy that works to keep these countries destitute.

Language Policy: Swimming in the Pool of Cheap Labor

Language policy has certainly taken a turn for the worse in the U.S. since the release of *Breaking Free*. Many Republicans and Democrats alike embrace the national movement towards English-only language and literacy policies and practices. Anti-bilingual advocates have argued that, in order to promote effective nationwide communications and meet the demands of modern technology and the economy, the United States is compelled to use a linguistic standard. These political voices have thus called for a mandatory English-only approach for all children in public schools throughout the country. At the forefront of this cause is Ron Unz, the chairman of the national advocacy organization English for the Children, and the originator of California's Proposition 227, which in 1998 effectively outlawed bilingual education in that state. After a similar victory in Arizona in 2000 he also attempted to win over Colorado. However, a wealthy parent spent a mountain of her own personal money on a press campaign to convince the middle-class White population not to support Unz's initiative, because if bilingual programs are dismantled then "those kids will be in class with your kids." This well-funded, racist plea worked, and Colorado voted no on the English-only referendum.

Unz demands that the United States replace bilingual education (which he describes as "a disastrous experiment") with a one-year Structured English Immersion Program. As the English for the Children publicity pamphlet states:

> Under this learning technique, youngsters not fluent in English are placed in a separate classroom in which they are taught English over a period of several months. Once they have become fluent in English, they are moved into regular classes.

In November 2002, after being bombarded with misinformation, Massachusetts voters decided the fate of bilingual education in K-12 public schools. English for the Children came to Boston in order to work to replace Transitional Bilingual Education, a three-year program, with one year of Structured English Immersion (Bartolomè & Leistyna, 2006). However, research clearly shows that it can take children from five to 7 years to become fluent and literate, able to learn sophisticated content in the second language, and thus able to handle the demands of standardized testing like the MCAS (Massachusetts Comprehensive Assessment System). This should come as no surprise as that's how long it took all of us in our first language experience. Effective immersion and bilingual programs take this fact into account, and they work from the basic premise that if knowledge is comprehensible in the first language (e.g., the language of math), then it will be easier to understand in the second language. The catch-up process in bilingual education consequently includes grade-appropriate content in the native language while the English improves. On the contrary, teachers under the Unz initiative can be sued and banned from working for 5 years if they use any language other than English in the classroom.

There is no defensible theory or body of research to support the claim that students need only one year (about 180 school days) to become fully fluent, literate, and able to learn content in another language. Regardless of Unz's rhetorical claims, the majority of students in California's Structured English Immersion Program did not achieve even intermediate fluency after 1 year. A progress report in California reveals the extent of the disaster:

> In 2002–2003, it [Ron Unz's Structured English Immersion] failed at least 1,479,420 children who remained limited in English. Only 42 percent of California students whose English was limited in 1998, when Proposition 227 passed, have since been redesignated as fluent in English—five years later! (Crawford, 2003, p. 1)

With 5 years of watered-down content, rather than intensive subject matter instruction in the primary language, these students will certainly be ill prepared for high-stakes standardized tests. In states like Massachusetts, students who do not pass the state's standardized test in high school will not graduate. Instead, they will be shown to the door and handed a Certificate of Attendance on their way out; that is, if they manage to stay in school under such conditions.

From a self-professed opponent of bilingual education, affirmative action, multiculturalism, multicultural education, and most other movements and policies that support a more participatory democracy, we hear statements from Unz (2000) such as:

> First and foremost, our public schools and educational institutions must be restored as engines of
> assimilation they once were. . . . In history and social studies classrooms, "multicultural education"
> is now widespread, placing an extreme and unrealistic emphasis on ethnic diversity instead of pass-
> ing on the traditional knowledge of Western civilization, our Founding Fathers, and the Civil and
> World Wars . . . current public school curricula which glorify obscure ethnic figures at the expense
> of the giants of American history have no place in a melting pot framework. (pp. 3–4)

What's particularly interesting about this rhetorical strategy that calls for "assimilative policies" is that the mainstream that supports English-only education in the U.S. is not the least
bit interested in the assimilation of racially subordinated groups into their neighborhoods,
places of work, educational institutions, clubs, and communities; that is, in equal rights and
universal access.

As has been historically the case in a xenophobic climate clouded with anti-immigrant
sentiments, the main concern of local folks is with "unwelcomed outsiders" taking their jobs
and affordable housing, and flooding public schools and other social services. The harsh reality is that beyond the concocted hype about the usurping of quality employment by "outsiders," the job opportunities that are intended for migrant workers, the majority of
immigrants, and the nation's own downtrodden consist of manual labor, cleaning crews, the
monotony of the assembly line, and farm jobs that require little-to-no English—as with the
Bracero Program (1942–1964) when more than 4 million Mexican farm laborers were
"legally brought" into the U.S. to work the fields and orchards. These workers spoke little-
to-no English, signed contracts that were controlled by independent farmers associations
and the Farm Bureau, and were immediately put to work without an understanding of their
rights. In 1964, when the Bracero Program was finally dismantled, the U.S. Department
of Labor officer heading the operation, Lee G. Williams, described it as "legalized slavery."

There is a new scramble by big business and politicians, both Republicans and
Democrats, to "legalize" undocumented workers. In response to a demand for and shortage
of low-wage jobs and low-skill workers, George W. Bush's administration is looking into
another guest-worker program. Thus, being pro-immigrant (Unz claims "Nearly all the people involved in the [English-only] effort have a strong pro-immigrant background") does
not necessarily mean being pro-social justice.

75% of all linguistic-minority students reside in low-income, urban areas that have
schools that are highly segregated and in rough shape. These students so often face harsh
racist and material conditions, incessant harassment, segregated school activities, limited
classroom materials, ill-prepared teachers, poorly designed and unenforced policies, and indif-
ferent leadership that dramatically disrupt their personal, cultural, and academic lives. The
leading voices of English-only education say virtually nothing about the socially sanctioned
and systemic practices that discriminate against certain groups of people and that generate antagonistic social relations and economic exploitation and abuse.

As the founder and chairman of a Silicon Valley financial services software firm, and
the 1994 GOP nominee for Governor of California, Unz's insistence that an English-only
approach will ensure "better jobs for their [linguistic-minority children's] parents" doesn't
seem to ring in solidarity with organized labor's concerns with the systematic exploitation

of workers, both documented and undocumented. Simply shifting to a one-year sink-or-swim Structured English Immersion Program for what would now be "legal" workers (who, by the way, won't be going to school as they'll be working long hours) will not eradicate the problems of economic abuse and subjugation. On the contrary, such conservative programs provide limited access to language and learning and prevent most linguistic-minority children from attaining academic fluency in either their native language or in English. A one-year Structured English Immersion Program is surely designed to fail in developing both fluency and literacy. Instead, these kinds of state and federal educational policies and practices reflect an implicit economic need to socialize immigrants and members of oppressed groups to fill necessary, but undesirable, low-status jobs.

White supremacy, classism, and other forms of discrimination embedded in neoliberal practices play a serious role in limiting one's access to social, economic, institutional, and legal power. Instead of addressing such issues, the English-only coalition serves up myths of meritocracy and life in a melting pot where the patterns of a "common culture" and economic success miraculously emerge if one is willing to submit to their agenda. Unz states that bilingual education is a place where children "remain imprisoned" and thus is about "guaranteeing that few would ever gain the proficiency in English they need to get ahead in America."[5] However, he neglects to recognize the fact that even in the cases where English is one's primary language, it does not guarantee economic, political, and integrative success. For example, Native Americans, Native Hawaiians, Chicano/as, and African Americans have been speaking English for generations in this country, and yet the majority of the members of these groups still remain socially, economically, and politically subordinated.

Class mobility in this country is more restricted than ever before, unless of course the direction is downward. Within these neoliberal economic shifts, the middle class is imploding into the working class, which in turn is imploding into the working poor who are literally relegated to life on the streets. Census data show that the gap between the rich and the poor in this country is the widest it's been since the government started collecting information in 1947. In fact, with the exception of Russia and Mexico, the United States has the most unequal distribution of wealth and income in the industrialized world. The richest 1% of Americans controls about 40% of the nation's wealth; the top 5% has more than 60%. While the nation's median household income is $44,389—down 3.8% from 1999—in 2002, the average income for the top 0.1% of the population was $3 million. The nation's wealthiest 10% own almost 90% of all stocks and mutual funds (Collins et al., 2004). While one in two Americans don't own stocks, the ubiquitous numbers from Wall Street imply that the market will help those in need and the country as a whole.

37 million people in this country live in poverty, a number that is up 1.1 million from 2003. Keep in mind the federal poverty thresholds: one person under 65 = $9,214, two people under 65 with one child = $12,207. According to the U.S. Department of Agriculture, there are 25.5 million people who rely on food stamps to avoid hunger—a number that is up 2 million from 2004. 6.8 million families live in poverty. 17% of the nation's children, or about 12 million kids, are compelled to endure inhumane economic conditions. And

yet, in this post-Katrina world—where federal malfeasance unwittingly exposed the raw poverty that exists in this country—the Bush administration and both Republican-run houses, just before Christmas 2006, pushed through $50 billion in spending cuts to such social programs as food stamps and Medicaid.

An Urban Institute study recently revealed that about 3.5 million people are homeless in the U.S. (a number projected to increase 5% each year); 1.3 million (or 39%) of them are children.

45.8 million Americans lack health insurance, which includes 9.2 million kids. "Overall, nearly 1 in 5 full-time workers today goes without health insurance; among part-time workers, it's 1 in 4" (Krim & Witte, 2004, p. A01). As compared with 2001, there were 5 million fewer jobs providing health insurance in 2004. These statistics are particularly interesting given that "the average compensation for the top health care executives at the top 10 managed healthcare companies, not including unexercised stock options, is $11.7 million per year" (Jackson, 2001).

Even the current tax system in this country is structured to perpetuate the class hierarchy. "People making $60,000 paid a larger share of their 2001 income in federal income, Social Security, and Medicare taxes than a family making $25 million, the latest Internal Revenue Service data show" (Ivins, 2005, p. 1).

Neoliberalism is particularly hard on women. On average, women make 77 cents to a man's dollar. Median income for men is $40,800; for women, it is $31,200.

The leading occupations for women are all lower-middle and working-class jobs. In addition, the majority of jobs at the bottom of the economic scale are held by women, especially women of color. "Minority women are even more likely to be low earners"—in 2003, 33.9% of Black women and 45.8% of Latinas earned low wages (Mishel, Bernstein, & Allegretto, 2005, p. 130).

While racism, like gender, can't simply be conflated with the economic base of capitalism, we certainly need to look at the ways in which it is used to exploit diverse groups within capitalist social relations. It is also crucial to look at the ways in which historically racism has served an important role in keeping at bay working-class unity and maintaining a system of labor exploitation.

In this age of downsizing, outsourcing, and offshoring, the current administration has bragged about creating new jobs for Americans, but it fails to inform the public that these are overwhelmingly part-time, adjunct, minimum-wage positions that provide no pension, union protection, or healthcare benefits. Part-time, temp, or subcontracted jobs currently make up 30% of the workforce ,and this number is rapidly increasing. As the federal minimum wage is currently $5.15 an hour—a wage that is sustained by powerful corporate lobbyists—full-time workers making minimum wage in the United States are paid about $10,712 a year. This makes it impossible to afford adequate housing throughout the country. It's no wonder that one out of every five homeless people is employed. It is important to note that contrary to popular myth, the majority of minimum-wage workers are not teenagers: 71.4% are over the age of 20.

Within this neoliberal reality, the average income in the United States is shrinking and workers are earning less, adjusting for inflation, than they did a quarter century ago. Real wages are falling at their fastest rate in 14 years. Meanwhile,

> median CEO pay at the 100 largest companies in Fortune's survey rose 14 percent last year to $13.2 million. Still, average CEO pay in *Business Week's* survey was $7.4 million. It would take 241 years for an average worker paid $30,722 to make that amount. (Sklar, 2003, p. 4)

The ratio of average CEO pay in the U.S. to the average blue-collar pay in the same corporation is 470 to 1.

The federal government provides $125 billion a year in subsidies and other forms of welfare to corporations, and this doesn't include the $427+ billion that is funneled through the Pentagon's military-industrial complex. Here the government socializes risk and investment while the public pays for the research and product development but privatizes the profits. The working class not only pays for "endless" wars with their tax dollars and by sustaining program cuts that fund these "adventures in capitalism," but also with the lives of their children, as they make up the majority of combat soldiers.

The massive budget cuts for war and other corporate exploits, and the frantic deficit spending that guts domestic funding for education, health care, and other public needs and services are part of a conscious effort to wipe out any money to sustain the public sector, paving the way for privatization.[6] One would think that in a democracy the media, in particular the airwaves (as they are owned by the people), would cover and problematize some of this neoliberal nonsense.

The Role of Corporate Media

While neoliberalism consists of a structural reality built on political and economic processes, institutions, and relationships, its proponents also rely on the formative power of culture to shape the kinds of meaning, desire, subjectivity, and thus identity that can work to ensure the maintenance of its logic and practice. Corporate bodies take very seriously the fact that culture shapes our sense of political agency and mediates the relations between everyday struggles and structures of power.[7] In fact, in this age of postmodern technologies that can saturate society with media messages, elite private interests have worked diligently to monopolize the means of production and distribution of information and ideas so as to be able to more effectively circulate, legitimate, and reproduce a vision of the world that suits their needs, a world where profit trumps people at every turn. Since the Democrats signed the *Telecommunications Act* of 1996 into law, radio waves have been largely monopolized by big business interests such as Clear Channel, and television is now largely controlled by five massive transnational corporations: Time Warner, Disney, News Corporation, General Electric, and Viacom. As the Federal Communications Commission continues to pass legislation that allows these conglomerates to further monopolize the use of public airwaves (McChesney, 2004)—while it buries research that clearly shows how such forces are breaking the law by neglecting to serve the needs of the general populace—such private interests have been effective in using this medium to disseminate messages that serve their ideological and economic imperatives in ways that reinforce classist, racist, and sexist stereotypes that serve to justify the inequities inherent in a capitalist system.

On the contrary, critical media literacy, as part of the larger project of critical pedagogy, emphasizes nurturing languages of critique that help us read into the values and beliefs that are embedded in the knowledge that we are exposed to, and inform our actions to transform the material conditions and symbolic systems that maintain the oppressive social code in the United States.

What to Do with All These Disposable People, Especially the Ones Who Get Out of Line?

Instead of confronting all of the aforementioned gross inequities and abuses of power, as part of class warfare the U.S. is developing and implementing repressive and punitive social policies to contain "disposable" and "unruly" populations.

Zero-tolerance policies and the criminalization of working-class, poor, homeless, and racially subordinated people feed into the growing prison-industrial complex. Prisons have been strategically used within the feudalism of today's capitalist social relations to lock up what is seen as superfluous populations that the powers that be have no immediate use for. The prison population in the United States has consequently skyrocketed over 200% since 1980. There are now over two million people in jail in the U.S., and although we have only 5% of the world's population, we have 25% of its prisoners. The U.S. surpassed Russia in the year 2000 and now has the world's highest incarceration rate. It is 5 to 17 times higher than all other Western nations. By the close of the millennium, 6.3 million people were on probation, in jail or prison, or on parole in this country.

Over 70% of prisoners in the U.S. are from non-European racial and ethnic backgrounds. African American males make up the largest number of those entering prisons each year in the United States. Racially subordinated women are also being incarcerated in epidemic proportions. As Loic Wacquant (2002) states, "The astounding upsurge in Black incarceration in the past three decades results from the obsolescence of the ghetto as a device for caste control and the correlative need for a substitute apparatus for keeping (unskilled) African Americans in a subordinate and confined position—physically, socially, and symbolically" (p. 23).

While the validity of these incarceration statistics is not in question in national discussions, there is great contestation as to why they exist. Conservatives endlessly wield racist and class-specific representations of violent groups that need to be contained. When young people are represented (as opposed to self-described) in the media, especially the poor and racially subordinated, they are overwhelmingly depicted as dangerous and untrustworthy. However, this representation is scripted outside of the reality that the proportion of racially subordinated workers earning low wages is substantial—30.4% of Black workers and 39.8% of Latino/a workers (Mishel, Bernstein, & Allegretto, 2005). The median income of racially subordinated families is $25,700, as compared with $45,200 for White families—(Collins et al., 2004). A consistent pattern in the data has shown that the unemployment rate for African Americans and Latino/as over the years has remained more than double that of Whites. While about 10% of White children live in poverty in the United States, over 30% of African American and Latino/a kids experience economic hardship.

Critical cultural workers and educators have been concerned with discrimination in employment and the judicial system, and have provided important analyses of the high levels of imprisonment and the correlation with unjust economic conditions, the dismantling of welfare, the driving down of wages, and the pursuit of neoliberalism and deregulation in the incessant search for cheaper labor. It is axiomatic that poverty produces crime, and the U.S. continues to have the highest child poverty rate among major industrialized countries, along with huge levels of working poor who are relegated to living below the poverty line regardless of their employment.

While progressive arguments that cogently connect incarceration with corporate class warfare and White supremacy should be at the forefront of national attention, it is also important to emphasize that there is an inextricable link between the astronomical numbers of racially subordinated and working-poor youth in prisons today and the public system of schooling. As revealed in the discussion about standards, high-stakes testing, and language policies, the economic and political forces that shape public education—institutions that reflect the larger social order—do not make an effort to create intellectually challenging, culturally responsive, humanizing, and thus inviting public spaces where youth can achieve academically and thrive professionally. As Ken Saltman (2000) observes:

> . . . urban, largely nonwhite institutions do not even feign to prepare students for entree into the professional class, the class that carries out the orders of the ruling corporate-state elite. These schools contain students who have been deemed hopeless and have been consigned to institutional containment. Many urban schools function as the first level of containment while the second level, America's largest growing industry, the prison system, awaits them. (p. 86)

For those throw-away masses, a callous social infrastructure, constant exposure to harsh material and symbolic conditions both inside and outside of school, exclusionary and distorted curricula, and apathetic and abusive educator attitudes and pedagogies work to virtually ensure the self-fulfilling prophesy of youth deviance. As one African American young man stated to me when I visited a local prison (after I moved away from the prison guards and into the crowd):

> This isn't rehabilitation . . . just look around. These are young people locked up all day and night long, for what, for smoking a joint, or getting in a fist fight in the street! There's no education here, there's no preparation for a future, there's no room here for healing—there's just time, a waste of time. This place breeds anger and hostility. Just look around, this is an entire generation that's being thrown away like the day's garbage, only this "garbage" is profitable! (Leistyna, 2003, p. 105)

Neoliberals have a new kind of incarceration that they are working to nationalize—the prison of the mind. While it sounds like science fiction, the drug industry in the United States is working closely with President Bush in order to screen the entire population for mental illness:

> Developed by the President's New Freedom Commission on Mental Health, the effort, critics charge,
> is a pharmaceutical industry marketing scheme to mine customers and promote sales of the
> newest, most expensive psychiatric medications . . . Under "New Freedom," mental health screen-
> ing of adult Americans is slated to occur during routine physical exams while that of young peo-
> ple will occur in the school system. Pre-school children will receive periodic "development
> screens." (Goldstein, 2004)

Not only is this scheme, which requires mandatory treatment, potentially highly profitable
for an industry that already makes more money than any other business in the country this
side of the oil industry and the likes of Exxon/Mobil, but it is also an ingenious and insid-
ious way to mark those people that society doesn't approve of as mentally disturbed
(Foucault, 1988). Take, for instance, a note that I just received from a former graduate student of mine who is currently teaching at a charter school in Florida:

> The school is currently in the Renaissance. As you will recall I lived in Italy and also in the Virgin
> Islands. Consequently, I began to discuss how Columbus' voyage was funded by expelling the Jews
> from Spain and how Columbus' crew behaved after naming the islands Virgin and the place Holy
> Cross. I made reference to Kirkpatrick Sale's *Conquest of Paradise*. We discussed how the anti-
> Semitism of the Renaissance had begun with Constantine in the 4th century and progressed through
> time until finally reaching the extermination of six million Jews. We discussed how Columbus put
> names on places that already had names. Finally I brought in diverse images of Renaissance gar-
> dens and used the Socratic method to reveal exactly how unnatural, unwelcoming and from the
> point of view of a Native American how insane the design of Renaissance gardens was. Well some-
> one did not like my anti-colonial stance nor my critique of the sacred Renaissance. I was removed
> from class, sent to the office, and told to go to the emergency room and get immediate psychiatric
> evaluation. The psychiatrist said exactly what the high school psychiatrist said when I was 16, "You
> made one terrible mistake, you told the truth to the wrong people."

Containment can thus be achieved via being institutionalized or through prescription
drugs.

This policy of mandatory mental health screening is also a way to justify medicating
youth in public schools. In the name of Attention Deficit Disorder, we are unnecessarily
doping our kids into conformity and complacency. As there is no scientific basis for diagnosing ADD, there is plenty of room for malice in diagnosing anyone that steps out of line.
Just go into any public school and look at the long line at the nurse's office after lunch.

Meanwhile, Ritalin has the same addictive qualities as the amphetamine cocaine. In
fact, it is listed as a Schedule II controlled substance by the Drug Enforcement Agency
(O'Meara, 2001). What better situation for satiating corporate greed than being allowed
to produce junkies who are not only controllable through psychotropic drugs, but who are
also addicted to your products?[8] Six million children, at the request of school officials and
doctors, are on these psychotropic drugs every day, and this number is dramatically increasing. While the drugs make kids robotic and lethargic and thus more manageable, they also
retard normal growth in children. As Michael Russell (2006) notes:

> We are overmedicating and under educating our youth, using Attention Deficit as an excuse. While
> there may be a small number of individuals whom the medication does help, many children are
> losing their identities to a small pill each day.

Of course, within the realm of neoliberalism, there is no encouragement to critically look at the commodified junk culture that has emerged under this economic logic; a culture saturated with frenetic media images, video games, and alienating ideas that create unrest and depression. There is no connection made between hyperactivity and the sugar and chemicals found in the corporate-generated junk food that kids have easy access to in schools across the nation (Schlosser, 2001; Zwillich, 2006); or any engagement with research that shows that fast-food chains target public schools ("Do Fast Food Chains Cluster Around Schools?," 2005). Nor is there any analysis of the psychological effects of a restrictive school structure, a boring standardized curriculum, and the anxiety generated by high-stakes testing.

Where Are We Now?:
In Even Greater Need for Critical Pedagogy

As we argued back in 1996 with the release of *Breaking Free: The Transformative Power of Critical Pedagogy*, progressive educators and community activists desperately need to continue to do the important work of informing and mobilizing the public to undo what is already largely under the control of private powers. Ultimately the long-term goal is to have a critically informed public vote out of office representatives that are sacrificing children to the corporate bottom line. In the meantime, there are things that teacher education programs and practitioners can do to work towards redemocratizing public schools and creating civic-minded students and a vibrant public sphere.

First and foremost, teacher education needs to be formulated in a way that helps to apprentice students into critical inquiry. Not to be confused with what's traditionally thought of as the "higher-order thinking skills" (problem-solving skills), *critical* in this sense implies being able to understand, analyze, pose questions, and affect the sociopolitical and economic realities that shape our lives. Developing critical consciousness isn't an exercise to get people to think in a certain way; rather, it is intended to get them to think more deeply about the issues and relations of power that affect them. Unlike the president who, at a White House ceremony honoring the 2002 National Teacher of the Year, declared, "When I picked the Secretary of Education, I wasn't interested in theorists . . ."—and previously, at the Fritsche Middle School in Milwaukee, Wisconsin in 2000: "We want our teachers trained so they can meet the obligations, their obligations as teachers"—civic-minded teacher education programs need to create the conditions within which people can think for themselves. Teachers shouldn't be mere practitioners who jump when they are told to jump; they need to be intellectuals and professionals who can make sense of the world around them so that their actions are informed. They need to be theorists.

Theory embodies existing ways in which people have interpreted, analyzed, and made generalizations about *why* the world works the way that it does. It is the *why* and *how* of what has been happening around us and not simply a focus on *what* is occurring and how to effectively respond. While understanding the ways in which existing theories explain social reality is enormously important, *theorizing* is the ability to actively engage bodies of knowledge and human practices for the logics and sociohistorical conditions that inform them so that they can be reworked. It encourages individuals to evaluate—based on their own experiences, expertise, and insight—the strengths and weaknesses of any conceptual and practical movement and to recontextualize and reinvent its possibilities for one's own predicaments (Leistyna, 2005).

Unfortunately, as revealed in the president's words, theory and theorizing are often discouraged and disarticulated from human agency, regardless of the fact that all sociocultural practices are sustained by some underlying assumptions and understanding. This disconnect is readily apparent in both mainstream and more radical pedagogical models, research methodologies, and social movements that call for materials, data, and strategies for social activism without adequately examining the realities that generate the particular political, symbolic, and material conditions that provoke such active responses. Instead of embracing the difficult reflective work that theorizing demands of us, there is often a premature call for "how to's" or for empirical research to replace rather than complement theory—as if descriptive or numerical patterns of behavior in the data will interpret themselves. Or, there is often passive acceptance of any given theory rather than critical engagement with its fundamental tenets. Theorizing is a pliable and ongoing process. As societies and lived experiences change within shifting social landscapes, theories as well as social activism should always be subjected to further critical exploration and recontextualization.

As an integral part of any political project, theorizing presents a constant challenge to imagine and materialize alternative political spaces and identities and more just and equitable economic, social, and cultural relations. It makes possible consciousness raising, coalition building, resistance, activism, and structural change. In such undemocratic times, it's not surprising that such a practice is often discouraged.

The assault on theorizing is in part connected to ways in which the university has been used as an indoctrinating force to deskill students by working to mold them into uncritical receivers and consumers of existing theory, but rarely viewing them as active and creative participants in the generative process of understanding. This is especially evident as, on a global scale, the academy is falling prey to the kinds of corporate logic that package thought as a commodity for exchange in the marketplace rather than inspiring the kinds of inquiry that probe that very logic and use of public energy and space. Within these corporate models of public education the production of technicians in all disciplines (areas of study which are artificially disconnected from one another) comes at the expense of transdisciplinary thinkers and producers of social knowledge about the world. As students are distracted or lured away from critically reading historical and existing social formations, especially those that maintain abuses of power, they often become the newest wave of exploited labor power and reproducers of oppressive social practices, whether they are conscious of it or not.

K-12 students also need to learn how to be more effective agents of change and need to engage in praxis. For example, if testing is such an important part of society as advocates of this industry claim, then students should also know more about testing; not just what's on the test and how to take it, but how the tests are generated and operate. This opens the possibility of an interdisciplinary approach where history, math, social studies, etc. are part of analyzing these tests. In the spirit of critical pedagogy, teachers should also teach to the test. But by this, I mean that they should engage the students in ideological analysis of the knowledge that they are being exposed to. It is important for young people to take a critical look, for example, at the history lessons that are taught in schools whose curricula and textbooks are generated by the current standards regime.

In these times of globalization—with 51 of the planet's 100 largest economies being corporations—critical education also needs to have an international scope. It needs to be connected to the transnational efforts to democratize global technologies, environmental resources, and media, information, and financial systems. Recognizing that globalization is a crisis in representative democracy, global justice activists have been experimenting with novel approaches for bringing together multiple identities, issues, and alliances—doing so, in part, to balance the demands of political unity and cultural diversity. The goal has been to search out new forms of democratic and revolutionary identification, to recognize differences and commonalities within struggles for economic and social justice, and to work through dialogue and action to sustain what has become a "movement of many movements." Such solidarity, as opposed to isolated localized efforts, may present the only way of combating transnational corporations that no longer need to negotiate with local labor organizations or area-specific human rights groups for living wages and realistic environmental protections—they just go elsewhere, leaving trade restrictions, unemployment, poverty, and political chaos in their path.

The goal of achieving unity in diversity while also maintaining an activist stance requires that we work through what need not be a contradiction between a Gramscian vision of civil society and war of position intended to use cultural and political practices on multiple fronts to lead to revolutionary change rather than just mere representation, while creating and protecting a Habermasian public sphere that can burgeon within a liberal democracy to serve as a venue for the free exchange of ideas—an exchange through which mobilization can germinate.

Rather than addressing these serious issues, conservative educators like Diane Ravitch, Lynne Cheney, and William Bennett—omnipresent spokespersons for the Republican Party—have aregued and continue to argue that attempts to reveal the underlying values, interests, and power relationships that structure educational policies and practices have corrupted the academic environment. Such efforts to depoliticize the public's understanding of social institutions, especially schools, in the name of neutrality are obviously a reactionary ploy to maintain the status quo. It is precisely this lack of inquiry, analysis, and agency that a critical philosophy of learning and teaching should work to reverse.

Or, perhaps the solution is to simply give these neoliberal nuts a taste of their own medicine: give them psychotropic drugs so as to make them passive and unable to hurt people, sit them down in front of the television and out of the way, and feed them junk food to their heart's content . . .

Notes

1.   When you consider the fact that NCLB is already underfunded by more than $40 billion, a chilling reality sets in: all of this rhetoric about accountability, efficiency, effectiveness, and excellence in public education is really an ideological trap intended to ensure that public schools fail, thus paving the way for their complete privatization. It's an interesting form of class warfare where you take taxpayers' money and use it to provide them with a poor education. The elite children don't attend these institutions; they go to private schools where there is no high-stakes testing. Some states are well aware of the fact that these new mandates cost far more to meet than they could ever possibly financially provide for and have thus decided to opt out of their eligibility for federal funding and go it on their own.

2.   Like the "Vallas Miracle" in Chicago and the "New York City Miracle" . . .

3.   This reference is taken from the White House web page at: www.whitehouse.gov/government/paige-bio.html

4.   For an excellent example of historical engineering by conservative forces, see any of the materials produced by E.D. Hirsch, Jr.'s Core Knowledge Foundation—"What Your 1–6th Grader Needs to Know: Fundamentals of a Good Education." See also Lynn Cheney's (2002) *America: A Patriotic Primer*.

5.   It is curious that so many mainstream politicians concerned with public education work so hard to eradicate multilingualism among racially and economically oppressed students, while simultaneously working to make certain that upper-middle-class and wealthy youth are able to speak international languages. Multilingualism, which is embraced in all the finest private schools in the country (where, by the way, the children of wealthy politicians go to school), is great for elite children but somehow bad for, and unpatriotic of, the poor.

6.   Keep in mind that the United States is over $8 trillion in debt, and instead of reining this debt in, the House raised the debt ceiling to $8.1 trillion. It is also important to note that the Bush administration has borrowed more money from foreign governments than all 42 of the presidential administrations that preceded it. China now owns $1 trillion of our national debt.

7.   Anticolonial activists have long recognized how material conditions, politics, and culture are interlaced and how subordination, resistance, and opposition take place in both the physical and symbolic realm.

8.   The "controllable" part is questionable given that these drugs are also linked with increased violence among youth. The two boys responsible for the violence in Columbine were on antidepressants. Of course, this angle of the story never entered the mainstream media.

References

Allington, R. (2002). *Big Brother and the national reading curriculum: How ideology trumped evidence*. Portsmouth, NH: Heinemann.

Bacon, D. (2000, April 1). School testing: Good for textbook publishers, bad for students. *Pacific News Service*. Retrieved September 17, 2006, from http://alternet.org/story/39/

Bartolomè, L. & Leistyna, P. (2006). Naming and interrogating our English-only legacy. *Radical Teacher, 75*, 2–9.

Bennett, W. (1993). *Book of virtues: A treasury of great moral stories*. New York: Simon & Schuster.

Bennett under fire for comments on blacks, crime. (2005, September 30). *CNN.com*. Retrieved September 15, 2006, from http://www.cnn.com/2005/POLITICS/09/30/bennett.comments/

Bollyn, C. (2005, October 24). Bush family financed by foreign money. *American Free Press, 43*. Retrieved September 17, 2006, from http://www.americanfreepress.net/html/bush_family_financed.html

Carlson, P. (2003, December 28). The relatively charmed life of Neil Bush: Despite Silverado and Voodoo, fortune still smiles on the president's brother. *Washington Post*, p. D01. Retrieved September 18, 2006, from http://www.washingtonpost.com/ac2/wp-dyn/A35297–2003Dec27

CBS News. (2004, August 25). The "Texas miracle." *60 minutes II*, New York: CBS. Retrieved September 17, 2006, from www.cbsnews.com/stories/2004/01/06/60II/main591676.shtml

Cheney, L. (2002). *America: A patriotic primer*. New York: Simon & Schuster Books for Young Readers.

Clarke, B. (2004, September 23). Leaving children behind: Exam privatization threatens public schools. *CorpWatch*. Retrieved September 15, 2006, from http://www.corpwatch.org/article.php?id=11543

Coles, G. (2000). *Misreading reading: The bad science that hurts children*.Portsmouth, NH: Heinemann.

Collins, C., Gluckman, A., Lui, M., Leonard-Wright, B., Offner, A., & Scharf, A. (Eds.). (2004). *The wealth inequality reader*. Boston: Dollars & Sense.

Collins, C., Hartman, C., & Sklar, H. (1999, December 15). Divided decade: Economic disparity at the century's turn. *United for a Fair Economy*. Retrieved September 17, 2006, from http://www.ufenet.org/press/archive/1999/Divided_Decade/divided_decade.html

Crawford, J. (2003, August 23). A few things Ron Unz would prefer you didn't know about: English learners in California. Retrieved September 17, 2006, from http://ourworld.compuserve.com/homepages/JWCRAWFORD/castats.htm

Do fast-food chains cluster around schools? (2005, August 24). *Associated Press*. Retrieved September 16, 2006, from http://www.msnbc.msn.com/id/9053465/

Fortune 500. (2006). *Fortune Magazine*. Retrieved September 16, 2006, from http://money.cnn.com/magazines/fortune/fortune500/

Foucault, M. (1988). *Madness and civilization: A history of insanity in the age of reason*. New York: Vintage.

Garza, C.L. (2006, March 23). Former First Lady's donation aids son: Katrina funds earmarked to pay for Neil Bush's software program. *Houston Chronicle*. Retrieved September 17, 2006, from http://chron.com/disp/story.mpl/headline/metro/3742329.html

Gluckman, A. (2002, January/February). Testing . . . testing . . . one, two, three: The commercial side of the standardized-testing boom. *Dollars & Sense: The Magazine of Economic Justice, 239*. Retrieved September 17, 2006, from http://www.dollarsandsense.org/archives/2002/0102gluckman.html

Goldstein, R. (2004, October 20). Critics see drug industry behind mental health plan. *Inter Press Service*. Retrieved September 17, 2006, from http://www.commondreams.org/headlines04/1020–20.htm

Goodman, A. (2004, March 12). *Democracy Now: No Bush left behind: When you're barred from banking, why not bank on education?* [Radio broadcast]. New York: Pacifica Radio. Retrieved September 15, 2006, from http://www.democracynow.org/article.pl?sid=04/03/12/1534244

Haney, W. (2000). The Texas miracle in education: Missing students and other mirages. *Education Policy Analysis Archives, 8*(41). Retrieved September 17, 2006, from http://epaa.asu.edu/epaa/v8n41/part5.htm

High-stakes testing and its effects on education. (2000, Winter). *TC Reports*. New York: Teachers College. Retrieved September 17, 2006, from http://www.tc.columbia.edu/news/article.htm?id=3811

Hoffman, T. (2005, October 4). The candid Bennett. *eSchool News: Ed-Tech Insider*. Retrieved September 17, 2006, from http://www.eschoolnews.com/eti/2005/10/001190.php

Horn, J. (2005, September 20). Hauling away the federal treasury. [Weblog entry]. *Schools Matter*. Retrieved September 17, 2006, from http://schoolsmatter.blogspot.com/2005/09/hauling-away-federal-treasury.html

Ivins, M. (2005, April 14). April 15th: You're getting screwed. *AlterNet*. Retrieved September 16, 2006, from http://www.alternet.org/story/21760

Jackson, D.Z. (2001, August 31). Who's better off this Labor Day? Numbers tell. *Boston Globe*. Retrieved September 16, 2006, from http://www.commondreams.org/views01/0831–01.htm.

Kohn, A. (2000). *The case against standardized testing: Raising the scores, ruining the schools*. Portsmouth, NH: Heinemann.

Kohn, A. & Shannon, P. (2002). *Education, Inc*. Portsmouth, NH: Heinemann.

Krim, J. & Witte, G. (2004, December 31). Average wage earners fall behind: New job market makes more demands but fewer promises. *Washington Post*, p. A01.

Lawrence, J. (2006, August 7). Congress full of fortunate sons—and other relatives. *USA Today*. Retrieved September 17, 2006, from http://www.usatoday.com/news/washington/2006–08–07-relatives-cover_x.htm

Leistyna, P. (2003). Facing Oppression: Youth Voices from the Front. In K. Saltman & D. Gabbard (Eds.), *Education as enforcement: The militarization and corporatization of schools* (pp. 103–126). New York: RoutledgeFalmer.

Leistyna, P. (Ed.). (2005). *Cultural studies: From theory to action*. Oxford, UK: Blackwell Publishing.

Leistyna, P., Woodrum, A., & Sherblom, S. (Eds.). (1996). *Breaking Free: The Transformative Power of Critical Pedagogy*. Cambridge, MA: Harvard Education Press.

McChesney, R. (2004). *The problem of the media: U. S. communication politics in the twenty-first century*. New York: Monthly Review Press.

McNeil, L. (2000). *Contradictions of school reform: Educational costs of standardized testing*. New York: RoutledgeFalmer.

Metcalf, S. (2002, January 28). Reading between the lines. *The Nation*. Retrieved December 24, 2006, from http://www.thenation.com/doc/20020128/metcalf

Miner, B. (2004/2005, Winter). Keeping public schools public: Testing companies mine for gold. *Rethinking Schools, 19*(2). Retrieved September 17, 2006, from http://www.rethinkingschools.org/archive/19_02/test192.shtml

Mishel, L., Bernstein, J., & Allegretto, S. (2005). *The state of working America, 2004/2005*. Ithaca, NY: ILR Press.

Molnar, A. (2005). *School commercialism*. New York: Routledge.

Molnar, A., Garcia, D., Bartlett, M., & O'Neill, A. (2006). *Profiles of for-profit education management organizations, 2005–2006*. Tempe, AZ: Arizona State University, Education Policy Studies Laboratory. Retrieved September 17, 2006, from http://www.asu.edu/educ/epsl/CERU/Documents/EPSL-0605–104-CERU.pdf

Ohanian, S. (2004, August 16). Grant to Bennett's K12 Inc. challenged. *eSchool News*. Retrieved September 15, 2006, from http://www.susanohanian.org/atrocity_fetch.php?id=2910

O'Meara, K.P. (2001, October 15). New research indicts Ritalin. *Insight Magazine*. Retrieved September 15, 2006, from http://www.resultsproject.net/New_Research_Indicts_Ritalin.html

Pearson (2005). *Performance 2005*. Retrieved September 16, 2006, from http://www.pearson.com/index.cfm?pageid=151

Pearson (2006, April 25). *Pearson enters teacher certification market*, Press release. Retrieved September 17, 2006, from http://www.pearsoned.com/pr_2006/042506.htm

Russell, M. (2006, June 10). ADD—Are children being unnecessarily medicated. EzineArticles. Retrieved December 24, 2006, from http://ezinearticles.com/?ADD---are-children-being-unnecessarily-medicated&id=216912

Saltman, K. (2000). *Collateral damage*. Boulder, CO: Rowman & Littlefield.

Saltman, K. (2005). *The Edison schools: Corporate schooling and the assault on public education*. New York: Routledge.

Scherer, M. (2001, May/June). That other Bush boy. *Mother Jones*. Retrieved September 17, 2006, from http://www.motherjones.com/news/outfront/2001/05/neilbush.html

Schlosser, E. (2001). *Fast food nation: The dark side of the all-American meal*. Boston: Houghton Mifflin.

Sklar, H. (2003, April 24). CEO pay still outrageous. *Knight Ridder/Tribune News Service*. Retrieved December 24, 2006, from http://www.ms.foundation.org/wmspage.cfm?parm1=192

Sturrock, C. (2006, June 30). States distort school test scores, researchers say. *San Francisco Chronicle*. Retrieved December 24, 2006, from http://www.sfgate.com/cgi-bin/article.cgi?file=/c/a/2006/06/30/MNG28JN9RC1.DTL

Suchak, B. (2001). Standardized testing: High-stakes for students and for corporate bottom lines. *Journal for Living*, 23, 36–41. Retrieved September 16, 2006, from http://www.nomoretests.com/ insider.htm

Texas NAACP (1995). TAAS Resolution Commitment. Retrieved September 16, 2006, from http://72.14.207.104/search?q=cache:zzHwpR6B1bIJ:www.texasnaacp.org/taasrc.htm+TAAS+exam,+english+and+spanish&hl=en&gl=us&ct=clnk&cd=10

The testing industry's big four. (2006). *Frontline*. Retrieved September 15, 2006, from http://www.pbs.org/wgbh/ pages/frontline/shows/schools/testing/companies.html

Unz, R. (2000, April/May). The right way for Republicans to handle ethnicity in politics. *American Enterprise*. Retrieved September 17, 2006, from http://www.onenation.org/0004/0400.html

Valadez, J. (Director). (2005, May 8). High stakes: The battle to save schools [Television series episode]. In S. Bedingfield (Executive Producer), *CNN Presents*. Lanham, MD: Cable News Network.

Wacquant, L. (2002, April/Mat). Deadly symbiosis: Rethinking race and imprisonment in twenty-first-century America. *Boston Review: A Political and Literary Forum*, 27(2), 23–31.

X U.S. Secretary of Education Bill Bennett and President Bush's brother Neil Bush. (2006). *Educational CyberPlayground*. Retrieved September 17, 2006, from http://www.edu-cyberpg.com/Culdesac/billbennett.html

Zwillich, T. (2006, June 20). Junk food in schools: Worst offenders. *WebMD Medical News*. Retrieved September 17, 2006, from http://www.medicinenet.com/script/main/art.asp?articlekey=62599

PART TWO

The Pedagogical Dimensions of Critical Pedagogy

CHAPTER 6

The Politics and Ethic of Performance Pedagogy

Toward a Pedagogy of Hope

NORMAN K. DENZIN

To invoke and paraphrase William Kittridge (1987, p. 87), today, in post-9/11 America—with Patriot Acts, Homeland Security Administrations, and a president who performs scripts of fear written by others—we are struggling to revise our dominant mythology to find a new story to inhabit, to find new laws to control our lives, laws designed to preserve a model of a free democratic society based on values learned from a shared mythology. Kittridge is clear, that only after reimagining our myths can we coherently remodel our laws, and hope to keep our society in a realistic relationship to what is actual and what is ideal. The ground upon which we stand has dramatically shifted. The neoconservatives have put into place a new set of myths, performances, narratives, and a new set of laws that threaten to destroy what we mean by freedom and democracy (Giroux, 2004).

Scholars in performance studies must ask a series of questions: "How can we use the aftermath of the crisis of 9/11 as a platform for rethinking what is meant by democracy and freedom in America today?" "Can we revise our dominant mythologies about who we are?" "Can we fashion a post-9/11 narrative that allows us to reinvent and reimagine our laws in ways that express a critical pedagogy of hope, liberation, freedom, and love?" "Can performance studies help us chart our way into this new space?" "Can we take back what has been lost?"

■   ■   ■

WAR IS PEACE
FREEDOM IS SLAVERY
IGNORANCE IS STRENGTH
Orwell, 1949, p. 17.

■   ■   ■

In this chapter I seek a politics and an ethics fitted to *a radical critical performance pedagogy*. I seek *a pedagogy of hope* crafted for life after 9/11. I want to contribute to a conversation that seeks to preserve a model of a free democratic society. In outlining this democratic pedagogy, I draw selectively from a series of performance texts written since 9/11.[1] In so doing I join four discourses, merging the performance turn in the human disciplines (Alexander, 2005; Conquergood, 1998), with theories of critical pedagogy (Giroux & Giroux, 2005) and critical race theory (Darder & Torres, 2004; Ladson-Billings & Donnor, 2005), connecting these formations to the call by indigenous scholars for a new ethics of inquiry (Smith, 2005), new pedagogies of hope, new models of democracy.

■   ■   ■

The "democratic character of critical pedagogy is defined largely through a set of basic assumptions" (Giroux & Giroux, 2005, p. 1): Pedagogical practices are always moral and political. The political is always performative. The performative is always pedagogical. Through performances, critical pedagogy disrupts those hegemonic cultural and educational practices that reproduce the logics of neoliberal conservatism. Critical pedagogy subjects structures of power, knowledge, and practice to critical scrutiny, demanding that they be evaluated "in terms of how they might open up or close down democratic experiences." Critical pedagogy and critical pedagogical theatre hold systems of authority accountable through the critical reading of texts, the creation of radical educational practices, and the promotion of critical literacy (p. 2). In turn, critical pedagogy encourages resistance to the "discourses of privatization, consumerism, the methodologies of standardization and accountability, and the new disciplinary techniques of surveillance" (p. 3). Critical pedagogy provides the tools for understanding how cultural and educational practices contribute to the construction of neoliberal conceptions of identity, citizenship, and agency.

■   ■   ■

The call to performance in the human disciplines requires a commitment to a progressive democratic politics, an ethics and aesthetics of performance (Pollock, 1998) that moves from critical race theory (Darder & Torres, 2004; Ladson-Billings & Donnor, 2005) to the radical pedagogical formulations of Paulo Freire (1998, 1999, 2001), as his work is reformulated and reinvented by Antonia Darder (2002), Kincheloe and McLaren (2005), Fischman and McLaren (2005), Giroux (2001, 2003), and Giroux and Giroux (2005) and others.

This performance ethic borrows from and is grounded in the discourses of indigenous peoples (Mutua & Swadener, 2004). Indigenous theories of ritual performance blend and blur with performative acts that critique, transgress, and bring dignity to human practices. This performance ethic honors difference and refuses commodification, as it draws from indigenous, feminist, queer, and communitarian formulations.

Within this radical pedagogical space, the performative and the political intersect on the terrain of a praxis-based ethic. This is the space of critical pedagogical theatre, which draws its inspirations from Boal's (1995) Theatre of the Oppressed. This ethic performs pedagogies that resist oppression. It enacts a politics of possibility (Madison, 1998) grounded in performative practices that embody love, hope, care, and compassion.

A postcolonial, indigenous participatory theatre is central to this discourse (Greenwood, 2001; Balme & Carstensen, 2001).[2] Contemporary indigenous playwrights and performers revisit and make a mockery of nineteenth-century racist practices. They interrogate and turn the tables on blackface minstrelsy and the global colonial theatre that reproduced racist politics through specific cross-race and cross-gender performances. They show how colonial performers used whiteface and blackface to construct oppressive models of whiteness, blackness, gender, and national identity (Kondo, 2000, p. 83; Gilbert, 2003).

Indigenous theatre nurtures a critical transnational, yet historically specific, critical race (and class) consciousness. It uses indigenous performance as a means of political representation and critique (Magowan, 2000, p. 311). Indigenous theatre reflexively uses historical restagings, masquerade, ventriloquism, and doubly inverted performances involving male and female impersonators to create a subversive theatre that undermines colonial racial representations (Bean, 2001, pp. 187–88). This theatre incorporates traditional indigenous and nonindigenous cultural texts into frameworks that disrupt colonial models of race and class relations. This theatre takes up key diasporic concerns, including those of memory, cultural loss, disorientation, violence, and exploitation (Balme & Carstensen, 2001, p. 45). This is a utopian theatre that addresses issues of equity, healing, and social justice.[3]

■ ■ ■ ■

Consider the following:

In *House Arrest* (2003) Anna Deavere Smith offers "an epic view of slavery, sexual misconduct, and the American presidency." Twelve actors, some in blackface, "play across lines of race, age and gender to 'become' Bill Clinton, Thomas Jefferson, Sally Hemings . . . and a vast array of historical and contemporary figures." (Kondo, 2000, p. 81)

In Native Canadian Bill Moses' play *Almighty Voice and His Wife* (1993) Native performers, wearing whiteface minstrel masks, mock such historical figures as Wild Bill Cody, Sitting Bull, and young Indian maidens called Sweet Sioux. (Gilbert, 2003, p. 692)

In Sydney, Australia aboriginal theatre groups perform statements of their indigenous rights demanding that politicians participate in these performance events "as co-producers of meaning rather than as tacit consumers." (Magowan, 2000, pp. 317–18)

Thus do indigenous performances function as strategies of critique and empowerment.

■ ■ ■ ■

The Decade of the World's Indigenous Peoples (1994–2004; Henderson, 2000, p. 168) has ended. Nonindigenous scholars have yet to learn from it; to learn that it is time to dismantle, deconstruct, and decolonize Western epistemologies from within, to learn that research does not have to be a dirty word, to learn that research is always already political and at least sometimes (even for postpositivists) moral.

Shaped by the sociological imagination (Mills, 1959), and building on George Herbert Mead's discursive, performative model of the act (1938, p. 460), critical pedagogy imagines and explores the multiple ways in which performance can be understood, including as imitation, or mimesis, as poiesis, or construction; as kinesis, movement, gendered bodies in motion, (Conquergood, 1998, p. 31; Pollock, 1998, p. 43). The researcher-as-performer moves from a view of performance as imitation, or dramaturgical staging (Goffman, 1959), to an emphasis on performance as liminality, construction, (McLaren, 1999), to a view of performance as embodied struggle, as an intervention, as a breaking and remaking, as kinesis, as a sociopolitical act, as a sensuous, material production that erupts in the moment of performativity "across the intersecting planes of identity, community, culture and politics" (Conquergood, 1998, p. 32; Pollock, 1998, p. 43).

Viewed as struggles and interventions, performances and performance events become gendered transgressive achievements, political accomplishments that break through "sedimented meanings and normative traditions" (Conquergood, 1998, p. 32). It is this performative model of emancipatory decolonized indigenous research that I develop here (Garoian, 1999; Gilbert, 2003; Kondo, 2000). Drawing on Garorian (1999), Du Bois (1926), Gilbert (2003), Madison (1998), Magowan (2000), Pollock (1998), and Anna Deavere Smith (2003), this model proposes a utopian performative politics of resistance (see below). Extending indigenous initiatives, this model is committed to a form of revolutionary, catalytic political theatre, a project that provokes and enacts pedagogies of dissent for the new millennium. This is a variant of forum theatre, Boal's *Theatre of the Oppressed*, his Rainbow of Desire, and Legislative Theatre used within a political system to produce a truer form of democracy (Jackson, 1995, p. xviii).

Life in America After 9/11

After the attack on the World Trade Center and the Pentagon on 9/11, a number of interpretive social scientists wrote about this event and its meanings in their lives. These personal narratives could be performed within the "mystory"[4] format.

Michelle Fine's (2002, p. 137) narratives text opens thusly:

"The mourning after"

12 September 2001

You can tell who's dead or missing by their smiles. Their photos dot the subways, ferries, trains and Port Authority Terminal, shockingly alive with joy, comfort and pleasure . . .
    The air in the City chokes with smoke, flesh, fear, memories, clouds and creeping nationalism . . . Now a flood of flags, talk of God, military and patriotism chase us all . . .

Two days later Fine writes:

> The Path train stopped. In a tunnel. No apparent reason. I couldn't breath. Anxiety . . . Is this
> an ok way to die? . . .
>
>   Lives and politics; grief and analysis. Those of us in New York seem to be having trouble writ-
> ing . . . U.S. politics then and now, racial profiling and anxious worries about what's coming next
> . . . Death, ghosts, orphans, analyses of U.S. imperialism, Middle East politics, and the terrors of
> terrorism sit in the same room. . . .

Several years have passed since Fine wrote these lines. They could have been written yesterday. "U.S. imperialism, Middle East politics, and the terrors of terrorism sit in the same
room." How do you write and perform the meaning of the present, when the nightmares
and terror that define the present have never been experienced before? How do you write
about an unending terror when each day starts with a new crisis, when lies are held up as
truths, and black has become white, and yes means no?

Turning to Annie Dillard, I seek my own meaning in these events. Dillard says that
divinity is not playful, that the universe was not made in jest, but in "solemn incompre-
hensible earnest. By a power that is unfathomably secret, and holy and fleet" (1974, p. 270),
and violent, I choose to believe this.

Ethics for Performance Studies

Any consideration of performance ethics must move in three directions at the same time,
addressing three interrelated issues: ethical pitfalls, traditional ethical models, and indigenous performance ethics connected to political theatre (Boal, 1995). Conquergood (1985,
p. 4) has identified four ethical pitfalls that performance ethnographers must avoid. He terms
them "The Custodian's Rip-Off," "The Enthusiast's Infatuation," "The Curator's
Exhibitionism," and "The Skeptic's Cop-Out."

Cultural custodians—or cultural imperialists—ransack their biographical past looking
for good texts to perform, and then perform them for a fee, often denigrating a family member or a cultural group, who regard such experiences as sacred. The enthusiast's—or
superficialist's—stance occurs when the writer and the performer fail to become deeply
involved in the cultural setting which they reperform. Conquergood (1985, p. 6) says this
trivializes the other because their experiences are neither contextualized nor well understood. Modifying Conquergood, the skeptic—or cynic—values detachment and being
cynical. This position refuses to face up to the "ethical tensions and moral ambiguities of
performing culturally sensitive materials" (p. 8). Finally, the curator—or sensationalist—
like the custodian, is a performer who sensationalizes the cultural differences that supposedly define the world of the other. He or she stages performances for the voyeur's gaze,
perhaps telling stories about an abusive, hurtful other (p. 7).

These four stances make problematic the questions of "How far into the other's world
can the performer and the audience go?" Of course we can never know the mind of an other,
only their performances. We can only know our own minds, and sometimes not well. This

means that the differences that define the other's world must always be respected. There is no null point in the moral universe (Conquergood, 1985, pp. 8–9).

■ ■ ■ ■

The second issue is implicit in Conquergood's four ethical pitfalls. He presumes a researcher who is held accountable to a set of universal ethical principles that are both duty and utilitarian based. Duty-based ethics assume that researchers and performers are virtuous, have good intentions, and are committed to values like justice, honesty, and respect. This is Conquergood's ideal performer. However, Conquergood is concerned with more than good intentions; he is concerned with the effects, or consequences, of a performance on a person or a community. Thus, he appears to implicitly endorse a utilitarian ethics based on consequences and pragmatic effects, not good intentions. This is the cost-benefit utilitarian model used by Human Subject Review Boards when they ask how this research will benefit society.

Both of these models have deficiencies. Carried to the extreme, the duty position can result in a moral absolutism, requiring that persons live up to an absolute standard, regardless of its human consequences. But who holds these values? Whose values are they? The utilitarian model is predicated on the belief that the ends justify the means (Kvale, 1996, p. 122); thus, the "wrongness or rightness of actions are judged by their consequences, not their intent" (Edwards & Mauthner, 2002, p. 20). Whose consequences are being considered? Whose means are being used? Best for whom?

It is necessary to contrast these two universalist models with feminist and critical pedagogically informed ethical models (Edwards & Mauthner, 2002, p. 21). Contingent feminist ethical models work outward from personal experience, and local systems of meaning and truth, to social contexts where experience is shaped by nurturing social relationships based on care, respect, and love. The researcher is an insider to the group, not an outsider. The desire is to enact a locally situated, contingent, feminist, communitarian ethic that respects and protects the rights, interests and sensitivities of research subjects is central to our task. Contingent ethical models have been adopted by professional social science associations that often navigate between universal normative models and contingent ethical directives (Edwards & Mauthner, 2002, p. 21). Such guidelines are then meant to guide the researcher when the kinds of pitfalls and dilemmas Conquergood identifies are encountered.

These professional guidelines do not include a space for culturally specific ethical ideas and values (Smith, 1995, p. 120). Within specific contexts, for instance the Maori, specific ethical values and rules are prescribed in cultural terms. These understandings include showing respect for others, listening, sharing, and being generous, cautious, and humble. Smith is quite explicit: "From indigenous perspectives ethical codes of conduct serve partly the same purposes as the protocols which govern our relationships with each other and with the environment."

■ ■ ■ ■

In contrast to social science codes of ethics and the protocols used by Human Subject Review Boards, critical pedagogy seeks to enact a situationally contingent ethic that is compatible with indigenous values. This ethic is predicated on *a pedagogy of hope*. It is based on values shared in the group. It blends intentions with consequences. It presumes that well-intended, trusting, honest, virtuous persons engage in moral acts that have positive consequences for others. This is a communitarian dialogical *ethic of care* and responsibility. It presumes that performances occur within sacred aesthetic spaces where research does not operate as a dirty word. It presumes that performers treat persons and their cares and concerns with dignity and respect. Indeed, the values that structure the performance are those shared by the community and its members. These values include care, trust, and reciprocity. Because of these shared understandings this model assumes that there will be few ethical dilemmas requiring negotiation.

A feminist, communitarian performance ethic is utopian in vision. While criticizing systems of injustice and oppression, it imagines how things could be different. It enacts a *performance pedagogy of radical democratic hope*.

■ ■ ■ ■

"What African American minstrels created was a new form of theater based in the skills of the performers, not their ability to conform to stereotypes" (Bean, 2001, pp. 187–88).

■ ■ ■ ■

An empowering performance pedagogy frames the third issue that must be addressed. The multivoiced performance text enacts *a pedagogy of hope*. A critical consciousness is invoked. The performance event engenders moral discernment that guides social transformation (Denzin, 2003, p. 112; Christians, 2000). The performance text is grounded in the cruelties and injustices of daily life. Like Boal's radical theatre, a documentary-drama format may be used, drawing on current events and media accounts of these events. A radical performance ethic is grounded in a politics of resistance. The performance must be ethically honest. It must be dialogical, seeking to locate dialogue and meaningful exchange in the *radical center*.

■ ■ ■ ■

The other always exists, as Trinh (1989) would argue, in the spaces on each side of the hyphen (Conquergood, 1985, p. 9). The performance text can only be dialogic, a text that does not speak about or for the other but which "speaks to and with them" (p. 10). It is a text that reengages the past and brings it alive in the present. The dialogic text attempts to keep the dialogue, the conversation—between the text, the past, the present, the performer, and the audience—ongoing and open-ended (p. 9). This text does more than invoke empathy; it interrogates, criticizes, and empowers. This is dialogical criticism. The dialogical performance is the means for "honest intercultural understanding."

If this understanding is to be created, the following elements need to be present. Scholars must have the energy, imagination, courage, and commitment to create these texts (see Conquergood, 1985, p. 10). Audiences must be drawn to the sites where these performances take place, and they must be willing to suspend normal aesthetic frameworks, so that coparticipatory performances can be produced. Boal is clear on this: "In the Theatre of the Oppressed we try to . . . make the dialogue between stage and audience totally transitive" (1995, p. 42). In these sites a shared field of emotional experience is created, and in these moments of sharing, critical, cultural awareness is awakened.

■ ■ ■ ■

Critical pedagogical theatre creates dialogical performances that follow these directives from Augusto Boal (1995, p. 42):

Directives from Boal:

Show How:

1.   Every oppressed person is a subjugated subversive.
2.   The Cop in our Head represents our submission to this oppression.
3.   Each person possesses the ability to be subversive.
4.   Critical Pedagogical Theatre can empower persons to be subversive, while making their submission to oppression disappear.

■ ■ ■ ■

The coperformed text aims to enact a *feminist communitarian moral ethic*. This ethic presumes a dialogical view of the self and its performances. It seeks narratives that ennoble human experience, performances that facilitate civic transformations in the public and private spheres. This ethic ratifies the dignities of the self and honors personal struggle. It understands cultural criticism to be a form of empowerment, arguing that empowerment begins in that ethical moment when individuals are lead into the troubling spaces occupied by others. In the moment of coperformance, lives are joined and struggle begins anew.

Ethical Injunctions:

Does this Performance:

1.   Nurture critical race consciousness?
2.   Use historical restagings and traditional texts to subvert and critique official ideology?
3.   Heal? Empower?
4.   Avoid Conquergood's four pitfalls?
5.   Enact a feminist, communitarian, socially contingent ethic?
6.   Present *a pedagogy of hope?*

Hope, Pedagogy, and the Critical Imagination

The critical imagination is radically democratic, pedagogical, and interventionist. Building on Freire (1998, p. 91) this imagination dialogically inserts itself into the world, provoking conflict, curiosity, criticism, and reflection. Extending Freire, performance autoethnography contributes to a conception of education and democracy as pedagogies of freedom.

As praxis, performance ethnography is a way of acting on the world in order to change it. Dialogic performances, enacting a performance-centered ethic, provide materials for critical reflection on radical democratic educational practices. In so doing, performance ethnography enacts a theory of selfhood and being. This is an ethical, relational, and moral theory. The purpose of "the particular type of relationality we call research ought to be enhancing . . . moral agency" (Christians, 2002, p. 409), moral discernment, critical consciousness, and a radical politics of resistance.

Indeed, performance ethnography enters the service of freedom by showing how, in concrete situations, persons produce history and culture, "even as history and culture produce them" (Glass, 2001, p. 17). Performance texts provide the grounds for liberation practice by opening up concrete situations that are being transformed through acts of resistance. In this way, performance ethnography advances the causes of liberation.

As an interventionist ideology, the critical imagination is hopeful of change. It seeks and promotes an ideology of hope that challenges and confronts hopelessness(Freire, 1999, p. 8). It understands that hope, like freedom, is "an ontological need." Hope is the desire to dream, the desire to change, the desire to improve human existence. Hopelessness is "but hope that has lost its bearings."

Hope is ethical. Hope is moral. Hope is peaceful and nonviolent. Hope seeks the truth of life's sufferings. Hope gives meaning to the struggles to change the world. Hope is grounded in concrete performative practices, in struggles and interventions that espouse the sacred values of love, care, community, trust, and well-being (Freire, 1999, p. 9). Hope, as a form of pedagogy, confronts and interrogates cynicism, the belief that change is not possible, or is too costly. Hope works from rage to love. It articulates a progressive politics that rejects "conservative, neoliberal postmodernity" (p. 10). Hope rejects terrorism. Hope rejects the claim that peace comes at any cost.

The critical democratic imagination is pedagogical, and this in four ways. First, as a form of instruction, it helps persons think critically, historically, sociologically. Second, as critical pedagogy, it exposes the pedagogies of oppression that produce and reproduce oppression and injustice (see Freire, 2001, p. 54). Thirdly, it contributes to an ethical self-consciousness that is critical and reflexive. It gives people a language and a set of pedagogical practices that turn oppression into freedom, despair into hope, hatred into love, doubt into trust. Fourth, in turn, this self-consciousness shapes a critical racial self-awareness. This awareness contributes to utopian dreams of racial equality and racial justice.

The use of this imagination by persons who have previously lost their way in this complex world is akin to being "suddenly awakened in a house with which they had only supposed themselves to be familiar" (Mills, 1959, p. 8). They now feel that they can provide themselves with critical understandings that undermine and challenge "older decisions that once appeared sound." Their critical imagination enlivened, persons "acquire a new way of thinking . . . in a word by their reflection and their sensibility, they realize the cultural meaning of the social sciences." They realize how to make and perform changes in their own lives, to become active agents in shaping the history that shapes them.

■ ■ ■ ■

A Performative Performance Studies

Following Conquergood (1998), Pollock (1998), Madison (1998), and Giroux (2000, p. 127), I am attempting to (re)theorize the grounds of performance studies, redefining the political and the cultural in performative and pedagogical terms. The discourses of postmodern (auto)ethnography provide a framework against which all other forms of writing about the politics of the popular under the regimes of global capitalism are judged.

In this model, a performative, pedagogical cultural studies becomes autoethnographic. The autoethnographer becomes a version of McLaren's reflexive flaneur/flaneuse and Kincheloe's (2001) critical bricoleur; the "primordial ethnographer" (McLaren, 1997a, p. 144), who lives "within postmodern, postorganized, late capitalist culture" (McLaren, 1997b, p. 295), and functions as a critical theorist, an urban ethnographer, an ethnographic agent, and a Marxist social theorist (McLaren, 1997a, pp. 164, 167; 2001, pp. 121–122).

The radical performance (auto)ethnographer functions as a cultural critic, a version of the modern antihero "reflecting an extreme external situation through his [her] own extremity. His [her] . . . [authoethnography] becomes diagnosis, not just of him [her] self, but of a phase of history" (Spender, 1984, p. ix). As a reflexive flaneur/flaneuse or bricoleur, the critical autoethnographer's conduct is justified because it is no longer just one individual's case history or life story. Within the context of history the autoethnography becomes the "dial of the instrument that records the effects of a particular stage of civilization upon a civilized individual." The autoethnography is both dial and instrument.

The autoethnographer functions as a universal singular, a single instance of more universal social experiences. This subject is "summed up and for this reason universalized by his [her] epoch, he [she] resumes it by reproducing him [her] self in it as a singularity" (Sartre, 1981, p. ix). Every person is like every other person, but like no other person. The autoethnographer inscribes the experiences of a historical moment, universalizing these experiences in their singular effects on a particular life. Using a critical imagination, the autoethnographer is theoretically informed in poststructural and postmodern ways. There is a commitment to connect critical ethnography to issues surrounding cultural policy, cultural politics, and procedural policy work (Willis & Trondman, 2000, pp. 10–11).

The commitment, as McLaren argues, is to a theory of praxis that is purposeful, "guided by critical reflection and a commitment to revolutionary praxis" (1997a, p. 170). This commitment involves a rejection of the historical and cultural logics and narratives that exclude those who have been previously marginalized. This is a reflexive performative ethnography. It privileges multiple subject positions, questions its own authority, and doubts those narratives that privilege one set of historical processes and sequences over another (McLaren, 1997a, p. 168; 1997b, p. 290).

Critical Performance Pedagogy

A commitment to critical performance pedagogy and critical race theory (CRT) gives performance studies a valuable lever for militant, utopian cultural criticism. In *Impure Acts*

(2000), Giroux calls for a practical, performative view of pedagogy, politics, and cultural studies. He seeks an interdisciplinary project that would enable theorists and educators to form a progressive alliance "connected to a broader notion of cultural politics designed to further racial, economic, and political democracy" (p. 128). This project anchors itself in the worlds of pain and lived experience, and is accountable to these worlds. It enacts an ethic of respect. It rejects the traditional denial by the West and Western scholars of respect, humanity, self-determination, citizenship, and human rights to indigenous peoples (Smith, 1995, p. 120).

Critical Race Theory

Such a project engages a militant utopianism, a provisional Marxism without guarantees, a cultural studies that is anticipatory, interventionist, and provisional. Such a project does not back away from the contemporary world, in its multiple global versions, including the West, the Third World, the moral, political, and geographic spaces occupied by First Nations and Fourth World persons, persons in marginal or liminal positions (Ladson-Billings and Donnor, 2005). Rather, it strategically engages this world in those liminal spaces where lives are bent and changed by the repressive structures of the new conservatism. This project pays particular attention to the dramatic increases around the world in domestic violence, rape, child abuse, crimes of hate, and violence directed toward persons of color.

Extending critical legal theory, critical race theory theorizes life in these liminal spaces, offering "pragmatic strategies for material and social transformation"(Ladson-Billings, 2000, p. 264). Critical race theory assumes that racism and White supremacy are the norms in American society. Critical race scholars use performative, story-telling, autoethnographic methods to uncover the ways in which racism operates in daily life. Critical race theory challenges those neoliberals who argue that civil rights have been attained for persons of color. Those who argue that the civil rights crusade is a long, slow struggle are also criticized. Advocates of CRT argue that racism requires radical social change. Liberalism and neoliberalism lack the mechanisms and imaginations to achieve such change. Critical race theorists contend that Whites have been the main beneficiaries of civil-rights legislation.

Strategically, CRT examines the ways in which race is performed, including the cultural logics and performative acts that inscribe and create whiteness and nonwhiteness (McLaren, 1997b, p. 278, p. 17). In an age of globalization and diasporic postnational identities, the color line should no longer be an issue—but sadly, it is.

Participatory, Performance Action Inquiry

Drawing on the complex traditions embedded in participatory action research, as well as the critical turn in feminist discourse, and the growing literature for and by indigenous peoples (Smith, 1999, 2005), critical performance pedagogy implements a commitment to participation and performance *with*, not *for*, community members. Amplifying Fine and Weis (2003, pp. 176–77), this project builds on local knowledge and experience developed at the bottom of social hierarchies. Following Smith's (1995) lead, participatory, performance work honors and respects local knowledge and customs and practices and incorporates those values and beliefs into participatory, performance action inquiry (Fine and Weis, 2003, p. 176).

Work in this participatory, activist performance tradition gives back to the community, "creating a legacy of inquiry, a process of change, and material resources to enable transformations in social practices" (Fine and Weis, 2003, p. 177). Through performance and participation, the scholar develops a "participatory mode of consciousness" (Bishop, 1998, p. 208). This helps shape the participant-driven nature of inquiry and folds the researcher as performer into the narrative and moral accountability structures of the group.

This project works outward from the university and its classrooms, treating the spaces of the academy as critical public spheres, as sites of resistance and empowerment (Giroux, 2000, p. 134). Critical pedagogy resists the increasing commercialization and commodification of higher education. It contests the penetration of neoliberal values into research parks, classrooms, and the curriculum. It is critical of institutional review boards that pass ever more restrictive judgment on human subject research.

A commitment to critical pedagogy in the classroom can be an empowering dialogical experience. The instructional spaces become sacred spaces. In them, students take risks and speak from the heart, using their own experiences as tools for forging critical race consciousness. The critical discourse created in this public sphere is then taken into other classrooms and pedagogical spaces, where a militant utopianism is imagined and experienced.

As a performative practice, this project interrogates and criticizes those cultural narratives that make victims responsible for the cultural and interpersonal violence they experience. These narratives blame and victimize the victim. But performance narratives do more than celebrate the lives and struggles of persons who have lived through violence and abuse. These narratives must always be directed back to the structures that shape and produce the violence in question. Pedagogically, the performative is political and focused on power. Performances are located within their historical moment, with attention given to the play of power and ideology. The performative becomes a way of critiquing the political, a way of analyzing how culture operates pedagogically to produce and reproduce victims.

Pedagogically and ideologically, the performative becomes an act of doing (Giroux, 2000, p. 135), a dialogical way of being in the world, a way of grounding performances in the concrete situations of the present. The performative becomes a way of interrogating how "objects, discourses, and practices construct possibilities for and constraints on citizenship" (Nelson & Gaonkar, 1996, p. 7; also quoted in Giroux, 2000, p. 134). This stance connects the biographical and the personal to the pedagogical and the performative. It casts the cultural critic in the identity of a critical citizen, a person who collaborates with others in participatory action projects that enact militant democratic visions of public life, community, and moral responsibility (Giroux, 2000, p. 141). This public intellectual practices critical performance pedagogy. As a concerned citizen working with others, he or she takes positions on the critical issues of the day, understanding that there can be no genuine democracy without genuine opposition and criticism (p. 136).

In turn, radical democratic pedagogy requires citizens and citizen-scholars committed to taking risks; persons willing to act in situations where the outcome cannot be predicted in advance. In such situations, a politics of new possibilities can be imagined and made to happen. Yet in these pedagogical spaces there are not leaders and followers; there are only coparticipants, persons jointly working together to develop new lines of action, new stories, new narratives in a collaborative effort (Bishop, 1998, p. 207).

■ ■ ■ ■

"We must find a new story to perform . . . we must preserve a model of a free democratic society"(Kittridge, 1987, p. 87).

A radical performance pedagogy means putting the critical sociological imagination to work, politically and ethically. This work involves pedagogies of hope and freedom. A performative cultural studies enacts these pedagogies reflexively and ethically. These practices require a performance ethics, which I have discussed in some detail.

Notes

1.   I call these war diaries, reports from the homeland and its battlefields. This essay extends arguments in Denzin (2003, 2005).

2.   This theatre often uses verbatim accounts of injustice and violence in daily life. See Mienczakowski (1995, p. 5; 2001; also Chessman, 1971) for a history of "verbatim theater" and Mienczakowski's extensions of this approach, using oral history, participant observation, and the methods of ethnodrama. A contemporary use of verbatim theatre is the play *Guantanamo: Honor Bound to Defend Freedom* (Riding, 2004). This anti-Iraq War play addresses the plight of British citizens imprisoned at Guantanamo. The "power of *Guantanamo* is that it is not really a play but a re-enactment of views expressed in interviews, letters, news conferences, and speeches by various players in the post-Sept 11 Iraq war drama, from British Muslim detainees, to lawyers, from U. S. Defense Secretary Donald H. Rumsfeld, to Jack Straw, Britain's foreign secretary." Nicolas Kent, the play's director, says he believes "political theater works here because the British have an innate sense of justice. When we do stories about injustice . . . there is a groundswell of sympathy . . . people are furious that there isn't due process. With Islamophobia growing around the world I wanted to show that we, too, think there is an injustice."

3.   At another level, indigenous participatory theatre extends the project connected to Third World popular theatre. This is political "theatre used by oppressed Third World people to achieve justice and development for themselves" (Etherton, 1988, p. 991), The International Popular Theatre Alliance, organized in the 1980s, uses existing forms of cultural expression to fashion improvised dramatic productions which analyze situations of poverty and oppression. This grassroots approach uses agitprop and sloganeering theatre (theatre pieces devised to ferment political action) to create collective awareness and collective action at the local level. This form of theatre has been popular in Latin America, in Africa, in parts of Asia, in India, and among Native populations in the Americas (pp. 991–992).

4.   Mystories are reflexive, critical, multimedia tales and tellings. Each mystory begins with the writer's biography and body; mystories relate epiphanic moments, turning-point experiences, and times of personal trouble and turmoil.

References

Alexander, Bryant. 2005. "Performance Ethnography: The Reenacting and Inciting of Culture." Pp. 411–441 in Norman K. Denzin and Yvonna S. Lincoln (Eds.), *Handbook of Qualitative Research*, 3/e. Thousand Oaks: Sage.

Balme, Christopher, and Astrid Carstensen. 2001. "Home Fires: Creating a Pacific Theatre in the Diaspora." *Theatre Research International*, 26, 1: 35–46.

Bean, Annemarie. 2001. "Black Minstrelsy and Double Inversion, Circa 1890." Pp. 171–191 in Harry J. Elam, Jr., and David Krasner (Eds.), *African American Performance and Theater History*. New York: Oxford University Press.

Bishop, Russell. 1998. "Freeing Ourselves From Neo-colonial Domination in Research: A Maori Approach to Creating Knowledge." *International Journal of Qualitative Studies in Education* 11:199–219.

Boal, Augusto. 1995. *The Rainbow of Desire: The Boal Method of Theatre and Therapy*. London: Routledge.

Chessman, Peter. 1971. "Production Casebook." *New Theatre Quarterly*. 1: 1–6.

Christians, Clifford. 2002. "Introduction." In "Ethical Issues and Qualitative Research" [Special Issue]. *Qualitative Inquiry* 8: 407–10.

Christians, Clifford. 2000. "Ethics and Politics in Qualitative Research." Pp. 133–155 in Norman K. Denzin and Yvonna S. Lincoln (Eds.), *Handbook of Qualitative Research*, 2/e. Thousand Oaks, CA: Sage.

Conquergood, Dwight. 1998. "Beyond the Text: Toward a Performative Cultural Politics." Pp. 25–36 in Sheron J. Dailey (Ed.), *The Future of Performance Studies: Visions and Revisions*. Annandale, VA: National Communication Association.

———. 1985. "Performing as a Moral Act: Ethical Dimensions of the Ethnography of Performance." *Literature in Performance*. 5: 1–13.

Darder, Antonia. 2002. *Reinventing Paulo Freire: A Pedagogy of Love*. Boulder, CO: Westview.

Darder, Antonia and Rodolfo D. Torres. 2004. *After Race: Racism after Multiculturalism*. New York: New York University Press.

Denzin, Norman K. 2005. "Emancipatory Discourses, and the Ethics and Politics of Interpretation." Pp. 933–958 in N. K. Denzin and Y. S. Lincoln (Eds.). *Handbook of Qualitative Research*, 3/e. Thousand Oaks: Sage.

Denzin, Norman K. 2003. *Performance Ethnography*. Thousand Oaks: Sage.

Dillard, Annie. 1974. *Pilgrim at Tinker Creek*. New York: Harper & Row.

Du Bois, W. E. B. 1926. "Krigwa Players Little Negro Theatre: The Story of a Little Theatre Movement." *Crisis*, 32 (July): 134–136.

Edwards, Rosalind, and Melanie Mauthner. 2002. "Ethics and Feminist Research: Theory and Practice." Pp. 14–31 in M. Mauthner, M. Birch, J. Jessop & T. Miller (Eds.). *Ethics in Qualitative Research*. Thousand Oaks: Sage.

Etherton, Michael. 1988. "Third World Popular Theatre." Pp. 991–992 in Martin Banham (Ed.), *The Cambridge Guide to Theatre*. Cambridge: Cambridge University Press.

Fine, Michelle and Lois Weis. 2003. *Silenced Voices and Extraordinary Conversations: Re-Imaging Schools*. New York: Teachers College Press.

Fine, Michelle. 2002. "The Mourning After." *Qualitative Inquiry*, 8: 137–145.

Fischman, Gustavo E., and Peter McLaren. 2005. "Rethinking Critical Pedagogy and the Gramscian Legacy: From Organic to Committed Intellectuals." *Cultural Studies—Critical Methodologies*. 5, 1.

Freire, Paulo. 2001. *Pedagogy of the Oppressed*, 30th Anniversary edition, With an Introduction by Donaldo Macedo. New York: Continuum.

Freire, Paulo. 1999. *Pedagogy of Hope*. New York: Continuum. (originally published 1992).

Freire, Paulo. 1998. *Pedagogy of Freedom: Ethics, Democracy, and Civic Courage*. Translated by Patrick Clarke, Foreword by Donaldo Macedo, Introduction by Stanley Aronowitz. Boulder, CO: Rowman & Littlefield Publishers, Inc.

Garoian, Charles R. 1999. *Performing Pedagogy: Toward an Art of Politics*. Albany: SUNY Press.

Gilbert, Helen. 2003. "Black and White and Re(a)d All Over Again: Indigenous Minstrelsy in Contemporary Canadian and Australian Theatre." *Theatre Journal*, 55: 679–698.

Giroux, Henry, and Susan Searls Giroux. 2005. "Challenging Neoliberalism's New World Order: The Promise of Critical Pedagogy." *Cultural Studies—Critical Methodologies*. 5, 1.

Giroux, Henry. 2004. *The Terror of Neoliberalism: Authoritarianism and the Eclipse of Democracy*. Boulder, CO: Paradigm Publishers.

Giroux, Henry. 2003. *The Abandoned Generation: Democracy Beyond the Culture of Fear*. New York: Palgrave.

Giroux, Henry. 2001. "Cultural Studies as Performative Politics." *Cultural Studies—Critical Methodologies*. 1: 5–23.

Giroux, Henry. 2000. *Impure Acts: The Practical Politics of Cultural Studies*. New York: Routledge.

Glass, Ronald David. 2001. "On Paulo Freire's Philosophy of Praxis and the Foundations of Liberation Education." *Educational Researcher*, 30: 15–25.

Goffman, Erving. 1959. *The Presentation of Self in Everyday Life*. New York: Doubleday.

Greenwood, Janinka. 2001. "Within a Third Space." *Research in Drama Education*, 6, 2: 193–205.

Henderson, James (Sakej) Youngblood. 2000. "Postcolonial Ledger Drawing: Legal Reform." Pp. 161–171 in Marie Battiste (Ed.), *Reclaiming Indigenous Voice and Vision*. Vancouver: UBC Press.

Jackson, Adrian. 1995. "Translator's Introduction." Pp. xviii-xxvi in Augusto Boal, *The Rainbow of Desire: The Boal Method of Theatre and Therapy*. London: Routledge.

Kincheloe, Joe L., and Peter McLaren. 2005. "Rethinking Critical Theory and Qualitative Research." Pp. 303–342 in Norman K. Denzin and Yvonna S. Lincoln (Eds.), *Handbook of Qualitative Research, 3/e*. Thousand Oaks, CA: Sage.

Kinechloe, Joe L. 2001. "Describing the Bricolage: Conceptualizing a New Rigor in Qualitative Research." *Qualitative Inquiry* 7:679–92

Kittridge, William. 1987. *Owning It All*. San Francisco: Murray House.

Kondo, Dorine. 2000. "(Re) Visions of Race: Contemporary Race Theory and the Cultural Politics of Racial Crossover in Documentary Theatre." *Theatre Journal*, 52: 81–107

Kvale, Steinar. 1996. *InterViews: An Introduction to Qualitative Research Interviewing*. London: Sage.

Ladson-Billings, Gloria. 2000. "Racialized Discourses and Ethnic Epistemologies," in Norman K. Denzin and Yvonna S. Lincoln (Eds), *Handbook of Qualitative Research, 2/e*. Thousand Oaks, CA: Sage.

Ladson-Billings, Gloria. and Jamal Donnor. 2005. "The Moral Activist Role of Critical Race Theory Scholarship." Pp. 279–301 in Norman K. Denzin and Yvonna S. Lincoln (Eds.), *Handbook of Qualitative Research, 3/e*. Thousand Oaks, CA: Sage.

Madison, D. Soyini. 1998. "Performances, Personal Narratives, and the Politics of Possibility." Pp. 276–286 in Sheron J. Dailey (Ed.), *The Future of Performance Studies: Visions and Revisions*. Annandale, VA: National Communication Association.

Magowan, Fiona. 2000. "Dancing with a Difference: Reconfiguring the Poetic Politics of Aboriginal Ritual as National Spectacle." *Australian Journal of Anthropology*, 11, 3: 308–321.

McLaren, Peter. 2001. "Che Guevara, Paulo Freire, and the Politics of Hope: Reclaiming Critical Pedagogy." *Cultural Studies—Critical Methodologies*, 1: 108–131.

McLaren, Peter. 1999. *Schooling as Ritual Performance*, 3/e. Lanham, MD: Rowman & Littlefield Publishers, Inc.

McLaren, Peter. 1997a. "The Ethnographer as Postmodern Flaneur: Critical Reflexivity and Posthybridity as Narrative Engagement." Pp. 143–177 in William G. Tierney and Yvonna S. Lincoln (Eds.), *Representation and the Text: Re-Framing the Narrative Voice*. Albany: State University of New York Press.

McLaren, Peter. 1997b. *Revolutionary Multiculturalism: Pedagogies of Dissent for the New Millennium*. Boulder, CO: Westview.

Mead, George Herbert. 1938. *The Philosophy of the Act*. Chicago: University of Chicago Press.

Mienczakowski, Jim. 2001. "Ethnodrama: Performed Research—Limitations and Potential." Pp. 468–476 in Paul Atkinson, Sara Delamont, and Amanda Coffey (Eds.), *Handbook of Ethnography*. London: Sage.

Mienczakowski, Jim. 1995. "The Theatre of Ethnography: The Reconstruction of Ethnography into Theatre with Emancipatory Potential." *Qualitative Inquiry*, 1: 360–375.

Mills, C. Wright. 1959. *The Sociological Imagination*. New York: Oxford.

Mutua, Kagendo and Beth Blue Swadener (Eds.). 2004. *Decolonizing Research in Cross-Cultural Contexts: Critical Personal Narratives*. Albany: SUNY Press.

Nelson, Cary, and Dilip Parameshwar Gaonkar. 1996. "Cultural Studies and the Politics of Disciplinarity." Pp. 1–22 in Cary Nelson and Dilip Parameshwar Gaonkar (Eds.), *Disciplinarity and Dissent in Cultural Studies*. New York: Routledge.

Orwell, George. 1949. *Nineteen Eighty-Four*. New York: Harcourt, Brace and Company.

Pollock, Della. 1998. "A Response to Dwight Conquergood's Essay: 'Beyond the Text: Towards a Performative Cultural Politics.'" Pp. 37–46 in Sheron J. Dailey (Ed.), *The Future of Performance Studies: Visions and Revisions*. Annandale, VA: National Communication Association.

Riding, Alan. 2004. "On a London Stage, a Hearing for Guantanamo Detainees." *New York Times*, 15 June, B2.

Sartre, Jean-Paul. 1981. *The Family Idiot: Gustave Flaubert, vol. 1, 1821–1857*. Chicago: University of Chicago Press.

Smith, Anna Deavere. 2003. *House Arrest and Piano*. New York: Anchor.

Smith, Linda Tuhiwai. 2005. "On Tricky Ground: Researching the Native in the Age of Uncertainty." Pp. 85–107 in Norman K. Denzin and Yvonna S. Lincoln (Eds.), *Handbook of Qualitative Research*, 3/e. Thousand Oaks, CA: Sage.

Smith, Linda Tuhiwai. 1995. *Decolonizing Methodologies: Research and Indigenous Peoples*. London: Zed Books.

Spender, Stephen. [1947] 1984. "Introduction." Pp. vii-xxiii in Malcolm Lowry, *Under the Volcano*. New York: New American Library.

Trinh, T. M-ha. 1989. *Woman, Native, Other*. Bloomington: Indiana University Press.

Willis, Paul and Mat Trondman. 2000. "Manifesto for Ethnography." *Ethnography* 1:5–16.

CHAPTER 7

From Social to Socialist Media

The Critical Potential of the Wikiworld

JUHA SUORANTA & TERE VADÉN

Introduction

Critical theorists in education claim that, at present, we are witnessing and living through the first steps of a true revolution in the art of digital communication and convivial tools for collaborative literacy and transformative learning:

> To dramatize the issues at stake, we should consider the claim that we are now undergoing one of the most significant technological revolutions for education since the progression from oral to print and book-based teaching. . . . Furthermore, the technological developments of the present era make possible the radical re-visioning and reconstruction of education and society argued for in the progressive era by Dewey and in the 1960s and 1970s by Ivan Illich, Paulo Freire, and others who sought radical educational and social reform. (Kellner, 2004, p. 10)

In the vast theoretical literature of critical pedagogy, issues of material, social, political, and cultural modes of production, with such related topics as class, gender, race, and popular culture as critical social formations, have been analyzed during the past decades. However, there have only been a few attempts so far to try to capture the effects of the vastly growing field of digital production, with its ever-evolving technologies, ideologies, and social codes (see Giroux, 2000; 2004; Kellner, 1995; 2004; Peters & Lankshear, 1996; Lankshear & Knobel, 2003).

In the debate, three general expectations towards digital media as a "teaching machine" can be discerned: threats (or even fears), promises, and possibilities. Firstly, new information and communication technologies have been seen as threats from the point of view of their implicit technical rationality, "technological determinism," and covert features of alienation. As Henry Giroux and Susan Searls Giroux (2004, p. 268) have put it, the central threat is not what new technologies enable and what they do not "but that such technologies, when not shaped by ethical considerations, collective debate, and dialogical approaches, lose whatever potential they might have for linking education to critical thinking and learning to democratic social change." In other words, "the real issue is whether such technology in its various pedagogical uses . . . is governed by a technocratic rationality that undermines human freedom and democratic values." Among the first to express these fears were Martin Heidegger, in his critique of enframing, and Herbert Marcuse, in his critique of technocracy (see Thomson, 2003).

Marcuse saw technocracy as a political state in which "technical considerations of imperialistic efficiency and rationality supersede the traditional standards of profitability and general welfare" (Marcuse, 1941, cited in Thomson, 2003, p. 61; see also Kellner, 1998). But what distinguishes Marcuse's critique of technology from Heidegger and also from most of his peers around the Frankfurt School was his insistence that technology holds a promise if its instrumentality can be thought of differently and modified by the abolition of class society and the associated principle of reducing people to things or mere resources to be optimized with maximal efficiency. Thus, it is "not only an ontological question of what technology is making of us; that question needs to be posed, to be sure, but we must also ask the political question of what we can make of technology" (Feenberg, 1998). This is also a line of thought in most critical educators who, in Marcuse's footsteps, "reject the hype and pretensions of techno-utopias and techno-fixes to the problems of education and society" (Kellner, 2004, p. 13), and instead want to evaluate the uses of information and communication technologies together with progressive pedagogical theories. To use a simile from Heidegger, who thought that the ultimate danger of technology does not lie in its possible breakdowns (nuclear disaster, climate change, etc.) but rather in the fact that technology does work smoothly in its own hermetic realm, one could say that the ultimate fear is that the information-technology-enhanced "teaching machines" work seamlessly together with technological rationality so that all emancipatory potential is finally lost.

On the other hand, digital technologies and their evolving applications have been seen as containing promises and ingredients of a new public sphere and "hyperpedagogy" (Dwight & Garrison, 2003) to be formed in cyberspace with diverse digital learning tools; for some this promises a new, enhanced, active citizenship. Referring to the 2,500-year-old Western teleological, dogmatic metaphysics with predetermined and rational educational ends, technological enthusiasts demand that digital learning tools "should free students to create their own unique essences in the learning process rather than have their essences proscribed by a teleological value system of predetermined fixed ends" (p. 724). The latter promise has also been seen in the framework of a Habermasian ideal communication consisting of open and free rational discussions in various web fora.

And thirdly, diverse spheres of digitally mediated communication—blogospheres, podspheres, wikispheres, etc. . . . contain possibilities to enlarge and enhance educational expertise into new areas of learning such as private enterprise, consulting, and digitally mastered distance education by using new information and communication technologies. Critical theorists have, for their part, asked for new emancipatory skills and literacies needed for comprehending various digital spaces and incorporating them in the settings of radical politico-social transformation and educational change. In terms of new possibilities, Kellner and Kahn (2006) maintain that

> people should be helped to advance the multiple technoliteracies that will allow them to understand, critique, and transform the oppressive social and cultural conditions in which they live, as they become ecologically-informed, ethical, and transformative subjects as opposed to objects of technological domination and manipulation. This requires producing multiple oppositional literacies for critical thinking, reflection, and the capacity to engage in the creation of discourse, cultural artifacts, and political action amidst widespread technological revolution. Further, as active and engaged subjects arise through social interactions with others, a notion of convivial technologies must come to be a part of the kinds of technoliteracy that a radical reconstruction of education now seeks to cultivate. (p. 10)

Besides these elementary questions, only a few have dared to ask the substantial question pertaining the critical or even revolutionary potential of social media. In the following chapter, we want to probe into this question by taking as an example the effects of Wikipedia and other wikis like it. Wiki software promises limitless and global open collaboration in terms of content production, discussion, and argumentation and thus ideally exemplifies the Habermasian potential of digital technology. However, we need to look further into the depths of the nature of such technology in order to find out how the much-hyped promise of wikis and other types of social media interacts with real-world constraints and conflicts. In a nutshell, not the form but the content—what is said and why—is crucial in evaluating digital media. The analysis of digital media in terms of communication theory or media theory has to be intertwined with an analysis of their political economy.

Wikipedia and Freedom

Wiki, from the Hawaiian word for "fast," is a web technology that enables users to modify existing web pages on the fly, to see the history of these changes, and to discuss the contents of the page with other users. The technology is best known for the fast-growing encyclopedia, Wikipedia.org, but is used also in many other projects of knowledge creation around the Internet. Wiki pages (or in the following, just "wikis," including different wikipedias), benefit from this technology of fast and easy creation and editing. However, it is only in connection with the hacker-originated culture of freedom on the net that the wiki technology gains its true potential.

The Wikipedia project has its roots in the hacker movement working in order to provide free software. The ambiguity of the word "free" merits further attention. Wikipedia is free in the sense of "gratis," but, more importantly, it is free in the sense of "free speech." The Wikipedia is licensed under the Gnu Free Documentation License (GFDL) innovated by Richard M. Stallman and the Free Software Foundation. In essence, the license says that one can use, distribute, and modify text licensed under the GFDL, provided that the redistributed and modified versions are also licensed under GFDL. This makes GFDL a so-called "copyleft license." It uses copyright law in order to give the users more rights: the rights of redistribution and modification.

A copyleft license guards the content from lock-in or privatization: no institution can take the content and commodify it. Ideally, this freedom is forever. In fact, like free software, free information under the GFDL has no exchange value but does have a potentially big use value. In this sense a combination of wiki technology and of copyleft licensing (such as exists in the case of the Wikipedia and many other wikis) provides, in a germ form, a new kind of "knowledge work." The social and political effects of such production are highly interesting, and well debated (e.g., Hardt & Negri, 2004; Zizek, 2002b, 2006b; Merten, 2000). From the economical point of view, the question of motivation is one of the most crucial: why do people engage in volunteer work like this without immediate economical rewards? The conditions under which voluntary nonalienated work is possible is of the utmost importance for the critical potential of open collaborative projects like the Wikipedia. Wikis may indeed prove to be something of a snapshot of future intellectual labor.

The Wikipedia has an obvious Gutenbergian potential. It is a free encyclopedia providing all the emancipatory potential of encyclopedias of the Enlightenment era, such as the *Encyclopédie ou dictionnaire raisonné des sciences, des arts et des métiers* (1751–72) by Denis Diderot and Jean D'Amelbert. It makes encyclopeadic knowledge accessible for free everywhere where the Internet is available, and in some cases even where it is not. CD-ROMs with a stable version of Wikipedia, and even printed editions and special wikibooks are being produced to overcome the lack of Internet infrastructure. If Gutenberg's revolution was about making printed media more abundant, the Wikipedia has the same effect multiplied to a different order of magnitude.

The Gutenbergian effect of Wikipedia, with its different language versions, is already being felt in educational institutions. Students borrowing material from the Wikipedia up to the point of "cheating" is a well-known phenomenon. Educators relying on the reproduction of ingested material in order to supervise the process of learning are having a hard time fighting this kind of use. More noteworthy is the fact that many teachers on different levels of education, from the primary to the university levels, are starting to feel that some topics that have traditionally been lectured (like 3D animation engines, TCP/IP protocol, and other "nerdy" subjects where the current state of Wikipedia is most advanced) are now better presented in the Wikipedia, and it is better to use the effort on something else. This wave will be felt during the next decades in all subjects in one way or another and will contribute to the changing nature of education and expertise.

However, this Gutenbergian potential is not the most interesting part of Wikipedia, with regard to issues of critical media literacy or pedagogy. The fact that the Wikipedia is free—in the sense of "free speech"—is, in our estimate, going to be much more influential. This second freedom has two important consequences that can, over time, completely change our views on things like education, literacy, and expert knowledge. Let us call these the "internal" and the "external" perspectives; internal meaning the process of creating wikipedia content, and external as concentrating on wikipedias as whole entities. We do not want to call these the "producer's" and "user's" perspectives, as the point is precisely that the division between these roles will be blurred (Peters & Lankshear 1996, p. 62).

The External Perspective: The Proliferation of Wikipedias

From the external perspective, the "free speech" freedom of Wikipedia makes possible limitless "forking"; that is, new modified versions based on the existing ones (for forks of Wikipedia, see http://en.wikipedia.org/wiki/Wikipedia:Mirrors_and_forks). We should, indeed, be talking of the class of wikipedias, in which the current Wikipedia, with its various language versions, is one case. In fact, the different language versions can already be classified as forks, since their content is different to an extent (see, e.g., the English and French articles on human reproductive organs). The reasons for forking Wikipedia have so far included reasons of editorial policy, attitudes on advertising, and most importantly, different rationalities or points of view behind the content. In essence, when talking about the forks of Wikipedia or the class of wikipedias in general, we are dealing with the politics of knowledge production.

Currently, Wikipedia has a policy of "Neutral Point of View" (NPOV): while discussing controversial issues, Wikipedia articles "must represent all significant views fairly and without bias." The NPOV is self-consciously a view, not the absence of all views. This means that like the encyclopaedias of the Enlightenment, the Wikipedia does contain a rationality of its own. The excessively scientific-positivist rationality of the Enlightenment has been amply criticized in the last 100 years or so. We have learned that, far from being a boon to all humanity, as it believed itself to be, Enlightenment rationality meant the suppression, if not worse, of different rationalities and people believing in them. While Wikipedia's NPOV is not as rabid as the more virulent forms of Enlightenment rationality, it is clear that the growing prominence of Wikipedified information will be corrosive towards certain types of communal, religious, and other rationalities. However, the possibility of forking the Wikipedia somewhat mitigates this negative aspect. In fact, certain Christian forks already exist.

Some kind of rationality is necessary for any kind of open collaborative project to work. In the case of open-source software, the criteria for an improvement of the code is quite straightforward. If the new code works better, it is better. In the case of Wikipedia, the NPOV provides the necessary goal-oriented rationality and makes it possible to decide what is an improvement over an existing version of an article. It is clear that the NPOV is not the only possible source for criteria of improvements. Consequently, different wikipedias, with different rationalities, are emerging. This possibility goes way beyond the Gutenbergian revolution. Editing wikipedia articles is easy. Given time, many political, gendered, geographical, and ethnic viewpoints will have wikipedias of their own. Already, a whole universe of different wiki-projects exists on the net, from the sustainability wiki of Finnish eco-villages to the gambling wikis of Las Vegas.

This radical proliferation of wikipedias will provide a wide spectrum for critical literacy. Not only are we able to learn from various points of view; we will also be able to formulate and argue for our own. The radical proliferation does not only concern points of view; the level of difficulty and need for active participation from the reader may be varied as well. Many Wikipedia articles are formed by providing a combination of short versions of longer articles. This fractal nature of wiki-information will also provide an active playfield for critical reason: sometimes understanding demands more information, sometimes less.

Limitless forking is not a value in itself; the Internet is already full of more or less useless information. However, in the hands of a group of committed individuals and intellectuals working towards a more or less shared goal in incremental steps, wikis provide essential possibilities. Free knowledge production in terms of copyleft does deliver—mutadis mutantis—something about Marx's ideas in his critique of the Gotha Program:

> In a higher phase of communist society, after the enslaving subordination of the individual to the division of labor, and therewith also the antithesis between mental and physical labor, has vanished; after labor has become not only a means of life but life's prime want; after the productive forces have also increased with the all-around development of the individual, and all the springs of co-operative wealth flow more abundantly—only then then can the narrow horizon of bourgeois right be crossed in its entirety and society inscribe on its banners: From each according to his ability, to each according to his needs! (Marx, 1875)

The Internal Perspective: Wikis as Ideal Communication

A wikipedia article comes not only with a button to the edit page, but also with a history and a discussion page. These two provide a unique perspective on how the content has been created, criticized, and cooperated on. The existence of the "edit" button already indicates a subtle but profound epistemological shift: knowledge comes with a past and a future; it is not immutable.

The birth of the public has also been credited to the Enlightenment. The newspaper, a medium in which argument based on the public use of one's reason (which is Kant's definition of adulthood and maturity in his "An Answer to the Question: What Is Enlightenment?" (1784)), has been celebrated as a cornerstone of democratic discussion and decision making. The newspaper has also been criticized by Kierkegaard and others as leveling down genuine expression. Now that commodified messages and mainstreamed content is taking over, the role of newspapers as an open and participatory public discussion forum (in the sense of Habermas or Dewey) is rapidly declining, even in so-called quality newspapers, caught in the pincers of tabloidization and concentration of ownership (see, e.g., Norris 2000, ch 4).

However, something of this public space is being recreated in the discussions around wikipedia content. The NPOV explicitly endorses Habermasian discourse, where the conditions of ideal communication are upheld by the guidelines of NPOV itself. These discussions have two aspects, the political and the epistemological.

On the epistemological side, the processual nature of wiki content emphasises the pragmatic and public aspects of knowledge, disregarding or circumventing aspects of authorship and credentials. The discussions on the reliability of Wikipedia articles often miss the interesting internal change: the reliability of a Wikipedia article is not (only or mainly) to be examined on the basis of the article as it stands, but also by looking at how it has been developed and what kind of criticism it has withstood. This widely distributed peer review gives wiki content a reliability that is different from that guaranteed by authors with institutional credentials. Currently, proposals are being made on how visual cues—for instance, color—could be used in highlighting well-established content on a wiki page (see Cross, 2006).

On the political side, the Wikipedia, and even more importantly, other open, collaborative wikis, are currently functioning as huge hotbeds for democratic discussion and education throughout the world. The wikis formed by special-interest groups or communities with common problems in the real world have the most to gain, as a preexisting goal and motivation works as a dynamo for collaborative knowledge creation. With the "edit," "history," and "discuss" buttons, information on a wiki page is obviously a collective process, not an individual's possession. This epistemological shift, togther with the proliferation of wikipedias, will have dramatic effects on education and learning. Community wikis and larger, open wikipedias are already building the public spheres of the future.

The Paradigm Shift in Education

The internal and external freedoms of wikipedias and the possibilities for forking and for collaborative and processual content creation together will cause a complete reevaluation of institutions of education. As noted, wikipedia content is already replacing the need for "information-delivery" lectures. What is the best way of using time when students and teachers are gathered together in a situation when wiki tools exist? What is the best way of using time when students and teachers are gathered together in a situation when a relatively completed wikipedia exists? In a few decades, there will be no need to lecture in order to transfer information. Rather, people gathered together can overcome the limitations of the cyberspace by discussing, criticizing, arguing, synthetizing, and building an understanding. What is the role of the teacher or any other expert in such a situation? These are the questions we should be asking ourselves while charting a route towards future critical pedagogy. Do we still need places like high-class higher education institutions with their campuses and associated infrastructure, or can we put them into better use, for the people's needs, in the Marxist sense of the word?

The situation resembles visions launched by many late-twentieth-century philosophers, who maintained that technologies of various kinds will play an important part in the democratic society to come. It seemed as if new information technologies were fulfilling some of the early prophesies of these and other democratic utopias. John Dewey's elementary pedagogical idea geared around the idea of "associated life," a cover term for all sorts of educational ideas and practices, old and new, in which people depend on one another and learn with one another (Bruffee, 1995). Ivan Illich (1974), for his part, talked about convivial society: networked communities with their own autonomous free street-corner learning clubs and learning webs, in which people can enjoy media and create their own contents and messages. Using Gilles Deleuze and Félix Guattari's (1987) concept of "rhizome," some thinkers claim that the basic division in the politico-educational arena is that between hierarchal democracy and rhizome-like democracy (Vail, 2005). The concept of rhizome refers to a "subterranean root-like stem that builds up a network of interconnections with no central organization" (Morss, 2003, p. 134). The division between a hierarcial tree-like democracy or organization and that of the rhizomeian democracy or organization not only has political implications in the ideas of "leaderless revolution" and networked dissidence but also educational implications in how to organize curricula in an era characterized by the end of foundational epistemology. In this situation, teaching cannot be easily seen as a authoritarian activity but more like "subversive activity" (Postman & Weingartner, 1971) in which teachers, along with their students, compare information from various sources, negotiate their knowledge and experiences together, and interpret the world.

When Jean-François Lyotard (1984, p. 53) claimed that "the age of the Professor" is ending, he meant that academic professionals and other experts (in their often exclusive ivory towers) are no longer "more competent than memory bank networks in transmitting established knowledge, no more competent than interdisciplinary teams in imagining new moves or new games." Think of the team compiling *Encyclopaedia Britannica* compared to the team compiling the Wikipedia. Lyotard gave only two options for the future of higher learning. The "teaching machines" and data banks providing and transmiting the necessary information constituted the passive or digestive version of the future of higher education; creative teamwork as the kernel of the production of new knowledge characterized the more active version. The latter option was, in Lyotard's view, an elitist version of the future, reserved only for the chosen ones inside academia.

Social media has totally changed this view. Lyotard did not take into account the opportunity for the use of social media, like wikis, in which the former "memory bank networks" could be used actively and be defined almost as "live" by-participants of human cooperation. This, however, is lived reality in the case of today's modes of cooperation between students and teachers, and between citizens and activists of various kinds in their daily studies and the search for the good and just society, as well as in pursuit of new ideas, information, innovations, social justice, peace, knowledge, love, and wisdom. Michel Foucault (1988) once dreamt about diverse methods of critical communication and broadcasting:

> I dream of a new age of curiosity. We have the technical means; the desire is there; there is an infinity of things to know; the people capable of doing such work exist. So what is our problem? Too

little: channels of communication that are too narrow, almost monopolistic, inadequate. We mustn't adopt a protectionist attitude, to stop "bad" information from invading and stifling the "good." We must rather increase the possibility for movement backwards and forwards. (p. 328)

It is relatively easy to see that these and other discourses have been reproduced in diverse techno-utopias, including our own "digital social creativity." These utopias are in sharp contrast with recent university policies and discourses in the Western world. We are repeatedly told that higher education is in crisis due to lack of public funding. As Mary Evans has put it in her *Killing Thinking: The Death of the Universities*, the end of the millennium "has not been a happy time, since those years have seen the transformation of teaching in universities into the painting-by-numbers exercise of the hand-out culture and of much research into an atavistic battle for funds" (Evans, 2004, p. ix).

The university system is regarded as our best resource, not only for intellectual vitality and creativity, but also more straightforwardly for our national economic competitiveness in global markets. Yet those potential resources are increasingly marginalized by cultures of assessment and regulation (Evans, 2004). The crucial hegemonic struggle concerns the language implicit in the use of new information and communication technologies. Whose language is it: technocrats, students, or teachers? Are there many languages, many vocabularies? Who has the power to define the leading vocabulary? There is a threat that the very same forces that are managerializing and thus ruining the critical potential of the universities will set the standards for the language proper. Thus an initial resistance would be urgent; it could start as "a refusal of a language now inflicted upon university staff" (p. 74). In this refusal "out would go consumers, missions statements, aims and objectives and all the widely loathed, and derided, vocabulary of the contemporary university. In could come students and reading lists." To the "in" list we would include the use of social media in various forms, and enough time for discussion, reflection, and debate.

It is said that the institution of education as an invention of the modern era was born to educate the people as citizens. At the same time as it was supposed to guide them, it also governed and disciplined them. But education—as well as literacy—is more or less a double-edged sword. As Raymond Williams nicely put it, if you teach people to read the Bible, you cannot, in principle, stop them from reading the radical press (Williams 2003). Whereas modern education emphasized obedience over authority, mostly "rote memorization, and what Freire called the 'banking concept' of education, in which learned teachers deposit knowledge into passive students, inculcating conformity, subordination, and normalization" (Kellner, 2004, pp. 10–11), the emphasis should be elsewhere in today's education, for it is practically impossible to control people's learning by the means of formal education. Therefore we should now reach for and foster digitalized ways to learn and communicate in cooperation with each other to make a progressive social change; these skills we can call "collaborative literacies."

> Modern education has imposed dominant forms of literacy associated with formal organizations, such as those of the school, the church, the work-place, the legal system, commerce, medical and welfare bureaucracies. . . . In dominant literacies there are professional experts and teachers through whom access to knowledge is controlled. To the extent that we can group these domi-

nant literacies together, they are given high value, legally and culturally. Dominant literacies are powerful in proportion to the power of the institution that shapes them. (Hamilton, 2005)

Another form of literacies, which Mary Hamilton names as "vernacular literacies" and we call "collaborative literacies," are those "which are not regulated or systematized by the formal rules and procedures of social institutions but have their origin in the purposes of everyday life" (Hamilton, 2005). Collaborative literacy practices develop, and are learnt informally. They are rooted in action but are not valued by formal social institutions. Often they develop in people's critical responses to authoritarian regimes and are part of the local and global protests against the institutions of power. Hamilton describes these literacies as follows:

> Vernacular literacies are as diverse as social practices are. They are hybrid in origin, part of a "Do-It-Yourself" culture and often it is clear that a particular activity may be classified in more than one way since people may have a mixture of motives for taking part in a given literacy activity. Preparing a residents association newsletter, for instance, can be a social activity, it can be part of leisure or political activity, and it may involve personal sense-making. They are part of a "Do-It-Yourself" culture that incorporates whatever materials and resources are available and combines them in novel ways. Spoken language, print and other media are integrated; literacy is integrated with other symbolic systems, such as numeracy, and visual semiotics. Different topics and activities can occur together, making it hard to identify the boundaries of a single literacy event or practice. This is in contrast to many school practices, where learning is separated from use, divided up into academically defined subject areas, disciplines and specialisms, and where knowledge is often made explicit within particular interactive routines, is reflected upon, and is open to evaluation through the testing of disembedded skills.

In order to develop collaborative and vernacular literacies as parts of political protests as well as projects of participatory democracy and lifelong transformative learning, we should increase physical spaces for people and groups to meet and exchange ideas, and expand access points for information (libraries, cyber cafes, bookshops, advice centres, Internet buses, community halls) so that citizens can engage in virtual or actual meetings with each other and with experts; strengthen open local government structures and forms of participatory democracy that facilitate social change and citizen action; support local media, which help to break the power of media giants; and provide structured opportunities to learn both content and process skills and link up with others interested in the same issues (Hamilton, 2005).

Social, Socialized, Socialist Media

The term "social media" can be taken to mean the online platforms and software people use in order to collaborate, share experiences, views, and so on, and to create their social identity. Correspondingly, "socialized media" would mean, in this context, such tools when they are owned, maintained, and managed by the community of users itself. Examples of this kind of self-management are many inside the hacker community. There are even cases of actively socializing previously private media. For instance, hackers have collected money in order to purchase the source code of computer programs so they can develop them freely and release them from the commodified world. The most famous example of this kind of commercial "socialization" is the 3D-animation software Blender (see http://en.wikipedia.org/wiki/Blender_%28software%29) that was made free in 2002 by the company that originally developed the software and has continued as an open-source project maintained by the Blender Foundation (The sum of 100,000 euros was collected in 7 weeks to keep the project running; now Blender code is released under the GPL.) Wikipedia itself has largely collected the money needed for its server park through fund-raising from its users.

What about the third step, the case of "socialist" media? Are there means enough for facilitating people's skills and opportunities to be part of the digitalized world, to participate in dialogue by using social media? And, more importantly, are these means themselves digital? It would not be hard to believe the contention forwarded by Zizek (2002a, p. 544) among others, that dialogue in both its traditional forms and in the form of social media takes us only to the gates of authentic and substantial democracy, or what Zizek, drawing on Lenin, refers to as "actual freedom," which undermines the very coordinates of the existing power relations.

Maybe we should start to organize strategies to take the hacker ideology of Free/Libre Open Source Software (FLOSS) to its next logical step. As Zizek puts it in his view of "cyber-communism":

> Is there not also an explosive potential for capitalism itself in the world wide web? Is not the lesson of the Microsoft monopoly precisely the Leninist one: instead of fighting its monopoly through the state apparatus (recall the court-ordered split of the Microsoft corporation), would it not be more "logical" just to socialize it, rendering it freely accessible? Today one is thus tempted to paraphrase Lenin's well-known motto, "Socialism = electrification + the power of the soviets": "Socialism = free access to internet + the power of the soviets." (Zizek, 2002b)

As the true believers of new technologies such as wikis claim (echoing the old axiom of technological determinism), anything that can be presented as digital code, as a series of ones and zeroes, can and will be copied with very little cost and no loss to the original. After the needed infrastructure is in place, digital information is not a scarce resource anymore. Consequently, cornucopian digital economy supposedly transcends the physical limitations of traditional economies.

Correspondingly, on the social level the digital world has been seen as the first germ of new forms of organization that will have radical political effects. Volunteer hacker organizations and the various civil society activities organized with the help of the Internet have been seen, on one hand, as providing fresh blood for the Habermasian ideal of democratic communication and, on the other hand, as completely new forms of civic self-organisation and self-management (for theories on hacker communities, see Castells, 1996 and Himanen, 2001. For instance, while looking for examples of the new multitudes that they advocate as the basic self-organizing models of future politics, Michael Hardt and Antonio Negri (2004, p. 301) turn to free and open-source software communities and related activities. When the self-organizational nature of hacker communities is combined with the observation that digital code is not a scarce resource, we get a cybercommunist utopia where volunteer organizations and communities of nonalienated labor manage themselves in a post-scarcity economy (e.g., Zizek, 2002a, 2006b; Merten, 2000).

One of the crucial consequences of digitalization has to do with the very conditions of material capitalist economy, in comparison to the "second economy" brought forth by the digital sphere. A whole school of writers (for an overview, see Lessig, 2004) have argued that, in addition to the capitalist economy, there exists another economy, variously called, the amateur economy, sharing economy, social production economy, noncommercial economy, participatory economy, p2p economy, or even gift economy. The problem these thinkers want to point out is that this second economy works with its own principles, and that an attempt to force it in the mode of the capitalist economy cannot hold and would be disastrous to its ideology.

The tension between the two economies escalates to two competing worldviews that can easily be discerned on various levels of society. Media researchers Colin Lankshear and Michelle Knobel (2006) have characterized these different mindsets, or attitudes. In mindset 1, emphasis is on business-as-usual, whereas mindset 2 tries to find new concepts, vocabularies, and practices in capturing the reality of social digital creativity. In mindset 1, the world is much the same as before, only now it is more technologized, whereas in mindset 2 the world is very different from before as a result of the emergence and uptake of digital electronic internetworked technologies. In the latter the world cannot be interpreted, understood, or responded to only in physical-industrial terms. The focus is not on individual intelligence as in mindset 1, but rather on collective intelligence. The authority "located" in individuals and institutions does not hold in the second mindset but demands distribution and collectivism; the word of the day is "hybrid expertise." Furthermore, former social relations of "bookspace" change into "digital media spaces."

The hope brought about by the emergence of the second economy lies in the promised post-scarcity and nonalienated mode of labor. Even if a cybercommunist utopia is still far away—What will the hackers eat? Will everyone be a hacker?—a change is already being felt inside the first economy. By adopting aspects of the second economy, the first economy tries to present itself "with a human face." Again the imitation is felt on many fronts: schools and universities want to augment themselves by providing access to informal learning with social media tools, presenting themselves as hubs of social interaction rather than formal institutions of power; nation-states want to shift the attention from traditional industry to competition in terms of design and high-quality experiences; and companies invite their customers to cocreate their future products in a process where innovation itself is supposedly dispersed and equalized. Again, Zizek (2006a) has his finger on the pulse when he discusses a new form of business in which "no one has to be vile." One step removed from the utopia of cybercommunism, Zizek calls this new ideal of capitalist economy in the disguise of the second economy "liberal communism." There are several rules—almost like Ten Commandments—of the new nomadic and frictionless capitalism, geared toward cultural industries.

First, give everything away free (free access, no copyright), but remember to charge for the additional services, which will make you rich. Second, do change the world; don't just sell things. Third, share, and be aware of social responsibility. Fourth, be creative: focus on design, new technologies, and science. Fifth, do not forget to tell all: have no secrets, endorse and practice the cult of transparency and the free flow of information; all humanity should collaborate and interact. Sixth, do not work: have no fixed nine-to-five jobs, but participate in smart communication. Seventh, go back to school for engaging in adult education. Eight, act as an enzyme: work not only for the market, but trigger new forms of social collaboration. Ninth, you should die poor and return all your wealth to those who need it, since you have more than you can ever spend; and tenth, cooperate with the state, since companies should be in partnership with the state. (Zizek, 2006a)

This is all good and well, as far as it goes. But like many other forms of the first economy simulating or appropriating features of the second one, the liberal communist economy conveniently forgets essential structural conditions of its own existence. For Bill Gates to give away huge sums of his fortune in charity, he first had to collect it by ruthless monopolistic practices. More generally, "Developed countries are constantly 'helping' undeveloped ones (with aid, credits, etc.), and so avoiding the key issue: their complicity in and responsibility for the miserable situation of the Third World. Outsourcing is the key notion. You export the (necessary) dark side of production—disciplined, hierarchical labor, ecological pollution to 'non-smart' Third World locations (or invisible ones in the First World)." (Zizek, 2006a). What liberal communism hides, deliberately or not, is the structural violence included in global capitalism.

Zizek points out that liberal communism can work only by masking the structural (economical, social, and political) violence on which its outsourced practices are based. He insists on a true universalism that overcomes all local (ethnic, national, gendered, etc.) identities. The local identities are not, for Zizek, a force against global capitalism, as it is only too happy to manipulate, create, and commodify such identities. However, we might ask, does not the utopia of cybercommunism itself contain an amount of structural violence, a violence that is familiar from earlier stages of cultural change? Is not cybercommunism, in this respect, a return to the square one?

Is the sometimes violent process of socializing the answer? Would it not be better if we could take another logical step—a quantum leap, or perhaps a leap of faith—from there, and start from the outset to talk about and invent what we would like to call—just for the sake of it—socialist media, instead of social, and socialized, media? What would the world be like, if there were exemplars of socialist media? And what would those examples be like?

Skeleton for a Socialist Media

Can we thus think of Wikipedia as an example of socialist media? Do we have other examples? To answer this question, we need to answer the following one: What are the definitive presumptions and characteristics of a socialist media?

Technical and Political Conditions

Besides the obvious technological infrastructure (servers, computers, and other devices) which is needed in organizing and using social media, basic energy—electricity—is rudimentary in the use of social media, as it is to the idea of progress and the modern world. But the crucial question is, who owns and provides energy? An answer to that basic question takes us from the digital realm to the realm of material production, and to the core of critical political economy.

The sad fact is that majority of the energy resources are owned by private international corporations. They are in many ways key players in the arena of international politics, directing foreign policies and making decisions about war and peace. But there is also a different idea for the ownership of such resources as energy. It is called "common wealth." The term comes from the Latin phrase "res publica," meaning "a democratic republic." In the theory of critical political economy, energy is considered to be a central part of common wealth, one that should not be owned by profit-making private companies, but rather by the state and the people. Unfortunately or not, this is a definitive precondition for social media ever to be a truly revolutionary force. Thus, the "social" and "political" still rule the "digital," for, imitating Zizek's "Leninist" formula, free access to the Internet still demands electrical supply.

This demand assumes, quite straightforwardly, that the state and the people take back their common wealth from the global players. Without this logical step, all efforts and activity towards open access are freedom without freedom. For without this ultimate and logical step to overcome private ownership of material resources, the ideology of FLOSS remains another one-issue social movement without authentic political aspect. But quite the reverse has been happening: "A substantial part of the Russian electricity sector created by Lenin to modernise the new Soviet economy is to be privatised with a series of floats expected on the London Stock Exchange" (Macalister, 2006). Lenin identified electricity and oil as key aspects of global imperial capitalism and tried to make a case against these imperial powers and their bourgeois defenders, which acted as cartels and monopolies. In his *Imperialism, the Highest Stage of Capitalism* (1916), Lenin stated that certain reactionary writers

> have expressed the opinion that international cartels, being one of the most striking expressions of the internationalisation of capital, give the hope of peace among nations under capitalism. Theoretically, this opinion is absolutely absurd, while in practice it is sophistry and a dishonest defence of the worst opportunism. International cartels show to what point capitalist monopolies have developed, and the object of the struggle between the various capitalist associations. This last circumstance is the most important; it alone shows us the historico-economic meaning of what is taking place; for the forms of the struggle may and do constantly change in accordance with varying, relatively specific and temporary causes, but the the substance of the struggle, its class content, positively cannot change while classes exist.

That said, we must of course emphasize the contradiction between the Leninist point of view and the idea of the role of a vanguard party leading the masses on one hand, and the digital revolution with the obvious fact that social media has no center, not to mention vanguards, controlling the digital development. This contradiction includes another one, that of ownership of natural resources by states or corporations, and intellectual resources of the people. In contrast to the Leninist idea, the key to emancipation in the sphere of social media and its sociopolitical consequences could be "oscillation and plurality . . . in the plurality and complexity of 'voices': an emancipation consisting in disorientation which is, at the same time, a liberation of dialect, local differences, and rationalities, each with its own distinctive grammar and syntax" (Peters & Lankshear, 1996, p. 60).

But we must add that there may be some glimpse of hope in the developments pointing in the opposite direction to that of the internationalization of capital. As an example, think of the case of Venezuela and its "Bolivarian revolution," part of a new trend for the nationalization of natural resources. Venezuela not only has large natural resources of oil, but also the political leadership and will to use those resources for the people's well-being rather than for the benefit of foreign investors. The same holds true in other Latin American countries like Chile and Bolivia.

Social and Individual Conditions

The physical energy—electricity—needed for running social media sites is one condition. Another is the less tangible energy and free time needed by individuals in order to contribute. For instance, the crown jewel of FLOSS, the GNU/Linux operating system, still receives more contributions from the U.S. and Europe than anywhere else. That this bias can be seen in many major open-collaboration projects, including Wikipedia, should direct our attention to the different possibiliites that present themselves to individuals in different socioeconomic settings. Also, the fact that cases like Blender and Wikipedia need substantial donations points to the importance of relative affluence.

Linus Torvalds, an inventor of the Linux operating system, was a student in the University of Helsinki (Finland) when he started the Linux project and consequently enjoyed the common benefits of the Finnish welfare state, including tuition-free access to the university and its resources. In addition, the Linux code was initially hosted by the Finnish University Network (FUNET). All of this points to the fact that nonalienated knowledge work on the Internet does seem to need a certain basis of affluence before it takes off. It often seems that the benefits of the free and public educational system in Finland will primarily go to the corporations, like the mobile phone company Nokia, and not to the public sector. Even so, these economic mega-players, exploiting the workforce and sucking the state, dare to claim that the state does not support their business enough in terms of radical tax cuts. What is thus needed is a countermove to free people's minds and intellectual resources from the slavery of the corporation.

Educationally speaking, there is a need for an altogether new social mentality and an ideology of a shared ownership. An urgent task of critical educators is to strengthen a sense of community and solidarity, as well as curiosity for different point of views. In this sense, social media has a revolutionary potential for increasing global understanding of difference and overcoming a capitalist drift of commodification and unification of the world.

There are several expressions of different forms of socialism, as Peters reminds us. They "revolve around the international labour movement and invoke new imperialism struggles

based on the movements of indigenous and racialised peoples" (Peters, 2004, p. 436). A starting point for the social condition of socialist media could be built around the concept of
"knowledge socialism." It refers to the politics of knowledge: on one hand to the question
of information domination and its means, and on the other hand to issues pertaining to intellectual property rights and intellectual resources in general, including questions of expert
knowledge versus amateur knowledge as explicated by Peters:

> In these discussions, issues of freedom and control reassert themselves at all levels: at those of con-
> tent, code and information. This issue of freedom/control concerns the ideation and codification
> of knowledge and the new "soft" technologies that take the notion of "practice" as the new
> desideratum: practitioner knowledge, communities of practice, and different forms of organisational
> learning adopted and adapted as part of corporate practice. Indeed, now we face the politics of the
> learning economy and the economics of forgetting that insists new ideas have only a short shelf
> life. . . . These questions are also tied up with larger questions concerning disciplinary versus infor-
> mal knowledge, the formalisation of the disciplines, the development of the informal knowledge
> economy, and the pervasiveness of informal education. Informal knowledge and education based
> on free exchange is still a good model for civil society in the age of knowledge capitalism. (p. 436)

In building a socialist media, a presumption that the mode of production shapes the context in which psychological and social processes take place and consciousness is formed
should be taken into account (Youngman, 1986, p. 101). Thus, the revolutionary potential of wikis. In the first place Wikipedia, or any other form of wiki, is not a technology but
praxis, a collective activity. It involves purpose and intention, and in this sense "knowledge arises and deepens within a continuous process of activity, conceptualisation, and
renewed activity" (p. 96). As knowledge can be defined in this instance as a social product, it always involves hegemonic battles over power to rule and regulate. In a capitalist society, the ruling elite owns the media and thus sets the ruling ideas. But inside this capitalist
realm there is the wikiworld evolving as yet another hegemonic battleground marking the
turn of a tide, for in the wikiworld people have unprecedented powers in their possessions.

The wikiworld is not only a counterhegemonic move but also a serious, hard-to-stop
mass activity. Wikipedia, and other wikis, are lived, educationally-laden social situations,
and if "hegemony is the result of lived social relationships and not simply the dominance
of ideas, then the experiences inherent in educational situations (i.e., the totality of knowledge, attitudes, values and relationships) is as significant as the purely intellectual content"
(Youngman, 1986, p. 105). In other words, the mere process of being in and part of the development of Wikipedia and other wikis is a critical learning experience towards the birth of
socialist media and the enfleshment of Marx's concept of general intellect:

> The development of fixed capital indicates to what degree general social knowledge has become
> a direct force of production, and to what degree, hence, the conditions of the process of social life
> itself have come under the control of the general intellect and been transformed in accordance
> with it. To what degree the powers of social production have been produced, not only in the form
> of knowledge, but also as immediate organs of social practice, of the real life process. (Marx, 1858)

Based on a close textual reading—a "short-circuiting"—of Lenin, Zizek refers to the idea
of general intellect as a huge "accounting apparatus" without which, says Lenin, socialism
is impossible. In order to make socialism happen, Lenin says that we need to make this mas-

sive apparatus, "even bigger, even more democratic, even more comprehensive. . . . This will be country-wide book-keeping, country-wide accounting of the production and distribution of goods, this will be, so to speak, something in the nature of the skeleton of socialist society." (Zizek, 2006b) To Zizek this marks "the most radical expression of Marx's notion of the general intellect regulating all social life in a transparent way, of the post-political world in which 'administration of people is supplanted by the 'administration of things.'" Zizek further notes that it is easy to criticize Lenin by referring to the horrors of real socialist experiment in Soviet Union, especially in Stalin's era, and the apparatus of social administration which grow "even bigger." But as Zizek asks: "Are, however, things really so unambiguous? What if one replaces the (obviously dated) example of the central bank with the World Wide Web, today's perfect candidate for the General Intellect?" What, indeed, if one replaces the example of the World Wide Web with the wikiworld, including the servers and the power plants?

Conclusion

As Kellner (2004) writes, the key question is not a moralistic one—whether social media are good or bad in the hands of critical educators. Rather it is a question of what critical educators can do with Wikipedia and other forms of social media in helping to create "a more democratic and equalitarian society and what their limitations are for producing more active and creative human beings and a more just society" (p. 16).

It goes without saying that Wikipedia and other wikis can be used in formal education. But the problem facing these uses is a certain tardiness and conservatism of the educational system. This holds true through the whole system, all the way from the public sphere to the corridors of the Ministry of Education and to the privacy of a single classroom. In some countries, like Finland, the state has for years launched various campaigns and initiatives relating to the use of computers and new information and computer literacies and skills, but the problem with these is that by the time the goals have been set and the campaigns started, the technologies and skills needed have already changed quite a few times. The system logic—or the grip of the state educational apparatus—does not hold in the wikiworld. Thus it is not wrong to claim that in many Western countries, not to mention some authoritarian regimes, the state has executed technocratic rationality in trying to govern and regulate the digital sphere educationally. It has acted as if it did not want people to liberate themselves in the area of digital literacy. Therefore, as Kellner and Kahn (2006) have stated in their critique of technoliteracy ruled from above, there must be another way:

> We cannot stress it enough: the project of reconstructing technoliteracy must take different forms in different contexts. In almost every cultural and social situation, however, a literacy of critique should be enhanced so that citizens can name the technological system, describe and grasp the technological changes occurring as defining features of the new global order, and learn to experimentally engage in critical and oppositional practices in the interests of democratization and progressive transformation. As part of a truly multicultural order, we need to encourage the growth and flourishing of numerous standpoints on technoliteracy, looking out for and legitimizing counter-hegemonic needs, values, and understandings. Such would be to propound multiple

technoliteracies "from below" as opposed to the largely functional, economistic, and technocratic technoliteracy "from above" that is favored by many industries and states. (p. 13)

Thus we would like to suggest that, in the future, the initiative could be to give more
and more to the hands of the learners, to the people—educators, students, activists,
parents—and their participatory cooperation. Real advances in the area of digital literacy
can be taken only if the power to learn is given to educative communities which can contribute locally and connect globally. No one knows what would be the consequences of this
change for public policy and for the state itself, and that can of course be frightening. It
may be that, "We have lost all certainty, but the openness of uncertainty is central to revolution" (Holloway, 2005, p. 215). Perhaps for the state's institutional players, this openness of uncertainty is their only chance of acting productively and doing their democratic
share. Otherwise, they do not have any role in the digital revolution. By giving their centralized power of defining the problems and solutions to the communities of digital practices, they could make a strong case for furthering not only peoples' digital literacies and
technological competencies, but also their self-regulated socio-political transformation. As
Giroux (2004) has aptly put it,

> one imperative of a critical pedagogy is to offer students opportunities to become aware of their
> potential and responsibility as individual and social agents to expand, struggle over, and deepen
> democratic values, institutions, and identities. They must help students unlearn the presupposi-
> tion that knowledge is unrelated to action, conception to implementation, and learning to social
> change. Knowledge in this case is more than understanding; it is also about the possibilities of self-
> determination, individual autonomy, and social agency. (p. 84)

Without such language of critique, hope, and possibility, it can be impossible to solve
the most daunting challenge confronting us in the twenty-first century: that of the gap
between our ability to be technologically correct, and our ability to morally and ethically
master the enormity of our actions and technologies. The filling of this gap is likely to be
the most daunting challenge confronting us (Bauman, 2002). Or is it just the opposite?
Should we be ready to turn the question concerning information technology's morality and
ethics into the question of how to act technologically incorrect and replace technocratic
"teaching machines"?

References

Bauman, Zygmunt (2002). Technological Development Without Ethics. Paper Presented to the Sixth
    Workshop of the McKinsey Bildet, Deutches Museum, Munich, February 19. http://www.allannoble.net/
    articles_by_zygmunt_bauman.htm (Retrieved October 11, 2006)

Bruffee, Kenneth (1995). Sharing Our Toys. *Change* 27 (1), 12–19.

Castells, Manuel (1996). *The Rise of the Network Society*. Oxford: Blackwell.

Cross, Tom (2006). Puppy Smoothies: Improving the Reliability of Open, Collaborative Wikis. *First Monday*,
    11 (9). http://www.firstmonday.org/issues/issue11_9/cross/index.html (Retrieved September 18, 2006)

Deleuze, Gilles & Guattari, Félix (1987). *A Thousand Plateaus: Capitalism and Schizophrenia*. Minneapolis:
    University of Minnesota Press.

Diderot, Denis & D'Alembert, Jean (1751). Encyclopédie, ou dictionnaire raisonné des sciences, des arts et des métiers. http://diderot.alembert.free.fr/ (Retrieved January 23, 2007)

Dwight, Jim & Garrison, Jim (2003). A Manifesto for Instructional Technology: Hyperpedagogy. *Teachers College Record, 105* (5), 699–728.

Evans, Mary (2004). *Killing Thinking. The Death of the Universities.* New York: Continuum.

Feenberg, Andrew (1998). Can Technology Incorporate Values? Marcuse's Answer to the Question of the Age. http://dogma.free.fr/txt/AF_Marcuse-Technology.htm (Retrieved October 21, 2006)

Foucault, Michel (1988) The Masked Philosopher. In *Politics, Philosophy, Culture: Interviews and Other Writings, 1977–1984.* Edited by Lawrence D. Kritzman. New York: Routledge.

Giroux, Henry. (2000). *Stealing Innocence. Corporate Culture's War on Children.* New York: St. Martin's Press.

Giroux, Henry. (2004). Academic Culture, Intellectual Courage, and the Crisis of Politics in an Era of Permanent War. In *Take Back Higher Education.* Edited by Henry Giroux and Susan Searls Giroux. New York: Palgrave Macmillan.

Giroux, Henry & Searls Giroux, Susan (2004). Neoliberalism Goes to College: Higher Education in the New Economy. In *Take Back Higher Education.* Edited by Henry Giroux and Susan Searls Giroux. New York: Palgrave Macmillan.

Hamilton, Mary (2005). Sustainable Literacies and the Ecology of Lifelong Learning. Working Papers of the Global Colloquium on Supporting Lifelong Learning Online, Milton Keynes, UK: Open University. http://www.open.ac.uk/lifelong-learning/papers/index.html (Retrieved October 7, 2006)

Hardt, Michael & Negri, Antonio (2004). *Multitude.* London: The Penguin Press.

Himanen, Pekka (2001). *The Hacker Ethic.* New York: Random House.

Holloway, John (2005). *Change the World Without Taking Power: The Meaning of Revolution Today.* London: Pluto Press.

Illich, Ivan (1974). Tools for Conviviality. http://opencollector.org/history/homebrew/tools.html (Retrieved October 15, 2006)

Kant, Immanuel (1784). An Answer to the Question: What Is Enlightenment? http://www.english.upenn.edu/~mgamer/Etexts/kant.html (Retrieved October 13, 2006)

Kellner, Douglas (1995). *Media Culture.* London & New York: Routledge.

Kellner, Douglas (1998). From 1984 to One-Dimensional Man: Critical Reflections on Orwell and Marcuse. http://www.uta.edu/huma/illuminations/kell13.htm (Retrieved October 21, 2006)

Kellner, Douglas (2004). Technological Transformation, Multiple Literacies, and the Re-visioning of Education. *E–Learning,* (1) 1. http://www.wwwords.co.uk/elea/content/pdfs/1/issue1_1.asp#2 (Retrieved January 23, 2007)

Kellner, Douglas & Kahn, Richard (2006). Reconstructing Technoliteracy: A Multiple Literacies Approach. http://www.gseis.ucla.edu/faculty/kellner/index.html (Retrieved October 6, 2006)

Lankshear, Colin & Knobel, Michelle (2003). *New Literacies. Changing Knowledge and Classroom Learning.* London: Open University Press.

Lankshear, Colin & Knobel, Michelle (2006). Blogging as Participation: The Active Sociality of a New Literacy. http://www.geocities.com/c.lankshear/work.html (Retrieved January 23, 2007)

Lenin, V. I. (1916). *Imperialism, the Highest Stage of Capitalism.* http://www.marxists.org/archive/lenin/works/1916/imp-hsc/ch05.htm (Retrieved October 7, 2006)

Lessig, Lawrence (2004). Free Culture. How Big Media Uses Technology and the Law to Lock Down Culture and Control Creativity. New York: The Penguin Press. http://free-culture.cc/freecontent/ (Retrieved January 24, 2007)

Lyotard, Jean-François (1984). The Postmodern Condition: A Report on Knowledge. http://www.marxists.org/reference/subject/philosophy/works/fr/lyotard.htm (Retrieved July 24 2006)

Macalister, Terry (2006). Soviet power falls to City of London with series of energy flotations. http://business.guardian.co.uk/story/0,,1830940,00.html (Retrieved October 7, 2006)

Marx, Karl (1858). The Grundrisse: Outlines of the Critique of Political Economy. http://www.marxists.org/archive/marx/works/1857/grundrisse/ch14.htm (Retrieved October 4, 2006)

Marx, Karl (1875). Critique of the Gotha Program. http://www.marxists.org/archive/marx/works/1875/gotha/ch01.htm (Retrieved October 21, 2006)

Marcuse, Herbert (1941). Some Social Implications of Modern Technology. Studies in Philosophy and Social Science, 9 (3), 414–439.

Merten, Stefan (2000). GNU/Linux—Milestone on the Way to the GPL Society. http://www.opentheory.org/gplsociety/text.phtml (Retrieved October 4, 2006)

Morss, John (2003). "Looking Allies": Gilles Deleuze as Critical Theorist. In Futures of Critical Theory: Dreams of Difference. Edited by Michael Peters, Mark Olssen, & Colin Lankshear. Lanham, MD: Rowman & Littlefield, 5127–139.

Norris, Pippa (2000). Virtuous Circle: Political Communications in Post-Industrial Societies. Cambridge: Cambridge University Press.

Peters, Michael (2004). Marxist Futures: Knowledge, Socialism and the Academy. (Editorial). Policy Futures in Education, 2 (3&4). http://www.wwwords.co.uk/pfie/content/pdfs/2/issue2_3.asp#1 (Retrieved October 12, 2006)

Peters, Michael & Lankshear, Colin (1996). Critical Literacy and Critical Texts. Educational Theory, 46 (1), 51–70.

Postman, Neil & Weingartner, Charles (1971). Teaching as Subversive Activity. New York: Delta.

Thomson, Iain (2003). From the Question Concerning Technology to the Quest for Democratic Technology: Heidegger, Marcuse, Feenberg. In Futures of Critical Theory: Dreams of Difference. Edited by Michael Peters, Mark Olssen, & Colin Lankshear. Lanham, MD: Rowman & Littlefield, 59–72.

Vail, Jeff (2005). Rhizome: Guerrilla Media, Swarming and Asymmetric Politics in the 21st Century. http://www.jeffvail.net/2005/07/rhizome-guerrilla-media-swarming-and.html (Retrieved October 20, 2006)

Williams, Raymond (2003). Television, Technology and Cultural Form. London & New York: Routledge.

Youngman, Frank (1986). Adult Education and Socialist Pedagogy. London: Croom Helm.

Zizek, Slavoj (2002a). A Plea for Leninist Intolerance. Critical Inquiry, 28(2), 543–566.

Zizek, Slavoj (2002b). A cyberspace Lenin: why not? International Socialism Journal, 95. http://pubs.socialistreviewindex.org.uk/isj95/zizek.htm (Retrieved October 7, 2006)

Zizek, Slavoj (2006a). No one has to be vile. London Review of Books, 28 (Retrieved October 4, 2006) http://lrb.co.uk/v28/n07/zize01_.html

Zizek, Slavoj (2006b). Repeating Lenin. http://www.marxists.org/reference/subject/philosophy/works/ot/zizek1.htm#49 (Retrieved October 13, 2006)

CHAPTER 8

Glocalizing Critical Pedagogy

A Case of Critical English Language Teaching in Korea

KIWAN SUNG

Introduction

With the dominance of political and academic discursive practices promoting globaliza-tion and internationalization as something good for everybody, English teachers in non-English speaking countries have been forced to conform to the practice of teaching language in a fragmented manner for a long time. That is, nowadays there are more quick-fix teaching methods using commercially developed instructional materials and test soft-ware to raise students' test scores for future job security. What is worse, most EFL practitioners in Korea accept such rigid practices as part of reality, unavoidable or even necessary steps to develop students' English language proficiency. However, such a distorted practice of teaching language for language's sake is problematic for many reasons and should be con-tested instead of being condoned without critical investigation.

Accordingly, this paper provides the historical backgrounds of English language teach-ing (ELT) in Korea, and documents experiences of implementing a graduate-level critical English language teaching (CELT) program for a period of 6 years. To be more specific, both positive aspects and recurring issues related to practicalizing critical pedagogy in a specific program are examined and discussed. In doing so, this chapter problematizes the current practice of unidirectionally espousing ESL theories and methods from ELT developed in English-speaking countries such as the U.S. or U.K. (Kachru & Nelson, 1996). Additionally, this chapter argues that EFL practitioners need to localize and engage in context-specific critical teaching practices linking English teaching to the issues of language, culture, power, and social justice to counteract the dominance of Western influences that use English teaching to monopolize ways of being and becoming.

Formation and Characteristics of ELT in Korea

The history of ELT in Korea is far from being clear-cut, because of complexities due to many political, sociocultural, and economical vicissitudes in the late 1800s and early 1900s. According to Moon (1976), English began to be taught in Korea at the turn of the twentieth century when the then-superpowers of the world vied to open the Korean Peninsula to secure a route to expand their military and economic powers. Vacillating along with the imperialistic powers manifested by China, Japan, the Soviet Union, Germany, and the U.S. and others, the Korean government changed its educational policies frequently to meet rather temporary needs in accordance with the political pendulum. For example, Dong Mun Hak was specially established by a German under the Office of International Trade and Commerce in order to train translators for English and Japanese. But it was closed when the first educational institute, Yook Young Gong Won, was established in 1886 on the order of the last Emperor Gojong of Korea; there, three Americans were in charge of modern education, in which English was one of the key subjects. However, Yook Young Gong Won was turned into Hansung English School in 1894 due to financial difficulties. Then, Hansung Foreign School was established in 1906, but was abolished in 1911 when the Educational Act for Chosun (the old name of Korea before the Japanese colonization in 1910) was enacted by the Japanese government. Consequently, English teaching was prohibited for a decade during the era of Japanese colonization; however, there were a few missionary schools established by the Westerners, which taught English to some extent. Accordingly, the early educational institutes established in Korea purported to bring modern education to Korea, and English was an important subject for utilitarian purposes—or, on a deeper level, to teach Western knowledge and the Bible to a group of selected Korean people (Hong, 1993).

It was not until after the 1919 Independence Movement that English teaching was again permitted as one of the softening policies to pacify the Koreans' resistance against the Japanese colonial regime. However, English was mostly taught through deeper structural analysis and rote learning of rules, using the Grammar-Translation Method (GTM) until it was banned again when World War II broke out. Such emphasis and reliance on linguistic elements and memorization have continued in ELT in Korea as a traditional and colonial legacy.

After the liberation from Japanese colonization and the ensuing internal Korean War of 1950–1952, English became a survival tool because the U.S. government and military ruled Korea. This had significant impacts on people's living, acting, and thinking. For instance, in order to improve the English proficiency of Korean government officials, military staff, and even students, a few organized English programs were founded. However, it was still taught by the traditional method, in which grammar and vocabulary learning, along with mechanical drilling and memorization, were dominantly used, based on highly structured curricular materials and instructional activities (Hong, 1993; Moon, 1976).

In the 1960s and 1970s, with the return of a few English professors who had studied in the U.S., ELT in Korea began to adopt theories and methods based on behavioral and cognitive views of language teaching and learning (Moon, 1976; Kim, 1995). In recent years, ELT in Korea has been influenced by contemporary theories, research results, and methods such as the Audiolingual Method in the 1970s, humanistic and affection-based teaching in the 1980s, and the Communicative Language Teaching (CLT) in the 1990s. As a matter of fact, in the 1990s, ELT in Korea started to assume its ownership as a discipline detaching itself from the traditional English literature and linguistics (Kwon, 2000a, 2000b). Kwon (2000b) observed that there is a growing trend in university curriculums in which more ELT courses related to acquisition and learning theories, teaching methods, and other skills-based subjects are offered even in English literature or linguistics programs. In the 1990s, the Korean Ministry of Education and Human Resources changed its national curriculum, in which English education is mandated, to enhance students' communicative competence. This encouraged people to accept the now popular idea of English for communication. Furthermore, English began to be taught from the third grade in elementary schools in 1997. Moreover, the government is experimenting in a few selected school districts with the idea of starting to teach English from the first grade in 2006. In addition, level- and stage-specific English teaching was implemented, and more native English-speaking teachers (NESTs) have been employed in both public schools and private institutes to meet the curricular mandates and learners' interests in learning English for communication (Kwon, 2000a).

However, some perennial problems continue to pose challenges in ELT in Korea. One of the most serious problems in ELT is the production and distribution of knowledge mostly through positivistic, reductionistic, and Cartesian-Newtonian research practices. According to Kim (2004), there are still many quantitative and descriptive research articles in *English Teaching*, a leading journal in Korea, while few articles rely on more interpretative, ideological, ethnographic, and narrative methods. However, despite several curriculum changes, there are some long-lasting problems, such as a lack of coherence between curricular contents and the mandated textbooks, rigid teaching methods to raise students' scores in high-stake tests such as the National College Entrance Exam (NCEE), teachers' lack of fluency in English, and large classroom sizes, which have significantly improved over the years (Han, 2005; Park, 2001; Sung, 2002).

In sum, like the rest of the world, the ELT in Korea surely subscribes to the ideology of English for communication and social mobilization, such as getting jobs or promotions (Kohn & Shannon, 2002; Pennycook, 1998; Sung, 2002). In such a context, many important educational concepts and issues are decontextualized, and individual efforts and development are highly valued due to Western influences. Furthermore, many do not problematize and examine the hegemonic equation of studying English for personal development and economic success (Gee, 1996). In other words, many do not understand that current practices of teaching English were neither neutrally nor naturally developed or spread, but were the result of the amalgam of many historical, political, sociocultural, and economical factors innately related to imperialism, neocolonialism, postmodernism, globalization, market theory, and technological progress (Canagarajah, 1999; Pennycook, 1995, 1998, 2001; Phillipson, 1992).

It is in this context described so far that I have engaged in particular sociocultural ways of delineating more relevant academic content and administrative and instructional procedures to embed critical theory and pedagogy in an M.A. graduate program in Korea. Accordingly, this chapter includes my journey of exerting efforts to develop a critical model of English teaching in order to debunk the over-reliance on the idea of teaching English as a mere tool for communication and jobs and, eventually, to move the field of ELT in Korea to claim ownership without constantly referring to English-speaking countries to verify the legitimacy of teaching English (Sung, 2004). I will describe some key factors in establishing a CELT program and highlight positive and negative experiences in implementing and operating it on a daily basis as director for five years and an adjunct for another year. In addition to interacting with faculty and students, I analyzed various curricular and instructional documents, works done by the teacher and students, notes from faculty and departmental meetings, ethnographic observations and data recorded in an on-the-spot or delayed manner, and many formal and informal talks and discussions with the teaching staff and students. Though these sources are not exhaustive, as an insider who developed this program with specific ideologies and objectives based on critical theory and pedagogy, I will present a reasonably understandable picture of what this particular program was like, and what challenges lie ahead in developing and improving similar programs in EFL contexts.

Background of Establishing a CELT Program

Explaining how and why I conceived of establishing a CELT program is closely related to my personal experiences as a teacher and student in both the Korean and U.S. academic contexts. On a personal level, having taught high school for over six years using traditional GTM or reading methods, and knowing what problems existed in ELT in Korea, I was more than ready to find new ways to teach English differently when I decided to study abroad. However, after going through the TESOL program for two years, I realized that, whether in the U.S. or in Korea, there is a large extent of aesthetic and ethical teaching in which traditional knowledge and the cultural heritage of the West, along with an emphasis on individual efforts and development to master Standard English (if it even exists) are highly emphasized (Morgan, 1997). In other words, there were always normative learning and language practices in English-speaking ESL programs imposed on students, consciously or unconsciously, based on hyperreal language standards which are thought to be used by highly educated middle-class White people in the West.

In such a context, despite the popular buzzword of teaching English for communication and valuing students' backgrounds, such as their cultures and languages, I felt that TESOL (or TESL, or ESL, or whatever acronyms it takes) predominantly followed the transmission model of delivering rather discrete knowledge and skills camouflaged as state-of-the-art theories and research. In this regard, Pennycook (1998) rightly views that the term TESOL (Teaching English to Speakers of Other Languages) itself as hegemonic, given that English is delivered by Western, mostly White, middle-class teachers, "to" others, who are lumped as "Other" and speak languages other than English.

It was a simple matter of luck that I switched over to the doctoral program in the College of Education at Penn State and, again by mere chance, started to take the courses from Joe Kincheloe, Henry Giroux, Pat Shannon, Ladi Semali, and Jamie Myers. I slowly began to realize that I had missed a lot under the pretext of teaching English in the right manner. I started to be more serious about the readings in and outside of class, and was truly surprised, awakened, and challenged academically and intellectually by these renowned scholars in the field of sociocultural and critical pedagogy, and from their writings and other critical works by Paulo Freire, Patti Lather, Peter McLaren, Donald Macedo, Alfie Kohn, Ira Shor, Elana Shohamy, Alastair Pennycook, and many others. That is how I stepped into the world of teaching English as a social and political act, which is still a dangerously subversive idea, as well as a missing piece in many ESL and EFL contexts where English is taught to help nonnative speakers of English (NNSEs) learn basic communicative language skills as a requirement for entering the job market (Phillipson, 1992; Tollefson, 1995).

After finishing my academic work, I secured a job at a small-sized industrial university located in Korea's sixth-largest city, home to about 1.35 million people, in the central part of the country. The school was established about three years before I joined and offered mostly engineering programs along with English, Japanese, Chinese, and business management, hotel management, and tourism programs. Therefore, this school was no more than an extension of a typical two-year junior college vocational school, where curriculums were expanded mostly with job-related language and technical-skills courses. As a matter of fact, in the first year, I was assigned to teach English Conversation, Reading, Writing, and TOEIC (Test of English as an International Communication) to the undergraduates who came to this school due to their low GPA and scores in the NCEE. However, despite such constraints, I always wanted to develop a program in which I could make use of the critical line of work in which I had been immersed over the years. In other words, I always wanted to establish a program where students use English as a critical tool, not only to learn diverse knowledge and cultures in relation to self, others, and the world but also to construct and distribute their own knowledge in their communities and world.

Characteristics of a CELT Program

English as a Medium of Instruction

There were a few things to consider in developing a CELT program in the context of ELT in Korea. For instance, it is very common that a student may not speak or write in English even though s/he has finished an advanced graduate degree in English, because the use of English is not required in almost all English programs. In other words, many students come out of these programs with a lack of both critical thinking as well as English proficiency, given that they go through programs focusing on aesthetic features of grand literature, so-called White canons, structural analyses of bits and pieces of the target language, or declarative knowledge on how to teach in the classroom. Therefore, English was used as a main medium of instruction and for all other work such as assignment and thesis writing, even though some Korean professors (including me) used Korean if necessary. This was done to make sure that the Korean students got beyond the threshold level of English by using the language all the time so that they became more confident in expressing their opinions in English.

Inclusion of NESTs

Despite the pressing needs of using English and designing a program for native English-speaking teachers (NESTs) who come to this country—as many as 20,000 per year (Kim, 2005)—there were and still are few programs for native speakers of English (NSEs) or NESTs who teach in public and private institutes. That is, despite so many unprepared, ill-prepared, and under-prepared teachers from various countries, there was no EFL program for these teachers, other than a couple of online programs offered outside of the country, or one or two teacher-certificate programs offered by a publisher like Oxford University Press. Thus, even though these teachers were aware of their lack of knowledge and skills in teaching EFL or of the incompatibility of adopting knowledge and skills from ESL contexts to EFL contexts, there was no program which could help these teachers develop their teaching skills. It was not until the 2000 that a couple of Korean ELT programs started to recruit foreign teachers. Therefore, despite my firm belief in bilingual, multilingual, and multicultural education, I compromised and offered all the courses in English. As a matter of fact, this particular CELT program was one of the first two programs which offered an M.A. degree and was the first to accept NESTs as students in Korea at the time of its establishment.

Focus on Technology

Another important component of the CELT program was technology. The reason that technology was included was because the use of multimedia can help students produce and share their own knowledge and understandings of various sociocultural phenomena in the world. Accordingly, the program was named TESOL-MALL (Teaching English for the Speakers of Other Languages-Multimedia-Assisted Language Learning), and the goals of the program, appearing on the official website (http://vod.wsu.ac.kr/tesol/introduction/ about_us.html), read as below:

> The TESOL-MALL Program educates professional English teachers in the globalization era to become specialists who will contribute to the development of English education and multimedia-related English education. This program offers an interdisciplinary curriculum and multimedia assisted language learning with highly qualified domestic and international faculty . . .
>
> The Masters of Arts Program in TESOL-MALL is open to both experienced and prospective language educators, both domestic and international, who wish to start or upgrade their ESL or EFL career in Korea or abroad. It is designed flexibly so as to accommodate the specific needs of each type of student and their varying career objectives while offering maximum interaction among a multilingual student population.

Differentiated Curriculum

As shown in the goals statement above, this CELT program operated under the critical framework of teaching and research by revising the curriculum on a yearly basis. In other words, the faculty and students were given opportunities to provide their interests in teaching and learning, and their opinions were reflected in the curriculum as much as possible. For example, until I left the program at the end of 2004, most courses were more in line with language acquisition theory courses, but there were two distinctive features; first, it had multimedia-assisted language learning components, and second, there were three courses specifically geared to critical pedagogy. *Postmodernity & English Language Teaching* was offered to help students investigate various pedagogical issues and practices, such as communicative language teaching and other progressive teaching, in the context of postmodernism and critical postmodernism. Relatedly, *Critical Sociolinguistics* provided students with the opportunity to examine a wide range of literature across the social sciences that views language acquisition and use as a social, rather than cognitive, phenomenon. Students were to read diverse literature from the fields of sociolinguistics, sociology, English as an international language (EIL), and cultural studies, so that they could make connections between the diversity of practices in ELT. In addition, in TESOL, *Methods of Alternative Inquiry*, students were guided to develop their research ideas for the M.A. paper using qualitative research methods such as content analysis, thick description, symbolic interactionism, discourse analysis, and historiography. As of 2006, there are several courses added due to the increase in students' interests and demands for specific CELT courses. They are *Literature, Film, and Issues in TESOL Education*; *Language Policy and Planning*; *Introduction to Critical English Language Teaching* (CELT); and *Media Literacy*. Among these, the two courses which particularly stand out are as follows:

Introduction to Critical English Language Teaching (CELT)

This course will survey theories and pedagogies in recent approaches to CELT. This course serves as an introduction to the courses of CELT 590 and CELT 500R. Literature surveyed in this course includes the theoretical and pedagogical concepts of situated learning, dialogism, inquiry education, project based curricula, communities of practice, post-structural and post-modern approaches to ELT, intertextuality, multiple modalities of representation, media literacy, and cultural studies approaches to ELT.

Cultural Studies in TEFL

This course examines methods of teaching culture in the EFL classroom by providing a framework for teaching culture and value systems in the second language classroom. The specific emphasis is on methods of cultural comparison, audio-visual materials and textbook evaluation, and situating the stories of EFL learners in local contexts.

The courses above are offered for two reasons. First, the introductory course for CELT is to induct the students into various theoretical and research discourses related to critical work in ELT or other educational contexts. Second, the cultural studies course helps students critically analyze various forms of texts in order to understand multilayered meanings and ideologies embedded in such texts.

In addition, from the informal talks and discussion with the head of the program, it was noted that he also wanted to include some traditional language-focused courses due to the increase of domestic and NESTs students who did not major in English and were in need of some foundational courses, such as *Pedagogical Grammar in TESOL*, and *Introduction to Linguistics*. Such revision is understandable since most ELT programs in Korea offer traditional linguistics and other skills courses, which require these students to be on par with students who study in English programs at other universities.

As a matter of fact, there is a clear curricular difference between this CELT program and many other ELT programs. For example, briefly comparing the latest CELT curriculum with two other renowned M.A. graduate English programs at K and E Women's Universities reveals that their programs do not include any critical courses, even though there are many courses on literature, linguistics, language skills, and methods, and a couple of courses on sociolinguistics and World Englishes. Obviously, the courses offered at these two universities followed the tradition of teaching English and focused on disciplinary fields of literature and applied areas of language based on psychological and cognitive orientations. That is, no course deals with sociocultural, sociopolitical, and critical lines of research and practices in a serious and in-depth manner in order to help students learn more than limited sets of literary, linguistic, and technical knowledge and skills mostly developed out of positivistic and reductionistic theory-making and research practices.

Instructional Support from External Faculty

In July of 2000, Jamie Myers from the Pennsylvania State University came and taught a course, *Design & Development of Interactive Instructional Programs*. He and I worked with a group of students to engage in multimedia inquiry projects in order to investigate diverse sociocultural issues based on their interests in and understandings of important phenomena at the time. That is, even though there were designated texts to read, the class moved along with student-chosen topics of inquiry throughout the course. The topics were important political and sociocultural issues, such as the possibility of reunification of North and South Koreas, the reasons for the popularity of Pokémon characters among children, the environmental issue of saving the Dong River in the eastern part of Korea, diverse views on the use of cellphones, issues of choice in the training of sports heroes, using children's literature in elementary schools, and the influence of the Japanese media in Korea. In doing so, the students were guided to use diverse texts, using multimedia to represent the results of their inquiries. In fact, the students spent a large amount of time finding relevant data and organizing them to critically analyze what factors contributed to such phenomena and how people made their own sense of these issues. This culminated with students designing web pages, and each group uploading their reports as an avenue for sharing their work with other groups, the program faculty, and school administrators. These students attested that they learned not only English but also how to use technology in order to construct their understandings of the phenomena. (See the student work at http://itss229.ed.psu.edu:16080/k-12/incountry/index.html; or refer to Sung, 2001).

For the next six years, there were steady offerings of summer or winter intersession courses taught by the faculty from collaborating and other universities, which enriched the quality and dimensions of the program. The intersession courses taught by the external faculty from collaborating universities were as follows:

- *Design & Development of Interactive Multimedia* (Dr. Jaime Myers)
- *Reading Other Ways* (Dr. Dan Hade)
- *Multiple America(s): Race and Ethnicity* (Dr. Myriam Espinosa-Dulanto)
- *A Critical Look at American Schools* (Dr. Deb Freedman)
- *Teaching of Writing* (Dr. Deborah Crusan)
- *Quantitative Research Methods* (Dr. Juhu Kim)
- *Qualitative Research: Engaging the Bricolage* (Dr. Joe Kincheloe)
- *Media Literacy and Cross-Cultural Communication* (Dr. Shirley Steinberg)
- *Whole Language* (Dr. Dan Hade)

The courses offered by invited faculty varied from scientifically and skills-based ones to critical approaches of teaching and research. That is, the students were given opportunities to take more traditional courses to keep up with students in other programs. However, in this CELT program, they always had valuable opportunities to link their understanding of English and its roles to diverse historical, sociocultural, political, and economic factors in a critical manner. In other words, the essence of this program lay in the fact that, for the first time, many domestic and foreign students were exposed to critical discourses in which the issues of power and inequality due to race, class, gender, sexuality, and other differences were related to English and the practice of teaching it. Especially, it provided somewhat vivid examples of discrimination and injustice when the faculty from English-speaking nations ruptured their unexamined assumptions and indirect knowledge coming from the West. That is, the students were enthusiastic or at least compelled to think about their teaching and learning practices by having engaged in truly collaborative inquiry work, read diverse children's literature for future use, understood roles of social markers and schooling in the age of technology, and, more importantly, learned new ways of researching in ELT. For instance, Joe's class on bricolage was new to the students, and there were a few students who were at first uneasy but came along to understand the "criticality" of educational research which can not be done in a monologic but multiple ways in real, situated contexts (Kincheloe, 2004).

Implication and Prospects of CELT in ELT in Korea

Positive and Negative Factors in CELT

As explained in detail above, there were a few reasons why critical pedagogy was possible in this specific CELT context. First, this program was developed in a fairly new university with no historical or academically competitive programs. Thus, there were few conflicts with existing programs, and little resistance from the administrators and other faculty in school since there was a great need for a graduate program, and most of the faculty were from engineering departments and did not know what specifics or details were needed in establishing English programs. It might have been difficult to establish such a program in a university with existing English literature or linguistics programs, where varying degrees of resistance from other faculty or internal barriers would have been probable. In addition, due to the fact that this was a new program, the University was generous about the scholarships and the expenses needed for inviting faculty from outside.

Second, the close linkage with cooperating schools was possible for many different aspects such as credit transfer programs, student and faculty exchange, continuous interaction for curricular and instructional collaboration, and special intersession courses from leading scholars in the critical and other progressive fields. Accordingly, the courses offered by these visiting scholars added depth to the curriculum, and exposed the students to different knowledge and understanding about the roles of English and English teachers, as well as various forces which shape current English teaching. In addition, there were opportunities for some students to study at collaborating programs in the States.

Third, despite the philosophical and pedagogical differences among faculty in the program, there was a relatively liberal academic atmosphere in which faculty members could discuss and do whatever it took for them to help students. Therefore, the students were not forced to think like or act like their professors, and could take some traditional skills or methods courses. In addition, because there were both Korean and foreign faculty, the students could seek emotional safety and academic help according to their needs. In other words, they could go to any faculty member and discuss their psychological or academic difficulties in their own languages or in English.

Fourth, given that this program was developed for both domestic and foreign students, the number of foreign students such as NSEs and a few students from China and Indonesia slowly increased, and the program became more internationalized when I left. In addition, there were an increasing number of Korean in-service teachers who joined the program to study in a competitive English program where they could learn in English along with NSEs. The head of the department, Rod Pederson, told me in the fall of 2006 that there were about 100 NSEs and in-service teachers who studied in the program. Such a composition of the students enriches the program by allowing for more meaningful and natural interaction given that English is always used to share knowledge and experiences in teaching and learning. In other words, the frequent interaction between NNSEs and NSEs was an indispensable asset in this program, and I still believe that more meaningful learning occurred when they talked, laughed, bonded, and shared so many diverse ideas in and outside the classroom. In fact, I myself learned much about English education from these students while in class and advising them.

Last but not least, the students were always immersed in a comfortable academic environment, able to utilize their learning and engage in the critical investigation of the issues related to ELT in Korea. For example, many students used more qualitative critical research such as case, narrative, or ethnographic studies for their M.A. theses, and in fact, only a couple of students—who seemed to rely more on outsiders rather than their peers or professors—adopted positivistic research methods. I advised 21 students over 6 years, and they all wrote M.A. theses in English except one who wanted to write hers in Korean, in order to publish it for Korean elementary teachers or parents who teach children's literature. They all did superb work linking ELT to the issues of power and identity with criticality in mind. That is, out of the 21 papers, 11 papers were in line with critical research studies such as the possibility of using critical or socially-oriented pedagogy in elementary, secondary, or university contexts; ways to enhance students' critical thinking and consciousness, using instructional materials, media, and culture critically; identity formation of a Korean student in the ESL class; sociocultural identity of English teachers who are Teacher Union members; and so on.

Among these papers, Whittle (2003) investigated how well TESOL programs in North America and in Korea prepared NESTs who taught in EFL settings. He surveyed both Korean and foreign students and also utilized different sources such as web sites, newspaper articles, and relevant documents, and even conducted numerous phone inquiries for his research. He found out that not many graduate TESOL programs in North America offer courses that are helpful to NESTs to prepare for teaching in EFL contexts. His findings also suggest that both NESTs and NNESTs in EFL settings have predominantly relied on theories and instructional activities originating from ESL contexts without considering contextual differences, such as sociocultural, curricular, and instructional factors. Accordingly, this kind of research would not have been possible without the criticality this particular researcher learned in the course. His work actually contributes to the field of ELT in Korea, suggesting a redesign of its programs to address the deficiencies he observed.

However, there were many struggles and obstacles to overcome in running this particular program. The most serious program was the institutional factor. That is, constant compromises had to be made given that the university mandates certain rules to follow. For instance, the university did not allow the initial proposal of at least 30 credits with a thesis requirement which accounts for 3–6 credits. Therefore, the required credits for this program were only 24 (27 for the paper or case study option), in line with most other Korean universities. So it was difficult to strike a balance between foundational language teaching subjects and the courses which are in line with critical theory or literacy.

Another was that the particular program belonged initially to the School of International Business Management and Foreign Language Communication. Then, it was shifted around the colleges in frequent restructuring processes to overcome low enrollment at the university. Once it was under the Department of English Language Communication, until it was separated as its own independent program called the Department of TESOL-MALL. A further difficulty was the fact that the teachers in this particular program were required to teach other English courses, mostly skills-based, in the undergraduate English programs. In fact, scheduling permitted most to teach only one graduate course, since they were assigned to teach three or four undergraduate courses. Therefore, it was always difficult to secure quality faculty members who were willing to juggle two different types of work in this fairly new school that was itself struggling to develop a reputation.

Another undesirable setback was the impossibility of establishing a doctoral program, despite the level of success this particular program achieved over such a short period time. Accordingly, from 2005 to late 2006, the current head of the program and I have engaged in many discussions to find ways to establish programs to meet the growing needs for such a program, but for many reasons such an effort and work were always unsuccessful for the few obvious reasons. The university does not meet the government's requirement for the faculty-to-student ratio to the extent that it can apply for a Ph.D. program. In addition, there were some internal power games and barriers among existing programs and the intermediating administrators, who interpret the establishment of a Ph.D. program as unnecessary or ineffective in a vocational school. Accordingly, it truly requires a strong will, tenacity, and even smart strategies to pursue the seemingly impossible and yet quite achievable goals of improving the current program to a varying degree. For example, a Ph.D. program may be possible if it is separate from the university and becomes an independent graduate program, as other universities have done.

There are always struggles facing any critical pedagogue; but s/he goes on, since if s/he does not, there may be no one to continue on the important projects of engaging our student in problematizing practices for better possibilities and hope for the marginalized (Freire, 1970; Pennycook, 2001; Simon, 1992).

Emergence and Increased Interests in CELT in Korea

The idea of English as a critical tool is extremely important and yet tacitly acknowledged or even resisted by the pure essentialists and dominant groups in ELT in Korea or other countries. For example, arguing that critical thinking is not well-defined and culturally problematic for ESL or EFL practitioners or learners, Atkinson (1997) states that critical thinking has been used in a reductive and exclusive manner in ELT. Therefore, he favors learners' cognitive endeavor, despite his awareness of the social dimensions of criticality. Such a position clearly represents a lack of understanding the difference between critical thinking and critical practices of teaching in English. That is, as many scholars refuted (e.g., Davidson, 1998; Gieve, 1998; Hawkins, 1998) Atkinson's view of teaching critical thinking solely based on the cognitive apprenticeships implies that learners should be pressed to think like people in Western countries, since the concept essentially belongs to the West. In addition, by denying the possibility of critical thinking in sociocultural contexts as Vygotsky (1986) and other scholars (e.g., Lave & Wenger, 1991; Zuengler & Miller, 2006) have presented, Atkinson seems to make an effort to turn the sociocultural tides backward. As a matter of fact, such a monologic view of critical thinking as cognitive domain is widespread in the mainstream ESL community, probably due to confusion over the difference between critical thinking and critical practices of teaching English (Canagarajah, 2006).

I never felt the denial of "criticality" in ELT more than in my own first-hand experience of publishing an article in the leading journal in Korea. I wrote a piece in 2002 titled "What is critical pedagogy?: The possibility of remapping English teaching in Korea." In this piece, I problematized the popular views on English in Korea by using a metaphor of "myths" and critiqued the limited practices of teaching English for jobs, using test-oriented curriculum and instruction; teaching only for practical and communicative English; relying on NSEs and on teaching Standard English blindly; sending students to study abroad with no clear educational goals and purposes; and implementing technological tools regardless of their instructional utilities. The results of the reviews done by the three anonymous readers were truly bipolar; I share the two reviewers' comments as below:

> This research tries to link critical pedagogy to English education in Korea. However, it is tedious and seems more appropriate for a general education journal than for an English education journal. It lacks relevance to English education and there are excessive explanations about general sociology and education. Therefore, I had a difficulty in understanding the paper overall and doubted whether I had to review this paper or not. Accordingly, it will be better to publish this paper in a general education journal. (*Original in Korean*)

This particular reviewer denies that English education is part of the field of education and is related to other disciplines such as philosophy, psychology, anthropology, sociology, cognitive science, and so on. Then, the reviewer gave the lowest point—E—for relevance, creativity, organization and development, and methodological appropriateness, except a C in the paper format. On the contrary, the other reviewer awarded all As (except for one C, for the paper format), and wrote:

This is an outstanding article on Critical Pedagogy, and the possibility of remapping English teaching in Korea. I cannot agree more with the research in that this is the time for English teaching professions in Korea to seriously discuss key issues of Critical Pedagogy and new ways to approach teaching/learning English. The research discusses in great depth English as medium for employment, supremacy of test-oriented curriculum and instruction, fallacy of practical English, phantom belief on native speakers, studying abroad as panacea, and technology as metanarrative in ELT. I too think that these are real important issues that we must talk about at this point. This article is truly worth reading, and I thank for the researcher to have said so eloquently what I had in mind. (*Original in English*)

In addition, the third reviewer said that the topic was new and innovative, and covered broad areas using relevant theories and research, especially linking critical pedagogy well with ELT by pointing out incorrect views about English due to the misunderstanding of the history of English teaching in Korea, and analyzing problems related to such views. Upon such sharp divisions in opinions over my paper, I appealed and wrote two letters to the chief editor, asking to reconsider the decision of "publishing after re-reviewing" or at least to change the particular reviewer who seemed to be ignorant about my line of work. What is surprising is that, despite my best effort to meet the irrational suggestions for revision, the same thing happened in the re-reviewing processes. One reviewer held my article until the last minute, and only with the chief editor's help, was the piece finally published. Though many researchers doing critical lines of work have had more excruciating experiences in mainstream educational contexts, my experiences of publishing this particular piece truly reflect the contentious nature of whose epistemologies or ontological perspectives count as important and are in power in ELT in Korea.

However, though my piece was probably one of the first pieces on critical theory and pedagogy published in the context of EFL in Korea, there are some scholars who are acutely aware of the importance of critical work in ELT. For example, Pennycook (1995) noted that the popular view of English as natural, neutral, and beneficial is the result of the historical construction and also of globalization and internationalization as well as of colonialism and neocolonialism. Such a one-sided view depoliticizes ELT in Korea or elsewhere as delivering limited sets of linguistic or cultural knowledge and skills to use in mostly consumer-oriented social worlds. In fact, considering ELT as an apolitical field is actually extremely political, in that it may conceal many discriminatory and hegemonic practices in teaching English. For example, while teaching English to NNSEs, culture becomes subservient to language and is introduced in bits and pieces, mostly those of dominant groups, without problematizing distorted practices of representing others through Othering (Bhabha, 1994; Kramsch, 1993). Another example is that, for a long time, one's native language was considered to be a stumbling block in learning English, as shown in the concept of L1 interference or noncognate language, which led to so many contrastive analyses of languages. Thus, NSEs have been held on the pedestal for NNSEs to imitate their pronunciation and behaviors, on the idea that they are standard bearers of the ideal target language. In such a context, some naïve and ignorant parents in Korea and in China are even said to have had doctors perform surgery on their children's tongue in the hopes that their children would be able to pronounce English sounds like NSEs (Markus, 2002; *The Korea Times*, 2004).

However, such hyperreal desire to imitate NSEs is no more than native-speakerism (Holliday, 2005), and perpetuates linguicism in which English is touted as a must, or as a key to master in order to succeed in the world (Phillipson, 1992; Pennycook, 1995).

As a matter of fact, critical theorists and scholars raise important questions over what constitutes and who produces knowledge in education and who benefits or is marginaliz-ing in teaching such knowledge in specific contexts (Giroux, 1988, 1992). These schol-ars question knowledge and practices produced in the context of rigid, lock-step theory-building and research and pedagogical practices which omit the issues of power, jus-tice, and many other important historical, sociopolitical, sociocultural, and economical fac-tors such as race, gender, class, sexuality, disabilities, religion, and other differences. Accordingly, from the mid-1990s, the field of ESL produced many scholarly works that were influenced by critical theory and literacy (e.g., Bae, 2004; Brown, 2001; Ellis, 2003; Gee, 1996; Kim, N., 2005; Lankshear & McLaren, 1993; Morgan, 1997; Norton & Toohey, 2004), linguistic imperialism and inequality in power in English teaching (Canagarajah, 1999; Tollefson, 1995), critical language awareness and critical discourse analysis (Fairclough, 1995), critical applied linguistics (Pennycook, 2001), and critical language testing (Shohamy, 2001; Spolsky, 1995). In fact, in one of the popular books on teaching, Brown (2001) acknowledges that language teaching is intricately linked with one's beliefs and that power relationships exist among teachers and students in the classroom. Therefore, he suggests, language teachers should be keen on embedding a political agenda in their teaching and on dealing with key sociocultural issues in a critical manner. However, such endorsements and statements should be taken with caution, given that there are many opponents, as well as those who embrace critical theory or pedagogy just because it is an "in" thing in ELT.

In a conference held in Korea, Widdowson (2002), who opposes critical views of lan-guage teaching and engaged in a heated debate on this issue with Pennycook, said that crit-ical theorists interpret things on their own and inculcate others accordingly. In addition, he explained that English is spread as a virtual, not actual, language that is adapted and nonconformative, depending on where it is used (Widdowson, 2003). His view is problem-atic given that it denies the forceful nature of language spread through governmental and institutional policies by a certain groups of people, and delineates particular communities with particular identities. Therefore, his own view rather reveals that he may not think that what he believes and presents is also partial and political and stems from his own under-standings of the world. In another conference, Ellis (2004) presented some reasonable but rather long and repetitive ideas about grammar teaching, but upon my question of why he included critical theory in his latest book on task-based learning and teaching (Ellis, 2003), he said that he did not remember including the topic. When I approached him and said that he indeed included critical theory after the presentation, he confided that if he did, he had probably done so in order to refute such a theory. However, based on my per-sonal conversation with him at the end of 2006, it seemed that he is very cognizant of the issue of power in language use, commenting that females are more skillful and adaptive in language use, maybe, due to the patriarchal structure of society. Accordingly, whether or not one refutes or denies critical theory, it will continue to have profound impacts on the way we think about language and language teaching.

In ELT in Korea, there has been some steady increase in CELT over the last several years. Kwon (2001) introduced different orientations of teaching English and presented the colonial and imperialistic influences on ELT in Asian regions. While Chang (1998) included the critical and dialectic paradigm in his classification of educational paradigms, Kim (2002) wrote about how culture in the context of language teaching can be taught in more meaningful and critical manners. Na and Kim (2003) observe that EFL teachers can utilize key concepts of critical literacy such as power, identity, critical awareness, and empowerment to help students deal with current changes, diverse identities in self and others, understand and interpret texts and worlds more critically, and problematize different power relationships in the social worlds. Pederson (2005) has also published critical pieces and emphasized the need of including key elements such as power, culture, identity, and agency in the context of teaching EFL in Korea. More emphatically, Kim (2004) calls for more critical work in ELT in Korea by stating that:

> With the critical perspectives, both teachers and students can understand the world's change by considering the diversity of English, recognize multiple identities which are formed in the process of using English, develop the ability of critically looking into the world and language, and be empowered to challenge the unequal relationship of power in the use of English. (p. 66; translated in English)

In conclusion, as I have documented and attested, a critical line of work is being actively practiced in ELT, and more is being done since there is now a sociocultural and postmodern turn in ELT everywhere (Canagarajah, 2006; Zuengler & Miller, 2006). For example, even after several years in the terrain of ELT in Korea, I had some encouraging comments about my latest piece on critical discourse analysis on discursive practices related to ELT in Korea (Sung, 2006). The reviewers said that my piece was not critical enough and should have included more broad spectrums related to the issues I chose.

I am deeply obliged to thank the faculty with whom I worked over the years, both those who agreed or disagreed to varying degrees on my pursuit of a critical approach to ELT; visiting colleagues who enriched the program so much; and my students, Korean and foreign, who shared many views and ideas with me in the hallway, in the classroom and office, and at restaurants or bars. They were truly motivated and came a long way to become the few and proud individuals who care about democracy, equality, and equity for all, and especially the marginalized, by being critical change agents wherever they work.

On a last note, I scrutinized the National Curriculum, which says that the ultimate goal of teaching Korean students is to develop their characters as democratic citizens who can engage in creative and critical thinking. Doesn't this mean that we all are violating the important goal of education in the name of teaching English to our students now? If so, it is high time, and also incumbent upon all teachers, that the disservice perpetrated against our students' right to learn valuable and critical knowledge in addition to language skills should be stopped once and for all.

References

Atkinson, D. (1997). A critical approach to critical thinking in TESOL. *TESOL Quarterly, 31*(1), 71–94.

Bae, G. (2004). Looking critically at the ESL classroom: Challenges and possibilities of critical pedagogy. *English Teaching, 59*(3), 333–356.

Bhabha, H. (1994). *The location of culture*. New York: Routledge.

Brown, H. D. (2001). *Teaching by principles: An interactive approach to language pedagogy*. White Plains, NY: Longman.

Canagarajah, A. S. (1999). *Resisting linguistic imperialism in English teaching*. Oxford, UK: Oxford University Press.

Canagarajah, A. S. (2006). TESOL at forty: What are the issues? *TESOL Quarterly, 40*(1). 9–34.

Chang, S. (1998). *Youngoerul oedukgae baewoogo garichilgotinga? [How to teach and learn English?]* Seoul: Shinasa.

Davidson, B. W. (1998). A case of critical thinking in the English language class. *TESOL Quarterly, 32*(1), 119–123.

Ellis, R. (2003). *Task-based language learning and teaching*. Oxford, UK: Oxford University Press.

Ellis, R. (2004, December). *Implicit and explicit knowledge and grammatical complexity*. The 2004 Applied Linguistics Association of Korea Conference, Seoul, Korea.

Fairclough, N. (1995). *Critical discourse analysis: The critical study of language*. London: Longman.

Freire, P. (1970). *Pedagogy of the oppressed*. New York: Seabury Press.

Gee, J. P. (1996). *Social linguistics and literacies: Ideology in discourses*. Bristol, PA: Taylor & Francis.

Gieve, S. (1998). A reader reacts. *TESOL Quarterly, 32*(1), 123–129.

Giroux, H. A. (1988). *Schooling and the struggle for public life: Critical pedagogy in the modern age*. Minneapolis, MN: University of Minnesota Press.

Giroux, H. A. (1992). *Border crossing*. New York: Routledge.

Han, H. (2005). Woori sidae Youngoe Damron: Gue weeseoneui gorideul [*Contemporary discursive practices on English: Circles of hypocrisy*]. Seoul: Tahaksa.

Hawkins, M.R. (1998). Apprenticing nonnative speakers to new discourse communities. *TESOL Quarterly, 32*(1), 129–132.

Holliday, A. (2005). *The struggle to teach English as an international language*. Oxford, UK: Oxford University Press.

Hong, J. (1993). A historical survey of English teaching. *English Teaching, 13*, 105–141.

Kachru, B. B., & Nelson, C. L. (1996). World Englishes. In S. L. Mckay & N. H. Hornberger (Eds.), *Sociolinguistics and language teaching* (pp. 71–102). New York: Cambridge University Press.

Kim, I. (1995). Development of theories of English language acquisition and learning in Korea. *English Teaching, 50*(2), 69–105.

Kim, J. (2004). A comparative analysis of research methodology and orientation in TEFL in Korea and around the world. *English Teaching, 59*(4), 45–70.

Kim, N. (2005). The role of ESL Social Studies class in ESL students' identity formation. *English Teaching, 60*(2), 307–331.

Kim, N. H. (2005). A study on the use of high-level foreign human resources in Korea. Seoul: Ministry of Education and Human Resources.

Kim, Y. (2002). A critical approach to culture education in EFL. *Foreign Languages Education*, 9(3), 243–264.

Kincheloe, J. L. (2004). *Critical pedagogy*. NY: Peter Lang.

Kincheloe, J. L. (2005). *Critical constructivism*. NY: Peter Lang.

Kohn, A., & Shannon, P. (Eds.). (2002). *Education, Inc.: Turning learning into a business*. Portsmouth, NH: Heinemann.

The Korea Times (2004). Korean Quest for Flawless English Drives Tongue Surgery for Toddlers. Retrieved Jan. 23, 2007, from the World Wide Web: http://times.hankooki.com/plaza/ap_news.php? cur_date=20040106&page=8

Kramsch, C. (1993). *Context and culture in language teaching*. New York: Oxford University Press.

Kwon, O. (2000a). Korea's English education policy changes in the 1990s: Innovations to gear the nation for the 21st century. *English Teaching*, 55, 47–91.

Kwon, O. (2000b, December). *English teaching in Korea: A retrospect and prospect at the turn of the century*. Paper presented at the 2000 Winter Conference of the Korea Association of Teachers of English, Busan, Korea.

Kwon, O. (2001, June). *Teaching English as a global language in the Asian context*. Paper presented at the 2001 Summer Conference of the Korea Association of Teachers of English, Seoul, Korea.

Lave, J., & Wenger, E. (1991) *Situated learning: Legitimate peripheral participation*. New York; Cambridge University Press.

Lankshear, C., & McLaren. (1993). *Critical literacy: Politics, praxis, and the postmodern*. Albany, NY; State University of New York Press.

Markus, F. (2002). Chinese find learning English a snap. *BBC News World Edition*. Retrieved Jan. 23, 2007, from http://news.bbc.co.uk/2/hi/asia-pacific/2161780.stm

Moon, Y. (1976). A historical review of the teaching of English in Korea. *Applied Linguistics*, 8(2), 203–222.

Morgan, W. (1997). *Critical literacy in the classroom: The art of the possible*. New York: Routledge.

Na, Y., & Kim, S. (2003). Critical literacy in the EFL classroom. *English Teaching*, 58(3), 143–163.

Norton, B., & Toohey, K. (Eds.) (2004). *Critical pedagogies and language learning*. New York: Cambridge University Press.

Park. J. (2001). *Woorieui youngoekyosiloe youngoenun itneunga? [Is there English in our English classroom?]*. Seoul: Hankook Munwha Sa.

Pederson, R. (2005). Applied Linguistics and Culture: Social Contexts of Identity and Agency. *English Teaching*, 60(1), 125–147.

Pennycook, A. (1995). English in the world/The world in English. In J. W. Tollefson (Ed.), *Power and inequality in language education* (pp. 34–58). New York: Cambridge University Press.

Pennycook, A. (1998). *English and the discourses of colonialism*. New York: Routledge.

Pennycook, A. (2001). *Critical applied linguistics: A critical introduction*. Mahwah, NJ: Lawrence Erlbaum Associates.

Phillipson, R. (1992). *Linguistic imperialism*. Oxford, UK: Oxford University Press.

Shohamy, E. (2001). *The power of tests*. New York: Longman.

Simon, R. (1992). Empowerment as a pedagogy of possibility. In P. Shannon (Ed.) *Becoming political* (pp. 139–151). Portsmouth, NH: Heinemann.

Spolsky, B. (1995). *Measured words*. New York: Longman.

Sung, K. W. (2001). Changing the terrain of English teaching: An inquiry approach using multimedia. *Multimedia-Assisted Language Learning, 4*(1), 57–85.

Sung, K. W. (2002). Critical theory and pedagogy: Remapping English teaching in Korea. *English Teaching, 57*(2), 65–89.

Sung, K. W. (2004). Still disenfranchised: Claiming the ownership of EFL. The 2nd Asia TEFL International Conference. Asia TEFL. 2004. Nov. 5–7. Olympic ParkTel, Seoul, Korea.

Sung, K. W. (2006). A critical analysis of current discursive practices in ELT in Korea. *Foreign Languages Education, 13*(3), 80–104.

Tollefson, J. W. (Ed.). (1995). *Power and inequality in language education* (pp. 34–58). New York: Cambridge University Press.

Vygotsky, L. S. (1986). *Thought and language*. Cambridge, MA: The MIT Press.

Whittle. C. (2003). Creating new centers: A survey on the necessity of developing MA-TESOL programs for EFL settings. Unpublished M.A. paper. Woosong University. Daejeon, Korea.

Widdowson, H. (2002). EFL: Defining the subject. The 2002 Applied Linguistics Association of Korea Conference. Dec. 7. Korea University. Seoul, Korea.

Widdowson, H. G. (2003). *Defining issues in English language teaching*. Oxford, UK: Oxford University Press.

Zuengler, J., & Miller, E. R. (2006). Cognitive and sociocultural perspectives: Two parallel SLA worlds? *TESOL Quarterly, 40*(1), 36–58.

CHAPTER 9

Critical Pedagogy and Popular Culture in an Urban Secondary English Classroom

JEFF DUNCAN-ANDRADE & ERNEST MORRELL

Introduction

Critical pedagogy is a hotly discussed and highly debated term in the academy. Its proponents draw upon important scholars (Freire, 1970; McLaren, 1994; Giroux, 2001; hooks, 1994; Darder, 1991; Kincheloe, 2004; Shor, 1992) to argue for an approach to education that is rooted in the experiences of marginalized peoples; that is centered in a critique of structural, economic, and racial oppression; that is focused on dialogue instead of a one-way transmission of knowledge; and that is structured to empower individuals and collectives as agents of social change. Increasingly, critical pedagogy has been discussed as a potential component of urban school reform. Again, educators and researchers look to critical pedagogy as they consider ways to motivate students, to develop literacies and numeracies of power, and to employ students and their communities in the struggle for educational justice. We certainly applaud these goals, but we also feel as though the field, at present, insufficiently explores the applications of critical pedagogy to urban education.

For the past dozen years we have been dedicated to the enterprise of designing and investigating classroom interventions that are built upon the core principles of critical pedagogy. In our collective efforts we have worked across multiple settings that range from English classrooms to basketball teams to summer research programs. Our goal in this research is to develop a grounded theory of practice (Strauss and Corbin, 1998); that is, a theory that begins with the core principles of critical pedagogy but uses empirical data from theoretically informed practice to develop a more nuanced and particular theory of critical pedagogy as it applies to urban education. In the following chapter we describe the applications of critical pedagogy to a secondary English class in a Northern California urban center where we co-taught for three years. We begin with the underlying principles that simultaneously honored the spirit of the discipline of secondary English, our commitment to academic excellence, and our belief in the practice of education for individual and collective freedom for all peoples.

Underlying Principles

Though we did not always agree with traditional definitions and measures of academic literacy, we remained committed to facilitating academic skills and academic achievement in our classrooms. We understood the promotion of academic literacy development and academic achievement to be part of our mandate, from the profession, from the students, and from their families. Without agreeing on much else, we could agree with our colleagues in the English department at North High, our on-site administrators, and state administrators that students needed to achieve academically in our schools. Regardless of our philosophical foundation, we understood that our students existed in a world where they would be expected to take and perform well on standardized tests that served as gatekeepers to post-secondary education and, by consequence, professional membership.

We also understood that our students would need to understand, interpret, and produce in the Language of Wider Communication (LWC) (Smitherman, 2001), or what others might refer to as Standard English; they needed to develop these linguistic competencies and literacy skills for academic advancement and professional employment but also for civic participation. If students were going to acquire capacities required of critical citizens, they needed strong literacy skills, which would include the ability to read and write in the LWC. Though critical literacy still existed as a goal of our pedagogy, we understood that critical literacy also demands a knowledge of and facility with the language of power. It is impossible to critique or refute texts that one does not understand; comprehension is an important prerequisite to critique. Through our reading of critical theory and our work with urban adolescents we came to understand the importance of studying dominant texts to the development and maintenance of a revolutionary consciousness for both teachers and the students in their classrooms (Freire, 1997).

As English teachers and former English students at the undergraduate and postgraduate levels, we also knew that our students would be expected to demonstrate knowledge of canonical literature in order to pass Advanced Placement exams or to succeed in college-level coursework in the discipline. Again, these literacies of power, though sometimes problematic, were important for our students and not unimportant for the development of critical consciousness. With respect to canonical literature, Nobel Laureate author and activist Toni Morrison reminds us that national literatures reflect what is on the national mind. Studying canonical texts is an important strategy for understanding the values and ideologies of dominant groups at various points in history. For example, we would often tell our students that literary texts such as *Scarlet Letter* and *Huckleberry Finn* offered more insights to the American psyche than most United States History texts. When engaging these texts, however, it became important to include critical literary theories and multicultural readings of canonical texts that empowered students as readers and did not defer to the authority of the texts.

Towards these ends, we made a concerned effort to incorporate canonical pieces from British and classical literature (the 12th-grade mandate in our district) with postcolonial literature and popular cultural texts. Our senior syllabus has included *Beowulf, Canterbury Tales, Othello, Pygmalion,* and *Heart of Darkness* in addition to popular films and hip-hip music, which we will mention later in this chapter. We also developed vocabulary units and units that prepared students for the SAT and ACT exams as well as the Advanced Placement examinations offered each Spring semester. Further, we placed a premium on academic writing, focusing on the genres of the expository essay and the research report, as well as academic speaking (or persuasive rhetoric) in the forms of presentation and debate. Though we did not use the language of rhetoric, we wanted students to be able to present themselves powerfully and persuasively across multiple written genres in addition to formal and informal oral presentations.

In no way, shape, or form did our focus on academic literacy compromise our commitment to critical pedagogy and to literacy education for individual freedom and social change. In fact, we felt that it was only within a pedagogy firmly committed to freedom and social change that we were able to motivate students to develop sophisticated academic literacies. On this point we were in accord with the Cuban ministers of education who centered all academic content within a framework of praxis-oriented pedagogy to increase students' sense of commitment to upholding the values of the Cuban revolution while simultaneously making connections with real local and global demands for knowledge accumulation and production (Kozol, 1978. Additionally, we were able to honor the existential experiences of our students and work toward the development of academic literacies by complementing the canonical literature with popular cultural texts from music, film, mass media, and sports. More importantly, though, we were able to situate all texts and curricula within a critical pedagogy that was explicitly aware of issues of power, oppression, and transformation; and that honored the nonschool cultural practices of the students and included the students in authentic dialogue about inequity and advocacy for justice.

One of the core foundational philosophical principles to classroom pedagogy and practice included a belief that multiculturalism was more related to pedagogy than curriculum. Although we were firm believers of foregrounding popular cultural texts in our curricula, we did not shy away from the "classics." The curriculum that we taught to a diverse population at North High included canonical texts such as *Beowulf, Canterbury Tales, Othello, Macbeth, Hamlet, The Odyssey,* Romantic poetry, and Joseph Conrad's *Heart of*

Darkness. We were able to apply multicultural readings to these texts, having the students pay close attention to the treatment of those who were distinguished as cultural "Others" such as the yeoman in *Canterbury Tales* or the natives in *Heart of Darkness.* We firmly believe that literacy educators can encourage a critical multicultural reading of any text (Nieto, 1992), even one several thousand years old like *The Odyssey.*

By the same token, we were wary of those educators and literary theorists who equated multiculturalism with simply offering texts written by or featuring people of color as protagonists. In our experiences as students and educators, we witnessed practices around these so-called "multicultural" texts that were equally, if not more disempowering of students of color than more traditional and less diverse texts. An oppressive rendering of a culturally diverse text is still oppressive.

This is not to suggest that the sole purpose of interacting with literary texts was to pick them apart or to tear them down. We believed that, to the extent that students were exposed to literature of other times and places, they would begin to make connections to their own everyday experiences while gaining an understanding of similarities across time and cultures. This certainly happened in our "Poet in Society" unit where students were able to make connections between classic poets such as Shakespeare and John Donne and contemporary hip hop artists such as the Refugee Camp. These connections also occurred during conversations of heroism and sexism in *The Odyssey* or of violence in *Beowulf.* Nothing promotes border crossing or tolerance more than helping students to arrive at an implicit understanding of what they share in common with those they have been taught to perceive as different. Noted anthropologist Clifford Geertz claims that the more we study the cultural practices of others, the more these practices seem logical to us (Geertz, 2000, p.16) and the more they help us to understand our own practices as equally unique and equally meaningful, one practice among many meaningful practices. Indeed, such cross-cultural literary study may allow us to see ourselves in others, even as we see these others as unique and different in important and extraordinary ways.

We would label these practices in our secondary English classrooms as critical pedagogy because they promoted a sense of empowerment over readings of traditional texts; creating classroom learning spaces where a 16-year-old student can see herself as having something to say to an author like Shakespeare is itself an empowering act that not only has implications for future readings of Shakespeare but future engagements with any texts that have the aura of immutability or ultimate authority. Hegemonic texts like local, state, and national legislation, corporate bylaws, labor-management agreements, professional contracts, mortgage offers, and school report cards to name a few, are those "sacred" texts that emerge in the everyday lives of citizens and that serve to limit, constrain, or control actions or thought. These are the very texts that need to be critiqued, contextualized, and ultimately rewritten by critically empowered and critically literate citizens, which is what we want our students to become and how we want them to act. These practices are also instantiations of critical pedagogy in that they encourage readings that are themselves critical of traditional approaches to multicultural readings, in that students are asked to find commonalities across multiple cultural contexts instead of solely highlighting differences that can be primarily ascribed to ethnic affiliation. Critically literate students should feel empowered to enjoy texts that more politically correct environments would pressure them to disdain. Our purposes as educators are not to replace one dominant ideology with another. Rather, we agree with Italian Marxist social theorist Antonio Gramsci's (1971) assertion that the ultimate goal of a proletariat education is to help make the students more critical consumers of all information that they encounter in their daily lives and to also give them the skills to become more capable producers of counterinformation; the goal is not to make them slaves to a different (and more politically correct) ideology.

We also endeavored as educators to question and expand the canon of what counted as literature; an important component of a critical pedagogy of urban secondary English necessarily entails questioning what actually constitutes a text worthy of study. While we respected and honored some of the current literary canon and encouraged our students to gain a mastery and appreciation of that literary canon, we also recognized that the canon was limiting in ways that were problematic and ultimately disempowering to our students. Particularly, the existing literary canon was problematic in its inclusions, but even more so in its exclusions. Our students were being given implicit and explicit messages about what texts were aesthetic or intellectual (coded definitions of the popular use of the term "literary") in ways that excluded, even condemned, the traditional and new media texts that they interacted with on a daily basis. Nowhere was this more evident than in the treatment of "popular culture" in secondary academic settings. Cultural theorists (Adorno & Horkheimer, 1999; Docker, 1994; Storey, 1998; Strinati, 2000) have pointed toward the hierarchy that has been articulated between elite culture and popular culture; where the former holds society's most idealized values and the latter is held as base, common, and unsophisticated. Clearly, one of the core purposes of industrial schooling (and literacy education in particular) has been to expose children to the "best" the culture has to offer to elevate them from their often vulgar and "un-American" backgrounds (Tyack, 1974). It's easy to understand why little popular culture has been sanctioned in traditional primary and secondary educational spheres. The irony here is that popular culture has always found a central place in the most elite of postsecondary educational institutions; and popular culture has consistently been a site of study by the most elite of society's philosophers and cultural theorists in the twentieth (and now twenty-first) centuries.

We sought to counter these traditions in our curriculum development and our pedagogies; and we sought to situate our work conceptually and empirically. To do so we chose a different tack, however; one more in line with the work of Russian psychologist Lev Vygotsky (1978), who drew from his cultural historical research and his experiments on language development, cultural transmission, and the relations between mothers and children to advocate for instruction that draws upon the everyday experiences or the known worlds of children. We do not agree with all aspects of Vygotskian cultural psychology; for instance we do not envision the hierarchical relationship between everyday activities and higher-order thinking skills as Vygotsky did, but we recognized the pedagogical potential of tapping into young people's everyday experiences as participants in popular culture to scaffold academic literacies. At the same time, we also draw from Freire and Macedo's (1987) dialectical relationship between reading the world and reading the word, where readings of the word informed readings of the world in a dialectic cycle. We wanted to make transitions to academic content, but we also felt it important to inform students' participation in their own worlds as a key component of the pedagogical enterprise within schools.

As teacher-researchers, we devoted significant time and resources to understanding the nature of youth involvement in popular culture and the extent to which systematic involvement with popular culture in academic settings could facilitate the development of academic skills and critical faculties. It is important to note that our definition of popular culture differed greatly from "popular" conceptions of the term. We drew upon the work of sociologists and cultural theorists who envisioned popular culture as a set of cultural practices that were both influenced by and influencing everyday culture and the culture industries that market and co-opt this culture. For instance, Frankfurt School theorists Max Horkheimer and Theodor Adorno believed that elite interests used the culture industries (film, radio, etc.) to promote dominant values. In a similar vein, Gramsci viewed emergent media fields as instruments of hegemony (Gramsci, 1971), and Louis Althusser viewed the media as an ideological state apparatus whereby the state could inculcate its citizens with ideologies that promote the reproduction of state interests. There have also been cultural theorists, notably from the Birmingham Centre for Contemporary Cultural Studies, who have identified mass culture as a site of working-class struggle and resistance. Most contemporary theorists acknowledge popular culture as both a site of resistance and dominant hegemony or even as a site of conflict between these forces (Storey, 1998).

As a result of this work, we developed classroom units that coupled the study of film, newspapers, magazines, and music with the study of traditional novels, poems, and plays. We also created opportunities for students to study their own everyday culture, whether as students attending urban schools or as citizens of a metropolitan community.

Finally, we were very much influenced by Paulo Freire's (1970) critiques of the banking metaphor for education, where teachers treat students as passive, empty receptacles and schooling becomes a process whereby knowledgeable experts "deposit" bits of information into the impoverished minds of students. Instead, Freire advocated a pedagogical practice centered upon dialogue, inquiry, and the real exchange of ideas between teachers and students who he felt had a great deal to offer one another. We took this idea of a dialogic or problem-posing pedagogy to heart when designing activities within our various units.

The final assignments for these units usually consisted of some sort of performance or presentation that allowed students to take ownership over the knowledge production process. There was also some form of interrogation built into these presentations that usually came from the remainder of the students who were not presenting. One common format was to divide a major work into sections or themes and divide the class into groups of five or six. Usually we would give the groups a week to work together on their particular section or theme. The groups would need to perform research, assign roles and responsibilities, prepare a presentation, rehearse that presentation, and anticipate possible questions and responses from the audience. As individual nonpresenting class members, responsibilities entailed preparing at least three questions of the presenting group that they could ask during the Q&A sessions. This would build upon work early in the year where we helped students understand the difference between critical questions and questions of fact.

Each group would then receive one class period in which to present. The hour-long periods were divided equally between group presentation and question and answer sessions. During the presentation, other class members were required to take copious notes, which would be handed in for grade at the end of the unit. Needless to say, there was a huge incentive for the groups to prepare themselves well. At the culmination of these activities, students would hand in outlines of their group's presentation along with a brief description of their role in the actual preparation and presentation. They would also hand in their notes and questions for the other groups. Final grades would be divided into thirds between preparation, presentation, and participation in other groups' presentations. We felt that this structure allowed us to evaluate the students' content knowledge while also encouraging dialogue and inquiry that are essential to any critical pedagogy.

We began with the fundamental knowledge of the disconnect among the skills and sensibilities we encouraged and our grading rubrics. Initially, we would call for active participation in discussions, but we would turn around and only grade final written products. This was a disservice to the students who worked diligently to contribute to the intellectual development of their peers and the class as a whole. Writing was not forgotten; only we sought to develop a grading system that honored skills no longer emphasized in many classrooms such as working well with classmates, presenting one's ideas orally, and engaging in respectful, yet critical conversations with teachers and classmates.

Pedagogical Practices

Savage inequalities in urban schools

Our first unit of the year strayed a bit from the traditional content of a high school English class. We began with a unit that brought together Jonathan Kozol's (1991) *Savage Inequalities* and the 1987 film *Stand and Deliver* in order to study the material conditions and pathways to academic achievement in urban schools. Briefly, *Savage Inequalities* is a book that offers a strong example of exposé journalism and the sociology of education research. Kozol visits several metropolitan areas throughout the country to document the drastic differences in spending, in curricular offerings, and in attitudes towards students in America's wealthiest and poorest schools. Kozol's thoroughly researched and rhetorically powerful tract shows a clear correlation between parental income, race, and quality of educational resources. He also shows very clearly that not only are the schools of the urban poor unequal, but they are in many cases inadequate and physically and psychologically unhealthy places for anyone's children to attend.

Stand and Deliver, by contrast, is a story of triumph in the face of adversity. It relates an account of Jaime Escalante, a computer engineer who becomes a substitute math teacher at an impoverished school in East Los Angeles. Within a few years' time, Escalante is able to help students who were failing Algebra to pass the Advanced Placement examination in Calculus.

By pairing the book with the film, we wanted our students to have a sense that young people around the country experience the harsh realities of urban schools, just as they do, but that there remain possibilities to transform and transcend those realities. After all, we were reading Kozol's *Savage Inequalities* in a school that was similar in every respect to the ones depicted in the text. Our classroom had no windows, often no heat in the winter, the carpet was held together in places by duct tape, and the moveable chalk board possessed only two of its original four wheels and a crack ran the full length of the board. In order to move the chalkboard, one needed to lift the side without its wheels and push it sideways. Also the classroom had no computers and the library had only one computer, which students could sign up for in 10-minute intervals. The Internet connection in the library was so slow, that it required more than 10 minutes to dial into America Online. We saw many a student kicked off that machine with their first page only partially loaded.

At the same time, however, we saw our goals as consistent with Jaime Escalante's (up to a point). We wanted our students to envision themselves as having academic potential, and we wanted to create a curriculum that enabled our students to compete on equal academic footing with their counterparts who were attending the nation's elite schools. Indeed, many of these students did go on to take the Advanced Placement examination in English, and a large percentage of them were able to matriculate to four-year universities where they were able to compete with peers who had attended better-funded, more highly regarded secondary institutions.

Our goals differed, though, to the extent that we foregrounded social critique and social praxis in our curriculum and pedagogy. We would not have been content, for instance, had our students achieved academically absent a language to make sense of the material conditions that separated their school from one of the wealthiest high schools in the nation, which was less than four miles away. While we wanted students to have a sense of their own agency to resist, to subvert, and to transcend, we also understood that agency is enacted within and against structural contexts. In this case, it would be dishonest to promote a pull-yourself-up-by-your-bootstrap approach within a structural context that facilitated academic underachievement. At the same time, it would be unconscionable to allow students an excuse to fail. Rather, we sought to encourage a critical dialogue whereby our students would understand that they possessed the individual and collective ability to achieve even within a structure that can only be labeled as oppressive. At the same time, we hoped that the dialogue would be generative in producing a transformational praxis. We hope that the life of our classroom, the lives of our students, our lives, and the words in this chapter serve as evidence of that praxis.

Toward these ends we created a space for discussion and action related to the conditions of urban schools. Naturally, a great deal of conversation pertained to comparisons between the conditions of schools in *Savage Inequalities* and *Stand and Deliver*. Students were critical of teachers and administrators who either contributed to inequitable conditions or stood idly by without trying to change them. We knew that this was a slippery slope because students often ended up indicting teachers and administrators that had significant power over them inside our school. We did our best to focus conversations on structural issues instead of individuals, but, honestly, several colleagues so closely resembled the antagonists from the book and film that not making comparisons required conscious effort. In those cases, we worked closely with students to steer them away from those teachers and administrators where possible, and/or to give them coping and support strategies until we could move them away from that person.

At the conclusion of the unit we wanted an assignment that moved from talk to action, so we placed student groups in the position of policy makers and had them consider the policy implications of the unit from local contexts to federal initiatives. Students researched school spending policies and interviewed administrators and local politicians. It just so happened that a wealthy nearby school was in the process of constructing a five million dollar stadium, while our students did not have books that they could take home with them in their math and science courses. Interestingly, students chose to interview peers and administrators in both the wealthy school and their own. Students also drew upon photographs, video footage, and other artifacts to exemplify the conditions of the various schools.

Students began using these critical media literacies for political advantage in fighting for social and educational justice. For example, when it looked as though the school was planning to serve lunch even though over an inch of sewage from a nearby backup covered the kitchen and cafeteria floor, the students called local media outlets to convene a press conference in the sewage-filled halls of the school. Both lunch and school were subsequently cancelled for the day.

Throughout the year a number of students became involved in city-wide politics, particularly urging council members to support an initiative to put "children first." Once the initiative was passed, two students continued to serve on the advisory board of the city council. Students, however, continued to experience the savage inequalities of North High for the rest of their tenure at the school. The wealthy school located up the hill finished their five million dollar stadium and, to this day, continues to score in the 99th percentile on state standardized tests. What did change noticeably, however, was the relationship between our students and the school. Everyone on campus, from the principal to the teachers, was on notice that if something was not right, the students would get to the bottom of it. This did not always make life enjoyable for us, their teachers, or for the students themselves. The stinging backlash became a frequent sensation. However, there is ample evidence and testimony to support the charge that the students felt empowered to challenge conditions that were seemingly innate and immutable.

Teaching hip hop music and culture

Other teachers and members of the larger society perceived many of the students in our classes as functionally illiterate and lacking in intellect. These detractors rely on traditional school-based measures (past school performance, test scores) to support their claims and their resultant behavior towards (more like against) these youth. These assessments, how-ever, ran counter to our observations of our students' sophisticated literacy practices that accompanied their participation in hip hop culture. The same students portrayed as unin-terested in literacy would come into our classrooms capable of reciting from memory the lyrics of entire rap albums. They voraciously read popular hip hop magazines, transcribed song lyrics, and several carried their own rap composition books. Even those students that were not so deeply involved with hip hop culture regularly listened to popular radio sta-tions whose programming was predominantly hip hop and accessed magazines and CDs.

To tap into this literacy-rich youth cultural activity, we developed a seven-week poetry unit that paired hip hop texts with canonical works of poetry. The goal of the unit was to scaffold students' heavy investments in hip hop into deeper understandings of school-based forms of poetry. We aimed to help students see the timelessness of the literary themes pres-ent in both canonical texts that they were mostly unfamiliar with and some of the music they listened to on a daily basis. We made explicit the fact that the literacy skills and knowl-edge that they exhibited in their interactions with hip hop texts were not far removed from the skills required to succeed in the analysis of poetry.

After pairing eight traditional poetry texts with eight rap songs, we divided our classes into groups of 4–5 students. Each group was responsible for preparing a class lesson on their pair of works. They were given relative autonomy for the form of their presentation, but each presentation was to have the following three elements:

i.   Analysis of the literary themes of each individual work (we gave students a list of common themes, but encouraged them to develop others as they saw them emerge in the work);

ii. Comparative analysis of the two works (how are the works similar, how are they different, how do the respective authors use similar or different devices to deliver their message, etc.);

iii. Guiding questions for class discussion (we had modeled complex, open-ended questions throughout the year, and encouraged students to design similar questions).

In addition to preparing their group presentation, each student was also expected to prepare an analysis of the other seven poem/song pairings so that they could participate in class discussions. We had worked hard all year on developing a classroom culture where stu-dent participation in dialogues about literary themes was normalized. This, along with the use of hip hop texts that drew students' attention, made the prospect of out-of-class prepa-ration more likely as the class came to enjoy challenging and broadening the literary analysis of their peers.

For the first two weeks of the unit, we spent class time going over poetic forms (son-net, haiku, free form, prose), poetic devices (rhythm, rhyme, meter, imagery, word choice, theme). We used examples from the eight pairings to teach these concepts, discussing with students their presence in music and traditional poetry. Students were also encouraged to bring examples from their favorite songs or poems that displayed the ideas we were learning. During this time, students also began developing their poetry portfolios, writing poems that employed the concepts and forms that were discussed.

During the second two weeks of the unit, students continued developing their own poems while they also worked in class with their groups and the teacher, preparing the analysis and presentation of their assigned pair. Class time was split between sharing and receiving feedback from peers on their poems and on preparing for their upcoming class presentations.

During the fifth and sixth weeks of the unit, each group was assigned one day to present their analysis and to lead the class in discussion about their pair. Presentations ranged from traditional stand-and-present approaches to more creative approaches where students brought in music videos, film clips, or utilized interactive activities.

The remaining week and a half was used for poetry readings. Each student was required to choose at least one poem that they would read in front of the class. These were often some of the most personally revealing and moving moments in the class. Putting the unit toward the end of the school year afforded many students the comfort level to risk sharing poems that revealed some of their most personal life experiences.

Race and justice in society unit

We started each spring semester with a unit on race and justice. We waited until the second semester for several reasons. Though the topic of race certainly cropped into earlier discussions, we wanted to ensure the development of a critical classroom culture and make certain that the students had prior experience with our brand of film study, which is described a bit later in more detail. The spring semester was also the time our department decided was ideal to teach Richard Wright's *Native Son*. The unit opened with a collective viewing of *A Time to Kill* and ended with a classroom court trial to decide the fate of Bigger Thomas. It is important to state up front that we watched film, not merely as entertainment, but as an intellectual activity. In the classroom, we watched with the lights on and notebooks out for about half of the period, and would spend the next half reviewing the segment, discussing interpretations and reactions to the text dealing with both the technical and thematic aspects of the film.

There is one particular incident we would like to recount that occurred during a viewing of a segment of *A Time to Kill* in which there are racial riots surrounding the trial of Carl Lee. Carl Lee Hailey is a Black man who is on trial for killing the two White men who raped his daughter and left her for dead and, as the trial approaches in the film, racial tensions escalate. The NAACP comes from up North to lobby on the side of Carl Lee, and the KKK comes from the Deep South to lobby on the side of the two White men that were killed.

As the racial tensions escalate in the movie, the class becomes more emotionally charged and begins to identify with the African Americans in the film and actually root for them. Students begin to chant with the protesters and yell disapproval at the screen. Obviously, this is more than a dispassionate viewing of a class assignment or an opportunity to sit back and be entertained. The class, in this example, is beginning to relate the film to their everyday lives as citizens in a racially charged society. They are also using this understanding to facilitate textual analysis as well as a critical engagement with the text. This is a film; the story is fictional and the characters are fictional, but the emotion surrounding the issues of racism and justice, where the students are upset with characters and clapping and cheering and pumping fists, shows that the students are politicizing this film and relating it to similar issues in their own lives. This relevance, we argue, leads to a deeper understanding that, in turn, facilitates a more personal and deeper analysis of the themes of race and justice found in the text.

Freeing Carl Lee, for these students, is victory for the African Americans, who are the oppressed group in the film. As members of oppressed groups within society, this perspective informs the students' identification with and analysis of the text. Several of the students have claimed that the torching of the Klan wizard is justice, and any exoneration of Carl Lee's actions is a victory for the oppressed—and the students clearly in this case identify themselves with this oppressed group. Their willingness to identify with this text enables them to bridge their worlds with the film text and to embrace the text at a critical level. Rather than looking at Carl Lee and the others as fictional characters, they are looking at what they represent to their own lives in creating that universal plane of knowledge. As they begin to relate the characters to their own everyday lives, they juxtapose the text against their everyday lives and bring their everyday life experiences into their critical interpretation of this text.

During the post-film discussion, Morrell asks whether the African American male who killed the Klan wizard was guilty of murder. The point gets made that the guilt of Blacks and Whites in the scene is not equivalent, since the Whites have power, privilege, and a stake in the status quo, while the Blacks in this scenario are largely reactionary. Morrell grants that Stump Sisson, the wizard, was wrong but suggests that he did not deserve to die; however, the boy who killed him was not necessarily guilty of first-degree murder. This type of interaction around the film and text helped to complicate simplistic notions of right and wrong and set the stage for future discussions and debates.

As we began to discuss our impending reenactment of the Bigger Thomas court trial, the connection was made between Clanton, Mississippi and the city where the school is located. One student recalls a recent incident between African Americans and Latinos at the school where the police were called to intervene. Another tells a story about how two Asian American friends of hers were victims of attacks by African Americans. A third asks for more details about the incident as the class listens attentively. Although we cannot agree on whether there can be a single concept of justice for all, the entire class agrees that what happened to the Asian American students was wrong.

Throughout the many times that we taught this unit, there were incidents similar to the one just described. Students had personal and meaningful transactions with the film that facilitated a healthy dialogic space and the completion of superior academic work. One class went so far as to create a newsletter that challenged the school's approach to issues of culture and power. These students interviewed their peers, teachers, and administrators, and candidates for the office of mayor. They also collected video footage of the campus climate that they offered to local news agencies. Most importantly, the students were able to learn about themselves and each other, and cross fairly entrenched racial and cultural lines to come together as a class committed to cultural acceptance and affirmation.

Critical English teachers can use films like *A Time to Kill* to promote reader-response or the use of critical literary theories (i.e., critical race, feminist, Marxist, postcolonial, psychoanalytic) in secondary English classrooms. Students can use film as a springboard to reflect upon their experiences as involuntary participants in a racialized society. Through the sharing of these personal transactions, students can acquire a sensitivity to and understanding of cultures different from their own. They can also use cultural studies to make sense of how society creates categories of self and other around a host of identifiers such as race, class, gender, sexuality, home language, and religion. Students can discuss how those classified as "Other" are portrayed and treated in popular media and in everyday life.

It is important to highlight that watching film together in a classroom is a social activity that is different from reading a text privately and then discussing it publicly. If film watching is done appropriately, this becomes a public viewing in a unique social space. The class members, as a community of practice, participate together in joint activity of making sense of this text. These young people are also able to come together as members of a common culture, a youth popular culture that frequently transcends race and class. The film text is a great equalizer, in that more students have a schema for the critical analysis of film and more experience with this literacy practice in their everyday lives.

It is also important to recognize the significance and power of the visual imagery associated with the film medium to engender critical dialogue about race. Sometimes it is more difficult for students to engage older texts such as *Huckleberry Finn* because they are from bygone eras that students can easily dismiss. More contemporary films that deal with the experiences of people of color, women, or people with disabilities have a greater chance of being perceived as relevant. These popular texts, however, can be used to create bridges with older, canonical texts, much as we did with *A Time to Kill* and *Native Son*.

By no means are we advocating that educators subordinate the popular to the canonical. Rather, we are encouraging the creation of meaningful links between the worlds of the students and the worlds of canonical texts. Many sociocultural theorists influenced by the work of Vygotsky have promoted authentic learning environments that draw upon the strengths that students bring from home and community and allow students to learn through legitimate peripheral participation in communities of practice. Moll (2000), for example, argues that educators become ethnographers who seek to understand and affirm the community's funds of knowledge when designing curricula. We agree with Moll and contend that any ethnographic investigations of the lives of young people would reveal that film plays a central role in their emergent understandings of themselves and their world.

Though we are absolutely convinced of the transformational possibilities associated with this innovative approach to English education, we want to address issues of appropriateness and communication. Because of the connotations of the medium and also because of its evocative nature, controversies and challenges are certain to arise. It is one thing to read about oppression or violence in a book; it is another experience entirely to watch these acts manifested through a film or video text. Teachers need to be prepared for the emotions that will be evoked by the visual text. They also need to be ready to communicate with other teachers, with administrators, with parents, and students about the importance of utilizing this medium to teach about issues related to diversity. Educators, however, should not shy away from these encounters, nor should they be apologetic about the use of film in their classrooms. The imperative of our movement demands that we push the envelope to discover novel approaches that allow us to accomplish our multiple goals of developing students who have the skills to function academically and professionally in a complex world, and also the sensitivities needed to function as critical citizens in a multicultural democracy.

Serious Voices for Urban Youth

It was during the final presentations of the Race and Justice Film Unit that one of the students stopped the discussion of the film to ask her classmates, "Do we have justice here at North High?" The response was swift and certain. The students knew that they did not, in fact, receive justice at their high school. Students shared narratives of receiving an inferior education, of being treated as prisoners and second-class citizens. They talked about being harassed by campus security, about being corralled into holding rooms when they were a few minutes late to class. One student commented on the greased fences to prevent students from climbing them doing school hours; the locked gates that went against the fire codes. "If there's a fire in here we're all gonna die, there's no way we can get out," a student correctly remarked.

Other comments addressed the lack of textbooks in Chemistry courses. So few, in fact, that students could not take the texts home. They would have to devote class time to writing down the problems they needed for homework. If, once at home, they required some sort of explanation, they were just out of luck. These comments continue in fervor and intensity, until Jasmine asks her classmates what they plan to do about this injustice. It is April of their senior year, six short weeks until their graduation. For these students, it is now or never; their final chance to leave a legacy to the students who will follow them.

What emerges from this discourse is a magazine project to which the students devoted their final six weeks as students of North High. The project ultimately became known as Serious Voices for Urban Youth, and included articles, poems, and drawings. The students selected themes and issues that they wanted to cover and selected peers to take on assignments. Some of these assignments included interviews with prospective mayoral candidates about the state of the high school, personal narratives about experiences in schools, portraits of inspiring teachers, letters of guidance and inspiration to successive classes at the school, and artwork depicting the conditions of the school.

Implications

We could have taught any of these units using more traditional methods and curriculum. This would, however, run counter to our philosophy that the most important ingredient of an effective classroom is engaging pedagogy and curriculum. Our sense about the development of this approach to teaching is that it must value the cultural sensibilities and interests of students. While this is not a particularly new idea, we would argue that the relative failure of this multicultural (Banks, 1994) or culturally relevant (Ladson-Billings, 1994) approach to education has been in the misapplication of these principles.

In short, the practice of multicultural education has employed an all-too-narrow definition of culture. The term "culture" in school curriculum has largely been a proxy for "race/ethnicity," and while this has resulted in some attention to a more ethnically and gender-diverse set of readings and perspectives, it has not considered other central aspects of culture. To understand this interpretation and application of modern multicultural and culturally relevant pedagogy theory, we can use John Dewey's notions about the importance of a democratic education.

In the early 1900s, Dewey suggested that educational theory had trapped teachers in a false binary when it came to pedagogy (Dewey, 1902). That is, Dewey believed that teachers were asked to choose between a classical curriculum or curriculum focused on the lived experiences of their students. More often than not, teachers select the former as it is traditional and, ergo, professionally more acceptable. Dewey's work argued that rather than thinking of curriculum as an either/or proposition, that it should always be a both/and endeavor. Dewey believed that the child should be at the center of the curriculum, such that school curriculum draws from the lived experiences of the child to expand into broader horizons. This approach does not attempt to replace the knowledge that children bring with them to school; it builds on it. Dewey believed that this would make the relevance of school immediately apparent to the students, given that they would be engaging school knowledge through the lens of their lived social reality. We agree, and developed our pedagogy and curriculum accordingly.

References

Adorno, T., & Horkheimer, M. (1999). The culture industry: enlightenment as mass deception. In S. During (Ed.), *The cultural studies reader*. New York: Routledge, 31–41.

Apple, M. (1990). *Ideology and curriculum*. New York: Routledge.

Appleman, D. (2000) *Critical encounters: Teaching literary theory to adolescents*. New York: Teachers College Press.

Aronowitz, S. and Giroux, H. (1991). *Postmodern education*. Minneapolis, MN: University of Minnesota Press.

Banks, J. (1994). Ethnicity, class, cognitive, and motivational styles: Research and teaching implications. In Kretovicks, J. and Nussel, E. (eds.), *Transforming urban education*. Boston: Allyn and Bacon.

Bartolome, L. (1994). Beyond the methods fetish: Toward a humanizing pedagogy. *Harvard Educational Review*, 64, 173–94.

Darder, A. (1991). *Culture and power in the classroom: A critical foundation for bicultural education*. Westport, CT: Bergin and Garvey.

Delpit, L. (1987). Skills and other dilemmas of a progressive Black educator. *Equity and Choice*, 3(2), 9–14.

Delpit, L. (1988). The silenced dialogue: Power and pedagogy in educating other people's children. *Harvard Educational Review*, 58(3), 280–298.

Delpit, L. (1995). *Other people's children: Cultural conflict in the classroom*. New York: The New Press.

Delpit, L., & Dowdy, J. K. (Eds.). (2002). *The skin that we speak*. New York: The New Press.

Dewey, J. (1902). The school and society and the child and the curriculum. Chicago: University of Chicago Press.

Docker, J. (1994). *Postmodernism and popular culture: A cultural history*. New York: Cambridge University Press.

Dyson, M. E. (1994). Be Like Mike? Michael Jordan and the pedagogy of desire. In H. Giroux & P. McLaren (Eds.), *Between borders: Pedagogy and the politics of cultural studies*. New York: Routledge.

Freire, P. (1970). *Pedagogy of the oppressed*. New York: Continuum.

Freire, P. (1997). *Teachers as cultural workers: Letters to those who dare teach*. Boulder, CO: Westview.

Freire, P., and Macedo, D. (1987). *Literacy: Reading the word and the world*. South Hadley, MA: Bergin and Garvey.

Gans, H. (1999). *Popular culture and high culture: An analysis and evaluation of taste*. New York: Basic Books.

Geertz, C. (2000). *Available light: Anthropological reflections on philosophical topics*. Princeton: Princeton University Press.

Giroux, H. (2001). *Theory and resistance in education: Towards a pedagogy for the opposition*. Westport, CT: Bergin & Garvey.

Gramsci, A. (1971). *Selections from the prison notebooks*. London: New Left Books.

Hall, S. (1998). Notes on deconstructing the popular. In J. Storey (Ed.). *Cultural theory and popular culture: A reader*. Athens, GA: University of Georgia Press, 442–453.

hooks, b. (1994). *Teaching to transgress: Education as the practice of freedom*. New York: Routledge.

Kincheloe, J. (2004). *Critical pedagogy primer*. New York: Peter Lang.

Kozol, J. (1991). *Savage inequalities: Children in America's schools*. New York: HarperCollins.

Kozol, J. (1978). *Children of the Revolution*. New York: Delacorte Press.

Ladson-Billlings, G. (1994). *The dreamkeepers: Successful teachers of African American children*. San Francisco: Jossey-Bass.

Lankshear, C., Peters, M., and Knobel, M. (1997). Critical pedagogy and cyberspace. In H.A. Giroux, C. Lankshear, P. McLaren, and M. Peters (Eds.), *Counternarratives: Cultural studies and critical pedagogies in postmodern spaces*. New York: Routledge, 149–188.

Lave, J. and Wenger, E. (1991). *Situated learning: Legitimate peripheral participation*. Cambridge, UK: Cambridge University Press.

Loewen, J. (1995). *Lies my teacher told me: Everything your American history textbook got wrong*. New York: Touchstone Press

Lyotard, J.F. (1984). *The postmodern condition: A report on knowledge*. Minneapolis, MN: University of Minnesota Press.

McLaren, P. (1994). *Life in schools: An introduction to critical pedagogy and the foundations of education.* New York: Longman.

McLaren, P. (1995). *Revolutionary multiculturalism: Pedagogies of dissent for the new millennium.* Boulder, CO: Westview.

Moll, L. (2000). Inspired by Vygotsky: Ethnographic Experiments in Education. In C. Lee and P. Smagorinsky (Eds.). *Vygotskian Perspectives on Literacy Research: Constructing Meaning through Collaborative Inquiry.* Cambridge, UK: Cambridge University Press, 256–268.

Montoya, M. E. (1997). Academic *Mestizaje:* Re/producing clinical teaching and re/framing wills as Latina praxis, *Harvard Latino Law Review,* 2: 349.

Morrell, E. (2004a). *Becoming critical researchers: Literacy and empowerment for urban youth.* New York: Peter Lang.

Morrell, E. (2004b). *Linking literacy and popular culture: Finding connections for lifelong learning.* Norwood, MA: Christopher-Gordon publishers.

Nieto, S. (1992). *Affirming diversity: The sociopolitical context of multicultural education.* New York: Longman.

Schumacher, J. (1996) (Director). *A time to kill* [Film]. Warner Brothers.

Shor, I. (1992). *Empowering education: Critical teaching for social change.* Chicago: University of Chicago Press.

G. Smitherman (2001). *Talkin that talk: Language, Culture and Education in African America.* New York: Routledge.

Storey, J. (1998). *An introduction to cultural theory and popular culture.* Athens, GA: University of Georgia Press.

Strauss, A. and Corbin, J. (1998). *Basics of qualitative research: Techniques and procedures for developing grounded theory.* Thousand Oaks, CA: Sage.

Strinati, D. (2000). *An introduction to studying popular culture.* New York: Routledge

Tyack, D. (1974). *The one best system: A history of American urban education.* Cambridge, MA: Harvard University Press.

Vygotsky, L. (1978). *Mind in society.* Cambridge, MA: Harvard University Press.

Williams, R. The analysis of culture. In J. Storey (Ed.). *Cultural theory and popular culture: A reader.* Athens, GA: University of Georgia Press, 48–56.

Wright, R. (1989). *Native Son.* New York: Harper Perennial.

Zinn, H. (1995). *A people's history of the United States.* New York: Harper-Perennial.

CHAPTER 10

Critical Pedagogy and Young Children's Worlds

ELIZABETH QUINTERO

We live today with multiple representations, some we call science, some we call art, precise, abstract, vivid, and evocative, each one proposing new connections. . . . Human beings construct meanings as spiders make webs—or as appropriate enzymes make proteins. This is how we survive. . . .

Bateson, 1994, p. 52

Multiple Representations—Why Critical Pedagogy and Critical Literacy?

Critical pedagogy and critical literacy allow all learners of all ages and all backgrounds to tell their own stories. Telling our own stories is intricately related to survival. Surviving is a complex task. There is physical survival. There is emotional survival. And, of course, there is historical and cultural survival. It may be that the only way to delve into survival is through personal story. What is story? What is literacy?

When we think of these questions and young children under the age of six or seven years old, the issue of what is real and what is fantasy becomes complicated. Young children, through their play, especially when immersed in an environment of literature, art, and story, can provide us with perspectives of possibility of what is and what can be. As they explore the possibilities they almost always begin with the personal story.

Centuries ago, the Middle Eastern poet Rumi asked, "Of these two thousand 'I' and 'we' people, which am I?" (1995, p.12) The contemporary poet, Francisco X. Alarcón, asks us if we can " . . . hear the voices between these lines?" (1997, p. 28) I believe that the personal voices of teachers, of students, of friends in our communities around the world are the voices we hear between the lines in all literacy events. For this reason, when I speak of literacy, all literacy is—or should be—critical literacy. This constructing of personal and communal meaning and taking action according to the meaning is the most authentic way to personalize literacy.

I define critical literacy, stemming from critical pedagogy, for all ages of learners as **a process of constructing and critically using language (oral and written) as a means of expression, interpretation, and/or transformation of our lives and the lives of those around us.** For young children this could be inventing a story, painting it, and writing some text about it. Or it could be drawing a picture of family members and labeling the picture in the home languages of the people in the picture. It could be using language and gestures to sort out an argument. And it could be extending information from a video game or a film, arguing with the information, and asking questions about the information.

In Faith Ringgold's *Tar Beach* and *Aunt Harriet's Underground Railroad in the Sky*, the character Cassie uses her imagination and her stories to overcome oppression and limitations.

Author, Lise Lunge-Larsen (1999) tells us:

> By living a life immersed in great stories and themes, children will see that they have the resources needed to solve life's struggles. And, while listening to these stories, children can rest for a while in a world that mirrors their own, full of magic and the possibility of greatness that lies within the human heart. (p. 11)

What are the "great stories"? Who decides? Is there room for family stories and cultural histories that differ from stories in the standard curriculum? (This the twenty-first century and we still need to ask this?) When children are exposed to stories, are they asking "What is really going on here?" (Macedo, 2006). Can we educators facilitate their asking this important question?

Children's author Tim Tingle, a Choctaw, writes, "In stories or in life, trouble comes." But these realities cut deeper than any fantasy. Even young children recognize the wicked characters as an archetype. Will the children who read books recognize the various people in them as the people in their lives or in their own families?

Literacy in the New World

It is a changing world. In my work with migrating families and their young children, I see interesting and complicated dynamics. Parental ethnotheories, which are the cultural belief systems parents and families have about their children's learning, give children a reality at home when they are very young. These beliefs relate to school expectations, pedagogical issues, all with the backdrop of worldwide media influences.

In early childhood education, we are blessed with and challenged by being the first stop on the educational journey that children make from home culture to the educational culture that will engage them for twelve or more years. I can't help but wonder: Will the Hmong children, who learned the history of their ancestors through oral storytelling and "reading" storycloths, use similar and/or different strategies to negotiate the literacy of the standard curriculum and the visual literacy in other media? Will Bangladeshi children, who learn to read and write the Qu'ran at their kitchen tables, and draw and write language experience stories at preschool, be able to sort out the "history" presented in their schools in the United Kingdom and the United States in a few years? Will they have critical skills to analyze which stories of South Asia and the Middle East are fabricated to suit one political agenda or another? I believe that this is possible when children's stories and family histories are addressed through critical literacy. Only when children are supported to be critical can they negotiate hyperreality and the current twenty-first-century changing world context.

The way I see it, never before has there been such an urgent need for educators to ask questions that have never before been asked—to children, about children, and for children; and for all of us. Steinberg and Kincheloe (2001) remind us that

> comments and analysis change our orientation to multicultural education in that we study not only the effects of oppression on the oppressed but its impact on the privileged as well. . . . It does mean that we see all human beings shaped by race, class, and general inscriptions of power. Indeed, part of what we would define as characteristic of a critically educated person is conscientiousness of the way power dynamics of race, class, gender, and other social dynamics have operated to help produce one's identity and consciousness. (p. 26)

To belong is to be recognized as a full participant in the practices that shape knowledge, identities, and action. Yet, to learn is to draw upon one's own and others' knowledge sources, to transform these, and formulate conceptual frames for future learning. Urban neighborhoods and schools have increasing numbers of people representing ethnic, racial, and religious diversity. Many students today in schools around our country have exquisitely complex stories of going and coming. They have gone from a home country for a myriad of reasons, and they have come to their new country with a multitude of experiences. The experts in our newest refugee and immigrant neighborhoods have much to teach other students, other families, and us educators.

Teachers and students can use multicultural story and critical literacy as a way to enter neighborhoods and begin to learn from other stories of the various groups of people. Furthermore, the study of our students' histories must be on-going and a part of literacy education. What does history mean when studying literacy curriculum and learning? Critical literacy is a process of both reading history (the world) and creating history (what do you believe is important?).

It is our responsibility as educators to challenge the sanctity of using an "early childhood Western lens, the over reliance on child development paradigms, psychology, and the exclusively Western ways of seeing the world" (Soto, 2000). Currently, a lot of research challenges the idea of child development, through ideas that examine development in context or the social, cultural, and economic factors that influence development. James, Jenks, and Prout (1998) challenge teachers and researchers to pay attention to children's experiences and to what situations might mean for children—not for the purposes of evaluating them in accordance with adult goals, but for the ways in which they inform us about how our practices contribute to children's unequal status. These authors call for inquiries that combine a focus on critically examining childhood with attention to children's lived experiences.

We teachers create the context for learners to pose questions and encourage the consideration of the strengths of students and their families and the consideration of the barriers they face daily. This process, combined with the mutual respect which becomes generative in this context, provides support for transformative action on the part of parents, children, teachers, and community members.

Critical Literacy with Young Children

I work with groups of student teachers in urban schools in one of the most diverse cities on earth. The teachers and I support students' multiple languages and recognize ways that multiple knowledge sources, identities, and language forms can contribute to the formation of new relationships and meanings. We respect the children's backgrounds, plan carefully for their current experiences in school, and prepare them for the future challenges of standardized testing, competitive learning programs, and a variety of future journeys including negotiating issues of hyperreality. Our work uses critical literacy as a framework. Again, to clarify, we define critical literacy as a **process of constructing and critically using language (oral and written) as a means of expression, interpretation and/or transformation of our lives and the lives of those around us.**

By using a critical literacy approach with children's literature and literacy activities, even the complex issues of a world in conflict and confusion can be addressed. This methodology supports child-choice of activities and gives children opportunity to use critical conversation, questioning, and symbolic play.

The problem-posing method of critical literacy was developed by Paulo Freire (1973) and critical pedagogists going back to the Frankfurt School of critical theory in the 1920s, initially for use with adult literacy students. This method leads students of any age, experience, or ability level to base new learning on personal experience in a way that encourages critical reflection and active participation. In other words, in every aspect of young children's pretend play or semi-structured play, when using their imagination, symbolizing, and action, this is critical literacy.

For example, in a kindergarten classroom, a student teacher worked with a group of children in a "Where I'm From" poetry activity. The class and teachers read some poems together; then the student teacher talked with one child and asked what she thought about the poem. She said she liked it. Then she asked her if she would like to work on a poem with her. "Yes!" she said. Two other girls overheard the conversation and said that they also wanted to work on the poem. So the student teacher asked the girls what they thought a poem was. One said, "It's like a song, it rhymes." Another added, "Yeah, it's like a story but it rhymes." The student teacher then told them that she was going to read them a poem that she had written about where she is from, about her home. As she read, the children listened attentively.

> I am from the comfy black leather sofa, the magazines-Filmfare, Movie, Society, Indian movies that took me to another world, and ah most importantly Hindi music that always filled the air.
>
> I am from congested streets, street vendors selling clothes, accessories and water chestnuts that gave a sweet aroma to the streets.
>
> I am from fast food restaurants, shops at every nook of the street, bakeries selling sweet bread and creamy fruit cakes.
>
> I am from Nani who had a special way of showing to each of us that we were her favorite grandchild.
>
> I am from "always have a sense of humor-it's one of the most valuable things you can have in life."
>
> I am from my mom's homemade dal, rice, paneer and roti

The student teacher reported that:

> When I said I was from "bakeries selling sweet bread and creamy fruit cakes," the girls said "yum!" I then asked them what they heard. S. excitedly said, "You are from crowded streets and movies!" O. added "sweet bread." L. said "you are from your mom's rice." I then told them I was going to act out something that I like doing at home and I pantomimed reading a book. They said "you are reading." I told them we were going to take turns and they would act out something that like doing at home which we then would make into our group poem. O. thought for a moment and hesitated before she started. She then pretended to read a book. S.and L. said, "you are reading a book" and O. said "yes." L. acted out stroking a cat. None of us could guess what she was doing and she finally said "I am from stroking a cat!" S. then said, "how can you be from stroking a cat?" L. said "well, that's what I do at home and that is where I am from." S. then acted out watching TV and O. guessed what she was doing. S. then said "I am from watching TV at home." I wrote down all their thoughts. We then read the poem together and then to the whole class.

These children are using a combination of pretend play, gesture, and poetry through critical literacy. The student teacher took the activity farther by questioning the children about what they see on television. They talked about what is real, what is pretend, who makes the stories on television, movies, and video games. The children were adamant about their belief that grown-ups make the stories on television, in movies, and even video games. They said that sometimes they like the stories, but often they have to change them because they are not good in their eyes.

The student teacher reported that she had been supported by the cooperating teacher, her mentor, in creating these lessons which are very much child-centered. They both agreed that critical literacy gives the children the chance to express their own views and opinions.

Another example of critical literacy and personal story, expressed through dramatic play and language in a kindergarten classroom, is documented by a student teacher:

Last week the Dramatic Play area was introduced as a choice during Choice Time. Three children are allowed there at a time. Two of the girls have chosen to go to Dramatic Play each day it has been open. On Friday, these two children and another girl chose Dramatic Play and went straight to the costume box. They stayed in the Dramatic Play area for the full half hour of Choice Time. Towards the end of the afternoon, I looked over and saw one of the children lying on her back on the floor grunting. She had on a long skirt, worn as a dress, and her legs were spread. At her feet knelt another girl with a doll in her hands, holding the doll by the head. The third girl stood next to the first girl wearing a stethoscope around her neck. After some more grunting and words of encouragement—"Come on, push, push!"—the girl who was kneeling held up the doll and exclaimed, "The baby's out! She had her baby!" The "doctor" said, "It's a girl!" I could almost imagine that the hustle and bustle of the other activities around the room were part of the chaos of a hospital. At least one (or maybe all three) of the children must have had an understanding of how a baby is born for their play to be so realistic.

They were able to express through their actions and oral language a very involved portrayal (interpretation) of a delivery room scene, something that may possibly play a role in their lives. Maybe one of the children has or will soon have a new baby sibling?

Another student teacher documented a sad case of a teacher (perhaps a whole school staff) not respecting a child and family's identity in terms of language or literacy. Here is the report:

I am student teaching in a Kindergarten class in East Harlem, P.S. 50.

The classroom is made up of a close to even split of 20 Hispanic and Black students, myself and my cooperating teacher. One 5 year old girl, whose name is Janna, is somewhat quiet and also hesitant to speak with teachers. Originally, I suspected this was probably related to language issues that collided between the Spanish I hear her mother speaking to her and the English we speak at school.

Mostly, I noticed that she really did not respond to me or the teacher when we called her name, Janna. Something did not feel right.

I asked my cooperating teacher if she was sure this was how she pronounced her name. She told me that no one had told her otherwise and that she thought Janna was simply "slow" because her family had not forced her to be more expressive with her language. Again, that did not feel like the right answer to me. I had observed Janna in many instances talking with other children and directing them on how to solve puzzles and discussing books at shared reading. "Slow" was not a word I could attach to a child that clearly had complex interactive language skills with her peers.

So, I decided to do some investigating. Knowing what little Spanish I do, combined with the knowledge I have about Hispanic culture, I decided to ask Janna about her life at home. During a writing exercise, Janna asked me to write her words about a picture with her mother in it. On a whim, I asked her if there was a name that mommy called her at home that was different from the one she is called at school. Her eyes grew big and a smile splayed across her face as she exclaimed to me, "HANNA! She calls me HANNA!" It was then that I understood what had happened.

Nearly every adult in the building had mispronounced her name, not knowing or not suspecting that the "J" sound should be switched to "H" because Spanish had always been her primary language at home. I said to her, "Oh! So mommy says your name differently than we do at school?" She nodded and I asked her if we could call her that at school as well, and to my surprise, the smile disappeared and she shook her head at once. She then told me, "We don't speak Spanish in school." It upset me that she would feel uncomfortable being called what is essentially her real given name, simply because the pronunciation does not match in both languages. I also felt annoyed that when I brought it to my cooperating teacher's attention, she said she too did not think it necessary to change our pronunciation of Janna's name.

Finally, consider the hopeful example of one small boy on a crowded subway train to see the power of story and imagination exemplified for a potentially more perfect world. The student teacher documented:

> I observed a child and his father riding the subway together. The train was very crowded and there was only enough room for the child to sit down, so the father stood in front of him. He put the child in the seat and gave him some paper and pen to draw. The child looked around for a while and then finally began drawing. The father asked the child what he was drawing and he said he was drawing the father riding the subway. The father replied, "But I'm standing, not sitting down." The child then said, "Not on this train, the train in my drawing has seats for everyone to sit down." This child has used some very important critical literacy through his imagination and his art.

References

Alarcón, F. (1997). *Laughing tomatoes and other spring poems: Jitomates risueños y otras poems de primavera.* San Francisco: Children's Book Press.

Bateson, Mary C. (1994). *Peripheral visions: Learning along the way.* New York: HarperCollins.

Freire, P. (1973). *Education for critical consciousness.* New York: Seabury.

James, A., Jenks, C., & Prout, A. (1998). *Theorizing childhood.* New York: Polity Press.

Lunge-Larsen, L. (1999). *The troll with no heart in his body and other tales of trolls from Norway.* Boston: Houghton Mifflin Company.

Macedo, D. (2006). Personal communication. El Paso, TX: Aug. 12, 2006.

Ringgold, F. (1991). *Tar beach.* New York: Crown Press.

Ringgold, F. (1995). *Aunt Harriet's underground railroad in the sky.* New York: Crown Publishers.

Rumi (Translated by Coleman Barks with John Moyne, A.J. Arberry, and Reynold Nicholson). (1995). *The essential Rumi.* Edison, NJ: Castle Books.

Soto, L. (2000). *The politics of early childhood education.* New York: Peter Lang.

Steinberg, S. & Kincheloe, J. (2001). Setting the context for critical multi/interculturalism: The power blocs of class elitism, white supremacy, and patriarchy. In S. Steinberg (Ed.), *Multi/intercultural conversations: A reader* (pp. 3–30). New York: Peter Lang.

Tobin, J. (2000). *Good guys don't wear hats: Children's talk about the media.* New York: Teachers College Press.

CHAPTER II

Escola Cidadã and Critical Discourses of Educational Hope

GUSTAVO E. FISCHMAN & LUIS A. GANDIN

Introduction

As teacher educators committed to the goals and principles of critical pedagogy, we usually share with our students the very passionate and articulate words written by Richard Shaull in the preface to *Pedagogy of the Oppressed:*

> Education either functions as an instrument which is used to facilitate the integration of generations into the logic of the present system and bring about conformity to it, or it becomes "the practice of freedom," the means by which men and women deal critically and creatively with reality and discover how to participate in the transformation of their world. (Freire, 1993, p. 15).

Many of our students are very concerned with issues of educational equity, committed to the development of anti-oppressive pedagogical practices, and if given the chance will embrace the notions of pedagogy as a practice of freedom. However, more often than we would like to admit, some of our students respond to what, for us, is an eloquent definition and a clear ethical orientation for our practice as educators, with high levels of skepticism, ironic comments, or straightforward rejection. Many of those students explain to us that they see Freire's ideas as an expression of a dreamlike utopianism that doesn't help them in becoming better teachers or in developing better and more efficient curricular plans.

Granted, some of these students reject critical pedagogy based on firm ideological or theoretical principles, but for others, their disbelief relates to their schooling experience, their lack of knowledge about other ways of teaching and learning, and their difficulties of imagining that other school is possible.

To demonstrate that other type of schooling is not only desirable but it is a reality for almost two decades is the main goal of this chapter. *Escola Cidadã* (Citizen School) is an ambitious and successful educational reform project implemented in the city of Porto Alegre, Brazil since 1989. This program involving thousands of students, their families and teachers, has been developed, organized, and implemented by following Freirean principles and in its almost 20 years of existence has functioned as a beacon of hope for many educators in the world.

This article is organized as follows: section one will discuss the political and pedagogical contexts of the Citizen School. This section starts with a brief discussion of the neoliberal educational reforms implemented in Latin America and Brazil during the 1980s and 1990s as a way of contextualizing the radical departure of the Citizen School and its emphasis on participation and democratization. Section two describes the local political and pedagogical context of *Escola Cidadã* and the processes involved in reeducating the City of Porto Alegre. The next section explains the three main goals of the Citizen School: democratization of access to schools; democratization of schools' administration; and democratization of knowledge. We conclude this article by discussing key dynamics through which the educators and citizens of Porto Alegre are engaging in the complex process of building a school that is academically, socially, and politically significant.

The Political-pedagogical Context of *Escola Cidadã:* Neoliberal Educational Reforms in Latin America

The vast literature which addresses the contemporary changes in educational systems associated with the processes of globalization and the reorganization of capitalism demonstrates, above all, that formal systems of schooling are positioned as one of the most important social policies of the state (Anyon, 2005; Ozga, 2000; Fischman et al., 2005; Rizvi & Lingard, 2000).

Echoing reforms in the U.S., the U.K., Canada, and Australia, many of the efforts aimed at reforming education in Latin America during the 1990s emphasized discourses in which the concepts of choice, accountability, efficiency, and decentralization figured prominently, signaling to societies and educational communities the notion that schools should operate with more autonomy, following a "business model" (Hursh, 2006). Many of these reforms had the paradoxical effect of reducing an already small degree of school autonomy, enabling central governments to acquire even greater control over the daily life of educational institutions. This is due, in part, to the way the decentralization process was conducted: without the necessary resources. Currently, after almost 20 years of reforms aimed at increasing school autonomy, federal and state departments of education have even more

power to determine school policies, curriculum, and evaluation. Moreover, highly centralized agencies have been created with the means to exercise a tighter control over the performance of individual schools, punishing and rewarding them (Ball et al., 2003).

The most alarming dynamic of this new type of control is that academic performances
are not driven by educational principles or needs but established as to meet the goals of
financial programs of economic adjustment (better known as Structural Adjustment
Programs, SAPs). The implementation of SAPs, devised and supervised by international
financial institutions such as the World Bank and the International Monetary Fund, has
required a significant reduction in the size of the state and public sector as well as in its
regulatory functions. This retrenchment of the state has been extended to many social services, including education, health, and related forms of welfare; and in most cases SAPs have
exacerbated the gap between rich and poor and created important challenges in the provision of basic services that were previously guaranteed by the state (Reimers, 2000).

In the particular case of Brazil, the educational policies of the 1990s also followed the
conceptual guidelines and constraints related to the implementation of SAPs. It is important to acknowledge that during this period the federal and state governments expanded
the number of buildings, teachers, and students; yet, what remains a source of great con-
troversy is the actual relevance of those educational policies in terms of equity and for
improving the educational outcomes of poor children.

Education in Brazil, as a rule, is centralized. In the majority of states and cities there
are no elections for the city or state council of education (traditionally a bureaucratic structure, with members appointed by the executive), let alone for principals in schools.
Departments of education in cities and states usually define the curriculum. Since the
resources are administered by centralized state agencies, schools usually have very little or
no autonomy.

Although recently Brazil has achieved a very high level of initial access to schools (close
to 98%), the indexes of failures and dropouts are frightening. Brazilian data have consistently shown over many years that only about 50% of the students in first grade passed to
second grade in their first attempt. Hence, although initial access is granted, the chance
of a poor child passing to second grade is very low. Furthermore, the dropout rate is
extremely high, close to 20% by fourth grade.

The high levels of educational exclusion that permeated almost all the educational
reforms in Latin America in the 1990s, coupled with the enormous disparities embedded
in the general performance of schooling in Brazil, are two key indicators of the vast challenges the citizens of Porto Alegre had to face in implementing the Citizen School Project.

The Local Context of *Escola Cidadã*: Reeducating the City of Porto Alegre

Located in the south of Brazil, Porto Alegre is the largest urban district and the capital city
of the State of Rio Grande do Sul. The city has a population of 1,400,000. Between 1989

and the end of 2003, the city was governed by a coalition of leftist parties under the general leadership of the Workers' Party. Among the many initiatives of the administration (such as the Participatory Budget (Santos, 1998)), the *Escola Cidadã* (Citizen School) stands out as an innovative urban educational reform project, because not only has it been successfully educating children and the citizenry of Porto Alegre, but also because, as described before, it has been doing so under severe economic constraints and against the dominant discourse and policies of educational reform not only in Brazil, but worldwide.

From its inception, the Citizen School Project has been organized around three main principles: 1) schooling is relevant and meaningful if it provides individual and social opportunities for learning to read the word and the world (Freire, 1997a) learning to read the word and the world is only possible when the educational community in general and educators in particular recognize the interdependence of the political dimensions of urban schooling and the pedagogical dimensions of political participation in the urban landscape; and 3) democratizing schools requires individual and collective efforts to create an educational project that is open and flexible in its structures while maintaining goals of creating participatory structures and practices.

Within the Citizen School Project, schools are transformed into laboratories for the practice of individual and social rights. At the center of this project are the following ideals: encouraging the development of autonomous, critical, and creative individuals; nurturing a model of citizenship which supports daily practices of solidarity, justice, freedom, and respect for diversity; and informing all curriculum practices with a commitment to the development of a less exploitative relationship with the environment. José Clóvis de Azevedo, former chair of the Department of Education of Porto Alegre, states that to achieve such ambitious goals it is necessary to recover the sense of schools as laboratories of democracy, a notion that directly counters technocratic attempts to run schools following commercial, or market-oriented models:

> We reaffirm our commitment to expand the humanist character of public schools and we oppose the submission of education to the values of the market and neo-liberal reforms in education. The market's main concern is to form consumers and customers, to turn education into merchandise submitted to profit-seeking rationales, naturalizing individualism, conformity, unfair competition, indifference and, consequently, the exclusion of those deemed a-priori unsuited to compete. (Azevedo, 1999a, p. 5 [our translation])

After almost 18 years, the educational reforms created in Porto Alegre and envisioned in Azevedo's statement are still a work in progress, based on a set of core principles. One of those principles is that schools that want to promote social justice will not be created by simply changing technical, administrative, and pedagogical aspects. Rather, new teaching methods, organizational changes, administration structures, and leadership must be coupled with a global political project as an effort to enact more democratic power relationships. Thus, the Citizen Schools Project is an ambitious project of educational transformation, which combines pedagogical innovation with a shift in the type of relationships cultivated within the school setting and the type of knowledge being taught.

To implement this transformation, the coordinators in the SMED (Municipal Department of Education) knew that they would have to incorporate many students (mostly the children of migrant families living in the poorest areas of the city) who had been excluded from the educational system; in short, they would have to build new schools. The number of schools increased from 29 in 1988 to 92 in 2004. In 1988, the municipal school system of Porto Alegre provided educational services to only 17,000 students and had a dropout rate of almost 10%. In 2004 the system has increased the coverage to 60,000 students[1], and the dropout rate fell to 2%. In a country like Brazil, where a large group of children are outside schools or simply drop out, these numbers represent a great achievement by itself.

The number of teachers also increased dramatically: in 1988 there were 1,700 teachers and in 2004 the municipal schools have 4,000 teachers. These teachers are among the best paid in public educational systems in Brazil, earning three times what a teacher in state public schools earns. Other indicators of the quality of this reform project are changes in curriculum and organizational structures that address the needs of a diverse urban population; high levels of community participation in the life of the schools; and the key role that schools play in the lives of local communities.

These are impressive results for a Brazilian municipal school district, one that had been surrounded and pressured by other educational models that operated from a completely different perspective. Furthermore, the results have been achieved following the core values of empowerment, collective work, respect for differences, solidarity, knowledge as a historical experience, and citizenship aimed at democratizing access to school, knowledge, and governance. Given these core values, since its conception and initial implementation in 1989, the Citizen School Project has been explicitly designed to radically change both the municipal schools and the relationship between communities, the state, and the educational system. This set of policies and the efforts to implement them are constitutive parts of a clear and politically explicit project aimed at developing institutions that will provide opportunities for not only better schooling for the students who have been traditionally excluded but also the provision of knowledge, opportunities for practice, and structures expected to support the constant expansion and strengthening of a social project of participatory democracy.

The Citizen School Project is not an isolated initiative. It is part of a larger program of radical transformation of the relationship between the state (in this case, the municipal state) and civil society. Perhaps the best known of those initiatives is a system of participatory decision-making program used to allocate up to one third of the funds from the municipal budget (*Orçamento Participativo*—Participatory Budget—or "OP"). As the prominent Portuguese sociologist Boaventura de Sousa Santos noted:

> The participatory budget promoted by the Prefeitura of Porto Alegre is a form of public government that tries to break away from the authoritarian and patrimonialist tradition of public policies, resorting to the direct participation of the population in the different phases of budget preparation and implementation, with special concern for the definition of priorities for the distribution of investment resources. (1998, p. 467)

The OP is at the core of the project of transforming the city of Porto Alegre and incorporating a historically excluded impoverished population into the processes of decision making. As a number of researchers have shown (Baiocchi, 1999; Santos, 1998; Abbers, 1998; Avritzer, 1999), not only have the material conditions of the impoverished population improved, but also the OP has generated an educative process that has forged new social organizations and associations in neighborhoods, and it is intimately related to and complements the Citizen School Project decision-making process, because the OP constitutes one of the organizing structural bases for hope.

Organizing the Participatory Structures of *Escola Cidadã*

One of the most salient characteristics of the Citizen School is to be organized around participatory structures that encourage educators, students, parents, community organizations, and individuals to participate in the decision-making process about the role that schools should play in the larger society. These decision-making processes require important levels of reflection upon the type of social, political, and educational practices they would like to see in operation in the municipality's schools. It is worth highlighting that in 1989, even amid a dramatic national financial and economic crisis, the Citizen School Project expressed the articulation of democratic ideals, community experiences, the legacy of the popular education movement, and a firm commitment to create a new model of schooling. The educational policies implemented by four subsequent different administrations of Porto Alegre's Department of Education infused a radical democratic spirit into the educational sphere by supporting the direct and active participation of students, teachers, administrators, staff, parents, and the community at large in the formulation, administration, and control of the municipal public policies.

In 1993, the Citizen School Project implemented a series of regional meetings designed to prepare a collective structure open to the participation of all the segments of the school community, called the "School Constituent Assembly." The goal of the School Constituent Assembly was to establish the guiding principles that would orient the construction of a democratic and emancipatory school. The School Constituent Assembly was attended by elected delegates, guaranteeing the participation of parents, students, teachers, and staff. The Assembly proclaimed that the democratization of schooling was the main goal of the Citizen School Project, and in order to achieve such goal the project had to create the structures that would guarantee democratization of access to schools, democratization of schools' administration, and democratization of knowledge. The next sections will expand and provide examples of what democratization of schools means for the Citizen School Project.

Democratizing access to municipal schools

As noted before, for the organizers of the Citizen School, the democratization of access to schools was a priority and something explicitly connected to the educational needs of the most impoverished neighborhoods of Porto Alegre, where the municipal schools are situ-ated. For the Popular Administration, guaranteeing access to public schooling for children of communities historically neglected by the state and its network of social services was the first step to promote social justice.

Accordingly, one of the first curricular and organizational reforms instituted to address the social and educational exclusion suffered by many students in Porto Alegre was abol-ishing the grade structure and establishing a "cycle of formation" system. These three cycles are three years long each, totaling nine years of education (which represented incorporat-ing one year of kindergarten to schooling, something not common at that time in Brazil). The education by cycles attempts to eliminate school-related mechanisms that perpetu-ate the exclusion of mostly poor students and students of color through failure and drop-ping out. The student's progress from one year to the other and the notion of "individual educational failure" was eliminated. The latter is meant to reframe the conception of fail-ure present in many educational systems that traditionally "solve educational failure" by blaming the student (or her/his family, or his/her race, culture, linguistic ability, social class, etc.) for her/his school performance, increasing the likelihood of dropping out of schools in later grades, without examining the role of the school in creating the very notion of stu-dent failure (Shepard & Smith, 1989). The fact that the concept of student's learning fail-ure was eliminated does not mean that assessment of the learning process of the students is not done. This assessment is very rigorous, and teachers organize dossiers that accom-pany students from one year to the following in order to help the next teacher to empha-size aspects that were not optimal in the learning process of the student.

The implementation of the cycles (Krug, 2001) as part of the process of elimination of school-related mechanisms of social and educational exclusion, though important, was not enough. The Citizen School also created several mechanisms that guaranteed the rein-clusion of students who had previously been excluded from the school system. One of those is the implementation of progression groups and learning laboratories (Gandin, 2006; Azevedo, 2000). In progression groups, students who come into a Citizen School from other school systems (e.g., state schools) having experienced multiple failures are provided spe-cial attention until they are integrated into a cycle at the appropriate educational level. Learning laboratories are not only a space where students with special needs are helped, but also a place where teachers conduct research activities (in the teacher-as-researcher model: Anderson, Herr, & Nihlen, 1994; Gandin, 2004) in order to improve the quality of the regular classes. A major emphasis of these mechanisms was the transformation of the school structure to improve access, participation, and learning.

Finally, the material conditions of the schools are excellent. All the schools are kept in prime condition, with good libraries, lighting, cooking facilities, and playgrounds. Almost all schools also have computer labs, or gymnasiums, dance floors or painting and sculpture studies. For those in the U.S. or Europe, most of those characteristics are a given in public schools, but in Brazil they are remarkable and a key component in strength-ening the bases for hope by guaranteeing access and permanence of students at the munic-ipal schools of the city of Porto Alegre.

Democratizing the administration of the municipal schools

The School Constituent Assembly mandated the establishment of mechanisms for the direct election of principals and assistant principals in the schools of Porto Alegre. This mechanism is aimed at the redefinition of power relationships inside schools. To be elected to occupy positions of leadership, candidates are required to present a feasible pedagogical and administrative program for the school. The proposed program has to state pedagogical goals and the means to achieve them; must obtain the support of staff, teachers, students, and parents; and has to be technically and financially responsible. In this manner, the goals, procedures, and norms for administrative and pedagogic relationships that are developed specifically for a given school require a process of consensus building through informed dialogue among teachers, students, educational authorities, parents, and members of the local community (Campos, 1998; Freitas, 2002; Dourado, 2002).

Another vital mechanism developed to democratize the exercise of power inside schools was the creation of School Councils, which are comprised of elected representatives (parents, students, employees, and teachers). The School Council is the highest level of decision making of the school and exercises considerable influence over administrative, financial, and pedagogic matters. The main responsibility is to define the general orientation of the school, to determine the administration's guidelines, and to allocate the school's resources. The school principal, who is a member of the Council, is also responsible for offering political and pedagogical coordination to the general project (Azevedo, 1999b).

These mechanisms of governance have impacted not only the administrative aspects of school life but also the sense of professionalism among teachers and principals; and perhaps, in a crucial manner, have opened real opportunities for deepening the bases for hope by emphasizing the importance of democratizing the access to knowledge.

Democratizing knowledge

Curriculum transformation is another crucial goal of Porto Alegre's project for transforming schools through more democratic practices. Curricular transformation is more than making sure that the students are going to be offered access to traditional knowledge required for an educated and enlightened citizenry. The Citizen School Project goes beyond the incorporation of new knowledge within the margins of an intact "core of humankind's wisdom." It is a radical transformation aimed at constructing a new epistemological understanding about what counts as knowledge. Thus the Citizen School Project goes beyond the mere episodic mentioning of the structural and cultural manifestations of class, racial, sexual, and gender-based oppression. It includes these themes as an essential part of the process of construction of knowledge.

To achieve this aim, the district of Porto Alegre implemented participatory research strategies to develop school curricula. One of the most effective tools for resolving the frequent disconnection between the cultural and social frameworks of communities and schools is the use of educational thematic units built around a central concern for the community. Teachers develop these units after conducting a social-anthropological diagnostic evaluation within their school communities.

These thematic units become a locally based and locally owned instrument designed to construct and distribute knowledge that is socially relevant for the communities served by each school. The critical incorporation of elements deemed relevant for the school community, complemented with pedagogical practices developed to strengthen the concept of radical democracy within *Escola Cidadã*, have given a new meaning to teaching and learning in Porto Alegre. Perhaps no other element better illustrates the meaning of what teaching is for the Citizen School Project than the role of the educator as defined by the School Constituent Assembly:

> The educator's role is to be next to the student, challenging the real and imaginary worlds brought to school by students, contributing to the life-world of the students in such a way that the "world" can be understood and reinvented by the student. The educator should also grow, learn, and experience together with the students, the conflicts, inventions, curiosity, and desires, respecting each student as a being that thinks differently, respecting each student's individuality. (SMED, 1999, p. 57 [our translation from Portuguese])

This program helps consolidate the mutual responsibility and obligations of the state and civil society, teachers, communities, and students by reinventing the concept of "schools for citizenship" where "achievement for all" is only the first step toward creating more democratic spaces in education. As Tarso Genro (former mayor of Porto Alegre and an ex-Federal Minister of Education) states:

> The truth about Escola Cidadã is that fundamentally, it is a rational and undetermined space. In it citizens—teachers and learners—are connecting with the values and legacies of the Enlightenment, tolerance, respect for human diversity and cultural pluralism, in dialogical coexistence, sharing experiences and knowledge and identifying history as open future. (Genro, 1999, p. 11 [our translation from Portuguese])

The "truth" defended by Genro implies that supporting and extending real and workable democratic reforms in schools like *Escola Cidadã* requires that controversial positions be debated fairly within political and social institutions as well as educational systems. The relative success of *Escola Cidadã* points to the urgent need for a greater understanding of the sociopolitical conditions facing many aggrieved communities within the social order, and the manifold challenges entailed in cultivating civic responsibility to ensure that public institutions embody community decisions with socially acceptable outcomes.

Developing Critical Discourses of Educational Hope: *Escola Cidadã* and the Possibilities Of Imagining and Building Another School

Our analysis and experiences working with teachers and students in many Citizen Schools has given us something that seems scarce in these times of neoliberal reforms: educational hope. Our pedagogical hopes are inscribed in the extraordinary potential and promise that happens when we implement participatory and democratic experiments within schools. These experiments are happening on a large scale in Porto Alegre and on smaller scales in many places around the world, from the cities of Rosario (Argentina) to Barcelona (Spain), Toronto (Canada) to Kerala (India) (Shugurensky & Lerner, 2005; Parker, 2000).

While the dominant trend in educational reform worldwide promotes privatization, high-stakes testing, quantitative indicators of accountability, and fragmented and shallow curricular packages that ultimately blame teachers and students for the lack of relevance of urban public schooling, the public municipal schools of Porto Alegre are an example of a realizable utopia, based on a critical discourse of hope.

The Citizen School is showing that it is possible to create an alternative space where articulations can be forged and where a new common sense around education can be created. It is possible to create a space where kids and the community feel connected to their schools and feel that their school serves them. Democratizing access, knowledge, and relationships in the current context of global capitalism is not easy, but the fact that *Escola Cidadā* is still operating after many years of structural adjustment in Brazil and has expanded its service to include an increasing proportion of the impoverished communities of greater Porto Alegre reflects the power of a critical discourse of hope and community organizing in the struggle for democracy.

Finally, we firmly believe that *Escola Cidadā*, with all its potential and limitations, is a good example of the possibility of developing a realistic pedagogical utopia, such as the one envisioned by Paulo Freire:

> Revolutionary utopia tends to be dynamic rather than static; tends to life rather than death; to the future as a challenge to man's creativity rather than as a repetition of the present; to love as liberation of subjects rather than as pathological possessiveness; to the emotion of life rather than cold abstractions; to living together in harmony rather than gregariousness; to dialogue rather than mutism; to praxis rather than "law and order"; to men who organize themselves reflectively for action rather than men who are organized for passivity; to creative and communicative language rather than prescriptive signals; to reflective challenges rather than domesticating slogans; and to values that are lived rather than myths that are imposed. (Paulo Freire, cited in Giroux & McLaren, 1997, p. 150)

Our discussion of *Escola Cidadā* was developed with the intent of showing the existence of pedagogical alternatives to the current models of educational reform. Developing pedagogical alternatives requires political commitment, creativity, and above all the development of a *critical discourse of educational hope*.

A critical discourse of educational hope, such as the one emerging from the Citizen School, is a collective construction, a historical and ontological requirement, and not an external characteristic of a pedagogical situation, something alien to the daily struggle of teachers and students (Fischman & McLaren, 2005). As such, only when hope is put in a concrete, practical experience of struggle, dialogue, and conflict, it attains its power. "Just to hope," Freire vehemently stated, "is to hope in vain" (1997a, p. 7):

> Hope is a natural, possible and necessary impetus in the context of our unfinishedness. Hope is an indispensable seasoning in our human, historical experience. Without it, instead of history we would

have pure determinism. History exists only where time is problematized and not simply a given. A future that is inexorable is a denial of history. (Freire, 1997b, p. 69)

A critical discourse of educational hope is not an illusion, a fantastic creation blinding us from reality, causing us to imagine impossible scenarios that will necessarily follow the typical Hollywood feel-good plot. A critical discourse of hope is not an apolitical and therefore ahistorical narrative. A critical discourse of hope that is not used as a basic component of the daily pedagogical and political conflicts of teachers, students, and their communities is ineffectual hope. A critical discourse of hope *is* an active, complex, participatory narrative.

Perhaps the most relevant lesson from the Citizen School is that another type of schooling is possible; and to obtain it, a critical discourse of educational hope is necessary. This new alternative school is a conflictive construction, a new institution in which students teachers, principals, families, and communities have no other possibility but to struggle to affirm themselves by increasing the opportunities for democratic dialogue and participation; be accountable for the success of everybody involved in teaching and learning; and establish common pedagogical and political goals, including the goals of accepting diversity and conflictive dialogue as intrinsic to the construction of a more efficient and democratic educational experience. It is up to them and to us as scholars and practitioners to imagine fruitful ways to identify the potential limitations, the spaces for hope, and those extraordinary times in which collective action demonstrate that history is always in the making.

Acknowledgments

We want to acknowledge the invaluable collaboration of the many teachers and principals who generously shared their time and knowledge with us. Gary Anderson, Ronald Glass, Michele Moses, and Pia Lindquist Wong offered very valuable comments, and we know that this chapter is a better one thanks to their criticisms. The mistakes, of course, remain, ours. Luis A. Gandin wants to acknowledge the support of Oakland University's School of Education and Human Services while he is serving as an invited Visiting Scholar in 2006/2007.

Notes

1.   It is important to note that in the Brazilian educational system, both the states and the cities maintain public schools. In Porto Alegre there are many students who attend state public schools, which explains the relatively small number of students in the municipal schools.

References

Abers, R. (1998). From clientelism to cooperation: Local government, participatory policy and civic organizing in Porto Alegre, Brazil. *Politics & Society*, 26 (4), 511–537.

Anderson, G. L., Herr, K. and Nihlen, A. (1994). *Studying your own school: An educator's guide to qualitative practitioner research.* Thousand Oaks, CA. Corwin Press.

Anyon, J. (2005). *Radical possibilities: Public policy, urban education, and a new social movement.* New York: Routledge.

Avritzer, L. (1999). Public deliberation at the local level: Participatory budgeting in Brazil. Unpublished manuscript.

Azevedo, J. C. (1998). Escola Cidadã: Construção coletiva e participação popular. In Silva, L.H. (Ed.), *A Escola Cidadã no contexto da globalização* (pp. 308–319). Petrópolis, Brazil: Vozes.

———. (1999a) Escola Cidadã: Construção coletiva e participação popular. Paper presented at The Comparative and International Education Society, Toronto, April 14–19.

———. (1999b). A democratização do Estado: A experiencia de Porto Alegre. In Silva, L.H. (Ed.), *Escola Cidadã: Teoria e Práctica.* Petrópolis, Brazil: Vozes.

———. (2000). *Escola Cidadã: Desafios, diálogos e travessias.* Petrópolis, Brazil: Vozes.

Baiocchi, G. (1999). Participation, activism, and politics: The Porto Alegre experiment and deliberative democratic theory. Unpublished manuscript.

Ball, S., Fischman, G., and Gvirtz, S. (Eds.). (2003). *Crisis and hope: The educational hopscotch of Latin America.* New York: Routledge.

Bowles, S. & Gintis, H. (1986). *Democracy and capitalism.* New York: Basic Books.

Campos, G.W. (1998). An anti-Taylorist approach for establishing a co-governance model for health care institutions in order to produce freedom and commitment. *Cad. Saúde Pública.* [online]. Vol. 14, no. 4 [citado 2006–08–28], pp. 863–870. Retrieved January 22, 2007 from http://www.scielo.br/scielo.php?script=sci_arttext&pid=S0102–311X1998000400029&lng=es&nrm=iso

Dourado, Luiz Fernandes. (2002). State reform and federal policies for higher education in Brazil in the 1990s. *Educ. Soc.* [online]. Vol. 23, no. 80 [citado 2006–08–28], pp. 234–252. Retrieved January 22, 2007 from http://www.scielo.br/scielo.php?script=sci_arttext&pid=S0101–73302002008000012&lng=es&nrm=iso

Fischman, G., & McLaren, P. (2005). Rethinking critical pedagogy and the Gramscian legacy: From organic to committed intellectuals. *Cultural Studies > Critical Methodologies,* 5(4), 425–447.

Fischman, G., McLaren, P., Sünker, H., & Lankshear, C. (Eds.). (2005). *Critical theories, radical pedagogies and global conflicts.* Lanham, MD: Rowman and Littlefield.

Freire, P. (1993). *Pedagogy of the oppressed* (New rev. 20th-Anniversary ed.). New York: Continuum.

———. (1997a). *Pedagogy of hope: Reliving the pedagogy of the oppressed.* New York: Continuum.

———. (1997b). *Pedagogy of the heart.* New York: Continuum.

———. (1999). *Pedagogy of freedom: Ethics, democracy, and civic courage.* Lanham, MD: Rowman & Littlefield.

Freitas, H. C. L. (2002). Formação de professores no Brasil: 10 anos de embate entre projetos de formação. *Educ. Soc.* [online]. Vol. 23, no. 80 [citado 2006–08–28], pp. 136–167. Retrieved January 22, 2007 from http://www.scielo.br/scielo.php?script=sci_arttext&pid=S0101–73302002008000009&lng=pt&nrm=iso

Gandin, D. (2004). *Planejamento como prática educativa.* Petrópolis, Brazil: Vozes.

Gandin, L. A. (2006). Creating real alternatives to neo-liberal policies in education: The Citizen School Project. In Apple, M. W. & Buras, K. (Eds.), *The subaltern speak: Curriculum, power, and educational struggles* (pp. 217–241). New York: Routledge.

Genro, T. (1999). Cidadã nia, emancipação e cidade. In Silva, L.H. (Ed.). *Escola Cidadã: Teoria e prática* (pp. 7–11). Petrópolis, Brazil: Vozes.

Giroux, H. & McLaren, P. (1997). Paulo Freire, postmodernism, and the utopian imagination: A Blochian reading. In Daniel, J. O., & Moylan, T. (Eds.), *Not Yet: Reconsidering Ernst Bloch* (pp. 138–162). London & New York: Verso.

Hursh, D. (2006). The crisis in urban education: Resisting neoliberal policies and forging democratic possibilities. *Educational Researcher, 35*(4), 19–25.

Krug, A. (2001). *Ciclos de Formação: uma proposta transformadora.* Porto Alegre: Mediação.

Ozga, J. (2000). *Policy research in educational settings: Contested terrain.* Buckingham, Open University Press.

Parker, W. et al. (2000). Making it work: Implementing multidimensional citizenship. In Cogan, J. & Derricott, R. (Eds.), *Citizenship for the 21st century: An international perspective on education* (pp. 151–170). London: Kogan Page.

Reimers, F. (2000) *Unequal schools, unequal chances: The challenges to equal opportunity in the Americas.* Cambridge, DRCS-Harvard University.

Rizvi F. & Lingard, B. (2000). Globalization and education: Complexities and contingencies. *Educational Theory, 50*(4): 419–426.

Santos, B.S. (1998). Participatory budgeting in Porto Alegre: Toward a distributive democracy. *Politics and Society, 26* (4), 461–510.

Schugurensky, D. and Lerner, J. (2005). Learning citizenship and democracy through participatory budgeting: The case of Rosario, Argentina. Paper presented at the conference '*Democratic Practices as Learning Opportunities.*' Teachers College, Columbia University, Nov. 4–5.

Shepard, L.A., & Smith, M.L. (1989). Flunking grades: A recapitulation. In Shepard, L.A., & Smith, M.A. (Eds.), *Flunking grades: Research and policies on retention* (pp. 214–235). London: Falmer Press.

SMED (1999). Ciclos de formação—Proposta político-pedagógica da Escola Cidadã. *Cadernos Pedagogicos,* 9 (1), 1–111

SMED (2000). *Boletim informativo—Informações educacionais.* Year 3, No. 7.

CHAPTER 12

Musicing Paulo Freire

A Critical Pedagogy for Music Education

FRANK ABRAHAMS

Introduction

"Boys and girls," the music teacher announces, "open your music books to page 123 and follow along with the recording." She pops a CD into the player and the children hear someone with a strong but chesty voice singing a South African song about tomato sauce. They see a picture of black children in a primitive kitchen stirring containers of what is presumably tomato sauce. The recording finishes, and she asks, "Who can tell me what the song is about?" Children quietly raise their hands and one child answers, "It's about tomato sauce." "That's correct" replies the teacher. She then asks, "What country do you think this song is from?" Children guess various places and finally someone says in an inquisitive and unsure tone, "Africa?" "That's right" the teacher says. "Let's listen again and see how many words you can pick up." She plays the recording again and proceeds to teach the song by rote—line by line until the children have it memorized. Throughout, she reminds them to sit tall in their seats and sing with a strong supported tone, always in their light, head voices and always reading from the textbook.

When the children have the words securely learned, their teacher again plays the accompaniment track as the children sing along. Later, they watch a DVD excerpt of the children from the textbook performing "Tomati So, So, So, So" and, with their teacher, the students learn the accompanying dance. For homework, the children are told to look on the Internet to learn more about South Africa and the music sung by children there. The students make some notations in their notebooks as the class is dismissed.

This is a familiar scene in American general music classrooms. Children learn folk songs, often in English translation, and may play native rhythms on classroom instruments. They frequently listen to or watch video performances of the music by artists from the culture they are studying. Singing, like the case described above, is nearly always in a Eurocentric style and from Western notation. While music teachers claim that these lessons broaden the child's worldview, the lessons are merely token attempts at including multiculturalism in music education.

The Context

Although music has been taught in schools for over 100 years, it remains on the fringe of the curriculum (Abrahams, 2006). Despite the inclusion of music and other arts in federal legislation, such as the Goals 2000: Education America Act (P. L. 103–227) and the No Child Left Behind Act of 2001 (P. L. 107–110), music and arts programs have been curtailed in many school districts and, most particularly, in urban areas. Understanding how a music education can empower children to perceive the world, and their significance in it, has escaped those who make the important decisions about what happens inside schools. For example, in 2006, Philadelphia eliminated 80 music teachers and their programs in order to make more time for reading. Similar statistics can be found for Los Angeles, Chicago, St. Louis, and New York City. In fact, the Center on Education Policy (2005) reported that 22% of districts surveyed in 2005–2006 indicated that instructional time in music had been reduced to allow more time for reading, language arts, and mathematics.

Music in schools remains marginalized for many reasons, such as the music industry's influence on students. A specific example can be seen at a magnet middle school in Newark, New Jersey that has a brand new set of the basal music series that the teacher can't use because the song material does not relate to her students' world. The students at this particular school understand the language and rhythms of hip hop and do not relate to songs about Aunt Rhody and her old gray goose. Neither can they relate to Mozart, Debussy, or Philip Glass. Their idols are Tupac Shakur and 50 Cent, artists who did not learn to rap in school music programs and who speak of issues in their music that are not authorized as appropriate conversation for children and their teachers in school. But children find a kindred spirit in those artists and make personal connections with their music.

Music teachers must share some of the responsibility for the dismal state of music education in many schools. Their curricula focus on the reproduction of music methodologies (Regelski, 2004) which are steeped in Western "art" music and a Eurocentric nineteenth-century aesthetic that is hardly relevant or interesting to children in school. Music educators, if they are to teach a music curriculum that is liberating, are challenged to analyze present traditions and practices. If educators are not reflective and analytical, they limit students to reproducing what went before. On the other hand, when music teachers realize that they are able to analyze, adapt, and manipulate the curriculum in an unlimited number of ways, they open possibilities for creative experiences that are both liberating and transformational.

Critical theorists acknowledge the power and influence that popular culture (or mass culture) has to shape peoples' attitudes and behaviors. Issues of struggle, power, culture, hegemony, and critical consciousness were important to the members of the Frankfurt School, and remain paramount to critical theorists today. The reproduction of "oppressive social patterns and the viability of social transformation" (Giroux, 1983), and particularly the role that schools play in that agenda, still appears frequently in critical theory writings. According to Meyer (1989) "habits of musical culture and style are an outward expression of belief. Forming the basis for a musical logic, they function as the 'rules of game,' thereby setting the standard against which musical individuality is compared and assessed" (p. 244). As Meyer explains it, "musical individuality is only possible in reference to some cultural or collective norm."

Horkheimer and Adorno (cited in Rose, 1990) believe that the mass production of popular culture turns music and the other arts into commodities and produces a mechanical world filled with standardized, stereotyped, and false images of mass culture. This, in turn, ensures the inequalities and injustices that subvert aesthetics, imagination, and intelligence. When this happens, the development of critical consciousness and emancipation is denied. Because dominant social classes control the media, they are able to impose their values on other social classes by prescribing social behavior and belief. The result for less-privileged classes of society is that "reality is thought of as a 'given' and essentially independent of the vagaries of human volition, rather than being socially constructed (Shepherd as quoted in Woodford, 1997, p. 45).

The Critical Pedagogy for Music Education Framework

Critical pedagogy means different things to different people (Kincheloe, 2005). For music educators, critical pedagogy seeks to break down the barriers that exist between the music students hear and love outside the classroom and the music their teachers want them to learn. When teachers connect school music to the child's own music, the music becomes empowering and offers more plentiful opportunities for meaningful musical experiences inside and outside of the classroom (Abrahams & Head, 2005).

From the perspective of critical theory, much of what teachers believe involves desires or needs that are implanted by the status quo into which those teachers were socialized. In the case of music education, this includes the world of music, musicians, and music education (Regelski, 1998). Rose (1990) studied music education in relation to cultural reproduction (Bourdieu, 1987; Bowles and Gintis, 1976), and the production of culture (Apple, 1982). She also looked at issues of hegemony (Gramsci, 1971) and found music education to be objectified through packaging and categorization for the purpose of reproducing and thereby perpetuating certain musical traditions and the underlying assumptions of these traditions.

Clearly, the school music program plays an important role as an agent of social and cultural production and reproduction. For instance, through music education, social barriers and inequalities can be overcome by experiencing music as a common language and a common expression (Rose, 1990). Gramsci (1971) points to the necessary development of a critical consciousness that defines people as both historical products and makers of history, so they understand their own experience within a wider construct of social and cultural hegemonic ideologies. Freire (1970, 1973, 1985, 1998) expressed belief in the power of individuals to come to a critical consciousness of their own existence through the process of conscientization—a process that goes beyond the ability to recall information to include understanding and the ability to act on the learning in such a way as to affect a change. To develop a critical consciousness of music in education (i.e., one that addresses the intrinsic and the extrinsic), an exploration of music tradition within a sociocultural framework is needed. Clearly, that does not happen in most school music classrooms. Schmidt (2002a) points out that schools no longer provide (if they ever did) the tools for critical thinking and transformative action. "Music education," he writes, "in its curricular and philosophical conception adheres to the same practice, continuing to foster a modern understanding of knowledge and its transmission" (p. 2).

As Rose (1990) notes, music, like other school subjects, has been used for the subtle domination of one group by another, noting that teachers generally have autonomy to choose which music is studied and which is not. Conversely, students are usually powerless to resist the selected music literature unless they can opt out of the music class entirely. Powerful relationships, which both inform and constitute dominant ideologies and traditions, exist in the classroom. For example, since music teachers control the curriculum, meaning all the experiences students have in the music program inside the music classroom and in the school building (Eisner, 2002), the teacher controls which cultures are taught along with which values are understood and perceived to be important (Schmidt, 2002b). In many situations where the Western canon comprises the substance of the musical diet, that diet is legitimized and reproduced. This may or may not reflect the interests, values, and backgrounds of students. Hence, certain or all individual and group intents are ignored, and an unconscious acceptance of a culture that may be irrelevant and foreign to these individuals and groups is fostered. This oversight inhibits the development and evolution of the students' social consciousness and transformation.

Recognizing the interconnections among education and schooling, society, aesthetics, and culture, Gates, Regelski, and others believe that critical theory might be an appropriate framework to inform music education. To that end, they established the MayDay group—an international think tank of music education philosophers, theorists, and practitioners. Meeting first in 1992, their goals (according to the MayDay Web site) are "to apply critical theory and critical thinking to the purposes and practices of music education and to affirm the central importance of musical participation in human life, and thus, the value of music in the general education of all people" (http://www.nyu.edu/education/music/may-day/maydaygroup/index.htm). As Gates explains, "Music, the person, the society and the culture are interlocked members of a musical life, and therefore of music education theorizing" (1999, p. 17).

The seven action ideals that drive the agenda of the MayDay group are:

1. Critically reflective music-making is basic to music education.
2. Consideration of music's social and cultural contexts is integral to good theory and practice.
3. Music teachers can influence cultural change.
4. Schools, colleges, and other musical institutions affect musical culture but need critical evaluation.
5. Research and study of music teaching and learning need an interdisciplinary approach.
6. The knowledge base of music educators should be both refined and broad.
7. Curriculum considerations are basic and should be guided by a critical, philosophical approach. (Gates, 1999, pp. 23–24)

Critical Pedagogy for Music Education

Critical Pedagogy for Music Education is not a traditional music teaching method, as it combines philosophy and pedagogy, theory and practice. Unlike the popular methodologies currently taught in summer workshops or in materials offered by the music industry, there are no specific teaching techniques or prescribed lists of musical repertoire for students to study and perform in the classroom. There are no required materials, such as instruments or tennis balls, and no prescribed scope and sequence. Instead, "critical pedagogy is a way of thinking about, negotiating, and transforming the relationships among classroom teaching, the production of knowledge, the institutional structures of the school, and the social and material relations of the wider community, society and nation state" (McLaren, 1998, p. 45). The focus is on developing the potential of both student and teacher. It is a perspective that looks toward expanding possibilities by acknowledging who the children and their teachers are, and building on their strengths while recognizing and assessing their needs. Critical Pedagogy for Music Education invites teachers to use many different teaching strategies to accomplish the mission, which is to empower children to be musicians.

When observing critical pedagogy in the music classroom, it is common to see children playing classroom instruments, using hand signs, moving, or reacting in some physical way to the sounds they hear. One might also see children working cooperatively in groups engaged in group problem solving or problem posing. There will be instances when children and their teachers engage in verbal or musical dialogue through discussion or improvisation to construct meaning in some creative way, and there will also be some hands-on activities that music teachers often include in their lessons. Children can be seen teaching their teachers in addition to the teachers instructing the children.

Critical Pedagogy for Music Education does not prescribe a particular curriculum but may be used with many. It encourages learning experiences that are multiple and liberating. Teachers play a key role in fostering such freedom since ultimately, the choices of what to teach and how to teach lie with individual teachers and their own particular students. They know each other best and collectively have the expertise to make thoughtful and informed decisions as to what is appropriate for themselves and their individual situations. Huff, as cited in Rose (1990), explains that teachers' actions and choices stem from their socialization process and are shaped by interactions with fellow participants within the context of school. Results of his study showed that teachers are actively constructing their own perspectives. In suggesting music education as a practice of liberation, Schmidt (2002b) notes that through conscientization (knowing that they know), teachers may effect change that will transform music education. The transformation of both teachers and students occurs when real learning takes place. "This new knowledge, discovered through dialogue and experienced in and with the world, has an impacting, changing force" (pp. 1–2). This notion was suggested by Paulo Freire (1998) when he wrote, "A correct way of thinking, that goes beyond the ingenuous must be produced by the learners in communion with the teacher responsible for their education" (p. 68).

Acknowledging that children come to the classroom with some prior knowledge gleaned from life experiences is an important concept. Applying critical pedagogy to American music education helps to connect music teaching to the mainstream goals of improved literacy that are so prominent in schools today and moves music education in schools from the fringe to a more prominent position in the curriculum. It also ensures that any musical knowledge gained, no matter how limited, is meaningful and retained longer in life.

Several key principles adapted from McLaren (2002) define Critical Pedagogy for Music Education (Abrahams, 2005). They are:

1. Music education is a conversation. Students and their teachers pose problems and solve problems together. In music classrooms, this means composing and improvising music in styles consistent with who the students are and the contexts in which they live.

2. Music education broadens the student's view of reality. The goal of music teaching and music learning is to effect a change in the way that both students and their teachers perceive the world.

3. Music education is empowering. When students and their teacher "know that they know," one can claim that the phenomenon of conscientization has occurred. In this view, music evokes critical action (Regelski, 2004) and critical feeling by engaging students in musical activities that are both significant and consistent with what musicians do when they are making music.

4. Music education is transformative. Music learning takes place when both the teachers and the students can acknowledge a change in perception. It is this change or transformation that teachers can assess.

5. Music education is political. There are issues of power and control inside the music classroom, the school building, and the community. Those in power make decisions about what is taught, how often classes meet, how much money is allocated to each school subject or program, and so forth. Those who use critical pedagogy are able to transcend the constraints that those in power place on them. They do this in their classrooms by acknowledging that children come to class with knowledge from the outside world and, as such, that their knowledge needs to be honored and valued.

A critical perspective allows music educators to view their role in the context of their own realities. Like their students, such realities include previous experiences, and their own conception of the political, cultural, and economic components of schooling. They can connect what they know with what their students bring to the classroom and, as a result, together they move from what organizational theorists Ouchi and Jaeger (1978) call the "is" to the "ought."

Four essential questions, gleaned from Habermas (1982), guide the development of music lessons grounded in critical pedagogy. They are: Who am I? Who are my students? What might they become? What might we become together? Believing that music education can be empowering and liberating, the approach extends Elliott (1995) and Small's (1998) conception of music as a verb, to that of a verb of power (Schmidt, 2002a). Music, by its very nature, has the power to liberate, transform, and effect change. This model enables students and their teachers to connect the music of the classroom to the music in their lives (Abrahams & Head, 2005). As a result, students come to better understand who they are and embrace the possibilities of who or what they might become. Music learning occurs when students and their teachers understand the making of meaning (McCarthy, 2000), and musical understanding occurs during the process of transformation.

Experiential learning (McCarthy, 1987, 2000) that honors the diversity of learning styles children present in the classroom, individual teaching styles, and constructivist theories (Wink & Putney, 2001), all contribute to the learning theory which grounds the Critical Pedagogy for Music Education view. As a result, classroom music lessons engage children in musical thinking. They begin with an exposition that introduces the main themes of the lesson. This is followed by a development section in which different ideas are explored and nurtured. Students are then encouraged to compose or improvise. The lesson ends with a recapitulation, where the themes are brought to a satisfying conclusion. In this lesson model, the teacher's role shifts from motivator to informer, to facilitator, and then to assessor (McCarthy, 1987). The students engage their musical intelligence or aptitude in four ways—using imagination, intellect, creativity, and the celebration of musical performance. Reading strategies used by teachers in general classrooms to help children meet standards of literacy are infused at appropriate points without compromising the integrity of the music lesson. Themes for all lessons come from social issues that are familiar to the students. Rather than focusing a lesson on an objective or a musical topic, such as theme and variation or ostinato, the lessons connect to the way children experience music in their lives outside of schooling. Lesson titles include "Music Builds Bridges and Defines Who We Are" (Abrahams & Head, 2005), or "Madonna, Mozart, Music, and Me," and "Rap the Chant, Chant the Rap" (Abrahams, 2005). Teachers can use the song "Bohemian Rhapsody" popularized by Queen as a metaphor for the Vietnam War.

Paulo Freire and Music Education

Applying the ideas and ideals of Paulo Freire to a Critical Pedagogy for Music Education frames a view of music education that is rich in dialogue and empowers students to be musicians. Such an empowerment affords the license to not only recreate the music of various cultures but to learn and perform it in a style that is authentic (Abrahams & Head, 2005). Informed by the musics they know, and the musics they learn, students reflect on who they are as cultural and social beings within the realities and contexts of their own particular heritages.

Freire suggested dialogue and problem posing as pathways to transformative learning and toward conscientization. He claimed that public schools have become places for social reproduction, prompting the necessary skills and social relations for the functioning of capitalism (Freire, 1985). As Schmidt (2002b) notes,

> Music education, because of its particular language, has the potential to reach and be a transforming power in different realities. Problems of language code, cultural and social stratification can find in music education a significant bridging point. Music education might be a significantly influential area in which individuals are challenged to recreate and reevaluate perceptions and understandings of social and cultural elements. (p. 4)

Citing Wallace and Wolf (1999) he continues, "Rules that are passed-on by social interactions determine people's actions." And Schmidt concludes:

> Music education by asking individuals to function in a different sphere, perhaps not as heavily permeated by rulings or structures of oral language, promises at least the possibility of new structures, nevertheless, ones embedded in dialogue and meaningful action. However, this can only be effective and become a tangible reality if music education and its professionals would engage in serious critical analysis of its practices. (p. 4)

Bowman (1993) extends these ideas when he writes, "Music education's tradition and connection to aesthetic education maintains this practice well and alive by considering only the western culture as valuable and erudite music as the 'best' music" (p. 13).

Critical pedagogy is concerned not only with the students and the change that occurs in them as a result of the learning but also with the change that occurs in the teacher. In critical pedagogy, not only do the teachers teach the students, but also the students, in turn, teach the teacher. This effects a transformation of both students and their teachers. When this occurs, Freire (1970) claims that true and meaningful learning has occurred. Allsup (1997) takes this further and states, "A fundamental purpose of performing art forms, engaging with them, and trying to create them is to provoke some kind of personal transformation" (p. 81).

The issue is a difficult one for music teachers. Those concerned with assessment and accountability wonder how they can measure student transformation. "Music educators interested in empowering students and providing a transformative education need to refuse the unwavering will [of rigid standards] to be who we are. Non-alienating methods of teaching require conscientization, but also the negation of who the dominant discourse tells us we are in society. Personal meaning, interpretation, self-social-cultural understanding and expression, as well as a wider knowledge of the world should come first in the conceptualization of music education" (Schmidt, 2002a, p. 9).

What kinds of changes constitute a transformation? According to Lamb (1996), teachers are reluctant to consider their own transformation, since that would involve critical reflection on their part and a willingness to open themselves to new realities. Schmidt (2001) writes, "Music teachers talk about the 'creative process' but when it gets down to the week before performance, product is always [the] bottom line. In a broader educational view testing and uniform assessment place learning plans in jeopardy. How to bring to terms a societal movement towards specialization of activities and knowledge, and critical understanding and perception of the world" is an important question (p. 25). What it comes down to is that if any change is to take place, students as well as their teachers must be fully engaged in a process of conscientization, or as Freire states, "of becoming critically conscious of the sociohistorical world in which one intervenes or pretends to intervene politically" (Macedo, 1994, p. xi–xii.)

Critical Pedagogy for Music in Action

McCarthy (2000) writes that education can only be effective if the learning is associated with a creative act, thus exercising the critical comprehension of the experience. Since schools are cultural and political spheres, they actively engage in the production of both cultural and societal norms, values, knowledge, and language. As such, it becomes necessary to examine music in education, and in particular, the role of music education in the formation of cultural ideals, attitudes, practices, and behaviors (Rose, 1990). According to Giroux (1983), schools are social sites with dual curricula—one overt and formal, the other hidden and informal. Additionally, if music education is to enable and empower students to be informed and critical thinkers, active creators and caring makers of their own cultural history, then it must look to both the implicit *and* explicit; the internal *and* external understandings, meanings and practices of music in education. According to Rose (1990), it is only through the process of developing a critical consciousness of music education that we can truly comprehend both the powers and possibilities of change, transformation, and emancipation that are inherent within music as an art form and within music in education (p. 26). Critical pedagogy seeks to identify possibilities in the classroom by offering schema to connect word to world, and by its unyielding urgency of transformation. It broadens the tenets of critical theory beyond the realm of critical thinking through problem posing and dialogue.

Critical pedagogy yields what Gates (1999) calls critically reflective musicianship. Critical pedagogy encourages students to become mindful of the musical results they are producing. "Values develop," Gates writes, "alongside knowledge and skill, and all these become the personal possession of each student and the collective possession of the society they are in the daily process of creating" (p. 17). Since music reflects thought and emotion (Langer, 1953; Meyer, 1957), it is as empowering as it is powerful; and as such, music provides the tools of language whereby emotion can be expressed in nonverbal ways. In this manner music connects to the realities of both individuals and communities who search for social change (Schmidt, 2002a).

Our definitions of our own personal culture's music and the culture in which we live are decisions of individual choice. These definitions, along with the music we identify as important to teach, can pose some controversial questions. Seeking answers, I asked my college music education students, who had completed two years of university study, if they were to teach students from a non-Western culture the music of the United States, what would constitute the musical literature selected for study? Would it be the folk songs from childhood? If so, whose songs? Would it be the spirituals from an enslaved South or the work songs of the Old West? Would they choose the lullabies from the "old country" their grandmothers sang to them, or might they choose jazz? How many would choose repertoire from the American musical theater? Would they select music by American composers, such as George Gershwin, Aaron Copeland, or Charles Ives? Perhaps it would it be barbershop, an indigenous musical form sung by a quartet of men traditionally designed to romance their girl; or hip hop, rap, and grunge music from the American urban neighborhoods that are popular among the American youth today.

On the same day as the Live 8 concerts that took place in Philadelphia and seven other cities around the world, I attended an American Independence Day concert at Longwood Gardens, a botanical garden just outside of Philadelphia. The concert was presented by a local community band before an audience of nearly 1,000 people. Most were Caucasian and appeared to be over 70 years old. The concert opened with the national anthem, followed by the march from *Raiders of the Lost Ark* by the contemporary film composer John Williams. The band played a Scott Joplin rag, and an arrangement of the American folk song "Shenandoah." They included a medley of music popularized during World War II by the Glenn Miller Band, and a medley of songs representing the various armed forces, where veterans in the audience and in the band stood and were applauded. This was followed by music from the American musical *West Side Story* by Leonard Bernstein, and an arrangement of "America the Beautiful." The traditional Sousa march "The Stars and Stripes Forever" concluded the program. During the final piece, towers of water sprung from fountains across the back of the stage. It brought the audience to their feet for a standing ovation.

While the older audience clearly enjoyed the concert at Longwood Gardens, it was promising to know that the Live 8 event, just miles away, was being enjoyed by nearly a million people, and Americans of all ethnicities were being linked by satellite to people all over the world in an effort to raise awareness for devastating conditions in Africa, during the same weekend when Americans celebrated their independence. This poses a good question for music educators as to what music defines American culture these days. It would be disappointing if children from varying parts of the world define American culture as a result of singing "Down in the Valley," a children's song that was sung by cowboys of the developing West, or the patriotic music in the program at Longwood Gardens. Many are offended by the lyrics of hip hop and rap and would be reluctant to claim it as the definitive music of American culture.

As advocates for music education begin to look more closely at the links between culture and music, ideals that detach music from its cultural context are being discarded in favor of a philosophy that is praxial. The profession's normative view of praxis emphasizes the relationship of culture to musical learning, particularly the understanding of cultural practices through music performance. To this end, music education serves to support culture, just as the reciprocal aim of culture is learning (Johnson, 2004). The disconnect, according to Allsup (2003), between the music children are taught in school and the recreational music students discover at home is in need of repair.

Musicing Freire

How might that multicultural experience presented to children at the opening of this chapter appear when viewed through the lens of a Freirian approach to Critical Pedagogy for Music Education? When my colleague Lynnel (Jenkins & Abrahams, 2006) teaches the lesson content described in the opening paragraph of this chapter, she uses strategies (Abrahams & Head, 2005) that are rich in Freirian ideals. She begins by asking students to bring a recording to class of a song that best defines who they are. Several students play their recordings and she engages students in a dialogue that explains how they frame their own being through the music they choose to hear. She engages their musical imaginations and honors their world. The discussions are significant and she learns quite a bit about her students, helping her to contextualize their social and cultural capitals as well as their collective habitus (Bourdieu, 1977). Next, she sings for them the song, "Tomati So, So, So, So" (a piece from her African heritage) and shares her experiences as a teacher in Kimberley, South Africa, where the children there taught her the song. The students learn an accompanying rhythmic pattern and learn to play the patterns on African drums. Lynnel takes this opportunity to teach the concept of ostinato—the phenomenon when a rhythmic or melodic pattern is repeated over and over. Then, using constructivist strategies, Lynnel challenges the children to find all of the musical devices they can in the song. This calls on the children to connect their world to the concept discussed in class and to engage their musical intellect. She has a map on the chalkboard of all the words that come to mind when they think about this music, as well as the music they brought to class. Then, in groups, the children write a rap using those words. After they are finished writing, the children choose African drums and other percussion instruments to accompany the original raps. This is both a creative step and a transition back to the world outside the classroom. In the end, the children perform for each other, engaging their musical creativity and celebrating their musical accomplishments through performance. All of the learning tasks are authentic, in that they mirror those steps composers follow when engaged in the act of their own professional music making. This is what Elliott (1995) and Small (1998) call musicing. This engagement with music as text becomes empowering and the conduit through which students read (in Freirean terms) or music the world.

Conclusion

Critical Pedagogy for Music Education yields what Gates (1999) calls critically reflective musicianship. Critical pedagogy encourages students to become mindful of the musical results they are producing. "Values develop," Gates writes, "alongside knowledge and skill, and all these become the personal possession of each student and the collective possession of the society they are in the daily process of creating" (p. 17). Since music reflects thought and emotion (Langer, 1953; Meyer, 1957), it is as empowering as it is powerful; and as such, music provides the tools of language whereby emotion can be expressed in nonverbal ways. In this manner, music connects to the realities of both individuals and communities who search for social change (Schmidt, 2002b).

McCarthy (2000) writes that education can only be effective if the learning is associated with a creative act, thus exercising the critical comprehension of the experience. Since schools are cultural and political spheres, they actively engage in the production of both cultural and societal norms, values, knowledge, and language. As such, it becomes necessary to examine music in education, and in particular, the role of music education in the formation of cultural ideals, attitudes, practices, and behaviors (Rose, 1990). According to Giroux (1983), schools are social sites with dual curricula—one overt and formal, the other hidden and informal. Additionally, if music education is to enable and empower students to be informed and critical thinkers, active creators and caring makers of their own cultural history, then it must look to both the implicit *and* explicit; the internal *and* external understandings, meanings and practices of music in education. According to Rose (1990), it is only through the process of developing a critical consciousness of music education that we can truly comprehend both the powers and possibilities of change, transformation, and emancipation that are inherent within music as an art form and within music in education (p. 26). Critical pedagogy seeks to identify possibilities in the classroom by offering schema to connect word to world and by its unyielding urgency of transformation. It broadens the tenets of critical theory beyond the realm of critical thinking through problem posing and dialogue.

Freire has much to offer music education, and Critical Pedagogy for Music Education is one means to bring Freirian pedagogy inside music classrooms. In *Pedagogy of the City*, Paulo Freire (1993) said that while education is not a lever for the transformation of society, it could be. Music education as it is currently delivered in many schools is not a lever for the transformation of children and their teachers; however, they could and should be. Curricula in music education should come as a result of students sharing their own cultural heritages when they teach their classmates and their teachers about who they are and how their own musical backgrounds fit into the larger world. Such a dialogic approach encourages students to come to terms with who they are and invites the other students and their teacher to share in that reality. Such a view of music education provides a conduit for children and their teachers to understand the world.

Critical pedagogy is an appropriate framework for music education. Its mission is to use knowledge to effect a change of perception for both the students and their teacher. For music education, a critical pedagogy approach to lesson planning and curriculum empowers teachers and their students to resist the hegemonic practices of music education in schools and of schooling itself. Finally, Critical Pedagogy for Music Education as a best teaching practice fosters transformational experiences that will move music education in the schools from the peripheral to a more worthy place in the center of all learning experiences.

References

Abrahams, Frank. "Critical Pedagogy for Music Education: A Best Practice to Prepare Future Music Educators." *Visions of Research in Music Education*, 7, no. 7 (2006).

———. "Transforming Classroom Music Instruction with Ideas from Critical Pedagogy." *Music Educators Journal*, 92, no. 1 (2005): 62–67.

Abrahams, Frank, and Paul D. Head. *Case Studies in Music Education*. 2nd ed. Chicago: GIA, 2005.

Allsup, Randall Everett. "Transformational Education and Critical Music Pedagogy: Examining the Link between Culture and Learning." *Music Education Research*, 5, no. 1 (2003): 5–12.

———. "Activating Self-Transformation through Improvisation in Instrumental Music Teaching." *Philosophy of Music Education Review*, 5, no. 2 (1997): 80–85.

Apple, Michael. *Education and Power*. Boston: Routledge & Kegan Paul, 1982.

Bourdieu, Pierre. "The Forms of Capital." In *Handbook of Theory and Research for Sociology of Education*, edited by J. Richardson, 241–158. New York: Greenwood Press, 1987.

———. *Outline of a Theory of Practice*. Cambridge: Cambridge University Press, 1977.

Bowles, Samuel, and Herbert Gintis. *Schooling in Capitalist America*. New York: Basic Books, 1976.

Bowman, Wayne. "The Problem of Aesthetics and Multiculturalism in Music Education." *Canadian Music Educator*, 34, no. 5 (1993): 1–15.

Center on Education Policy. "NCLB: Narrowing the Curriculum?" Washington, DC: Center on Education Policy, 2005.

Eisner, Elliot. *The Educational Imagination: On the Design and Evaluation of School Programs*. 3rd ed. Upper Saddle River, NJ: PrenticeHall, 2002.

Elliott, David. J. *Music Matters: A New Philosophy of Music Education*. New York: Oxford University Press, 1995.

Freire, Paulo. *Pedagogy of Freedom*. Boston: Rowman & Littlefield, 1998.

———. *Pedagogy of the City*. New York: Continuum, 1993.

———. *The Politics of Education*. New York: Bergin & Garvey, 1985.

———. *Education for Critical Consciousness*. New York: Herder and Herder, 1973.

————. *Pedagogy of the Oppressed*. New York: Continuum, 1970.

Gates, J. Terry. "Action for Change in Music Education: The Mayday Group Agenda." In *Music Education as Praxis: Reflecting on Music-Making as Human Action*, edited by Marie McCarthy, 14–25. College Park: University of Maryland, 1999.

Giroux, Henry. "Public Philosophy and the Crisis in Education." *Harvard Educational Review*, 54, no. 2 (1983).

Gramsci, Antonio. *Selections from the Prison Notebooks of Antonio Gramsci*. Edited by Q. Hoare & G. Smith. New York: International Publishers, 1971.

Habermas, Jurgen. *Lifeworld and System: A Critique of Functionalist Reason*. Englewood Cliffs, NJ: PrenticeHall, 1982.

Jenkins, Lynnel Joy, and Frank Abrahams. *Best Teaching Practices in Music Education*. Princeton: Rider University, 2006.

Johnson, Bob L., Jr. "A Sound Education for All: Multicultural Issues in Music Education." *Educational Policy*, 18, no. 1 (2004): 116–41.

Kincheloe, Joe L. *Critical Pedagogy*. New York: Peter Lang, 2005.

Lamb, Roberta. "Feminism as Critique in Philosophy of Music Education." In *Critical Reflections on Music Education: Proceedings of the Second International Symposium on the Philosophy of Music Education*, edited by Lee R. Bartel & David J. Elliott, 237–63. Toronto: Canadian Music Education Research Centre, 1996.

————. "Feminist Pedagogy in Music Education." *Theory into Practice* 35, no. 2 (1996): 124–31.

Langer, Suzanne K. *Feeling and Form: A Theory of Art*. New York: Scribner, 1953.

Macedo, Donaldo P. *Literacies of Power: What Americans Are Not Allowed to Know*. Boulder, CO: Westview Press, Inc, 1994.

McCarthy, Bernice. *About Teaching: 4mat in the Classroom*. Wauconda, IL: About Learning, Inc., 2000.

————. *The 4mat System: Teaching to Learning Styles with Right and Left-Mode Techniques*. Barrington, IL: Excel, 1987.

McLaren, Peter. *Life in Schools: An Introduction to Critical Pedagogy in the Foundations of Education*. 4th ed. Boston: Allyn & Bacon, 2002.

————. "Che: The Pedagogy of Che Guevara: Critical Pedagogy and Globalization Thirty Years after Che." *Cultural Circles*, 3 (1998): 29–103.

Meyer, Leonard B. *Style and Music Theory, History, and Ideology*. Philadelphia: University of Pennsylvania Press, 1989.

————. *Emotion and Meaning in Music*. Chicago: University of Chicago Press, 1957.

Ouchi, William. G., and Alfred M. Jaeger. "Type Z Organization: Stability in the Midst of Mobility." *Academy of Management Review* (1978): 305–14.

Regelski, Thomas A. *Teaching General Music in Grades 4–8: A Musicianship Approach*. New York: Oxford University Press, 2004.

————. "Critical Theory as a Basis for Critical Thinking in Music Education." *Studies in Music from the University of Western Ontario*, 17 (1998): 1–19.

Rose, Andrea M. "Music Education in Culture: A Critical Analysis of Reproduction Production and Hegemony." University of Wisconsin, 1990.

Schmidt, Patrick. "Looking for a Broader Road: College Music Education Curriculum through Social Lenses." Paper presented at the MayDay Group, Columbus, OH, 2002a.

————. "Music Education as Liberatory Practice: Creating New Frameworks for Learning Music through a Freirian Perspective." Paper presented at the Paulo Freire Institute, Los Angeles, CA, 2002b.

————. "The Applications of a Dialoguing and Problem Posing Pedagogy for the Teaching of History and Philosophy of Music Education to Graduate Music Education Majors: An Action Research." Westminster Choir College of Rider University, 2001.

Small, Christopher. *Musicking: The Meanings of Performing and Listening*. Middletown, CT: Wesleyan University Press, 1998.

Wallace, Ruth A., and Alison Wolf. *Contemporary Sociological Theory: Expanding the Classical Tradition*. 6th ed. Upper Saddle River, NJ: PrenticeHall, 1999.

Wink, Joan, and LeAnn G. Putney. *A Vision of Vygotsky*. Boston: Allyn & Bacon, 2001.

Woodford, Paul G. "Transfer in Music as Social and Reconstructive Inquiry." In *On the Sociology of Music Education*, edited by Roger Rideout, 43–54. Norman: University of Oklahoma, 1997.

CHAPTER 13

Reflections on the Violence of High-Stakes Testing and the Soothing Nature of Critical Pedagogy

VALERIE J. JANESICK

Introduction

Violence is so omnipresent in contemporary society that we may overlook it when it is staring us in the face. Television, movies, popular magazines, advertising, the Internet sites, some rap recordings, and PlayStation games, to name a few areas of violence, are filled with moments, if not hours, of scenes depicting violence. Many argue that because violence is so regular and relentless, we have trained ourselves to be numb in the face of violence. In this paper I wish to discuss the violence of high-stakes testing as one form of violence staring us in the face. In this volume of essays, each writer is connecting to the question of how we have evolved after a generation of critical pedagogy. Thus I will also discuss that on the one hand, in the case of high-stakes testing, critical pedagogy has been pushed to the margins. On the other hand, critical pedagogy can be thought of as the framework behind and inspiration for a grassroots movement, led by citizens such as Monty Neill at www.fairtest.com, which has developed across the U.S. and which is demanding assessment reform. Thus we have two orientations operating simultaneously. As a result there is no end to the information available in print and nonprint media on the topic of high-stakes testing, assessment reform, and authentic assessment. In fact, the World Wide Web has so many sites devoted to critiques of high-stakes testing, data showing the harm of high-stakes testing, sites for assessment reform state by state, and authentic assessment techniques to replace the faltering high-stakes testing approach, that I will only be able to describe and explain the context of the top sites to clarify how critical pedagogy is alive and well today.

Why is High-Stakes Testing a Form of Violence?

The term violence, as defined in the dictionary, lists as one definition "injury by distortion, infringement, or profanation." When we look at the many cases of one-shot high-stakes testing advocated by the government through the No Child Left Behind (NCLB) Act, there is no alternative but to call this violence. Distortion of the reporting of scores to secure money from the government, the infringement on actual class time and curriculum for study, and the profanation of and arrogance about the use of class time for drilling for the test all converge to elucidate the violence of high-stakes testing. The emotional pain and cost of the stress of testing have also been documented in the literature (see Horn & Kincheloe, 2001; Janesick, 2006; Kohn, 2000; McNeil, 2000; Meier, 2000; Minkin, 2004; Ohanian, 1999). It is amazing to me that, as educators, we speak about creating a caring environment in our schools, yet we often behave in another manner when it comes to high-stakes testing.

Since the 1990s, I have been increasingly concerned about the continuing emphasis on high-stakes testing despite what we know of its harmfulness and biases. Furthermore, the systemic attack on public education which began in the 1980s with the Reagan administration has not abated. In fact, it has intensified as a corporate model of profiteering and has replaced an emphasis on learning, child development studies, and research which clearly shows how disadvantaged populations in particular have suffered due to high-stakes standardized tests. Of course, if we assume that schools reflect society, one only has to look around at the politics of the day. I have written earlier (2006) that it is no wonder that schools are being cast as mini-corporations with a one-size-fits-all model of education and testing. Intrusion into the field of education is easy for politicians who act as bullies under the guise of leaving no child behind. Look at this vignette recently reported in the *St. Petersburg Times* (Florida) of February 10, 2005, written by Lane De Gregory. It is captured here as an indication of the violence and depravity of high-stakes testing. A lengthier description and explanation can be found in Janesick (2006):

> The title reads "For sick kids FCAT just another exam." Here we learn about George Purvis Jr. who is in a small room on the hospital's fifth floor. Injured in a biking accident, he must drag himself to take the 10th grade Florida Comprehensive Assessment Test, FCAT, even though he cannot hold a No. 2 pencil required for the test. Luckily he is a creative fellow as he used tape to wrap around the pencil until he could grasp the pencil to fill in the 54 bubbles on the test paper. Of course he had to ignore the violent spasms in his back and literally scratch out an essay with his weakened left hand. Did you know this fact? Each year in Florida, many sick and injured kids take the FCAT: kids on dialysis, kids in casts, with transplants, a new bone marrow, broken necks, kids with Chemo drips and kids crippled with burns. George Purvis has made significant strides in his reha-

bilitation. He no longer needs a diaper or a wheel chair. He stumbles in the shower and his dad ties his shoes. When he took his FCAT, he piled the tape around the pencil two inches thick and one inch long.

His test taking event totally exhausting him, he returns to the hospital bed to rest and await the next battery of tests in two weeks.

Keep this case in mind as we wind through this essay and think about alternatives to high-stakes testing, grounded in critical pedagogical practice.

As a result of dissatisfaction with typical tests, high-stakes testing, and an emphasis on rote and repetition in classrooms indicating a misplaced nostalgia for the olden days, many professionals, researchers, and educators began to ask questions in the 1980s and 1990s (Wiggins, 1993, 1998) and onwards about a better way to assess student work. Consequently, the authentic assessment movement evolved and is alive and well today. Educators and researchers relentlessly began to concentrate on authentic assessment to see whether students could explain, apply, and critique their own responses and justify the answers they provided. In addition, authentic assessment is dynamic and looks at what students should be able to do and continually learn and how students progress through their studies. It is most like the process in the arts with critique, feedback, redirection, and reconstruction. Authentic assessment stands in contrast to typical tests. Typical tests are known by the following traits:

Characteristics of Typical Tests

1. Usually require one and only one correct response, and this only on a particularly assigned day decided upon by bureaucrats;
2. Usually are disconnected from the learner's environment;
3. Usually are constructed by a bureaucrat removed from the learner's environment;
4. The test maker may, in fact, not be knowledgeable about or trained in the field in which questions are being constructed;
5. Usually are simplified for ease in scoring;
6. Provide a one-shot, one-time score.

Many educators were dissatisfied with this approach to testing and evaluating students. Thus a new way of defining and viewing assessment took shape. This new approach is called authentic assessment.

What is Authentic Assessment and How Does It Encompass Critical Pedagogy?

There are numerous books and articles on authentic assessment. Many writers have devoted their lives to examining assessment, offering strong criticism for standardized tests, and giving reasonable alternatives to uniform standardized tests. Writers such as Grant

Wiggins, Alfie Kohn, Joe Kincheloe, Ray Horn, and Susan Ohanian have numerous books and articles on authentic assessment. Wiggins (1998) suggests the following standards for authentic assessment which many in our field concur with. An Assessment Task is authentic when:

1. It is realistic. Thus, the assessment task should follow closely the ways in which a person's abilities are "tested" in the real world. For example, as a former dancer, in ballet class I practiced dance exercises such as pliés, jetés, turns, exercises, etc. But these are merely exercises. The realistic assessment task would be found in the actual performance of the ballet. In the ballet *Swan Lake*, as a cast member, I was forced to show what I could do. This is a realistic test, an authentic assessment measure.

2. It requires judgment and innovation. Here the learner must use knowledge and skills to solve problems. In addition the learner has to present a rationale for the judgments made.

3. It asks the student to "do" the subject. Back to the ballet dancer, the dancer must put all the steps together and perform a role in an actual ballet. This includes the whole person, emotions, thoughts, feelings, and all.

4. It replicates or simulates actual "tests" in the workplace, personal life, and civic life. Since each learner is at a unique stage of growth and development at any given time, you can easily see why authentic assessment is more sensible than contrived standardized tests. For one thing, one size does not fit all learners. Common sense surely indicates this.

5. It assesses the student's ability and skills to effectively and efficiently use a repertoire of many skills to complete a problem or task. In terms of accessing more than verbal or mathematical skills, authentic assessment relies on all the many intelligences a person can develop.

6. It allows many opportunities to practice, rehearse, consult, get feedback, and refine actual performances and productions. Thus we have performance, feedback, performance revision, feedback, performance, etc. In other words, students must learn something and get better at doing the task at hand. In many ways this is like the artist who has constant critique for improvement. To use dance as an example once again, after each performance the director of a ballet or performance piece typically reads "critique notes." Thus, built in to the concept of feedback is the assumption that the learner will work to improve the next performance test.

The reason authentic assessment is important is obvious. Every teacher is forced to assess the achievement and progress of learners. Since teachers deal with assessment issues constantly, educators in every arena want to find a realistic, workable, authentic system of assessment. The basic tenets of authentic assessment are congruent with and exemplify the critical pedagogy discussed in this text. A person who puts into action the tenets of critical pedagogy is often a person who uses the tools of authentic assessment. These include but are not limited to critical thinking, emancipatory thinking, dialectical thinking, higher-order thinking skills, and viewing each student as a thinking, human caring person. I have often thought that a person who practices critical pedagogy in action is also a critical public intellectual. As a public intellectual I have learned from critical pedagogy that every educational activity is also a moral ethical activity and is also an opportunity to empower any learner or any teacher.

Some examples of authentic assessment techniques which reflect critical pedagogy include but are not limited to portfolios which exhibit what a learner can do at various stages of learning; journal writing to show what a student has learned; constructing videos, CDs, or other electronic media vehicles; mentor-protégé evaluations; peer evaluations; staging a performance; or dance, drama, poetry, photography, and all forms of narrative artistic expression, to name a few. By showing what a learner can do, we go beyond the drill-and-repetition method for schooling and society. There are many authentic tasks that can be developed for the purposes of the critical pedagogy practitioner. The point is that teachers and learners together demonstrate on a regular basis that one size fits few, and there are multiple ways of knowing our world.

On the Soothing Nature of Critical Pedagogy and Grassroots Citizens in Action

When I think of critical pedagogy I think of how soothing it is to know that because of critical pedagogy, I can counter the violent effects of high-stakes testing by offering a valuable alternative, that of authentic assessment. Not only that, but organized groups of citizens coming together to demand assessment reform in schools and therefore in society are alive and well and very active today, contributing to this soothing nature. There is a grassroots movement of parents, educators, and students concerned about these issues, and the organization responsible for this is FAIRTEST. This group, composed of subgroups from each and every state of the U.S., has raised these serious questions to a wide audience through their web site, www.fairtest.org. This web site offers the history of the standards movement, reform movement, testing movement, and criticism of those movements. It also catalogues the activities of the states which are members of the ARN, Assessment Reform Network. States are listed and evaluated as to what level of high-stakes testing is being done and how citizens have organized to fight this mindless and rampant testing. Particularly, for example, in California, Ohio, and Iowa, citizens fight high-stakes testing by removing students from the classroom on those high-stakes testing days, writing letters to the editor, and holding meetings in public places to confront administrators about the ethics of standards and testing. On the Ohio website, a list of activities is described, such as organizing a march on the legislature. In fact, FAIRTEST lists samples of letters to editors, descriptions and accounts of meetings, and how to get organized in your state. Do look at this web site, for it offers all of us examples of actual citizens coming together to build community through showing their deep concern for education. By doing so, critical pedagogy is also critical action.

With FAIRTEST as the leader in monitoring what goes on nationally, it was not long before students also joined the discussion. In fact, students own and operate the site Students Against Testing, with the address of www.nomoretests.com. For example, if you check this site you will see that the students have a section on the site with a listing of 100 things to do INSTEAD of standardized testing. I will not list all 100 activities, but to name a few they describe writing your autobiography, designing your own web page, building your own furniture, dissecting and rebuilding a computer, taking a bike trip, interviewing your school janitor, helping someone, interviewing a community member and doing an oral history project, reading the newspaper, and making history. The students who work on this site also use humor to teach about what has gone wrong with standardized tests. In fact, they spoof testing with their own "Best Standardized Test EVER." Here are a few examples from the spoof page.

1. The "Texas Miracle" proved that:
   a. Country music makes kids smarter
   b. All we need to do is kick out the low scoring and minority students
   c. Testing is the same as learning
   d. Y'all can't think for y'allselves
2. The scores of students most accurately reveal:
   a. Their parent's income
   b. Their ability to learn and explore the world
   c. The number of nose hairs they have
   d. How many doses of Prozac they were given the week before
3. True or False (and nothing in between!)
   _____ In the end, we need tests to hold schools accountable
   _____ The 4th Grade MCAS exam is longer than the Massachusetts Bar Exam [true]
   _____ There's nothing I can do to change the testing craze in our schools
   _____ Tests are graded accurately and carefully by well-trained staff at testing corporations
   _____ One day, you'll discover the reason you had to take so many tests

EXTRA CREDIT: (hint: you just might get even more state money if you do this!)

1. Create your own educational system.
2. List everything you'd do right now if you didn't have to take this or any other test.

Obviously, you can see they are tapping into their humorous creative side, given these examples. On the other hand, they have diligently scoured databases to list, for example, the organizations opposed to high-stakes testing, much like the ARN has done. They have also summarized the research around high-stakes testing and its problems to make it understandable to students and parents who may be prompted to act on the information.

It is really amazing to me that government employees and businessmen have the audacity to meddle in the work of professional educators, and in that process demean and criticize the nearly entirely female workforce. Would they do this in the field of Medicine or Law, for example? Would they try to do this in Engineering or the Arts? The fact is that the field of Education is easy to pick on. The reverie these sometimes-critics revert to in terms of how good the "good old days were" is astonishing when you look at the evidence. Were there ever any good old days? In addition, the media seem to love stories about failures in public schools. Is it not surprising that the failures in private schools receive little, if any, press coverage? For example, in a recent situation in the state of Florida, a faith-based private charter-type school was found to be ludicrously wanton in use of public funds, with nothing to show for it. The empty promise of higher achievement was not met, and in fact the students in this publicly funded private venture actually were described as below standard. Oddly enough, this particular case in Florida was only covered by the local news media on a regular basis and only once covered on CNN. The CNN report was brief and nondescriptive. This is not surprising given the planned attack on public education which began in the Ronald Reagan era of the 1980s. Reagan and his paid employees and subsequent leaders to the present day have attempted to:

1. Denigrate public education in order to move toward an agenda of privatization and corporatization of public schools;
2. Erase the U. S. Department of Education, which met with such opposition that Reagan and his boys had to give this one up—but I imagine this will be returning;
3. Develop an ongoing agenda of failure stories rather than success stories about public education, and at the same time, report little on private schools and their failures—check out your daily newspapers to see if there are any education success stories;
4. Use high-stakes testing as the only measure of effectiveness, and when this itself was found problematic, dumb down the test to appear that more students were passing the tests, or—as in the case of students dropping out of schools—simply falsely report the number of dropouts;
5. Marginalize people and programs which offered solid evidence of the waste of high-stakes testing; for example the web-scrubbing by the Bush Administration of the ERIC database of educational research in April, 2002, which basically erased all the research which "does not agree with the administration's policy on education and testing"; furthermore, in remarkably poor taste, the Bush team members went on to actually name researchers and label them as "unscientific," despite the fact that those researchers did meticulous "scientific" work;
6. Remove teachers from actually teaching the subject matter of the curriculum in order to prep for high-stakes testing and live by the corporate creed of, "You pass the test, you get the big money, and if not we publicize and name your schools as failures";
7. Use high-stakes tests as a cover-up for what is really going on with dropouts, special-needs learners, minority students, and children whose native language is not English;

8. Foist on the public the erroneous belief that more tests make better schools, despite no evidence of this;

9. Cover up the reporting of the profits and sometimes conflicts of interest of individuals and companies which make millions of dollars from the testing business, such as in Florida, where the Florida test (FCAT) was owned and operated by Neil Bush, the brother of the governor of Florida, and after an uproar the test was sold to Macmillan, where his mother sits on the board;

10. Deny research which shows clearly all the problems earlier described with high-stakes testing and its effects; in other words, denial trumps science;

11. Attempt to lead the public into thinking that one size fits all when it comes to testing;

12. Along with this, attempt to paint all regions of the U.S.—Northeast, Southeast, Deep South, Southwest, West, Northwest, North Central, and Midwest—as equal in terms of curricula;

13. Cause states to lower the bar for testing requirements.

Sadly, even with the voices of those who write about the problems with high-stakes testing, the public is largely unaware of what is the nature and harm of high-stakes testing. Likewise and not surprising, the public is largely unaware of authentic assessment and critical pedagogy. In the meantime, hopeful signs continue to spring up that states which have experienced the violence of high-stakes testing are taking control of their lives and saying, "No more of this." If you go to the FAIRTEST site, you may be interested in web links to those sites from the states that are fighting the violence of high-stakes testing.

For example, The Florida Coalition for Assessment Reform (FCAR). At www.fcar.org, you find the historical record for monitoring, exposing weaknesses, and publicizing the problems with high-stakes testing and the NCLB law. Members of FCAR work to do the following:

1. Monitor the uses and abuses of the FCAT;

2. Advocate for Florida's children;

3. Promote public policies that support constructive, authentic assessment;

4. Increase public awareness of alternatives to high-stakes testing;

5. Publicize the onerous burdens and the negative effects of NCLB.

So you can see why there is hope in the quagmire. Similarly, the state of Ohio has a site constructed by activist educators and parents at www.stophighstakestesting.org, also called www.stopopts.com, which is focused on its title, Stop the Ohio Proficiency Tests. At this sophisticated site, citizens may find sample letters to send to Congress, businessmen, and particular textbook companies which have recently changed textbooks to match the state tests, thus insuring a brain-dead student population. These textbook makers do not allow for the use of creativity or imagination in the learning process. Sadly, they have trivialized learning for children by reducing schooling to memorizing facts, drilling for the facts, and trying to get that one right answer. Thus, the books and tests are actually formulated to keep children from exercising critical and higher-order thinking skills.

To use just one more example, let us turn to the state of California. California educators and citizens organized the comprehensive site of www.calcare.org, where you will find that this Coalition for Authentic Reform in Education is battling against high-stakes testing, ethical improprieties in the administration and scoring of the standardized SAT-9 test used in California, exposing the harmful effects felt by children, as well as cogently describing the arguments on cultural bias in the test. Furthermore, educators and administrators joined the movement and in fact began a careful process of reviewing textbooks and refusing those textbooks which took a one-size-fits-all approach and which attempted to use only drill-and-repetition as a learning method. California teachers have posted their success stories as well on the site, which clearly demonstrated the value of critical pedagogy.

Thus we see examples of citizens in action across the nation. The common ground of these citizens, state by state, is that they narrate a story of finding feasible alternative courses of action and indicate that the current policy in terms of high-stakes testing is not working. Although most research has been done on minority students, English as a Second Language students, and students with disabilities, high-stakes testing also harms all children. It is through these citizens' initiatives that we find the soothing nature of critical pedagogy. They are not turning back. They are only going forward and I urge you to become active in your state on these issues.

Hope for the future

One might think that because of the notoriety and prevalence of high-stakes testing, it is almost impossible to change this existing situation. Yet, if it were not for high-stakes testing, we may not have seen this rise in citizens' action. As you visit the web sites mentioned in this article, you may be surprised at what you find. Instead of apathy, you will find action. Instead of lack of information and secrecy, you will find openness and mounds of critical data to support authentic assessment and assessment reform to replace the violence of high-stakes testing. Most obvious, you will find that students, teachers, administrators, and parents are no longer bystanders in the educational process. They are active participants. This, it seems to me, is the heart and soul of critical pedagogy. Yes, we have a long way to go. Yes, we cannot afford to lose momentum. Yet, to paraphrase the words of the great philosopher-teacher Lao Tzu, a journey of a thousand miles begins with a single step.

References

Horn, R. and J. L. Kincheloe. (2001) *American Standards: Quality Education in a Complex World, The Texas Case*. New York: Peter Lang Publishing.

Janesick, V. J. (2006) *Authentic Assessment Primer*. New York: Peter Lang Publishing.

Janesick, V. J. (2000) *The Assessment debate: A Reference Handbook*. Santa Barbara, CA: ABC-CLIO Publishers.

Kohn, A. (2000) *The Case against Standardized Testing: Raising the Scores, Ruining the Schools*. Portsmouth, NH: Heinemann.

Kohn, A. (1999) *The Schools Our Children Deserve: Moving Beyond Traditional Classrooms and "Tougher Standards."* Boston: Houghton Mifflin.

McNeil, L. (2000) *Contradictions of School Reform: Educational Costs of Standardized Testing*. New York: Routledge.

Meier, D. (2000) *Will Standards Save Public Education?* Boston: Beacon Press.

Meier, D., A. Kohn, L. Darling-Hammond, T.R. Sizer, & G.Wood. (2004) *Many Children Left Behind: How the NCLB Act is Damaging Our Children and Our Schools*. Boston: Beacon Press.

Minkin, M. (2004) Test Ban Entreaty: An Interview with Alfie Kohn. *Hope Magazine*. Jan-Feb. pp. 1–3.

Ohanian, S. (1999) *One Size Fits Few: The Folly of Educational Standards*. Portsmouth, NH: Heinemann.

Wiggins, G. (1998) *Educative Assessment: Designing Assessments to Inform and Improve Student Performance*. San Francisco: Jossey-Bass Publishers.

Wiggins, G. (1993) *Assessing Student Performance: Exploring the Purpose and Limits of Testing*. San Francisco: Jossey-Bass Publishers.

Websites, listed in order of giving the reader the most information:

1. FAIRTEST, www.fairtest.org

   The National Center for Fair & Open Testing (FAIRTEST) works to end the misuses and flaws of standardized testing and to ensure that evaluation of students, teachers, and schools is fair, open, valid, and educationally beneficial. This organization is a center of information on all aspects of testing. It catalogues the latest action steps taken in every state and reports on coalitions to fight unfair tests. It also contains various fact sheets on the NCLB and offers many solutions for parents, teachers, and students in reference to fair testing. FAIRTEST also has position statements, tracks research on this topic, and offers a sounding board for all persons interested in actually assessing student progress. It focuses on building capacity, not draining capacity. It also has many related links to professional organizations with those organizations' formal statements against high-stakes testing.

2. Alfie Kohn, www.alfiekohn.org

   This site offers books, articles, recent research studies, and key activities and information on assessment reform. In addition, there are key arguments posted for any person to use on the problems of high-stakes testing. Also, links to other sites are available here.

3. Students Against Testing, www.nomoretests.com

   This web site provides updates by students doing research about the perils of over-testing, and provides updates on NCLB. It is a refreshing documentation of student activism from elementary grades through college years. There are databanks, summaries of recent findings on testing and its harmful effects, and creative and refreshing humorous pieces on the perils of high-stakes testing.

CHAPTER 19

Pedagogy of Testimony

Reflections on the Pedagogy of Critical Pedagogy

LUIS HUERTA-CHARLES

El proceso de conscientización ocurre entre sujetos (entre conciencias), y a través de experiencias.

[The conscientization process happens among subjects (among consciences), and through experiences.]

Antón de Schutter (1981)

Through the actual experience of something, we intuitively apprehend its essence; we feel, enjoy and understand it as reality, and we thereby place our own being in a wider, more fulfilling context . . . such an experience . . . is called *vivencia*.

Fals-Borda & Rahman (1991)

En la realidad concreta, las experiencias vividas y las luchas sociales son las que concientizan a las personas, grupos o clases sociales.

[In the concrete reality, the lived experiences and the social struggles conscientize individuals, groups or social classes.]

Anton de Schutter (1981)

This chapter attempts to analyze and share a professor's living testimony regarding teaching *about* and *from* a critical pedagogy perspective in a teacher education program at a major university in the Southwest of the United States. In this teacher education program, critical pedagogy has been integrated as an essential part of its framework and conceptual pillars. Using the framework of the testimonies, this professor's reflections document how prospective and in-service teachers have difficulties in understanding the main concepts of critical pedagogy, as well as how they see this theory as being disconnected from and alien to the practices they perform in the school settings through the practicum and student teaching. Finally, this professor's pedagogy is contextualized as a way of helping teachers to understand critical analyses in order to incorporate them into their actual teaching practices.

Why Critical Pedagogy?

At least during the last two decades, critical pedagogy has been a theoretical and political perspective that has gained, little by little, a place in the educational debate (Apple, 2000a, 2000b, 2006; Doyle & Singh, 2006; Giroux, 1997, 2006a; Kincheloe, 2004; McLaren, 1995, 1998, 2003, 2006). As a way to involve teacher candidates in the pursuit of social justice within society, some colleges of education have integrated critical pedagogy as a major component of the curricular framework for their teacher preparation program (Huerta, Scott, & Horton, 2001). This is important because within the critical pedagogy perspective there is a hope that teachers will become agents of social change.

It is also important because, at the moment, we are living in times of dehumanized neoliberal politics that have brought about suffering to many people and the enrichment of the few; consequently, it is affecting the living conditions of millions of people around the world (Apple, 1998, 1999; Chomsky, 1995,1999; Giroux, 2004, 2005; McLaren, 1998, 2000; Purpel, 1999). These politics are part of a new type of economic relation to production called "new capitalism." It is a new form of capitalism that is immersed in a globalized context, where a new world has been taking shape after the collapse of the socialist alternative.

Bárcena and Mèlich (2000) indicates that this capitalism is also a new form of totalitarianism—as in the ones that Hitler and Stalin built—because one of the main characteristics of totalitarianism is its capacity to pulverize our thinking, judgments, and moral reflective categories while it is manufacturing the public consent. The totalitarian thinking shows itself as the only existing option, and we are seeing this right now when the new capitalism proclaims itself the only alternative to our world (Gee, Hull, & Lankshear, 1996). The new globalized neoliberal capitalism, with all its frightening outcomes, is making more people suffer and creating more unequal societies throughout the world (Dussel, 2002).

This new global and dehumanized capitalism became the dominant force for controlling the world during the 1980s and 1990s. It has constructed a particular, individualist, unhistorical, and social Darwinist worldview, in which harmful effects have been expressed through very concrete politics that are modifying the working conditions in which human beings are been dehumanized; and now, they are not even valuable enough for exploitation, as if they are disposable people (Bales, 1999; Forrester, 1997, 2000). Other concrete effects we have seen in these times include fierce competitions for the markets, an increase in the number of temporary jobs and consequently the elimination of most of the full-time jobs, reduced wages, increasing unemployment, destruction or weakening of unions around the world, less protective labor contracts, and reduction—if not destruction—of the welfare state (Apple, 2000a; Chomsky, 1999; Dussel, 2002; Forrester, 1997, 2000; Gee, Hull, & Lankshear, 1996; McLaren, 1998, 2000, 2006).

It is important to notice that, at the same time that the new capitalism has been transforming the production and working conditions, it has also been manufacturing the public social consent regarding itself, through several discourses, institutions, and social practices in order to make us accept as a "given" reality this kind of capitalism, along with its social inequalities.

For these reasons, it is imperative for us to be aware and willing to fight back against all these situations derived from these unjust neoliberal politics. At the same time, it is why it is important that critical pedagogy becomes part of the teacher's education programs. In using critical pedagogy in the colleges of education, we can prepare teachers to be the agents for constructing a more just and, as Freire (2003, 2004) says, less ugly society; a society based on the ethics of humanization and solidarity, and not on the ethics of the markets. This context makes it crucial for critical educators to try to incorporate this perspective into our classes and into our pedagogy; because we need to have teachers that have the courage to place the preservation of human life as a criterion of truth and ethical action in the midst of this dehumanized and profit-led society (Dussel, 1985, 2002, 2003). It seems that the most revolutionary act in these times is to place the human being as the center of every politics and every action we take as society. As I previously mentioned, there is a growing demonstration from the business world that human beings are now disposable, not even valuables to be exploited. At the same time, these politics of disposability privilege specific groups while trying to dispose of the poor minorities and working-class people (Bales, 1999; Giroux, 2006b), or what Bauman (2004) calls the "wasted humans."

The Dilemma of Critical Pedagogy

Even though critical pedagogy has extended enormously the deep understanding we now have of our world and the ways in which we can transform it, it still has to face a great dilemma if we want to keep applying it in educating teachers to be social change agents: It has to reflect on and modify its pedagogical ways of helping teachers to access its discursive construction. In a study carried out with students from a critical-pedagogy-based teacher education program (Huerta, Scott, & Horton, 2001), students still felt lost after taking several classes based on the foundational principles of this perspective. One student expressed the following view during one of the focus-group interviews we did while conducting this study:

> I took the class last semester, I had to buy and read all the four books that the professor included in the syllabus, but I still do not understand what the heck critical pedagogy is.

Some ended their classes thinking that critical pedagogy would become another subject that they would "have to teach." Other students mentioned that the professors that taught the critical pedagogy classes were not modeling to them, or at least they were not using in the classroom, critical pedagogy in action. Because of all of the doubts the students had regarding the critical pedagogy content, professors lectured on the topic and made them work in small groups without giving closure to the activities. Therefore, instead of giving closure by emphasizing the perspectives of critical pedagogy, the professors gave the students the impression that "anything" goes. Graduate students at the master level, which mainly were in-service teachers, commented that the critical pedagogy's language was so abstract that they could not grasp the meaning of what was taught to them in the classes. One said that:

> Critical pedagogy is for teaching in university classrooms, but in the real world, in our classrooms (the classrooms where they were teaching at that time) we cannot use a single thing from the books.

It is possible that some members of academia may attribute these students' criticisms to their lack of analytical reading skills in developing an understanding of the books content or to alienation they are still being subjected to. Regardless of how we interpret their criticisms, the fact remains that after taking several critical pedagogy classes, these students didn't develop enough insight to think critically and challenge their misconceptions or wrong assumptions. However, if we do not listen to and reflect critically on those kinds of comments and criticisms, we will be forgetting that one of the main purposes of critical pedagogy is helping individuals to achieve conscientization. If we, as critical educators, do not listen to them, we are going to be following the same totalitarian way of thinking that Bárcena and Mèlich (2000) mention above.

These narratives show us something important that we, critical educators, need to reconsider: more and more the language, the theoretical discourse of critical pedagogy is becoming a kind of exclusionary tool that keeps teachers distanced from the possibility of having real experiences with critical practices. Similar criticisms were stated by Apple (2000a, 2000b; Apple & Buras, 2006) when he pointed out that:

> The discourse of critical pedagogy has become too theoretical, abstract, esoteric, and out of touch with the conflicts and struggles that teachers, students, and activists act on. (2000a, p. 247)

Within the critical pedagogy field, some authors have addressed these criticisms, mentioning that this language is necessary in order to offer teachers a new language of hope and possibility. Constructing a new language helps us name reality, and name it differently, in order to be able to transform it. In this debate, Giroux (1992) mentions that teachers are not dumb and they are able to understand the language of critical pedagogy. I have no doubt in their abilities; however, we cannot forget that teachers have been living manipulation processes in schools and at a societal level that deploy onto them a particular way of seeing the world—from a neoliberal perspective—which also molds the understanding they have regarding their own practice. Most of the time they have not had the opportunity, nor the support, for critically thinking about their own practice and the impact it has in changing and shaping a more just society.

In one of the doctoral classes that I taught, I saw the difficulties my students had in understanding basic critical concepts that may look simple to others working in the field of critical pedagogy. In that class we were reading a new book by Apple and Buras (2006), *The Subaltern Speaks*, and I asked my students to read the introduction and the first two chapters for that day. It is important to mention that all of these doctoral students were professionals working in different areas such as justice and health with most of them teaching at different levels. When we started to discuss the readings, one student asked me if I could clarify for her the concept of hegemony and the subaltern that the authors were discussing in the chapters. Several other voices supported her question. That was an indicator for me that most of the class had difficulties understanding the readings. I asked students to raise their hand if they, too, had not grasped the concepts that the other student had asked about. Some of them hesitated to raise their hands as if they were fearful of being exposed in front of the class. I invited them to let me know if I needed to spend more time on those topics or just try to answer the other student's question. I told them that I needed to know if the discussion we were about to have would make sense to them or not. All hands went up telling me that they wanted to understand the concepts because they were fighting with the complexity and abstractness of the discourse.

The students had read the chapters but not understood them. They had tried to establish connections with their previous experiences, but they still had complications in grasping the meaning of these concepts. The student that had asked the question told us that specifically Chapter 2 had made her reflect a lot on her own experience and, at times, disagree or feel angry with the criticisms put forward by the authors. In the chapter the authors talk about homeschooling, women's labor, and the ways in which the Right have captured the discourse of subalternity, allowing conservative and privileged people to place themselves as the "the new oppressed." This student is currently an elementary school teacher, but previously she had homeschooled her own children. Her discomfort in struggling to understand the concepts pushed her to ask more questions in order to make meaning of the main ideas in the reading; and, because she put herself in the front of the discussion, the other students started to engage in the conversation, too.

This situation showed me how my students were engaged in reading and thinking seriously on the readings, but they still needed to clarify the meaning of the ideas. Without thinking that the students are dumb, I recognized that the content was complex and abstract for them because of the apparent lack of previous experiences they had in connection to this theory. At the same time, this situation could become a temptation for the university professor to spend the whole class lecturing and continuing the process of students' domination, reinforcing the perception that we are the "controllers" of the knowledge. In this sense, Fals-Borda and Rahman (1991) state that having the power of controlling which knowledge is valid and *the* way we should approach it, is also a form of oppression that limits people's opportunities of being self-aware of the processes that are oppressing them.

Helping our students understand the structure of the ideas, what is behind the "thing" under analysis, as Kosik (1976) mentions regarding the necessary dialectical thinking for understanding our reality, implies that critical educators must change the relationship we have with our students from one where we are in control of the learning and teaching processes into one that places us in a subject-to-subject relationship of collaboration in constructing knowledge and learning. Taking this risk will help us to face one of the challenges that Freire (2004) presents to us: the need to be congruent, reducing the gap between what we say, talk about, and what we do. In working to be congruent we must recognize that there is an implicit power relationship in everyday situations; for example, we cannot talk about social justice while treating secretaries and custodial staff with disrespect or while ignoring students' contributions and questions during class.

My Pedagogical Experience Using Critical Pedagogy: My Pedagogy of Testimony

In the story I was sharing in the previous section, some of my students engaged in the conversation, putting themselves in the center of the analysis. They were trying to establish connections between the content that was under discussion and their previous experiences and teaching practices. I also was under analysis when I tried to share with them my personal connections; this sharing helped me reconstruct my pedagogy. We as university professors must consider ourselves also as projects (Freire, 2004), as in a state of constant transformation, struggling always to become committed individuals trying to make a better world and a more just society for all. If we do not consider that, we are not being consistent with what Freire (1996, 2003, 2004) indicates is our ontological task: the search for becoming fully human.

It is important to clarify that I did not believe that my pedagogy is just my way of teaching. Instead, my pedagogy involves a worldview where my students and myself are active learners constructing our knowledge, establishing connections between the new knowledge and our previous experiences. That means that I consider my students as colearners and coteachers, because they also teach me how to read their expressions and their understandings without being disappointed when they misunderstand something. For instance, in my classes, I have learned to read my students' facial and bodily expressions when they do not understand what is being discussed. They do not want to show themselves in front of the class as the ones that did not comprehend the readings. For that reason, seeing them restlessly writing notes down during the discussion is an indicator for me that they feel not ready to engage in the conversation. However, instead of feeling frustration for that, I feel compelled to look for alternative ways to engage them in the analyses. I also try to find out if their silence is a creative silence, through which they are making meaning while they observe or are silent during the conversation. In that way, they are also helping me to become a better teacher for them.

My pedagogy is, at the same time, my testimony of how I believe I am constructing a better society. Therefore, my pedagogy goes far beyond the idea of having a set of teaching strategies; it becomes a solid vision of what kind of individual I want to help educate in order to construct a better society. This includes ideas on how to assist the students in becoming agents of social change, supporting them as they acquire dispositions that make them caring and committed individuals that value and respect the other, and consequently fight any kind of discrimination and oppression. Simultaneously, my pedagogy tries to be rigorous about the knowledge my students are learning. As Freire (1998) says, the professional education of teachers requires a solid political preparation, but it also requires a technical-instrumental one because just politically educating teachers is not enough. Nevertheless, for me education involves a political and academic dimension.

In *Teachers as Cultural Workers*, Freire (1998) says that testimonies are the best way of calling students' attention towards the validity of what is presented, towards the firmness of the struggle we are fighting for in constructing a better world. He says that we

> must take advantage of every opportunity to give testimony [of our] commitment to the realization of a better world—a world more just, less ugly and substantially more democratic . . . (Freire, 2004, p. 8)

And he goes further,

> I seek to give testimony of the consistency between what I preach and what I do, between the dream of which I speak and my practice, the faith I embrace and the authentic manner in which, while educating myself with them, I educate them in an ethical and democratic perspective. (p. 13)

At the same time that I offer my students the testimony of my congruence between what I say and what I do through my pedagogy, I also incorporate testimonies from the field of what I have observed and believe are critical practices and opportunities where we miss the critical analysis of our pedagogical practice. Therefore, there are two types of testimonies I share in my classes: one is the personal and the other is from the field. In one hand I hold my personal testimony of being congruent in front of the class by not acting in ways that contradict the ideas I am sharing with them from the class content. This should not be something false, like a play, because students are so intelligent that they can identify when we are pretending to be congruent but at the same time are not walking our talk. In my other hand I hold the testimonies from the field that I share through narratives that tell stories about classrooms and interactions that I have witnessed while connecting with students and colleagues.

Giving personal testimony is complex because at the beginning of the interactions I have to face students' challenges in terms of a content that is making them feel uncomfortable, and on the other hand, challenges about my positioned teaching when I share with them my critical and political perspective for constructing a better world. In one of my classes, for instance, one student told me that she didn't believe that education was political, that I was trying to indoctrinate them toward a specific partisan perspective. The other students were silent because the comment was told using a challenging tone and posture. This became a great opportunity to see if what I was saying about respecting their voices and listening to their opinion as important in the learning process was the truth. They were just looking at me and then back looking to the other student. I asked the student if she could share with us her ideas about education not being political in nature; so that I could better understand where her comments came from. Then, she told us that neither Democrats nor Republicans should interfere with the education of our children in schools, that we should teach them only what the curriculum indicates. Some other students supported her comment saying something like "yeah," or "right." However, that helped me to read what their ideas about politics and education were. They were seeing that connection in the way in which the neoliberal and globalized capitalism makes us think about politics and democracy. If we see education as disconnected from politics, then it could be truth that the NCLB politics are neutral and acting only on behalf of minority students, which I think is not happening in many cases.

I told them that even our most simple actions in our classrooms are political and morally charged. I told them a story from one of the classrooms that I visited when I was observing one of my student-teachers in a Head Start classroom. Having visited the fire station that day, the children were divided into centers where they revolved around firefighters. In the dramatic play area, some children where making a cardboard fire truck, painting it, and pretending to be the firefighters. Just five children were allowed per center. Suddenly, one little Anglo girl came into the dramatic play area and tried to take the helmet off of the head of an African American boy. They started to fight for the helmet: "Give it to me!" "No, I have it first!" My student teacher came into the area and asked them, "Who had it first?" The little boy said, "I had it," and she told the little girl to wait for him to finish playing with it. The little girl moved away into the computer station, but my student stayed with the little boy, telling him that they need to share while they are playing. After 3 minutes of listening to her, the little boy stood up and went to the little girl to give her the helmet. However, the girl told him "I do not want it; besides, you already have a black mask on you." The boy tried to push her for her comment, and the student teacher came again and told her, "That is not nice to say to anyone, you need to say 'I'm sorry' to him." She did that and she moved to another area. I started following her. She went into the block area where she tried to get some wooden blocks; the other children told her, "You are not in this area." Then, she left the blocks on the floor and kicked down the zoo and the road that the other kids were building. The children started calling the teacher and she said, "I'm sorry, I'm sorry" and moved to another area.

After that story, my testimony from the field, several students started to point out that the little girl was learning that saying "I'm sorry" was enough for justifying any wrong action she was doing. At this moment the students began to see that curriculum and teachers' actions are not neutral. They also indicated that even with the most simple of our everyday actions we are shaping the beliefs and prejudices of the future citizens of our country. From there I tried to move the analysis to a more global level, to the political nature of education. Without blaming my student teacher for what happened in that classroom, I asked the class if they can imagine what kind of individual we were educating in the story of the little girl. That was the kind of political action I was talking about when I said that education was political and that we need to be aware of our own actions and worldviews and the way in which they influence our teaching practices.

I used a story, a testimony from the field in order to be congruent with the challenging comment that my student had posed in front of the class, as my way of responding to her. After that, I was able to engage in an open and honest conversation with them, because they began to feel comfortable sharing their testimonies from their own practice. Giving testimony implies being congruent with the ideas from the theory and the pedagogy that we are using in our classes. In that way, I tried to make the class reflect on the topic of the political nature of education without openly confronting or putting down my students' ideas. I also read what the other students were teaching me when they supported her comment. I needed to make them think critically and reflect on the global issues of politics and educations through the context of a real situation that happened in a classroom, without undermining my ability to construct a safe environment where they participate and ask questions.

The testimonies from the field are stories, narrative situations that allow us to establish a significant connection between the theory and the practice. Testimonies should promote, among the people listening to and sharing them, a critical praxis that connects action and reflection in order to transform the world. The stories I use have a sequence of events that allow my students to establish a connection between the dialectic of the extraordinary and the ordinary, between what is expected and what came to pass (Bruner, 1990, 1996, 2002). Therefore, I always keep in mind that stories, my testimonies, are not innocent (Bruner, 1996, 2002); in fact they are political because through them I express my perspective, and as Beverley (2005) expresses, my ethical and epistemological stance to my students. I like to think, following Bruner (2002), that narratives are instruments for finding problems, not solving them.

In my testimonies, I promote with my students the necessity to give meaning to our actions and to the world. Testimonies also ask my students to take a posture in front of an unethical or oppressive situation that makes them identify their values before a specific testimony (Beverley, 2005). Taking into account that the testimonies help us make meaning of the world, the stories must help us *name* what we see around us which is not just, such as hunger, passivity, extreme poverty, and silences (Greene, 1995). Through testimonies, students are asked to reject unnecessary human suffering and to struggle for constructing something different by making our voices sound clearly and strongly in order to be heard. In analyzing the testimonies, we get a different perspective; we reflect and imagine that things could be different in order to achieve our freedom, taking control of our own actions in the world. Therefore, stories are windows of opportunities (Clandinin & Connelly, 2000) to reflect critically on the way in which we can change our world.

Testimonies help us as teachers and educators reject and transform what is dehumanizing and alienating us. Using a pedagogy of testimony helps us to connect in a very accessible and simple way—without being simplistic, because oversimplifying the analysis hides the truth (Freire, 2003)—the theory with the practice at micro and macro levels of analysis. In my experience, testimonies bridge the connections between the "abstract" content from university classrooms and the "real world" of schools. In that way, testimonies help me show my students how complex concepts, such as hegemony, subalternity, domination, oppression, and praxis itself, illuminate and happen in our daily actions at our schools and in our personal lives.

Students also share their testimonies when they feel that we have constructed a safe environment for them to show themselves as individuals. This is because testimonies from the practice are personal; sharing their own elaborations requires them to exhibit themselves in front of the whole class. In that way, students are trying to make meaning of the content we are analyzing, connecting it with their previous personal and professional experiences. Therefore, an important part of my pedagogy of testimony is to encourage them to analyze their own testimonies, where they can somehow apply the central knowledge, skills, and attitudes from our class in the analysis of their experiences. In that way, there is hope in that they are going to be able to figure out ways to better serve and help people from minority groups and the communities they are working in.

I also believe that, in analyzing their testimonies, prospective teachers will learn to read and understand their world, and consequently they will be able to help their students in their classes to read theirs (Freire & Macedo, 1987). If we, critical educators, want to change the schools and the ways in which the schooling system oppresses and excludes diverse people from being fully human beings, then we need to make it accessible to the classroom teachers in order to be able to interrupt the right to continue taking over our public schools (Apple, 2006; Apple & Buras, 2006).

A Tentative Closure

Where are we now in the development of critical pedagogy? Even in the light of the tremendous conceptual accomplishments critical pedagogy has achieved, we must continue to develop the critical analyses that are so needed in these times. Critical pedagogy has been developed from a diversity of perspectives (McLaren, 2003; Kincheloe, 2004) with the purpose of facing oppression and any kind of discrimination, in order to put the human being as the center of our ethical commitment towards the oppressed and dispossessed (Dussel, 2002; Freire, 2004), facing the ethics of the free markets.

What needs to be done in these times? I think that we have to consolidate an answer to the essential challenge that Freire (2004) and Apple (2000a, 2000b) presented to critical pedagogy: the necessity of making it simple. Again, let me emphasize that I conceive simple as being different than simplistic, as Freire (2003) clearly indicates. The call to make critical pedagogy simple was a task that Freire (2004) committed himself to. He explicitly stated his commitment toward that task when he wrote the pedagogical letters that integrate the basic text of his *Pedagogy of Indignation*. He said that, in writing the letters, he wanted them to be

> free of arrogance, which intimidate and make communication not viable; of sufficiency, which prevents the sufficient themselves from recognizing their insufficiency; of excessive certainty of being right; of theoristic elitism, full of refusals and ill disposition towards practice. (p. 13)

That has to become one of the main challenges that critical pedagogy has to face in the times to come, especially if we want to face the simplistic and plain-language politics that the Right is deploying into our public schools and through the media. These simplistic politics have been so effective in our daily life that they have manipulated teachers' schools' and communities' common sense, leading them to believe that the results of the standardized tests are really the expressions of educational quality. I am imaging it as a twofold task: on one hand we need to keep developing the critical analyses, but at the same time, on the other hand, we need to keep looking for ways to reach more teachers and people in the communities, making theory accessible enough for engaging them in the analysis of their reality and, with that, helping them to become conscious of their world in order to transform it. Likewise, we have to continue giving testimony of our praxis, of our commitment toward the oppressed and different. In other words, we as critical educators have to be congruent with the theory we are promoting; we have to connect the theory we talk about with our practice. We need to break down the ivory tower of academia and get closer to the teachers and the communities that we serve, which most of the times are the ones that are suffering the harsh effects of the new capitalism.

I want to follow Maxine Greene's idea, because in using testimonies my students and myself

> can see from many vantage points, make sense from different sides. I want us to work together to unconceal what is hidden, to contextualize what happens to us, to mediate the dialectic that keeps us on the edge, that may be keeping us alive. (1995, p. 115)

It is time that we listen again to what Marx expressed in his 11th thesis on Feuerbach: we have interpreted the world in many and varied ways, the point now is to transform it. We have the duty to keep trying and the responsibility to give our testimony of living ethically (Freire, 2004).

References

Apple, M. W. (1998, Spring). Knowledge, pedagogy, and the conservative alliance. *Studies in the Literary Imagination, 31*(1), 5–23.

——— (1999). Between Neo and Post: Critique and transformation in critical educational studies. In C. A. Grant (Ed.), *Multicultural research: A reflective engagement with race, class, gender and sexual orientation* (pp. 54–67). London & Philadelphia: Falmer Press.

——— (2000a). The shock of the real: Critical pedagogies and rightist reconstructions. In P. P. Trifonas. (Ed.) *Revolutionary pedagogies: Cultural politics, instituting education, and the discourse of theory* (pp. 225–250). New York & London: RoutledgeFalmer.

——— (2000b, Spring). Can critical pedagogies interrupt rightist policies? *Educational Theory, 50* (2), 229–254. University of Illinois at Urbana-Champaign.

——— (2004). *Ideology and curriculum* (3rd ed.). New York & London: RoutledgeFalmer.

——— (2006). *Educating the "Right" way: Markets, standards, God, and inequality* (2nd ed.). New York: Routledge.

Apple, M. W. & K. L. Buras. (Eds.). (2006). *The subaltern speaks: Curriculum, power, and educational struggles*. New York: Routledge.

Bales, K. (1999). *Disposable people: New slavery in the global economy*. Berkeley, CA: University of California Press.

Bárcena, F., and Mèlich, J.-C. (2000). *La educación como acontecimiento ético: Natalidad, narración y hospitalidad* [Education as ethical event: Birthrate, narrative and hospitality]. Barcelona, Spain: Paidós.

Bauman, Z. (2004). *Wasted lives: Modernity and its outcasts*. Cambridge, UK: Polity Press.

Beverley, J. (2005). Testimonio, subalternity, and narrative authority. In N. K. Denzin and Y. S. Lincoln (Editors), *The Sage handbook of qualitative research* (3rd, ed.) (pp. 547–557). Thousand Oaks, CA: Sage Publications.

Bruner, J. S. (1990). *Acts of meaning*. Cambridge, MA: Harvard University Press.

——— (1996). *The culture of education*. Cambridge, MA: Harvard University Press.

——— (2002). *Making stories: Law, literature, life*. Cambridge, MA: Harvard University Press.

Chomsky, N. (1999). *Profit over people: Neoliberalism and global order*. New York: Seven Stories Press.

——— (1995). Democracia y mercados en el nuevo orden mundial [Democracy and markets in the new world order]. En N. Chomsky y H. Dieterich. *La sociedad global: Educación, mercado y democracia* (pp. 15–47) [The global society: Education, market and democracy]. Mexico: Joaquin Moritz.

Clandinin, D. J. and F. M. Connelly. (2000). *Narrative inquiry: Experience and story in qualitative research*. San Francisco: Jossey-Bass.

Doyle, C. and A. Singh. (2006). *Reading and teaching Henry Giroux*. New York: Peter Lang.

Dussel, E. (1985). *Philosophy of liberation* (A. Martinez & Ch. Morkovsky, trans.). Eugene, OR :Wipf & Stock.

——— (2002). *Ética de la liberación en la edad de la globalización y de la exclusión* [Ethics of liberation in times of globalization and exclusion]. Madrid, Spain: Editorial Trotta.

——— (2003). *Beyond philosophy: Ethics, history, Marxism, and liberation theology*. (E. Mendieta, Ed.). Lanham, MD: Rowman & Littlefield.

Fals-Borda, O. & M. A. Rahman. (1991). *Action and knowledge: Breaking the monopoly with participatory action-research*. New York: The Apex Press.

Forrester, V. (1997). *El horror económico* [The economic horror]. Buenos Aires, Argentina: Fondo de Cultura Económica.

——— (2000). *Una extraña dictadura* [A strange dictatorship]. Buenos Aires, Argentina: Fondo de Cultura Económica.

Freire, P. (1970/1993). *Pedagogy of the oppressed*. New York: Continuum.

——— (1996). *Pedagogy of hope*. New York: Continuum.

——— (1998). *Teachers as cultural workers: Letter to those who dare teach*. Lanham, MD: Rowman & Littlefield.

——— (2003). *El grito manso* [The gentle cry]. Buenos Aires, ARG: Siglo XXI Editores.

——— (2004). *Pedagogy of indignation*. Boulder, CO: Paradigm Publishers.

——— and D. Macedo. (1987). *Literacy: Reading the word and the world*. Westport, CT: Bergin & Garvey.

Gee, J. P., G. Hull, and C. Lankshear, (1996). *The new work order: Behind the language of the new capitalism*. Boulder, CO: Westview Press.

Giroux, H. A. (1992). *Border crossings: Cultural workers and the politics of education*. New York: Routledge.

———— (1997). *Pedagogy and the politics of hope: Theory, culture, and schooling: A critical reader*. Boulder, CO: Westview Press.

———— (2004). *The terror of neoliberalism: Authoritarianism and the eclipse of democracy*. Boulder, CO: Paradigm Publishers

———— (2005). *Against the new authoritarianism: Politics after Abu Ghraib*. Manitoba, Canada: Arbeiter Ring Publishing.

———— (2006a). *America on the edge: Henry Giroux on politics, culture, and education*. New York: Palgrave Macmillan.

———— (2006b). *Stormy weather: Katrina and the politics of disposability*. Boulder, CO: Paradigm Publishers.

Greene, M. (1995). *Releasing the imagination: Essays on education, the arts, and social change*. San Francisco: Jossey-Bass.

Huerta, L., Scott, D., and Horton, J. K. (2001/April). *How do we know preservice teachers are comprehending, willing, and able to apply critical pedagogy in their classrooms?* Round table presented at the American Educational Research Association Annual Meeting. Seattle, WA.

Kincheloe, J. L. (2004). *Critical pedagogy primer*. New York: Peter Lang.

Kosik, K. (1976). *Dialectics of the concrete: A study on problems of man and world*. Dordrecht, Holland: Reidel Publishing Co.

McLaren, P. (1995). *Critical pedagogy and predatory culture*. New York: Routledge.

———— (1998, Fall). Revolutionary pedagogy in post-revolutionary times: Rethinking the political economy of critical education. *Educational Theory, 48 (4)*, 431–462.

———— (2000). *Che Guevara, Paulo Freire, and the pedagogy of revolution*. Lanham, MD: Rowman & Littlefield.

———— (2003). *Life in schools: An introduction to critical pedagogy in the foundations of education* (4th ed.). Boston: Allyn & Bacon.

———— (2006). *Rage and hope: Interviews with Peter McLaren on war, imperialism, and critical pedagogy*. New York: Peter Lang.

Purpel, D. (1999). *Moral outrage in education*. New York: Peter Lang.

Schutter, A. de. (1981). *Investigación participativa: Una opción metodológica para la educación de adultos* [Participatory research: A methodological option for adult education]. Michoacán, MX: CREFAL

CHAPTER 15

Critical Pedagogy and Teacher Education

Radicalizing Prospective Teachers

LILIA I. BARTOLOMÉ

The task of successfully preparing teachers in the United States to effectively work with an ever-increasing culturally and linguistically diverse student body represents a pressing challenge for teacher educators. Unfortunately, much of this practice of equipping prospective teachers for working with learners from different backgrounds revolves around exposing these future educators to what are perceived as the best practical strategies to ensure the academic and linguistic development of their students. Gaining access to and actively creating methods and materials for the classroom is certainly an important step towards effective teaching. However, this practical focus far too often occurs without examining teachers' own assumptions, values, and beliefs, and how this ideological posture informs, often unconsciously, their perceptions and actions when working with linguistic-minority and other politically, socially, and economically subordinated students.

"Ideology" is used here to refer to the framework of thought constructed and held by members of a society to justify or rationalize an existing social order. As Antonia Darder, Rodolfo Torres, and Marta Baltodano (2002) point out, what is important is that ideology be understood as existing at the deep, embedded psychological structures of the personality. Ideology more often than not manifests itself in the inner histories and experiences that give rise to questions of subjectivity as they are constructed by individual needs, drives, and passions, as well as the changing material conditions and social foundations of a society. (p. 13)

In this paper, I discuss the importance of infusing teacher education curricula with critical pedagogical principles in order to prepare educators to aggressively name and interrogate potentially harmful ideologies and practices in the schools and classrooms where they work. I maintain that teachers need to develop political and ideological clarity in order to increase the chances of academic success for all students. I also argue that it is imperative that these educators instill in their students in K-12 public schools the same kind of critical consciousness that enables them to read and act upon the world around them.

"Political clarity" refers to the ongoing process by which individuals achieve ever-deepening consciousness of the sociopolitical and economic realities that shape their lives and their capacity to transform such material and symbolic conditions. It also refers to the process by which individuals come to understand the possible linkages between macro-level political, economic, and social variables, and subordinated groups' academic performance in the micro-level classroom (Bartolomé, 1994). "Ideological clarity" refers to the process by which individuals struggle to identify and compare their own explanations for the existing socioeconomic and political hierarchy with the dominant society's. The juxtaposing of ideologies should help teachers to better understand if, when, and how their belief systems uncritically reflect those of the dominant society and thus maintain unequal and what should be unacceptable conditions that so many students experience on a daily basis (Bartolomé, 2000).

One effective way to ensure that pre-service teachers begin to develop and increase their political and ideological clarity is by having teacher education classrooms explicitly explore how ideology functions as it relates to power. It is also important for prospective teachers to examine the political and cultural role that counterhegemonic resistance can serve to contest and transform the exclusionary, harmful, and fundamentally undemocratic values and beliefs that inform dominant educational practices in the United States. In what follows, I first explain why it is necessary for teacher educators to recognize, better understand, and challenge the ideological dimensions of prospective teachers' beliefs and attitudes toward subordinated students. Next, I share research results from my work at Riverview High School that illustrate the powerful potential of teachers' who critically understand the ideological and material obstacles faced by youth in schools and their proactive responses as defenders of their students. Finally, I identify key critical pedagogical principles that, interwoven into teacher education coursework and field experiences, have the potential to help develop in prospective teachers, much like the teachers in my research study, the ability to assume counterhegemonic stances so as to create a "more equal playing field" for all students.

Changing Demographics and the Clashing of Ideologies

The dramatic increase in low-income, non-White and linguistic-minority students in U.S. public schools signals the urgent need to understand and challenge the ideological orientations of prospective teachers in teacher education programs. One current challenge is to adequately prepare the overwhelmingly White, female, and middle-class pre-service teacher population to work with these students, as they are quickly becoming the majority in many of the largest urban public schools in the country (Gomez, 1994). While the nation's school population is made up of approximately 40 percent minority children, nearly 90 percent of teachers are White (National Center for Education Statistics, 1992). In addition, the social-class differences between teachers and students continue to grow. For example, 44 percent of African American children and 36 percent of Latino children live in poverty, and yet increasingly teachers are coming from White lower-middle and middle-class homes and have been raised in rural and suburban communities (Zimpher, 1989). There are also significant differences in teacher-student language backgrounds. Despite the fact that by 1994 there were already approximately 5 to 7.5 million nonnative English-speaking students in public schools around the country—a number that has continued to rise—the majority of teachers in the U.S. are monolingual English speakers.

Given the social-class, racial, cultural, and language differences between teachers and students and our society's historical predisposition to view culturally and linguistically diverse students through a deficit lens that positions them as less intelligent, talented, qualified, and deserving, it is especially urgent that educators critically understand their ideological orientations with respect to these differences and begin to comprehend that teaching is not a politically or ideologically neutral undertaking. It is also important to acknowledge that minority academic underachievement and high "drop out," suspension, and expulsion rates cannot be addressed in primarily methodological and technical terms dislodged from the material, social, and ideological conditions that have shaped and sustained such failure rates.

What We Know about Teachers' Ideological Orientations

Increasing, teachers' ideological awareness and clarity require that educators compare and contrast their personal explanations of the wider social order with those propagated by the dominant society. Unfortunately, transforming educators' conscious and unconscious beliefs and attitudes regarding the legitimacy of the dominant social order and of the resulting unequal power relations among cultural groups at the school and classroom level has, by and large, historically not been acknowledged in mainstream teacher education programs as a significant step towards improving the educational processes for and outcomes of low-SES, non-White, and linguistic-minority students.

However, more progressive literature on teacher education suggests that prospective teachers, regardless of their ethnic background, tend to uncritically and often unconsciously hold beliefs and attitudes about the existing social order that reflect dominant ideologies that are harmful to so many students (Bloom, 1991; Davis, 1994; Freire, 1997, 1998a, 1998b; Gomez, 1994; Gonsalves, 1996; Haberman, 1991; Macedo, 1994; Sleeter, 1992). Furthermore, these educators tend to see the social order as a fair and just one. John Farley (2000) explains that one dominant ideological belief that Blacks and Latinos are responsible for their own disadvantages "appears deeply rooted in an American ideology of individualism, a belief that each individual determines his or her own situation" (p. 66). When people believe that the system is fair, that is, that African Americans and Latinos have the same opportunity as White Americans, they will usually do two things: 1) they blame the minorities themselves for any disadvantages they experience rather than blaming White racism or other oppressive aspects of the system; and 2) they oppose policies designed to increase minority opportunities such as bilingual education and affirmative action.

Prospective and experienced educators alike often resent having to take courses that challenge some of the dominant ideologies they unconsciously hold (Gonsalvez, 1996). Interestingly enough, even when teachers recognize that certain minority groups have historically been economically worse off, have academically underachieved, and have higher mortality rates than Whites, their explanations for such inequalities are usually underdeveloped or nonexistent (Bartolomé, 1998; King, 1991).

Unfortunately, this lack of political and ideological clarity often translates into teachers uncritically accepting the status quo as "natural." It also leads educators down an assimilationist path to learning and teaching, rather than a culturally responsive, integrative, and transformative one, and perpetuates deficit-based views of low-SES, non-White, and linguistic-minority students. Educators who do not identify and interrogate their negative, racist, and classist ideological orientations often work to reproduce the existing social order (Bartolomé, 1998; Bloom, 1991). Even teachers who subscribe to the latest teaching methodologies and learning theories can unknowingly end up perverting and subverting their work because of unacknowledged and unexamined dysconscious racism (King, 1991) and other discriminatory tendencies.

Recent literature on effective teachers of minority students describes the teachers as caring, knowledgeable, and skilled practitioners. The research also alludes to the teachers' ability to recognize the subordinate status accorded to low-SES and non-White students, and describes the teachers' efforts to validate the cultures and identities of children in school (Beauboeuf, 1997; Garcia, 1991; Howard, 2000; Ladson-Billings, 2000; Nieto, 2000a, 2000b). However, much of this literature stops short of naming teachers' beliefs and attitudes as "ideology" and instead treats these dispositions as individually motivated and thus apolitical constructs.

In the section that follows, I share the results of a study I conducted with a colleague (Bartolomé & Balderrama, 2001) that captures how some teachers figure out that teaching is not an apolitical undertaking, develop a critical understanding of how asymmetrical power relations play out in schools, and devise strategies on their students' behalf for short-circuiting potential inequalities they may experience. Though the teachers studied vary in terms of their personal political orientations (they self-identified across the conservative-liberal spectrum) and the degree to which they engage in critical forms of education, these educators share some important counterhegemonic beliefs to dominant oppressive practices, a strong sense of student advocacy, as well as a commitment to creating more just and humane schooling conditions for their students. In this paper, I not only describe their efforts, but I also work to expand them by offering critical pedagogical insights intended to compound and magnify their success.

The Study

Riverview High School

The educators interviewed for this research project all work at Riverview High School (pseudonyms have been used for the names of all participants and the school). This high school has been in existence for 100 years and is located in the coastal southern California community of Rancho Nacional, approximately 18 miles north of the Mexican border.

Riverview High School has an impressive academic track record over the past two decades. In 1994, *Redbook Magazine* recognized it as a "Best High School," and in 1996 the school was named a "California Distinguished School." In addition, approximately 70 percent of each graduating class attend either community or four-year colleges, and receive millions of dollars in scholarship monies. Furthermore, past research on effective schools has included Riverview in its sample (for an example of this research, see Lucas, Henze, & Donato, 1990).

Riverview High School is culturally and linguistically diverse. The student enrollment is 70 percent Mexicano/Latino, and 8 percent Filipino American. The descriptor "Mexicano/Latino" is used here because historically the Latino population in Riverview has been predominantly of Mexican ancestry. However, I also want to acknowledge those Latino students who may not be of Mexican ancestry. At the same time, the term "Mexicano" is utilized instead of the more common Mexican American or Chicano because a significant number of these students are first-generation Americans or recent immigrants. The rest of the student body is made up of smaller numbers of Whites, African Americans, and Pacific Islanders. In addition, 62 percent of all Riverview students come from homes where a language other than English is spoken (the majority being Spanish speakers). According to school records, non-English and limited-English proficient students comprise 23 percent of the current enrollment (Riverview High School Profile Information, 1996). The school offers regular and honors-level courses in bilingual (English/Spanish) and sheltered instructional settings, as well as bilingual counseling services (English, Spanish, and Tagalog) for students not proficient in English. The majority of Riverview students come from low-income homes that receive federal assistance and are thus eligible for free nutrition and lunch services.

The four exemplary educators

Four Riverview High School educators, identified as exemplary by administrators and colleagues, were invited to discuss their experiences with Mexicano/Latino students (and other low-SES, non-White, and linguistic-minority students) and how to effectively prepare them academically. The four educators ranged in experience (8 to 25 years) and consisted of: one White female principal, Dr. Peabody; one Chicano history teacher, Mr. Tijerina; one White female English teacher, Mrs. Cortland; and one White male math teacher, Mr. Broadbent. The educators were similar in age (mid to late 50s). Two of the teachers taught exclusively or primarily in English, and Mr. Tijerina had experience in both English mainstream and English-Spanish classroom settings.

The interview protocol consisted of open-ended questions intended to elicit teacher explanations and views about their own experiences with and beliefs about low-SES, non-White, and linguistic-minority students and factors related to educating them. In addition, my research associate and I asked these educators about their personal histories and the life journeys that led them to teaching. They were also asked to describe their personal school experiences as students as well as their experiences with non-White people growing up. Additionally, we asked them to discuss their teacher preparation experiences, their current teaching at Riverview, their conceptions of effective teaching, as well as their explanations for Riverview High's touted effectiveness.

Awareness of asymmetrical power relations

The preliminary findings suggest that, in general, the educators interviewed attribute the academic and social success of their students to the school personnel's ability to create and sustain a caring, just and level playing field—a "comfort zone" as they call it—for learners who have historically not been treated well in educational institutions or in the greater society. The teachers, albeit to different degrees, question particular dominant ideologies such as meritocratic explanations of the existing social order, and they reject deficit views of their students. They also generally resist romanticized and White-supremacist views of White, middle-class (mainstream) culture. In addition, the participants report having engaged in what I label as "cultural border crossing," where they personally experienced being positioned as low status or witnessed someone else's subordination. The fourth and final finding of this study suggests that the educators see themselves as cultural brokers or advocates for their students and perceive this aspect of their work as key in helping their students figure out the school culture in order to succeed therein.

'There is no equal playing field" —Questioning meritocratic explanations of the social order

Across interviews, the educators questioned the validity of meritocracy—the myth that you get ahead simply by virtue of your hard work and talents—as well as the "meritocratic" explanation of the existing social order that works to justify why Mexicanos/Latinos and other minorities are at the "bottom" and Whites are on the "top" of the academic, socioeconomic, and political ladder. For example, Mr. Broadbent explained that Mexican American academic failure could be partly countered if teachers somehow get their working-class students to see "how the other half lives" and question their "lot in life." He made the point that life is not fair and that those most capable, often because of working-class limitations, are not exposed to the outside world and, as a result, often do not feel confident enough to "grab for it." He pointed out that often such opportunities are not based on merit or ability but rather on sheer luck. Mr. Broadbent shared that had his father not been moved up from enlisted man to officer, he too might not "have been pushed by someone who had seen it"— the good life:

> He wasn't a college graduate, but he got a taste of the better life when he was in the army after the war. He got raised up from an enlisted man to an officer. And so he saw how the other half lived.

He attributed his father's career ascension to a fluke of good luck. Mr. Broadbent pointed out that kids, through no fault of their own, are often put into a disadvantaged position unless concerted efforts are made to "level the playing field." He shared that, as a math teacher, he constantly talks to students about college and immediate careers that require mathematical expertise so that they can begin to think about their life opportunities beyond high school.

While Mr. Broadbent's analysis of the problems facing his students is by no means radical in its assessment, more critical forms of education would call for addressing with students how social class is a structure of capitalist social relations and thus a systemic inequity. He is nonetheless successful with his disenfranchised students because he acknowledges to some degree (even if his theory is limited to luck and a lack of exposure) that there is a problem.

Mrs. Cortland also questioned the meritocratic notion of success and achievement of the "most able," particularly as commonly subscribed to in schools. She cited an incident during which the vocal music choir she advises was almost eliminated from a competition because "they [couldn't] afford to compete." Mrs. Cortland explained that her student group, "An International Affair" (self-named because of its diverse make-up), received "superior" scores at local and county competitions. Based on their superior county scores, the group was invited to compete in a festival held in Las Vegas. She explained that in order to compete, the students were required to raise funds; she wryly noted that in a more affluent part of the district, parents had recently held a golf tournament and raised more than $30,000 for their children's trip to Australia. She juxtaposed that reality with the fundraising obstacles faced by her working-class Riverview students:

> As we began to do the fundraising, I noticed that the kids—a month before it was time to go— knew we were nowhere near the [needed] amount of money. Then I thought, "Well, we're going! It doesn't matter; we're going because we said we were going!" But they began to come up with all these excuses, "Well, my mom doesn't really want me to go" or "I have to work." So I said, "No! Money is not the issue. I will find sponsors for all these kids." And so, that sunk in, that we were not going to be limited because we live in the thirteenth poorest city in the United States. And for the majority of these kids, I mean $100 . . . that's the groceries for the month for the entire family! So when I took the burden away so we could just concentrate on doing it, not only did we go, we won first place. We won the "Spirit of Las Vegas Award!"

Mrs. Cortland discussed, at great length, how "competition requires more than merit," and pointed out that "the level of excellence can only be assessed to the direct tie it has to the pocketbook." However, she refused to give in to the constraints that were imposed on her students because of their racial and economic backgrounds and fought to reveal the contradictions that inform current public educational practices:

> Am I supposed to tell these kids, "You're as good as you can get but we can't test your excellence or allow you to evolve any further because we don't have the money?" No, we shouldn't have to worry about that if the charge in the curriculum is to create students who meet or exceed the [standards]. Then it can't be tied to the economy, it can't be tied to the color of their skin and it can't be tied to whether or not they've had this experience before in their lives.

Similarly, Dr. Peabody questioned the merit system, as she acknowledged that racism is a very real obstacle in the lives of her students of color. She reported reminding White teachers and peers that:

> Even if you were oppressed as an Anglo, being poor or whatever, what I know is that the worst day or the worst part of all of that is never as challenging as [that encountered by] a Black person or Brown person. That whole color issue brings in a whole different thing.

She admitted that a big part of her job is continuously trying to change the racist lenses of some of her teachers. Dr. Peabody explained that there aren't too many teachers that she would consider purposely racist, and she avoids using the term "racist" in the school context because "it isn't that they're deliberately that way." This isn't an attempt to act as an apologist for White people's discriminatory behavior. Rather, her comment appears to represent a more profound understanding of how racism works and thus a more strategic way to confront it. As an example, she spoke of an incident where the California Scholarship Federation Honor Society (CSF) advisor did not encourage her students to participate in a district-wide CSF scholarship competition because the advisor did not believe that her minority students were qualified to compete against White students from more affluent schools. Dr. Peabody recalled this incident with indignation:

> I mean, every flag in my head just went off. I just went through the ceiling . . . that's a deficit model, that is—"How could these kids compete with anybody else?"

She went on to describe how she confronted the teacher and used CSF alumni college graduation information to prove to this teacher just how qualified and outstanding her minority CSF students truly were.

The educators in this sample articulated their belief that other factors, such as racism and economic restrictions, often assume greater importance than pure merit and ability in their students' lives. They relate this reality in a matter-of-fact tone, yet they do not fall into negative or deterministic views of their students' life chances.

"You have to love brown [people]!" —
rejecting deficit views of minority students

A second belief shared by these educators is their rejection of deficit views of their students. As evident in the above story about Dr. Peabody's experience with the California Scholarship Federation Honor Society (CSF) advisor, she is very aware of the deficit model that's in place in schools, and she insists that all students be encouraged to be their best regardless of their background. Dr. Peabody was disgusted with the proposition that her students, even if given a fair shake, couldn't compete against White students from more affluent communities.

Mr. Broadbent stated that there were many positive aspects of Mexican culture, such as demonstrating respect for elders (a practice, in his opinion, fast becoming uncommon in mainstream American culture), that he believed the students should maintain. He discussed the importance of helping his students see themselves in a positive light and learn about mainstream culture in an effort to better themselves. While exploring the deficit-model orientation and its implications, Mr. Broadbent de-emphasized issues of culture and race and focused on social class. He explained that the belief that one could improve one's class status is where self-esteem, confidence, and motivation would come from. He argued that this approach to helping his students wasn't so much a matter of trying to assimilate them into the White mainstream—which he recognized as having its own flaws—as much as it is about introducing them to middle-class culture. Later, he mentioned that, because of his own experience growing up as a working-class youth, he identified and felt comfortable teaching and mentoring working-class Riverview students who he felt were not deficient but rather economically deprived.

Mr. Tijerina similarly discussed positive aspects of many of the cultures present in the school. He emphasized the highly desirable values and ways of behaving that Mexicanos/Latinos tend to bring to school. He described these students as generally hard-working, family-oriented, and desirous to improve their lot in life as well as their families'. He argued that they are, however, unsure as to how to go about this and are often in need of teachers' guidance. However, unlike Mr. Broadbent's sole focus on socioeconomic status, Mr. Tijerina targeted issues of ethnicity and racism when discussing deficit beliefs and obstacles facing his students. He maintained that effective teachers of Mexicano/Latino students and other minorities have to be conscious of their own racist beliefs and tendencies to view the kids as less than, and to try to make them like, White students. He explained that to be effective teachers of these students, you have to discard deficit notions and "you have to like people of color—you have to authentically like dark colors, you have to love brown!" He elaborated:

> I think we have the feeling here [at Riverview] that minorities aren't inferior. I think there's a difference between the patronizing that goes on in some schools where they really think a person is inferior to some degree, but "Hey, you can make it if you try harder." The White people here, I don't think they feel that here. I think that they feel that our kids are equal—they have the same brains as kids in [more affluent, predominantly White schools such as] Playa Dorada or Buena Vista

or any place else. They do have the same brains, only the background is definitively disadvantaged
. . . for lots of reasons.

While Mr. Broadbent emphasized socioeconomic status and Mr. Tijerina focused on race
and ethnicity in their arguments against deficit perspectives of low-SES, non-White students, and linguistic-minority students, both share the common belief that the academic
problems that many of these students have are not a result of their culture or language. In
fact, these educators distinguished between the very real economically and socially restrictive life circumstances their students live and their students' innate potential. The two seem
to believe that their students "do have the same brains" but that, through no fault of their
own, they have experienced difficult life conditions which are often the direct result of living in poverty and being discriminated against. They see their students' chief problem as
not having money, respect, and access. However, they do not restrict their students' academic potential because of their racial or low socioeconomic standing.

While this is extremely important, it is also key that educators look at the relationships
between racism and social-class stratification, so that class does not obscure the harmful
effects of racism and vice versa. This is particularly important for Mr. Broadbent—being
White—as the lethal role that racism plays in society and in schools is so often neglected
by White educators who focus more on issues of social class. It is also important for Mr.
Tijerina—a Chicano—to not bypass economics in pursuit of the abuses of racism and ethnocentrism. While not conflating race and class, there is an inextricable link between these
two constructs that needs to be fully explored by educators.

"They play this game, 'All these (White and middle-class) students are smart and wonderful'"!—Interrogating Romanticized Views of Dominant Culture

The educators in this study refuse to blindly accept dominant White culture as superior or
highly desirable to emulate. They question the superordinate and romanticized status typically conferred on "mainstream," middle-class, White culture. Mr. Tijerina explained that
he actually preferred working with Mexicano/ Latino students instead of the more affluent
White students in other schools:

> I would not teach in [more affluent White schools such as] Playa Dorada or Buena Vista. See, I
> like these kids and I don't think I would like being in a White school because the students are, by
> my standards, they're disrespectful. I think they're *muy igualados*. *Muy igualados* is a good way to
> describe them. ["Igualado," in Mexican colloquial language, refers to someone who is in a subor-
> dinate position but acts as if equal or better to a superior. Mr. Tijerina's example refers specifically
> to students who assume equal or superior status with their teachers in behaving as equals and come
> across as improper, disrespectful, and impolite.] They are *muy igualados*, like you owe them and
> "You're here to teach me," you know, "Teach me, we pay your salary" kind of an attitude. The kids
> here are just very, very respectful and they're very accepting and tolerant of each other.

He emphasized the importance of maintaining traditional Mexicano/Latino cultural values and belief systems and incorporating them into the mainstream high school culture. For example, he mentioned that Mexicano/Latino students, by custom, demonstrate their respect for teachers and peers by cordially greeting others when they encounter them in hallways and other school sites, and he compared their behavior with his observations of White, middle-class students who he describes as often being rude, self-absorbed, and accustomed to ignoring people.

He also mentioned that Mexicano/Latino students (and other minority students) tend to be more accepting of diversity than White mainstream youth. He provided as proof the fact that Riverview High School houses the district Special Education program and explained that Mexicano/Latino students have positively and affectionately received their Special Education peers into the school, unlike what usually occurs in other schools.

Mr. Tijerina argued that mainstream middle-class White culture (with its lack of familial loyalty and overemphasis on individualism) would benefit tremendously if aspects of Mexicano/Latino culture were incorporated into it. He shared his belief that many dimensions of middle-class White culture serve to dehumanize people and yet promote the erroneous and arrogant belief that Whites are superior. He stated that if the mainstream could adopt traditional Mexican values of respect, humility, and acceptance of difference, it might become more humane and reduce the feelings of disconnection and alienation that so many of its own members feel. Mr. Tijerina added that these humanistic values and worldviews are also present in other cultural groups at Riverview High School such as Filipinos, Pacific Islanders, and the Vietnamese.

Beliefs about the superiority of White, middle- and upper-middle-class culture were also debunked by Mrs. Cortland when she spoke of the hypocrisy, dishonesty, arrogance, and disrespectful behavior often exhibited by many of the affluent White students she had worked with in the past. She pointed out that while White students, their parents, and their teachers lie to themselves about just how superior they and their students are in comparison to poorer, non-White students, she found many of them to be seriously lacking in important human qualities such as respect and empathy for others. Mrs. Cortland shared her views regarding the "psychological game" that she observed White people play:

> They [the students and their teachers] played this "game"—"All these students are smart and wonderful." And the kids would come and go, "We'll pretend we are smart and wonderful."

She also shared first-hand experiences in teaching this type of student when she began to substitute teach at the most affluent school in the district, Buena Vista High School. Mrs. Cortland highlighted the cruel and inhuman reaction of the "Anglo kids" to the news that their teacher had taken ill and would not be returning to school:

> And I mean, the lady I took over for, I think she had a nervous breakdown. They never told me but I walked in and the first class was what they called 122 English and [they were] all Anglo kids. [When the assistant principal left me in the classroom], they [the students] all stood on their desks and sang, "Ding-Dong the Witch Is Dead" and thought it was funny.

Both Mrs. Cortland and Mr. Tijerina explicitly challenge and reject romanticized perceptions of White mainstream culture. Their attitude seems to be that they "know better" than to believe unrealistic and uncritical views of White, middle-class culture. Too often, the norm in schools and in society is to compare poor, non-White, and linguistic-minority students to that invisible, yet highly romanticized, White, middle-class standard. These educators are not impressed by nor buy into myths of White superiority, or, conversely, to myths about Mexicano/Latino or working-class inferiority. On the contrary, they very realistically name the invisible center—middle-class White culture—and they point out numerous undesirable aspects of it. As such, they are able to help students maintain their cultures and prevent their uncritical assimilation of negative, Anglo cultural beliefs and practices.

While affirming diversity is extremely important in gaining the respect and attention of students, educators should not stop there. From a critical pedagogical perspective, students should also examine their own cultural backgrounds for strengths and weaknesses so as to be able to transform any unjust beliefs and practices that lie within; e.g., sexism, homophobia, religious intolerance. However, it is important to note that when I asked Mr. Tijerina about his tendency to romanticize Mexican culture to his students, his response was that he did so purposely. He explained that, throughout their lives, Mexicano/Latino and other subordinated students are only exposed to negative and racist views of their cultures. He maintained that it would be counterproductive to engage them in a critique of their home cultures because all they ever are exposed to about their ethnic group is primarily negative. Mr. Tijerina explained that students urgently needed to learn about the positive aspects and important contributions of their cultures—cultures too often portrayed in schools and by the mass media as inferior and valueless. He admitted that his portrayals of Mexican culture, history, music, etc., might be a bit romanticized but argued that Mexicano/Latino students first need to develop a positive ethnic identity before critiquing it. Furthermore, he pointed out that trying to politicize young students could be counterproductive because they are developmentally young.

Mr. Tijerina presents a provocative point of view. Nevertheless, despite the legitimacy of his claims and his expertise with this age group and population, it is important to devise ways to develop students' political and ideological clarity in developmentally appropriate ways so that they too can theoretically make sense of the world around them and work to transform what they feel is unjust and unacceptable.

'These experiences have shown me that if you are a person of color, it is more difficult for you to achieve" — Witnesses of Subordination and Cultural Border Crossers

A "border crosser" refers to an individual who is able and willing to develop empathy with the cultural "Other" and to authentically view as equal the values of the "Other" while conscious of the cultural group's subordinated social status in the greater society. A border crosser is someone who will critically consider the positive cultural traits of the "Other" and, at the same time, is able to critique the discriminatory practices of his/her culture that may be involved in the creation of the cultural "Other" in the first place. In other words, a border crosser, while embracing the cultural "Other," must also divest from his/her cultural privilege that often functions as a cultural border itself (Bartolomé, 2002).

My definition of a "cultural border crosser" differs from more conventional definitions that merely focus on a person's ability to successfully interact and exist in an alternative social, economic, or ethnic cultural reality, without dealing with the real issues of asymmetrical power relations and subordination. Members of the dominant culture typically tend to border cross without compromising their position of cultural and social privilege. This type of border crosser can travel the world, study the "Other" in a detached and curious manner without ever recognizing that cultural groups occupy different positions of power and status and that many cultural perceptions and practices result from such power asymmetries. Often, these types of ideologically and politically "blind" border crossers assume "tourist" or "voyeur" perspectives that are very much tainted by their unconscious deficit and White supremacist ideologies (Bartolomé, 2002).

The third finding of this study reveals that the educators in this sample crossed ethnic and socioeconomic borders and came to the realization that some cultural groups, through no fault of their own, occupy positions of low social status and are marginalized and mistreated by members of higher-status groups. This realization enabled the individuals to authentically empathize with the cultural "Other" and take some form of action to equalize asymmetrical relations of power and eradicate the stigmatized social identities imposed on subordinated students.

These educators had been, at some point in their lives, profoundly affected by experiences with subordination and injustice. They all reported personally experiencing or witnessing someone else's unfair treatment. For example, Mrs. Cortland grew up as a lower-middle-class girl in an affluent White community and, early on, learned to discern social class and status differences. Mrs. Cortland shared her experiences of marginalization and explained that more affluent peers never fully accepted her family. She described one particularly hurtful memory when her father could not afford to buy her sister the "popular" shoes (also the most expensive) worn by her cohort at school. Mrs. Cortland recalled the discomfort of belonging to a "lower" class in comparison to her more affluent White community and being viewed as less despite her superior academic performance in school. Although this anecdote might not constitute, in the minds of many readers, an example of serious subordination, the important point is that Mrs. Cortland learned, at an early age, to question the myths of a "level playing field" and meritocracy. Her experience taught her that her lower socioeconomic status marked her as socially less valuable than her more affluent peers, despite her strong intellectual abilities and merit.

Mr. Tijerina spoke of his life experiences as a working-class Chicano who grew up in Rancho Nacional and attended Riverview High School approximately 35 years ago. As a working-class minority, he was forced to cross social and cultural borders in order to survive what was at that time a middle-class White school culture.

He reported that during his generation's attendance at Riverview High School (from 1960–1964), Mexican Americans constituted approximately 30 percent of the student body. Despite their numbers, they generally were not visible in the mainstream high school culture. He vividly remembered the second-class citizenship to which the majority of Mexican American students were relegated. He related the condescending attitude directed at Mexicans as well as the outright disrespectful treatment they experienced. The maximum insult was to be called a "dirty Mexican" and told to "go back to Mexico." He explained that these derogatory comments lay just under the surface of Mexican and White interactions and were frequently utilized by White students at the slightest, real or perceived, provocation.

Mr. Tijerina explained that throughout his young life, he was always conscious of the low prestige ascribed to his working-class status and Mexican ethnicity. He attributed his resilience and resistance to the strong pride he felt in being Mexicano (a value his father instilled in him) and to his increasing conscious understanding of racism and its manifestations. His later experiences with progressive Chicano organizations in the 1970s and 1980s provided him with opportunities to formally study White supremacist ideology and the practice of colonialization.

The high school principal, Dr. Peabody, attributed her early cultural border-crossing experiences to growing up as one of a few Whites in inner-city, predominantly African American, Pittsburgh. As a working-class White girl growing up in an African American community, she explained that she learned about the advantages of cultural pluralism early on:

> Essentially my own story is that I grew up in a Black innercity ghetto in Pittsburgh . . . to be a White person in a Black innercity ghetto is a whole other interesting thing . . . At the time I didn't think much about it because I was there. But it turned out later to be a real strength. I learned about different people and different cultures. I did not think it was unusual to have Black friends and eat in their house—or Jewish or Puerto Rican friends—because I did it all the time.

Although, like Mr. Tijerina, she too experienced firsthand what it means to be relegated to low status, given her position as a "minority" White person in her African American community, she recognized the lifelong privilege and preferential treatment she received by virtue of being White. She told of her exposure to racism and discrimination as chiefly a result of her close work with people of color.

She also shared her belief in allowing people of color to "use" her position as a White person (perceived by other Whites as a more legitimate spokesperson) to carry their messages (e.g., support for bilingual education, allowing students to demonstrate against an anti-immigrant proposition). Dr. Peabody shared her conscious decision to utilize her privileged position as a White woman to become a change-agent in school settings.

> In my career when I started in Riverview School District, they [the Mexicanos/ Latinos] used me. I allowed myself to be used. So they used to me to be the carrier at of their messages . . . I have a lot of credibility [as perceived by others because of her whiteness] and because I am a very strong personality, I [cannot] be swayed off course.

Dr. Peabody explained that her own working-class background helped her understand Riverview High School and the surrounding community. Her identification and feelings of solidarity with working-class Mexican culture were also evident in her relationship with a parent she met during her first principalship in the district. She explained that the parent became a real advocate for her and that she came to realize, "Oh my God, she's more like my grandmother than most White [middle-class] women!" Dr. Peabody's feelings of solidarity with working-class, non-White, and linguistic minorities have led her to assume the role of advocate and cultural broker for her students, parents, and communities.

The cultural border-crossing experiences of the educators in this study were substantively different from typical "tourist" or "voyeur" White border-crossing experiences. Personally experiencing or witnessing someone else's subordination left a permanent impression on these educators. They learned early on that some folks are seen and treated as low status simply because of their race, ethnicity, and class. Given their "baptism of fire" during their border-crossing experiences, these educators learned to more clearly discern and understand unequal power relations among cultural groups, and consequently they worked toward reducing and preventing their reproduction at Riverview High School.

Although the scope of this study did not allow for student interviews, it is important to note that any continuation of this important effort to reduce and prevent the reproduction of unequal power relations and abusive practices in schools should include generating dialogue with students in the classrooms (and with members of the community) about oppressive practices by allowing them to share their own feelings and experiences if they so choose. When teachers assume the role of cultural broker for their students, it is the first step in being able and willing to create this critical dialogical space.

'You're here to encourage them, to help them go to college, to help them do all those good things—that's what you're here for"—Educators as Dedicated Cultural Brokers

All of the educators in this study mentioned the need to mentor and "show students the way" to a better life as part of their professional responsibility as teachers and administrators. Given their clarity in understanding the hierarchy of social status generated within the asymmetry of power and economic relations, they shared their commitment to helping their low-SES, non-White, and linguistic-minority students, typically depicted as low status and deficient by the greater society, to better understand school culture in order to succeed socially and academically therein. Though they did not employ the term "cultural broker," they all spoke about their role in helping students more effectively navigate school and mainstream culture.

Mr. Broadbent seemed particularly preoccupied with the students' inability to see beyond their experiences in Riverview High School and the Rancho Nacional community. He spoke often of the need to get the students to see "how the other half lives" so as to motivate them to do well in school. One of his greatest frustrations was his perceived inability to help the students see their high school experience as a stepping-stone toward college or a good-paying job. One of the strategies he employed for helping students both see the bigger picture and assume control over their learning process has been to teach them the "rules of the game" in very explicit ways. For example, when teaching math and computer technology courses, he often explicitly links the skills and knowledge bases taught with immediate job opportunities in an effort to help students demystify "high-tech" jobs, see the immediate relevance of the classes, and view these employment opportunities as possible for them.

While it is important to recognize that students should be encouraged to reach higher in their aspirations, the idea that not being able to "see" a better life is in large part what keeps subordinated students down can easily be misinterpreted. If it's just a matter of seeing the virtues of a middle-class reality—with the help of a teacher—that leads to success, this puts the onus on students subsequent to their exposure to knowledge, career opportunities, and a taste of "how the other half lives," and again disregards the systemic and ideological obstacles that get in their way. In other words, simply seeing the good life does not ensure getting access to it, regardless of how hard one tries. It is important that educators heed Mr. Broadbent's call to raise as much awareness and confidence in students as possible in order to increase their chances of success. However, critical pedagogues also encourage keeping an eye on and working to eradicate the deeper ideological and material barriers that subordinated students face.

Mr. Broadbent repeatedly spoke of the importance of being open and honest with students and not withholding vital information from them. Again, because his particular subject matter—math and computer technology—can easily be misrepresented as being too abstract and difficult, he reported making a conscious effort to teach the courses in accessible and student-friendly ways. He explained that the Navy is a good example of an institution where power is maintained by a select few precisely by withholding information from the majority. As part of his strategy for establishing honest, caring, and trusting relations with students, he highlighted his ability to communicate with his students.

> I think for the most part, I've been able to talk to the kids. I don't talk down [to them] and unlike in the Navy where people are trying to hide something from you just so that they can have power, I tell the kids straight out what I think [and expect in class] and I don't hide anything from them.

Mr. Broadbent explained that his job consists not only in imparting strong mathematics knowledge for immediate and later use but also in mentoring kids around life in general. He likened his role as teacher to his own father's role as parent, "I'm like a stepfather for many of my kids, especially the boys who don't have a dad at home." He shared that in this parent-mentor role he exhibits authentic concern and caring for students. However, he added that simply caring for students is not enough and that teachers need to "back-up" their caring with real action in the form of solid content instruction and honest teacher-student communication.

Mr. Tijerina similarly emphasized the importance of teachers assuming a mentoring role vis-à-vis their students. He shared his opinion that, the majority of Riverview High School students are "good kids" who, because of their unfamiliarity with school culture, require teacher guidance in figuring out the "rules of the game" in school and in the outside world. He mentioned that students not only receive help from teachers but also from top quality counselors at Riverview High who provide assistance and counseling in three languages: English, Spanish, and Tagalog. He pointed out that the counselors do an outstanding job getting students into college precisely because they demystify the concept of "college." For example, the counselors take students and parents on college visits and invite former Riverview graduates to share their college experiences. In addition, the counselors assist students in filling out applications, writing statements of purpose, and practicing interview strategies for getting accepted into the college of their choice.

Mr. Tijerina also shared his techniques for helping students understand school culture. He explained that he explicitly discusses his class rules and even role-plays with students in order for them to clearly understand academic and behavioral expectations. He is particularly explicit when it comes to grading:

> I tell them, "You can see your grades whenever you want"; we have folders on all the students' work. I say, "Hey, you can see them whenever you want, you know, here's your total. I grade you on the curve or on a class scale, or on a standard scale, whichever is best for you." I treat them like adults. "I'm not trying to cheat you. I'm not trying to trick you."

Mr. Tijerina is adamant in his belief that, as teachers of young people, particularly youth who don't understand the school culture clearly, it is important that teachers be open, sincere, honest, as well as encouraging. He added:

> [As a teacher], you're not here to put down students or to give them "F's." You're not here to confuse them. You're not here to threaten them. You're not here to be dishonest with them. You're here to encourage them, to make them feel good, to help them, to help them go to college, to help them do all those good things—that's what you're here for.

The educators in this study articulated the importance of explicitly assisting their students in better understanding both school and mainstream culture. In school, they reported that they consciously work to assist students in effectively dealing with both the explicit and hidden aspects of the school curriculum. These teachers mentioned the importance of demystifying grading and evaluation procedures and the college application process as strategies for helping their students become confident, empowered learners. They reported striving to provide their students with practices and knowledge bases that are typically unavailable to working-class youth—the very cultural capital that many middle-class and more privileged parents regularly provide their own children in order to insure their competitive advantage (Stanton-Salazar, 1997; Stanton-Salazar, Vásquez, & Mehan, 2000).

One way to expand the important work that these educators have been doing is to move beyond simply helping students to better understand and navigate school and mainstream culture, by engaging them in strategies to theorize for themselves and actively work to democratize and transform such cultural practices. One gets the impression in Riverview that the goal, as well-intentioned as it may be, is to protect students, guide them, help them develop greater ethnic pride, and get them into college. Education is believed to be the great equalizer and thus the key for subordinated students to enter into a better life. Many of the teachers proudly listed off names of students who have returned to the community after completing college and have assumed positions of leadership, but they did not address strategies for encouraging such student behavior. Furthermore, although the teachers hinted at the importance of preparing their students for future advocacy and leadership roles, there was no mention of explicit efforts to encourage students to develop counterhegemonic beliefs and practices.

Rather than embracing a pedagogy of temporary "comfort zone," critical educators need to generate an explicit and developmentally appropriate pedagogy of getting in with the intent of, once you're in, transforming the very abusive dominant ideological forces that created and maintain society's margins in the first place. While learning and appropriating from the successes of these four remarkable people in this study is important, any critical democratic pedagogy should include a transformative politic that works to combat the very social order that gives rise to impoverished and disenfranchised communities.

Implications for Teacher Education

It is evident that the four educators in this study understand that teaching is not an apolitical undertaking. They questioned, albeit to various degrees, the dominant culture's explanations of the existing social order. They also report rejecting deficit ideologies and respecting and valuing non-White, linguistic-minority, and working-class cultures. In addition, the educators resist romanticizing White, middle-class mainstream culture, and reject total assimilation as a goal for their students. Furthermore, because they also perceive that their students are not operating on a level playing field, these educators highlight their willingness to assume roles as advocates and cultural brokers for them. These findings suggest the power that teachers and other educators, as change-agents, possess and can potentially wield in their work for creating more just and democratic schools. And, as these educators have achieved great successes with their students, I believe that there are lessons to be learned here, regardless of the questions that I have raised.

In the following section, I would like to conclude by discussing possible implications of my findings for teacher preparation. My comments focus specifically on transforming teacher education coursework and practicum experiences by infusing key critical pedagogical practices. As Pepi Leistyna and Arlie Woodrum (1996) correctly explain, "Critical pedagogy is primarily concerned with the kinds of educational theories and practices that encourage both students and teachers to develop an understanding of the interconnecting relationship among ideology, power, and culture" (p. 3). In order for teachers to better understand this three-way relation, two important critical pedagogical principles need to inform the curriculum: a critical understanding of dominant ideologies, and exposure to and development of effective counterhegemonic discourses to resist and transform such oppressive practices (Darder, Torres, & Baltodano, 2002).

Explicit Study of Ideology

The aforementioned research reveals that the exemplary educators in Riverview questioned three common dominant ideologies about the existing social order: the myth of meritocracy, deficit views of minority students, and the superiority of White mainstream culture. An important implication of this pattern of political clarity, given the success of these educators, is the need to incorporate into teacher education programs learning experiences that will formally and explicitly examine ideology. In this way educators can see what's currently in place in a society, where one actually stands and why, and what can be done to contest existing social injustices that are part and parcel of mainstream sociocultural practices. Darder et al. (2002) point out that the study of ideology

> serves as a starting point for asking questions that will help teachers to evaluate critically their practice and to better recognize how the culture of the dominant class becomes embedded in the hidden curriculum that is informed by ideological views that silence students and structurally reproduce the dominant cultural assumptions and practices that thwart democratic education. (p. 13)

This could include exposing students to (and encouraging them to provide insight given their own experiences) alternative explanations for the academic underachievement of minorities, to the myth of meritocracy and how such a theory works to explain and justify the existing social (dis)order, and to how assimilationist models reinforce antagonistic social relations and fundamentally undemocratic practices. What I am suggesting is that the teacher education curriculum (coursework and practicum experiences) be deliberately designed and carried out to expose prospective teachers to a variety of ideological postures so that they can begin to perceive their own ideologies in relation to others' and critically examine the damaging biases they may personally hold, and the inequalities and injustices present in schools and in the society as a whole.

The end result, hopefully, will be the preparation of teachers, like the educators in the sample, who are not afraid to assume counterhegemonic positions in an effort to better understand and change current inequalities in schools. However, the means for bringing about such teacher political and ideological clarity can, and should, vary from program to program, as context-specific adaptation in crucial. In other words, even though it is important to provide pre-service teachers with critical pedagogical strategies, particular instructional programs and specific teaching methods, it is erroneous to assume that blind replication of these programs and methods will, in and of themselves, guarantee successful student learning.

Additionally, the border-crossing experiences of the target teachers, during which they personally experienced or witnessed someone else's subordination, need to be replicated or simulated in coursework and practicum experiences. These curricular experiences should be organized in ways that increase the likelihood that prospective teachers learn about the realities of subordination and marginalization (similar to what the educators learned via their own cultural border-crossing experiences). I am in no way suggesting that teacher educators brainwash their students to think in an ideologically uniform way. Nor am I suggesting that it is necessary to mistreat prospective teachers so they can, as the target teachers in the study have done, experience subordination first-hand in order for them to grasp the concept of asymmetrical power relations. The idea is simply to open up students to a wide range of experiences so that they can expand, hold up to a critical light, and adjust their own ideological lens in ways that make the classroom more inclusive, exploratory, and transformative.

Educating teachers to understand the importance of their role as defenders and cultural advocates for their students also needs to be addressed and encouraged in coursework and practicum experiences. As stated earlier, cultural brokers can create the necessary self-empowering conditions within which students play an active role in their own learning—in which they have a voice in the overall institutional process.

There are teacher preparation programs around the country that provide learning experiences with the potential to help prospective teachers increase their cultural awareness. For example, many teacher education programs require that students learn a second language so that they can better communicate with linguistic-minority students. A few innovative programs actually go as far as presenting their students with opportunities to study abroad in order to develop multilingual and multicultural competencies as well as cross-cultural sensitivities. However, most teacher preparation programs do not offer courses and practicum experiences that will enable students to identify and understand the role of ideology (hegemonic and counterhegemonic) in teaching. There are programs that require prospective teachers to visit, observe, and student-teach in low-income and culturally diverse schools in order to learn about "cultural differences," but even these programs are rarely deliberately designed to ensure that prospective teachers study what structurally produces such oppressed communities and engage in generating alternative ideological positions regarding the low social status and academic achievement of subordinated populations.

Despite good intentions on the part of many teacher educators, and the tremendous potential of many of their learning activities to increase political and ideological clarity, prospective teachers are generally left to their own devices when making sense of cross-cultural and cross-socioeconomic class experiences. Often, the unanticipated end result of many of these learning experiences is that the majority of students emerge ever-more bound to their unquestioned ethnocentric ideologies, precisely because they go into these learning situations without explicitly identifying and questioning the ideological lenses that filter their perceptions. For example, I have had student-teachers that completed part of their student teaching in Mexico. While there, they witness poverty and mistreatment of indigenous people and of the poor; a common reaction has been to denounce those practices in Mexico and to rejoice upon returning to the U.S. "where these things don't happen." A well-conceptualized teacher education program would foresee and plan for this type of student reaction. At the very minimum, debriefing sessions designed to deal with dominant ideologies and resulting social hierarchies in Mexico and in the U.S. would serve to increase students' understanding of oppression. This would also require an in-depth analysis of the devastating effects that international trade "agreements" like NAFTA have on the people, economics, and politics of both nations. Unfortunately, educators are rarely encouraged to explore how nations, like the U.S. and Mexico, via a long history of foreign and economic policies, are intertwined socially, politically, and culturally.

Assuming a Counterhegemonic Stance: Subverting the System for the Good of the Students

Interestingly enough, during cross-cultural learning experiences, I have witnessed a small minority of participating students, on their own, identify abusive asymmetrical power relations at work and consequently assume the role of student defender. For example, I have had prospective teachers describe to me how learning a second language placed them in a position of vulnerability that allowed them to see the world from the eyes of a second-language learner. They experienced the fragility one feels when attempting to acquire a new language and understand, firsthand, the difficulty in learning a second language. Similarly, after working in low-income schools in this country and abroad, many students have approached me, irate and indignant about the life and school conditions of low-SES, non-White students. For many of these students, their anger and indignation serve as a catalyst that propels them to question what they previously considered to be a fair social order and to take some type of action to "subvert the system" and do right by their students.

The concept of "subverting the system" brings to mind a young woman I worked with years ago in a public university teacher education program. Similar to a great number of students in teacher education programs, this young woman came into the program with unexamined beliefs about the social order and status quo. She came into the program, though largely unaware of it, with an uncritical acceptance of the social order as just and fair. Given her unexamined ideological orientation and rather sheltered life experiences, she demonstrated little comprehension of the very real inequities confronting subordinated students in schools and the larger society.

I distinctly remember her initial discomfort with Paulo Freire's (and other critical pedagogues') writings and, in particular, her rejection of the notion that teachers of subordinated students often have to work in ways that teach against the grain in order to do right by the children. The young woman voiced her disbelief and discomfort with this critical notion and argued that it was not necessary for teachers to resort to subversive behavior since the key function of schools is precisely to help students. The student recalled her own experience as a middle-class White public-school student, and maintained that school systems were fair places and that students who failed to succeed did not take full advantage of the opportunities afforded them. However, later in the semester—while completing her student-teaching experience in a predominantly African American and Mexicano/Latino urban elementary school—she came into class and shared that she had engaged in her first act of conscious resistance against school rules, rules which she felt worked to hurt and further subordinate her students.

She explained that the urban elementary school in which she student-taught had very few green areas. The young woman voiced her opinion that she found the lack of grassy areas and vegetation to be especially unacceptable, given that the school was supposed to service young children. The student-teacher then went on to describe one area of the school that had a small tree and small plot of grass that was off-limits to students. On a particularly warm day, she decided she wanted to read a story to her students under the shade of that small tree. Although she was well aware that students were not allowed in this area, she consciously broke the rule in order to, as she explained, provide her students with an optimal storybook reading experience. She angrily pointed out that White students in middle-class and suburban schools take for granted learning opportunities such as sitting on the grass and having a story read to them, while her children (poor Mexicanos/Latinos and African Americans) were prohibited from sitting on the only patch of green grass available at the school.

Although this particular student's act of subversion was not particularly radical or extreme, my point is that it is precisely this outrage and sense of student advocacy—reflective of increased political and ideological clarity—that I believe that all teachers, but in particular teachers of subordinated students, must possess in order to do right by the young people that they serve. Such prospective teachers, like the experienced educators described in this article, have in part surmised that their previously held ideological explanations for the existing social order (e.g., that the social order is fair and based on ability and merit, that if people work hard enough they can overcome oppression, etc.) were not adequate for explaining the grave inequities, injustice, and subordination they witnessed. Unfortunately, in my experience as a teacher educator, the majority of prospective teachers are not quite so perceptive or flexible in their thinking to consider alternative ideological explanations without assistance from teacher education personnel.

Concluding Thoughts

Prospective teachers, all educators for that matter, need to begin to develop the political and ideological clarity that will guide them in denouncing discriminatory school and social conditions and practices. This clarity is crucial if teachers truly wish to better instruct, protect, and advocate for their students. It is also indispensable if educators endeavor to nurture youth into being critical thinkers capable of acting upon the world. According to Freire (1998a, 1998b), beyond technical skills, teachers should also be equipped with a full understanding of what it means to have courage—to denounce the present inequities that directly harm certain populations of students—and effectively create psychologically healthy, culturally responsive, humanizing, and self-empowering educational contexts. Critical pedagogy challenges us to see through the dense fog of ideology and to become courageous in our commitment to defend subordinated student populations—even when it is easier not to take a stand—and equip them with critical transformative tools. Freire (1997) states:

> What keeps a person, a teacher able as a liberatory educator is the political clarity to understand
> the ideological manipulations that disconfirm human beings as such, the political clarity that would

tell us that it is ethically wrong to allow human beings to be dehumanized . . . One has to believe that if men and women created the ugly world that we are denouncing, then men and women can create a world that is less discriminating and more humane. (p. 315)

In the spirit of the realistic yet hopeful educators in this study, critical pedagogy reminds us of the importance of clearly identifying obstacles in order to work collaboratively with students and communities to come up with equally clear and realistic strategies for overcoming them.

Note

1.   Sections of this chapter first appeared in Bartolomé L. & Balderrama, M. (2001). The Need for Educators with Political and Ideological Clarity: Providing Our Children with "the Best." In M. De la Luz Reyes & J. Halcón. *The Best for Our Children: Critical Perspectives on Literacy for Latino Students*. New York: Teachers College Press (pp. 48–64). This chapter also constitutes an expanded version of my 2002 chapter, Creating an Equal Playing Field: Teachers as Advocates, Border Crossers, and Cultural Brokers. In Z. F. Beykont (Ed.) *The Power of Culture: Teaching Across Language Differences*. Cambridge, MA: Harvard Education Publishing Group.

References

Bartolomé, L. I. (1994). Beyond the Methods Fetish: Toward a Humanizing Pedagogy. *Harvard Educational Review*, 64(2), pp. 173–194.

Bartolomé, L. I. (1998). *The Misteaching of Academic Discourses: The Politics of Language in the Classroom*. Boulder, CO: Westview Press.

Bartolomé, L. I. (2000). Democratizing Bilingualism: The Role of Critical Teacher Education. In Z.F. Beykont (Ed.) *Lifting Every Voice: Pedagogy and Politics of Bilingualism*. Cambridge, MA: Harvard Education Publishing Group (pp.167–186).

Bartolomé, L. I. (2002). Creating an Equal Playing Field: Teachers as Advocates, Border Crossers, and Cultural Brokers. In Z. F. Beykont (Ed.) *The Power of Culture: Teaching across Language Differences*. Cambridge, MA: Harvard Education Publishing Group (pp. 167–192).

Bartolomé, L. I. & Balderrama, M. (2001). The Need for Educators with Political and Ideological Clarity: Providing Our Children with "the Best." In M. Reyes & J. J. Halcón (Eds.) *The Best for Our Children: Latina/Latino Views on Literacy*. New York: Teachers College Press (pp. 48–64).

Beaubouef, T. (1997). Politicized Mothering among African-American Women Teachers: A Qualitative Inquiry. Unpublished doctoral dissertation, Harvard Graduate School of Education, Cambridge, MA.

Bloom, G. M. (1991). The Effects of Speech Style and Skin Color on Bilingual Teaching Candidates' and Bilingual Teachers' Attitudes toward Mexican-American Pupils. Unpublished doctoral dissertation, Stanford University, Stanford, CA.

Darder, A., Torres, R., & Baltodano, M. (2002). Introduction. In A. Darder, R. Tones & M. Baltodano. *The Critical Pedagogy Reader*. New York: RoutledgeFalmer.

Davis, K.A. (1994). Multicultural Classrooms and Cultural Communities of Teachers. *Teaching and Teacher Education*, 11, pp. 553–563.

Farley, J. E. (2000). *Majority-Minority Relations* (fourth edition). Upper Saddle River, NJ: Prentice Hall.

Freire, P. (1997). *Mentoring the Mentor: A Critical Dialogue with Paulo Freire*. New York: Peter Lang.

Freire, P. (1998a). *Pedagogy of Freedom: Ethics, Democracy, and Civic Courage*. Lanham, MD: Rowman & Littlefield.

Freire, P. (1998b). *Teachers as Cultural Workers*. Boulder, CO: Westview Press.

Garcia, E. (1991). Effective Instruction for Language-minority Students: The Teacher. *Boston University Journal of Education*, 173(2), pp. 130–141.

Gomez, M. L. (1994). Teacher Education Reform and Prospective Teachers' Perspectives on Teaching "Other People's Children." *Teaching and Teacher Education*, 10(3), pp. 319–334.

Gonsalves, R. (1996). Resistance in the Multicultural Education Classroom. Unpublished manuscript, Harvard Graduate School of Education, Cambridge, MA.

Haberman, M. (1991). Can Culture Awareness Be Taught in Teacher Education Programs? *Teacher Education*, 4(1), pp. 25–31.

Howard, G. R. (2000). *We Can't Teach What We Don't Know: White Teachers, Multiracial Schools*. New York: Teachers College Press.

King, J. E. (1991). Dysconscious Racism: Ideology, Identity, and the Miseducation of Teachers. *Journal of Negro Education*, 60(2), pp. 133–157.

Ladson-Billings, G. (2000). Fighting for Our Lives: Preparing Teachers to Teach African-American Students. *Journal of Teacher Education*, 51(3), May/June, pp. 206–214.

Leistyna, P. & Woodrum, A. (1996). Context and Culture: What Is Critical Pedagogy? In P. Leistyna, A. Woodrum, & S. Sherblom (Eds.) *Breaking Free: The Transformative Power of Critical Pedagogy*. Cambridge, MA: Harvard Education Publishing Group.

Lucas, T., Henze, R., & Donato, R. (1990). Promoting the Success of Latino Language-minority Students: An Exploratory Study of Six High Schools. *Harvard Educational Review*, 60(3), pp. 3 15–340.

Macedo, D. (1994). *Literacies of Power: What Americans Are Not Allowed to Know*. Boulder, CO: Westview.

National Center for Education Statistics. (1992). *American Education at a Glance*. Washington, DC: Office of Education Research and Improvement.

Nieto, S. (2000a). Placing Equity Front and Center: Some Thoughts on Transforming Teacher Education for a New Century. *Journal of Teacher Education*, 51(3), May/June, pp. 180–187.

Nieto, S. (2000b). Bringing Bilingual Education out of the Basement, and Other Imperatives for Teacher Education. In Z. F. Beykont (Ed.) *Lifting Every Voice: Pedagogy and Politics of Bilingualism*. Cambridge, MA: Harvard Education Publishing Group, pp.187–207.

Riverview High School Profile Information (1996). National City, CA.

Sleeter, C. (1992). Restructuring Schools for Multicultural Education. *Journal of Teacher Education*, 43(2), pp. 141–148.

Stanton-Salazar, R. D. (1997). A Social Capital Framework for Understanding the Socialization of Racial-minority Children and Youths. *Harvard Educational Review*, 67(1), pp. 1–40.

Stanton-Salazar, R. D., Vásquez, O. A., & Mehan, H. (2000). Re-engineering Academic Success through Institutional Support. In S.T. Gregory (Ed.) *The Academic Achievement of Minority Students: Perspectives, Practices, and Prescriptions*. Lanham, MD: University Press of America, pp. 213–247.

Zimpher, N. (1989). The RATE Project: A Profile of Teacher Education Students. *Journal of Teacher Education*, 40(6), pp. 27–30. (First published in *Teacher Education Quarterly*, 39, no. 1 (2004), 97–122.

PART THREE

The Political
Dimensions of
Critical Pedagogy

CHAPTER 16

The Future of the Past

Reflections on the Present State of Empire and Pedagogy

PETER MCLAREN

Hand-in-hand with his threat warnings, Bush keeps telling us how his War on Terror has made us so much safer, bragging that there hasn't been a terrorist attack in the United States in the five years since the one of September 11, 2001. Marvelous. There wasn't a terrorist attack in the United States in the five years before that day either.

(Blum, 2006)

In the twenty-first century, leaders of the dominant capitalist states have declared a permanent war on terror. Antidemocratic laws which grant extrajudicial powers to hold citizens and immigrants without trial are moving modern democracies towards capitalist sovereignty congealed in the shape of totalitarianism. The Patriot Act was extended in the United States, eviscerating basic Constitutional rights. Civil society is becoming militarized in the direction of a permanent security state, while political leaders on the right betray an unvarnished contempt for any kind of criticism of US foreign or domestic policy. Where comity among nations was once lauded as a virtue, it is now seen as a weakness. The world's only superpower seeks to rule by intimidation and brutality.

Marx's critique of political economy and his materialist conception of history cannot be so easily discarded into the rag-and-bone shop of social history. Just as in Marx's day, the development of capitalism is concomitant with the growth and consolidation of common-place understandings of how freedom of the market translates into democratic freedom. The prevailing categories and forms of thought used today to justify foreign and domestic pol-icy in capitalist societies—such as those of "democracy"' and "freedom"—are shaped by the social relations of the societies that employ them. They have contributed to the perpetu-ation of a class-divided, racialized, and patriarchal social order. These forms of thought man-ifest a certain universality and often reveal the imprint of the ruling class (echoing Marx's famous dictum that the ideas of the ruling class prevail in every epoch as the ruling ideas). The market as a category in the vernacular of the ruling class is not conceived of as a cru-cible of exploitation but as a means of opportunity, a means of leveling the playing field, a means of achieving freedom and democracy. But Marx showed that precisely what we need is freedom from the market.

Marx demonstrated how the formal equality of political rights can exist, hand-in-hand, with brute exploitation and suffering. The separation of economic and political rights is the very condition of the impossibility of democracy, a separation that liberals have been stunningly unable to challenge in their discourses of reform. In fact, as Ellen Meiksins Wood (1995) and others have pointed out, the constitutive impossibility of democracy in a soci-ety built upon property rights significantly accounts for why democracy can be invoked against the democratic imperatives of the people in the gilded name of the global imperium. Property and the market must be served by ensuring that there is too little, not too much, democracy, and this cause can be advanced by leaders making sure that the world exists in a constant state of conflict. This, of course, can only occur when citizens are convinced that "freedom is not free" and that war will always be necessary to defend it (including "preven-tative wars" waged against those who are deemed to pose a threat sometime in the near or distant future). This is precisely how the United States secures its suzerainty: by ruling through the market, allowing limited autonomy to nations that adhere to the rules of the market and agree to keep their populaces subjugated as cheap labor. And by sending its war-rior class into furious battle in those recalcitrant arenas where there is resistance to the rulers of the market as well as to the market rules, and hence to the conditions of freedom and democracy and its imperial agents and guardians. This is the real meaning of the freedom of the market. The market generates the conditions for the "winners" to create the neces-sary ideologies for justifying violence on the grounds of "us-against-them" theories of "inherent" competition and violence within the human species. And it provides them with the most formidable weapons available to carry out such violence and, in the case of the United States, to achieve the status (at least for the time being) as the organizing center of the world state.

A Reflection on Education under Attack

In 2006, the Governor of Florida, Jeb Bush, approved a law (known as the Florida Education Omnibus Bill) barring the teaching of "revisionist" history in Florida public schools, including "postmodern viewpoints of relative truth." One chilling passage in the bill states: "American history shall be viewed as factual, not constructed, shall be viewed as knowable, teachable, and testable, and shall be defined as the creation of a new nation based largely on the universal principles stated in the Declaration of Independence." In a directive that brings to mind a cult of anti-intellectualism, teachers are charged to concentrate on the history and content of the Declaration and are instructed to teach the "history, meaning, significance and effect of the provisions of the Constitution of the United States and the amendments thereto" and to emphasize "flag education, including proper flag display and flag salute" and on the necessity of teaching "the nature and importance of free enterprise to the United States economy" (Craig, 2006). When seen in conjunction with President George W. Bush's 2003 attack on "revisionist historians" who challenged his justifications for using force against Saddam Hussein, and his 2005 warning on Veteran's Day in which he proclaimed that it is "deeply irresponsible to rewrite the history of how the war began" (Zimmerman, 2006), this inflammatory public demand for interpretive orthodoxy is designed to ward off any and all challenge to conventional understandings of history, understandings awash in information of suspicious provenance. In such a climate that is witnessing concerted attempts to blur the distinction between fact and value, collapsing them into official versions of events that carry the force of unbreachable dogma, disagreement can easily be equated with misinterpretation and misrepresentation, or even tantamount to deliberate falsification.

The accolades heaped by the corporate media upon Ronald Reagan after his death was an index of just how little Americans know—or want to remember—about their presidents. Reagan's administration helped to establish the murderous Contra terrorists, who deliberately targeted innocent civilians, including women and children, in their attempt to overthrow Nicaragua's Sandinista rebels. And what about Gerald Ford? Ford gave the Indonesian dictator Suharto permission to invade East Timor, resulting in the massacre of 200, 000 people, one third of the population of the country. Ford blocked the UN security council from enforcing its resolution respecting the right of self-determination and demanding the withdrawal of the Indonesian army. Ford also provided military and economic aid, including training for repressive internal security forces, to more than a dozen Latin American dictatorships, including that of Chile's infamous Augusto Pinochet. He sent large-scale arms aid and security assistance to numerous other brutal dictators, including Ferdinand Marcos in the Philippines and the Shah of Iran. He also allied with both the Mobutu dictatorship of Zaire and the apartheid regime in South Africa to arm rebel groups against the internationally recognized government of Angola (Zunes, 2006) . And while these accounts barely scrape the surface of the horrendous policies of Reagan and Ford, it was difficult, if not impossible, to find any mention of them in the mainstream media accounts of Reagan and Ford's historical 'legacies.' After the deaths of these two "great" presidents, how many classroom discussions in the nation's schools centered around their egregious foreign and domestic policies? One wonders if the Florida Education Omnibus Bill is even necessary?

Reflections on Multicultural Education

The field of multiculturalism has, regrettably, overemphasized contingency and the reversibility of cultural practices at the level of the individual at the expense of challenging the structural determinations and productive forces of capital, its laws of motion, and its value form of labor—a move that has replaced an undialectical theory of economic determination with a poststructuralist theory of cultural determination, one that underestimates the ways in which the so-called autonomy of cultural acts are already rooted in the coercive relationships of the realm of necessity. Here, multiculturalists and antiracist scholars have often failed to acknowledge the considerable extent to which objective surplus labor grounds both cultural practices and social institutions. It is essential, therefore, that current realities we are witnessing in the national and international political arenas be understood in terms of their historical specificity and in terms of their functional imperatives for nation-states "administering a commodity-centered economy and its class-determining division of social labor" (San Juan, 2002). Despite the current rhetoric of positive nationalism, i.e., equal opportunity for all, these politics occlude both the racialized ideologies and economic interests of the capitalist class. But we also want to emphasize that we do not wish to limit counterhegemonic struggles against racism, patriarchy, and capitalist exploitation to a productivist framework of unilinear labor struggles involving the proletariat. Nor do we see the antiglobalization movement begun in Seattle as the global vanguard. Rather, we see current liberation struggles led not by the whitestream anticapitalist vanguard, but by the world's most destitute: groups such as South Africa's *abantu abahlala emijondolo* (shack-dweller movement) and the new movements of nondocumented workers throughout the world, including the United States.

A deepened understanding of the impact of global capitalism on aggrieved communities is essential for understanding the emergence of an acutely polarized labor market and the fact that disproportionately high percentages of people of color are trapped in the lower rungs of domestic and global labor markets. Difference in the era of global capitalism is crucial to the workings, movements, and profit levels of multinational corporations, but those types of complex relations cannot be mapped out without attending to capitalist class formations. Severing issues of difference from class analysis therefore conveniently draws attention away from the crucially important ways in which people of color (and more specifically women of color) provide capital with its superexploited labor pools—a phenomenon that is on the rise all over the world with the internationalization of migrant labor. In our call for a materialist analysis of the intersections of race, class, ethnicity, and gender, we are not arguing that proponents of cultural studies, post-Marxists or postcolonial theorists have all made their peace with capital, but they have exercised a "solidarity of defeat" in so far as they have limited their work to bad-faith reforms that have sidestepped the struggle against capital and pursued analysis compatible with the demands of neoliberal capitalism. Post-Marxists who are quick to celebrate the politics of difference, particularity, and historicity when they are discussing race quickly substitute these terms for those of universalizing, totalizing, or essentializing when they are discussing Marxist theory.

Joel Kovel (2002) has discussed the practice of prioritizing different categories of race, class, gender, species, etc., which he refers to as "dominative splitting." Kovel describes the process of establishing the priority of such categories as follows:

> Here we must ask, priority in relation to what? If we intend prior in time, then gender holds the laurel—and, considering how history always adds to the past rather than replacing it, would appear as at least a trace in all further dominations. If we intend prior in existential significance, then that would apply to whichever of the categories was put forward by immediate historical forces as these are lived by masses of people: thus to a Jew living in Germany in the 1930s, anti-Semitism would have been searingly prior, just as anti-Arab racism would be to a Palestinian living under Israeli domination today, or a ruthless aggravated sexism would be to women living in, say, Afghanistan. As to which is politically prior, in the sense of being that which whose transformation is practically more urgent, that depends upon the preceding, but also upon the deployment of all the forces active in a concrete situation . . . If, however, we ask the question of efficacy, that is, which split sets the others into motion, then priority would have to be given to class, for the plain reason that class relations entail the state as an instrument of enforcement and control, and it is the state that shapes and organizes the splits that appear in human ecosystems. (p. 123)

Kovel warns that we should not talk of "classism" to go along with "sexism," "racism," and "speciesism" because, he argues, "class is an essentially man-made category, without root in even a mystified biology." He maintains that historically the difference arises because "class"

> signifies one side of a larger figure that includes a state apparatus whose conquests and regulations create races and shape gender relations. Thus there will be no true resolution of racism so long as class society stands, inasmuch as a racially oppressed society implies the activities of a class-defending state. Nor can gender inequality be enacted away so long as class society, with its state, demands the super-exploitation of women. (pp. 123–124)

As I have acknowledged elsewhere (Scatamburlo-D'Annibale & McLaren, 2003, 2004), class is part of the "triptych formulation" that presumes to explain identity formation via intersecting relations of class, race, and gender in which people experientially locate themselves. Yet this formulation often reduces class to "classism" and fails to acknowledge its strategic centrality as a universal form of exploitation that provides the ground from which racialized and gendered social relations are produced. It fails to appreciate the conceptual fecundity of understanding race and racism within the context of class rule (which is not the same thing as reducing race and gender to class since the primacy of class most often means putting the fight against racism and sexism at the center of the struggle for socialism). That is to say, I stress the explanatory primacy of class for analyzing the structural determinants of race, gender, and class oppression (Meyerson, 2000). To reduce identity to the experience that people have of their race, class, and gender location is to fail to acknowledge the objective structures of inequality produced by specific historical forces that mediate the subjective understandings of both individuals and groups. It is similarly a failure to acknowledge that while relations of oppression on the basis of race, class, and gender invariably intersect, their causes can be effectively traced in capitalist societies to the social relations of production. It is necessary to acknowledge that most social relations constitutive of difference—including those of race, ethnicity, gender, etc.—are considerably shaped by the relations of production and that there is undoubtedly a racialized and gendered division of labor whose severity and function vary depending on where one is situated in the capitalist global economy.

That racism and sexism are necessary social relations of oppression for organizing contemporary capitalist formations (neocolonialist, fascist, imperialist, subimperialist) seems to escape the collective imaginations of those who theorize difference in a truncated and exclusively culturalist manner. (Of course, capitalism can also survive quite well in relations of relative gender and racial equality. Capitalism has, after all, been multiculturalized.) Indeed, we find it remarkable that so much of contemporary social theory, including strands of postcolonial theory (ostensibly concerned with marginalized peoples, i.e., the subaltern), have largely abandoned the problems of class, labor exploitation, and socialist struggle at a time when colonialism is reasserting itself in the form of global trade rules and structural adjustment programs.

The Birth Pangs of a New Social Movement

In the United States, an anti-immigration bill sponsored by Rep. James Sensenbrenner which criminalizes undocumented immigrants and makes living and working in the United States illegally a felony has outraged and angered many immigrant communities across the United States. A compromise bill, the Kennedy-McCain immigration bill, while an improvement, is little more than an echo of the "bracero" program of the 1940s, a binational temporary contract labor program initiated in 1942 by the United States and Mexico.

A Marxist analysis of race can be accused of ignoring, understating or even denigrating the importance of anti-racist struggle. In my recent work, I stress the *explanatory primacy* of class for analyzing the *structural determinants* of race, gender and class oppression. I attempt to highlight how class operates as a universal form of exploitation whose abolition is central to the abolition of all manifestations of oppression. One must abolish a class-defending state in order to make real headway in eliminating racism and patriarchy. I take the position that forms of oppression based on categories of difference do not possess relative autonomy from class relations but rather constitute the ways in which oppression is lived and experienced within a class-based system. It is important to specify how all forms of social oppression function within an overarching capitalist system. We must use a multi-pronged approach in our social struggle. We must choose to organize against racism, sexism, class oppression and white supremacy *simultaneously* as part of a larger anti-imperialist project directed towards the struggle for socialism. Forms of non-class domination such as racism must often be fought in advance of the class struggle. Certainly we cannot make headway in fighting class oppression without fighting racism and sexism. And clearly, racism and sexism must be fought against, despite whether or not we have traced their existence to capitalist relations of exploitation., In order for Euro American workers to participate in their own class liberation, it's absolutely imperative that they reject in the strongest possible way the system of white-skin privilege. Marxists certainly shouldn't naturalize whiteness, nor should they simplify race by reducing it to class. At the same time, race is more than a social construct delinked from capitalist social relations of production.

At great personal risk, immigrants have taken part in a surge of protests against anti-immigration, transforming the political landscape in the United States. Millions are rallying against the government, asking important questions about the nature of this system and how they can participate in the fight for a better world. *Juntos en la lucha*, students and I marched together with over half a million immigrants, mostly from Mexico and other South and Central American countries during a day of protest that was billed "A Day Without Immigrants" and "The Great American Boycott." We walked four miles through Koreatown and the Mid-Wilshire district of downtown Los Angeles, to La Brea Avenue. We witnessed numerous signs that read "We are all immigrants" and "No human being is illegal." In a show of support, Seventh Street wholesale fruit stands, meatpacking plants, and garment factories closed down in order to allow their nondocumented employees to march. Elsewhere throughout the city, factories, restaurants, construction, landscaping, transportation, and many other industries and services ground to a halt. After noticing several signs that read, "Si por que soy Mexicano dicen que soy 'illegal' revisa la historia real pues estoy en mi tierra natal" ("If because I am Mexican they say that I am illegal, revisit the real history, I am in my native country"), we remembered the fact that for the past 156 years, the United States has occupied Mexico, and that even George W. Bush's ranch in Crawford, Texas, stands on stolen Mexican land. The Minutemen, a vigilante citizen group that hunts immigrants along the border with Mexico (which Mexicans call "la linea" or "the line"), have already set off on a cross-country trek through rural and urban communities in Arizona, New Mexico, Texas, Arkansas, Tennessee, Georgia, Alabama, and Virginia. Some Minutemen have sported T-shirts with the emblem, "Kill a Mexican today?" and others have organized "for profit" human safaris in the desert (Robinson, 2006). Jim Gilchrist, the pugnacious and brawny founder, wears a bulletproof vest in addition to having three or more bodyguards nearby at all times. Yet while clearly trying to inspire fear among undocumented workers, Minutemen are being challenged by crowds chanting: "¡Bush escucha! ¡Estamos en la lucha!" and "¡El pueblo unido jamás será vencido!" ("Bush listen up! We are in struggle!" and "The people united will never be defeated!").

While conservative politicians and the unprincipled pettifoggers who work for them no longer are speaking of conquering land, resources, and/or people adjacent to the southwest US border, they nevertheless view themselves and the Anglo-American constituencies they represent as living at the cusp of an inevitable "brown wave" of immigration that could wash over them inexorably and extinguish their identities. Consequently, there is a strong emphasis on nationalism, and the acculturation and assimilation of Latina/os to the American Way of Life. The American way of life reinforces the self-validating attributes of gender, kinship or parentage, skin color, and the naturalizing markers demarcating

them from the subjugated and subordinated peoples, thereby serving as a functioning principle of the imperial nation-state, one that seeks an "asymmetrical distribution of social
wealth and power" (San Juan, 2002, p. 93). According to E. San Juan, the object of
nationalism signifies a community "just like us" which is inextricably linked to the nation-
state's formation of classes and social groups.

San Juan elaborates on this position by unfolding the core roots of American national
identity. He asserts that the development of American "patria" takes place along two primary dimensions: the systematic inclusion and exclusion of certain segments of the population, and the political management of social life forms according to the hierarchization
of morals and codes of conduct (93). These identity formations are made manifest across
multiple dimensions. The media, the electorate, pop culture, and education work symbi-
otically to sustain and proliferate hegemonic interpretations of what it means to be
"American." Tensions do arise, however, when such formations are threatened by dramatic
demographic shifts in the population that no longer are able to secure a static or unyielding social configuration. It is precisely when the geopolitical landscape becomes destabi-
lized that we witness an inversion in dominant discourses. The "colonizers" claim to be the
"colonized" and consequently, a spate of systematic and sustained political initiatives make
their way into the legislative body as a necessary precaution or defense against the inclusion of "other" cultural arrangements.

We must work against neoliberal economic imperialism that, on the one hand, creates
the need for cheap, exploitable, and deportable labor, and that on the other creates the conditions that cause the displacement of workers worldwide and which, in the context of the
United States, encourages the formerly privileged sectors of the White working class to
engage in the most repugnant forms of racism and to scapegoat immigrants of color. And
we struggle against conditions that allow nondocumented immigrants to be deported,
because the threat of deportation is the club that employers hold over the heads of nondocumented workers to keep them in a condition of dependency and helps to ensure their
silence in the process of their superexploitation (Amoo-Adare, in press).

An op-ed in the *Wall Street Journal* received widespread attention when Shelby Steele,
an African American neoconservative scholar from Stanford University's Hoover Institute,
lamented that the US allows itself to be hampered in its foreign policy objectives by the
paralysis of White guilt. Such guilt, claimed Steele, is the engine that drives anti-
Americanism, which in turn is a "construct of Western sin." Steele described White guilt
as a "vacuum of moral authority visited on the present by the shames of the past." He believes
such guilt was spawned after the "collapse of white supremacy as a source of moral authority, political legitimacy and even sovereignty" which according to Steele occurred sometime after World War II. But a price was exacted—"a kind of secular penitence in which
the slightest echo of past sins brings down withering condemnation." As "the greatest embodiment of Western power," the United States is, according to Steele, currently stigmatized
as an ugly imperialist and racist regime because it cannot dissociate itself from its past sins.
Steele writes that "White guilt makes our Third World enemies into colored victims, people whose problems—even the tyrannies they live under—were created by the historical

disruptions and injustices of the white West. We must 'understand' and pity our enemy even as we fight him." Consequently, White guilt forces us to fight Islamic extremism with "managerial minimalism" detached from the "passions of war."

The argument that the United States fights its wars in a minimalist fashion and does not have "enough ferocity to win" is one that we find difficult to swallow, especially when you consider the brutal and sweeping ruthlessness of its military campaigns over the last half century. We suppose Steele would like the military to act with a type of dispassionate passion, a cold, calculated killing machine able to ratchet up the kill ratio of its troops without so much as a twinge of White guilt. Perhaps along with blasting limbs from bodies, the military could also blast away any of the coordinates of reason that might be holding back its troops, unhinging the gates of our White conscience for the sake of a morally frictionless annihilation of the enemy—murder with an excess of efficiency. Steele would like us not to have a second thought about why we are killing so many people of color, and why we are attacking so many nations of non-Christians or those who might have a different opinion about the free market than American business leaders. Steele also uses his theory of White guilt to explain why we are so impotent in "truly regulating the southern border" against illegal immigrants.

Reflections on Educating Inside the Beast

Here, in the world's imperial heartland, education has become an epicenter of debate over the meaning of citizenship and the role and status of the United States in world history. Science is under attack in the high schools; theories of evolution are being challenged by those of creationism and intelligent design, and privatization is destroying what is left of public schools.

An emphasis on testing resulting in a teaching-to-the-test mania, strict accountability schemes, prepackaged and scripted teaching for students of color, and a frenetic push towards more standardized testing—what Kozol refers to as "desperation strategies that have come out of the acceptance of inequality" (2005, p. 51)—has been abundantly present since the mid-1990s. But what has this trend produced? As Jonathan Kozol points out, the achievement gap between Black and White children has substantially widened since the early 1990s, about the same time as we began to witness the growing resegregation of schools (when the courts began to disregard the mandates of the Brown decision). This has led to what Kozol calls "apartheid schooling." Kozol reports that in 48% of high schools in the country's largest districts (those that have the highest concentrations of Black and Latina/o students), less than half of the entering ninth graders graduate in 4 years. There was a 75% increase between 1993–2002 in the number of high schools graduating less than half of their ninth-grade class in 4 years. In the 94% of districts in New York State where the majority of the students are White, nearly 80% of students graduate from high school in 4 years. In the 6% of districts where Black and Latina/o students make up the majority, the percentage is considerably less—approximately 40%. There are 120 high schools in New York (enrolling nearly 200,000 minority students) where, Kozol notes, less than 60% of entering ninth graders make it to the twelfth grade. This statistic prompted Kozol to exclaim: "There is something deeply hypocritical about a society that holds an eight-year-old inner-city child 'accountable' for her performance on a high-stakes standardized exam but does not hold the high officials of our government accountable for robbing her of what they gave their own kids six or seven years earlier" (p. 46).

Reflections on Our Providential History

The history of the United States is deeply providential. The increasing ranks of Americans who profess to serve no other king but Jesus see themselves as moral stewards of a country preordained by God to save humanity. Besotted with the White man's burden of uplifting the ignorant masses of the third world so that they might join the ranks of the civilized, evangelical Christians (including and perhaps especially those "power puritans" and "opportunistic ayatollahs" who serve at the helm of the Bush administration) betray a Messianic vision rooted in bad theology, rapture politics, and the covenant God has apparently made with consecutive White House administrations throughout history (no doubt more favorably rewarding Republican administrations). With so many professed Christians braying about how important moral values are in the United States, it might come as a surprise that

> in 2004, as a share of our economy, we ranked second to last, after Italy, among developed countries in government foreign aid. Per capita we each provide fifteen cents a day to official development assistance to poor countries. And it's not because we were giving to private charities for relief work instead. Such funding increases our average daily donation by just six pennies, to twenty-one cents. It's also not because Americans were too busy taking care of their own, nearly 18 percent of American children lived in poverty (compared with, say, 8 percent in Sweden). In fact, by pretty much any measure of caring for the least among us you want to propose—we come in nearly last among the rich nations, and often by a wide margin. The point is that (as everyone already knows) the American nation trails badly in all these categories, categories to which Jesus paid particular attention. And it's not as if the numbers are getting better: the US Department of Agriculture reported last year that the number of households that were "food insecure with hunger" had climbed more than 26 percent between 1999 and 2003. (McKibben, 2005, p. 32)

The attack by right-wing law makers on public schools is in part a condemnation of ungodly secular humanism that is seen as robbing the moral authority of the state of its imprimatur granted by God. The same callow calculus cloaked in a sacred rage has had a hand in defining what is to be considered unpatriotic and anti-American, especially after September 11, 2001.

What we are may see in so-called progressive, critical classrooms throughout the United States is not a pedagogy steeled in opposition to oppression, but rather an ersatz critical pedagogy, a domesticated approach to Freirean teaching that stresses the centrality of engaging student experiences and histories. This situation provokes the following sempiternal questions: Are these histories and experiences self-evident? If not, how are the histories of the oppressed written, and who writes them? How are experiences interpreted, and whose interpretation counts the most? What languages of critique are employed at under-standing the formation of student subjectivities? What languages of possibility? Experiences, after all, are the "effects" of discursive regimes which, in turn, are given birth in a vortex of contending social forces, cultural formations, linguistic fields, ideological structures, insti-tutional formations, and which are overdetermined by social relations of production. Those pedagogies that affirm (through dominant narratives and discourses that unprob-lematically valorize democracy and freedom) student experiences but fail to question how these experiences are produced conjecturally in the formation of subjectivity and agency, accept a priori the sovereignty of the market over the body politic; and this, in turn, helps to resecure a pliant submission to the capitalist law of value. And they are often the soft-focus pedagogies of the give-advantage-to-the-already-advantaged, self-empowerment variety. These dominant pedagogies systematically negate rather than make meaningful alternative understandings of the relationship between identity-formation and social rela-tions of production. They are not only reflective but also productive and reproductive of antagonistic social relations, dependent hierarchies of power, and privilege and hege-monic strategies of containing dissent and opposition.

Reflections on a Pedagogy for Life: Paulo Freire in Urgent Times

Motivated by a desire to anchor their students in a coherent worldview and provide them with an enduring stability, teachers especially become an easily breached conduit for the official narratives of the state, whether these be providential, imperialist, triumphalist, cap-italist, or a combination of all of these. The moral panic surrounding the meaning of patri-otism in the post-9/11 United States has produced confusion among teachers and students alike—proclivities easily leveraged by the Bush administration through the corporate media that amplify, echo, mirror, and appease official government narratives at times of national crisis. Loyalty to the office of the President, to the troops fighting our imperial-ist wars, and to whatever laws have been put in to place to protect us from the hirsute ter-rorists has become the highest desideratum.

For over a century, the US government has intervened both forcibly and covertly to topple the governments of numerous countries, including Nicaragua, Guatemala, the Philippines, Panama, South Vietnam, and Chile. For instance, to cite just one of dozens of examples, when the US overthrew Jacobo Arbenz, the left-leaning president of Guatemala, and imposed a military regime, a 30-year civil war ensued in which hundreds of thousands died. One reason that you find some of the most open political rebellions against US policies in Latin America is because this is a region where the US has frequently intervened and where populations have been brutally victimized as a result.

It should come as no surprise that South America has become the site from which some of the most prescient analyses of US imperialism and capitalist exploitation have been devel-oped. At this moment in history, the work of Paulo Freire threatens to explode the culture of silence that informs our everyday life as educators in the world's greatest imperialist democracy, a key overarching saga of which has been the successful dismantling of public schooling by the juggernaut of neoliberal globalization and the corporatization of the public sphere. As critical pedagogy's conscience-in-exile, Freire sought through the pedagogical encounter to foist off the tyranny of authoritarianism and oppression and bring about an all-embracing and diverse fellowship of global citizens profoundly endowed with a fully claimed humanity. Yet instead of heeding a Freirean call for a multivocal public and international dialogue on our responsibility as the world's sole superpower, one that acknowledges that we as a nation are also changed by our relationship to the way we treat others, we have permitted a fanatical cabal of politicians to convince us that dialogue is weakness, an obstacle to peace, that probity is a trait that is secondary to achieving "results," and univocal assertion is a strength.

I have taken inspiration for my work from Paulo Freire, and I, like many other educators, have spoken out—and continue to speak out—against acts of imperialist aggression by the United States government. I have done so in numerous books, articles, and speeches over the past 30 years. The broader context for these writings has been my work in critical pedagogy that involves, among other things, publishing critiques of mainstream educational policy and practice and revealing how such policy and practice is underwritten by the politics of neoliberal capitalist globalization. I have also engaged in anticapitalist, antiracist and antiimperialist activism as part of my ongoing struggle for a socialist alternative to capitalism.

Those who live and write a critical pedagogy are open to attack by both right-wing and liberal critics. I have been challenging the efforts of right-wing politicians and conservative social critics who are attempting to pass a bill in various state legislatures throughout the United States that, under the pretext of establishing political neutrality in the classroom, is designed to curtail the rights of professors in universities to speak out against social and political injustice. Right-wing critics charge that professors like me, who follow a Freirean example, "indoctrinate" students with left-wing propaganda. If passed, "The Academic Bill of Rights"will expressly forbid professors from using the classroom to supposedly "propagandize" their views. In other words, the classroom will become even more of a politically contested site than it is at present, with neoconservatives trying to shut down critical dialogue surrounding initiatives of right-wing politicians. There are many educators who have put themselves at greater risk in their attempts to resist injustice in various educational arenas, and that underscores the rabid intensity of the right in their assault on critical approaches to teaching and learning.

Charges of indoctrinating students were addressed by Paulo Freire, specifically in his magisterial book, *Pedagogy of Hope* (1994), and they serve as an excellent resource for teachers, especially those in the United States that are being labeled as "traitors" and "supporters of terrorism" because they use the classroom as forums for critical dialogue about the war in Iraq and other controversial issues. It is important for teachers to return to the work of an educator who we still use as a compass for our pedagogical life, a life that does not end when the door to the classroom is closed for the day, but one which we have integrated into our hearts and minds, and adapted to the everyday rhythm of our lives.

Freire observes that educational practice reveals a "helplessness to be 'neutral'" (1994, p. 77). There is, Freire argues, no "educational practice in zero space-time" (1994, p. 77); that is, there is no neutral practice. This is because educators are disposed to be ethical agents engaged in educative practice that is directive, political, and indeed has a preference. Freire writes that as an educator, he must "live a life full of consistency between my democratic option and my educational practice, which is likewise democratic" (1994, p. 79). He agrees that we find authoritarianism on both the right and the left of the political spectrum. Both groups can be reactionary in an "identical way" if they "judge themselves the proprietors of knowledge, the former, of revolutionary knowledge, the latter, of conservative knowledge" (1994, p. 79). Both forms of authoritarianism are elitist. Freire underscores the fact that we cannot "conscientize" students without at the same time being "conscientized" by them as well. Teaching should never, under any circumstances, be a form of imposition. On the other hand, we cannot shrink from our democratic duty and fear to teach because of manipulation. We always run this risk and must do so willingly, as a necessary act, as a leap across a dialectical divide that is necessary for any act of knowing to occur. This is why critical educators stress the idea of the hidden curriculum as a way of self-examination, of remaining coherent, of remaining tolerant and at the same time of becoming critically disposed in their teaching. As Freire reminds us, tolerance breeds openness and critical disposition breeds curiosity and humility.

Knowing is a type of dance—a movement, but a self-conscious one. Criticality is not a line stretching into eternity; it is a circle. In other words, knowing can be the object of our knowing, it can be self-reflective, and it is something in which we can make an intervention. We inherit cognition as a species, but we acquire other skills along the way, and we need to grow integrally and with coherence.

Freire reminds us that teaching cannot be reduced to the one-way transmission of the object of knowledge, or a two-way transaction between the teacher and the student, but is rather a form of dialectical transformation of both the teacher and the student, and this occurs when a teacher knows the content of what is to be taught and a student learns how to learn. Teaching occurs when educators recognize their knowing in the knowing of the students.

Freire argues that teachers must challenge students to move beyond their commonsense beliefs and assumptions regarding their self-in-the-world and their self-with-the-world, but must do so by respecting the commonsense knowledge that students bring into the classroom. Freire notes: "What is impermissible—I repeat myself, now—is disrespect for the knowledge of common sense. What is impermissible is the attempt to transcend it without starting with it and proceeding by way of it" (1994, p. 83). Yet at the same time we have a duty to challenge students' feelings of certainty about their own experiential knowledge. Freire asks:

> What kind of educator would I be if I did not feel moved by a powerful impulse to seek, without
> lying, convincing arguments in defense of the dreams for which I struggle, in defense of the "why"

of the hope with which I act as an educator? What is not permissible to be doing is to conceal truths, deny information, impose principles, eviscerate the educands of their freedom, or punish them, no matter by what method, if, for various reasons, they fail to accept my discourse—reject my utopia. (1994, p. 83)

Freire makes it clear that we reject a "focalist" approach to students' experiential knowledge and approach a student's experiential knowledge contextually, inserting our respect for such knowledge "into the larger horizon against which it is generated—the horizon of cultural context, which cannot be understood apart from its class particularities, and this indeed in societies so complex that the characterization of those particularities is less easy to come by" (1994, p. 85). Students' experiences must be understood within the contextual and historical specificities in which such experiences are produced. They must be read dialectically against the larger totality in which they are generated. For Freire, the regional emerges from the local; the national emerges from the regional; the continental emerges from the national, and the worldwide emerges from the continental. He warns: "Just as it is a mistake to get stuck in the local, losing our vision of the whole, so also it is a mistake to waft above the whole, renouncing any reference to the local when the whole has emerged" (1994, p. 87). We are universalists, yes, because we struggle for universal human rights, for economic justice worldwide, but we begin from somewhere, from concrete spaces and places where subjectivities are forged and commodified (and, we hope, decommodified), and where critical agency is developed in particular and distinct ways. And when Freire speaks of struggling to build a utopia, he is speaking of a concrete as opposed to an abstract utopia, a utopia grounded in the present, always operating "from the tension between the *denunciation* of a present becoming more and more intolerable, and the '*annunciation*,' announcement, of a future to be created, built—politically, esthetically, and ethically—by us women and men" (1994, p. 91). Utopias are always in motion; they are never pregiven, they never exist as blueprints which would only ensure the "mechanical repetition of the present," but rather they exist within the movement of history itself, as opportunity and not as determinism. They are never guaranteed.

While it is vitally important that we, as educators, never underestimate knowledge produced from our daily, commonsense experience (since such a rejection of popular knowledge amounts to a form of nearsightedness that is sectarian, elitist, and that occasions epistemological error), by the same token it is important not to engage in the "mythification of popular knowledge, its superexaltation" (p. 84). And while it is important to dream of a better world—since dreaming is "a necessary political act, it is an integral part of the historico-social manner of being a person . . . part of human nature, which, within history, is in permanent process of becoming" (pp. 90–91)—we need to remember that "there is no dream without hope."

Critical educators are in the process of creating their own dreams of a world that is arching towards social and economic justice, and can see those dreams reflected in the mirror of Freire's pedagogical dream, one that is inspired by a hope born of political struggle and a belief in the ability of the oppressed to transform the world from "what is" to "what could be," to reimagine, re-enchant, and recreate the world rather than adapt to it. The reverse mirror image of this dream is the one that drives the "neutral" pedagogy that neoconservatives are struggling to bring about in the United States. Pressuring professors to be silent about politics in their classrooms by threat of legal action is itself an abridgement of academic freedom; it is an attempt to remove politics from the classroom by means of imposing politics—and a narrow politics, I might add—on the education process itself. Academic freedom means freedom from having my curriculum scrutinized by a political act of adjudication, by the establishment of some crude political scale from "liberal" to "conservative" that actually prevents critical knowledge from thriving.

Neoconservative educators in the United States defend the freedom to choose to be poor or rich, the freedom to be sick or healthy, the freedom to vote or not to vote—but truly free choice is a choice in which I do not merely choose between two or more options presented to me on a grid preapproved by legislative fiat. Rather, it is the freedom to change the very grid in which those choices are lodged. That is what the concept of freedom means in the practice of critical pedagogy, in the struggle for social justice. And that is what makes Freire's work so important, as important today as it ever was—perhaps even more.

Possibly the greatest reproach that Freire addressed to the authoritarian culture of his time concerned the devitalization and devaluation of human life; the fragmentation and commodification of subjectivity; and the erection of barriers to freely associated labor, joyful participation in social relations, and the self-development of the subject—an indictment that we must extend to all of capitalist society. It would be difficult for progressive educators in the United States not to interpret Freire's message as a call to overthrow the political curates with whom most Americans took refuge after 9/11, priests of disorder who dragged the country deep into some sulfuric swampland populated by church-going elementals and hairy-knuckled demons clutching Bibles—an inferno fit for politicians that even Dante could not imagine. It is surely striking how Freire's eviscerating pedagogical commentary, by planting the seed of catharsis and thereby placing in our hands the responsibility to overcome the political amnesia that has become the hallmark of contemporary teaching, cannot be officially welcomed into the classrooms of our nation by the guardians of the state. For they have witnessed the unnerving intimacy and camaraderie Freire was able to forge among his admirers worldwide and the extent to which they were challenged by the disseminating force of his liberatory language of hope and possibility. And while teacher education programs have not been able to root him out of the philosophy of teaching, they have cannily managed to domesticate his presence. They have done this by transforming the political revolutionary with Marxist ideas into a friendly sage who advocates a love of dialogue, separating this notion from that of a dialogue of love. Hence, the importance of reclaiming Paulo Freire for these urgent times. Freire was critical of teachers who, while turning their podiums in the direction of history, refused to leave their seminar rooms in order to shape it.

Of particular significance for teachers is Freire's last book, *Teachers as Cultural Workers: Letters to Those Who Dare Teach*. It is significant because it serves as an exhortation to a mindfulness of where we are going as educators, of what kind of world we are living in, of what kind of world we would like to see in its place. I would like to reflect upon some of the themes of this book as a way of addressing the challenge we face as citizens in a desperate and uncertain future. One of the central themes is the importance of a pedagogy powered by love.

For Freire, love is preeminently and irrevocably dialogical. It is not an attachment or emotion isolated from the everyday world; it viscerally emerges from an act of daring, of courage, of critical reflection. Love is not only the fire that ignites the revolutionary but also the creative action of the artist, wielding a palette of sinew and spirit on a canvas of thought and action, its explosion of meaning forever synchronized with the gasp of human freedom. Freire writes:

> We must dare in the full sense of the word, to speak of love without the fear of being called ridiculous, mawkish, or unscientific, if not antiscientific. We must dare in order to say scientifically, and not as mere blah-blah-blah, that we study, we learn, we teach, we know with our entire body. We do all of these things with feeling, with emotion, with wishes, with fear, with doubts, with passion, and also with critical reasoning. (1998, p. 3)

On the topic of love, Freire also writes:

> To the humility with which teachers perform and relate to their students another quality needs to be added: *lovingness*, without which their work would lose its meaning. And here I mean lovingness not only toward the students but also toward the very process of teaching. I must confess, not meaning to cavil, that I do not believe educators can survive the negativities of their trade without some sort of "armed love," as the poet Tiago de Melo would say. Without it they could not survive all the injustice or the government's contempt, which is expressed in the shameful wages and the arbitrary treatment of teachers, not coddling mothers, who take a stand, who participate in protest activities through their union, who are punished, and who yet remain devoted to their work with students.
>
>   It is indeed necessary, however, that this love be an "armed love," the fighting love of those convinced of the right and the duty to fight, to denounce, and to announce. It is this form of love that is indispensable to the progressive educator and that we must all learn. (1998, pp. 40–41)

In addition to the quality of lovingness, Freire adds to the characteristics of the progressive teacher those of humility, courage, tolerance, decisiveness, security, the tension between patience and impatience, joy of living, and verbal parsimony, often inflecting some of these terms with nuance and poetic meaning. For instance, Freire denotes humility as the characteristic of admitting that you don't know everything; for critical citizens it represents a "human duty" to listen to those considered less competent without condescension, a practice intimately identified with the struggle for democracy and a distain for elitism.

Another example is that of tolerance. For Freire, tolerance is not understood as "acquiescing to the intolerable" or "coexistence with the intolerable" nor does it mean "coddling the oppressor" or "disguising aggression." Freire claims that tolerance "is the virtue that teaches us to live with the different. It teaches us to learn from and respect the different."

Freire elaborates:

> On an initial level, tolerance may almost seem to be a favor, as if being tolerant were a courteous, thoughtful way of accepting, of *tolerating*, the not-quite-desired presence of one's opposite, a civilized way of permitting a coexistence that might seem repugnant. That, however, is hypocrisy, not

tolerance. Hypocrisy is a defect; it is degradation. Tolerance is a virtue. Thus if I live tolerance, I should embrace it. I must experience it as something that makes me coherent first with my historical being, inconclusive as that may sound, and second with my democratic political choice. I cannot see how one might be democratic without experiencing tolerance, coexistence with the different, as a fundamental principle. (1998, p. 42)

Freire's dialectics of the concrete (to borrow a phrase from Marxist philosopher Karil Kosik) is very unlike the methodology of the educational postmodernists who, in their artful counterposing of the familiar and the strange in order to deconstruct the unified subject of bourgeois humanism, mock the pieties of monologic authoritarianism with sportive saber slashes across the horizon of familiarity and consensus. Whereas postmodern "resistance" results in a playful hemorrhaging of certainty, a spilling forth of fixed meanings into the submerged grammars of bourgeois society, remixed in the sewers of the social as "resistance" and rematerialized in the art-house jargon of fashionable apostasy, Freire's work retains an unshakable modernist faith in human agency consequent upon language's ineradicable sociality and dialogical embeddedness. What Freire does have in common with the postmodernists, however, is a desire to break free of contemporary discourses that domesticate both the heart and mind. He is not content to remain with the postmodernists in the nocturnal world of the subconscious; rather, he is compelled to take his critical pedagogy to the streets of the real. Freire writes:

> To the extent that I become clearer about my choices and my dreams, which are substantively political and attributively pedagogical, and to the extent that I recognize that though an educator I am also a political agent, I can better understand why I fear and realize how far we still have to go to improve our democracy. I also understand that as we put into practice an education that critically provokes the learner's consciousness, we are necessarily working against myths that deform us. As we confront such myths, we also face the dominant power because those myths are nothing but the expression of this power, of its ideology. (1998, p. 41)

Ultimately, Freire's work is about establishing a critical relationship between pedagogy and politics, highlighting the political aspects of the pedagogical and drawing attention to the implicit and explicit domain of the pedagogical inscribed in the political. While Freire extolled the virtues of socialism, and drew substantively from various Marxist traditions, he was also critical of dogmatic, doctrinaire Marxists whom he saw as intolerant and authoritarian. In fact, he chastised the practice of some "mechanistic Marxists" whom he claimed believed "that because it is part of society's superstructure, education has no role to play before the society is radically transformed in its infrastructure, in its material conditions" (1998, p. 67). In fact, Freire argues that by refusing to take education seriously as a site of political transformation and by opposing socialism to democracy, the mechanistic Marxists have, in effect, delayed the realization of socialism for our times.

Political choices and ideological paths chosen by teachers are the fundamental stuff of Freirean pedagogy. Freire goes so far as to say that educators "are politicians" and that "we engage in politics when we educate" (1998, p. 68). And if it is the case that we must choose a political path, then let us, in Freire's words, "dream about democracy" while fighting "day and night, for a school in which we talk to and with the learners so that, hearing them, we can be heard by them as well" (1998, p. 68).

This is the central challenge of Freire's work and one that, especially at this difficult time in world history, requires a dauntless courage, a hopeful vision, and a steadfast commitment as we struggle within and against these troubling times.

Reflections on a Revolutionary Socialist Pedagogy

On a recent trip to Caracas, Venezuela, to support the Bolivarian revolution, I had the opportunity to reflect upon what a socialist pedagogy might mean for the deepening development of a Freirean-based critical pedagogy. At Miraflores Palace, President Hugo Chavez offered me and my colleague, some brief words of hope. Initially he cautioned us that a monster was living in Washington, a monster that has been a disaster for the entire world; in order to bring about a better world we must remain united in our attempts to defeat this monster. While thanking us for the pedagogical work we have been doing, he nevertheless implored us to work harder, and to be inspired by the example of the Bolivarian revolution. By enfranchising Venezuela's vast working class through an attack on neoliberalism and by channeling increased oil revenues into social projects aimed at increasing educational opportunities and medical treatment for the poor, Chavez is creating the conditions of possibility for a robust push towards socialism. Two thirds of the population of Venezuela who voted for Chavez did so with an understanding that he intends to build socialism of the 21st century. Chavez is working towards Latin American integration to defeat the Monroe Doctrine and he is getting more control of economic sectors. Chavez seeks an integration of the continent and a "complementation" of economies.

A few days later we were present at a taping of *Aló Presidente*, Chavez's weekly television address to the people of Venezuela, and were sitting next to the great Nicaraguan poet of the revolution, Ernesto Cardenal. Responding to an attempt by President Chavez to imagine a new relationship of solidarity and anti-imperialist struggle between people of good will in the United States and those in Venezuela, Cardenal called President Chavez a prophet who was proclaiming a desire for a mystical union among people from opposing nations based on love:

> Mr. President, you have said some things that are very important and moreover are also prophetic . . . when I was a monk my teacher prophesized that one day the people of the United States and the people of Latin America were going to unite but not with an economic union, nor political, nor military, but a mystic union, of love, of two peoples (or nations) loving each other. I have now heard this from you and I want this to be revealed because it is something that hasn't been heard. I have heard it from my teacher and now you have made it a prophecy. [translated by Nathalia Jaramillo]

How Freirean, indeed!

We were impressed by the Bolivian Missions. These missions consist of anti-poverty and social welfare programs. We were fortunate to be able to visit many of them. In one year, the Chavez government was able to graduate 1.43 million Venezuelans from *Mission*

Robinson, a program launched in June 2003. Volunteers who worked for *Mission Robinson* teach reading, writing, and arithmetic to illiterate adults using the *Yo Si Puedo* (Yes I Can) method developed in Cuba. This method uses a combination of video classes and texts which, in only seven weeks, brings students to a basic literacy level. Indigenous peoples are taught to read and write in Spanish and in their own languages, in line with the indigenous rights outlined in the 1999 Bolivian Constitution, Articles 199, 120 and 121 (*Mission Robinson International* has just been launched in Bolivia). *Mission Robinson II* provides basic education up to the sixth grade and *Mission Robinson III* teaches functional literacy and links these efforts to the creation of production units. *Mission Ribas*, a two-year remedial secondary school program (it teaches Spanish, mathematics, world geography, Venezuelan economics, world history, Venezuelan history, English, physics, chemistry, biology and computer science), targets five million Venezuelan dropouts. This program has a Community and Social-labor Component, where groups use their personal experience and their learning to develop practical proposals to solve community problems. I was fortunate enough to join in a group discussion of this component of the program in Barrio La Vega, and were especially impressed with the efforts of students to design a day care center. Unemployed graduates of *Mission Ribas* (known as "lanceros") are encouraged to enroll in *Mission Vuelvan Caras* (About Face), where they receive training in endogenous development, and are eventually incorporated into the formal economy. *Mission Sucre* provides a scholarship program in higher education to the most impoverished sectors of Venezuela, graduating university professionals in three years as opposed to the traditional five years. Our work in an international think-tank based in Caracas, *Centro International Miranda*, has six areas of focus in helping to further the Bolivarian revolution. One of these areas is critical pedagogy.

What is needed now are pedagogies that connect the language of students' everyday experiences to the larger struggle for autonomy and social justice carried out by groups in pursuit of genuine democracy and freedom outside of capital's law of value, organizations working towards building socialist communities of the future. That is something taught by Bolivarian educators who are struggling to build a socialist future in a country deeply divided by class antagonisms.

In our pursuit of locally rooted, self-reliant economies; in our struggles designed to defend the world from being forced to serve as a market for corporate globalists; in our attempts at decolonizing our cultural and political spaces and places of livelihood; in our fight for antitrust legislation for the media; in our challenges to replace indirect social labor (labor mediated by capital) with direct social labor; in our quest to live in balance with nature; and in our various efforts to replace our dominant culture of materialism with values integrated in a life economy, we need to develop a new vision of the future, but one that does not stray into abstract utopian hinterlands too far removed from our analysis of the present barbarism wrought by capital. Our vision of the future must go beyond the present but still be rooted in it; it must exist in the plane of immanence, and not some transcendent sphere where we engage in mystical union with the inhabitants of Mount Olympus. It must attempt to "speak the unspeakable" while remaining organically connected to the familiar and the mundane. We cannot deny the presence of the possible in the contradictions we live out daily in the messy realm of capital. We seek, therefore, a concrete utopia where the subjunctive world of the "ought to be" can be wrought within the imperfect, partial, defective, and finite world of the "what is" by the dialectical act of absolute negation.

Not only must we understand our needs and our capacities—with the goal of satisfying the former and fully developing the latter—but we need to express them in ways that will encourage new cultural formations, institutional structures, and social relations of production that can best help meet those needs and nurture those capacities to the fullest through democratic participation. Equally important is realizing, through our self-activity and subjective self-awareness and formation, that socialism is a collective enterprise that recognizes humankind's global interdependence, that respects diversity while at the same time building unity and solidarity. These very principles underlay the ongoing work in Venezuela's literacy and educational programs taking place in the barrios. Meeting several of the leaders and coordinators of these programs in Barrio La Vega, Sector B, emphasized for me the importance of working towards socialism as an endpoint, but not in some teleological sense. Rather, the struggle could best be animated by the words of Antonio Machado's (1962, p. 826) poem: "Caminante no hay camino, se hace el camino al andar" ("Traveler, there is no road. The road is made as one walks").

Michael Lebowitz (2005) talks about the possibility of "another kind of knowledge" that might exist in a world that is able to transcend capitalism—a socialist world. He urges us to think about what it would be like to operate in a world by means of a direct social knowledge that cannot be communicated through the indirect medium of money: a knowledge tacitly based upon recognition of our unity and solidarity:

> It is a different knowledge when we are aware of who produces for us and how, when we understand the conditions of life of others and the needs they have for what we can contribute. Knowledge of this type immediately places us as beings within society, provides an understanding of the basis of all our lives. It is immediately direct social knowledge because it cannot be communicated through the indirect medium of money. (p. 64)

This is a knowledge, affirms Lebowitz, "which differs qualitatively and quantitatively from the knowledge we have under dominant social relations" (p. 65). It is different precisely because knowledge is no longer treated as a scarce commodity; there is no longer a monopolization and restriction on knowledge as private gain. This type of knowledge, writes Lebowitz, has to be based on certain values; values that are, he notes, enshrined in the Constitution of the Bolivarian Republic of Venezuela, especially Article 299 that is based on "ensuring overall human development"; Article 20, which stipulates that "everyone has the right to the free development of his or her own personality"; and Article 102, where the focus is upon "developing the creative potential of every human being and the full exercise of his or her personality in a democratic society" (pp. 66–67). Such development can only occur through participation (as set out in Article 62) in democratic social formations that enable self-management, comanagement, and cooperation in many forms (as set out in Article 70). Lebowitz's example of Venezuela and its Constitution is a good one, and one that critical educators everywhere would do well to consider for deepening their approach to their own particular struggles.

Reflections on Critical Pedagogy for a Better Society

We are currently living in what Antonio Gramsci called a "war of position"—a struggle to unify diverse social movements in our collective efforts to resist global capitalism—in order to wage what he called "a war of maneuver"; that is, a concerted effort to challenge and transform the state, to create an alternative matrix for society other than value. Part of our war of position is taking place in our schools.

While there is much talk about labor today, and the decline of the labor movement, what is important for educators to keep in mind is the *social form that labor takes*. In capitalist societies, that social form is human capital. Schools are charged with educating a certain form of human capital, with socially producing labor power, and in doing so enhancing specific attributes of labor power that serve the interests of capital. In other words, schools educate the labor-power needs of capital—for capital in general, for the national capital, for fractions of capital (manufacturing, finance, services, etc.), for sectors of capital (particular industries, etc.), or for individual capital (specific companies and enterprises, etc.); they also educate for functions of capital that cut across these categories of capital. General education, for instance, is intentionally divorced from labor-power attributes required to work within individual capitals and is aimed at educating for capital in general. Practical education tries to shape labor-power attributes in the direction of skills needed within specific fractions or sectors of capital. Training, on the other hand, involves educating for labor-power attributes that will best serve specific or individual capitals (Rikowski, 2005).

It is important to note that Rikowski has described capital not only as the subsumption of concrete, living labor by abstract alienated labor, but also as a mode of being, as a unified social force that flows through our subjectivities, our bodies, our meaning-making capacities. Schools educate labor power by serving as a medium for its constitution or its social production in the service of capital. But schools are more than this; they do more than nourish labor power because all of capitalist society accomplishes that. In addition to producing capital in general, schools additionally *condition* labor power in the varying interests of the marketplace. But because labor power is a living commodity, and a highly contradictory one at that, it can be reeducated and shaped in the interests of building socialism; that is, in creating opportunities for the self-emancipation of the working class.

Labor power, as the capacity or potential to labor, doesn't have to serve its current master—capital. It serves the master only when it engages in *the act of laboring for a wage*. Because individuals can refuse to labor in the interests of capital accumulation, labor power can therefore serve another cause—the cause of socialism. Critical pedagogy can be used as a means of finding ways of transcending the contradictory aspects of labor-power creation and creating different spaces where a dereification, decommodification, and decolonization of subjectivity can occur. Critical pedagogy is an agonistic arena where the development of a discerning political subjectivity can be fashioned (recognizing that there will always be socially and self-imposed constraints).

Revolutionary critical pedagogy is multifaceted in that it brings a Marxist humanist perspective to a wide range of policy and curriculum issues. The list of topics includes the globalization of capitalism, the marketization of education, neoliberalism and school reform, imperialism and capitalist schooling, and so on. Revolutionary critical pedagogy (as I am developing it) also offers an alternative interpretation of the history of capitalism and capitalist societies, with a particular emphasis on the United States.

Revolutionary classrooms are prefigurative of socialism in the sense that they are connected to social relations that we want to create as revolutionary socialists. The organization of classrooms generally tries to mirror what students and teachers would collectively like to see in the world outside of schools—respect for everyone's ideas, tolerance of differences, a commitment to creativity and social and educational justice, the importance of working collectively, a willingness and desire to work hard for the betterment of humanity, and a commitment to antiracist, antisexist, and antihomophobic practices.

If, within the social universe of capital, we are inevitably lashed to the very conditions we as critical educators hope to abolish, then there is no sense in trying to strike a delicate equipoise between capital and labor. The time has come to look beyond the value form of labor and seek alternatives to capitalism. Those of us who work in the field of education cannot afford to sit on the sidelines and watch this debate over the future of education as passive spectators. We need to take direct action, creating the conditions for students to become critical agents of social transformation. This means subjecting social relations of everyday life to a different social logic—transforming them in terms of criteria that have not already seeped in the logic of commodification. Students can—and should—become resolute and intransigent adversaries of the values that lie at the heart of commodity capitalism. This implies a new social culture, control of work by the associated producers, and also the very transformation of the nature of work itself.

Critical educators need to move beyond the struggle for a redistribution of value, because such a position ignores the social form of value and assumes a priori the vampire-like inevitability of the market. We need to transcend value, not redistribute it, since we can't build a socialist society on the principle of selling one's labor for a wage. Nor will it suffice to substitute collective capital for private capital. We are in a struggle to negate the value form of mediation, not to produce it in different degrees, scales, or registers. We need freedom, not to revert to some pristine substance or abstract essence prior to the point of production, but the freedom to learn how to appropriate the many social developments formed on the basis of alienated activity, to realize our human capacities to be free, to be a self-directed subject and not merely an instrument of capital for the self-expansion of value, and to be a conscious and purposeful human being with the freedom to determine the basis of our relationships. Here, subjectivity would not be locked into the requirements of capital's valorization process.

Revolutionary critical pedagogy operates from an understanding that the basis of education is political, and that spaces need to be created where students can imagine a different world outside of capitalism's law of value (i.e., social form of labor), where alternatives to capitalism and capitalist institutions can be discussed and debated, and where dialogue can occur about why so many revolutions in past history turned into their opposite. It looks to create a world where a new mode of distribution can prevail, not based on socially necessary labor time, but on actual labor time; where alienated human relations are subsumed by authentically transparent ones; where freely associated individuals can successfully work towards a permanent revolution; where the division between mental and manual labor can be abolished; where patriarchal relations and other privileging hierarchies of oppression and exploitation can be ended; where, to paraphrase Marx, we can truly exercise the principle "from each according to his or her ability and to each according to his or her need." It looks to create a world where we can traverse the terrain of universal rights unburdened by necessity, moving sensuously and fluidly within that ontological space where subjectivity is exercised as a form of capacity building and creative self-activity within and as a part of the social totality: a space where labor is no longer exploited and becomes a striving that will benefit all human beings, where labor refuses to be instrumentalized and commodified and ceases to be a compulsory activity, and where the full development of human capacity is encouraged(Hudis, 2005). It also builds upon forms of self-organization that are part of the history of liberation struggles worldwide, such as the 1871 Paris Commune, Cuba's *Consejos Populares* formed in 1989, those that developed during the civil rights, feminist, and worker movements, and those organizations of today that emphasize participatory democracy.

Critical pedagogy is by no means commensurate with the attention it excites in the academic literature, yet it continues to provide an important site of praxis-making which can be used to educate and agitate about crucial issues that affect our collective future. We need more than powerful exhortations; we need actions that can transform existing concrete situations into socialist solutions. We can't blithely conjure exploitation out of existence with benevolent abstractions—with words that are treated as revolutionary acts in themselves, no matter how universal their reach (Amoo-Adare, in press). Neither can we comfortably rest in our assurance that populism is the answer.

Reflections on Bad Faith Rebels

We would do well to avoid the pretentiousness and arrogance—not to mention competitiveness—that inflicts some educators with the disease of presenting themselves as a living litmus test for true radical praxis. Every so often these educators feel it necessary to announce their radical credentials to the world, marking their territory with stale ink from an acerbic pen. Such educators, often under the cover of "solidarity," attempt to set the boundaries of what counts as radical politics. Highlighting their closeness to grassroots communities, they ready themselves for a progressive purge of the field which, in their mind, is to dismiss the contributions of anyone who uses language that ruptures the accessible tropes of what counts as good journalism.

This type of grandstanding was not useful twenty years ago, and it is even less useful today. To minimize the contributions of critical theory to the project of educational transformation because its scholarly language appears too removed from everyday life is to slide into a reactionary form of populism or "basism" which Paulo Freire warned us against decades ago.

Dismissing those who choose to engage in conceptual work that addresses issues of theory or philosophy as unworthy and unqualified to join the ranks of the "real" activists, these so-called "radicals" try to stigmatize critical theorists as failed revolutionaries hopelessly trapped in rhetorical paralysis (despite the nature of the grassroots work in which such theorists might be engaged outside of the academy), often as an attempt to inflate their own contributions to the field. Everything must have an immediate connection to people "on the ground," it must be laden with a workable strategy. Working out difficult issues that deal with philosophical principles and concepts is just, well, a form of elitism. According to the reactionary populists, writing about conceptual developments in critical social theory doesn't permit educators to feel transformed. In the words of one reactionary populist, such writing doesn't help teachers to feel "free" enough. These educators partake of a woeful misreading of the concept of freedom, at least from the standpoint of revolutionary critical pedagogy. To feel free is not to get yourself into a particular state of mind. It's not a characteristic of "affect." From the perspective of revolutionary critical pedagogy, to "feel free" actually requires human beings to "be free" from necessity, and this goal has many paths, and requires the participation of many educators, and the key task is the transformation of social relations of production. For many reactionary populists, to be of service to the struggle for social justice mandates that first and foremost you must be all about sharing experiences and making affective connections with teachers and students and community members on the ground. Sharing experiences and making connections is all well and good, but doing so without understanding how such experiences are mediated and shaped by larger social relations is really missing the point. All too frequently, these "radical" educators dismiss the language of philosophy or theory because, they bloviate, it is too removed from everyday discourse. This, of course, ignores the insight of Marx that abstractions are often the best way to grasp the concrete. The so-called liberating language of the reactionary populist in many cases becomes a language filled with thoughts and ideas but looted of concepts and analysis.

It's also an example of what Sartre called "bad faith."

Critical educators strive for "another kind of knowledge" that might exist in a world that is able to transcend capitalism—a socialist world. What would it be like to operate in a world by means of a direct social knowledge that cannot be communicated through the indirect medium of money: a knowledge tacitly based upon recognition of our unity and solidarity? (Lebowitz, 2005) We need to take to the streets alongside those whose stolid persistence and arduous years of unmerited suffering have earned them the right to fight back. We need to find ways of fighting back together.

For those who have ears, you can listen to the groans of Marx in his grave; he stubbornly refuses to die because his mission is not yet completed. The more his adversaries pronounce him dead, the more he bangs his fist against his crypt, reminding us that capitalism never sleeps, and neither should we until our job as its gravediggers is complete. For critical educators, Marx is no longer the backdrop on the shallow stage of history or a portent of failed worker states; nor is he heralded as the unsung savior of humankind, fulsomely celebrated by those who possess the correct interpretation of his texts. Rather, he offers to educators a way to move forward in the struggle to make classrooms spaces of social critique and social transformation, where teachers and students alike can exercise a dialectical pedagogy of critique and hope, grounded in an exploration of what it means to labor and to educate one's labor power for the future purpose of selling it for a wage, and understanding this process from the perspective of the larger totality of capitalist social relations. And further, to cultivate the necessary political agency to move from understanding the world to changing it.

Undoubtedly, critical pedagogy remains a source of hope and possibility for educators engaged in struggles against oppression in their classrooms. The time has come for teachers and educators to embrace critical pedagogy with a renewed interest and sense of urgency. While critical pedagogy comes under increasing attack by reactionary ideologies and ideologues, its message only becomes more urgent and important in these troubled and dangerous times.

Note

* This essay draws from several recent essays, including a chapter in the fifth edition of *Life in Schools* (2006), and an introduction to a special issue of the journal *Ethnicities*, edited by Peter McLaren and Nathalia E. Jaramillo (2006).

References

Amoo-Adare, A. (in press). An interview with the Dirty Thirty's Peter McLaren. *Chopbox Magazine*.

Arellano, G.(2006, May 3). The anti-immigrant all-stars. *LA Weekly*, p. 18.

Blum, W. (2005, July 14). The anti-empire report. Retrieved January 15, 2007 from http://www.killinghope.org

Blum, W. (2006, September 25). The anti-empire report. Retrieved January 15, 2007 from http://members.aol.com/bblum6/aer37.htm

Burgos, R. (2002). The Gramscian intervention in the theoretical and political production of the Latin American Left. *Latin American Perspectives, 29*(1), 9–37.

Craig, B. (2006, June 1). New Florida law tightens control over history in schools. *George Mason University's History News Network*. Retrieved January 15, 2007 from http://hnn.us/roundup/entries/26016.html

Freire, P. (1998). *Teachers as cultural workers: Letters to those who dare teach* (Expanded ed.). (D. Macedo, D. Koike, and A. Oliveira, Trans.). Boulder, CO: Westview Press.

Freire, P. (1994). *Pedagogy of hope: Reliving pedagogy of the oppressed*. (R. R. Barr, Trans.). New York: Continuum.

Gonzalez, M. (2004). Postmodernism, historical materialism and Chicana/o cultural studies. *Science & Society, 68*(2), 161–186,

Gramsci, A. (1971). *Selections from the prison notebooks*. New York: International Publishers.

Gulli, B. (2005). The folly of utopia. *Situations, 1*(1), 161–191.

Hudis, P. (2005, March). *Directly and indirectly social labor: What kind of human relations can transcend capitalism?* Paper presented at series "Beyond Capitalism," Chicago, IL.

Kincheloe, Joe. (2005). *Critical Pedagogy: A Primer*. New York: Peter Lang Publishing.

Kosik, K. (1976). *Dialectics of the concrete: A study on problems of man and world*. Boston: D. Reidel Publishing Company.

Kovel, J. (2002). *The enemy of nature: The end of capitalism or the end of the world?* New York: Zed Books.

Kozol, J. (2005, September). Still separate, still unequal: America's educational apartheid. *Harper's Magazine, 311*(1864), 41–54.

Lebowitz, M. A. (2005, July/August). The knowledge of a better world. *Monthly Review, 57*(3), 62–69.

Machado, A. (1962). *Manuel y Antonio Machado: Obras Completas.* Madrid: Editorial Plenitud.

Marx, K. (1992). *Capital: A critique of political economy,* (Vol. 1). (B. Fowkes, Trans.). New York: Penguin Classics. (Original work published 1887)

Mayo, P. (2004). *Liberating praxis: Paulo Freire's legacy for radical education and politics.* Westport, CT: Praeger.

McKibben, B. (2005, August). The Christian paradox: How a faithful nation gets Jesus wrong. *Harper's Magazine, 311*(1863), 31–37.

McLaren, P. & Jaramillo, N. (2006). Juntos en la lucha. *Ethnicities, 6*(3), 283–296

McLaren, P. & Jaramillo, N. (2005). God's cowboy warrior: Christianity, globalization, and the false prophets of imperialism. In P. McLaren (Ed.), *Capitalists and conquerors: A critical pedagogy against empire* (pp. 261–333). Lanham, MD: Rowman and Littlefield.

Meyerson, G. (2000). Rethinking Black Marxism: Reflections on Cedric Robinson and others. *Cultural Logic, 3*(2). Retrieved January 15, 2007, from http://clogic.eserver.org/3–1&2/meyerson.html

Miller, J. (2006, May 15). Forget the Middle East: The U.S. Harbors the World's Most Dangerous Terrorists. *The Baltimore Chronicle & Sentinel.* Retrieved January 15, 2007, from http://baltimorechronicle.com/ 2006/042506Miller.shtml

Rikowski, G. (2005, February). "Distillation: Education in Karl Marx's social universe." Paper presented at lunchtime seminar at the School of Education, University of East London, Barking Campus.

Robinson, W. (2006). "*¡Aqui estamos y no nos vamos!: The struggle for immigrant rights in the U.S.* Unpublished paper.

San Juan, E. (2002). *Racism and cultural studies: Critiques of multiculturalist ideology and the politics of difference.* Durham, NC: Duke University Press.

Scatamburlo-D'Annibale, V. & McLaren, P. (2004). Class dismissed? Historical materialism and the politics of 'difference.' *Educational Philosophy and Theory, 36*(2), 183–199.

Scatamburlo-D'Annibale, V. & McLaren, P. (2003). The strategic centrality of class in the politics of race and 'difference.' *Cultural Studies/Critical Methodologies, 3*(2), 148–175

Somerville, J. (2005). The philosophy of Marxism: An exposition. [Special Issue]. *Nature, Society, and Thought, 18*(1).

Steele, S. (2006, May 2). White guilt and the Western past: Why is America so delicate with its enemy? *The Wall Street Journal.* Retrieved January 15, 2007, from http://www.opinionjournal.com/editorial/ feature.html?id=110008318

Wood, E. M. (1995). *Democracy against capitalism: Renewing historical materialism.* Cambridge, UK: Cambridge University Press.

Zavarzadeh, Mas'ud. (2003). The pedagogy of totality. *Journal of Advanced Composition, 23*(1), 1–52.

Zimmerman, J. (2006, June 7). All history is revisionist. *Los Angeles Times.* Retrieved January 20, 2007 from http://www.latimes.com/news/opinion/commentary/la-oe-zimmerman7jun07,0,5940045.story? coll=la-news-comment-opinions

Zunes, Stephen. (2006, December 31). Gerald Ford's foreign policy legacy. Retrieved January 20, 2007 at http://www.commondreams.org/views06/1231-20.htm

CHAPTER 17

Red Lake Woebegone

Pedagogy, Decolonization, and the Critical Project

SANDY GRANDE

"The pure products of America go crazy"

—William Carlos Williams

The English translation of *Pedagogy of the Oppressed* made its debut around the same time I did, in 1970. Now, it seems almost providential that I was born into a world where Freire had already made his mark, transforming consciousness on the necessary conditions for humanity. As the daughter of Quechua (Peruvian) immigrants, I am especially indebted to his articulation of a radical pedagogy in defense of the "third world." In Freire's time it was truly revolutionary for him to proclaim that the world's poor were human too. Sadly, nearly 40 years later, it seems that we have no greater understanding of this powerful entreaty—either as a moral imperative or political assertion. On the contrary, the world's "oppressed" seem to only grow in numbers and yet are somehow more invisible. They struggle against the domestication of colonization into tropes of "globalization" and "disadvantage." As they depart this world, they fall as Pachamama's children, and return to her belly. It is there where they meet the ancestors again, and Machucha (grandfather) Paulo.

Maybe together their wisdom will save the rest of us from falling . . . When a body catch a body comin' thro' the rye . . .

Though educators the world over mourned Freire's passing in 1997, perhaps it was God's grace that spared him from witnessing the recent atrocities of 9/11, the war in Iraq, Abu Ghraib, Hurricane Katrina, and the seemingly endless spate of school massacres. On some level, these events speak to our failure to realize Freire's dream: to dismantle the contradictions between oppressor and oppressed. On the other hand, the legions of Freireian scholars on the front lines who work to "demystify" the tragedies as products of the dangerous liaisons between "capitalists and conquerors" speak to the power of his legacy.

Staring down threats of political treason and academic exile, scholars such as Michael Apple, Paula Allen, Noam Chomsky, Ramin Farahmandpur, Henry Giroux, Jane Kenway, Peter McLaren, and Valerie Scatamburlo slice through the vapid, sound-bite analyses of pundits and proselytes who blame everything from video games to the "Axis of Evil" for the woes of the world. Freire's progeny "write back," calling attention to the rampant excesses of capital. Their collective analyses shine a glimmer of integrity against the backdrop of political chop shops masquerading as "think tanks" and academic fashionistas interested only in selling the latest brand of scholarship. Through the maelstrom of marketeering, their critiques have stood the test of time, carefully tending and cultivating the seeds Freire planted in the decades before. Thus, contrary to proclamations that Marxism is dead, in this time of globalization and empire building, the voices of critical theorists have only grown more relevant, rescuing us from the bourgeois humanism that is the bedfellow of capitalism.

Despite its seeming import, indigenous scholars have been reluctant to engage critical theory. Against the immediate needs and political urgencies of their own communities, engagement in abstract theory seems indulgent—a luxury and privilege of the academic elite. Though this impulse is rational, the lack of engagement with critical theory has ultimately limited possibilities for indigenous scholars to build broad-based coalitions and political solidarities. Such a limitation has serious implications, particularly since indigenous communities remain under siege from the forces of global encroachment. Communities either unable or unwilling to extend borders of coalition and enact *transcendent* theories of decolonization will only compound their vulnerability to the whims and demands of the "new global order."

As indigenous communities continue to be transformed by movement, access, border crossing, and transgression, it becomes even more pertinent for indigenous scholars to abandon what Robert Allen Warrior[1] refers to as the "death dance of dependence." That is, the vacillation between wholesale adoption of Anglo-Western theories and the declaration that Native scholars need nothing outside of themselves to understand their world or place within it.[2] In other words, as the sociocultural geography of Indian Country expands, so too must the intellectual borders of indigenous intellectualism. While there is nothing inherently healing, liberatory, or revolutionary about theory, it is one of our primary responsibilities as educators to link the lived experience of theorizing to the processes of self-recovery and social transformation.

That being said, this is not a call for indigenous scholars to simply join the conversation of critical theorists. Rather, the chapter is intended to spark an indigenous conversation that can, in turn, engage in dialogical contestation with critical and revolutionary theories. The aim is to define a *Red Pedagogy* that examines points of tension and intersection between critical theory and indigenous knowledge, articulating possibilities for coalition.

This chapter is a narrative about the Ojibwe peoples of the Red Lake community and their encounters with colonization, a story that provides a framework from which to explore the relationship between *Red Pedagogy* and the critical project. The discussion begins with a look at the current state of critical pedagogy, examining schools not only as a site of political struggle but also of youth violence. This analysis is engaged from the perspective of revolutionary critical pedagogy, where schools are theorized as places where the broader relations of power, domination, and authority are played out. Next, the history of Red Lake is recounted from an indigenous perspective, which offsets the criticalist perspective of *capitalism* as the central struggle concept, replacing it instead with *colonization*. Finally, points of tension and intersection are delineated between the indigenous project of sovereignty and the critical project of socialist democracy. The hope is that possibilities for broad-based coalition and solidarity will emerge between these two important projects.

Critical Pedagogy Today

Critical pedagogy is first and foremost an approach to schooling (i.e., teaching, policy making, curriculum production) that emphasizes the political nature of education. As such, critical pedagogy aims to understand, reveal, and disrupt the mechanisms of oppression imposed by the established order, suturing the processes and aims of education to emancipatory goals. Leading scholar Henry Giroux (2001) underscores its emancipatory aim, asserting that critical pedagogy must be envisioned as "part of a broader ethical and political project wedded to furthering social and economic justice and making multicultural democracy operational" (p. 3).

Beyond these basic principles, the project's ever broadening theoretical foundation has greatly diversified the field. According to McLaren, leading exponents of critical pedagogy have always "cross-fertilized" their work with "just about every transdisciplinary tradition imaginable, including theoretical forays into the Frankfurt School . . . the work of Richard Rorty, Jacques Lacan, Jacques Derrida, and Michel Foucault" (p. 11–12). With such transdisciplinary beginnings, it is not surprising that critical pedagogy has emerged as a kind of "big tent" for a variety of educator/scholars working toward social justice and greater equity (Lather, 1998). Most recently, postmodern, post-structuralist, postcolonial, feminist, Marxist, and critical race theorists have all developed their own versions of critical pedagogy.

Such differences have given rise to intellectual tensions among scholars. Lather (1998) notes that "as an ensemble of practices and discourses with competing claims of truth, typicality, and credibility" there have always been tensions among critical scholars (p. 487). Though at times petty and unproductive, the publicly aired differences and ongoing interchanges between such scholars have helped to push the field, engaging the dialogical praxis that defines critical praxis.

Despite the potential allure of theories that valorize difference and heterogeneity—particularly for those marginalized by the homogenizing project of White supremacy—many critical scholars resist the reduction of critical pedagogy to depoliticize postmodern theory. As McLaren (2002) notes, in their effort to try to be everything to everyone, some postmodern theorists have (re)cast the net of critical pedagogy so wide and so cavalierly that it has come to be associated with everything from "classroom furniture organized in a 'dialogue friendly' circle to 'feel-good' curricula designed to increase students' self-image" (p. 13). Thus while critics recognize the ways in which postmodernists have helped to expose the hidden trajectories of power (particularly within processes of representation and identity), critical scholars maintain that they have been "woefully remiss in addressing the constitution of class formations and the machinations of capitalist social organization" (Scatamburlo-D'Annibale & McLaren, 2002, p. 4). Specifically, insofar as some postmodernists have distanced themselves from the labor/capital problematic, they are viewed by radical educators as advocating procapitalist forms of schooling.

In the wake of the relentless march of global capitalism, Marxist and other radical scholars view such a stance as insufficient. They are especially critical of the abandonment of emancipatory agendas and the struggle against capitalist exploitation, arguing that apolitical postmodernists have substituted the project of radical, social transformation with a politics of representation. As Scatamburlo and McLaren (2002) note, to remain "enamored with the 'cultural' and seemingly blind to the 'economic,'" in this moment of late capitalism is not simply an act of ignoring, but one of complicity (pp. 4–5). It requires turning a blind eye to the roughly 2.8 billion people (nearly half the world's population) living on less than two dollars a day (McQuaig, 2001, p. 27), and the 100 million people in the industrial world living below the poverty level (Sactamburlo-D'Annibale & McLaren, 2002).[3] Such statistics are clear indicators that the inherent contradictions of capitalism are "taking us further away from democratic accountability" and closer toward what "Rosa Luxemburg referred to as an age of 'barbarism'" (McLaren & Farahmandpur, 2001, p. 277).

Thus, from the vantage point of Marxist scholars we do not simply need an education for equity and social justice but rather an anticapitalist education for a socialist democracy. Advocates of radical forms of critical pedagogy thus insist on a theory and praxis of schooling with an unabashed emancipatory intent; one that is future-centered and forward-looking to a time when "wage labor disappears with class society itself" (McLaren, 2002, p. 30). In accordance with these aims, critical scholars have articulated a *"revolutionary critical pedagogy"* (Allman, 2001) or the synthesis of contemporary Marxist scholarship with a rematerialized critical pedagogy.[4]

McLaren and Farahmandpur (2001) define the core principles of revolutionary critical pedagogy as follows: (1) to recognize that capitalism, despite its power, is a "historically produced social relation that can be challenged (most forcefully by those exploited by it)" (McLaren & Farahmandpur, 2001, p. 272); (2) to foreground historical materialist analysis which "provides critical pedagogy with a theory of the material basis of social life rooted in historical social relations" and assigns primacy to uncovering the structures of class conflict and the effects produced by the social division of labor (McLaren, 2002, p. 26)[5]; (3) to reimagine Marxist theory in the interests of the critical educational project, and (4) to understand that Marxist revolutionary theory "must be flexible enough to reinvent itself" and not operate "as a universal truth but (rather) as a weapon of interpretation" (McLaren & Farahmandpur, 2001, pp. 301–302). Beyond these commitments, McLaren and Farahmandpur (2001) define the following elements of revolutionary critical praxis:[6]

1. A revolutionary critical pedagogy must be a *collective process*. One that involves utilizing a Freirean dialogical learning approach.
2. A revolutionary critical pedagogy must be *critical*; that is, it works to locate the underlying causes of class exploitation and economic oppression within the social, political, and economic infrastructure of capitalist social relations of production.
3. A revolutionary critical pedagogy is profoundly *systematic* in the sense that it is guided by Marx's dialectical method of inquiry, which begins with the "real concrete" circumstances of the oppressed masses and moves towards a classification, conceptualization, analysis, and breaking down of the concrete social world into units of abstractions to get at the essence of social phenomena. It then reconstructs and makes the social world intelligible by transforming and translating theory into concrete social and political action.
4. A revolutionary critical pedagogy is *participatory*, involving building coalitions among community members, grassroots movements, church organizations, and labor unions.
5. A revolutionary critical pedagogy is a *creative process*; incorporating elements of popular culture (i.e., drama, music, oral history, narratives) as educational tools to politicize and revolutionize working-class consciousness (p. xvii).

In addition, Allman (2001, pp. 177–186) defines the more affective or "vital powers" necessary for revolutionary struggle:

> [We need] principles of mutual respect, humility, openness, trust and co-operation; a commitment to learn to "read the world" critically and expend the effort necessary to bring about social transformation; vigilance with regard to one's own process of self-transformation and adherence to the principles and aims of the group; adopting an "ethics of authenticity" as a guiding principle; internalizing social justice as passion; acquiring critical, creative, and hopeful thinking; transforming the self through transforming the social relations of learning and teaching; establishing democracy as a fundamental way of life; developing critical curiosity; and deepening one's solidarity and commitment to self and social transformation and the project of humanization. (McLaren, 2002, p. 31)

Such principles are clearly relevant to indigenous students and educators and their need for pedagogies of disruption, intervention, affirmative action, hope, and possibility.

Revolutionary Critical Pedagogy and Indigenous Praxis

Insofar as the project for colonialist education has been imbricated with the social, economic, and political policies of U.S. imperialism, an education for decolonization must also make no claim to political neutrality. It must engage a method of analysis and social inquiry that troubles the imperialist aims of unfettered competition, accumulation, and exploitation. Moreover, beyond an approach to schooling that underscores the political nature of education, Native students and educators require a praxis that enables the dismantling of *colonialist* forces. That is, they need a pedagogy that cultivates a sense of political agency and spiritual solidarity.

Toward this end, the frameworks of revolutionary critical theory provide indigenous scholars new ways to think about critical issues such as sovereignty and self-determination. In particular, their foregrounding of capitalist relations as the axis of exploitation helps to frame the history of indigenous peoples as one of dispossession and not simply cultural oppression, and their trenchant critique of postmodernism reveals the "problem" of identity (social representation) as a dangerous distraction from the imperatives of social transformation. That being said, the Western foundation of critical pedagogy also presents significant tensions for indigenous pedagogy and praxis. The radical constructs of democratization, subjectivity, and citizenship all remain defined through Western epistemological frames. As such, they carry certain assumptions about human beings and their relationship to the natural world, the view of progress, and the primacy of the rational process. The implications of such tensions are myriad and significant, giving rise to competing notions of governance, economy, and identity.

It is important to note however, that within *Red Pedagogy* the aporias of critical pedagogy are not theorized as deficiencies but rather as points of tension, helping to define the spaces-in-between the Western and indigenous thought-worlds. Revolutionary scholars themselves acknowledge "no theory can fully anticipate or account for the consequences of its application but remains a living aperture through which specific histories are made visible and intelligible."[7] In other words, no theory can be, nor should be, everything to all peoples—differences in the material world necessitate differences in the discursive realm. Therefore, while revolutionary critical theory may serve as a vital tool for indigenous educators and scholars, the basis of *Red Pedagogy* remains distinctive, rooted in indigenous knowledge and praxis.

While critical indigenous scholars do not equivocate the ravages of capitalism, a *Red* critique of critical pedagogy decenters capitalism as the main struggle concept and replaces it with colonization. Comparatively, the colonialist project is understood as profoundly multidimensional and intersectional; underwritten by Christian fundamentalism, defined by White supremacy, and fueled by global capitalism. This fundamental difference shifts the pedagogic goal from the "transformation of existing social and economic relations" through the critique and transformation of capitalist social relations of production (i.e., *democratization*) to the transformation of existing colonialist relations through critique and transformation of the exploitive relations of imperialism, (i.e. *sovereignty*). This is not to say that the political/pedagogical projects of democratization and sovereignty are mutually exclusive; on the contrary, in this new era of empire, it may be that sovereignty extends democracy its only lifeline.

Perhaps nowhere else is this more visible than in the playing field of American education, where the dreams of democracy hit the concrete walls of youth culture. The daily headlines document the evidence of this violent collision—predatory teachers, desensitized students, school massacres—all indications of an institution's own struggle with empire. Students instinctively rebel against a colonialist education that paints the ruling class as heroes—but they know they aren't—and the colonized as immaterial—but they know they matter. In the end, all students sense the fundamental contradictions of conquest: How is it possible for democracy to grow from the seeds of tyranny? For the good life can be built upon the deaths of thousands? They rage against the machine, searching for answers, and when they don't get them they submit to the anesthetizing accoutrements of capital. Within this context, critical scholars work in their interest, to do what they can to provide explanations for the real and symbolic violence that fills their lives.

School as Sites of Violence

Simplistic analyses of school violence have dominated the media circuits, with pundits from across the political spectrum denouncing the moral degeneration of youth and lamenting the loss of innocence. Conservatives blame the deterioration of family values, loss of school prayer, and the dilatory effects of progressive education and permissive parenting. Liberals indict school bullies, violent video games, high-stakes testing, and the loss of various social programs. Ultimately, however, the phenomenon of school massacres is explained through models of individualized deviance, dismissed as a crisis of pathological families and youth. The location of deviance is individualized in order to assuage any notion that the incidents might be pervasive or endemic to society, confirming the nightmare that "it could happen anywhere."

In contrast, critical scholars link school violence to profound alienation, connecting the "existential experiences of youth" to the larger social, economic, and cultural formations that are "the basis of specific historical relations of domination and resistance" (Frymer, 2005, p. 1). From a Marxist perspective, alienation is not simply an experience of estrangement but also a "material and ontological condition of distorted historical being formed within the capitalist relations of production" (p. 5). For instance, workers are viewed as alienated or "estranged" in a variety of ways: from the product and process of labor, from other workers, and from themselves—commodified as objects to be bought and sold on the market like any other commodity (p. 4). Building upon this framework, critical theorists construct students as laborers whereby student alienation is understood as "both a material and cultural phenomenon" (p.2) directly linked to the larger structures of American schooling and late capitalist society.

In particular, Freire defines alienation as the negation of subjectivity; that is, the separation of the subject from their "ontological vocation of active human participation in the world" (Freymer, 2005, p. 4). Thus, as Frymer (2005) notes, the "ultimate significance of social and economic domination is the establishment of a class of dehumanized and alienated objects" (p. 4). That is, "the oppressed are turned from potentially active subjects to dominated objects; from critically reflective actors who participate in society democratically to passive instruments of elite authoritarian control."

Frymer (2005) furthermore argues that in this moment of late capitalism or "spectacle phase"[8] of capitalism, youth alienation transcends class, race, gender, and sexuality. He writes, "The advanced development of commodity capitalism has changed the landscape of alienation" so that even privileged (by race, class, gender, or sexuality) youth have difficulty finding "meaningful bases of authentic existence and rebellion" (p. 9). Matza (1999) concurs, noting that the postmodern crisis has infiltrated the experience of youth ranging from "suburban meaninglessness to inner-city war zones" (p. ix).

Frymer (2005) theorizes that through new suburban and rural estrangement, adolescents struggle to "maintain the integrity of self in the face of the larger alienated society" (p. 10). The exclusively male perpetrators of recent school massacres are viewed as "vulnerably masculine 'outsiders' [who] form anomic detachment, nihilism, anger, and resentment in response to the perceived mediocrity, meaninglessness, and absurdity of life in the society of the spectacle." He furthermore posits that, "regardless of the new possibilities globalization provides, estranged school shooters see no alternative to the closed worlds of status hierarchy, or the mediated diversions from boredom in the hollowed-out world of suburbia or rural towns."

Thus, beyond the class hierarchies that determine a child's worth through her parent's relationship to production and/or labor, schools also replicate capitalism's suppression of difference. For instance, in the case of Dylan Klebold, while individual pathology was undoubtedly at play, he and Eric Harris were also casualties of suburban banality, sanitized homogenity and prisoners of privilege. They violently raged against the machine, stealing what they saw as their only moment of relevancy in an otherwise virtual existence. Homogeneity is the wake of capital, leveling everything in its path to the least common denominator. Without difference or, alternatively, when sameness abounds, opportunities to step outside oneself— to transcend—are greatly diminished. What else can the loss of self-transcendence breed but a profound narcissism?

The analysis of critical scholars provides significantly more insight to the issue of youth violence, situating it as a by-product of the various distortions (i.e., dehumanization and commodification) formed by capitalist relations of production. A *Red* critique builds upon this analysis, but instead of limiting its focus to the forces of production and labor, it views objectification as the product of a more pervasive social system: colonization.

Red Lake: Same Country, Different Nation

The Red Lake school shooting is the one school massacre that Minnesota reporter Mike Mosedale remarked occurred in the "same country, different nation" (Mosedale, 2005). At first, he notes that "the story arc conformed to the now-familiar pattern" with initial coverage "focusing on the development of the narrative through eyewitness accounts" and later shifting to the development of "a profile of the killer" (p. 2). The killer in this instance was

Jeff Weise, a sixteen-year-old troubled teen and displaced member of the Red Lake Ojibwe nation.[9] The media capitalized on the tabloid drama that was Jeff's life—the mother who committed suicide; the brain-damaged, alcoholic mother; the "NativeNazi" web moniker; and the infamous yearbook picture with his hair sculpted into devil's horns—which all sated the liberal desire to pathologize and contain the criminality.

Despite the severity of his individual family circumstances, Weise—more than any other perpetrator—was depicted as a product of his environment. It made sense to the outside world that such an event would happen *there*—a poor Indian reservation, forgotten, isolated and "deprived" of all the "free market" had to offer. While reservation communities are indeed victims of capitalism, a brief look at the history of Red Lake tells a different, fuller narrative. It is the story of what happens when capital meets conquest:

A Brief History of Red Lake[10]

Nineteenth century

1842   The first (Protestant) mission is established at Red Lake (abandoned 1857).

1843   The Red Lake Indians, known to be thrifty farmers, were especially successful this year, supporting many families who fled to Red Lake to escape starvation. Their land was notoriously fertile and in addition to growing corn, wheat, potatoes, and rye they were very rich in timber.

1851   United States purchases 5 million acres of land from the Indians for $230,000, to be paid over 20 years without interest.

1852   The Governor issues an order abolishing literary and religious schools, establishing instead manual labor and/or training schools.

1858   A Catholic mission is opened at Red Lake by Rev. Lawrence Lautischar, who occupies a portion of the house owned by Joseph Jourdain, a French trader.

1864   The Ojibwe send a delegation to Washington to amend the treaty of 1863 which provided for the ceding of approximately 8 million more acres of land.

1868   Migration and unrest among the Ojibwe cause many schools to be abandoned. Following the Civil War, there was a significant decrease in government supervision and assistance.

1877   An Episcopal mission and government boarding school were founded.

1885   The vastness of the reservation makes it difficult for the Indians to protect it from pine thievery. They request government protection against unlawful depredation.

1887   The General Allotment (Dawes) Act was passed by Congress, authorizing the president, at his discretion, to survey and break up the communal land holdings of tribes into individual allotments.

1889   The Dawes Commission is charged with negotiating a treaty with all Ojibwe
        bands in Minnesota. The Indians complain about numerous unfulfilled prom-
        ises in past treaties. The Red Lake Ojibwes launch a fierce objection to their
        land being broken up into privately owned allotments, advocating continuing
        to hold their land in common. After several council meetings, they come to
        an agreement. In exchange for 3 million more acres of land, the Red Lake
        Indians are allowed to maintain their land in common.

1893   As a community, Red Lake begins to prosper. They had more hotels, stores, and
        trading posts than any nearby village.

1896   The government opens the "surplus" ceded reservation land for settlement to
        homesteaders.

This era of Red Lake history is remarkable within Indian Country only in that Red Lake
Ojibwes fared significantly better than most tribes! Their geographic location and tenacious
leaders protected them from the worst of nineteenth-century policies aimed at the cultural
genocide of indigenous peoples. However, while they were protected, they did not manage
to escape completely. As with most tribes, their slow demise began with a period of
missionization.

Perhaps at no other time in U.S. history did the church and state work so hand-in-hand
to advance the common project of White supremacy. During this time, missionary groups
acted as the primary developers of schools, while the federal government worked as the not-
so-silent partner, providing economic and political capital to the churches through policies such as the Civilization Fund.[11] Indeed, the work of teachers, political leaders, and priests
was hardly distinguishable; saving souls and colonizing minds became part and parcel of the
broader project of colonization. The joint mission was to "invalidate the totality of Indian
life" (Deloria, 1999, p. 23) and replace it with Christian and democratic values: White
supremacy, monotheism, patriarchy, democracy and capitalism.

The movement away from mission schools toward "manual labor schools," which
commenced in Red Lake in 1852, was common across Indian Country. In addition to providing vocational training, such schools introduced the concept of forced labor as an integral part of Indian education, transforming the "moral" project of civilizing Indians into a
for-profit enterprise. Specifically, churches were endowed with hundreds of acres for children to plow, maintain, and harvest, with dioceses often yielding considerable profits from
the "free" labor. This shift in the central aim of Indian education was highly conscious and
purposeful. In his annual report (1881), Commissioner of Indian Affairs Hiram Price
argued that previous attempts to civilize Indians failed because they did not teach "the necessity of labor" (Spring, 2001, p. 173). He maintained this ethic could only be taught by making Indians responsible for their own economic welfare, achievable through teaching
proper appreciation for private property.

Therefore, Price, along with other federal and school officials, advocated for an allotment program, attacking the tribal way of life as socialistic and contrary to the values of

civilization. Richard Pratt, founder of the Carlisle Indian school, laid the "failure" of Indian assimilation at the feet of the missionaries and their failure to advocate for the disintegration of tribes. In a letter to the Commissioner of Indian Affairs, he wrote: "Pandering to the tribe and its socialism as most of the Government and mission plans do is the principal reason why the Indians have not advanced more and are not advancing as rapidly as they ought to" (Spring, 1996, p. 173).

Thus, as the (White) population grew, and the federal government increasingly realized the value of Indian land, full-scale appropriation of Indian territory commenced. Senator Dawes, a self-proclaimed "friend to the Indian," advocated for a reallocation of tribal lands based on Locke's theory of property, arguing that the normative deficiency of tribalism constituted proper grounds for the dissolution of tribal lands. In a speech to the U.S. Senate, Dawes articulated the difference between tribal and "civilized" societies:

> The head chief told us that there was not a family in the nation that had not a home of its own. There is not a pauper in that nation, and that nation does not owe a dollar. It built its own capitol, in which we had this examination, and built its schools and hospitals. Yet the defect of the system was apparent. They have got as far as they can go, because they hold their land in common. It is (the socialist writer) Henry George's system, and under that there is no enterprise to make your home better than that of your neighbors. There is no selfishness, which is at the bottom of civilization. Till these people will consent to give up their lands, and divide them among their citizens so that each can own the land he cultivates, they will not make much progress.[12]

Based on this reasoning, Dawes and his counterparts convinced Congress that Indian "civilization" could only be achieved through teaching Indians the virtues of private property.[13] In 1887, the General Allotment or Dawes Act (24 Stat., 388)[14] was passed. Though it took years to put into affect, by the end of the allotment period the aggregate Indian land base was reduced from approximately 138 million to 48 million acres, or by nearly two-thirds. In addition, tribes were divested of their right to determine their own membership; the trust doctrine was irrevocably violated; and specious identification procedures created various "classes" of Indians, establishing enduring and, at times, violent divisions among "fullbloods," "mixed-bloods," "assimilated," and "traditional" Indians.

While the Red Lake Ojibwes managed to stave off allotment, surviving the immediate impact, the collateral damage from Dawes has been festering like a cancer, metastasizing through every organ of the tribal body. Over time the loss of aggregate land base through ceded lands impacted family and kinship relations by either breaking up or consolidating their habitats. Arguably more destructive was the introduction of the Western value of land as property. Once land is treated as property—especially in a manner that differentially awards individual tribal members based on gender and blood quantum—the relational basis of land and kinship becomes vulnerable to the logic of commodification. Particularly following decades of spiritual erosion, the time was ripe to play Indian against Indian, convincing "mixed-bloods" and young males that tribal ways were inferior to the "civilized" world of private property. Though the tribal leaders of Red Lake resisted this notion, the seeds of Indian as inferior and White as superior were planted, left dormant to fester and divide the community for centuries to come.

Moreover, just as the denigration of traditional spiritual and governance structures reached unprecedented heights, the government opened the ceded lands to homesteaders, bringing further White cultural encroachment to Indian territory. The sum of nineteenth-century policy and practice clearly marks tribalism—not socialism—as the primary target, and U.S. policies of colonization—not capitalism—as the first weapon of mass destruction. This trajectory continues throughout the twentieth century.

Twentieth century

1900–1940	Boarding school period.
1901	Smallpox epidemic breaks out in Ponemah.
1908	Public school education begins.
1918	Red Lake General Council established.
1902	In agreement with the adult male Indians, over 250,000 acres of land are sold to the U.S. government for $1 million. Of this amount, $250,000 is to be paid in 15 annual installments. This was later "amended" so that instead of paying $1 million dollars, the U.S. government offered the land for pubic sale to homesteaders with the proceeds of land to be credited to the Red Lake Indians but deposited in the U.S. Treasury.
1934	The Indian Reorganization Act is passed.
1935	Red Lake Public High School established.
1953	House Concurrent Resolution 108 (67 Stat. B 132)—a.k.a. the Termination Act—was passed by Congress. By the mid-1960s, 109 Indian Tribes and over 12,000 individual Indians lost official recognition of their treaty status as legally recognized tribes. In addition, over 2.5 million acres of reservation land formerly protected by the trust relationship between treaty tribes and the federal government passed into non-Indian control.
1958	Revised Constitution and bylaws adopted. In accordance with the IRA, the new Constitution required direct election of tribal leaders.
1959	Roger Jourdain is the first elected Tribal Chairman.
1979	After the Jourdain-led tribal council fired the secretary-treasurer, a riot erupted. Armed dissidents chased away the police before setting fire to his home and about a dozen other buildings. In the melee that followed, two teenagers died of accidental gunshot wounds.
1986	A chief judge on the reservation is shot to death in connection with a dispute related to the Bureau of Indian Affairs in the twentieth century; deterioration of tribal ways continued through decimation from disease, boarding schools, and more insidious policies of colonization. More tribal land is ceded through increasingly specious financial dealings with the government, inviting even more homesteaders and therefore greater depreciation of sovereignty. Though Red Lake, once again, escaped the most

destructive policy of this era—Termination—it may have been a Pyrrhic victory. That is, like many tribes, they were forced to make "deals with the devil" in order to save the soul of their community.

To understand the full impact of Termination, it is necessary to go back to 1934 and the passage of the Indian Reorganization Act. While the Indian Reorganization Act (IRA) put an end to allotment policies (providing for the purchase of new lands and the restoration of some unallotted lands), virtually all provisions were contingent upon a tribe's pledge to "reorganize." That is, to adopt "Western-style constitutions," form and elect tribal councils, and implement a variety of economic development plans (e.g., Western conservation measures, community and educational loan programs).

Thus, the net effect of the IRA was that it dramatically increased federal supervision over Indian nations. As Hauptman (1992) notes, "even when the majority of an Indian nation valued the opportunity to rebuild . . . many viewed the increased federal supervision as . . . (an) unpleasant trade-off" (pp. 328–329). Indeed, there is ample evidence that "reorganization" was primarily fueled by the growing desire of the federal government to gain "lawful" and "credible" access to tribal resources. Specifically, through the establishment of "puppet governments" federal officials and their corporate accessories secured access to Indian resources,[15] paving the way for the future control and appropriation of Indian peoples. For instance, there is evidence that through Dawes, the government knowingly assigned "mixed-blood" status to several Whites in order to gain a foothold in Indian Country, essentially buying the favor of newly enrolled (White) members through the promise of Indian land. In short, the insider trading, double-dealings, and unholy alliances orchestrated by Dawes make Jack Abramoff look like the real "friend to the Indians."

Insofar as this scandal affects Red Lake, there has always been some speculation that Roger Jourdain, a "mixed-blood," was a puppet of the federal government, encouraged to run for tribal chairman in exchange for land on the reservation. Despite speculation, Jourdain went on to serve as chairman for 30 years, during which time the tribe often benefited from his close ties with Washington insiders. For example, Jourdain is typically credited for saving Red Lake from Termination by lobbying his friends in Washington. During his tenure, the tribe made great strides in capital improvements, including improved housing and infrastructure. Perhaps it was also his "protected" status that allowed him the freedom to call attention to issues like sovereignty through very public and controversial policies such as requiring non-band members to carry passports, barring the news media from the reservation during difficult times, and issuing the first tribal nation license plates in the country. Overall, however, Jourdain's tenuous allegiances and abrasive style led his 30-year term to be characterized by scandal and unrest. Mosedale (2005) remarks that "to his opponents, he was an outright autocrat who ran roughshod over anyone who disagreed with him" (p. 5). Many felt that his administration bore more resemblance to old-style city machine politics, defined by its heavy-handed patronage and nepotism (Mosedale, 2005).

The ensuing tensions culminated in 1979, when Jourdain fired tribal secretary-treasurer Stephanie Hanson under suspicious circumstances. Reportedly, Jourdain was upset that

Hanson had requested a legal opinion from the United States Department of the Interior Field Solicitor's office regarding a proposed, but not adopted, resolution concerning chairman Jourdain's business account. Her subsequent termination ignited deep and long-standing tensions in the community. According to court records, armed men, led by tribal member Harry Hanson, entered the Red Lake Law Enforcement Center (LEC), taking over the building. The prisoners were released, and two BIA officers, a police dispatcher, and two BIA jailers were taken hostage. In the ensuing melee, several buildings were burned and two teenagers died of gunshot wounds.

After the siege ended, the Red Lake tribal council sued the U.S. government for damages, charging federal officials with negligent unilateral withdrawal of law enforcement in the middle of an insurrection. In addition, the plaintiffs charged that the FBI and the BIA had negligently failed to make adequate plans prior to the uprising despite warnings that trouble was brewing. As a result, Roger Jourdain and his cohorts were awarded damages totaling $849,562.62 by the U.S. District Court. In 1991, the U.S. Court of Appeals reversed the district court's judgment, concluding that the damages were not proximately caused by the [U.S.] government's negligence.

Twenty-first century

2002   Red Lake is involved in a suit against the U.S. Bureau of Land Management with regard to mismanagement of the forest.

2005   Jeff Weise, an Ojibwe teen from Red Lake, goes on a shooting rampage at Red Lake High School. He killed nine people, wounded several more, and then committed suicide. Among the dead was Weise's grandfather, Daryl "Dash" Lussier, one of the tribal police officers who kept order during the 1979 uprising. A few days later, his friend and cousin, Louis Jourdain, was arrested and charged with conspiracy to commit murder. Eventually, federal prosecutors dropped the conspiracy charge, and Jourdain pled guilty to sending threatening messages over the Internet. U.S. District Judge Donovan Frank sentenced Jourdain, but barred the public from the courtroom, and sealed the sentence so it could not be made public.

2006   On March 21, peoples of Red Lake quietly commemorate the one-year anniversary of the school shooting; no reporters were allowed on school grounds.

2006   In July, Buck Jourdain, tribal chairman and father of alleged coconspirator Louis Jourdain narrowly wins re-election as tribal chairman. Tribal secretary Judy Roy won the popular vote with on-reservation voters, but when absentee ballots and votes from the Twin Cities were counted, Jourdain won the election by 69 votes. The results of the election were contested under charges that Jourdain attempted to buy votes and misused tribal funds for campaign purposes. Jourdain vigorously denied all charges. The election board called for a new election, even though some questioned its authority (as opposed to the tribal council) to do so. Subsequently, after long debate, the tribal council voted 6–2 to install Buck Jourdain as tribal chairman for a second term.

In the context of the long history of colonization, the eruption of Jeff Weise hardly seems remarkable. In fact, what might be remarkable is that such an event is not a more regular occurrence in Indian Country, particularly when one considers Red Lake has long been considered one of the strongest, most resilient communities in Indian Country. Their resistance to Allotment, Termination, and the IRA is legendary. Which raises the question, what does it mean to be a strong indigenous nation in a time of "globalization" (a.k.a. colonization, world domination, empire)?

While Red Lake was strong enough to resist Allotment what they are left with is "common land" held in trust by the U.S. government, which doesn't have the same (or any) value in the eyes of lending institutions (i.e., collateral). This condition leaves individual tribal members little access to capital and therefore wholly dependent on federal subsidies. Such dependency, compounded by over 200 years of whitestream domination, has left tribal peoples exhausted, dispirited, miseducated, and therefore vulnerable to the modes and desires of the "outside" world. Those stripped of the benefit of their traditional ways—language, stories, cultural knowledge, memories—have few resources to resist the current onslaught of slogans, jingles, and signs that assert the (White) supremacy of everything they are not and don't have. Thus, while the vast, "commonly held" lands once protected the Ojibwes from White encroachment and against cultural invasion, the 20th century influx of satellite television, cell phones, the Internet, and other accoutrements of spectacle capitalism has rendered the community isolated but not insulated.

The legacy of colonization is felt most acutely among Indian youth, caught at the crossroads of colonialism in this supposedly postcolonial time. Consider that one out of six American Indian teens attempt suicide, 54% of American Indian youth lives below the poverty line, and 70% of American Indian children in Minnesota live with a single parent or other relative. Ojibwe scholar Scott Lyons remarks on the Red Lake tragedy: "From the very moment of his birth, Jeff's life was defined by violence—the violence of community poverty, the violence of racism, the violence of little respect and few opportunities, the violence of guns, security systems, punitive politics and a growing militarism. Until these acts of everyday violence are put to an end, how can we ever expect our children to live peacefully?"

Amidst this despair, Jeff Weise lashed out, stealing life from a world where he and his people were already presumed dead. The history of colonialization reduces the momentary larger-than-life gunman to the child that he was. He was the child of great warriors and dignified leaders as well as the child of dispossession, disenchantment, and imperial greed. Among the other casualties was Jeff Weise's grandfather, Daryl "Dash" Lussier, a celebrated tribal police officer who helped to keep order during the 1979 uprising. Among the accused was Louis Jourdain, son of current tribal Chairman Buck Jourdain, a distant relative to legendary tribal chairman Roger Jourdain. Moreover, the Jourdain family name can be traced back to the French fur trader and host to the first Catholic missionary, Joseph

Jourdain. The story of Red Lake reveals how tightly and intricately the tangled webs of empire have been woven, holding Native communities captive well beyond the simple bonds of capitalism.

Red Pedagogy:
Where There Is Resistance There Is Power

Audre Lorde's essay, *The Master's Tools Will Not Dismantle the Master's House*, is one of the most quoted essays in academic history and, I would also venture to say, one that needs rethinking. While it is self-evident that indigenous knowledge is essential to the process of decolonization, I would also argue that the Master's tools are necessary. Otherwise, to take Audre Lorde seriously means to create a dichotomy between the tools of the colonizer and those of the colonized. Such a dichotomy leaves the indigenous scholar to grapple with a kind of "Sophie's Choice" moment where one feels compelled to choose between retaining their integrity (identity) as a Native scholar by employing only indigenous knowledge or to "sell out" and employ the frames of Western knowledge. What does it mean for indigenous scholars to engage Western knowledge? Does it signify a final submission to the siren's song, seducing us into the colonialist abyss with promises of empowerment? Or is it the necessary first step in reclaiming and decolonizing an intellectual space—an inquiry room—of our own? Such questions provoke beyond the bounds of academic exercise, suggesting instead the need for an academic exorcism.

The demon to be purged is the specter of colonialism. As indigenous scholars, we live within, against, and outside of its constant company, witnessing its various manifestations as it shape-shifts its way into everything from research and public policy to textbooks and classrooms. Thus, the colonial tax of Native scholars not only requires a renegotiation of personal identity but also an analysis of how whole nations get trans- or (dis)figured when articulated through Western frames of knowing. As Edward Said observes, "institutions, vocabulary, scholarship, imagery, doctrines, even colonial bureaucracies and colonial styles" all support to the "Western discourse" (Said, 1985, p. 2). In other words, is it possible to engage the grammar of empire without replicating its effects?

At the same time indigenous scholars entertain these ruminations, Native communities continue to be impacted and transformed by the forces of colonization, rendering the "choice" of whether to employ Western knowledge in the process of defining indigenous pedagogies essentially moot. In other words, by virtue of living in this world and having to negotiate the forces of colonization, indigenous scholars are given no choice but to know, understand, and acquire the grammar of empire as well as develop the skills to contest it. The relationship between the two is not some liberal dream of multicultural harmony but rather the critical and dialogical tension between competing moral visions.

Such is the premise and promise of *Red Pedagogy*. It is an indigenous pedagogy that operates at the crossroads of Western theory—specifically critical pedagogy—and indigenous knowledge. In bridging these epistemological worlds, *Red Pedagogy* asks that as we examine our own communities, policies, and practices, we take seriously the notion that to know ourselves as revolutionary agents is more than an act of understanding who we are. It is an act of reinventing ourselves, of validating our overlapping cultural identifications and relating them to the materiality of social life and power relations (McLaren, 1997). As such, *Red Pedagogy* is, by definition, a space of engagement. It is the liminal and intellectual borderlands where indigenous and nonindigenous scholars encounter one another, working to remember, redefine, and reverse the devastation of the original colonialist "encounter."

As with any "conversation," language is important. As indigenous scholar Haunani-Kay Trask writes, "Thinking in one's own cultural referents leads to conceptualizing in one's own world view which, in turn, leads to disagreement with and eventual opposition to the dominant ideology" (1996, p. 54). Thus, where a revolutionary critical pedagogy compels students and educators to question how "knowledge is related historically, culturally and institutionally to the processes of production and consumption," a *Red Pedagogy*, compels students to question how Western knowledge is related to the processes of colonization and how indigenous knowledge can inform the project of decolonization. In short, a *Red Pedagogy* aims to create awareness of what Trask terms "disagreements," helping to foster discontent about the "inconsistencies between the world as it is and as it should be" (Alfred, 1999, p. 132).

Within this context, it is important that indigenous sovereignty not be viewed as a separatist discourse. On the contrary, *it is a restorative process*. As Deloria suggests, indigenous peoples must learn to "withdraw without becoming separatists . . ." we must be "willing to reach out for the contradictions within our experience" and open ourselves to "the pain and the joy of others" (Warrior, 1995, p. 124). This sentiment renders sovereignty a profoundly spiritual project involving questions about who we are as a people. Indeed Deloria and Lytle (1984) suggest that indigenous sovereignty will not be possible until "Indians resolve for themselves a comfortable modern identity" (p. 266).

This "resolution" will require indigenous peoples to engage the difficult process of self-definition, to come to consensus on a set of criteria that defines what behaviors and beliefs constitute acceptable expressions of their tribal heritage (Deloria & Lytle, 1984, p. 254). While this process is necessarily deliberative, it is not (as in revolutionary pedagogies) limited to the processes of "*conscientizagão*."[16] Rather, it will remain an inward- and outward-looking process, a process of reenchantment, of ensoulment, that is both deeply spiritual and sincerely mindful.

The guiding force in this process must be the tribe, the people, the community; the perseverance of these entities and their connection to indigenous lands and sacred places is what inherits "spirituality" and, in turn, the "sovereignty" of Native peoples. As Lyons notes, "rather than representing an enclave, sovereignty . . . is the ability to assert oneself renewed—in the presence of others. It is a people's right to rebuild its demand to exist and present its gifts to the world . . . an adamant refusal to dissociate culture, identity, and power from the *land*" (Lyons, 2000, p. 457). In other words, the vision of tribal stability, of community stability, not only rests in the desire and ability of indigenous peoples to listen to each other but also to the land. The question remains whether the ability to exercise spiritual sovereignty will continue to be fettered if not usurped by the desires of a capitalist state intent on devouring the land.

Finally, from the standpoint of *Red Pedagogy, the primary lesson in all of this is pedagogical.* In other words, as we are poised to raise yet another generation in a nation at war and at risk, we must consider how emerging conceptions of citizenship, sovereignty, and democracy will impact the (re)formation of our national identity, particularly among young people in schools. As Mitchell (2001, p. 5) notes, "the production of democracy, the practice of education, and the constitution of the nation-state" have always been interminably bound together. The imperative before us as citizens is to engage a process of unthinking our colonial roots and rethinking the relationship between indigenous sovereignty and radical democracy. For teachers and students, this means that we must be willing to act as agents of transgression, posing critical questions and engaging dangerous discourse. Such is the epistemological basis of *Red Pedagogy.* In particular, *Red Pedagogy* offers the following seven precepts as a way of thinking our way around and through the challenges facing American education in the twenty-first century and our mutual need to define decolonizing pedagogies:

1. *Red Pedagogy* is primarily a pedagogical project. In this context, pedagogy is understood as being inherently political, cultural, spiritual, and intellectual.

2. *Red Pedagogy* is fundamentally rooted in indigenous knowledge and praxis. It is particularly interested in knowledge that furthers understanding and analysis of the forces of colonization.

3. *Red Pedagogy* is informed by critical theories of education. A *Red Pedagogy* searches for ways it can both deepen and be deepened by engagement with critical and revolutionary theories and praxis.

4. *Red Pedagogy* promotes an education for decolonization. Within *Red Pedagogy* the root metaphors of decolonization are articulated as equity, emancipation, sovereignty, and balance. In this sense, an education for decolonization makes no claim to political neutrality but rather engages a method of analysis and social inquiry that troubles the capitalist-imperialist aims of unfettered competition, accumulation, and exploitation.

5. *Red Pedagogy* is a project that interrogates both democracy and indigenous sovereignty. In this context sovereignty is broadly defined as "a people's right to rebuild its demand to exist and present its gifts to the world . . . an adamant refusal to dissociate culture, identity, and power from the land" (Lyons, 2000).

6. *Red Pedagogy* actively cultivates praxis of collective agency. That is, *Red Pedagogy* aims to build transcultural and transnational solidarities among indigenous peoples and others committed to reimagining a sovereign space free of imperialist, colonialist, and capitalist exploitation.

7. *Red Pedagogy* is grounded in hope. This is, however, not the future-centered hope of the Western imagination, but rather a hope that lives in contingency with the past—one that trusts the beliefs and understandings of our ancestors, the power of traditional knowledge, and the possibilities of new understandings.

In the end, a *Red Pedagogy* is about engaging the development of "community-based power" in the interest of "a responsible political, economic, and spiritual society." That is, the power to live out "active presences and *survivances* rather than an illusionary democracy." Vizenor's notion of survivance signifies a state of being beyond "survival, endurance, or a mere response to colonization," and of moving toward "an active presence . . . and active repudiation of dominance, tragedy and victimry." In rethinking the stories of such tragic figures as Jeff Weise, Dylan Klebold, and Eric Harris, I find the notion of survivance to be poignant and powerful. It speaks to our collective need to decolonize, to push back against empire, and reclaim what it means to be a people of sovereign mind and body. The peoples of Red Lake, Columbine, Lancaster County, and the Ninth Ward serve as a reminder to all of us that just as the specter of colonialism haunts the collective soul of America, so too does the more hopeful spirit of indigeneity.

Notes

1. Robert Allen Warrior, *Tribal Secrets: Recovering American Indian Intellectual Traditions* (Minneapolis, MN: University of Minnesota Press, 1995), 123.

2. Ibid., 124.

3. Even more problematic is the fact that the casualties caused by capitalism continue to mount. For example, in 2001 there were 1.3 million more poor people in the United States than in 2000.

4. Leading advocates of revolutionary critical pedagogy include Paula Allman (who penned the term), Peter McLaren, Mike Cole, Terry Eagleton, Ramin Farahmandpur, Dave Hill, Jane Kenway, Helen Raduntz, Glen Rikowski, and Valerie Scatamburlo-D'Annibale. Others whose work has greatly influenced the formation of revolutionary critical pedagogy include Teresa Ebert, Paulo Friere, Martha Gimenez, Antonio Gramsci, Henry Giroux, Rosemary Hennessy, Chrys Ingraham, Karl Marx, and Ellen Meskins Wood.

5. Unlike other contemporary narratives that focus on one form of oppression or another, Scatamburlo–D'Annibale & McLaren (2002) note that the power of historical materialism resides in "its ability to reveal (a) how forms of oppression based on categories of difference do not possess relative autonomy from class relations but rather constitute the ways in which oppression is lived/experienced within a class based system and (b) how all forms of social oppression function within an overlapping capitalist system" (p. 14).

6. These principles are articulated by Farahmandpur (2002) in the foreword of McLaren's seminal text *Life in Schools*, p. xvii.

7. McLaren & Farahmandpur, p. 301.

8. Debord defines the spectacle phase of capitalist society as one in which everyday life is increasingly governed by the images, messages, and fantasies of consumer society.

9. Jeff Weise was actually raised in the Twin Cities, but after his mother committed suicide he moved to Red Lake to live with his grandfather.

10. Sources for this compiled history include: Don Trent Jacobs (ed.) Unlearning the Language of Conquest. University of Texas Press: Austin, TX. 2006; Erwin Mittelholtz. "Chronological history of Red Lake and vicinity." Beltrami Historical Society: http://uts.cc.utexas,edu. Mike Mosedale, "Same country, different nation," City Pages; and Red Lake Net News, http://www.rlnn.com.

11.   In 1819, Congress passed an act to fund the "civilization" of Indians. In its first year of inception, expenditures did not exceed $10,000, but by 1880 appropriations reached $130,000 and continued to rise exponentially throughout the decade.

12.   Quoted in Janey B. Hendrix, "Redbird Smith and the Nighthawk Keetoowahs," *Journal of Cherokee Studies*, 8, no. 1 (Spring, 1983), p. 32.

13.   Wilkins & Lomawaima (2002) write, "Policymakers had such abiding faith in the deeply transformative powers of America's Protestant mercantile culture that they believed the mere prospect of private property ownership would magically transform tribal Indians into ruggedly individualistic, Christian, self-supporting yeoman farmers" (p. 108).

14.   Depending upon various criteria established by the Dawes Commission and Bureau of Indian Affairs (BIA), individual (male) tribal members received 160-, 80-, or 40-acre land parcels. More specifically, land was allotted according to the following formula: "(1) To each head of family, one-quarter of a section; (2) To each single person over eighteen years of age, one-eighth of a section; (3) To each orphan child under eighteen years of age, one-eighth of a section; and, (4) To each single person under eighteen now living, or who may be born prior to the date of the order of the President directing an allotment of the lands embraced in any reservation, one sixteenth of a section" (U.S. 24 Stat: 388–391). Allotments were held in trust by the government for a period of 25 years, during which time "the Indian owner was expected to learn proper business methods" (Deloria & Lytle, 1984, p. 8). At the end of the trust period, the allotees received free and clear title to their land and were "awarded" U.S. citizenship, which placed them under state jurisdiction. The Secretary of the Interior also had full discretion to either shorten or extend the trust period, dependent upon his determination of any individual Indian's "competency" to manage his or her own affairs. Graduation from an Indian school, possession of a sufficient degree of White blood, and/or demonstration of "self-sufficiency" were all considered legitimate grounds for determining "competency" (Wilkins & Lomawaima, 2002, p. 283). Finally, after all allotments were dispensed, the balance of reserve territory was declared "surplus" and opened to non-Indian homesteading, corporate utilization and/or incorporation into national parks and forests (Churchill & Morris, 1992).

15.   For instance, the American Indian Policy Review Commission (the Abourezk Commission) found that while 595,157 acres of land were restored under the IRA, that government agencies condemned 1,811,010 acres of Indian land during this same period. (American Indian Policy Review Commission, *Final Report*, vol. 1. Washington, D.C.: U.S. Government Printing Office, 1976, 309–310.

16.   "Conscientizagão" is a Freiean term that refers to the development of critical social consciousness, wherein dialogue and analysis serve as the foundation for reflection and action.

References

Alfred, Taiaiake. 1999. *Peace, Power, Righteousness: An Indigenous Manifesto*. Oxford: Oxford University Press.

Allman, Paula. 2001. *Critical Education Against Global Capital: Karl Marx and Revolutionary Critical Education*. Westport, CT: Bergin & Garvey.

American Indian Policy Review Commission: *Final Report*. 1976. Washington, D.C. : U.S. Government Printing Office.

Churchill, Ward and Glenn T. Morris. 1992. "Table: Key Indian Cases." In *State of Native America: Genocide, Colonization and resistance*. M. Annette Jaimes, ed., Boston: South End Press.

Deloria, Philip. 1999. *Playing Indian*. New Haven, CT: Yale University Press.

Deloria, V. Jr., & Lytle, C. 1984. *The Nations Within: The Past and Future of American Indian Sovereignity*. Austin: University of Texas Press.

Deloria, V. Jr. 1983. *American Indians, American Justice*. Austin: University of Texas Press.

Frymer, Benjamin. 2005. "Freire, alienation, and contemporary youth: Toward a pedagogy of everyday life." *InterActions: UCLA Journal of Education and Information Studies*. 1.2.

Giroux, H. 2001. "Pedagogy of the Depressed: Beyond the New Politics of Cynicism." *College Literature* 28.3 (Fall): 1–32.

Hauptman, Laurence M. 1992. "Congress, Plenary Power, and the American Indian, 1870–1992." In *Exiled in the Land of the Free: Democracy, Indian Nations and the U.S. Constitution*, eds. Chief Oren Lyons, and John Mohawk. Santa Fe, NM: Clear Light Publishers 318–336.

Hendrix, Janey B. 1983. "Redbird Smith and the Nighthawk Keetowahs." *Journal of Cherokee Studies* 8, no. 1 (Spring): 32.

Lather, P. 1998. Critical Pedagogy and Its Complicities: A Praxis of Stuck Places. *Educational Theory*, 48 (4), 431–462.

Lyons, S.R. 2000. "Rhetorical Sovereignty: What do American Indians Want from Writing?" *College, Composition and Communication*, 51:3 (February): 447–468.

Matza, David. 1999. "Introduction." In Davis, N. *Youth Crisis: Growing up in the High-Risk Society*. Westport, CT: Praeger.

McLaren, Peter. 2002. *Life in Schools: An Introduction to Critical Pedagogy in the Foundations of Education*. 4th ed. Boston: Allyn and Bacon.

McLaren, Peter. 1997. *Revolutionary Multiculturalism: Pedagogies of Dissent for the New Millennium*. Boulder, CO: Westview Press.

McLaren, Peter. and Ramin Farahmandpur. 2001. "The Globalization of Capitalism and the New Imperialism: Notes Toward a Revolutionary Pedagogy." *The Review of Education, Pedagogy, Cultural Studies* 23: 271–315.

McQuaig, Linda. 2001. *All You Can Eat: Greed, Lust and the New Capitalism*. Toronto: Penguin Books.

Mitchell, K. 2001. "Education for Democratic Citizenship: Transnationalism, Multiculturalism, and the Limits of Liberalism." *Harvard Educational Review* 71, no. 1 (Spring): 51–78.

Mosedale, Mike. 2005. "Same Country Different Nation." *City Pages*, Minneapolis, Minnesota. Vol. 26: 1274. (May 4).

Said, E. 1985. Orientalism Reconsidered. *Race and Class*, 26 (1), 1–15.

Scatamburlo-D'Annibale, V. and P. McLaren. 2002."The Strategic Centrality of Class in the Politics of 'Race' and 'Difference.'" *Cultural Studies/Critical Methodologies* 3, no. 2 (May): 148–175

Spring, Joel. 2001. *The American School: 1642–2000*. 5th ed. Boston: McGraw-Hill.

Spring, Joel. 1996. *The Cultural Transformation of a Native American Family and its Tribe 1763–1995*. New York: Lawrence Erlbaum.

Trask, Haunani-Kay. 1996. "Feminism and Indigenous Hawaiian Nationalism." *Signs: Journal of Women in Culture and Society* 21, no. 4 (Summer): 906–916.

Vizenor, G. 1993. The Ruins of Representation. *American Indian Quarterly*, 17, 1–7.

Warrior, R.A. 1995. *Tribal Secrets: Recovering American Indian Intellectual Traditions*. Minneapolis: University of Minnesota.

Wilkins, David E., and K. 2002. Tsianina Lomawaima. *Uneven Ground: American Indian Sovereignty and Federal Law*. Norman: University of Oklahoma Press.

CHAPTER 18

The Poverty
of Critical Pedagogy

Toward a Politics of Engagement[1]

GREGORY MARTIN

Critical pedagogy is in crisis. This is not an isolated crisis affecting a specific aspect of the educational Left. It is a worsening crisis of legitimacy produced under the impact of the collapse of the former Soviet Union, capitalist restructuring, the weak nature of bourgeois democracy (its period of decline, its limits, its emasculation), and the breakdown of the academic Left as a whole to its lowest level of degeneracy. Against the backdrop of neo-liberalism and its unrelenting drive to open up educational systems for global competition and surplus accumulation, we have seen the wholesale erosion and degradation of public education (Hill, 2003, 2006). Even if such a past never truly existed, universities and public colleges are no longer refuges from the discipline of capital's law of value. Although most state workers including academics are "*not* [wholly] governed by market conditions" in that they rely for wages "from *public funds* rather than directly from *private capital*" (Frankel, 1978, p. 34), one of the basic features of the changing role of universities has been the "full Monty" opportunism of careerist academics. By all indications, neo-liberalism has produced a qualitative shift in consciousness, enabling the bourgeoisie to consolidate its alliance with an upper echelon of knowledge workers. This alliance takes a variety of philosophical forms, but economically and ideologically it acts in interests that are aligned to the capitalist state. With regards to both teaching and research, this includes blocking the production of reliable knowledges that are necessary for praxis and the radical transformation of capitalism (Ebert, 1997; Kelsh, 1998; Kelsh & Hill, 2006). What has emerged most clearly is that the restrictive character of education and pedagogy is tied up with homogenizing the aspirations of students (potential workers) within the social universe of capital.

It comes as a relief, though, that gentrification has not infected the borderlands of the bourgeois academy. Radical pedagogues such as Paula Allman, Mike Cole, Dave Hill, Debra Kelsh, Peter McLaren, Glenn Rikowski, Ramin Farahmandpur, Valerie Scatamburo-D'Annibale, and Helen Raduntz have reestablished the theoretical content of the main concepts or "building blocks" of a Marxified critical pedagogy, as well as the connections between them. Although this newer work is at its early stages, the fate and fortune of "revolutionary critical pedagogy" (Allman, 2001) depend upon the development of living, breathing examples of how it can be socially researched and enacted through embodied methodological praxis (see Rikowski, 2002; Martin, 2005). Viewed from this perspective, I believe that the understandings and social implications of Marxism as a mode of political discourse and as an axis of working-class political organization ought to be enlarged and fleshed out by linking theory, politics, and practice through the development of praxis (McLaren, 1999, p.lxiv), or what Marx defined as "revolutionary, critical-practical activity" (cited in Dunayevskaya, 2001).

In this chapter I argue that Marxist academics—as producers of counter-hegemonic knowledge—ought to develop a more reflexive orientation to community, which requires a new relation between theory and practice (Hudis, 2003; see also Martin, 2005, in press). One of the single most important tasks facing the class struggle wing of the educational Left is its ability to work hand-in-hand with activist social movements toward collective goals of a humane and ecologically sustainable society. A critical dialogical engagement between the academy and the "street" will help to create new spheres in which interventionist knowledge can be produced. In the discussion that follows, I provide a quick anatomy of the crisis of critical pedagogy and its discontents. I then discuss how critical pedagogy is currently being reconfigured toward a more engaged and sustained program of revolutionary social action before providing an anecdotal account based upon my experience as an academic/activist within the context of a grassroots social movement in Los Angeles.

The Present Crisis

In this period of dislocation, transition, and class collaboration, the crisis of critical pedagogy is symptomatic of the emergence of intensified "forms of ideological subjection," which are intimately tied up with the reproduction of labor power (Althusser, 1971, p. 133; see also Hill, 2004, 2005; Rikowski, 2000a, 2000b). Arising out of disruptions in the flow of exchange value on a national and global scale, these ideologies are associated with capital's attempt to raise the rate of domination and exploitation within all spheres of social life (intensive management regimes, direct attacks on wages and working conditions, and a corresponding assault on the social wage and "cradle to grave" welfare state). But if you press your nose closer to the glass, Harry Cleaver argues that this potentially explosive situation is clearly "a crisis from the point of view of both classes" (Radical Chains, 1994). Given that the interests of the capitalists (exploiters) and proletarians (exploited) are inherently antagonistic, the capitalist control of consciousness is never total.[2] As a result of this awareness, it is obvious that, for monopoly capital, the crisis of critical pedagogy is to be "gotten over" as quickly as possible because struggles over "truth" and "knowledge" are "part of larger struggles over such things as property and political power" (Katz, 1991, p. 225).

Under the impact of a growing crisis toward the end of a prolonged period of economic upswing, critical pedagogy "is one site relaying the conflict" resulting from tectonic shifts in the material terrain of capitalism (declines in profitability, inflation/deflation, soaring raw-material prices, inter-imperialist rivalries, and war) (Ebert, 1997). What is alarming here is that critical pedagogy in its current manifestation has been scrubbed clean of its social consciousness and is no longer a material force for social change. In advertising its contemporary relevance to the development of human capital, critical pedagogy has been reduced to a shopping basket of critical thinking, problem solving and self-motivational skills susceptible to the private profit needs of big business. If the proof of the pudding is in the eating, then let us look at what we have eaten, with the attempt to turn students away from critical theory toward "a new form of pragmatism" that emphasizes contingency and indeterminacy as the material basis of everyday life (Zavarzadeh & Morton, 1994, pp. 3–4).

On a political level, the question of ethics in a postmodern world is put forward to explain the refusal of critical theory, which is not "appreciative" of knowledge that is viewed through the prism of multiple and hybrid effects (Zavarzadeh & Morton, 1994; Sahay, 1998). In essence, critique that enables the production of reliable "knowledge of the social totality" upon which a transformative politics could be grounded is replaced with "a kind of 'ethical' knowledge" of the local and contingent (Zavarzadeh & Morton, 1994, p. 4; see also Kelsh, 1998). Local and contingent knowledge viewed in this light liquidates the belief that historical materialist critique of capitalism is possible or even desirable (Ebert, 1996; Sahay, 1998). As Ebert (1996) writes:

> Materialist critique is a mode of knowing that inquires into what is not said, into the silences and the suppressed or missing, in order to uncover the concealed operations of power and socio-economic relations connecting the myriad details and representations of our lives. It shows that apparently disconnected zones of culture are in fact materially linked through the highly differentiated, mediated, and dispersed operation of a systematic logic of exploitation. In sum, materialist critique disrupts "what is" to *explain* how social differences—specifically gender, race, sexuality, and class—have been systematically produced and continue to operate within regimes of exploitation, so that we can change them. It is the means for producing transformative knowledges. (p. 7)

The effect of some forms of postmodernism on critical pedagogy is therefore unsettling. It is like visiting a familiar town where all the street signs have been renamed. Here, on the ground, as Molyneux (1995) argues, " . . . it mitigates against any attempt to consciously make history or change society by rendering history and society unintelligible."[3]

At the same time, the crisis of critical pedagogy has certainly not unfolded according to a simple, mechanistic, linear model of cause and effect. Ebert (1997) further argues that the ongoing struggle between capital and labor at the point of production and distribution is characterized by two opposing but historically connected tendencies that shape the contours of class struggle. On the one hand, there exists an opportunistic layer of knowledge workers who are institutionalizing pedagogical work that fits what she terms the "practical and pragmatic" interests of capitalism "founded upon *consumption* practices—and the identities derived from them." On the other, " . . . there is the assertion of the class solidarity of working people (articulated, in part, in the work of resistance knowledge workers) who oppose transnationalism . . . in support of a collective internationalism based on *production* practices and class struggle" (p. 13). That the working class is able to achieve some success is what inevitably compels the bourgeoisie to create and perfect new forms of control.

In this new phase of development and unstable compromise (which must be constantly negotiated, modified, and renewed), the struggle over education cannot be divorced from social problems—unemployment, climate change, alienation—confronting society. Drawing inspiration from Paulo Freire's (1993) problem posing method, critical educators such as Henry Giroux (1992) and Peter McLaren (2000) argue that these problems are not only political but also inherently pedagogical. With a view to rescuing the concept of human agency, Giroux (1988) argues that making "the pedagogical more political and the political more pedagogical" will enable individuals working together within social movements to evaluate and change existing knowledge and power relations (p. 127). Within the total integrated sphere of social reproduction, what matters here is that the problems facing education do not bode well for public education or radical social change, particularly in a world in which the traditional institutions of the working class (trade unions and political parties) have either disintegrated, retreated or become so thoroughly embourgeoisified that they have abandoned even the pretense of building socialism.

Critical Pedagogy

Critical pedagogy, developed by Paulo Freire and rebooted by Paula Allman, Peter McLaren, and the British Hillcole Group, amongst others, is actually more than 30 years old. In the politically barren landscape of education, it has a long and solid pedigree in terms of the theoretical and empirical tools it provides activist teachers, students, and cultural workers for coordination and empowerment (Darder, Torres, & Baltodano, 2002; Kincheloe, 2004; Kincheloe and Steinberg, 1998; Steinberg and Kincheloe, 1998). As carefully demonstrated by Peter McLaren (2000, 2003, 2005), the ancestral DNA of revolutionary critical pedagogy reveals that it grew out of the disillusionment with critical pedagogy, which mutated under the influence of liberal/deconstructive/post-Marxist approaches to social change over the past two turbulent decades. Stripped of its Marxist concepts (class, ideology, exploitation, and revolution), critical pedagogy was hollowed out and politically paralyzed. What I want to emphasize is that as critical pedagogy was influenced by some more fashionable theories of the postmodern Left, it underwent a metamorphosis. But what it grew into dimmed its transformative potential. Thus, some forms of postmodernism is much like Darwin's ichneumon wasp, which lays its eggs inside the living caterpillar (Gould, 1984). Having taken up residence, the infant ichneumon injects a powerful paralyzing agent and then proceeds to feed off the blood and soft tissue of the caterpillar, slowly devouring it from the inside out (Gould, 1984). Likewise, postmodernism, having invaded the revolutionary body of critical pedagogy, thereby remade it.

Indeed, without invoking a particular theoretical strand, a politically diverse group of academics takes comfort in the idea that critical pedagogy has been subject to evolutionary change and that the fossilized thinking of Marxism has been exorcised along with its antagonistic binaries of class. Such comfort, of course, is false. Given that theory does not stand apart from subjectivity and political consciousness, Lenin (1970) argued that the struggle over abstract ideas is connected to the most intimate, sensuous, and material level of class struggle. So far as this is concerned with the impotent rage of non-critical postmodernism and the rise of oppositional tendencies and activist social movements at multiple geographical scales, we can talk about a crisis of categories. As the autonomist Marxist Harry Cleaver (Radical Chains, 1994) points out:

> The categories of marxist analysis are the categories of class relations, capital is a class relation— a class relation of struggle. All the categories of marxist analysis in the three volumes of *Capital* and elsewhere are those of that social relation—which is the class struggle. The only movement of the categories is a movement that occurs as part of the class struggle.

As such, what we are witnessing today is a form of class struggle that has emerged out of the movement of categories as the academic Left, in search of a happier narrative, cuts itself free from Marxism and the burden of foundational truths in favor of more entrepreneurial "readings" of social reality (Zavarzadeh & Morton, 1994). Witness the rise of demi-celebrity theorists who, manufactured by the culture industry, can command six figure salaries and are swept up into assuming their derelict roles on the academic conference circuit, signing autographs for obsessive fans. Capitalism is always in need of new modes of individualism that secure the "freedom" of the subject (capital) and "democracy" (Ebert, 1995). Basically, the primary effect of postmodernism, which reduces political praxis to particularized and localized acts of consumption in the cultural sphere, is to obscure the class link to power relations (Ebert, 1996; Sahay, 1998). Such a stance relies on the dominant fiction of post-structuralist and post-Marxist narratives that historical materialist critique is a totalitarian act, which is not appreciative of local knowledge, e.g., the particular experiences of women and indigenous peoples. Whilst I cannot directly address all the complex and far-reaching issues raised in this argument, the Marxist drive to totalize through its insistence on reading history in class terms is framed as a form of philosophical impossibility that imposes a false closure on meaning. My concern here is with the mind-boggling claim that any materialist critique that brings about class consciousness is an imposition from the "outside," constituting a form of "indoctrination" that is a totalitarian act (Sahay, 1998). By denouncing revolutionary critical pedagogy as a "totalizing act," critics such as Chet Bowers (2005) and Patti Lather (2001) suggest that it leads straight to the gulag. Within this organizing narrative, the concept of totality is readily dismissed as untenable, unethical, and reductionist, as it is not appreciative of local knowledge.

It is a sad story when leftists buy into such vastly oversimplified rhetoric and pitiful logic, especially when it is capitalism that is degrading and vulgar in all realms of human life, including its mass psychology that promotes a deeply ingrained sense of "powerlessness," thereby inducing people to conform to the uncritical dream of the market. As Marxist feminists such as Amrohini Sahay argue, such an "appreciative" politics is not really a compassionate act, but rather an opportunistic narrative on the part of a few privileged intellectuals because it forecloses the rights to struggles that are concerned with the relation of the "inside" to its "outside." In all of its exuberant nihilism, "a praxis of undecidability" (Lather, 2001, p. 191) serves as an alibi to ensure the unavailability of any systemic knowledge of the "outside," which might work to critique a system of domination that produces difference (Sahay 1998). In other words, it fails to provide the most oppressed and exploited people on this planet with a theory of the "big picture," which might enable them to translate their daily free-floating frustrations with the "system" into a coherent set of ideas, beliefs and feelings that provide the basis for action (Ebert, 1996). In effect, by presenting historical materialist critique as authoritarian rather than as democratizing in the fullest sense of the term, these self-appointed guardians of minority identity are actually shoring up support for the regime of profit, which produces differing social relations of exploitation such as race, gender, and sexual orientation (Sahay, 1998).

The overall effects of non-critical postmodern ethics on critical pedagogy have thus been dire. By the early 1990s, it was an open secret that critical pedagogy was in bad shape. Perhaps ironically, it was the stinging criticisms of its theoretical content that led to a resurgence of interest in the relationship between Marxism and pedagogy (Rikowski, 1996, 1997). After a few wrong turns and internecine squabbles, critical pedagogy has recently been revamped to connect with the educational imperatives of activist labor and social movement organizations. Expanding upon Marx's value theory of labor, Glenn Rikowski (2001) has identified the latent explosive potential of labor power (our capacity to labor in the form of epistemological paradigms, skills, dispositions and attitudes) as being at the heart of its theoretical arsenal. Without going into the rich tangle of detail, he argues that a revolutionary critical pedagogy is more about changing our internal social relations than it is about propagating a particular set of ideas. Here, individual human development is organically tied to collective forms of action based in the real, everyday, material struggles of the working class (Martin, 2005). With regard to tactics and strategy, a revolutionary critical pedagogy must also exist within an organizational framework if it is to intervene in the actual class struggle to change the world. Organization, in the broadest sense of the concept, allows for social mobilization and revolutionary praxis when confronted with the armed force and legal authority of the bourgeois state.

At the same time, the development of revolutionary critical pedagogy is context dependent on local, spatial and historical conditions. This makes its implementation on the ground a challenge for scholars and activists alike. However, rather than impose a one-size-fits-all approach, radical pedagogues working within this revived tradition have eloquently articulated how this legacy might have a message or two for a new generation of political activists coming to the fore. For obvious reasons, what Paula Allman (2001) has termed a "revolutionary critical pedagogy" is not easy to achieve. In her groundbreaking book *Critical Education Against Global Capitalism,* Allman (2001) sketches out the key principles of revolutionary critical pedagogy. These are cited in point form below:

- Mutual respect, humility, openness, trust, and cooperation . . .
- Commitment to learning to "read the world" critically and to transforming conventional and dominant educational relations, based at least at the level of understanding why the transformations are necessary . . .
- Vigilance with regard to one's own process of self-transformation and adherence to principles and aims the group is attempting to fulfill . . .
- Honesty, truth . . . required from every member of the group once the process of learning has begun . . .
- Passion (italics in the original, pp. 178–180)

Allman's key principles are also followed by several objectives or aims:

- Critical, Creative and Hopeful Thinking . . .
- Transformation of Self and the Social Relations of Learning and Teaching . . .
- Democratizaton . . .
- Embracing and Internalizing the Principles . . .
- Unquenchable Thirst for Understanding, or Genuine Critical Curiosity . . .
- Solidarity and Commitment to Self and Social Transformation and the Project of Humanization (italics in the original, pp. 180–183)

Regrettably, some of the educational Left has denounced this unsweetened version of critical pedagogy as being "outmoded," "too theoretical," and overtly "romantic." Whilst I do not want to dismiss the impressive rearguard actions by progressive educators, for the most part these efforts at pedagogical reform somehow pay pointless homage to the Right and have been too imprecise and too inconsistent. Indeed, rather than embark on a clear, systematic process of change, the soul-destroying pragmatics of some of the bourgeois educational Left has assisted in a regression to domination, symptomatic of the effects of imperialism.

Teaching Against the Grain: Revolutionary Critical Pedagogy in the Present

Given that my work is influenced by the Freirean pedagogical tradition and Marxist Humanist currents, I believe that engaging in processes and practices that are transformative (rather than merely reproductive) requires a revolutionary critical pedagogy, which emphasizes the central importance of class struggle in the fight against the oppression and exploitation of capital. Whereas conservative and liberal pedagogies exist to solicit and recruit individuals into the status quo by offering an ebullient accommodation with those subject locations that invite identification with this predatory force (although this is certainly not the *intended* outcome of the latter), a revolutionary critical pedagogy challenges the ideology that works to naturalize and secure it.

As an antidote to the poison of bourgeois ideology and practices that are hegemonic under capitalism, a revolutionary critical pedagogy can serve as the basis for the development of what McLaren refers to as "critical subjectivity" (cited in Pozo, 2003). Critical subjectivity springs from social struggle analysis and strategies that grow out in direct relation to power, poverty, and difference, which are effects of the dialectical relationship between the ideological superstructure and the underlying economic base of society. The construction of critical subjectivities does not take place in an ideological vacuum but is a dynamic and ongoing exercise, which requires breaking down the structures of bourgeois thought and politics. Marx (1978) used the idea of the "camera obscura" to explain how ideology turned material reality "upside-down" (p. 154). To circumvent these effects, Ebert (1996) argues that a useful and practical tool for developing class consciousness is a critique of ideology. A critique of ideology can sweep away the cobwebs of the dominant ideology by revealing the hidden and ugly contradictions it works to deny. As Ebert clarifies:

> Critique of ideology inquires into the social and historical struggles over meaning. It interrogates the operation of difference in relation to its outside, to the social contradictions of specific regimes of exploitation, paying special attention to the contesting ways diverse superstructural articulations of difference are related to the divisions of labor and property. It investigates how codes, tropes, and signifying practices are *used* to help achieve and maintain the social, cultural, political, and juridical forms—in short, the superstructure—required by the existing relations of production. It examines how they operate to secure ideologically necessary subject positions and how these subject positions are represented as natural. (p. 176)

Although ideology critique plays a critical role in the development of revolutionary thought, a danger exists in emphasizing this form of social investigation if it becomes the object and not the subject of knowledge. It is a classic case of the divorce of thought from action, which leads to an ending that is a forgone conclusion: idealism. I raise this issue because, in practical terms, too often cognitive practice neglects the practice of activity Marx intended to emphasize, action. If revolutionary critical pedagogy is to be a factor in the effort to transform society, I believe that we must develop our political ideals and social commitments by expanding our knowledge and using the achieved knowledge to generate further knowledge through reflection and action. Through such social praxis, which Freire (1993) defines as the dialectical synthesis of "reflection and action upon the world in order to transform it," a revolutionary critical pedagogy can enable us to change the social structure of knowledge and power (p. 33). What is important to emphasize here is that a revolutionary critical pedagogy does not view knowledge as an innate psychological attribute of individuals, but rather as a social relation, the content of which is mediated by material practice within inherited structures. Here, the advantage of such social praxis is that it provides the practical basis for students/laborers to overcome their political alienation (individuality) by discovering their shared historical role and interest (McLaren & Farahmandpur, 2000, 2001a, 2001b).

One of the principal aims of a revolutionary critical pedagogy is to enable the most exploited and oppressed individuals and groups to mobilize their collective resources in order to overcome the limits placed upon their historically devalued literacies, knowledges, and social competencies. By positioning working-class and oppressed peoples as producers of their own knowledge, a revolutionary critical pedagogy interpellates them as historical agents who can work together (at the level of reproduction) to lay the practical foundations for credible new institutions of popular power, capable of changing their objective life situations. Thus, when looking at the possibilities for political action in activist social movement organizations, a revolutionary critical pedagogy can provide the basis for working-class regroupment and international solidarity by developing alternative conceptions of social identity and subjectivity based upon a continuous cycle of reflection and action that is grounded in the suppressed knowledges, skills, and social competencies of the working class and oppressed nationalities. The transformation of individualized, tacit, and everyday knowledge about capitalism into collective, explicit, and radical knowledge within activist and participatory modes of social organization has direct relevance to understanding the democratic process and the potential for creating a world community in which all activity is oriented toward the full satisfaction of human and ecological needs, whether through efforts to build citywide and neighborhood protest campaigns, or via major mobilizations to establish or reestablish internationalist organization, which is the aim of all revolutionary pedagogy.

Toward a Pedagogy of Engagement

Although I am inspired by the scholarly work of Marxism, I believe that in its most academic incarnations it has gotten bogged down in the language games of the bourgeois academy. This is not to say that the entire field of academic Marxism falls into this category, but all too often it is reduced to mind-numbingly boring and futile debates between competing bureaucrats of "expert" knowledge. Within this context, I believe that it is incumbent upon politically committed leftists to find positions for themselves within the various radical social movements that have arisen as a defensive reflex against the horrors of capitalism (Martin, in press; Moss, 2004). To this end, when I arrived as a doctoral student at the University of California, Los Angeles (UCLA) in the late 1990s, I was interested in bridging the two by expanding my involvement in some of the struggles and organizations of the working class. Although I did not have any organic roots in Los Angeles, I began to look around to find out what the most militant and emergent social forces were doing to confront the appalling inequality in this city, which exhibits all the ugly contradictions of modern capitalism. One of the ways geographic segregation gets reproduced in Los Angeles is through the decrepit and racist bus system, and having personally relied upon increase in bus ridership. Always on the offensive, the BRU also forced the MTA to replace its dilapidated fleet of diesel fuel buses with new Compressed Natural Gas (CNG) buses. Significantly, the BRU has publicly stated that these victories have " . . . generated more than 1,000 new green jobs for Black, Latino, Asian/Pacific Islander, and white workers, many of whom are women, as the bus fleet expanded. This is an expansion of public sector union jobs in an era of privatization and union-busting" (Clean Air, nd). As Robin Kelley (1996) puts its, at a time when many leftists, and Civil Rights leaders "are busy begging the Democratic Party" not to abandon the working class, the BRU is building a progressive political alternative in the form of a grassroots social movement which is connecting the struggle over public transportation to a range of other pressing issues including environmental justice, labor struggles, privatization, and the problems of capitalism.

Here, strategic and tactical concepts that arise out of the everyday spatial, temporal and sensuous class struggle of ordinary workers (janitors, security guards, housewives) are developed to fit concrete reality and not abstract theory. For example, while the BRU and its members self-identify as working class through both individual and collective forms of address, the organization has developed an "inclusive" stance toward class. Rejecting the white male laborism of the traditional trade union movement, the BRU has attempted to create a shared system of meaning by striving to implement a culture inside the organization that is multilingual (all meetings are conducted in English, Spanish, and Korean, and all flyers are considered public education and are printed in these languages), antiracist, and supportive of women's liberation in its day-to-day work (Martin, 2005). Attending to the ethnic and linguistic diversity of its social base has strengthened an instinctive sense of working class solidarity within the organization, which appears to emerge more from its diversity than from any kind of homogeneity. In fact, it provided the legal basis for the BRU's role as "class representatives" for 450,000 transit dependent bus riders in Los Angeles.

What is important to remember here is that the primary political actors in the struggle of the BRU are not the trained organizers who helped to build the organization from the ground up, but rather the hundreds of ordinary, spirited men and women who are its ultimate resources of knowledge and power (Martin, in press). One of the strengths of learning organizations such as the BRU is that it does not reduce education to a potentially alienating tool designed to teach its members how to sit still and "get along" while its elected officialdom acts as a mediator with the state. Motivated by the idea of carrying out its struggle at a deeper and wider political level, it fuses critique with agency by connecting individual understanding and development to personal and social transformation. To kick-start the process, the BRU actively encourages members to use their own unique and immediate experiences of oppression and subordination as a starting point to transform their situation. This includes the use of educative process and practices in the everyday activities of the BRU, which provide structured opportunities "to read the world critically" through dialogue, shared problem solving, and collective action.

To take just one example, full-time paid organizers (exposed to Freire's writings) actively promoted "dialogue" and "problem-posing" to facilitate the process of what Freire (1993) called "conscientization" and the empowerment of members at monthly meetings.

it to get to school and work, my attention was drawn to the Bus Riders Union/Sindicato de Passajeros (BRU/SDP).

The Bus Riders Union is an intergenerational, multiracial, multilingual, gendered, working-class political movement in Los Angeles, built to fight against the government for civil rights in the form of a first-class, clean-fuel, mass public transit system. Keeping the Civil Rights torch alight, which was sparked 50 years ago when Rosa Parks refused to give up her seat to a white passenger on a bus in Montgomery, Alabama (hot on the heels of the Baton Rouge bus boycott), the BRU operates as a democratic organization with both a Principles of Unity and a set of bylaws. It also welcomes a variety of cultural and political perspectives, e.g., ethnic/nationalist, feminist, gay and lesbian, and socialist. Established in 1993 as an experimental project of the Labor Strategy Community Center, a "think tank/act tank" also based in Los Angeles, the BRU claims to represent an estimated 3,000 dues-paying and 50,000 self-identified members, representing 450,000 Los Angeles bus riders (Mann, 1999, 2002). Critics might argue that these numbers rely upon a relaxed definition of membership, but at a time when most Americans are soundly asleep at the wheel about the threat of capitalism the BRU is involved in a collective experiment to build a left organizational form. In fact, although popular accounts of the BRU give it a larger-than-life portrayal, its homegrown success has spun off variants in other parts of the United States as well as in Canada.

The BRU's roots sprouted in the 1990s, when members of the Center for Community Justice got together and initiated its Public Transportation Group, which developed a tactical plan to mobilize the power of the urban poor in the fight over social priorities to improve the bus system. This organizing project was based on what the Group learned after broad consultation, listening to people and learning from them about the quality of mass transit for low-income people in Los Angeles. Unlike the heavily subsidized Metrolink rail system built to serve a White ridership (as high as 70%), which lives in the relatively wealthy suburbs of the region, the bus system is notoriously overcrowded and unreliable as well as a major source of air pollution. According to one of the BRU's political leaders, an inside joke at the Metropolitan Transport Authority (until it was publicized by the BRU) described the public bus system as, "a third class bus system for Third World People" (Mann, 1996, p. 17). Indeed, the massive transfer in public funds away from the bus system toward rail is perceived to express not only the class content of such "economic conversion" but also the strong racial character of the state apparatus and its resulting two-tiered segregated public transportation system in Los Angeles (p. 24).

What instantly captured my interest was that the BRU developed a number of innovative processes and practices to identify, capture, integrate, archive and leverage the dispersed, local, everyday knowledge of thousands of bus riders, to make otherwise unreasonable demands on the state. Indeed, its piéce de résistance came in 1994, when the BRU filed a class action civil rights lawsuit, which forced the MTA to improve and expand the dismal public transportation system in Los Angeles. The landmark civil rights Consent Decree that the BRU won in October of 1996 had a number of provisions including the requirement that the MTA reduce monthly bus fares, which translated into a 10 percent

As a public gathering in which individuals could both express and critically discuss their everyday lived experiences, emotions, and creative insights, I found that monthly meetings had the potential to recognize and spread new ideas rapidly throughout the organization as well as to develop local literacies around global issues (climate change, the war in Iraq). Each meeting was always chaired and monitored by members of the BRU leadership (one woman and one man for gender balance). Members were first updated with campaign developments and tactical plans before they were asked to discuss a range of social issues that were openly discussed and debated (e.g., Valley secession, the occupation of Palestine), with the voices of women, people of color, and non-English speakers always prioritized (The Bus Riders Union Asks, 2002). What matters here is that, recognizing who drove the entire process, full-time organizers held "Open Mic" sessions to allow for new knowledge and insights to emerge. Creating participation structures such as Open Mic sessions for open-ended dialogue allowed for interaction, the building of solidarity amongst peers, and for the development of action competencies through the "inculcation of conscious political subjects capable of participating in the production and not merely the assimilation and (re)privitization of resistant knowledges" (Sahay, 1993). Indeed, as a situated form of literacy activity, Open Mic sessions at the BRU allowed for learning to be "more evenly shared" in an "interactive," "multi-voiced" framework, where "expertise is distributed" within the organization (Gutierrez, Larson, Rymes & Stone, 2000, p. 8). Here, in terms of its established "purpose" and "result," Open Mic was a form of critical literacy related to Freire's (1993) concept of "praxis" (pp. 106–107). To put it more precisely, literacy events such as Open Mic constituted the "movement of inquiry" directed toward freedom from the real, brutal conditions of life through continuous acts of reflection and action (1993, p. 66).

Rather than place limits on the space of political agency, this form of grassroots critical pedagogy constitutes a bottom-up approach to the creation of knowledge and acknowledges the organic skills, literacies, and social competencies of BRU members. Such knowledges, skills, and perspectives can be derived formally, informally, or incidentally through everyday work routines, social practices, norms, and action, or even through the role of social memory as "historical knowledge" that is handed down to generations of activists (Foley, 1999; see also Houston and Pulido, 2002, for an example in their discussion of the Local 11 chapter of the Hotel and Restaurant Employees Union's struggle against unfair labor practices at the University of Southern California). With every activity seen to constitute some sort of pedagogical value, whether it was going out to organize on buses or standing on street corners, the BRU had developed a range of knowledge-creation techniques to capture and transform any individualized, tacit, and everyday learning that occurred "naturally" into a form of explicit, radical, and collective knowledge that the organization could act upon, such as "shared story telling," "role playing," "brainstorming," "face-to-face dialogue," and "group work" (Foley, 1999, 2001). One of the most effective of these knowledge creation strategies was the Union's use of Civil Rights Diaries, handed out to thousands of riders. These detailed declarations documented the problems that users of the bus system judged most important (overcrowding, run-down buses) and were used as testimony in legal action against the Metropolitan Transport Authority. As a spatial mapping of traveling problems, these diaries captured practical everyday knowledges and perspectives, which enabled the organization's intelligence to grow.

A Call to Action

Despite claims to the contrary, revolutionary politics is not a lost cause, not even in the repressive aftermath of the 9/11 terrorist attacks. Rather than wander in putative introspection around a decaying ivory tower, I believe that in a period of ideological lockdown it is the responsibility of academic activists to act with courage and not to succumb to fear, blind pessimism, or despair. As bearers of what Giroux (1988) terms "dangerous memory," it is incumbent upon the class struggle wing of the educational Left to resist the corporatization of the university by engaging in direct social action through forms of community organization at the grassroots level, even if it does involve an element of risk. After all, as rightist forces aligned with the bourgeois state rail against Left bias in universities, the liberal notion of academic freedom will not be defended if it is not connected to the struggles and interests of ordinary people around the world. Clearly, this will require resisting our normalized identities in the workplace in terms of being a "professional" or career progression, including the impulse of many academics to work too hard (let's not forget that most work beyond the 40-hour university workweek). Without neglecting our teaching and research responsibilities, we might consider avoiding activities organized to yield a profit in favor of "new forms of labour power expenditure, and hence new forms of labour, based on human *need*—forms that crash beyond the value-form of labour, cutting short the formation of capital" (Rikowski, 2000a). Following this line of thinking, activist academics, or "organic intellectuals," to borrow Gramsci's (1971) use of the term, could use their *left* over time and energy to engage in voluntary labor or extra-academic activity, which by its very nature confronts the law of value that constitutes the substance of capital's social universe (Rikowski, 2002). What matters here is that the development of theoretical and empirical insights cannot take place abstractly within a test-tube situation but must be built and tested through actual experiments in building new forms of political life oriented to socialist ideals. With the various discourses of postmodernism morally and politically exhausted, I believe that at this historical juncture, we need a revolutionary critical pedagogy based in hope that can bridge the politics of the academy with forms of grassroots political organizing capable of achieving social and ecological transformation.

Notes

1.   This title takes inspiration from the historical facts of class-based resistance and struggle that are guiding a new generation, young and old, mobilizing around anti-racist, feminist, queer, ecological, anti-war and anti-imperialist movements worldwide as well as E. P. Thompson's (1978) book *The Poverty of Theory*, London: Merlin Press.

2.   Today, plenty of discontent exists at the base of capitalist society and the contemporary relevance of Marx and Engel's (1967) writings is best captured in a famous quote from the *Communist*

Manifesto, "Society as a whole is more and more splitting up into two great hostile camps, into two great classes directly facing each other: Bourgeoisie and Proletariat" (p. 80). Engels specified the meanings of these terms in a footnote, "By bourgeoisie is meant the class of modern Capitalists, owners of the means of social production and employers of wage labour. By proletariat, the class of modern wage-labourers who, having no means of production of their own, are reduced to selling their labour-power in order to live" (Marx & Engels, 1967, p. 79). Thus, in this chapter, the terms 'proletariat,' 'worker' and 'working class' are all abstract concepts used to refer to those who do not own the means of production and have only their labor power to sell. Conceived in this way, they are inclusive concepts that are against the exclusive ideology and practice of white male laborism rampant in the Western Trade Union movement (Sears & Mooers, 1995).

3.   In contrast to the bourgeois moralizing of the postmodern left, Marx and Engels (1967) argued that ethics are relational and constructed through the immediate and concretely sensuous class struggle to create a communist future, where "we shall have an association, in which the free development of each is the condition for the free development of all" (p. 105).

References

Allman, P. (2001). *Critical education against global capitalism: Karl Marx and revolutionary critical education*. Westport, CT: Bergin & Garvey.

Althusser, L. (1971). *Lenin and philosophy and other essays*. New York: Monthly Review Press.

Apple, M. (2000). The shock of the real: Critical pedagogies and rightist reconstructions. In P. Trifonas, (Ed.), *Revolutionary pedagogies: Cultural politics, instituting education, and the discourse of theory* (pp. 225–250). New York: RoutledgeFalmer.

Bowers, C. (2005). How Peter McLaren and Donna Houston, and other 'green' Marxists contribute to the globalization of the West's industrial culture. *Education Studies, 3* (1), 185–195.

Clean Air, Clean Lungs, Clean Buses Campaign—History & Analysis (nd). The Bus Riders Union. Retrieved August 11, 2006, from http://www.busridersunion.org/engli/Campaigns/cleanair/cleanairhistory.htm

Cole, M., Hill, D., McLaren, P., & Rikowski, G. (2001). *Red chalk: On schooling, capitalism & politics*. London: Tufnell Press.

Darder, A., Torres, R., & Baltodano, M. (2002). *The critical pedagogy reader*. New York: RoutledgeFalmer.

Dunayevskaya, R. (2001). *Marxism & freedom: From 1776 until today*. New York: Humanity Books.

Ebert, T. (1996). *Ludic feminism and after: Postmodernism, desire, and labor in late capitalism*. Ann Arbor, MI: The University of Michigan Press.

Ebert, T. (1997). Quango-ing the university. *The Alternative Orange, 5*(2), 5–47.

Fight transit racism, billions for buses and environmental justice campaigns. (n.d.). The Bus Riders Union.

Foley, G. (1999). *Learning in social action: A contribution to understanding informal education*. New York: Zed Books.

Foley, G. (2001). *Strategic learning: Understanding and facilitating organizational change*. Sydney: Centre for Popular Education.

Frankel, B. (1978). *Marxian theories of the state: A critique of orthodoxy*. Melbourne: Arena Publications Association.

Freire, P. (1993). *Pedagogy of the oppressed*. New York: Continuum. (Original work published 1970)

Giroux, H. (1988). *Teachers as intellectuals: Toward a critical pedagogy of learning*. New York: Bergin and Garvey.

Giroux, H. (1992). *Border crossings: Cultural workers and the politics of education*. New York: Routledge.

Gould, S. (1984). Nonmoral nature. *The Unofficial Stephen Jay Gould Archive*. Retrieved August 12, 2006, from http://www.stephenjaygould.org/library/gould_nonmoral.html

Gramsci, A. (1971). *Selections from the prison notebooks of Antonio Gramsci*. New York: International Publishers.

Gutierrez, K., Larson, J., Rymes, B., & Stone, L. (2000). Constructing classrooms of learners: Literacy learning as social practice. Unpublished manuscript.

Hill, D. (2003). Global neo-liberalism, the deformation of education and resistance. *Journal for Critical Education Policy Studies*, *1*(1): Retrieved May 12, 2006, from http://www.jceps.com/index.php?pageID=article&articleID=7

Hill, D. (2004). Books, banks and bullets: controlling our minds—the global project of imperialistic and militaristic neoliberalism and its effect on education policy. *Policy Futures*, *2*(3). Retrieved February 3, 2006, from http://www.wwwords.co.uk/pdf/viewpdf.asp?j=pfie&vol=2&issue=3&year=2004&article= 6_Hill_PFIE_2_3–4_web&id=203.196.46.160

Hill, D. (2005). Globalisation and its educational discontents: Neoliberalism and its impacts on education workers' rights, pay and conditions. *International Studies in Sociology of Education*, *15*(3), 257–288.

Hill, D. (2006). Education services liberalization. In E. Rosskam, (Ed.), *Winners or Losers? Liberalizing Public Services* (pp. 3–54). Geneva: International Labour Office.

Houston, D., & Pulido, L. (2002). The work of performativity: Staging social justice at the university. *Society and Space*, *20*(4), 401–424.

Hudis, P. (2003). The future of dialectical Marxism: Toward a new relation of theory and practice. Paper presented at Rethinking Marxism Conference, University of Massachusetts at Amherst.

Katz, A. (1991). The university and revolutionary practice: A letter toward a Leninist pedagogy. In D. Morton & M. Zavarzadeh (Eds.), *Theory/pedagogy/politics: Texts for change* (pp. 222–239). Chicago: University of Illinois Press.

Kelley, R. (1996, February 5). Freedom fighters (the sequel). *The Nation*. Retrieved January 25, 2007, from http://www.busridersunion.org/LangIndy/Resources/NewsArticles/pdfs/1990s/Robin%20D.G.%20Kelley%20Freedom%20Riders%20the%20nation%202-5-96.pdf

Kelsh, D. (1998). Desire and class: The knowledge industry in the wake of poststructuralism. *Cultural Logic*, *1*(2). Retrieved January 9, 2001, from http://www.eserver.org/clogic/1–2/kelsh.html

Kelsh, D., & Hill, D. (2006). The culturalization of class and the occluding of class consciousness: The knowledge industry in/of education. *Journal for Critical Education Policy Studies*, *4*(1). Retrieved September 28, 2006, from http://www.jceps.com/index.php?pageID=article&articleID=59

Kincheloe, J. (2004). *Critical pedagogy primer*. New York: Peter Lang Publishing.

Kincheloe, J., and Steinberg, S. (1998). *Unauthorized methods: Strategies for critical teaching*. New York: Routledge.

Laclau, E., & Mouffe, C. (1985). *Hegemony & socialist strategy*. New York: Verso.

Lather, P. (2001). Ten years later, yet again: Critical pedagogy and its complicities. In K. Weiler (Ed.), *Feminist engagements* (pp. 183–195). New York: Routledge.

Lenin, V. I. (1970). *What is to be done?* London: Panther.

Mann, E. (1996). *A new vision for urban transportation: The Bus Riders Union makes history at the intersection of mass transit, civil rights, and the environment.* Los Angeles: Strategy Center Publications.

Mann, E. (1999). Class, community and empire: Toward an anti-imperialist strategy for labor. In E. Meiksins Wood, P. Meiksins & M. Yates, (Eds.), *Rising from the ashes? Labor in the age of "Global" capitalism* (pp. 100–109). New York: Monthly Review Press.

Mann, E. (2002). *Dispatches from Durban: Firsthand commentaries on the World Conference Against Racism and post-September 11 movement strategies.* Los Angeles: Frontline Press.

Martin, G. (2005). You can't be neutral on a moving bus: Critical pedagogy as community praxis. *Journal for Critical Education Policy Studies, 3*(2). Retrieved August 12, 2006, from http://www.jceps.com

Martin, G. (in press). Marxist political praxis: Class notes on academic activism in the corporate university. In A. Green & G. Rikowski (Eds.), *Dialogues in Marxism and education: Volume 1. Openings.* London: Palgrave Macmillan.

Marx, K. (1978). The German ideology, Part I. In R. Tucker (Ed.), *The Marx-Engels Reader* (pp. 146–200) (Second Edition). New York: Norton.

Marx, K., & Engels, F. (1967). *The communist manifesto.* Ringwood, Victoria: Penguin Books. (Original work published 1848)

McLaren, P. (1999). *Schooling as a ritual performance: Toward a political economy of educational symbols and gestures* (Third Edition). Lanham, MD: Rowman & Littlefield.

McLaren, P. (2000). *Che Guevara, Paulo Freire, and the pedagogy of revolution.* Boulder, CO: Rowman and Littlefield.

McLaren, P. (2003). *Life in schools: An introduction to critical pedagogy in the foundations of education* (Fourth Edition). New York: Longman.

McLaren, P. (2005). *Capitalists & conquerors: A critical pedagogy against empire.* Boulder, CO: Rowman & Littlefield.

McLaren, P., & Farahmandpur, R. (2000). Reconsidering Marx in post-Marxist times: A requiem for postmodernism? *Educational Researcher, 29*(3), 25–33.

McLaren, P., & Farahmandpur, R. (2001a). Educational policy and the socialist imagination: Revolutionary citizenship as a pedagogy of resistance. *Educational Policy, 13*(3), 343–378.

McLaren, P., & Farahmandpur, R. (2001b). Teaching against globalization and the new imperialism: Toward a revolutionary pedagogy. *Journal of Teacher Education, 52*(2), 136–150.

McLaren, P., & Farahmandpur, R. (2005). *Teaching against globalization and the new imperialism: A critical pedagogy.* Lanham, MD: Rowman & Littlefield.

Molyneux, J. (1995). Is Marxism deterministic? *International Socialism Journal, 68.* Retrieved December 4, 2006, from http://pubs.socialistreviewindex.org.uk/isj68/molyneux.htm

Moss, P. (2004). A 'politics of local politics': Praxis in places that matter. In D. Fuller & R. Kitchin (Eds.), *Radical theory/critical praxis: Making a difference beyond the academy* (pp. 103–115). Praxis(e)Press. Retrieved October 2, 2004, from http://www.praxis-epress.org

Pozo, M. (2003, December 3). Toward a critical revolutionary pedagogy: An interview with Peter McLaren. *St. John's University Humanities Review, 2*(1). Retrieved June 30, 2004, from http://dissidentvoice.org/Articles9/Pozo_McLaren-Interview.htm

Radical Chains. (1994). 'Autonomist' & 'Trotskyist' views: Harry Cleaver debates Hillel Ticktin on capitalism's present crisis . . . danger and opportunity. *Radical Chains, 4,* 9–17. Retrieved December 12, 2001, from http://www.hrc.wmin.ac.uk/guest/radical/RC-DEBAT.HTM

Rikowski, G. (1996). Left alone: End time for Marxist educational theory? *British Journal of Sociology of Education, 17*(4), 415–451.

Rikowski, G. (1997) Scorched Earth: Prelude to rebuilding Marxist educational theory, *British Journal of Sociology of Education, 18*(4), 551–574.

Rikowski, G. (2000a, September). *Messing with the explosive commodity: School improvement, educational research, and labour-power in the era of global capitalism. If we aren't pursuing improvement, what are we doing?* Paper presented at the British Educational Research Association Conference, Cardiff University. Retrieved December 3, 2006, from http://www.leeds.ac.uk/educol/documents/00001610.htm

Rikowski, G. (2000b, September). *That other great class of commodities: Repositioning Marxist educational theory*. Paper presented at the British Educational Research Association Conference, Cardiff University[CLC9]. Retrieved December 3, 2006, from http://www.leeds.ac.uk/educol/documents/00001624.htm

Rikowski, G. (2001). *The battle in Seattle: Its significance for education*. London: Tufnell Press.

Rikowski, G. (2002, March). Methods for researching the social production of labour power in capitalism. Paper presented at Research Seminar, University College Northampton, UK. Retrieved December 3, 2006, from http://www.ieps.org.uk.cwc.net/rikowski2002b.pdf

Sahay, A. (1993). Toward a critique-al practice [and against the (re)vision-ism of the (post)modern liberal ethos], *The Alternative Orange, 3*(1), 6–7, 20–21.

Sahay, A. (1998). Transforming race matters: Towards a critique-al cultural studies. *Cultural Logic, 1*(2). Retrieved June 6, 2002, from http://eserver.org/clogic/1–2/sahay.html

Sears, A., & Mooers, C. (1995). The politics of hegemony: Democracy, class, and social movements. *Transformation: Marxist boundary work in theory, economics, politics and culture, 1*, 216–242.

Steinberg, S., & Kincheloe, J. (1998). *Students as researchers: Creating classrooms that matter*. London: RoutledgeFalmer.

Strauss, J. (2005). The Labour aristocracy and working-class politics. Retrieved July 4, 2006, from http://www.dsp.org.au/links/back/issue28/Strauss.htm

The Bus Riders Union asks the U.S. and Israeli governments: Let the Palestinian people go! (2002). Bus Riders Union.

Zavarzadeh, M., & Morton, D. (1994). *Theory as resistance: Politics and culture after (post)structuralism*. New York: The Guilford Press.

CHAPTER 19

Frantz Fanon and a Materialist Critical Pedagogy

NOAH DE LISSOVOY

In U.S. schooling, the racist disparities in the allocation of resources, and the cultural coding of standards and evaluation, approach a kind of apartheid. Not only does a "second-generation" de facto segregation relegate most students of color to substandard facilities and instructional materials; in addition, public education is increasingly in the grip of a hyper-reductionistic "accountability" movement which impoverishes the curriculum while also constructing the performance of low-income students, through the tool of the standardized test, as failure. Increasingly militarized schools aggressively enroll youth of color and poor White students into global projects of conquest and empire building; at the same time, these imperialist adventures correspond to the almost complete abandonment by the state of its already limited commitments to its own constituents, and to the basic social institutions which serve them.

In understanding these conditions, and the colonial relationships which produce them, the work of Frantz Fanon (1925–1961) is a crucial starting point. Fanon was a brilliant psychiatrist and revolutionary theorist, originally from Martinique, who was active as a leader and intellectual in the Algerian independence movement. His work has been influential in resistance movements throughout Africa and the rest of the world, and has also been indispensable in understanding the cultural and psychological dynamics of colonialism and racism, as well as decolonization itself. In contrast to the dominant ways in which social inequality is understood, Fanon's work analyzes cultural life as inextricably linked to politics, and to histories of violence, power, and exploitation. Fanon demonstrates that these histories traverse a range of registers, from the physical and psychical to the cultural and economic, and he describes a project of resistance that comprises all of these dimensions. For critical educators in North America, these insights are crucial resources for challenging the technicist framework of educational reform, the reification of race and culture and their separation from material relationships of domination, as well as overly economistic analyses of social oppression.

In this essay, I contrast Fanon's work with other critical analyses of oppression in society and culture and consider the implications of his thought for critical pedagogy and liberatory educational projects. In particular, I describe how both Marxist and postmodernist approaches in educational theory can benefit from a consideration of Fanon's insights, and the ways in which his work challenges presuppositions of both of these traditions. In the course of this discussion, I outline a "Fanonian" materialist perspective which links the cultural, political, and economic in a complexly dialectical conception. This understanding returns, I believe, to the original Marxist sense of the material as constituted by the historical organization of social relationships of production. This framework suggests a form of decentered humanism that is global in its commitments and revolutionary in its intentions, which I believe crucially extends the possibilities for critical pedagogy in the present.

Racism, Colonialism, and Dialectical Analysis

In Fanon's analysis of the historical processes of colonialism and anticolonial struggle, a Manichean opposition organizes colonial society into a rigid binary:

> The originality of the colonial context is that economic reality, inequality, and the immense difference of ways of life never come to mask the human realities. When you examine at close quarters the colonial context it is evident that what parcels out the world is to begin with the fact of belonging to or not belonging to a given race, a given species. In the colonies the economic substructure is also superstructure. The cause is the consequence; you are rich because you are white, you are white because you are rich. This is why Marxist analysis should always be slightly stretched every time we have to do with the colonial problem (1963, p.40).

In this account, a dynamic of domination mediates the opposition between colonizer and colonized which differs from the naturalized order of exploitation within metropolitan capitalism. Economic position is identified first of all with racial assignation, rather than being essentially an effect of social class. Fanon articulates here what he calls a "stretched" dialectic of oppression. There are several aspects of this analysis that are important. First of all, the central contradiction in classical Marxism between labor and capital is pulled apart to encompass a different one: the opposition between two "species," as Fanon puts it—Black and White, the contradiction of colonial racism. This represents a displacement of the class contradiction, but in addition, the nature of the opposition that Fanon describes is different. The logic that mediates the relationship between colonizer and colonized is one of violence, rather than incorporation. Colonial society is organized to begin with by the absolute separation of White and Black, instead of by the intimate relationship, in production, that defines the contradiction between classes. Nevertheless, this is not some entirely different social universe from that described by classical Marxism: the fact of belonging to a particular race is still connected to political economy: "You are rich because you are white." And as in a Marxist frame, a central antagonism systematically produces social reality, even if it is not the antagonism between capital and labor.

Fanon's text produces an asymmetry, since it focuses the language of Marxist critique on a phenomenon usually thought of as analytically secondary in this theoretical tradition—namely, racism. This rhetorical asymmetry itself conveys the complexity of the colonial context. In its very deployment of the language of Marxism, Fanon's narrative ironically evokes its own distance from this methodology (as traditionally understood), and appropriates its own "distortedness" as oppositional and productive. In fact, this distortion of the Marxist dialectic is also a moment of its development and advance. Fanon teaches us the importance of critical readings that are caught in the tension between successfully recuperating their objects and registering the resistance of reality to this recuperation: an off-balance dialectic for a world that is itself also essentially off-balance.

This stretched dialectic can allow us to make sense of phenomena in education that appear incoherent from the perspective of a simple model of reproduction of class society (which has dominated critical sociology of education). Power in schools operates not only to order, organize, and produce, but also to violate, refuse, and expel (Devine, 1996). This power also operates differentially—socializing differently raced students differently. Zero-tolerance disciplinary policies, "tough love" retention schemes, and high school exit exams are all examples of popular educational initiatives designed to preserve advantages for White students through the partial or complete expulsion of the students of color that they disproportionately target (Dohrn, 2001). These aspects of education appear anomalous within a system that is thought to be oriented toward the socialization and incorporation of students as disposers of labor power or as the functional citizen-subjects of bourgeois hegemony. However, from Fanon's perspective these processes can be understood as systematic—the expression of an organized violence and colonialism. They should suggest to us that the essence of domination in education is represented as much in the subjection of students of color as through the ideological interpellation of students generally.

The relevance of Fanon's analysis to contemporary education is especially evident in the rapid militarization of schooling that is presently occurring. As a result of more and more aggressive recruiting tactics, and the articulation between schools and the military that the No Child Left Behind Act makes automatic (in furnishing the names of high school students to recruiters as a matter of policy), students of color and poor White students are pressed with even greater energy into the service of neocolonialist projects (Furumoto, 2005). While preparation for military service has arguably always been one function of schools, the contemporary institutionalization of recruitment as a central schooling function is new, and inflects in a new way our sense of the very idea of citizenship for which schools are taken to be a preparatory mechanism, as Henry Giroux (2003) describes in relation to patriotism more generally. This process of militarization—of the invasion and reorganization of the space of civil society by the war machine—reflects at some distance the actual imperialist invasions of the post-9/11 era, and the destruction and distortion of the social that they have occasioned in Afghanistan and Iraq. These invasions are also powerful testimony to the continuing significance of the problematic of colonialism, as described by Fanon, in contemporary global society.

For Marxists, not to attend to the complexities Fanon describes is either to deny the basic salience of his account or to restrict the frame of reference of socialist theory to a Eurocentric framework. As Fanon points out, "the dialectical strengthening that occurs between the movement of liberation of the colonized peoples and the emancipatory struggle of the exploited working classes of the imperialist countries is sometimes neglected, and indeed forgotten" (1967b, p. 144). What is in order is precisely an extension of left analysis, an exploration of the relationships between different systems of social oppression. Such an exploration would not posit any arbitrary unity but would nevertheless persistently attempt to conceptualize the whole. Racism, in Fanon's account, produces a social order: colonialism. Likewise, while capitalist exploitation is usually thought of in terms of economic production, it is also a moment of social *violence* in creating "free" workers as such (Marx, 1976). The production of racial and class positions, their intersection and distinctiveness, must itself be carefully thought out, not in order to equalize or identify them but rather to begin to glimpse the total universe they point to together.

Rethinking Difference: A Materialist Framework

The idea of difference has been ubiquitous in recent theory, both in the academy generally and in education in particular. In philosophy, a preoccupation with difference has been one of the hallmarks of postmodernism; in education, it has been a crucial organizing principle of theories of multiculturalism. This emphasis has often been counterposed to an old-fashioned universalistic tendency to "synthesize . . . differences into a unitary, univocal whole" (Flax, 1990, p. 4) and to imagine liberation and education in terms of a series of unifications: of the class, of the society, of the teacher and students, etc. In this way, difference has been thought of as tracing the boundaries of a sequence of experiences, cultures, and identities which the modernist language of the left is refused or erased. However, this conceptualization of difference is marked by a certain idealism, since it tends to understand differences as either marking static identities (e.g., "cultures"), or as infinitely variable, the space of the free play of language and subjectivity. On the other hand, the "old" Left has sometimes been too happy to cede this conceptual terrain to the postmodernists as a secondary dimension that does not affect the underlying contradictions that determine social life. In Fanon, this false opposition is exploded; he demonstrates the historic, dynamic, and dialectical processes that difference is the product of, and the continuous and violent process of differentiation that ties subjects always to the social totality. Cultures do not simply congeal into the categories that they are often assumed to be in educational discourse, but are always the constructed and historical products of struggle, and their fates are inextricably bound up with the political aspirations of the people: "There is no other fight for culture which can develop apart from the popular struggle" (1963, p. 233). It is in this sense that Fanon's conception of difference can be understood as materialist, as opposed to the purely discursive, symbolic, and ideal conceptions that predominate in much cultural and educational theory.

This understanding of the material dimensions of difference poses an implicit challenge even to forms of progressive education, such as multiculturalism, which seek to honor differences and to challenge inequities through a reframing of cultural valuations and affective relationships. The problem is that the very emphasis on the emotional and ethical concern of teachers for their students tends to overlook the *economy* of caring itself—the materiality of relationships in education which are themselves caught up in a circulation that produces both scarcity and surplus. The emphasis on caring and expectations tends to admonish teachers to transform their relationships to students without recognizing the fact that this attention and concern is itself a key resource systematically distributed in favor of dominant groups. Furthermore, and paradoxically, caring does not merely describe an affective state of the teacher, but in fact is already differentially attached to students as a kind of right—what Cheryl Harris (1995) describes more generally as a "property interest in whiteness." The disparity in concern cannot be fixed by merely switching the disposition of the teacher, since this relationship is not simply a matter of attitude, but is already crucially determined by the differential valuation of students in the discursive practice that is schooling, and within which pedagogy is made coherent. Elaborating from Fanon, we might say that a schooling system, like a society, is either racist or it is not, and that all (neo)colonial systems are racist. It is not a matter of adjusting an attitude, but rather of struggling against an overarching social logic and set of relationships. Even the category of love, in teaching, has to be understood materially; it is part of the structure of racism in education that in this libidinal economy, as in the dollar economy, resources are plundered and redistributed across the social topography in ways that impoverish learning spaces for students of color.

However, postmodernists who have emphasized the radical implications of difference have been impatient with appeals to the "material." Judith Butler (1993) argues that *matter* and *material* are already discursive formations to begin with, since even the outside of discourse (i.e., the material) can only be thought by means of or through discourse. This critique contains a misreading of the category of materialism within Marxism. In Marxism, the content of materiality is not located in a naturalistic substratum outside of analysis, but rather in a particular organization of social relationships (Marx & Engels, 1970). This organization is real, and given by history, in a way that defies idealistic and ideological characterizations of it. To insist on the materiality of social life is to insist on the total dynamic of these relationships produced and reproduced in history. This dynamic includes discourse, not as a mere effect, but as an aspect, just as it includes the physical. What distinguishes a materialist perspective from others is that it recognizes, in the different dimensions of life, not merely an indifference and chaos that only acquire sense within language, but rather the registers of a fluid but immanent social *logic* that traverses them, as it does language as well.

In caricaturing materialism as a mere essentialization of the "economy," narrowly conceived, common misunderstandings of this perspective ignore the way that materialist analysis *brings together* different dimensions of experience and reveals their shared participation in a historical process that cannot be identified with any single dimension. In this regard, both to push against common and narrow understandings of materialism, and to clarify the political possibilities of difference and democracy, an analysis is necessary which takes up the problems of power and otherness within a focus on the embodied ecology of political life. In this regard, I take the writing of Fanon as a fundamental political analysis, and one that should be located at the center of the materialist tradition. For example, Fanon's theory upsets the immaterialism of the dominant psychoanalytic paradigms in finding the sense of psychopathology at the level of the body itself:

> At the extreme, I should say that the Negro, because of his body, impedes the closing of the postural schema of the white man—at the point, naturally, at which the black man makes his entry into the phenomenal world of the white man (1967a, p. 160).

This reframing of neurosis in terms of the corporeal, and specifically the *raced* body, is at the same time an understanding of individual suffering as essentially social. For colonized people, Fanon argues, "every abnormal manifestation . . . is the product of [their] cultural situation" (1967a, p. 152)—that is, of the logic of racism. The social, the psychological, and the economic as well, express a logic of domination based not only on the marginalization of different voices, but on the active organization of violence against Black bodies and souls.

Unlike the common understanding of difference as a sphere of competition for relative degrees of sanction or legitimacy, especially in education, Fanon describes difference as the index of an absolute cleavage of the social, the axis of a historical and active brutalization. In this context, existential problems are immediately determinate political ones, physical ones, embodied ones, and no longer can theoretical consciousness "flatter itself that it is something other than consciousness of existing practice," in the terms of Marx and Engels (1970, p. 52). In other words, even as a matter of rhetoric, difference has to be understood as a historical process, concretely and violently lived out (and through). And identity as a function of difference is recast from a structure of choices to a historical problem, inherently linked to the production not only of psyches, but also cultures and economies: "This European opulence is literally scandalous, for it has been founded on slavery, it has been nourished with the blood of slaves and it comes directly from the soil and from the subsoil of that underdeveloped world" (Fanon, 1963, p. 96). Difference here is not an arbitrary effect of identification but the result of racism, colonialism, and capitalism as encompassing structures and processes. If oppression is a matter of material production in this way, then resistance to it must be a material production of another kind. And if domination always acts on living bodies—reducing, immobilizing, and violating them—then resistance is a matter as well of the release, as Fanon puts it, of a "muscular tension" (p. 54). Negation is a necessary moment of liberatory movement in the context of a society in which all positivities are given as a result of exploitation.

However, there is a strong positivist streak in progressive and some left-liberal approaches to difference in education, which are often organized around an extension of the idea of *success* or achievement, and an insistence on its possibility for all students. In these accounts, the caring of culturally relevant teachers for their students is expressed in a commitment to and belief in the success of all:

> Rather than aiming for slight improvement or maintenance, culturally relevant teaching aims at another level—excellence—and transforms shifting responsibility into *sharing* responsibility. As they strive for excellence, such teachers function as *conductors* or *coaches*. *Conductors* believe that students are capable of excellence and they assume responsibility for ensuring that their students achieve that excellence (Ladson-Billings, 1994, p. 23).

This is definitely an urgent emphasis against the low expectations that teachers have consistently been shown to demonstrate in relation to students of color. However, this framing of the issue risks ignoring the logics that overdetermine the very idea of excellence around which teacher expectations are supposed to be structured.

Success and *excellence* in U.S. schooling are not isolable qualities but instead are part of economies of achievement that encompass them. As both a concept and a process, success both requires and conceals the *opposite* that is part of its very structure. In systems of educational assessment, competition, and credentialing, as well as in the larger logic of social life under capital, *success* means the privilege of a triumph against that which negatively constitutes it, namely "failure." Failure is the necessary condition of success, not simply as it happens, but as the essential anatomy of the idea. Therefore, it is necessary for critical educators to recognize not only that all students are capable of achievement, but that achievement is itself constructed as the property of a particular class and color. In this sense, "excellence" is part of a discourse that systematically excludes children of color from the privileges of achievement (De Lissovoy & McLaren, 2003).

The discursive economy of "success" reveals both the structure of ideology in capitalism as well as the Manichean logic of colonialism. In capitalism, the "success" of a few is predicated on the immiseration of the majority, a fact that never emerges in the celebrations of those who are singled out as "excellent." At the same time, the success/failure couple is fundamentally tied to the logic of racism, and the material and symbolic privileges of "achievement" are awarded on this basis. The only analysis that is adequate is one that can encompass the relationship between these two systems, as Fanon's does. In the simple deploring of inequities that characterizes mainstream thinking about education and the tinkering with policies and initiatives that aim to temper the disparities around the edges, the dominant understanding dooms itself to failure as far as real transformation is concerned, since this understanding does not confront the logic that produces both the "problems" and the "solutions" at once.

Fanon reveals this contradiction in reference to education itself, a topic he does not otherwise write much about, in a passage in "Letter to a Frenchman":

> That I should say for example: there is a shortage of schools in Algeria, so that you will think: it's a shame, something has to be done about it.
>
> That I should say: one Arab out of three hundred is able to sign his name, so that you will think: that's too bad, it has to stop.

Listen further:

> A school-mistress complaining to me, complaining about having to admit new Arab children to her school every year.
>
> A school mistress complaining that once all the Europeans were enrolled, she was obliged to give schooling to a few Arab children (1967b, p. 49).

Here a reflexive condemnation of educational inequality is immediately exposed by the fundamental racism that underlies this inequality. If this racism is usually less dramatically overt in the U.S., it nevertheless continues to organize, at a structural level, the system of public schooling. For change to be a possibility, the structure and logic of racial domination must be exposed and analyzed, rather than the mere fact of differential privilege (Leonardo, 2005). The irony of efforts aimed at improving the educational resources, opportunities, and competitiveness of students of color is that the system of opportunity and competition is organized around their exclusion. In that regard, critical pedagogy has to *deconstruct* normative ideas of success and excellence at the same time as asserting that they are possible for all students.

Elite and Subaltern:
Revolutionary Leadership and Educational Authority

The complexity of Fanon's analysis of oppression described above reappears in his discussion of liberatory movements, and reappears as well for critical pedagogy in its effort to imagine a truly oppositional and democratic form of teaching. Fanon shows how the contradiction of racism, in the colonial situation, appears to displace that of capital and labor as the essence of the social, and to become the content, in a way, of class struggle itself. However, the contradiction between bourgeoisie and proletariat nevertheless persists in latent form, and reemerges in the postcolonial period, as new forms of indigenous elitism restore the urgency of the struggle against capitalism as such. Likewise, Fanon describes a similarly double-jointed structure in the movement of liberation, which succeeds in organizing the people into a coherent organization and yet contains within itself the incipient contradictions of class and power between elite and subaltern that must themselves be confronted in the course of the struggle.

Being attuned to these difficulties is crucial for critical pedagogy as well. Critical pedagogy must be able to interrogate itself, in a principled way, with regard to the forms of leadership it proposes in classrooms, and must also be vigilant with regard to efforts aimed at assimilating its own principles, in distorted form, to (neo)liberal currents in education (McLaren, 2000). This attention to both the internal and the external contradictions of liberatory projects, and a steadfast commitment to think through them, is essential in educational movements no less than in politics generally. On the one hand it is possible, as some have suggested, that critical pedagogy may sometimes reproduce in its own practice some of the authoritarianism it aims to combat. On the other hand, it is also clear that this tradition is vulnerable to being co-opted by a range of purposes quite alien to it. An interesting case is the effort to use the tools of critical pedagogy for the education of the elite, for example in the training of future managers in MBA programs (see Currie & Knights, 2003). This development may represent a remarkable contradiction, but it also shows the originality and fluidity of capital and cautions the tradition of critical education to be vigilant against appropriations that erase or subvert its political commitments.

The dilemmas described above have often overtaken the process of liberation, as those in whose name it is undertaken are silenced and erased in the very pronouncements of its "leaders." Fanon is famous as a theorist of anticolonial struggle, but in his central work, *The Wretched of the Earth* (1963), he is equally concerned with sketching out the way this revolution has been typically betrayed by the nationalist bourgeoisie, once it attains power:

> The people who for years on end have seen this leader and heard him speak, who from a distance in a kind of dream have followed his contests with the colonial power, spontaneously put their trust in this patriot. Before independence, the leader generally embodies the aspirations of the people for independence, political liberty, and national dignity. But as soon as independence is declared, far from embodying in concrete form the needs of the people in what touches bread, land, and the restoration of the country to the sacred hands of the people, the leader will reveal his inner purpose: to become the general president of that company of profiteers impatient for their returns which constitutes the national bourgeoisie (p. 166).

This contravention of the goals of the movement is not a random turn of events, but is connected to the logic itself of the revolution, to its organization around an elite cadre who claim the authority to speak immediately for the desires of the mass. In this context, a materialist commitment holds to the lived experience of the people against the assimilation of their aspirations to the projects of the powerful.

The dynamics of this political assimilation have been studied by historiographers of formerly colonial societies. Ranajit Guha (1988) has described how official narratives of the nationalist movement in India reproduce the elitism, at the level even of rhetorical structure, of colonial British accounts of Indian history. Guha shows that both the colonial and the nationalist accounts ignore the decisive contribution of subaltern political activity—the purposive insurgency of *the people* themselves. The lesson here is that is that any reading of social reality, or project for its transformation, needs to acknowledge the gaps and impasses that partly structure its own pronouncements. Such pronouncements upon and about the subjectivity of the oppressed, which construe this subjectivity as consolidated, knowable, and transparent, may conceal an effort to assimilate, through misrecognition, the experience of the other (Spivak, 1988). Similarly, Dipesh Chakrabarty (2000) has criticized the historicist underpinnings of Eurocentric liberal and left accounts of postcolonial societies, in which the latter appear as underdeveloped or deformed versions of a particular experience of European modernity.

In the context of contemporary neoliberalism, the *class* dimension of the elitism of bourgeois nationalist movements is exposed again in perhaps an even more marked fashion than in Fanon's day (Bond, 2005). As the programs of once-radical organizations are accommodated to the universe of global capital (e.g., in the case of the African National Congress in South Africa or the Workers' Party in Brazil), it becomes clear that the claim to speak for the people must be critiqued for the way that it rhetorically erases the contradiction between the capitalist state and the masses. Indeed, neoliberalism's success as a class offensive has importantly come from its ability to represent itself as a progressive process of social transformation—represented in a parade of new initiatives and institutions aimed at "development" and even "empowerment."

These senses of elitism are important for liberatory projects in education to confront in their own sphere. To begin with, the idea that through the intervention of critical teachers, students can be transformed from the passive objects to the active subjects of history, may share a common structure with the elite narratives of nationalism and modernity that have been interrogated by the theorists mentioned here (De Lissovoy, 2004). "Empowerment" itself, as it is often imagined in education, may assume the same universal and unified subject that elite accounts of national development emphasize with regard to politics. The idea that through liberatory education students discover their true selves and voices may assume an original *lack* in students that is already *dis*empowering. In this context, educators need to be wary of understanding subaltern or oppressed students transparently. They need to be wary of believing that they can know or decide who students ultimately are. Lisa Delpit (1995) has criticized progressive educators for a facile assumption that they understand, by virtue of a critical orientation, the needs of students of color. Educators involved in liberatory projects need to be sensitive to the inherent complexities that are involved without thereby giving up on radical praxis and the movements of resistance it enables.

On the other hand, in the neoliberal moment, there is an external crisis for critical pedagogy to the extent that its initial radical commitments have been significantly diluted as it has been incorporated into the academy and, to a lesser extent, into schools themselves. Partly, this has resulted from a watering down in mainstream contexts of the Freirean tradition as expressed in an overemphasis on an ill-defined notion of dialogue and a purposeless imperative to "cooperation." There is also the proliferation of the ambiguous discourse of "social justice," which now organizes teacher education programs and entire colleges of education across the U.S., while reserving for itself a determined vagueness which often acts to obfuscate the very social forces that support the injustices that social-justice efforts presumably aim to eliminate. The language of social justice, *in practice*, frequently operates in a way that prevents a militant interrogation of power, to the extent that it projects an image of progressiveness while undercutting the more charged and difficult task of naming and investigating systemic racism, for example, as a concrete problem (as opposed to "inequity"), not to mention capitalism or imperialism (as opposed to "corporatization"). This, too, is an interested misrecognition, as the generous intentions of professional intellectuals and educators are taken to be an accurate reflection of the desires, needs, and historical vocation of the people. As in the problematic traced by Fanon, an apparently unifying language of elevated and collective purpose conceals the differential location of elite and subaltern; indeed, this language can even become a tool for the consolidation of the elite purchase on power.

The Politics of Dialogue

Education scholars tend to diagram the problem in the current state of affairs in schools and society and then rather easily move to a proposal for a better situation or system. For example: basic resources and opportunities to learn are unequally distributed in schools—therefore, we should demand that more opportunities be provided to those who lack them (Oakes & Saunders, 2004). With regard to pedagogy itself, new teachers are exhorted to engage in critical curriculum building and to become agents of reform against the narrowing of the meaning of instruction (Cochran-Smith, 1991). What is often missing is a narration of the process of liberatory practice itself, which is always a moving *towards* the liberatory, never the creation of a static image of it, and which is always the story at the same time of the persistent system of obstacles that this movement encounters. Without recognizing the determined systems of interests that are constitutively opposed to the equalization of conditions and opportunities, theorists unwittingly doom their proposals from the start. Educators must be able to recognize the global projects of neoliberalism, capitalism, White supremacy, and colonialism, as well as those classes and institutions that represent their interests in the arena of schooling, if we are to have a chance at overcoming the effects of these systems. Outside of this sensibility to the dynamic *economies* of both oppression and resistance, democracy becomes an ideological figment.

In his description of the stages of anticolonial movement, Fanon narrates a praxis informed by this dynamic sensibility. Fanon's praxis is a dialectical movement in that its truth does not belong to one formulation but develops through a series of positions, which as concrete engagements with an overdetermining social and psychic reality are never fully successful. To be colonized is to be forced to identify with the oppressor; to resist this, the colonized person must assert his or her absolute difference; to do so is to discover that this difference is empty and immediately recuperated in the logic of domination; against this recuperation, the self must be asserted again, not as a simple negation of the oppressor but as something new; but with what resources can that be imagined? Homi Bhabha writes that "Fanon is the purveyor of the transgressive and transitional truth. He may yearn for the total transformation of Man and Society, but he speaks most effectively from the uncertain interstices of historical change" (1994, p. 40). There is no solution outside of the active working through of the problem.

It is important to distinguish this open-ended praxis from an ethic of complete indeterminacy. In the focus on the crossing of borders and the creation of new meanings, which has become an important focus in critical pedagogy, we need to ask through what *process* the educator's understanding becomes an active incitement to dialogue. How do the relationships of power and the stakes of different articulations come to be at issue in the space of teaching? In the terms of Paulo Freire, this is the problem of "codification," i.e., the production of the "*objects* which mediate the decoders in their critical analysis" (1997, p. 95)—how the essential contradictions of a historical situation are thematized in a way that makes them available for exploration and critique by students. In political terms, the point is that a theory of liberation, and liberatory teaching, involves not only specifying principles of democratic relationships and the forms of understanding they produce, but also envisioning the program that enacts these principles. Critical pedagogy's response to the current criminalization of youth, for example, must include more than an insistence on resuscitating a culture of democratic deliberation; it should include projects which investigate and confront federal legislation and municipal ordinances, sentencing guidelines, media representations, and artifacts of popular youth culture as well—not in a reflexive gesture of protest, but as a curriculum of engagement which initiates problems and possibilities rather than resolving them.

In addition, democratic pedagogy as material practice has to be able to envision the process of the teacher's own involvement as a coparticipant in the space of narration and critical self-interrogation. In Giroux's terms:

> By being able to listen critically to the voices of their students, teachers also become border-crossers through their ability both to make different narratives available to themselves and to legitimate difference as basic condition for understanding the limits of one's own knowledge (1992, pp. 34–35).

But far from being a latent capacity that teachers simply need to make use of, this sensibility is the result of a difficult process of self-criticism and transformation which a theory of liberatory pedagogy must also be able to conceptualize. There are two important processes to theorize in this regard: 1) the existential crisis teachers have to pass through in the transition from official authoritarian identifications to a revolutionary commitment; and 2) the actual dynamic movement of interruption and reframing of the teacher's voice in the classroom dialogue. In particular, recognizing teachers' *inclusion* in the discursive space of teaching suggests rethinking the shape and limits of the authority that is reserved for them even within critical approaches in pedagogy.

Fanon provides a crucial conceptualization of this process in his notion of a "fighting culture" which unifies intellectuals, militants, and the people in a common struggle for liberation. The organizational principle of this culture is a process of democratic dialogue, which importantly calls the intellectuals away from the comfort of their own sureties and into a profound (and destabilizing) dialogue with the people. This is the turning point in the oppositional movement, as Fanon describes it in *The Wretched of the Earth*, as different sectors are drawn together in an encompassing project. Hussein Adam (1999) emphasizes that, for Fanon, this is a deeply decentralized process, not directed from above, through which the slow development of the nation takes place in a genuinely consultative fashion. In Fanon's description in *A Dying Colonialism* of the importance of radio in the course of the Algerian struggle, even the interruption of revolutionary broadcasts by the French creates a space for the participation of the masses in imagining and constructing the missing voice of the movement:

A real task of reconstruction would then begin. Everyone would participate, and the battles of yesterday and the day before would be re-fought in accordance with the deep aspirations and the unshakable faith of the group. The listener would compensate for the fragmentary nature of the news by an autonomous creation of information (1965, p. 86).

Here the very gaps in communication create the space for the emergence of a more powerful movement and adherence of the people. Nigel Gibson (1999) argues that Fanon intends to emphasize that the French jamming of the broadcasts disrupted the very authority of the movement, as the leaders present in any audience were forced to negotiate, along with other listeners, the meanings of what they had listened to. In contrast, perhaps, to a notion of leadership as deriving its authority from an underlying and seamless communion with the people, in this account this authority must be continually and locally renegotiated in creative fashion.

This is an important lesson for critical educators to learn, or relearn. It is possible that conceptions of democracy that emerge from the educational context may have a tendency toward authoritarianism, given the structures of institutional power that usually set the stage for the encounter between teachers and students in schools. And in the present context, in which teachers are instruments of a hyper-authoritarianism at the level even of the fundamental organization of cognition (through micromanaged and prepackaged curricula and assessment schemes), it may be important for conceptions of democratic educational engagement to start from models outside of formal instruction. It is crucial for critical pedagogy to always remember its affiliation to the larger movement, and the moment of decentered and collective struggle, and to some extent to internalize this metaphor even in its own approach to dialogue and solidarity in teaching situations. Fanon's emphasis on the complementary roles of participants in the movement, including peasants, intellectuals, workers, etc., recalls Rosa Luxemburg's (2004) insistence that the only authority that really counts, in the process of learning through struggle, is the "mass ego" of the working class (as opposed to the authority of the professional cadres), which can only authentically learn through its own mistakes and experiments.

It might be salutary for critical educators, most of whom have been formed through the experience of a wielding a strong and institutionally guaranteed power in the space of dialogue (that of the teacher), to remind themselves that the teaching situation is only one moment of potential struggle, and that the position of the critical teacher is the position of only one kind of participant in it. In this light, the point of critical pedagogy is less for the teacher (as leader) to steer the students' learning toward the proper (critical) analysis, than to provoke both students and teachers to kinds of investigation that can increase the knowledge and possibilities for the collective movement, in which both are participants and leaders in a democratic "life in common" (Hardt & Negri, 2004). For example, youth-led movements against militarization of schools and the impoverishment of curriculum by standardized testing regimes are opportunities for engagement and learning in which teachers can act as crucial resources without occupying the position of leadership. At the purely methodological level, this suggests the importance for critical pedagogy of rediscovering the radical potential in the decentralized and Deweyan notion of curriculum as project and activity—reconceptualized in this case, however, as *revolutionary* project and activity within the context of a wider movement.

Conclusion: Materialism as Humanism

The vulgar version of materialism is the idea that there is no truth except in the cold, hard reality of things themselves. This simple objectivism, however, is not what Marxism means by materialism. In materialism, the relevant opposition is not between ideas and things, but rather between ideology and the social relationships from which it derives. The mistake of bourgeois philosophy is to suppose that truth exists prior to and apart from human history. Materialism is fundamentally an analytical and ethical responsibility to history, and coincides with a humanism that registers the suffering that has marked this history. In this tradition, Fanon condemns the violent and distorted idealism of Europe:

> Leave this Europe where they are never done talking of Man, yet murder men everywhere they find them, at the corner of every one of their own streets, in all the corners of the globe. For centuries they have stifled almost the whole of humanity in the name of a so-called spiritual experience (1963, p. 311).

An authentic humanism must see past these myths to the historical violence they have concealed and must materially intervene to disrupt it. The liberatory philosophy that emerges in this project is necessarily grounded in this concrete imperative: "It is simply a very concrete question of not dragging men toward mutilation, of not imposing upon the brain rhythms which very quickly obliterate it and wreck it" (p. 314). Fanon's challenge presses European left traditions to recognize their own myopias, which have often pressed the violence of colonialism, slavery, and racism into the background. The prioritization of these histories, and of the lessons they offer, represents a tremendous expansion of the possibilities of both materialism and humanism, since attention to them reveals vastly more of the concrete logic that has characterized the historical exploitation of human beings, and since the overcoming of these forms of violence opens new and unimagined possibilities for what human being and human solidarity might be.

As Fanon shows, humanism expresses a political project in the context of the materiality of social relationships and revolutionary aspiration. This is an extrapolation of humanity from a historical kindredness which is at the same time both difference and connection. The coherence of liberation, in this perspective, comes not from a scientific glimpse of the continuous essence of oppression, but from the combination of struggles which find in their commonalities and simultaneity the possibility of a shared project and the outlines of a shared opponent. This historical and political solidarity returns to the category of *class* its original political character, indeed its human, practical, and processual aspect (Przeworski, 1986). For educators, this means a continuous process, in collaboration with students, of making connections: between the racism of reductionistic, test-based "accountability" initiatives and the racism of a militarized society that uses youth of color and poor Whites as cannon fodder; between the bottom-line logic of global neoliberal structural adjustment and the gutting of a stripped-down public education system by a vicious "compassionate" conservatism; between the demonization of Brown people in distant "rogue" states and the vituperation against immigrants in the U.S. heartland. In studying their own and others' experiences, students and teachers can trace for themselves the shape of Fanon's "stretched" dialectic, and the complicated imbrication of oppressions that it exposes in the contemporary context.

This essay has described how Fanon's concrete analysis of the forms of oppression in the African colonial context enlarges the meanings of liberatory praxis and dialectical analysis in critical pedagogy and beyond. While Fanon's work has been indirectly important to critical pedagogy in its influence on Freire and other theorists, I believe that it should occupy a central position in this tradition's sense of its guiding exponents and of its historical forebears. Indeed, without reference to the arguments and analyses of Fanon, I believe it will be difficult for critical educators to resolve the tremendous dilemmas that neoliberalism, racism, and globalization pose for education—not only taken separately (if this is possible), but more importantly in their complex imbrications and interrelationships. Fanon provides indispensable insights into the complexities of praxis, and a profoundly dialectical analysis of the shifts, stages, and mutations that such struggle must recognize and traverse. For educators, oppositional movement is coincident with the building of solidarity in teaching, and in this regard Fanon's exposition of the principles of revolutionary-democratic dialogue is especially relevant. In the context of education as well as social life generally, Fanon's work doubles and deepens materialist analysis, and unfolds new spaces for a more complete and expansive humanism, the vision of which we cannot afford to do without.

References

Adam, H. M. (1999). Fanon as a democratic theorist. In N. C. Gibson (Ed.), *Rethinking Fanon: The continuing dialogue* (pp. 119–140). Amherst, NY: Humanity Books.

Bhabha, H. K. (1994). *The location of culture*. London: Routledge.

Bond, P. (2005). *Talk left, walk right: South Africa's frustrated global reforms*. KwaZulu-Natal, South Africa: University of KwaZulu-Natal Press.

Butler, J. (1993). *Bodies that matter: On the discursive limits of sex*. New York: Routledge.

Chakrabarty, D. (2000). *Provincializing Europe: Postcolonial thought and historical difference*. Princeton, NJ: Princeton University Press.

Cochran-Smith, M. (1991). Learning to teach against the grain. *Harvard Educational Review, 61*(3), 279–310.

Currie, G., & Knights, D. (2003). Reflecting on a critical pedagogy in MBA education. *Management Learning, 34*(1), 27–49.

De Lissovoy, N. (2004). Affirmation, ambivalence, autonomy: Reading the subaltern subject in postcolonial historiography and critical pedagogy. *Journal of Postcolonial Education, 3*(1), 5–23.

De Lissovoy, N., & McLaren, P. (2003). Educational "accountability" and the violence of capital: A Marxian reading. *Journal of Education Policy, 18*(2), 131–143.

Delpit, L. (1995). *Other people's children: Cultural conflict in the classroom*. New York: The New Press.

Devine, J. (1996). *Maximum security: The culture of violence in inner-city schools*. Chicago: University of Chicago Press.

Dohrn, B. (2001). "Look Out Kid/ It's Something You Did": Zero tolerance for children. In W. Ayers, B. Dohrn & R. Ayers (Eds.), *Zero tolerance: Resisting the drive for punishment in our schools* (pp. 89–113). New York: The New Press.

Fanon, F. (1963). *The wretched of the earth* (C. Farrington, Trans.). New York: Grove Press.

Fanon, F. (1965). *A dying colonialism* (H. Chevalier, Trans.). New York: Grove Press.

Fanon, F. (1967a). *Black skin, white masks* (C. L. Markmann, Trans.). New York: Grove Press.

Fanon, F. (1967b). *Toward the African revolution* (H. Chevalier, Trans.). New York: Grove Press.

Flax, J. (1990). *Thinking fragments: Pschoanalysis, feminism, and postmodernism in the contemporary West*. Berkeley, CA: University of California Press.

Freire, P. (1997). *Pedagogy of the oppressed* (M. B. Ramos, Trans.). New York: Continuum.

Furumoto, R. (2005). No poor child left unrecruited: How NCLB codifies and perpetuates urban school militarism. *Equity and Excellence in Education, 38*(3), 200–210.

Gibson, N. C. (1999). Radical mutations: Fanon's untidy dialectic of history. In N. Gibson (Ed.), *Rethinking Fanon: The continuing dialogue* (pp. 408–446). Amherst, NY: Humanity Books.

Giroux, H. A. (1992). *Border crossings: Cultural workers and the politics of education*. New York: Routledge.

Giroux, H. A. (2003). *The abandoned generation: Democracy beyond the culture of fear*. New York: Palgrave Macmillan.

Guha, R. (1988). On some aspects of the historiography of colonial India. In R. Guha & G. C. Spivak (Eds.), *Selected subaltern studies* (pp. 37–44). Oxford, UK: Oxford University Press.

Hardt, M., & Negri, A. (2004). *Multitude: War and democracy in the age of empire*. New York: Penguin Press.

Harris, C. I. (1995). Whiteness as property. In K. Crenshaw, N. Gotanda, G. Peller & K. Thomas (Eds.), *Critical race theory: The key writings that formed the movement* (pp. 276–291). New York: New Press.

Ladson-Billings, G. (1994). *The dreamkeepers: Successful teachers of African American children*. San Francisco: Jossey-Bass Publishers.

Leonardo, Z. (2005). The color of supremacy: Beyond the discourse of "White Privilege." In Z. Leonardo (Ed.), *Critical pedagogy and race* (pp. 37–52). Malden, MA: Blackwell Publishing.

Luxemburg, R. (2004). Organizational questions of Russian social democracy. In P. Hudis & K. B. Anderson (Eds.), *The Rosa Luxemburg reader* (pp. 248–265). New York: Monthly Review Press.

Marx, K. (1976). *Capital* (Vol. I). New York: Penguin Books.

Marx, K., & Engels, F. (1970). *The German ideology*. New York: International Publishers.

McLaren, P. (2000). *Che Guevara, Paulo Freire, and the pedagogy of revolution*. New York: Rowman and Littlefield.

Oakes, J., & Saunders, M. (2004). Education's most basic tools: Access to textbooks and instructional materials in California's public schools. *Teachers College Record, 106*(10), 1967–1988.

Przeworski, A. (1986). *Capitalism and social democracy*. Cambridge, UK: Cambridge University Press.

Spivak, G. C. (1988). Can the subaltern speak? In C. Nelson & L. Grossberg (Eds.), *Marxism and the interpretation of culture* (pp. 271–313). Chicago: University of Illinois Press.

CHAPTER 20

Critical Pedagogy

Democratic Realism,
Neoliberalism, Conservativism,
and a Tragic Sense of Education

WILLIAM B. STANLEY

The Context of Education Reform

The history of critical pedagogy is rooted in theories that recommend education as a form of countersocialization to promote democracy and social justice. Countersocialization is a necessary response to mainstream education, which functions to legitimate a social order defined by extreme disparities of wealth, income, political power, and oppression based on class, gender, ethnicity, and cultural status. In its strongest form (Brosio, 2004; Hill, McLaren, Cole, & Rikowski, 2002; Wood & Foster, 1997), critical pedagogy is shaped by a neo-Marxist critique of capitalism that views education as part of a wider effort to bring about a radical transformation of the American political and economic system.

Any society will use its educational system to help preserve its institutions, values, and political structure, and the evidence is overwhelming that mainstream education (like mainstream media) largely functions to legitimate the dominant social order. Those who control education policy at the federal and state levels are often quite explicit about their intentions (e.g., William Bennett, Clarence Paige, and Margaret Spellings). In this process, federal and state education policies and curricula generally mask and rationalize how the dominant social order contributes to political, cultural, ethnic, and economic oppression.

More ominously, the recent expansion of federal executive power in response to the "war on terrorism" has created a political climate that can only further erode the democratic culture in which education functions (Drew, 2006).

Not surprisingly, the impact of an education theory in direct conflict with the dominant culture's commitment to the ideologies of individualism, capitalism, American exceptionalism, and conservative cultural traditions, has been limited. The marginalization of critical pedagogy in American educational discourse and practice is only one element of wider efforts to suppress left-liberal (particularly radical) political, cultural, and economic reform efforts since the late nineteenth century. It is worth noting, however, that many left-liberal critics have also found certain radical proposals for reform both unrealistic and ill-conceived (e.g., Dewey, 1933, 1934, 1935a, 1935b, 1937; Dewey & Childs, 1933; Niebuhr, 1933; Gitlin, 1995, 2006; Isaac, 2003; Lasch, 1989; Stanley, 1992; Whitson & Stanley, 1996), a point we will return to later.[1]

With justification, critical educators often lament our mainstream opponents' failure to invest the intellectual effort required to understand critical pedagogy, and their tendency to reject any radical analysis of mainstream education out of hand. It can be exasperating to hear critics dismiss Marxism as a discredited and bankrupt theory, irrelevant to the educational problems of the twenty-first century. If you need proof of this, they say, just look at the collapse of Marxist governments in the U.S.S.R. and Eastern Europe since the end of the Cold War and China's embrace of capitalism. The survival of the Cuban and North Korean regimes hardly serve as models for other nations. And so on.

To what extent, however, do critical educators reciprocate in kind? Do not most of us tend to view capitalism as a discredited economic system, or worse, the major source of injustice and oppression in the modern world? Do we not also tend to dismiss liberalism as a political philosophy that fails to provide an adequate critique of the dominant social order while simultaneously serving to legitimate it? To what extent do we ever take seriously (except as a problem to be overcome) the conservative or neoliberal theories employed to justify our dominant culture, economic, and political institutions?

Certainly critical educators claim solid theoretical and evidentiary grounds for the positions they take. Still, something is not quite right with our prevailing analysis of mainstream education and society. To what extent do we attack a theoretical caricature of our opponents? How likely is it that small groups of critical educators (and their political allies) are the only ones who really understand what is wrong with our society and educational system? Does it make sense to assume that all the advocates of mainstream society and education theories have been either wrong or worse, that the employment of such theories is no more than a cynical attempt to maintain the status quo? Why do dominant political, economic, and cultural assumptions persist and elicit such widespread popular support among all classes and ethnic groups? Is it reasonable to reduce popular support for mainstream education and institutions to mass false consciousness?

To address such questions, we need to take seriously those conservative and neoliberal theories that shape, however indirectly, the consciousness of the many groups who oppose radical changes in education. If we push past the superficial analysis of the "culture wars" and American foreign policy that dominate mainstream talk radio, television, and other mainstream news media, political debate, and most of the current education reform debates, we find far more substantive disagreements regarding conceptions of social justice and the good society that are central to critical pedagogy.

In an effort to explore these questions, I first summarize three theoretical traditions that continue to shape conservative and neoliberal theory: *democratic realism* as expressed in the work of Walter Lippmann and Richard Posner, *neoliberal theory* represented by Frederick Hayek, and Leo Strauss's *political philosophy* as contrasted with the Straussian legacy of his American intellectual progeny. A summary of these ideas provides a sense of the complex, multiple, and often-contradictory intellectual traditions deeply embedded in our institutions and discursive practices.

While most critical educators have some awareness of these conservative and neoliberal authors, one seldom encounters a critical colleague who has actually read them or has an in-depth familiarity with their work. More frequently, my colleagues wonder why one would even bother to read these authors. A conservative or neoliberal educator who adopted the same stance toward Marx, critical theory, or other important critical traditions would be considered uninformed. How might one even have a dialog with a person whose grasp of Marx and critical theory was a distorted caricature? Yet the conservative and liberal scholars discussed here are rarely mentioned by most critical educators except in passing as apologists for capitalism or examples of discredited ideas we should avoid.

Following my overview of the conservative and neoliberal schools of thought, I examine a *tragic* intellectual tradition embodied in the work of Henry Adams, Reinhold Niebuhr, Christopher Lasch, Robert Westbrook, and others. This tragic left-progressive tradition emphasizes the inherent limits of human agency, cognition, and social reform. As we shall see, these tragic intellectual scholars share several insights raised by their conservative and liberal opponents. Nevertheless, they have not given up their quest for a more just and democratic society. Finally, I suggest how the conservative, neoliberal, and tragic traditions discussed here problematize the concept of countersocialization at the heart of critical pedagogy and might inform our future conceptions of critical education reform.

Democratic Realism

Democratic realism gained wide public attention through Walter Lippmann's work during the 1920s and 30s. Lippmann, a prominent journalist, former Socialist, and progressive intellectual, questioned the very possibility of participatory democracy as envisioned by Dewey and other progressives. Using the newly emerging methodologies of the social sciences, democratic realists concluded that most voters behaved irrationally, were motivated by narrow self-interests, and lacked the adequate knowledge and competence to participate in meaningful deliberation regarding public policy (Westbrook, 1991, 300–318).

Lippmann echoed the earlier work of historian Henry Adams (1934), who concluded that our culture's liberal faith in democratic institutions, like open elections, a free press, and public schools, was unable to guarantee liberty (Diggins, 1991, p. 23). Diggins traces the origins of Adams' skepticism to the roots of the early republic. The Founding Fathers themselves were well aware of the role of factions, passion, and irrationality in human politics. They had designed a political system of checks and balances to secure liberty because they did not believe human reason or principles were capable of doing so alone (pp. 18–19).

In *Public Opinion* (1922), Lippmann argued that late nineteenth-century industrialization and urbanization had fundamentally transformed the widespread network of small communities that once provided the context for participatory democracy. This loss of community undermined the capacity of individuals to acquire directly the knowledge necessary to determine their interests and contribute to informed public policy decisions. In addition, the exponential expansion of social and scientific knowledge, and the increasing complexity of modern society, were now largely beyond the access or comprehension of the masses.

Lippmann noted how easily government could employ highly effective propaganda techniques to shape public opinion. While popular consent remained critical in a democratic society, it was no longer generated by the masses but manufactured from above by government and business interests. Citizenship was largely reduced to the right (albeit uninformed) to vote. Under such conditions, the success of government no longer depends on the level of public participation but on a society's ability to provide a high level of security, goods, and services.

Lippmann, like Dewey, thought a scientific habit of mind could overcome the constraints impeding our understanding of modern society and believed the recently created social sciences offered the best way to acquire an accurate understanding of modern society and the knowledge required to make complex policy. However, only an enlightened elite (of disinterested experts), not the masses, had the capacity to secure the knowledge necessary to make complex public policy decisions that served the general public interest. In his next book, *The Phantom Public* (Lippmann, 1925), he even came to doubt the capacity of elites to acquire the scientific knowledge to resolve our increasingly complex policy problems.

Traditional liberal democratic practices and institutions (education, a free press, citizen participation in policy decisions) were no longer effective and could not restore the requisite conditions for popular democracy that modern industrial society had destroyed. In reality, the average person had neither the time nor interest to acquire the knowledge necessary for making complex public policy decisions. The masses' understanding of reality had been reduced to a cluster of distorted representations (what Lippmann called "stereotypes") that bore little resemblance to actual conditions. Under such circumstances, the minimum level of popular participation possible was desirable in modern democratic societies.

Dewey (1925) praised Lippmann's accurate analysis of current social and political conditions but rejected his critique of education's ability to develop the reflective citizenship skills required for full participation in our political process. According to Westbrook (1991, pp. 300–318), Dewey's critique of Lippmann was both obscure and inconclusive. While he raised some strong theoretical objections, Dewey never adequately addressed the practical problems that Lippmann raised regarding the core assumptions of liberal democracy. To the extent that Lipmann's analysis was accurate in the 1920s and 30s, his views should be even more persuasive in our contemporary culture saturated by mass media at a level Lippmann could only glimpse toward the end of his life.

Although he never cites Lippmann, Richard Posner (2003) recently proposed a theoretical extension of democratic realism applied to our complex postindustrial society. Posner makes a case for what he calls "Type II" democracy, as contrasted to the stronger "Type I" form of deliberative democracy supported, albeit in different ways, by various left progressives (e.g., Barber, 1992; Dewey, 1916) and critical pedagogy. While deliberative democracy does provide some guidelines relevant to judicial decision-making and other elite-level deliberations, he rejects Dewey's conception of Type I democracy and education for democracy applied to the masses as naïve and unworkable (Posner, 2003, pp. 107–133).

Posner's conception of Type II democracy is shaped by his own limited interpretation of pragmatism fused with the theory of classical liberal intellectuals like Hayek, Mill, but particularly Schumpeter (1942), to develop a theory that views deliberative democracy as a quixotic, and even counterproductive, approach to governing modern societies. Posner (2003, pp. 14–19, 204–205, 384–387) argues that our political system functions much like a free-market economy, wherein politicians compete to sell their candidacy to voters much as entrepreneurs do with products or services. Like Lippmann, Posner (pp. 183–184, 204–206) considers modern society far too complex for the mass of humanity to make meaningful contributions to public policy decisions. He acknowledges that even elite technocratic groups never have access to all the knowledge necessary for a full understanding of social issues. However, the current American political system does provide a workable structure (analogous to Mill's "marketplace of ideas") wherein we are able to sort highly complex technical information in a way that has the best potential for developing effective public policy (pp. 14–15, 349–350, 386–387).

Posner (like Lippmann), argues the right to vote in free elections is a critical element of democracy, something necessary to build public confidence, legitimate public policy, and ensure that politicians must compete for public support. While the average person is unlikely to have the competence to make complex policy decisions, she is qualified to determine, over time, if elected officials are acting in the public interest. In this respect, Posner (2003) seems to have more faith than Lippmann does in the competence of the masses to make good choices regarding their political representatives. Even if a case could be made that the public often selects candidates unwisely, voting would remain a necessary condition for the success of Posner's Type II model of democracy (pp. 222–223).

Clearly, Posner would oppose critical pedagogy's support of education for social transformation, given its focus on developing an illusionary and unworkable conception of participatory democracy that can only lead to student cynicism. Instead, schools should help students understand how our Type II democracy works, how it might be improved, and why it is the preferred political system.

Hayek's Theoretical Foundation for Neoliberalism

Frederick Hayek was a relatively obscure Austrian economist living in London when he published his most influential work, *The Road to Serfdom*, in 1944. His central argument was that the knowledge necessary for centralized economic planning envisioned by socialism was not available, even to groups of experts. Thus, the advocacy of centralized planning was both irrational and impossible absent a market to price capital goods. Our current social and economic order was a spontaneous and natural result of human evolution and had developed the way it had for good reason. Even the more modest level of economic planning advocated by Keynesians and the New Deal would eventually require a level of coercion that led to the loss of freedom (pp. 16–31). Written at a time when centralized economic planning was the dominant perspective reinforced by the New Deal and successful wartime planning in England, America, and the U.S.S.R., Hayek's was a distinct minority view.

Nevertheless, the book's success made Hayek famous and he gradually gained iconic status among conservatives and classical liberals. The publication of *The Road to Serfdom* also proved to be a major event in American intellectual history (Foner, 1998, p. 235). *Reader's Digest* published a condensed version in 1945, and Hayek was invited to give a public tour to promote his ideas in the spring of that year. Hayek had provided a new theoretical argument for the superiority of the market system, but one that also saw it as essential to the preservation of human freedom. He had also predicted the inevitable failure of socialism. The eventual collapse of the Eastern bloc in 1989, the move toward a market economy in China and South East Asia, and the globalization of capitalism all seemed to confirm Hayek's prescience.

Hayek's ideas were one aspect of Austrian economic theory developed concurrently by Ludwig von Mises and others. Oscar Lange's (1938) contribution to the "socialist calculation debate" offered what many on the Left thought to be a persuasive socialist rebuttal of Hayek's views before his book was published in 1944 (Blaug, 1993; Caldwell, 2004, pp. 214–220). Lange (1938) argued that a "trial and error" process would enable socialist planners to determine the correct accounting prices (pp. 72–83). Lange's work also helped to promote the "Walrasian general equilibrium theory as the appropriate framework" for dealing with this issue (Blaug, 1993, p. 56). Lange and Hayek continued this debate until shortly before Hayek's death in 1993, and the issue remains controversial (Blaugh, 1993; Lavoie, 1985; Caldwell, 1997, 2004). While Hayek was never able to establish completely the technical microeconomic elements of his theory, his work posed a serious challenge that socialist economists have not been able to resolve (Blaugh, 1993; Caldwell, 2004).

Although often labeled a conservative, Hayek explicitly rejected conservatism. He acknowledged that it was sometimes necessary to make alliances with conservatives to resist the drift toward social engineering and planned societies, but one should not confuse conservatism with classical liberalism. It is worth quoting Hayek at length on this point:

> Conservatism, though a necessary element of any stable society, is not a social program; in its paternalistic, nationalistic, and power-adoring tendencies it is often closer to socialism than true liberalism; with its traditionalistic, anti-intellectual, and often mystical propensities, it will never,

except in short periods of disillusionment, appeal to the young and all those who believe that some changes are desirable if this world is to become a better place. A conservative movement, by its very nature, is bound to be a defender of established privilege and to lean on the power of government for the protection of privilege. The essence of the liberal position, however, is the denial of all privilege. (Hayek, 1944/1956, p. xi)

Neither was Hayek a doctrinaire proponent of laissez-faire economics. He endorsed the value of a social safety net to provide all citizens with essential needs (food, clothing, and shelter), laws establishing a minimum wage and maximum working hours, and antitrust regulations (Foner 1998, p. 236). His concern was to prevent the safety net from becoming a hammock.

Hayek's hostility to conservatism and socialism derives from his insights regarding the limits of human cognition and knowledge (1944/1956). These limits are not, as Lippmann argued, merely an artifact of the increasing complexity of modern society. Human knowledge is a product of our cultural institutions and conventions, which have evolved. We are incapable of thinking outside the concepts and constraints of current cultural knowledge. In other words, social life and the mind itself are governed by rules or background assumptions, most of which we are unaware. This tacit dimension of human knowledge is something we have but can never fully articulate (Hayek, 1937/1948, pp. 57–76, 1983).

Hayek shared Hume's conception of human reason as an outcome rather than the basis for civilization and culture (Livingston, 1991, pp. 161–163). Reason is always convention laden, and any attempt to try to escape this dilemma by an appeal to foundational knowledge was futile. Hayek's views are in direct conflict with the "critical theory" so central to critical pedagogy. For example, the Frankfurt School viewed social institutions as original sources of oppression and saw the task of philosophy as freeing us from the constraints and distortions of dominant social forces. In contrast, Hayek's view was that "reason, being the outcome of social institutions and embedded in them, cannot, without absurdity, be conceived in opposition to them." This does not mean that critique of social institutions is impossible, "only that such criticism must presuppose the background of social institutions as having original authority to discipline judgment" (p. 164).

More importantly, any attempt by government to interfere with the natural (evolved) social order was likely to make things worse (Hayek 1944/1956). Hayek (1937/1960) also argued that human values, like human intelligence, had evolved over time as the result of the interactions. Human liberty, consequently, should take precedence over general claims to social welfare, inasmuch as individual liberty was a prior condition for the creation of any concept of social welfare. For Hayek, the liberal or progressive emphasis on the need for a conception of "social justice" to drive public policy was among the most powerful threats to individual liberty that had emerged in recent years. From Hayek's perspective, the emphasis on social justice at the heart of critical pedagogy could only work to invert the "original and authentic concept of liberty, in which it is properly attributed only to individual actions"(p. 387).

In other words, Hayek asserted that our lack of knowledge adequate for central planning of the economy was not merely a technical problem. We also lack agreement on the priority of social ends and values that should orient social planning. Inevitably, any attempt to centralize social and economic planning would require the imposition of a code of values not shared by the masses.

It is important to recall that Hayek was reacting to the growing influence of scientific reasoning on public policy in the twentieth century. For many on the Left, only a science freed of capitalist influence could provide an adequate guide for policy. From Hayek's perspective, this sort of scientism reflected the positivist impulse to apply the methods of the natural sciences to the social sciences (Caldwell, 2004, pp. 232–260). However, positivism promoted a false sense of science and knowledge. In this regard, Hayek's work was supported by and related to his intellectual colleague Michael Polanyi (1940, p. 19). The market had evolved as an institution best suited for coordinating and maximizing the disparate tacit knowledge of the millions of individuals to determine pricing by prioritizing social values and preferences. Absent this mechanism for maximizing individual choice, we would lose both the rational basis for economic activity and our democratic freedoms (Hayek, 1944/1956). A market economy was inherently the best way to maximize individual freedom and the potential of our social institutions, including schooling.

Milton Friedman (1963), a colleague of Hayek's at the University of Chicago in the 1950s, extended Hayek's ideas in the post-World War II era. His theories are often applied to the neoliberal economic reforms of the past four decades in America and the United Kingdom, but also in Australia, Canada, Chile, China, Japan, Korea, Russia, Eastern Europe, New Zealand, Singapore, Taiwan, and much of Western Europe (Harvey, 2005). But it is important to recall that Friedman went well beyond Hayek in advocating the privatization of almost all social services (including schooling), and Hayek had some strong reservations concerning his colleague's ideas (Caldwell, 2004; Ebenstein, 2003).

Leo Strauss and Neoconservatism

Much attention has been given to the alleged influence of Leo Strauss, a relatively obscure political philosopher, on the neoconservative movement and policy of the Reagan and both Bush administrations. The actual extent of Strauss's influence on American politics and policy is a matter of considerable debate, and it is important to separate Strauss's own work from his American followers, many of whom distort and oversimplify his ideas (Drury, 1999; Deutsch & Murley, 1999; Lilla, 2004a, 2004b; Norton, 2004; Smith, 2006).

Strauss was a prolific scholar and only a summary of his key ideas is possible in this context. For Strauss (1965), the fundamental theological-political problem was rooted in the question, "How should I live?" In Western civilization, philosophy and religion (revelation) have provided competing answers to this question. The tension between these two sources of knowledge is irreconcilable, as neither can refute the other. Yet this fundamental tension has been a primary source of our cultural development. According to Strauss (Drury, 1988; Strauss, 1953, 1958b), the Enlightenment was a modernist attempt to eliminate or reduce significantly this tension by isolating politics from religion.

The Enlightenment succeeded all too well in creating the illusion of a solution to the theological-political problem in the form of modern philosophy and liberalism, both of which distort our perception of the human condition. The fundamental questions and insights understood by the ancients were now seen as mere outmoded artifacts of their time and place. We have forgotten the need to choose between philosophy and religion as fundamental to human existence. A return to the study of our ancient philosophical and religious traditions, particularly the Socratic tradition and Talmud, can act as a counterweight to modernity and help us avoid its worst effects (Strauss, 1948/1968, 1965).

This assumption brings us to a second focus of Strauss's work: the role philosophy plays in society. Philosophy is essential to the full realization of human society, but, as Socrates illustrates, philosophy is also dangerous to the philosopher and social order (Strauss, 1952). Philosophy is dangerous, because it recognizes that the tension between revelation and reason cannot be reconciled. Their recognition of this aporia places philosophers in a permanent state of openness where fundamental questions remain irresolvable. At the same time, society and the masses require authority and certain fundamental beliefs (i.e., Plato's noble lie) for stability and continuity. Consequently, philosophers require protection from political and religious constraints, and the knowledge that no foundations for such beliefs exist must be kept to the philosophers themselves. How can philosophy accomplish these conflicting aims and serve the social order?

Strauss (1952) claimed that, over time, philosophers developed a capacity for what he called esoteric reading and writing. Esoteric knowledge was available in the Great Books and other works of the ancients and only accessible to those with the requisite skills and knowledge. However, a second form of knowledge (exoteric) was accessible to the masses and contained in the great books of the Western tradition. This exoteric form of knowledge provided the traditions and beliefs individuals and society required to maintain social order. Combining esoteric and exoteric knowledge in their writing and teaching enabled philosophers to be free intellectually, while remaining politically responsible. A successful revival of ancient philosophy would require the application of both forms of knowledge.

Natural Right and History (1953), Strauss's most influential work in America, argued for a link between the concept of natural right and the founding of United States political culture. Strauss linked the "self-evident truths" and "inalienable rights" of the Declaration to classical natural-rights theory originating with Greek philosophy and early Jewish and Christian religious traditions. According to Strauss, there is a clear distinction between nature and human conventions, and true (natural) justice is derived from the rules of nature best explicated in ancient Western philosophical and religious traditions. Without such rules, we would lack the standards and capacity to fully understand and criticize our conventions and institutions.

Modern thought, starting with Machiavelli, rejected natural-right tradition as a standard in favor of the interests of the prince (Strauss, 1958b). One can trace the decline of Western thought from this point on, as political science emerged to replace political philosophy. Liberalism gradually emerged as the modern political system representing a historicist conception of human rights that attempted to exclude religion and reduce rights to a set of orientations and procedural constraints. Strauss (1953, 1958b, 1959) argued that the modernist liberal move away from natural rights leads to relativism and eventually nihilism, which is a serious threat to any society. While Strauss decried the danger of relativism and nihilism, one needs to keep in mind insight regarding the lack of foundational knowledge described earlier, i.e., the inability to reconcile reason and revelation. Of course, this paradox or parallax view was accessible to only the philosophical elite (Strauss, 1952, 1959).

There is little doubt that Strauss's impact on American neoconservative discourse and public policy has been significant, but it has been subject to a variety of interpretations and distortions (Drury, 1988, 1999; Lilla, 2004a, 2004b; Norton, 2004; Smith, 2006). Strauss's actual impact on his contemporary intellectual colleagues is difficult to sort out. Many of the early neoconservatives were former leftists who became strong anticommunists (e.g., Daniel Bell, Nathan Glazer, Gertrude Himmelfarb, Irving Kristol, Norman Podhoretz, and Seymour Martin Lipset), in reaction to events of the Cold War, revelations concerning the Soviet Union and the American Communist Party, and liberalism's perceived weaknesses in the face of these developments. In contrast, Strauss's key ideas can be traced to his early work in the 1930s, although they were certainly reinforced by the Cold War.

Strauss's most direct impact was on his American students and the students of those students. Many of these intellectual progeny went on to positions in higher education (mainly in political science departments), where they established a powerful school of thought in political philosophy. Other Straussians, including some who first went to higher education, moved on to become political consultants, journalists, or to important positions in the Reagan and Bush administrations (Drury, 1999; Norton, 2004; Smith, 2006). A partial list of those who studied with Strauss or with the students of Strauss gives some indication of his influence, (e.g., Robert Bork, Francis Fukuyama, Alan Keys, William Kristol, Carns Lord, Clarence Thomas, and Paul Wolfowitz). Influential academic Straussians include Allan Bloom, Martin Diamond, Joseph Cropsey, and Ralph Lerner at the University of Chicago; Harvey Mansfield at Harvard; Harry Jaffa at Claremont College; Willmore Kendall at the University of Dallas; Stanley Rosen at Boston University; and Stephen Salkever at Swarthmore.

Lilla (2004a, 2004b) contends that, while Strauss himself is an intellectual worthy of study, his influence in America has been far different from that in Europe. Strauss came to America in 1938 and taught at the New School for a decade. However, his major impact occurred while teaching at the University of Chicago from 1949 to 1968. In stark contrast to most European universities, Strauss's students in Chicago had little or no philosophical background and tended to interpret his ideas within the postwar American cultural and political context. Most ignored his important earlier work and used *Natural Right and History* (1953) as their touchstone. For many, his complex ideas became instead a sort of catechism or script that blocked reinterpretation or, put another way, prompted Straussians to interpret events within the framework of a single narrative. Strauss's influence on his students was exacerbated by the events of the late 60s; the overall impact was intellectually stultifying (Lilla, 2004a, 2004b).

For Straussian neoconservatives, America (and the West in general), is in crisis. The greatest danger is the spread of cultural relativism and nihilism that makes us vulnerable to our internal and external enemies. For some (e.g., Lord, 2004), the "barbarians within" (a focus of the culture wars) are seen as even more dangerous than our external enemies. Internal barbaric influences include public education, liberal university professors, the mainstream press, leftist intellectuals, multiculturalists, lax immigration policies, the decline of moral standards, and ignorance or abandonment of our constitutional heritage. These negative influences are both a primary cause of the many problems we face and a symptom of our cultural decline. Some neoconservative Straussians have found Strauss's connection between natural rights and America's founding an important source for resolving our current cultural and political crisis (Jaffa, 1984).[2]

Notwithstanding its vulgar, ethnocentric, and simplistic elements, neoconservatives often enlist rightist populism to help resist relativism and return us to our naïve awareness of ancient fundamental wisdom regarding right and wrong. More ominously, many neoconservative Straussians promote America's "civilizing" mission to spread democracy to other nations, arguing that we have nothing to fear from other democracies, only totalitarian regimes (Drury, 1999; Norton, 2004; Ricks, 2006). In this context, it is worth noting that left progressive Christopher Lasch (1989) also draws on similar populist traditions to support his critique of the left.

Where traditional conservatives have been anti-intellectual in criticizing their opponents, neoconservatives are counterintellectual (Lilla, 2004b). A key insight for neoconservatives is that the best way to counter liberal cultural elites is to replace them with their own alternative neoconservative cultural elite. Consider how effective neoconservatives have been in creating their own think tanks, media outlets, political consultants, professional organizations, a powerful Straussian school of thought in the revival of political philosophy, K-12 education policy, and the successful prosecution of the culture war. Their influence on the current Bush administration's foreign policy, particularly Paul Wolfowitz, is another negative Straussian consequence.

However, Lilla (2004b) and Smith (2006) disagree with critics like Drury (1999) and Norton (2004) who argue that Strauss's ideas lead directly to neoconservative public and foreign policy in America. The intelligence distortions regarding WMD were not derived from Strauss's interpretation of Plato's "noble lie." Rather, many American Straussians have distorted his ideas and adapted them to Republican Party ideology and the culture wars. In contrast, Strauss himself is an important, relevant, and underappreciated philosopher whose works are worthy of attention.

The Tragic View of Education

Liberals and left progressives alike tend to exhibit a confidence that human reason can provide the knowledge and values required to address the major problems we face at the start of the twenty-first century. However, the theoretical insights posed by the conservatives and classical liberals discussed above call our attention to constraints on human cognition and action. One theme running through all these works is the problem of acquiring and disseminating the knowledge we need to solve human problems. There is a good deal of elitism in the assumptions of Lippmann, Posner, Strauss, and others regarding the masses' inability to understand the deeper knowledge essential to human survival. At best, only a privileged few have the competence to acquire and comprehend such knowledge. More importantly, each of these authors recognizes that humans cannot have, or at least demonstrate, access to foundational knowledge.

On the other hand, it is interesting to note the many similar insights espoused by a left-progressive tradition that also questions the limits of human reason, foundational knowledge, and our assumptions regarding human progress (Diggins, 1991; Niebuhr, 1932; Lasch, 1989; Westbrook, 2005). To the extent theoretical and cultural pluralism are intrinsic to the human condition and foundational knowledge an illusion, then critical educators need to acknowledge the real limits of human reason and our assumptions regarding education reform and progress.

Nicholas Burbules (1990) summarized the tragic sense of education 15 years ago in a thoughtful essay. Burbules points out why our educational aims are always in doubt and that "uncertainty, confusion, [and] failure" are a given (pp. 469–470). Burbules cites Hook's (1974) observation that the tragic sense of life is reflected in the "defeat of our plans and hopes, the realization that in much grief there is not much wisdom, and that we cannot count . . . [on] time alone to diminish our stupidities and cruelties" (p. 11). As educators, we need to understand that "everything we do impinges in a harmful way on someone, somewhere; that for every policy, however well-intentioned, there are unavoidable bad consequences" (Burbules, 1990, p. 473).

The tragic tradition invoked by Burbules has deep roots in American history. Henry Adams (1934) came to accept a tragic sense of life following his nineteenth-century study of American history to ascertain the meaning of human existence threatened by the rise of scientific thought. After decades of study, he found no fundamental truths or causal patterns in history and concluded that human "experience ceases to educate" (p. 294). Human knowledge was indeterminate and there was no going back to Enlightenment assumptions regarding reason and values.

Theologian Reinhold Niebuhr (1932, 1933) was among those left intellectuals who, following World War I, gradually lost faith in the capacity of liberalism, human intelligence, and science to bring about the reforms necessary for a just social order. Niebuhr's own experiences working with the poor in Detroit reinforced his skepticism. Once an advocate of nonviolence, Niebuhr came to question the efficacy of that policy, given the limits of reason, religion, and education to constrain narrow and predatory self-interest. He came to see human conflict as inevitable, something no social order can eliminate. Since some level of conflict and injustice are intrinsic to human existence, they must be confronted with power, which will include coercion and, on occasion, violence (Niebuhr, 1932).

Niebuhr understood that modern science, for all its insights, is incapable of providing the human "nerve and will" to resist social injustice. On the other hand, the utopian faith of the Social Gospel movement in the late nineteenth century and the progressive ideas that had guided American social reform movements in the early twentieth century were both naïve and counterproductive because they were based on false assumptions regarding the possibility of human progress.

Niebuhr was especially skeptical regarding the application of ideals and absolutes to social reform. While human ideals can be identified, they are always partial and illusory (Niebuhr, 1932, p. 81). Furthermore, we are incapable of acting consistently on such ideals in the real world. In practice, no form of government or approach to education was capable of getting people to work together toward the good of all. The optimistic appeal of left progressives like Dewey to disinterested social intelligence as the basis for social reform ignored the harsh realities of social life and also denied the masses' need for morale, which can only be "created by the right dogmas, symbols, and exceptionally potent oversimplifications" (Niebuhr, 1933, pp. 203–205).

Niebuhr was not a defeatist and remained an activist on behalf of social justice throughout his life. Instead, he espoused what he called "Christian realism," the need to maintain a consciousness of human limits and possibilities as we go about our social reform work. We should continue to act for social justice motivated primarily by hope and love, not science and social engineering. Too often progressive reformers overestimated human finitude, acting on the illusion that they were making progress and blind to their own selfish motivations. Even on those occasions when people are able to rise above self-interest and act with the best intentions, the policies they create generally have unintended negative, and often ironic, consequences. History contains a long record of reform efforts that, in effect, strengthened the status quo.

The work of Christopher Lasch is a more recent example of a writer working in the tragic tradition (Lasch, 1989). Lasch described the optimistic faith in human progress as a messianic creed that has seduced liberals and many critics of liberalism as well. In short, a faith in human progress had become the dominant ideology of modernism. Lasch was responding to the liberal, progressive, and totalitarian efforts to construct blueprints for the good society and apply science and social engineering to bring about a new, and presumably improved, social order.

Lasch (1989) argued that authentic selfhood involves hope, which he described as the capacity to accept the limits of human existence without despair. Lasch took pains to distinguish hope from optimism: "Hope implies a deep-seated trust in life that appears absurd to those who lack it." The hopeful are always prepared for the worst, but "their trust in life would not be worth much if it had not survived disappointments in the past" and an awareness that more were in store in the future. Indeed, "a blind faith that things will somehow work out for the best furnishes a poor substitute for the disposition to see things through even when they don't" (1989, p. 81).

Modernist reform efforts are generally motivated by an elitist conception (however well intentioned) of what was in the best interest of the masses (Lasch, 1989). The elite's ideological commitment to progress and belief that they have the knowledge to act in the interest of the masses (including the design of education reform) only intensify their reform efforts and exacerbates the unintended (including antidemocratic) consequences their policies. Our various beliefs in foundational knowledge and progress continue to have a powerful influence, because the tragic conception of human existence cuts too close to the bone for most Americans, who, despite episodes of self-doubt, tend to cling to foundationalism, resist all forms of relativism, and take progress for granted. The large number of educators across the political spectrum who, whatever their other differences, refuse to give up claims of privileged access to foundations for epistemological and/or axiological knowledge illustrates this point.

Conclusion

Our current educational debates are part of the continuing attempt to respond to the jarring challenges posed by modernism. American society and the world are still adjusting to the effects of modernism. While there is no going back to a premodernist society and culture, we continue to struggle over what social order would best serve human interests in the modern era. We find absent the secure comforts of tradition or theology afforded our premodern predecessors (Diggins, 1991).

Critical pedagogy's focus on education as countersocialization to help create a just democratic society is only one among many attempts to clarify the purpose of education for social justice in the wake of modernism. It is clear that schools alone are in no position to create a new democratic social order. The real question is this: what sort of education would best enable students to function in the present society and contribute to the creation of a just and democratic social order? The summaries of conservative, neoliberal, and tragic viewpoints above provide one indication of how difficult it is to answer this question.

I remain firmly committed to the continued relevance of critical pedagogy. It is not possible to provide a curriculum necessary to the realization and preservation of a democratic social order absent a genuine critical perspective. A genuine critical perspective is only possible within a theoretical framework that acknowledges the reality of theoretical pluralism and both intrinsic and structural constraints on human agency. To accomplish this shift in emphasis, critical pedagogy will need to replace its current focus on countersocialization based on an assumed theoretical superiority with a more modest critical conception of "socialization" to maximize the potential for human agency and competence to work for a democratic social order.

Dewey (1929) described how modern societies are driven to eliminate uncertainty from human knowledge and policy. Our search for foundational knowledge was illusory and a major source of human misery and dissatisfaction. In other words, our most noble aims, including our attempts to design education for a democratic society, were always constrained by the limits of human cognition and social contexts. In a direct response to Counts' (1932) social-reconstructionist call to use schools to "build a new social order," Dewey (1937) rejected countersocialization as a misguided approach to education and social reform. Those supporting education as countersocialization, he said:

. . . rest their adherence to the theory, in part, upon the fact that there is a great deal of indoctrination now going on in the schools, especially with reference to narrow nationalism under the name of patriotism, and with reference to the dominant economic regime. These facts unfortunately are *facts. But they do not prove that the right course is to seize upon the method of indoctrination and reverse its object. (p. 328)*

We must constantly bear in mind that we are teaching "other people's children." We need to resist the progressive tendency to act as if we alone know what is best for the masses, what must be done, while simultaneously preaching about the value of participatory democracy. As humans, we simply do not have access to this kind of knowledge, and to assume we do can quickly become just another form of elitist dogmatism. Neoliberal theory can (and mainly does) function " . . . as a political project to re-establish the conditions for capital accumulation and to restore the power of economic elites." Nevertheless, neoliberalism can also serve "as a utopian project to re-establish the conditions for capital accumulation" and democracy (Harvey, 2005, p. 19). Although it is difficult, we must try to distinguish between our roles as educators and political activists.[3] Dewey was a socialist in his political life but not in the classroom. What he did recommend was a form of education that would enable citizens in a democratic society to apply human intelligence to the solution of social problems. Dewey, unlike the reconstructionists and many contemporary critical educators, believed it was possible to cultivate the formation of the democratic mind by attending to requirements of competence for social action, without the need to direct instruction toward a specific conception of social welfare or conception of a preferred social order.

Dewey's views should be filtered through the harsh reality of democratic realism, neoliberalism, conservatism, and the tragic-progressive critique of education. With respect to democratic realism, left progressives like Robert Westbrook (2005), acknowledge "the anemic state of American Democracy . . ." and that the "prospects for a more expansive democracy are gloomier today than they were in the early nineteenth century" (p. 199). Many other left progressives argue that we need to reconsider the theoretical grounds for social and political reform as we attempt to apply our ideas globally.[4]

To acknowledge the tragic limits on human agency is not to argue for either complacency or despair. Dewey's arguments for deliberative democracy grounded by critical pragmatism should remain the "regulative ideal" for critical educators (Westbrook, 2005, pp. 218–240). To make this claim is to rely on a faith in democracy underdetermined by theory (Menand, 2004; West, 1999, p. 186; Westbrook 2005). As Lasch (1989, p. 81) and Westbrook (2005, p. 240) remind us, we can supplement our theoretical limitations with a concept of democratic hope.

Lasch (1989) cautioned that we not confuse hope with the optimism associated with a modernist belief in progress. Rather we should contrast hope with pessimism. Democratic hope "implies a deep-seated trust in life that appears absurd to those who lack it." Those holding this view are prepared for the worst eventualities. "Their trust in life would not be worth much if it had not survived disappointments in the past, while the knowledge that the future holds further disappointments demonstrates the continuing need for hope." In contrast, "a blind faith that things will work out for the best furnishes a poor substitute for the disposition to see things through when they don't" (p. 81).

We have good reason to believe the only effective path to education for social transformation lies in enabling our students themselves to develop the competencies required for active participation in work necessary to construct a democratic social order. We can hope but will never know in advance if this approach will work. When it occurs, significant political and social transformation generally results from multiple factors, including institutional failure, deep cultural conflicts, effective organization of powerful opposition groups, and the implied threat (or actuality) of major social disruption and/possible violence. This sort of political activism is normally well beyond the theoretical scope and potential of K-12 educators. What we do know is that, while critical pedagogy can play an important role, it is competent citizens, not critical K-12 schoolteachers or professors, who are in the best position to preserve a democratic social order and determine the shape of the democratic society to come.

Notes

1. Eric Lott (2006) provides a scathing critique of the tendency of former radicals and left progressives to move toward what he sees as a more centrist position, which undercuts a left critique of American culture and politics.

2. See Willmore Kendall (1985) for a Straussian critique of Jaffa's position.

3. For a very different view, see the case developed by Brennan (2006) and Lott (2006) that educators should be political activists who reject liberalism and attempts to work to build wider educational and political coalitions as complacency and accommodation.

4. See, for example, the variety of theoretical positions reflected in the work of Agamben, 1995/1998; Anderson, 2006; Gitlin, 1995, 2006; Grey, 2000; Hardt & Negri, 2000; Isaac, 2003; Nussbaum, et al., 1996; Westbrook, 2005; and Zizek, 2003. For a contrary view of this theoretical trend, see Brennan, 2006; Harvey, 2005; and Lott, 2006.

References

Adams, H. (1934). *The education of Henry Adams*. New York: Modern Library.

Agamben, G. (1998). *Homo sacer: Sovereign power and bare life*. (D. Heller-Roazen, Trans.). Stanford, CA: Stanford University Press. (Original work published 1995)

Anderson, A. (2006). *The way we argue now: A study in the cultures of theory*. Princeton, NJ: Princeton University Press.

Barber, B. (1992). *Aristocracy of everyone: The politics of education and the future of America*. New York: Ballantine.

Blaug, M. (1993). Hayek revisited. *Critical Review, 7*(1), 51–60.

Bloom, A. (1987). *The closing of the American mind: How higher education has failed democracy and impoverished the souls of today's students*. New York: Simon and Schuster.

Brennan, T. (2006). *Wars of position: The cultural politics of left and right*. New York: Columbia University Press.

Brosio, R. (2004). Essay review: Critical education against global capitalism: Karl Marx and revolutionary critical education. *Educational Studies, 34*, 446–464.

Burbules, N.C. (1990). The tragic sense of education. *Teachers College Record, 91*, 469–479.

Caldwell, B. (2004). *Hayek's challenge: An intellectual biography of F. A. Hayek.* Chicago: University of Chicago Press.

Counts, G. S. (1932). *Dare the school build a new social order?* New York: John Day.

Deutsch, K. L., & Murley, J. A. (Eds.). (1999). *Leo Strauss, the Straussians, and the American regime.* Lanham, MD: Rowman and Littlefield Publishers, Inc.

Dewey, J. (1916). *Democracy and education: An introduction to the philosophy of education.* New York: The Macmillan Company.

Dewey, John. 1929. *Experience and Nature.* LaSalle, Illinois: Open Court.

Dewey, J. (1934). Can education share in the social reconstruction? *The Social Frontier, 1*(1), 11.

Dewey, J. (1935a). The need for orientation. *Forum, 93*, 334.

Dewey, J. (1935b). The crucial role of intelligence. *The Social Frontier, 1*(5), 9.

Dewey, J. (1937). Education and social change. *The Social Frontier, 2*, 235–238.

Dewey, J., & Childs, J. L. (1933). The social-economic situation and education. In W. H. Kilpatrick (Ed.), *Educational frontier* (pp. 71–72, 318–319). New York: D. Appleton-Century.

Diggins, J. 1991. *The Rise and Fall of the American Left.* New York: W. W. Norton.

Drew, E. (2006). Power grab. *The New York Review of Books, 53*(11), pp. 10, 12, 14–15.

Drury, S. B. (1988). *The political ideas of Leo Strauss.* New York: St. Martin's Press.

Drury, S. B. (1999). *Leo Strauss and the American right.* New York: St. Martin's Press.

Ebenstein, Alan. (2003). *Hayek's journey: The mind of Friedrich Hayek.* New York: Palgrave Macmillan.

Foner, E. (1998). *The story of American freedom.* New York: W. W. Norton and Company.

Friedman, M. (1963). *Capitalism and freedom.* Chicago: University of Chicago Press.

Gee, J. (1992). *The social mind.* New York: Bergin and Garvey.

Gitlin, T. (1995). *The twilight of common dreams: Why America is wracked by culture wars.* New York: Metropolitan Publishers.

Gitlin, T. (2006). *The intellectuals and the flag.* New York: Columbia University Press.

Grey, J. (1998). *Hayek on liberty* (3rd ed.). New York: The New Press.

Grey, J. (2000). *Two faces of liberalism.* New York: The New Press.

Halstead, T., & Lind, M. (2001). *The radical center and the future of American politics.* New York: Doubleday.

Hardt, M., & Negri, A. (2000). *Empire.* Cambridge, MA: Harvard University Press.

Harvey, D. (2005). *A brief history of neoliberalism.* New York: Oxford University Press.

Hayek, F. (1948). Economics and knowledge, In *Individualism and the economic order* (pp. 33–56). Chicago: University of Chicago Press. (Original work published 1937).

Hayek, F. (1956). *The road to serfdom.* London: Routledge. (Original work published 1944)

Hayek, F. (1983). *Knowledge, evolution, and society.* London: Adam Smith Institute.

Hayek, F. (1960). *The constitution of liberty.* London: Routledge. (Original work published 1937)

Hill, D., McLaren, P., Cole, M., & Rikowski, G. (Eds.). (2002). *Marxism against postmodernism in educational theory*. New York: Lexington.

Hook, S. (1989). The closing of the American mind: An intellectual best seller revisited. *American Scholar*, 58, 123–35.

Isaac, J. C. (2003). *The poverty of progressivism: The future of American democracy in a time of liberal decline*. Lanham, MD: Rowman and Littlefield Publishers, Inc.

Jaffa, H. V. (1984). *American conservatism and the American founding*. Durham, NC: Carolina Academic Press.

Kendall, W. (1985). *The conservative affirmation in America*. Chicago: Gateway Expectations.

Kristol, I. (1983). *Reflections of a neoconservative*. New York: Basic Books.

Kristol, I. (1994). *Neoconservativism: Autobiography of an idea*. New York: Free Press.

Lange, Oscar. 1938. *On the Economic Theory of Socialism*. New York: Augustus M. Kelley Publishers.

Lasch, C. (1989). *The true and only heaven*. New York: W. W. Norton and Company.

Lavoie, Dan. 1985. *Rivalry and Central Planning: The Socialist Calculation Debabe Reconsidered*. New York: Cambridge University Press.

Lilla, M. (2004a). Leo Strauss: The European. *The New York Review of Books*, 51(16), 58–63.

Lilla, M. (2004b). The closing of the Straussian mind. *The New York Review of Books*, 51(17), 55–59.

Lippmann, W. (1922). *Public opinion*. New York: Harcourt Brace.

Lippmann, W. (1925). *The phantom public*. New York: Macmillan.

Livingston, D. W. (1991). Hayek as Humean. *Critical Review*, 5, 159–177.

Lord, C. (2004). *The modern prince: What leaders need to know now*. New Haven, CT: Yale University Press.

Lott, E. (2006). *The disappearing liberal intellectual*. New York: Basic Books.

Menand, L. (2004, August 30). The Unpolitical Animal. *The New Yorker*, 80, 92–94.

Misak, C. (2000). *Truth, politics, morality: Pragmatism and deliberation*. London: Routledge.

Niebuhr, R. (1932). *Moral man and immoral society*. New York: Scribner and Sons Publishers.

Niebuhr, R. (1933, March 1). After capitalism—what? *World Tomorrow*, pp. 203-205.

Norton, A. (2004). *Leo Strauss and the politics of American empire*. New Haven, CT: Yale University Press.

Nussbaum, M. C., and respondents. (1996). *For love of country: Debating the limits of patriotism*. Boston: Beacon Press.

Parker, W. C. (2003). *Teaching democracy: Unity and diversity in public life*. New York: Teachers College Press.

Polanyi, M. (1940). *The contempt of freedom: The Russian experiment and after*. New York: Arno Press.

Posner, R. (2003). *Law, pragmatism, and democracy*. Cambridge, MA: Harvard University Press.

Richardson, G. H., & Blades, D. W. (Eds.). (2006). *Troubling the canon of citizenship education*. New York: Peter Lang.

Ricks, T. E. (2006). *Fiasco: The American military adventure in Iraq*. London: Penguin Press.

Schumpeter, J. (1942). *Capitalism, socialism, and democracy*. New York: Harper & Brothers.

Smith, S. B. (2006). *Reading Leo Strauss: Politics, philosophy, Judaism*. Chicago: University of Chicago Press.

Stanley, W.B. (1992). *Curriculum for utopia: Social reconstructionism and critical pedagogy in the postmodern era*. Albany, NY: State University of New York Press.

Strauss, L. (1952). *Persecution and the art of writing.* Westport, CT: Greenwood Press.

Strauss, L. (1953). *Natural right and history.* Chicago: University of Chicago Press.

Strauss, L. (1958a). *Liberalism, ancient and modern.* New York: Basic Books.

Strauss, L. (1958b). *Thoughts on Machiavelli.* Chicago: University of Chicago Press.

Strauss, L. (1959). *What is political philosophy?* New York: Free Press.

Strauss, L. (1965). *Spinoza's critique of religion.* New York: Schocken Books.

Strauss, L. (1968). *On tyranny.* Ithaca, NY: Cornell University Press. (Original work published 1948)

West, C. (1999). The limits of neopragmatism. In C. West (Ed.), *The Cornel West reader* (pp. 183–187). New York: Basic Books.

Westbrook, R. (1991). *John Dewey and American democracy.* Ithaca, NY: Cornell University Press.

Westbrook, R. (2005). *Democratic hope: Pragmatism and the politics of truth.* Ithaca, NY: Cornell University Press.

Whitson, J. A., & Stanley, W. B. (1996) Re-Minding education for democracy. In W. C. Parker (Ed.), *Educating the democratic mind* (pp. 309-336). Albany, NY: State University of New York Press.

Wood, E., & Foster, J. (1997). *In defense of history: Marxism and the postmodernism agenda.* New York: Monthly Review Press.

Zizek, S. 2003. *The Puppet and the Dwarf: The Perverse Core of Christianity.* Boston: M.I.T. Press.

Afterword

Reinserting Criticity into Critical Pedagogy

DONALDO MACEDO

Joe L. Kincheloe and Peter McLaren's edited text, *Critical Pedagogy: Where Are We Now?* could not have been more timely, given the strangulation of democratic ideals by George W. Bush's administration—an administration that in other contexts, for example, in Latin America, would have been correctly labeled as a junta led by the triumvirate composed of former Secretary of Defense Donald Rumsfeld, Vice-President Dick Cheney, and President George W. Bush. The assault on civil liberties through the enactment of the Patriot Act that was overwhelmingly enacted by a rubber stamp Congress has not only undermined the Constitution, it has also limited guaranteed freedom of association and speech. In the name of "security," most Americans willingly accepted President Bush's directive for neighbors to spy on neighbors, for citizens to lose protection from racial and ethnic profiling, and for citizens and noncitizens alike to be jailed without being charged with a crime and without the right to legal counsel if one is characterized as an "enemy combatant." The administration was so callously blatant in its assault on civil liberties that, according to Walter Pincus, "FBI and Justice Department investigators [said] that 'traditional civil liberties may have to be cast aside if they are to extract information about the Sept. 11 attacks and terrorist plans.'"[1]

Against a reactionary landscape that smacks of Eastern Bloc totalitarianism that the American propaganda apparatus used to aggressively denounce during the Cold War years, one should not be surprised that critical pedagogy would be attacked since schools, more and more, are coerced into high-stakes tests and state mandates that, for all practical purpose, have put teachers and students alike under siege. The draconian accountability measures designed to address a fabricated educational crisis have not only renewed the question, "Is there any Left left?" but they have also exposed anew the fault line of some liberal educators who, while embracing critical pedagogy as a tenet, have on the other hand summarily undermined any political project in critical pedagogy they consider too radical. In other words, most liberal educators remain paradoxical with respect to their discourse which proclaims the virtues of social justice, freedom, and democracy to the degree that they happily maintain privileges extracted from the very structures engaged in discriminatory practices and the violation of democratic principles they purport to denounce.

The uneasiness of liberals regarding a critical educational project is abundantly clear when Derek Bok, the former president of Harvard University, critiqued Henry Giroux at length in his new book on higher education, *Our Underachieving Colleges*, by labeling Giroux's educational proposals—which embrace "pedagogical practices informed by an ethical stance that contests racism, sexism, class exploitation, and other dehumanizing and exploitative social relations . . ."[2]—as a form of indoctrination. According to Bok, "[s]ince these political goals are matter of legitimate debate, the vision of a university committed to promoting Giroux's agenda is deeply unsettling. Could students who disagree with the agenda feel entirely free to express opposing views? Would appointments and promotions committees in Giroux's university evaluate candidates on their intellectual merits or be swayed by how closely the candidates' teaching and writing conformed to his political vision?"[3]

While Derek Bok is unsettled by Giroux's pedagogy that promotes social justice and an "ethical stance that contests racism, sexism, class exploitation, and other dehumanizing and exploitative social relations," he is ominously silent with regard to Harvard Professor Samuel P. Huntington, whose anti-immigrant tirades against Mexicans are blatantly racist: "[t]he superiority of the 'Anglo-American race' justified its members conquering and ruling Mexicans."[4] Is Bok concerned that Huntington's racist vision of Mexicans could prompt him to block the appointment of the world-renowned Mexican author, Carlos Fuentes, from gaining a teaching position at Harvard, particularly when Fuentes eloquently contradicts him by arguing that "people and their culture perish in isolation, but they are born or reborn in contact with other men and women, with men and women of another culture, another creed, and another race. If we do not recognize our humanity in others, we shall not recognize it ourselves?"[5] Would Bok consider Fuentes' pronouncements also a form of multicultural indoctrination? Bok was also astutely silent concerning the sexist treaties by another Harvard professor, Harvey C. Mansfield, whose book *Manliness* is an obscene attack on women. Is Bok unsettled by Mansfield's view of women as inferior and that he could also aggressively attempt to prevent women from teaching at Harvard? Does Bok think that former Harvard President Summers was doctrinaire and sexist when he pontificated about women's genetic inferiority in science? This is where Bok's liberalism collapses under the weight of its de facto conservative ideology.

While one may question Derek Bok and Harvard University's liberal credentials, the university is often cited by the Right as the bastion of liberalism, and the liberal label is also used as an effective character-assassination method when political figures are associated with Cambridge, Massachusetts. Thus, the Right has conveniently collapsed liberals with left politics and, in the process, reduced drastically the spaces for any political posture to the left of center, given that a centrist position is now considered left in American politics, as Hillary Clinton and John Kerry exemplify. Within this political entrapment, any radical educational proposal based on a radical democracy that envisions a world that is less discriminatory, more just, and less dehumanizing and more humane is always typecast as extremist and is routinely devalued and dismissed.

The devaluation process manifests itself, for instance, over language use, where a critical language is often associated with theory giving rise to a false binarism between theory and practice. The whitewashing of language via euphemism as a process of not naming reality for what it is constitutes a mechanism used by both conservative and liberal educators to conceal the dominant ideology from which both groups reap benefits and privileges for their complicity with the dominant structures. That is why terms such as oppression, ruling class, and praxis are seldom found in the popular press and the mainstream educational literature and become, for instance, disenfranchised, affluent people, and practice, respectively. While the mass media and educational institutions make abundant references to middle-class and working-class issues, they simultaneously deny the existence of class in the United States, as the Democrats try to avoid the label of "class warfare" at all cost. What would not be allowed is the reference to the proletariat as a class category to the degree that it has been associated with Marxism, a taboo term in American open society. The proletariat's euphemistic replacement, the working-class, fails to capture the substance and complexity encapsulated in what it means to be workers "possessing neither capital nor means of production . . . [who] . . . must earn their living by selling their labor"[6] under exploitative conditions and antagonistic working relations with owners who control the means of production. The term working-class also conjures up a false reality in which the inhabitants of the middle-class category would have to be classified as nonworkers. Most liberals have an aversion to critical language and viscerally dismiss the use of critical language by falsely labeling it as too theoretical (meaning not practical enough). This was evident during a discussion with a liberal colleague concerning the role of language in class demarcation when, after exhausting her arguments to deny the existence of class in the United States, she proclaimed: "That's why I don't do theory"—a remark that forced me to point out to her that she, in fact, does theory. Her problem does not lie with the theory per se but with the fact that she does bad theory. Bad theory involves its denial by those who falsely claim to be engaged in practice only, particularly when the denial of theory truncates questions that could unveil the raison d'être of the very denial of theory.

The false dichotomy manufactured by both conservatives and most liberals regarding theory vs. practice represents yet another pedagogy of entrapment through which the ideals of social justice, democracy, and liberation that undergird critical pedagogy are undermined. For example, while many liberals conveniently adopt a Freirean discourse as an alternative to the conservative domesticating education, many of these same liberals have an aversion to theory and a critical language which, invariably, reduces Freire's leading ideas of democracy, social justice, and liberation to a method. According to Stanley Aronowitz, the North American fetish for methods has allowed Freire's philosophical ideas to be "assimilated to the prevailing obsession of North American education, following a tendency in all human and social sciences, with methods—of verifying knowledge and, in schools, of teaching, that is, transmitting knowledge to otherwise unprepared students."[7]

The fetish for methods among many who claim to be critical pedagogues not only debases critical pedagogy of its criticity, but it also works insidiously against educators' adhering to Freire's own pronouncement against the importation and exportation of methods. In a long conversation I had with him about this issue he said: "Donaldo, I don't want to be imported or exported. It is impossible to export pedagogical practices without reinventing them. Please, tell your fellow American educators not to import me. Ask them to recreate and rewrite my ideas." And recreating and rewriting Freire's ideas inevitably involves taking a detour through Freire's theories, a path that many pseudo-critical educators arrogantly reject while falsely boasting to be educators of action.

Joe Kincheloe's and Peter McLaren's edited volume, *Critical Pedagogy: Where Are We Now?* cleverly avoids the temptation of falling into a reductionistic language of critique while exposing the challenges that critical pedagogy is now facing. Hence, its authors passionately yearn for a language of possibility that moves us beyond where we are now by painstakingly unveiling the contradictions that have somewhat paralyzed the political project of critical pedagogy. In doing so, we need to remain always vigilant in our understanding that critical pedagogy is never an arrival point that could be easily turned into a new form of methodological rigidity laced with benevolent oppression—all done under the guise of democracy and liberation. What the authors of this must-read volume make clear is that critical pedagogy is not a method neatly prepackaged for consumption by educators who pretend to be agents of change. Critical pedagogy is a state of becoming, a way of being in the world and with the world—a neverending process that involves struggle and pain but also hope and joy shaped and maintained by a humanizing pedagogy that, according to Freire, "is a path through which men and women can become conscious about their presence in the world. The way they act and think when they develop all of their capacities, taking into consideration their needs, but also the needs and aspirations of others."[8]

Notes

1.   Alexander Cockburn, "Green Lights for Torture," *The Nation*, May 31, 2004, p. 9.

2.   Derek Bok, *Our Underachieving Colleges* (Princeton, New Jersey: Princeton University Press, 2006), p. 62.

3.   Ibid., p. 63.

4.   Samuel P. Huntington, *Who Are We: The Challenges to America's National Identity* (New York, NY: Simon & Schuster, 2004), p. 55.

5.   Carlos Fuentes, "The Mirror of the Other," *The Nation*, March 30, 1992, p. 411.

6.   *The American Heritage Dictionary*, p. 990.

7.   Stanley Aronowitz, "Paulo Freire's Radical Democratic Humanism," in Peter McLaren and Peter Leonard, eds., *Paulo Freire: A Critical Encounter* (London: Routledge, 1993), p.8.

8.   Paulo Freire and Frei Betto, *Essa Escola Chamada Vida* (São Paulo: Editora Scipione, 1989), p.8.

Contributors

FRANK ABRAHAMS is professor of music education and chair of the Music Education Department at Westminster Choir College of Rider University in Princeton, New Jersey. A pioneer in the development of Critical Pedagogy for Music Education, he has published articles in the *Music Educators Journal, Update: Applications of Research in Music Education, Arts Education Policy Review,* and *Visions of Research in Music Education*—an on-line journal where he serves as editor. Abrahams has lectured extensively in Brazil including the Paulo Freire Institute in Recife. In Brazil his articles are published in *Revista da ABEM,* the journal of the Brazilian Music Educator's Association.

LILIA I. BARTOLOMÉ is Associate Professor in the Applied Linguistics Graduate Program at the University of Massachusetts Boston. As a teacher educator, Bartolomé examines teacher ideological orientations around their work with linguistic minority students as well as their actual classroom practices with this student population. Her publications include a special co-edited issue of *Radical Teacher:* "Naming and Interrogating Our English-only Legacy," and the following books, *Immigrant Voices: In Search of Pedagogical Equity* (co-editor and co-authored with Henry Trueba, 2000), and *Dancing with Bigotry: The Poisoning of Culture* (co-authored with Donaldo Macedo, 2000).

KATHLEEN S. BERRY is a professor of education at the University of New Brunswick, Canada where she teaches literacies and drama in the Department of Critical Studies. She has located herself in critical pedagogy since she was four, first by chance and now by choice. She has recently published chapters on counter-memory, research as bricolage, critical media studies, and whiteness in Canada. She is the author of many articles and chapters and of *The Dramatic Arts and Cultural Studies* (Garland, 2000), and *Rigour & Complexity in Educational Research* (Open University Press, 2004 with Joe Kincheloe). She wears intellectual and emotional armor when facing the opposition to Critical Studies entering the fields of education.

NOAH DE LISSOVOY is assistant professor of social foundations of education in the College of Education and Human Development at the University of Texas at San Antonio. His work focuses on the investigation of oppression and resistance in schooling and society and the development of contemporary theories of liberatory pedagogy and praxis. His articles have appeared or will be forthcoming in *The Journal of Education Policy*, *The Review of Education, Pedagogy and Cultural Studies*, *The Journal of Postcolonial Education*, and other journals, as well as in several edited collections on pedagogy and politics. Prior to graduate study, he taught in the Los Angeles Unified School District, where he was also a union representative and education activist.

NORMAN K. DENZIN is Distinguished Professor of Communications, Research Professor of Communications, Cinema Studies, Sociology, Criticism and Interpretive Theory at the University, of Illinois at Urbana-Champaign. He is the author, co-author, or co-editor of over 50 books and 200 professional articles and chapters. He is founding President of the International Association of Qualitative Inquiry (2005–), and Director of the International Center of Qualitative Inquiry (2005–). He is past editor of *The Sociological Quarterly*, founding co-editor of *Qualitative Inquiry*, and founding editor of *Cultural Studies<>Critical Methodologies*, and *Studies in Symbolic Interaction: A Research Annual*.

JEFF DUNCAN-ANDRADE, is Assistant Professor of Raza Studies and Education Administration and Interdisciplinary Studies, and Co-Director of the Educational Equity Initiative at San Francisco State University's Cesar Chavez Institute. In addition to these duties, he teaches an 11th grade Urban Sociology course at East Oakland Community High School, where he continues his research into the uses of critical pedagogy in urban schools.

GUSTAVO E. FISCHMAN is associate professor in the divisions of Educational Leadership and Policy Studies and Curriculum and Instruction at Arizona State University. His research interests are in the areas of comparative and international education, gender studies, and qualitative studies in education. Dr. Fischman is the author of *Imagining Teachers: Rethinking Gender Dynamics in Teacher Education* (2001) and the Associate Editor for the online journals *Education Policy Analysis Archives* (EPAA) and *Education Review*.

LUIS A. GANDIN is a Professor of Sociology of Education at the School of Education of the Federal University of Rio Grande do Sul in Porto Alegre, Brazil. He is Visiting Scholar and Professor at the School of Education and Human Services of Oakland University. He is the editor of *Journal Currculo sem Fronteiras* (Curriculum without borders) and has published four books in Brazil and Portugal, several book chapters, and many articles in academic journals. Gandin's research interests are in the areas of sociology of education, educational policy, curriculum theory, and progressive educational reforms.

HENRY A. GIROUX currently holds the Global TV Network Chair Professorship at McMaster University in the English and Cultural Studies Department. He has published many books and articles. His most recent books include: *Take Back Higher Education* (co-authored with Susan Searls-Giroux), *America on the Edge: Henry Giroux on Politics, Culture, and Education*, and *Beyond the Spectacle of Terrorism, The Giroux Reader, Stormy Weather: Katrina and the Politics of Disposability*, and, *The University in Chains: Confronting the Military-Industrial-Academic Complex*. His primary research areas are cultural studies, youth studies, critical pedagogy, popular culture, media studies, social theory, and the politics of higher and public education.

SANDY GRANDE is a professor at Connecticut College. Her current research examines the intersections between critical theory and American Indian intellectualism. Her approach is profoundly inter- and cross-disciplinary and has included the integration of critical, feminist and Marxist theories of education with the concerns of American Indian and environmental education. She is the author of the highly acclaimed *Red Pedagogy: Critical Theory and American Indian Education* (2004).

LUIS HUERTA-CHARLES is an assistant professor of Early Childhood/Bilingual Education in the Department of Curriculum and Instruction at New Mexico State University. He is co-editor (with Marc Pruyn) of *Teaching Peter McLaren: Paths of Dissent* (Peter Lang, 2005). His research interest focuses on the processes of early biliteracy, bilingual education and teacher education related to socially justice practices in the Borderlands. He has been also engaged in developing a research approach centered on viewing research as praxis within communities as a way of making real Marx's eleventh thesis on Feuerbach.

VALERIE J. JANESICK is Professor of Educational Leadership and Policy Studies, University of South Florida, Tampa. She teaches classes in Qualitative Research Methods, Curriculum Theory and Inquiry, Foundations of Curriculum, Ethics and Educational Leadership and Program Evaluation. Her most recent book is *Authentic Assessment: A Primer* (Peter Lang, 2006).

JOE L. KINCHELOE is the Canada Research Chair of Critical Pedagogy at the McGill University Faculty of Education. He is the founder of the Paulo and Nita Freire International Project for Critical Pedagogy at McGill University. Kincheloe is the author of numerous books and articles about pedagogy, education and social justice, racism, class bias, and sexism, issues of cognition and cultural context, and educational reform. His books include: *Teachers as Researchers, Classroom Teaching: An Introduction, Getting Beyond the Facts: Teaching Social Studies/Social Sciences in the Twenty-first Century, The Sign of the Burger: McDonald's and the Culture of Power, City Kids: Understanding Them, Appreciating Them, and Teaching Them, and Changing Multiculturalism* (with Shirley Steinberg). His co-edited works include *White Reign: Deploying Whiteness in America* (with Shirley Steinberg et al.) and the Gustavus Myers Human Rights award winner: *Measured Lies: The Bell Curve Examined* (with Shirley Steinberg).

PEPI LEISTYNA is an Associate Professor of Applied Linguistics Graduate Studies at the University of Massachusetts Boston, where he coordinates the research program and teaches courses in cultural studies, media literacy, and language acquisition. Leistyna has published articles in various scholarly journals and his books include: *Breaking Free: The Transformative Power of Critical Pedagogy; Presence of Mind: Education and the Politics of Deception; Defining and Designing Multiculturalism; Cultural Studies: From Theory to Action*, and *Corpus Analysis: Language Structure and Language Use.* His recent documentary film with the Media Education Foundation is called *Class Dismissed: How TV Frames the Working Class.*

DONALDO MACEDO is Professor of English and Distinguished Professor of Liberal Arts and Education at the University of Massachusetts Boston. He has published extensively in the areas of Creole languages, critical literacy, bilingualism, and multiculturalism. His publication include *Literacy: Reading the Word and the World* (with Paulo Freire, 1987), *Literacies of Power: What Americans Are Not Allowed to Know* (1994), *Howard Zinn on Democratic Education* (with Howard Zinn, 2005). His work has been translated into many languages.

GREGORY MARTIN is a Lecturer in the School of Education and Professional Studies at Griffith University, Gold Coast Campus. His research interests include Marxist theory, critical pedagogy and socially critical action research. He is currently a member of Australia's National Tertiary Education Union and the Gold Coast branch of Socialist Alliance.

PETER MCLAREN is Professor of Urban Schooling at the Graduate School of Education and Information Studies, University of California, Los Angeles. He is the author and editor of over forty books on critical pedagogy and critical social theory. His writings have been translated into 20 languages. McLaren lectures worldwide. He serves the Bolivarian Revolution in Venezuela as an international advisor for Centro Internacional Miranda in Caracas, and through the Catedra Peter McLaren at the Bolivarian University. McLaren's work is the topic of two book-length studies, *Teaching Peter McLaren: Paths of Dissent*, edited by Marc Pruyn and Luis Huerta-Charles (Peter Lang), and *Peter McLaren, Education, and the Struggle for Liberation: The Educator as Revolutionary*, edited by Mustafa Eryaman. His most recent book, *Pedagogy and Praxis in the Age of Empire* is co-authored with Nathalia Jaramillo.

ERNEST MORRELL is an assistant professor in the Urban Schooling division of the Graduate School of Education and Information Studies at the University of California at Los Angeles. His work examines the possible intersections between urban adolescent literacies and the "sanctioned" literacies of dominant institutions such as schools. English teachers. Morrell is the author of *Linking Literacy and Popular Culture: Finding Connections for Lifelong Learning* (Christopher-Gordon) and *Becoming Critical Researchers: Literacy and Empowerment for Urban Youth* (Peter Lang). His newest books are: *Critical Literacy and Urban Youth* and *Critical Pedagogy in Urban Contexts: Toward a Grounded Theory of Praxis* (Peter Lang).

ELIZABETH QUINTERO, is Professor of Early Childhood and Childhood Education, director of Early Childhood Masters program, and chair of doctoral committee in the Department of Teaching and Learning, School of Education at New York University. Dr. Quintero's research, teaching and service involve critical literacy in multilingual, multicultural communities. She is author of *Problem Posing with Multicultural Children's Literature: Developing Critical Early Childhood Curricula* (Peter Lang) and co-author of *Becoming a Teacher in the New Society: Bringing Communities and Classrooms Together* (Peter Lang 2003) and co-author of *Teachers' Reading/Teachers' Lives* (1997).

WILLIAM B. STANLEY is Professor and Dean of Education at Monmouth University, NJ. He is the author of numerous articles, book chapters, two edited books, including *Curriculum for Utopia* (1992) and *Critical Issues in Social Studies for the 21st Century* (2002). His research interests include curriculum theory, critical approaches to education reform social studies education, and social studies education.

SHIRLEY R. STEINBERG is the Director of the Paulo and Nita Freire International Project for Critical Pedagogy at McGill University. She also teaches cultural and youth studies in the Department of Integrated Studies in Education. Her most recent book (with Donaldo Macedo) is *Media Literacy: A Reader*. The founding editor of *Taboo: the Journal of Culture and Education*, she has edited *Teen Life in Europe, Multi/intercultural Conversations: A Reader*, and the award-winning *International Encyclopedia of Contemporary Youth Culture* (with Priya Parmar and Birgit Richard). With Joe Kincheloe, she has written and edited many books. Her areas of research are critical media literacy, critical pedagogy, youth studies, and social drama.

KIWAN SUNG received his MA(TESOL) and Ph.D.(Language & Literacy) at The Pennsylvania State University. He studied second language acquisition and learning and critical literacy and pedagogy. He has published and translated 3 books and written more than 30 articles and also presented his work at both domestic and international contexts. He now teaches at Kyung Hee University. He also serves as secretary general for the Korea Association of Multimedia-Assisted Language Learning and as broad members for other professional organizations.

JUHA SUORANTA is Professor of Adult Education at the University of Tampere, Finland. He holds Adjunct Professorship in media education at the University of Tampere and in music education in Sibelius Academy (Helsinki, Finland). He has studied research methodology, theory of radical adult education and foundations of critical pedagogy.

TERE VADÉN is Assistant Professor of Hypermedia at the University of Tampere, Finland. He holds Adjunct Professorship in theoretical philosophy at the University of Tampere and in the philosophy of cognitive science at the University of Lapland (Rovaniemi, Finland). He has focused in his research on the philosophy of cognitive science, Finnish philosophy and social media.

ERIC J. WEINER is Associate Professor at Montclair State University. His current research interests are language and imagination, adult literacy, critical pedagogy, and epistemology. His work can be found in *TC Record*, *Educational Foundations*, *Journal of Adolescent and Adult Literacy*, and *Educational Philosophy and Theory*. . His first book *Private Learning, Public Needs: The Neoliberal Assault on Democratic Education* (Peter Lang) was published in 2005.

PHILIP WEXLER lives in Jerusalem, where he is Professor of Sociology of Education at the Hebrew University. He works in the areas of sociological and anthropological theory, social psychology, sociology of education and sociology of knowledge and religion, as journal editor, member of editorial boards, and researcher. He is the author of a number of books, including: *Critical Social Psychology*; *Social Analysis of Education*; *Becoming Somebody*; *Holy Sparks*; *Mystical Society*; and, most recently, *Mystical Interactions* (Cherub, 2007); and *Symbolic Movement: From the Critique of Liberalism to New Age Sociology of Education* (Sense, 2007).

Index

Studies in the Postmodern Theory of Education

General Editors
Joe L. Kincheloe & Shirley R. Steinberg

Counterpoints publishes the most compelling and imaginative books being written in education today. Grounded on the theoretical advances in criticalism, feminism, and postmodernism in the last two decades of the twentieth century, Counterpoints engages the meaning of these innovations in various forms of educational expression. Committed to the proposition that theoretical literature should be accessible to a variety of audiences, the series insists that its authors avoid esoteric and jargonistic languages that transform educational scholarship into an elite discourse for the initiated. Scholarly work matters only to the degree it affects consciousness and practice at multiple sites. Counterpoints' editorial policy is based on these principles and the ability of scholars to break new ground, to open new conversations, to go where educators have never gone before.

For additional information about this series or for the submission of manuscripts, please contact:

> Joe L. Kincheloe & Shirley R. Steinberg
> c/o Peter Lang Publishing, Inc.
> 29 Broadway, 18th floor
> New York, New York 10006

To order other books in this series, please contact our Customer Service Department:

> (800) 770-LANG (within the U.S.)
> (212) 647-7706 (outside the U.S.)
> (212) 647-7707 FAX

Or browse online by series:
> www.peterlang.com